D1259734

Poems

A CONCISE
ANTHOLOGY

Poems

A CONCISE ANTHOLOGY

Edited by
Elizabeth Renker

broadview press

BROADVIEW PRESS – www.broadviewpress.com

Peterborough, Ontario, Canada

Founded in 1985, Broadview Press remains a wholly independent publishing house. Broadview's focus is on academic publishing; our titles are accessible to university and college students as well as scholars and general readers. With over 600 titles in print, Broadview has become a leading international publisher in the humanities, with world-wide distribution. Broadview is committed to environmentally responsible publishing and fair business practices.

Library and Archives Canada Cataloguing in Publication

Poems (Broadview Press)
    Poems : a concise anthology / edited by Elizabeth Renker.

Includes bibliographical references and index.
ISBN 978-1-55481-147-2 (paperback)

    1. English poetry. 2. American poetry. I. Renker, Elizabeth, editor II. Title.

PR1174.P63 2016   821.008   C2016-900011-7

Broadview Press handles its own distribution in North America
PO Box 1243, Peterborough, Ontario K9J 7H5, Canada
555 Riverwalk Parkway, Tonawanda, NY 14150, USA
Tel: (705) 743-8990; Fax: (705) 743-8353
email: customerservice@broadviewpress.com

Distribution is handled by Eurospan Group in the UK, Europe, Central Asia, Middle East, Africa, India, Southeast Asia, Central America, South America, and the Caribbean. Distribution is handled by Footprint Books in Australia and New Zealand.

Broadview Press acknowledges the financial support of the Government of Canada through the Canada Book Fund for our publishing activities.

Typeset: Eileen Eckert
Cover design: George Kirkpatrick

PRINTED IN CANADA

Chronological Table of Contents

Readings shaded in gray below are available on the anthology's companion website:
http://sites.broadviewpress.com/poemsconcise/
Passcode: BVPC4862&

Note on formatting: square brackets in the table of contents indicate that the original poem was untitled and is generally referred to instead by its first line.

Language Poets   653

Poems in Conversation

The Poems in Conversation units are carefully designed to serve as selected reading lists, lesson plans, and paper and presentation topics that work well for students. Additional Poems in Conversation units appear on p. 723.

The Seduction Lyric and Its Variants

Colonization and Diaspora

The Modern Predicament

Experiments in Dramatic Monologue

Elegies

Acknowledgments

My delightful and fascinating intellectual exchanges with many students, colleagues, friends, and family members have influenced and improved this volume, among them Eric Anderson, Caroline Angell, Paula Bernat Bennett, David Brewer, Peter J. Canepa, Emily Corey, Tim Dean, Raybecca Elder, Jon Erickson, Ashley Fournier, Ben Friedlander, Anthony Geraci, Dori Grabinsky, Kathy Fagan Grandinetti, Mark Grimsley, Gordon McConville Hewes, Beth Hewitt, Patrick Houston, Andrew Hudgins, Robert Hughes, Alex Kinsel, Jack Lynch, John H. Maher, Jasmine McCloskey, Brian McHale, Andrew Mikac, Robert Miklitsch, Max Orr, Dexter A. Payne, Daniel Pacheco, William Pietrykowski, Eliza Richards, David Riede, Lacey Ross, Tim Sergay, Mitchell Snay, Michael D. Snediker, Ben Teater, Jon Billy Theiss, Matthew Vadnais, Hilary Wesenberg, Meagan Winkelman, and Andreá N. Williams; all those who responded to my crowdsourced poetry and music polls; and all my students in "Poetry/Alternative: The History of English Poetry and Alternative Music," an upper-division elective I have taught at The Ohio State University over the past decade. I offer my sincere and profound thanks to all the musicians who videoconferenced with my classes to talk about lyrics and poetry, including Rivers Cuomo of Weezer, Matt Berninger of The National, Richard Edwards of Margot and the Nuclear So and So's, Jack Tatum of Wild Nothing, Peter Silberman of The Antlers, and Cameron McGill; to the musicians who generously visited class in person, especially Erik Kang and Ed McGee; and to Dawn Barger of Post Hoc Management.

The superb staff at the Rare Books and Manuscripts Library of The Ohio State University Libraries, especially Lisa Iacobellis and Rebecca Jewett, provided generous assistance with access to primary materials.

The publisher thanks Brett McLenithan for assistance with song lyrics.

Broadview Press also wishes to thank all the readers who provided helpful commentary on early plans for this volume:

Matthew Darling, Gannon University
John Garrison, Carroll College
Jeff Grieneisen, State College of Florida
Michael Hettich, Miami Dade College
Ginger Jones, Louisiana State University, Alexandria
Robert Kern, Boston College
Damien Kortum, Laramie County Community College

Amy Levin, Northern Illinois University
Mark Long, Keene State College
Daniel Martinez, New Mexico Highlands University
Miranda Miller, Northern Wyoming Community College
James Pollock, Loras College
Sandra Pyle, Point Park University
Kevin Rabas, Emporia State University
Christian Sheridan, Bridgewater College
Jill Treftz, Marshall University
Cathy Wagner, Miami University (Ohio)
Tana Welch, Florida State University

Contributors

The glossary, annotations, and headnotes for this anthology incorporate some material initially prepared for the following Broadview anthologies: *The Broadview Introduction to Literature*, edited by Lisa Chalykoff, Neta Gordon, and Paul Lumsden; *The Broadview Anthology of Poetry*, edited by Herbert Rosengarten and Amanda Goldrick-Jones; and *The Broadview Anthology of British Literature*, edited by Joseph Black et al. The publisher gratefully acknowledges the contributions of the editors of these anthologies.

EDITORIAL COORDINATOR	Marjorie Mather
EDITORIAL ASSISTANT	Tara Bodie
CONTRIBUTING WRITERS	Laura Buzzard
	Paul Johnson Byrne
	Brad DeVetten
	Rose Eckert-Jantzie
	Emily Farrell
	Travis Mason
	Virginia Philipson
	Nora Ruddock
PRODUCTION COORDINATOR	Tara Lowes
PROOFREADERS	Joe Davies
	Judith Earnshaw
DESIGN AND TYPESETTING	Eileen Eckert
PERMISSIONS COORDINATOR	Merilee Atos
COVER DESIGN	George Kirkpatrick

Note to Readers

The features of *Poems: A Concise Anthology* are carefully designed to meet the classroom needs of both students and instructors—in one efficient volume.

To Students

A brief informative introduction to each poet (called a "headnote") provides a quick overview that will enhance your understanding of the poems.

A glossary in the back of the book will help you to understand key literary terms.

The headnotes will sometimes call your attention to other poets in this anthology or to key literary terms. As you prepare for class, think about those poetic comparisons and key terms. Applying what you are learning in this way on a regular basis will build your comprehension and retention of the larger body of material.

Helpful footnotes to each poem explain unfamiliar references.

The first section of the table of contents, called the "Chronological Table of Contents," lists all the poems in this book in historical order. This long chronological sweep illustrates how the art of poetry has developed over time. Poets respond to the poetic tradition that has been shaped by writers from the past as well as to the innovations of their peers in the present. They also often respond to evolving social and historical conditions. For these reasons, you will find it helpful to pay attention to the historical moment in which a poet is writing. Doing so will give you some clues to where the poem falls in the history of the art form as well as to important social context. We provide dates of publication at the end of each poem.

Alone in the current textbook market, this anthology incorporates contemporary song lyrics from the genres often called progressive, alternative, or indie, as well as rap and hip-hop. Songs are a form of oral and performance poetry dating back to the ancient world as well as one of the most vital forms of poetry in our culture today.

The "Poems in Conversation" section of the table of contents groups poems and songs from the chronological section in thematic units. This section is designed to help you generate ideas and topics for papers and presentations.

The "Conversations" will also help you understand poems from across the centuries in relation to one another.

A companion website provides supplementary readings; the passcode is included with the purchase of the anthology and appears at the top of the table of contents.

To Instructors

This volume includes a broad range of fully annotated selections from across the long history of poetry in English. The contents judiciously balance an extensive array of works that will support teaching traditional canons as well as multiple alternate lesson plans.

Selections include recently reclaimed works, such as poems by women who long fell from historical view (for example, Lydia Sigourney, Charlotte Smith, and Sarah Morgan Bryan Piatt). They also include lesser-known individual poems that have become newly central to poetic history (such as some of Emily Dickinson's Civil War poems and Elizabeth Barrett Browning's *Aurora Leigh*) and poems that speak to areas of deepening recent focus (such as the legacies of slavery, colonization, and diaspora and concepts of nature that range from the traditional foci of Romanticism to animal studies and eco-poetics). Experimental and conceptual works, including an entire section on Language poetry, are well represented. Poets' poets who are still rarely anthologized (such as Weldon Kees and his entire "Robinson" sequence) appear here as well.

Headnotes to each poet are designed for pedagogical usefulness. Instructors new to particular poets or to teaching poetry classes will find that the headnotes provide efficient grounding in the most current scholarship. When assigned as part of the homework, the headnotes will provide a quick, helpful conceptual framework that students can apply while reading the poems in order to gain a firmer footing in what to "read for," a difficulty that students frequently face with reading assignments.

The first section of the table of contents, the "Chronological Table of Contents," offers a rich and extensive selection of poems suited to a literary-historical course framework.

The second section of the table of contents, called "Poems in Conversation," offers a selected list of conceptual and thematic teaching units readily adaptable to lesson plans. The "Conversations" also serve as a ready-made list of fruitful paper and presentation topics for the undergraduate classroom. Instructors might find it pedagogically valuable as the term develops to ask students to create their own "Conversations" from the contents of this anthology or by incorporating additional poems and songs that are not included in this volume. Such assignments will work beautifully with digital humanities formats that students themselves might design and share. Unique in the textbook market, this volume incorporates contemporary song lyrics from the genres often called progressive, alternative, or indie as well as rap and hip-hop. Songs are a form of oral and performance poetry dating back to the ancient world as well as one of the most vital forms of poetry in our culture today. Students can readily apply their training in the close reading of poems to song lyrics in this volume as well as to their broader media worlds.

A companion website provides supplementary readings, which are listed in the table of contents. The passcode is included with the purchase of the anthology and appears at the top of the table of contents.

—Elizabeth Renker

The Exeter Book

C. 970–1000 CE

"Saga hwæt ic hatte (Say what I am called)": thus do many of the riddles compiled in the Exeter Book challenge the reader to identify their true subjects. Named for the cathedral in which it has resided for nearly a millennium, the Exeter Book is one of just four extant manuscripts consisting entirely of Anglo-Saxon writing. In some respects, the group of "elegies," serious meditative poems that constitute a portion of the Exeter Book, are as ambiguous as the riddles they accompany. Most, such as *The Wanderer* and *The Wife's Lament*, are monologues spoken by an unidentified character whose situation is unclear but who seems to be cut off from human society and the comforts of home and friendship. That the riddles were transcribed alongside these elegies and other serious works suggests that, though probably intended primarily as entertainments, the riddles were also esteemed for their poetry. Undoubtedly they are much more than cunning descriptions of objects in terms intended to suggest something else: their elaborate extended metaphors prompt the reader to consider even the most mundane articles in a different light, challenging fixed habits of mind and perception and revealing unlooked-for connections between things apparently unlike.

The Wife's Lament[1]

I make this song of myself, deeply sorrowing,
my own life's journey. I am able to tell
all the hardships I've suffered since I grew up,
but new or old, never worse than now—
ever I suffer the torment of my exile.   5
    First my lord left his people
over the tumbling waves; I worried at dawn
where on earth my leader of men might be.
When I set out myself in my sorrow,
a friendless exile, to find his retainers,   10
that man's kinsmen began to think
in secret that they would separate us,
so we would live far apart in the world,
most miserably, and longing seized me.

---

1   *The Wife's Lament* Translation by R.M. Liuzza, copyright Broadview Press.

15   My lord commanded me to live here;[1]
I had few loved ones or loyal friends
in this country, which causes me grief.
Then I found that my most fitting man
was unfortunate, filled with grief,
20 concealing his mind, plotting murder
with a smiling face. So often we swore
that only death could ever divide us,
nothing else—all that is changed now;
it is now as if it had never been,
25 our friendship. Far and near, I must
endure the hatred of my dearest one.
     They forced me to live in a forest grove,
under an oak tree in an earthen cave.[2]
This earth-hall is old, and I ache with longing;
30 the dales are dark, the hills too high,
harsh hedges overhung with briars,
a home without joy. Here my lord's leaving
often fiercely seized me. There are friends on earth,
lovers living who lie in their bed,
35 while I walk alone in the first light of dawn
under the oak-tree and through this earth-cave,
where I must sit the summer-long day;
there I can weep for all my exiles,
my many troubles; and so I can never
40 escape from the cares of my sorrowful mind,
nor all the longings that seize me in this life.
     May the young man always be sad-minded
with hard heart-thoughts, yet let him have
a smiling face along with his heartache,
45 a crowd of constant sorrows. Let to himself
all his worldly joys belong! let him be outlawed
in a far distant land, so my friend sits
under stone cliffs chilled by storms,
weary-minded, surrounded by water
50 in a sad dreary hall! My beloved will suffer
the cares of a sorrowful mind; he will remember

---

1   *live here* Or, "take up a dwelling in a grove" or "live in a (pagan) shrine." The precise
    meaning of the line, like the general meaning of the poem, is a matter of dispute and
    conjecture.
2   *earthen cave* Or "an earthen grave" or barrow.

too often a happier home. Woe to the one
who must wait with longing for a loved one.[1]

—10th century

Exeter Book Riddles[2]

Riddle 23

I am a wondrous thing, a joy to women,
Of use to close companions; no one
Do I harm, except the one who slays me.
High up I stand above the bed;
Underneath I am shaggy. Sometimes   5
Will come to me the lovely daughter
Of a peasant—will grab me, eager girl, rushing to grip
My red skin, holding me fast,
Taking my head. Soon she feels
What happens when you meet me,   10
She with curly hair. Wet will be her eye.

Riddle 33

Creature came through waves, sailed strangely
As if a ship's stem, shouting at land,
Sounding loudly. Its laughter horrible,
Chilling to all. Sharp were her sides.
She was spiteful, sluggish in battle,   5
Biting in her bad works, smashing any ship's shield wall.
Hard in her taking, binding with spells
Spoke with cunning of her own creation:
"My mother is of the dearest race of women,
And my mother is my daughter too,   10
Grown big, pregnant. It is known to men of old
And to all people that she stands
In beauty in all lands of the world."

---

1   *May the young man ... loved one* These difficult lines have been read as a particular re-
    flection, imagining the mental state of her distant beloved, or as a general reflection on
    the double-faced nature of the world; here, following the reading of some critics, they
    are taken as a kind of curse.
2   *Exeter Book Riddles* Translations by R.M. Liuzza, copyright Broadview Press.

Riddle 81

Not silent is my house; I am quiet.
We are two together, moving
As our Maker meant. I am faster than he is,
Sometimes stronger; he runs harder, lasts longer.
5 Sometimes I rest; he must run on.
He is my house all my life long
If we are parted death is my destiny.

—10th century

Solutions to the Exeter Book Riddles are provided on p. 772.

Geoffrey Chaucer

c. 1343–1400

Geoffrey Chaucer is generally considered the father of English poetry, a title bestowed by John Dryden, who held his forebear "in the same degree of veneration as the Grecians held Homer, or the Romans Virgil." Together with William Langland and the anonymous author of *Sir Gawain and the Green Knight*, Chaucer was among the first poets to craft sophisticated literary expressions in a Middle English vernacular. But whereas Langland and the *Gawain* poet wrote in an unrhymed alliterative style characteristic of Old English verse, Chaucer's poetry reflects the fashions and influences of the Continent and is written in a dialect more closely related to modern English.

Though Chaucer wrote some short poems (such as "To Rosemounde"), he is best known for his longer works, most notably *The Parliament of Fowls* (1380), an early dream vision; *Troilus and Criseyde* (c. 1385), a masterly romance of great psychological complexity; and *The Canterbury Tales*, generally considered his masterpiece. Frequently hilarious, sometimes bawdy, and often revealing, *The Canterbury Tales* presents itself as a series of stories told by a group of pilgrims on their way from London to Canterbury. Chaucer worked on *The Canterbury Tales* during the last decades of his life, producing 24 tales totaling over 17,000 lines, but leaving the work unfinished when he died.

To Rosemounde

A Balade

Madame, ye ben of al beaute shryne°	*shrine*
As fer as cercled° is the mapamounde,°[1]	*rounded / map of the world*
For as the cristal glorious ye shyne,	
And lyke ruby ben your chekes rounde.	
Therwith ye ben so mery and so jocounde°	*pleasant, joyful* 5
That at a revel° whan that I see you daunce,	*festival*
It is an oynement° unto my wounde,	*ointment*
Thogh ye to me ne do no daliaunce.[2]	
For thogh I wepe of teres ful a tyne,°	*barrel*
Yet may that wo myn herte nat confounde;°	*destroy* 10

---

1   *ye ben of al ... mapamounde* You are the shrine of all beauty throughout the world.
2   *Thogh ... daliaunce* Even though you give me no encouragement.

Your semy° voys that ye so smal out twyne°   *small, high / twist out*
Maketh my thoght in joy and blis habounde.°   *abound, be full of*
So curtaysly I go with love bounde
That to myself I sey in my penaunce,
15   "Suffyseth me to love you, Rosemounde,
Thogh ye to me ne do no daliaunce."[1]

Nas never pyk walwed° in galauntyne[2]   *immersed*
As I in love am walwed and ywounde,°   *wound*
For which ful ofte I of myself devyne°   *discover, understand*
20   That I am trewe Tristam[3] the secounde.
My love may not refreyde° nor affounde,°   *grow cold / founder, grow numb*
I brenne° ay in an amorous plesaunce.°   *burn / desire*
Do what you lyst,° I wyl your thral be founde,[4]   *wish*
Thogh ye to me ne do no daliaunce.

25   tregentil————————//—————————chaucer[5]

—c. 1477

---

1   *daliaunce* Sociable interaction, or more explicitly, amorous or sexual exchange.
2   *Nas ... galauntyne* No pike was ever steeped in galantine sauce.
3   *Tristam* Tristan, lover of Isolde, often presented as the ideal lover in medieval romance.
4   *I ... founde* I will remain your servant.
5   *tregentil ... chaucer* Although the words appear joined (or separated) by a line or flourish
     in the manuscript, the status of *tregentil* is uncertain. It may be an epithet (French: very
     gentle) or a proper name.

Sir Thomas Wyatt

c. 1503–1542

Thomas Wyatt lived his entire adult life amidst the political intrigue and turmoil that accompanied the reign of King Henry VIII, and was twice imprisoned in the Tower of London. Even his poems on subjects far from the machinations of the king and his courtiers—subjects such as love and idyllic country life—can carry a subtext about the court's political dramas. Wyatt wrote in many poetic forms, but is best known for the artistry of his satires and songs and, along with Henry Howard, Earl of Surrey (1517–47), for introducing the Italian sonnet to England.

Few of Wyatt's poems were printed in his lifetime, but many appeared in Richard Tottel's 1557 volume *Songes and Sonettes* (later to become known as *Tottel's Miscellany*). Some years later, the Elizabethan critic George Puttenham summarized Sir Thomas Wyatt's importance to the English literary tradition in terms that remain broadly accepted today: "[Wyatt and Surrey] travailed into Italie, and there tasted the sweet and stately measures and stile of the Italian Poesie.... They greatly pollished our rude & homely maner of vulgar Poesie, from that it had been before, and for that cause may justly be said the first reformers of our English meetre and stile."

[The long love that in my thought doth harbour][1]

The long love that in my thought doth harbour	
And in mine heart doth keep his residence	
Into my face presseth with bold pretence	
And therein campeth, spreading his banner.	
She that me learneth° to love and suffer	*teaches* 5
And will° that my trust and lust's negligence	*wishes*
Be reined by reason, shame,° and reverence,	*modesty*
With his hardiness° taketh displeasure.	*daring*
Wherewithal unto the heart's forest he fleeth,	
Leaving his enterprise with pain and cry,	10
And there him hideth and not appeareth.	
What may I do when my master feareth,	
But in the field with him to live and die?	
For good is the life ending faithfully.	

—1557

---

1   [*The long love ... doth harbour*] This poem is an adaptation of Sonnet 140 from the Italian poet Petrarch's *Rime sparse* (*Scattered Rhymes*).

[Whoso list to hunt, I know where is an hind][1]

Whoso list° to hunt, I know where is an hind,°   *likes / female deer*
But as for me, alas, I may no more:
The vain travail hath wearied me so sore.
I am of them that farthest cometh behind;
5   Yet may I by no means my wearied mind
Draw from the deer: but as she fleeth afore,
Fainting I follow. I leave off therefore,
Since in a net I seek to hold the wind.
Who list her hunt, I put him out of doubt,
10   As well as I may spend his time in vain:
And, graven with diamonds, in letters plain
There is written her fair neck round about:
"*Noli me tangere*, for Caesar's I am,[2]
And wild for to hold, though I seem tame."

—1557

---

1   *[Whoso list ... an hind]* This poem is an adaptation of Sonnet 190 from Petrarch's *Rime sparse* (*Scattered Rhymes*).

2   *Noli me tangere* Latin: Touch me not; words spoken by Christ after his resurrection; *for Caesar's I am* It was thought that Caesar's deer wore collars with this inscription to ensure they would not be hunted. Wyatt's readers who identified the deer with Anne Boleyn (whom Wyatt knew and perhaps loved) would have read the lines as suggesting that the "hind" belongs to Henry VIII.

Edmund Spenser
1552?–1599

Best known for his epic poem *The Faerie Queene* (1590–96), Edmund Spenser was an extraordinarily accomplished poet in other forms as well. In 1579 Spenser used the pseudonym "Immerito" on his first significant publication, *The Shepheardes Calender*, a set of illustrated pastoral poems for each month of the year. He spent the following decade working on the first three books of *The Faerie Queene* (1590), an allegorical examination of the virtues set in a magical romance world. This work was politically as well as poetically motivated: the poem was a bid for more direct royal patronage from Queen Elizabeth I. Its central if often absent figure is Prince Arthur, the future British king, who is seeking the always absent heroine, the "Faerie Queene" Gloriana—an allegorical "mirror" of Queen Elizabeth I in her public role as ruler. Spenser had hoped to write twelve books, but completed only six, the second set of three books being published in a 1596 edition. Spenser won a pension from the queen, but Elizabeth's patronage seems to have gone no further, perhaps because his satirical "Mother Hubberds Tale," included in his *Complaints* (1591), angered the authorities.

In between the two installments of *The Faerie Queene*, Spenser wrote several other volumes, including *Colin Clouts Come Home Againe* (1595), a sometimes satirical anti-court pastoral; and *Astrophel* (1596), an elegy for fellow poet Philip Sidney. During this time he also completed his *Amoretti* (1595), a series of sonnets commemorating his courtship of Elizabeth Boyle, issued with *Epithalamion*, a marriage hymn celebrating their union. Spenser died early in 1599 and is buried in Westminster Abbey, next to Chaucer.

from *Amoretti*[1]

1

Happy ye leaves° when as those lilly hands,	*pages*
which hold my life in their dead doing° might,	*death-dealing*
shall handle you and hold in loves soft bands,°	*bonds*
lyke captives trembling at the victors sight.	
And happy lines, on which with starry light,	5
those lamping° eyes will deigne sometimes to look	*blazing*
and read the sorrowes of my dying spright,°	*spirit*
written with teares in harts close bleeding book.	

---

1   *Amoretti* Italian: Little Loves.

And happy rymes bath'd in the sacred brooke,
10   of *Helicon*[1] whence she derivèd is,
when ye behold that Angels blessèd looke,
my soules long lackèd foode, my heavens blis.
Leaves, lines, and rymes, seeke her to please alone,
whom if ye please, I care for other none.

75

One day I wrote her name upon the strand,°   *shore*
but came the waves and washèd it away:
agayne I wrote it with a second hand,
but came the tyde, and made my paynes his pray.°   *prey*
5 Vayne man, sayd she, that doest in vaine assay,°   *attempt*
a mortall thing so to immortalize.
for I my selve shall lyke to this decay,
and eek° my name bee wypèd out lykewize.   *also*
Not so, (quod° I) let baser things devize   *said*
10   to dy in dust, but you shall live by fame:
my verse your vertues rare shall eternize,
and in the hevens wryte your glorious name.
Where whenas° death shall all the world subdew,   *whenever*
our love shall live, and later life renew.

—1595

---

1   *Helicon* One of the mountains sacred to the Nine Muses, the goddesses of the arts and
sciences. The sacred spring that flows from Helicon is the Hippocrene.

Sir Walter Ralegh

c. 1554–1618

Known as an explorer, courtier, writer, and adventurer—and as a knight and captain of the Queen's Guard who was later accused of treason—Sir Walter Ralegh was a controversial figure. A great portion of his writing has been lost over the centuries, but the remaining works reveal a dynamic voice imaginatively relaying his experiences and boldly critiquing the social and political climate in which he lived.

Ralegh was a student at Oxford and a soldier in France and Ireland before becoming a favorite of Elizabeth I in the early 1580s. A secret marriage to one of Elizabeth's ladies-in-waiting caused him to fall out of favor, and in 1592 he was imprisoned for several months in the Tower of London. Before and after his imprisonment Ralegh made attempts to establish colonies in what is now Virginia and the Carolinas, and he undertook several expeditions to the New World, including a 1595 voyage to Guiana in search of the legendary golden city of El Dorado. After his tumultuous relationship with Elizabeth I, Ralegh found a less sympathetic ruler in James I, who had him condemned under dubious charges of treason and imprisoned in the Tower from 1603 to 1616. Upon his release Ralegh embarked on another failed search for El Dorado. During this expedition, his crew attacked a Spanish settlement in contradiction of James's diplomatic policy, and when Ralegh returned home he was executed for his defiance.

Ralegh's poetry is characterized by an intensely personal treatment of such conventional themes as love, loss, beauty, and time. The majority of his poems are short lyrics—many of them occasional, written in response to particular events. Although he wrote throughout his eventful life, he was most prolific during the period of his long imprisonment, producing poetry, political treatises, and an unfinished *History of the World* intended to chronicle life on Earth from the time of creation to Ralegh's own era.

The Nymph's Reply to the Shepherd[1]

If all the world and love were young,
And truth in every shepherd's tongue,
These pretty pleasures might me move
To live with thee and be thy love.

---

1   *The Nymph's ... Shepherd* Response to Christopher Marlowe's "The Passionate Shepherd to His Love" (1599), below.

5   Time drives the flocks from field to fold
    When rivers rage and rocks grow cold,
    And Philomel becometh dumb;[1]
    The rest complains of cares to come.

    The flowers do fade, and wanton° fields   *unrestrained, unruly*
10 To wayward winter reckoning yields;
    A honey tongue, a heart of gall,°   *bitterness, rancor*
    Is fancy's spring, but sorrow's fall.

    Thy gowns, thy shoes, thy beds of roses,
    Thy cap, thy kirtle,° and thy posies   *tunic or skirt*
15 Soon break, soon wither, soon forgotten—
    In folly ripe, in reason rotten.

    Thy belt of straw and ivy buds,
    Thy coral clasps and amber studs,
    All these in me no means can move
20 To come to thee and be thy love.

    But could youth last and love still breed,
    Had joys no date nor age no need,[2]
    Then these delights my mind might move
    To live with thee and be thy love.

                                                        —1600

---

1   *Philomel becometh dumb* I.e., the nightingale does not sing. In classical mythology,
    Philomela, the daughter of the king of Athens, was transformed into a nightingale after
    being pursued and raped by her brother-in-law, Tereus, who tore out her tongue.
2   *Had joys ... no need* If joys had no ending and aging did not bring with it its own needs.

Christopher Marlowe
1564–1593

As Tennyson wrote, "if Shakespeare is the dazzling sun" of the English Renaissance, then his fellow poet-playwright Christopher Marlowe "is certainly the morning star." Marlowe's plays heralded a new dawn for English drama in their use of blank verse (unrhymed iambic pentameter): by demonstrating its potential to capture the dynamic cadence of natural speech in plays such as *Tamburlaine the Great* (1587) and *Doctor Faustus* (1592?), he helped to make blank verse a standard form for playwrights of the period. Marlowe's facility with language extended to poetry, and he was known for his translations of Latin poets as well as for his original work. "The Passionate Shepherd to His Love," based in part on Virgil's Second Eclogue, is perhaps his most famous English poem.

Despite his success as a writer, Marlowe was dogged by controversy throughout his career. Not only was he a party to a homicide (of which he was acquitted on grounds of self-defense), he was also arrested for coining money and arraigned before the Privy Council on charges of blasphemy and heresy, both serious transgressions in Elizabethan England. Marlowe's troubles came to a brutal head when at 29 he was fatally stabbed in what may have been a planned assassination connected with his apparent service to the Crown as a government agent. The enigmatic circumstances of his life and death have contributed to Marlowe's reputation as a man who—as Thomas Kyd attested—was "intemperate and of a cruel heart," skeptical of religion, scornful of decorum, and "bold unto recklessness." Whatever the truth may be, Marlowe produced an extraordinary body of work that emits what William Hazlitt described as "a glow of the imagination, unhallowed by anything but its own energies."

The Passionate Shepherd to His Love

Come live with me and be my love,
And we will all the pleasures prove°   *try*
That valleys, groves, hills, and fields,
Woods, or steepy mountain yields.

5   And we will sit upon the rocks,
    Seeing the shepherds feed their flocks,
    By shallow rivers to whose falls
    Melodious birds sing madrigals.[1]

    And I will make thee beds of roses
10 And a thousand fragrant posies,
    A cap of flowers, and a kirtle°   *tunic, skirt*
    Embroidered all with leaves of myrtle;

    A gown made of the finest wool
    Which from our pretty lambs we pull;
15 Fair linèd slippers for the cold,
    With buckles of the purest gold;

    A belt of straw and ivy buds,
    With coral clasps and amber studs:
    And if these pleasures may thee move,
20 Come live with me, and be my love.

    The shepherd swains° shall dance and sing   *rustic lovers*
    For thy delight each May morning:
    If these delights thy mind may move,
    Then live with me and be my love.

                                                                      —1599

---

1   *madrigals* Part-songs for several voices, often with pastoral or amatory associations.

William Shakespeare

1564–1616

As his fellow poet-playwright Ben Jonson declared, William Shakespeare "was not of an age, but for all time." Without doubt, the "Bard of Avon" has proved worthy of this monumental phrase: nearly four centuries after his death, Shakespeare's histories, comedies, tragedies, and romances continue to be staged the world over.

Today, Shakespeare's name is connected less with a flesh-and-blood human being—the son of a glover, born in the small town of Stratford-on-Avon, who left for London to pursue a career in the theater after fathering three children—than with an extraordinary body of work. Shakespeare's oeuvre includes as many as 38 plays, many of them masterpieces; two narrative poems, *Venus and Adonis* (1593) and *The Rape of Lucrece* (1594), both much admired in Shakespeare's lifetime; and 154 sonnets, which were not necessarily conceived as a sequence but were published as one in 1609, perhaps without Shakespeare's consent.

In the sonnets the chief object of the poet's desire is not a chaste fair-haired lady but an idealized young man who prefers the praises of a rival poet and who occupies the center of a psychologically complex love triangle in which the poet-speaker and a promiscuous "dark lady" are entangled. Because of their intensely intimate expression of love, lust, jealousy, and shame, the sonnets have been the subject of endless biographical speculation, yet it is by no means certain whether the poet-speaker is Shakespeare himself or a persona constructed for dramatic effect. The enduring power of the sonnets resides not merely in what they mean but in how they produce meaning, that is, in the emotional and intellectual tensions and continuities across the sequence.

Sonnets

18

Shall I compare thee to a summer's day?
Thou art more lovely and more temperate:
Rough winds do shake the darling buds of May,
And summer's lease hath all too short a date:
Sometime too hot the eye of heaven shines,   5
And often is his gold complexion dimmed;
And every fair° from fair sometime declines,   *beauty*
By chance, or nature's changing course, untrimmed:
But thy eternal summer shall not fade,

10 Nor lose possession of that fair thou ow'st,°   *own*
   Nor shall death brag thou wander'st in his shade
   When in eternal lines to time thou grow'st:
       So long as men can breathe or eyes can see,
       So long lives this, and this gives life to thee.

29

   When in disgrace with fortune and men's eyes
   I all alone beweep my outcast state,
   And trouble deaf heav'n with my bootless° cries,   *unavailing*
   And look upon myself, and curse my fate,
5 Wishing me like to one more rich in hope,
   Featured like him,[1] like him with friends possessed,
   Desiring this man's art° and that man's scope,   *skill*
   With what I most enjoy contented least;
   Yet in these thoughts myself almost despising,
10 Haply° I think on thee, and then my state,   *By chance*
   Like to the lark at break of day arising,
   From sullen° earth sings hymns at heaven's gate;   *dark, gloomy*
       For thy sweet love remembered such wealth brings
       That then I scorn to change my state with kings.

73

   That time of year thou mayst in me behold,
   When yellow leaves, or none, or few do hang
   Upon those boughs which shake against the cold,
   Bare ruined choirs[2] where late the sweet birds sang;
5 In me thou seest the twilight of such day
   As after sunset fadeth in the west,
   Which by and by black night doth take away,
   Death's second self[3] that seals up all in rest;
   In me thou seest the glowing of such fire
10 That on the ashes of his youth doth lie,
   As the deathbed, whereon it must expire,
   Consumed with that which it was nourished by;
       This thou perceiv'st, which makes thy love more strong,
       To love that well, which thou must leave° ere long.   *lose*

---

1   *Featured like him* With physical attractions like his.
2   *choirs* Parts of churches designated for singers.
3   *Death's second self* Sleep.

116

Let me not to the marriage of true minds
Admit impediments;[1] love is not love
Which alters when it alteration finds,
Or bends with the remover[2] to remove.
O no, it is an ever-fixèd mark,   5
That looks on tempests and is never shaken;
It is the star to every wand'ring bark,°   *boat*
Whose worth's unknown, although his height be taken.[3]
Love's not Time's fool, though rosy lips and cheeks
Within his bending sickle's compass° come;   *sweep* 10
Love alters not with his brief hours and weeks,
But bears it out even to the edge of doom.
    If this be error and upon me proved,
    I never writ, nor no man ever loved.

130

My mistress' eyes are nothing like the sun;
Coral is far more red than her lips' red;
If snow be white, why then her breasts are dun;°   *grayish-brown*
If hairs be wires, black wires grow on her head;
I have seen roses damasked,° red and white,   *parti-colored* 5
But no such roses see I in her cheeks;
And in some perfumes is there more delight
Than in the breath that from my mistress reeks.
I love to hear her speak, yet well I know
That music hath a far more pleasing sound;   10
I grant I never saw a goddess go;°   *walk*
My mistress when she walks treads on the ground.
    And yet, by heaven, I think my love as rare
    As any she[4] belied with false compare.

—1609

---

1   *impediments* Cf. the marriage service in the Book of Common Prayer (c. 1552): "If any
of you know cause, or just impediment, why these two persons should not be joined
together in holy Matrimony, ye are to declare it."

2   *remover* One who changes, i.e., ceases to love.

3   *Whose ... taken* Referring to the "star" of the previous line, most likely the North Star,
whose altitude can be reckoned for navigation purposes using a sextant, but whose es-
sence remains unknown.

4   *any she* Any woman.

Thomas Campion
1567–1620

Thomas Campion was both a poet and a composer who, as he wrote in the introduction to one of his volumes of lyric poems, "chiefly aymed to couple [his] Words and Notes louingly together."

Campion was born in London and attended Cambridge and Gray's Inn, one of England's four Inns of Court for the study of law. While he never did take up a legal profession, he had an active social life at the Inns of Court and formed many friendships with musicians and poets. His first collection, *Poemata* (1595), was a volume of Latin verse, but it was *A Booke of Ayres* (1601), his first book in English, that cemented his reputation as a lyric poet. Written in collaboration with the lutist Philip Rosseter, *A Booke of Ayres* was the first of several volumes of lyrics with lute accompaniment that Campion would produce. He followed it with the manifesto *Observations in the Art of English Poesie* (1602), in which he championed the use of classical meters and deplored the "vulgar and unarteficiall custome of riming"—although he frequently disregarded this philosophy and used traditional English rhyme and meter in much of his own work.

In 1605, Campion completed a medical degree at Caen University in France. He practiced medicine for the rest of his life, but he continued to write songs and poetry, as well as the libretti for several elaborate masques that were performed at important court weddings. His last book, *Third and Fourth Booke of Ayres*, was published in 1617, three years before his death.

[There is a garden in her face]

There is a garden in her face,
Where roses and white lilies grow;
    A heav'nly paradise is that place,
Wherein all pleasant fruits do flow.
5   There cherries grow, which none may buy
    Till cherry ripe[1] themselves do cry.

Those cherries fairly do enclose
Of orient pearl[2] a double row,
    Which when her lovely laughter shows,
10 They look like rosebuds filled with snow.

---

1   *cherry ripe* Cry of a London street seller.
2   *orient pearl* High-quality pearl.

Yet them nor peer nor prince can buy,
Till cherry ripe themselves do cry.

Her eyes like angels watch them still;
Her brows like bended bows do stand,
   Threat'ning with piercing frowns to kill
All that attempt with eye or hand   15
   Those sacred cherries to come nigh,
   Till cherry ripe themselves do cry.

—1617

Thomas Nashe

c. 1567–1601

Thomas Nashe was educated at Cambridge and made his living as a pamphleteer, playwright, and poet in London. One of a circle of young writers that included Christopher Marlowe, Nashe was a clever satirist, and his writings involved him in several literary and political controversies. The 1597 play *The Isle of Dogs* was found to be seditious by authorities and resulted in Nashe fleeing London. (Nashe's co-writer Ben Jonson was briefly imprisoned.) While some of Nashe's satires attacked specific individuals, many were more general in nature, pointing out the hypocrisies of his society. *The Unfortunate Traveller* (1594) tells the story of Jack Wilton, a sometime soldier and servant, as he travels around England and Europe from 1513 to the 1530s. Though the story is fictional, Nashe incorporates real historical situations and people, making many satirical comments on recent religious and political events and attitudes.

The poem below, now famous as an independent work, was written as part of Nashe's 1600 play *Summer's Last Will and Testament*.

A Litany in Time of Plague

Adieu, farewell, earth's bliss;
This world uncertain is;
Fond are life's lustful joys;
Death proves them all but toys;
5 None from his darts can fly;
I am sick, I must die.
  Lord, have mercy on us!

Rich men, trust not in wealth,
Gold cannot buy you health;
10 Physic himself must fade.
All things to end are made,
The plague full swift goes by;
I am sick, I must die.
  Lord, have mercy on us!

15 Beauty is but a flower
Which wrinkles will devour;
Brightness falls from the air;

Queens have died young and fair;
Dust hath closed Helen's[1] eye.
I am sick, I must die.
   Lord, have mercy on us!   20

Strength stoops unto the grave,
Worms feed on Hector[2] brave;
Swords may not fight with fate,
Earth still holds ope her gate.   25
"Come, come!" the bells do cry.
I am sick, I must die.
   Lord, have mercy on us.

Wit with his wantonness
Tasteth death's bitterness;   30
Hell's executioner
Hath no ears for to hear
What vain art can reply.
I am sick, I must die.
   Lord, have mercy on us.   35

Haste, therefore, each degree,
To welcome destiny;
Heaven is our heritage,
Earth but a player's stage;
Mount we unto the sky.   40
I am sick, I must die.
   Lord, have mercy on us.

—1600

---

1   *Helen's* Helen of Troy, a famously beautiful woman in Greek legend and the daughter of
   Zeus and Leda.
2   *Hector* A Trojan hero of Greek mythology.

John Donne

1572–1631

John Donne was an innovator who set out to startle readers with his disdain for convention, writing poems that challenged expectations about what was appropriate in poetic subject matter, form, tone, language, and imagery.

As with the speaker of his "Holy Sonnet 19," in Donne "contraries meet in one." Some critics and readers try to resolve these "contraries" by separating Donne's career in two: in early life, a witty man-about-London whose love poems combine erotic energy with high-minded argument; in later life, a learned minister famous for his religious verse and his sermons. But Donne frequently blurs the differences between the sacred and the secular, sometimes presenting erotic love as a form of religious experience, and sometimes portraying religious devotion as an erotic experience. His poetic voice, moreover, ranges across a multitude of roles and postures, from misogynist cynicism to tender idealism and devout religious passion.

Donne was the son of a prosperous ironmonger, and his family was Catholic at a time when the government viewed all Catholics with suspicion. Donne studied at Oxford and Cambridge but took no degree—perhaps because graduation required accepting the Church of England's 39 "articles of religion." In 1592 he began legal studies in London, and over the next few years wrote many of the love lyrics for which he later became famous; like most of his poems, these were circulated in manuscript but not published during his lifetime.

Donne eventually converted to Anglicanism, and in 1615 he became a clergyman. In 1621, he was appointed Dean of St. Paul's Cathedral in London, where he attracted large audiences for his intellectually challenging and emotionally stirring sermons. His *Poems* first appeared in 1633, two years after his death.

The Flea

Mark but this flea, and mark in this,
How little that which thou deny'st me is;
It sucked me first, and now sucks thee,
And in this flea, our two bloods mingled be;[1]
5 Thou know'st that this cannot be said
A sin, nor shame, nor loss of maidenhead,
    Yet this enjoys before it woo,

---

1   *mingled be* The speaker's subsequent argument hinges on the traditional belief that blood mixed during sexual intercourse.

And pampered swells with one blood made of two
And this, alas, is more than we would do.

Oh stay, three lives in one flea spare,   10
Where we almost, yea more than married are.
This flea is you and I, and this
Our marriage bed, and marriage temple is;
Though parents grudge, and you, we're met,
And cloistered in these living walls of jet.   15
  Though use° make you apt to kill me,   *habit*
  Let not to that, self murder added be,
  And sacrilege, three sins in killing three.

Cruel and sudden, hast thou since
Purpled thy nail, in blood of innocence?   20
Wherein could this flea guilty be,
Except in that drop which it sucked from thee?
Yet thou triumph'st, and sayest that thou
Find'st not thy self, nor me the weaker now;
  'Tis true, then learn how false, fears be;   25
  Just so much honour, when thou yield'st to me,
  Will waste, as this flea's death took life from thee.

             —1633

The Good-Morrow

I wonder by my troth, what thou, and I
Did, till we loved? were we not weaned till then?
But sucked on country pleasures, childishly?
Or snorted we in the seven sleepers den?[1]
T'was so; But this, all pleasures fancies be.   5
If ever any beauty I did see,
Which I desired, and got, t'was but a dream of thee.

And now good morrow to our waking souls,
Which watch not one another out of fear;

---

1 *seven sleepers den* Seven Christian youths were said to have hidden in a cave near Ephesus
 to avoid persecution by the Roman Emperor Decius, and to have slept for almost 200
 years.

10 For love, all love of other sights controls,
And makes one little room, an every where.
Let sea-discoverers to new worlds have gone,
Let maps to other, worlds on worlds have shown,
Let us possess one world, each hath one, and is one.

15 My face in thine eye, thine in mine appears,
And true plain hearts do in the faces rest;
Where can we find two better hemispheres
Without sharp North, without declining West?
What ever dies, was not mixed equally;[1]
20 If our two loves be one, or, thou and I
Love so alike, that none do slacken, none can die.

—1633

from *Holy Sonnets*

10

Death be not proud, though some have called thee
Mighty and dreadful, for thou art not so,
For, those, whom thou think'st thou dost overthrow
Die not, poor death, nor yet canst thou kill me.
5 From rest and sleep, which but thy pictures be,
Much pleasure, then from thee, much more must flow,
And soonest our best men with thee do go,
Rest of their bones, and soul's delivery.
Thou art slave to Fate, Chance, kings, and desperate men,
10 And dost with poison, war, and sickness dwell,
And poppy, or charms, can make us sleep as well,
And better than thy stroke; why swell'st thou then?
One short sleep past, we wake eternally,
And death shall be no more; death, thou shalt die.

---

1   *What ever ... equally* According to medieval science, unless the elements in nature were in
     perfect equilibrium, they were subject to flux and mortality; such equilibrium could not
     be achieved on earth.

14

Batter my heart, three personed God; for you
As yet but knock, breathe, shine, and seek to mend;
That I may rise and stand, o'erthrow me, and bend
Your force, to break, blow, burn and make me new.
I, like an usurped town, to another due,   5
Labour to admit You, but oh, to no end,
Reason Your viceroy in me, me should defend,
But is captived, and proves weak or untrue.
Yet dearly I love You, and would be loved fain,
But am betrothed unto Your enemy: 10
Divorce me, untie, or break that knot again,
Take me to you, imprison me, for I,
Except you enthrall me, never shall be free,
Nor ever chaste, except you ravish me.

—1633

A Valediction: Forbidding Mourning

As virtuous men pass mildly away,
    And whisper to their souls to go,
Whilst some of their sad friends do say,
    The breath goes now, and some say, no:

So let us melt, and make no noise,   5
    No tear-floods, nor sigh-tempests move,
'Twere profanation of our joys
    To tell the laity our love.

Moving of th'earth° brings harms and fears,   *earthquake*
    Men reckon what it did and meant,   10
But trepidation of the spheres,[1]
    Though greater far, is innocent.

---

1   *the spheres* According to Ptolemaic theory, a concentric series of spheres revolved around
     the earth; the heavenly bodies were set into these spheres. Enveloping all the rest was an
     outer sphere known as the "*Primum Mobile*" ("First Mover"), thought to give motion to
     the other spheres, and to introduce variations into the times of the equinoxes.

Dull sublunary[1] lovers' love
    (Whose soul is sense) cannot admit
15 Absence, because it doth remove
    Those things which elemented it.

But we by a love, so much refined,
    That our selves know not what it is,
Inter-assured of the mind,
20   Care less, eyes, lips, and hands to miss.

Our two souls therefore, which are one,
    Though I must go, endure not yet
A breach, but an expansion,
    Like gold to airy thinness beat.

25 If they be two, they are two so
    As stiff twin compasses[2] are two,
Thy soul, the fixed foot, makes no show
    To move, but doth, if th'other do.

And though it in the centre sit,
30   Yet when the other far doth roam,
It leans, and hearkens after it,
    And grows erect, as that comes home.

Such wilt thou be to me, who must
    Like th'other foot, obliquely run;
35 Thy firmness draws my circle just,
    And makes me end, where I begun.

                          —1633

---

1   *sublunary* Beneath the moon, hence earthly (as opposed to heavenly) and therefore cor-
    ruptible and subject to change.
2   *twin compasses* Single drawing compass (with twin "feet").

Lady Mary Wroth
1587–1653?

Lady Mary Wroth wrote the first work of prose romance and the first ama-
tory sonnet sequence published by a woman in English. Her work was ad-
mired by a number of poets of her day—Ben Jonson proclaimed that her
verse had made him "a better lover, and much better poet"—and although
her reputation faded during the ensuing centuries, today she is recognized
as a significant Jacobean writer and pioneer.

Born Mary Sidney, Wroth was a member of an illustrious political and
literary family. She was educated by tutors and was already an accomplished
scholar and musician by the time of her arranged marriage in 1604. The
marriage was unhappy; when her husband died in 1614, Wroth was left with
crushing debts, but was also free to pursue more openly a long-time illicit
affair with her cousin, William Herbert. This affair, and financial constraints,
may have limited Wroth's access to court and spurred her to write more seri-
ously.

Wroth published *The Countess of Montgomery's Urania* in 1621. A ground-
breaking work, *Urania* exploits a genre traditionally written by men—pasto-
ral romance—in untraditional ways to examine the social situation of women
in court society. Appended to *Urania* was a sequence of 83 sonnets and 20
songs entitled *Pamphilia to Amphilanthus*. These poems highlight love's ten-
sions and contradictions with great poetic skill; the climax of *Pamphilia to
Amphilanthus* is a technical *tour de force*, a "corona" or "crown" of 14 sonnets
in which the last line of each poem becomes the first line of the next.

from *Pamphilia to Amphilanthus*

Song [Love, a child, is ever crying]

Love, a child, is ever crying,
    Please him, and he straight is flying;
    Give him, he the more is craving,
    Never satisfied with having.

His desires have no measure,
    Endless folly is his treasure;
    What he promiseth he breaketh;
    Trust not one word that he speaketh.

5

He vows nothing but false matter,
10 And to cozen° you he'll flatter;   *deceive*
Let him gain the hand, he'll leave you,
And still glory to deceive you.

He will triumph in your wailing,
And yet cause be of your failing:
15 These his virtues are, and slighter
Are his gifts, his favours lighter.

Feathers are as firm in staying,
Wolves no fiercer in their preying.
As a child then leave him crying,
20 Nor seek him, so giv'n to flying.

77[1]

In this strange labyrinth how shall I turn?
    Ways° are on all sides while the way I miss: *Paths*
    If to the right hand, there in love I burn;
    Let me go forward, therein danger is;
5 If to the left, suspicion hinders bliss;
    Let me turn back, shame cries I ought return,
    Nor faint, though crosses° with my fortunes kiss;   *troubles*
    Stand still is harder, although sure to mourn.[2]
Thus let me take the right, or left-hand way,
10   Go forward, or stand still, or back retire:
    I must these doubts endure without allay°   *relief*
    Or help, but travail[3] find for my best hire.
Yet that which most my troubled sense doth move,
Is to leave all, and take the thread of Love.[4]

—1621

---

1   *77* First sonnet in the 14-poem sequence *A Crown of Sonnets Dedicated to Love*, part of
     the larger sequence of *Pamphilia to Amphilanthus*.
2   *sure to mourn* Sure to make me mourn.
3   *travail* Take pains to; possibly meant as a pun on "travel," which was the word used in an
     early edition of the poem.
4   *thread of Love* Referring to the myth of Ariadne, who gave her beloved Theseus a spool
     of thread to unwind behind him as he traveled through the labyrinth of the Minotaur; by
     following the thread he could find his way back out.

Robert Herrick

1591–1674

Of the "sons of Ben" who basked in the genius of poet and playwright Ben Jonson in 1620s' London, Robert Herrick is the poet most familiar to modern readers—more so, to many readers, than Jonson himself. Herrick's major collection, *Hesperides* (1648), contains over 1,400 poems, including epigrams, epistles, odes, eclogues, and other lyric forms. Whether playful or earnest, many of his poems are exhortations in the *carpe diem* tradition: since all things are subject to "Time's trans-shifting," we must seize every fleeting chance for happiness, but we must do so with due regard for the classical virtue of moderation. The opening line of "To the Virgins, to Make Much of Time"—"Gather ye rosebuds while ye may"—has entered the English language as a familiar emblem of the *carpe diem* mentality.

Although *Hesperides* was published during the English Civil Wars (1642–51), Herrick, a staunch Royalist, often seems insensible to the political upheaval embraced by his more rebellious contemporaries, such as Milton. Partly because its light bucolic tone did not match the seriousness of the time, *Hesperides* achieved little notice during Herrick's life; in the nineteenth century, however, the Romantic attraction to pastoral and rural themes made Herrick popular with anthologists. More recent critics, appreciating his cunning and delicate artistry, have accorded him a high status among seventeenth-century poets.

Delight in Disorder

A sweet disorder in the dress
Kindles in clothes a wantonness:
A lawn[1] about the shoulders thrown
Into a fine distraction;
An erring lace, which here and there   5
Enthralls the crimson stomacher:[2]
A cuff neglectful, and thereby
Ribbons to flow confusedly:
A winning wave, deserving note,
In the tempestuous petticoat;   10

---

1   *lawn* Shawl or scarf of finely woven cotton or linen.
2   *stomacher* Decorative garment worn over the breast and stomach and secured by lacing.

A careless shoestring, in whose tie
I see a wild civility:
Do more bewitch me than when art
Is too precise in every part.

—1648

To the Virgins, to Make Much of Time

Gather ye rosebuds while ye may,
    Old time is still a-flying;[1]
And this same flower that smiles today,
    Tomorrow will be dying.

5 The glorious lamp of heaven, the sun,
    The higher he's a-getting;
The sooner will his race be run,[2]
    And nearer he's to setting.

That age is best, which is the first,
10   When youth and blood are warmer;
But being spent, the worse, and worst
    Times still succeed the former.

Then be not coy, but use your time,
    And while ye may, go marry;
15 For having lost but once your prime,
    You may for ever tarry.

—1648

---

1   *Old ... a-flying* Paraphrase of the Latin *tempus fugit* ("time flies").
2   *his race be run* The sun's movement was pictured in Greek mythology as the chariot of
    Phoebus Apollo racing across the sky.

George Herbert
1593–1633

George Herbert was born in Wales to a well-connected family and was educated at Trinity College in Cambridge, becoming a university orator, a member of Parliament, and later an Anglican priest. Deeply religious, he bemoaned the number of "love poems that are daily writ and consecrated to Venus" and the much smaller number of poems that "look toward God and Heaven." His own poems masterfully employ the many dimensions of poetic form and content to express his Christian devotion.

He crafted the poem "Easter Wings," for example, so that its shape on the page would depict two pairs of wings, while the text of "The Altar" visually represents an altar. Such typographical "pattern poems" influenced nineteenth- and twentieth-century poets including Lewis Carroll, E.E. Cummings, bpNichol, and others, and Herbert's work is a precursor to the "concrete poetry" movement of the 1950s. *The Temple* (1633), Herbert's major collection, was published in the year of his death.

Herbert had immense influence on the devotional poets of the 1600s, but by the nineteenth century his reputation had waned. In the twentieth century he rejoined the poetic mainstream when T.S. Eliot praised his fusion of emotion and intellect. Herbert was, Eliot wrote, "an anatomist of feeling and a trained theologian too; his mind is working continually both on the mysteries of faith and the motives of the heart."

The Altar

A broken A L T A R, Lord thy servant rears,
Made of a heart, and cemented with tears:[1]
    Whose parts are as thy hand did frame;
    No workman's tool hath touched the same.[2]
5   A H E A R T alone
          Is   such   a   stone,
          As   nothing   but
          Thy pow'r doth cut.
          Wherefore° each part
10   Of my hard heart
          Meets in this frame,
          To praise thy name.
    That, if I chance to hold my peace,
    These stones to praise thee may not cease.[3]
15 O let thy blessed S A C R I F I C E be mine,
And sanctify this A L T A R to be thine.

                                   —1633

The Collar

I struck the board,° and cry'd, No more.   *table*
            I will abroad.
    What? shall I ever sigh and pine?
My lines and life are free; free as the rode,
5   Loose as the winde, as large as store.
            Shall I be still in suit?[4]
Have I no harvest but a thorn
To let me bloud, and not restore
What I have lost with cordiall fruit?
10   Sure there was wine
    Before my sighs did drie it: there was corn

---

1   *A broken ... tears* See Psalms 51.17: "The sacrifices of God are a broken spirit: a broken and a contrite heart, O God, thou wilt not despise."
2   *No ... same* See Exodus 20.25: "And if thou wilt make me an altar of stone, thou shalt not build it of hewn stone: for if thou lift up thy tool upon it, thou hast polluted it."
3   *That ... cease* In Luke 19.40, Jesus says of his disciples, "if these should hold their peace, the stones would immediately cry out."
4   *in suit* Petitioning for favor.

Before my tears did drown it.
Is the yeare onely lost to me?
Have I no bayes to crown it?
No flowers, no garlands gay? all blasted? 15
All wasted?
Not so, my heart: but there is fruit,
And thou hast hands.
Recover all thy sigh-blown age
On double pleasures: leave thy cold dispute 20
Of what is fit, and not. Forsake thy cage,
Thy rope of sands,
Which pettie thoughts have made, and made to thee
Good cable, to enforce and draw,
And be thy law, 25
While thou didst wink[1] and wouldst not see.
Away; take heed:
I will abroad.
Call in thy deaths head[2] there: tie up thy fears.
He that forbears 30
To suit and serve his need,
Deserves his load.
But as I rav'd and grew more fierce and wilde
At every word,
Me thoughts I heard one calling, *Child*: 35
And I reply'd, *My Lord*.

—1633

---

1   *wink* Here, close both eyes.
2   *deaths head* A skull, an emblem of mortality seen by the penitent as a reminder of immin-
    ent death.

Easter Wings

Lord, who createdst man in wealth and store,
Though foolishly he lost the same,
Decaying more and more,
Till he became
Most poor:
  5
With thee
O let me rise
As larks, harmoniously,
And sing this day thy victories:
Then shall the fall further the flight in me.
  10

My tender age in sorrow did begin:
And still with sicknesses and shame
Thou didst so punish sin,
That I became
Most thin.
  15
With thee
Let me combine,
And feel this day thy victory:
For, if I imp¹ my wing on thine,
Affliction shall advance the flight in me.
  20

—1633

1   *imp* Graft feathers from one falcon onto the wing of another, a technique used in falconry to mend damaged wings and improve flight.

John Milton
1608–1674

Missionary poet, Puritan sage, and radical champion of religious, domestic, and civil liberties, John Milton is among the most influential figures in English literature, a writer who, as the critic Matthew Arnold wrote, was "of the highest rank in the great style." In *Paradise Lost* (1667), his culminating achievement, Milton at once works within and transforms the epic tradition of Homer, Virgil, and Dante, casting off "the troublesome and modern bondage of rhyming" for majestic blank verse (unrhymed lines of iambic pentameter).

Milton was a Puritan, a Protestant who wanted to "purify" and simplify English religion, and, like other Puritans during the English Civil Wars (1642–51), he supported rebellion against the king—a support he expressed in an array of tracts and polemics. However, his religious opinions diverged from Puritanism to become increasingly heretical in his later years. Denounced for his pamphlets advocating divorce, which were prompted by his troubled marriage, Milton wrote the *Areopagitica* (1644), one of history's most rousing defenses of a free press. He later reconciled with his wife only to lose her in childbirth, the first in a series of personal crises that saw the death of his son, his second wife, and their infant daughter, as well as the complete loss of his sight. Despite these blows, Milton continued late into his life to produce poetry of vast ambition.

Note to readers: Milton's poem "Lycidas" appears on the anthology's companion website. The URL and passcode appear in the Table of Contents.

On Shakespeare

What needs my Shakespeare for his honoured bones
The labour of an age in pilèd stones,
Or that his hallowed relics should be hid
Under a star-ypointing pyramid?
Dear son of memory,[1] great heir of Fame,   5
What need'st thou such weak witness of thy name?
Thou in our wonder and astonishment
Hast built thyself a livelong monument.
For whilst to th'shame of slow-endeavouring art,
Thy easy numbers flow, and that each heart   10

---

1   *memory* Mnemosyne, mother of the Muses.

Hath from the leaves of thy unvalued° Book   *invaluable*
Those Delphic[1] lines with deep impression took,
Then thou our fancy of itself bereaving,
Dost make us marble with too much conceiving;
15   And so sepùlchered in such pomp dost lie,
That kings for such a tomb would wish to die.

—1632

How Soon Hath Time

How soon hath Time, the subtle thief of youth,
      Stol'n on his wing my three and twentieth year!
      My hasting days fly on with full career,
      But my late spring no bud or blossom show'th.
5   Perhaps my semblance might deceive the truth,
      That I to manhood am arriv'd so near,
      And inward ripeness doth much less appear,
      That some more timely-happy spirits endu'th.
Yet be it less or more, or soon or slow,
10   It shall be still in strictest measure ev'n
      To that same lot, however mean or high,
Toward which Time leads me, and the will of Heav'n;
      All is, if I have grace to use it so,
      As ever in my great task-Master's eye.

—1645

[When I consider how my light is spent][2]

When I consider how my light is spent,
      Ere half my days, in this dark world and wide,
      And that one talent[3] which is death to hide,
      Lodged with me useless, though my soul more bent
5   To serve therewith my maker, and present

---

1   *Delphic* Apollo, god of poetry, had his temple at Delphi.
2   *[When ... spent]* Milton became blind in 1651.
3   *talent* Reference to the biblical parable of the talents; see Matthew 25.14–30. In this parable, a master gives varying amounts of money to three servants: five talents, two talents, and one talent, respectively. The servants that received larger sums invest the money, double it, and are celebrated, while the servant with one talent buries it for safekeeping and is punished for his failure to collect interest.

My true account, lest he returning chide,
Doth God exact day-labour, light denied,
I fondly° ask; but patience to prevent   *foolishly*
That murmur, soon replies, God doth not need
   Either man's work or his own gifts; who best   10
   Bear his mild yoke, they serve him best, his state
Is kingly. Thousands at his bidding speed
   And post° o'er land and ocean without rest: *ride*
   They also serve who only stand and wait.

      —1673 (written c. 1652–55)

Anne Bradstreet
1612–1672

A member of an affluent and well-connected English family, Anne Bradstreet was broadly educated at home in languages, literature, philosophy, the sciences, and history. At 18, she left England with her husband and parents aboard the *Arbella*, a ship headed for New England. The Massachusetts Bay Colony's governor, John Winthrop, famously called this Puritan settlement "a city on a hill," a place that he hoped would model "Christian Charity" for the rest of the world. The intensely focused Puritan worldview and the challenging physical conditions of daily life in this "wilderness"—a frequent term these English people used for the lands on which they settled, lands already populated by indigenous peoples—shaped Bradstreet's young adulthood. Twenty years later, her poetry collection *The Tenth Muse Lately Sprung Up in America* (1650) was published in London by her brother-in-law, apparently without her knowledge. She was the first published poet writing in the new English colonies.

Certainly Bradstreet found herself very far removed from the material comforts of her old life. Initially, she wrote, her "heart rose up" in protest at the "new world and new manners" that she found there. However, she continued to write under the difficult conditions of colonial life, while also raising eight children in the country so different from her birthplace. Although she composed poems on a broad and impressive range of historical and intellectual topics, she is best known for her lyrics (a term that often designates short poems expressing an individual speaker's feelings or private thoughts) that explore her familial devotion; her roles as a woman and a female poet; her relationship with nature; and her strong Puritan faith—as well as her doubt.

The Author to Her Book[1]

Thou ill-formed offspring of my feeble brain,
Who after birth didst by my side remain,
Till snatched from thence by friends, less wise than true
Who thee abroad, exposed to public view,
5 Made thee in rags, halting to th' press to trudge,

---

1   *The Author to Her Book* This poem appeared in the second edition of her poems (1678), published after her death. Scholars believe that it recounts her reaction to discovering that her brother-in-law had published *The Tenth Muse* in 1650 without her knowledge. It was common for poets at this time, and for women in particular, to disclaim any ambition to publish so as not to appear vain; nevertheless, there is no evidence that Bradstreet knew that her brother-in-law was seeking publication for her book.

Where errors were not lessened (all may judge).
At thy return my blushing was not small,
My rambling brat (in print) should mother call,
I cast thee by as one unfit for light,
Thy visage° was so irksome in my sight;   *face* 10
Yet being mine own, at length affection would
Thy blemishes amend, if so I could:
I washed thy face, but more defects I saw,
And rubbing off a spot still made a flaw.
I stretched thy joints to make thee even feet,   15
Yet still thou run'st more hobbling than is meet;°   *appropriate*
In better dress to trim thee was my mind,
But nought save homespun cloth i' th' house I find.
In this array 'mongst vulgars may'st thou roam.
In critic's hands beware thou dost not come,   20
And take thy way where yet thou art not known;
If for thy father asked, say thou hadst none;
And for thy mother, she alas is poor,
Which caused her thus to send thee out of door.

—1678

Before the Birth of One of Her Children[1]

All things within this fading world hath end,
Adversity doth still our joys attend;
No ties so strong, no friends so dear and sweet,
But with death's parting blow is sure to meet.
The sentence past is most irrevocable,   5
A common thing, yet oh, inevitable.
How soon, my Dear, death may my steps attend,
How soon't may be thy lot to lose thy friend,
We both are ignorant, yet love bids me
These farewell lines to recommend to thee,   10
That when that knot's untied that made us one,
I may seem thine, who in effect am none.
And if I see not half my days that's due,
What nature would, God grant to yours and you;
The many faults that well you know I have   15

---

1   *Before the Birth ... Children* It was routine for women of Bradstreet's time to die in child-
     birth. Bradstreet here confronts that prospect.

Let be interred in my oblivious grave;
If any worth or virtue were in me,
Let that live freshly in thy memory
And when thou feel'st no grief, as I no harms,
20 Yet love thy dead, who long lay in thine arms.
And when thy loss shall be repaid with gains
Look to my little babes, my dear remains.
And if thou love thyself, or loved'st me,
These O protect from step-dame's injury.
25 And if chance to thine eyes shall bring this verse,
With some sad sighs honour my absent hearse;
And kiss this paper for thy love's dear sake,
Who with salt tears this last farewell did take.

—1678

Here Follows Some Verses upon the Burning of Our House July 10th, 1666

Copied Out of a Loose Paper.

In silent night when rest I took
For sorrow near I did not look
I wakened was with thund'ring noise
And piteous shrieks of dreadful voice.
5 That fearful sound of "Fire!" and "Fire!"
Let no man know is my desire.[1]
I, starting up, the light did spy,
And to my God my heart did cry
To straighten me in my distress
10 And not to leave me succorless.[2]
Then, coming out, beheld a space[3]
The flame consume my dwelling place.
And when I could no longer look,
I blest His name that gave and took,[4]
15 That laid my goods now in the dust.
Yea, so it was, and so 'twas just.

---

1   *That fearful ... desire* I.e., My desire is that no man hear the sound of someone shouting "Fire!"
2   *succorless* Without assistance.
3   *beheld a space* I.e., watched a while.
4   *His ... took* See Job 1.21 in the Bible's Old Testament.

It was His own, it was not mine,
Far be it that I should repine;°   *fret*
He might of all justly bereft
But yet sufficient for us left.   20
When by the ruins oft I past
My sorrowing eyes aside did cast,
And here and there the places spy
Where oft I sat and long did lie:
Here stood that trunk, and there that chest,   25
There lay that store I counted best.
My pleasant things in ashes lie,
And them behold no more shall I.
Under thy roof no guest shall sit,
Nor at thy table eat a bit.   30
No pleasant talk shall e'er be told,
Nor things recounted done of old.
No candle e'er shall shine in thee,
Nor bridegroom's voice e'er heard shall be.
In silence ever shalt thou lie,   35
Adieu, Adieu, all's vanity.
Then straight I 'gin my heart to chide,
And did thy wealth on earth abide?
Didst fix thy hope on mould'ring dust?
The arm of flesh didst make thy trust?   40
Raise up thy thoughts above the sky
That dunghill mists away may fly.
Thou hast a house on high[1] erect,
Framed by that mighty Architect,
With glory richly furnished,   45
Stands permanent though this be fled.
It's purchased and paid for too
By Him who hath enough to do.
A price so vast as is unknown,
Yet by His gift is made thine own;   50
There's wealth enough, I need no more,
Farewell, my pelf,[2] farewell my store.
The world no longer let me love,
My hope and treasure lies above.

—1867 (written 1666)

1   *Thou ... high* See John 14.2 in the Bible's New Testament.
2   *pelf* Ill-gotten wealth.

Andrew Marvell
1621–1678

Andrew Marvell's poems are complex. Full of paradox and irony, they frequently employ naive or ambivalent personae who present debates or balance competing claims. Marvell was known primarily as a politician and satirist during his lifetime, and his reputation as one of the best lyric poets of his era was not fully established until the twentieth century.

The son of a clergyman, Marvell grew up in Hull in northeast England. At age 12 he was admitted to Cambridge, where he studied for seven years and where he published his first poems, written in Latin and Greek. Instead of completing his degree, Marvell left England in 1642 for four years of travel in continental Europe, perhaps to wait out the period of the English Civil Wars. In 1650, he began working as a tutor to the 12-year-old daughter of Thomas, Lord Fairfax, the recently retired commander-in-chief of Cromwell's army. It was likely during his two years on the Fairfax estate that Marvell composed many of his most famous works, including the sensuous and witty "To His Coy Mistress."

The Garden

1

How vainly men themselves amaze
To win the palm, the oak, or bays,[1]
And their uncessant labours see
Crowned from some single herb or tree,
5 Whose short and narrow vergèd shade
Does prudently their toils upbraid,
While all flow'rs and all trees do close
To weave the garlands of repose.

2

Fair Quiet, have I found thee here,
10 And Innocence, thy sister dear!
Mistaken long, I sought you then
In busy companies of men.

---

1   *the palm, the oak, or bays* Wreaths or garlands; the traditional rewards signifying military (palm leaves), civic or political (oak leaves), or poetic (bay laurel leaves) achievement.

Your sacred plants, if here below,
Only among the plants will grow.
Society is all but rude,°   *ignorant*   15
To this delicious solitude.

3

No white nor red[1] was ever seen
So am'rous as this lovely green.
Fond lovers, cruel as their flame,
Cut in these trees their mistress' name.   20
Little, alas, they know, or heed,
How far these beauties hers exceed!
Fair trees! wheres'e'er your barks I wound,
No name shall but your own be found.

4

When we have run our passions' heat,   25
Love hither makes his best retreat.
The gods, that mortal beauty chase,
Still in a tree did end their race.
Apollo hunted Daphne so,
Only that she might laurel grow.   30
And Pan did after Syrinx speed,
Not as a nymph, but for a reed.[2]

5

What wondrous life is this I lead!
Ripe apples drop about my head;
The luscious clusters of the vine   35
Upon my mouth do crush their wine;
The nectarine, and curious peach,
Into my hands themselves do reach;
Stumbling on melons, as I pass,
Ensnared with flow'rs, I fall on grass.   40

---

1   *white nor red* Colors traditionally associated with female beauty.
2   *Apollo ... reed* Reference to two classical myths associated with erotic pursuit and trans-
     formation. While being chased by Apollo, the god of poetry, Daphne was transformed
     into the laurel tree that became Apollo's sacred emblem. Syrinx, chased by Pan, god of
     flocks and shepherds, was transformed into a reed, the basis of the pan-pipe, emblem
     of pastoral poetry.

6

Meanwhile the mind, from pleasures less,
Withdraws into its happiness:
The mind, that ocean where each kind
Does straight its own resemblance find;[1]
45 Yet it creates, transcending these,
Far other worlds, and other seas,
Annihilating all that's made
To a green thought in a green shade.

7

Here at the fountain's sliding foot,
50 Or at some fruit-tree's mossy root,
Casting the body's vest aside,
My soul into the boughs does glide:
There like a bird it sits, and sings,
Then whets,° and combs its silver wings;   *preens*
55 And, till prepared for longer flight,
Waves in its plumes the various light.

8

Such was that happy garden-state,
While man there walked without a mate:
After a place so pure, and sweet,
60 What other help could yet be meet?[2]
But 'twas beyond a mortal's share
To wander solitary there:
Two Paradises 'twere in one
To live in Paradise alone.

9

65 How well the skilful gardener drew
Of flowers and herbs this dial[3] new,
Where from above the milder sun
Does through a fragrant zodiac run;

---

1   *that ocean ... own resemblance find* Alluding to the Renaissance belief that the ocean
     contains a counterpart for every plant and animal on land.
2   *help ... meet* See Genesis 2.18 in the Bible's Old Testament: "And the Lord God said, It
     is not good that the man should be alone; I will make him an help meet for him."
3   *dial* Floral sundial.

And, as it works, the industrious bee
Computes its time as well as we. 70
How could such sweet and wholesome hours
Be reckoned but with herbs and flowers!
            —1681 (probably written in the early 1650s)

To His Coy Mistress

Had we but world enough, and time,
This coyness Lady were no crime.
We would sit down, and think which way
To walk, and pass our long love's day.
Thou by the Indian Ganges' side 5
Should'st rubies find: I by the tide
Of Humber[1] would complain. I would
Love you ten years before the Flood:
And you should, if you please, refuse
Till the conversion of the Jews.[2] 10
My vegetable love should grow[3]
Vaster than empires, and more slow.
An hundred years should go to praise
Thine eyes, and on thy forehead gaze.
Two hundred to adore each breast: 15
But thirty thousand to the rest.
An age at least to every part,
And the last age should show your heart.
For Lady you deserve this state;
Nor would I love at lower rate. 20
But at my back I always hear,
Time's wingèd chariot hurrying near:
And yonder all before us lie
Deserts of vast eternity.
Thy beauty shall no more be found; 25
Nor, in thy marble vault, shall sound

---

1   *Humber* River in northern England; it flows alongside Hull, Marvell's home town.
2   *conversion of the Jews* Event supposed to usher in the final millennium leading to the end of time.
3   *vegetable love should grow* His love (or its physical manifestation) would grow slowly and steadily: Aristotle (384–322 BCE) defined the vegetative part of the soul as that characterized only by growth.

My echoing song; then worms shall try
That long preserved virginity:
And your quaint honour turn to dust;
30 And into ashes all my lust.
The grave's a fine and private place,
But none I think do there embrace.
Now therefore, while the youthful glew
Sits on thy skin like morning dew,[1]
35 And while thy willing soul transpires
At every pore with instant fires,
Now let us sport us while we may;
And now, like am'rous birds of prey,
Rather at once our time devour,
40 Than languish in his slow-chapt[2] pow'r.
Let us roll all our strength, and all
Our sweetness, up into one ball:
And tear our pleasures with rough strife,
Thorough° the iron gates[3] of life.   *Through*
45 Thus, though we cannot make our sun
Stand still,[4] yet we will make him run.

—1681

1   *youthful glew ... morning dew* This wording appears in Marvell's original manuscript, but there are many early variants on the final words in each line of this couplet, most made by printers. "Glew" may mean "sweat," or be a variant spelling of "glow."
2   *slow-chapt* Slowly devouring; "chaps" are jaws.
3   *gates* "Grates" in the 1681 printed edition with manuscript corrections, but many editors see "gates of life" as a typically Marvellian inversion of the biblical "gates of death" (see Psalm 9.13).
4   *sun / Stand still* Refers both to the love poetry convention in which lovers ask for time to stop when they are together, and to Joshua 10.12–14, in which Joshua made the sun and moon stand still while his army slaughtered the Amorites.

Thomas Gray

1716–1771

A scholar and a recluse who produced only a handful of poems, Thomas Gray nevertheless occupies a pivotal position in the history of English literature. His reputation is secured by his "Elegy Written in a Country Churchyard" (1751), which brought him immediate (and unwelcomed) fame. Gray had published only a few poems—all anonymously—before the "Elegy." The poem, which draws on traditions that include landscape poetry, the funeral elegy, and graveyard poetry, received immediate and widespread praise from both critics and readers. It went through 12 editions by 1763, appeared in several periodicals, was imitated, parodied, and translated into numerous languages, and became arguably the most quoted poem in English.

After the success of the "Elegy" six of Gray's poems were published in an illustrated collection (1753), and he turned to writing more elaborate poetry. In 1757, he was offered the Poet Laureateship, which he declined, and he published two odes, "The Progress of Poesy" and "The Bard"—complex, allusive poems that puzzled many readers. In later years he traveled, studied more and wrote less, and, in 1768, accepted a professorship of modern history at Cambridge, but never delivered a lecture. In temperament, he described himself as melancholic and others described him as socially withdrawn, but his letters reveal a lively wit and superior intellect.

Elegy Written in a Country Churchyard

The curfew tolls the knell of parting day,
The lowing herd wind slowly o'er the lea,[1]
The plowman homeward plods his weary way,
And leaves the world to darkness and to me.

Now fades the glimm'ring landscape on the sight,   5
And all the air a solemn stillness holds,
Save where the beetle wheels his droning flight,
And drowsy tinklings lull the distant folds;

Save that from yonder ivy-mantled tow'r
The moping owl does to the moon complain   10
Of such as, wand'ring near her secret bow'r,
Molest her ancient solitary reign.

---

1   *lea* Meadow or area of grassland.

Beneath those rugged elms, that yew-tree's shade,
Where heaves the turf in many a mould'ring heap,
15 Each in his narrow cell for ever laid,
The rude° forefathers of the hamlet sleep.   *unlearned*

The breezy call of incense-breathing morn,
The swallow twitt'ring from the straw-built shed,
The cock's shrill clarion or the echoing horn,
20 No more shall rouse them from their lowly bed.

For them no more the blazing hearth shall burn,
Or busy housewife ply her evening care:
No children run to lisp their sire's return,
Or climb his knees the envied kiss to share.

25 Oft did the harvest to their sickle yield,
Their furrow oft the stubborn glebe° has broke;   *soil*
How jocund° did they drive their team afield!   *merrily*
How bowed the woods beneath their sturdy stroke!

Let not Ambition mock their useful toil,
30 Their homely joys, and destiny obscure;
Nor Grandeur hear, with a disdainful smile,
The short and simple annals of the poor.

The boast of heraldry, the pomp of pow'r,
And all that beauty, all that wealth e'er gave,
35 Awaits alike th' inevitable hour.
The paths of glory lead but to the grave.

Nor you, ye Proud, impute to these the fault,
If Mem'ry o'er their tomb no trophies raise,
Where through the long-drawn aisle and fretted[1] vault
40 The pealing anthem swells the note of praise.

Can storied urn or animated bust
Back to its mansion call the fleeting breath?
Can Honour's voice provoke the silent dust,
Or Flatt'ry soothe the dull cold ear of Death?

---

1   *fretted* Carved with decorative patterns.

Perhaps in this neglected spot is laid 45
Some heart once pregnant with celestial fire;
Hands that the rod of empire might have swayed,
Or waked to ecstasy the living lyre.

But Knowledge to their eyes her ample page
Rich with the spoils of time did ne'er unroll; 50
Chill Penury repressed their noble rage,[1]
And froze the genial current of the soul.

Full many a gem of purest ray serene
The dark unfathomed caves of ocean bear:
Full many a flow'r is born to blush unseen 55
And waste its sweetness on the desert air.

Some village-Hampden[2] that with dauntless breast
The little tyrant of his fields withstood;
Some mute inglorious Milton[3] here may rest,
Some Cromwell[4] guiltless of his country's blood. 60

Th' applause of list'ning senates to command,
The threats of pain and ruin to despise,
To scatter plenty o'er a smiling land,
And read their hist'ry in a nation's eyes,

Their lot forbade: nor circumscribed alone 65
Their growing virtues, but their crimes confined;
Forbade to wade through slaughter to a throne,
And shut the gates of mercy on mankind,

The struggling pangs of conscious truth to hide,
To quench the blushes of ingenuous shame, 70
Or heap the shrine of Luxury and Pride
With incense kindled at the Muse's flame.

---

1   *rage* Ardor, enthusiasm.
2   *Hampden* John Hampden (1594–1643), member of Parliament who defied Charles I
     and died early in the ensuing civil war.
3   *Milton* John Milton (1608–74), English poet and dramatist.
4   *Cromwell* Oliver Cromwell, military and political leader during the English Civil Wars
     (1642–51) and Lord Protector of England (1653–58).

Far from the madding crowd's ignoble strife,
Their sober wishes never learned to stray;
75 Along the cool sequestered vale of life
They kept the noiseless tenor of their way.

Yet ev'n these bones from insult to protect
Some frail memorial still erected nigh,
With uncouth rhymes and shapeless sculpture decked,
80 Implores the passing tribute of a sigh.

Their name, their years, spelt by th' unlettered muse,
The place of fame and elegy supply:
And many a holy text around she strews,
That teach the rustic moralist to die.

85 For who to dumb Forgetfulness a prey,
This pleasing anxious being e'er resigned,
Left the warm precincts of the cheerful day,
Nor cast one longing ling'ring look behind?

On some fond breast the parting soul relies,
90 Some pious drops the closing eye requires;
Ev'n from the tomb the voice of nature cries,
Ev'n in our ashes live their wonted fires.

For thee who, mindful of th' unhonoured dead,
Dost in these lines their artless tale relate;
95 If chance, by lonely Contemplation led,
Some kindred spirit shall inquire thy fate,

Haply some hoary-headed swain[1] may say,
"Oft have we seen him at the peep of dawn
Brushing with hasty steps the dews away
100 To meet the sun upon the upland lawn.

"There at the foot of yonder nodding beech
That wreathes its old fantastic roots so high,
His listless length at noontide would he stretch,
And pore upon the brook that babbles by.

---

1   *hoary-headed swain* I.e., white-haired farmer.

"Hard by yon wood, now smiling as in scorn,   105
Mutt'ring his wayward fancies he would rove,
Now drooping, woeful wan, like one forlorn,
Or crazed with care, or crossed in hopeless love.

"One morn I missed him on the customed hill,
Along the heath and near his fav'rite tree;   110
Another came; nor yet beside the rill,
Nor up the lawn, nor at the wood was he;

"The next with dirges due in sad array
Slow through the church-way path we saw him borne.
Approach and read (for thou can'st read) the lay,   115
Graved on the stone beneath yon aged thorn."

THE EPITAPH

Here rests his head upon the lap of earth
A youth to fortune and to fame unknown.
Fair Science° frowned not on his humble birth,   *learning*
And Melancholy marked him for her own.   120

Large was his bounty and his soul sincere,
Heav'n did a recompense as largely send:
He gave to Mis'ry all he had, a tear,
He gained from Heav'n ('twas all he wished) a friend.

No farther seek his merits to disclose,   125
Or draw his frailties from their dread abode,
(There they alike in trembling hope repose)
The bosom of his Father and his God.

—1751

Charlotte Smith
1749–1806

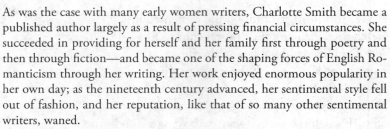 As was the case with many early women writers, Charlotte Smith became a published author largely as a result of pressing financial circumstances. She succeeded in providing for herself and her family first through poetry and then through fiction—and became one of the shaping forces of English Romanticism through her writing. Her work enjoyed enormous popularity in her own day; as the nineteenth century advanced, her sentimental style fell out of fashion, and her reputation, like that of so many other sentimental writers, waned.

Smith first turned to writing in 1784. Desperate for money while her husband was in debtor's prison (where she had spent seven months with him), she composed *Elegiac Sonnets*. The volume was extremely popular, and she later repeatedly rearranged and enlarged the collection. By 1851 her sonnets had gone through ten editions. Both Wordsworth and Coleridge learned from her, admiring her more in their youth than they were later willing to admit.

In 1788 her first novel, *Emmeline*, was published, and from then on she published almost a novel a year. Although she was known primarily as a novelist and, in the later part of her life, as a children's author, she continued to write poetry. In her last years she suffered from arthritis, which made writing difficult. *Beachy Head*, one of her finest poems, was published the year after her death. Smith's poems were crucial to a new surge of interest in the sonnet form in the Romantic era. Wordsworth wrote that she was "a lady to whom English verse is under greater obligations than are likely to be either acknowledged or remembered."

from *Elegiac Sonnets*

Sonnet LXX

[On being cautioned against walking on an headland overlooking the sea, because it was frequented by a lunatic]

Is there a solitary wretch who hies°   *hastens*
To the tall cliff, with starting pace or slow,
And, measuring, views with wild and hollow eyes
Its distance from the waves that chide below;
5   Who, as the sea-born gale with frequent sighs
Chills his cold bed upon the mountain turf,

With hoarse, half-utter'd lamentation, lies
Murmuring responses to the dashing surf?
In moody sadness, on the giddy° brink,   *dizzying*
I see him more with envy than with fear;   10
He has no *nice felicities* that shrink
From giant horrors; wildly wandering here,
He seems (uncursed with reason) not to know
The depth or the duration of his woe.

—1784

Phillis Wheatley

c. 1753–1784

Born in Africa, Phillis Wheatley was kidnapped and sold into slavery in 1761, when she was about seven years old. A Boston man, John Wheatley, purchased her as a companion for his wife and became the little girl's master. The Wheatleys allowed her to learn to read, to write, and to pursue studies in Latin and other subjects, very unusual conditions for a slave at this time. Brilliant and talented, she wrote an array of poems, many of which were Christian elegies, that were published in book form in London in 1773 as *Poems on Various Subjects, Religious and Moral*, when Wheatley was about 20 years old. Since no one at the time believed that a young African slave woman could write such accomplished verse, the book opened with a statement signed by a committee of distinguished men in Boston, including the Governor, who had "examined" Phillis to see if she was truly capable of writing these poems. Their signed statement assured readers that "Phillis, a young negro girl, who was but a few years since, brought an uncultivated barbarian from *Africa* ... has been examined by some of the best judges, and is thought qualified to write them." Her master freed her later that year. The rest of her short life was difficult, including a troubled marriage, poverty, and the deaths of two children. She was unable to publish her second volume of poems before she died at 31.

The conventional Christian attitudes in many of her poems were non-threatening to her white audience and thus gave her access to publication and recognition. The mere fact that she had written such poems astonished white society and challenged routine ideologies about African "barbarians." Wheatley's command of the poetic and rhetorical conventions of her time powerfully defied her era's assumption that the African race was innately inferior.

Long neglected by literary history, Wheatley is now widely recognized as an important historical figure: the first African-American to publish a book, she was also a woman, a slave, and a poet. The selections here demonstrate Wheatley's complex socio-political engagement with colonial discourses of slavery, race, and political freedom. Wheatley stands as the first figure in a long tradition of American poetry by people of African descent, poets who negotiated in diverse ways the challenges of speaking in a society that does not treat them as equal or even as human.

To the Right Honorable William, Earl of Dartmouth[1]

His Majesty's Principal Secretary of State for North America, etc.

Hail, happy day, when smiling like the morn,
Fair *Freedom* rose New England to adorn;
The northern clime beneath her genial ray,
Dartmouth congratulates thy blissful sway;
Elate with hope her race no longer mourns,   5
Each soul expands, each grateful bosom burns,
While in thine hand with pleasure we behold
The silken reins, and Freedom's charms unfold.
Long lost to realms beneath the northern skies
She shines supreme, while hated faction dies;   10
Soon as appeared the *Goddess* long desir'd,
Sick at the view, she languish'd and expir'd;
Thus from the splendor of the morning light
The owl in sadness seeks the caves of night.

No more *America*, in mournful strain   15
Of wrongs, and grievance unredress'd complain,
No longer shall thou dread the iron chain,
Which wanton *Tyranny* with lawless hand
Had made, and with it meant to enslave the land.
Should you, my lord, while you peruse my song,   20
Wonder from whence my love of *Freedom* sprung,
Whence flow these wishes for the common good,
By feeling hearts alone best understood,
I, young in life, by seeming cruel fate
Was snatch'd from Afric's fancy'd happy seat;   25
What pangs excruciatingly must molest,
What sorrows labour in my parent's breast?
Steel'd was that soul and by no misery mov'd
That from a father seized his babe belov'd;

---

1   *To the Right…Dartmouth* Wheatley composed this poem in 1772 at the suggestion of the
     Secretary of State's colonial representative, Thomas Wooldridge, who then sent the poem
     directly to Dartmouth, whose role as Secretary of State for North America gave him sig-
     nificant political influence. Scholar Vincent Carretta points out that Wheatley's hopes in
     the poem, that England will address America's "grievances," were soon to be disappointed.
     Wheatley complexly invokes familiar discourse of the colonies as enslaved by the "iron
     chain" of British tyranny.

30 Such, such my case. And can I then but pray
Others may never feel tyrannic sway?

For favors past, great Sir, our thanks are due,
And thee we ask thy favors to renew,
Since in thy pow'r, as in thy will before,
35 To sooth the griefs, which thou didst once deplore.
May heav'nly grace the sacred sanction give
To all thy works, and thou forever live
Not only on the wings of fleeting *Fame*,
Though praise immortal crowns the patriot's name,
40 But to conduct to heav'n's refulgent fane°   *temple*
May fiery coursers sweep th' etherial plain,
And bear thee upwards to the blest abode,
Where, like the prophet, thou shalt find thy God.

—1772

On Being Brought from Africa to America[1]

'Twas mercy brought me from my *Pagan* land,
Taught my benighted soul to understand
That there's a God, that there's a *Saviour* too:
Once I redemption neither sought nor knew.
5 Some view our sable race with scornful eye—
"Their colour is a diabolic dye."
Remember, *Christians*,[2] Negroes, black as *Cain*,[3]
May be refined, and join th' angelic train.

—1773

---

1   *On Being Brought ... America* Scholar Henry Louis Gates, Jr. calls this "the most reviled poem in African-American literature" for its apparent gratitude for the slave trade. Gates and Carretta remind us that Wheatley's very complex and vulnerable position as a poet requires that we scrutinize the rhetorical occasion she faced in writing for an audience that saw her as an "uncultivated barbarian" who had to prove both her intelligence and her fundamental humanity.

2   *Remember, Christians* Carretta points out that Wheatley presents fellow Christians with a challenge and a choice about how they view Africans. Christianity was the dominant religion in England and in the American colonies at this time and held tremendous social and political power.

3   *Cain* In Genesis 4.1–15, the son of Adam and Eve, who murdered his brother Abel and was cursed and marked by God as punishment. Christians at this time sometimes construed this "mark" as the racial origin of non-Caucasians. The American system of enslaving people of African descent relied heavily on biblical justifications.

William Blake
1757–1827

"I labour upwards into futurity," wrote William Blake on the back of one of the "tablets" of his visionary art. Blake's genius was largely unrecognized during his own lifetime, but the mysterious and powerful poetry that he crafted—perhaps most memorably in *Songs of Innocence and Experience* (1789, 1794)—would eventually be recognized as having revolutionary significance.

As a child living above his parents' hosiery shop in London, Blake once received a thrashing for declaring he had seen the face of God. Apprenticed at 14 to a highly respected engraver, he spent seven years learning the trade that would earn him his keep. As an adult, Blake claimed to communicate daily with the spirit of his brother Robert, who had died of tuberculosis; the unique style of "illuminated printing" that Blake later devised came to him in a visitation from Robert. Etching words backwards into copper plates so that they would reverse to normal upon printing, Blake in 1788 created his first illuminated texts. Over the next 20 years he would produce an extraordinary series of works in which he used both words and images to express his artistic vision. The Bible was a tremendous imaginative reserve upon which Blake drew all of his life, and one vision to which he often returns is that of an earthly Eden triumphing over forces of repression. He also had associations with decidedly non-mystical movements calling for political reforms, although he never fully participated in any organization, religious or political.

Against the grain of the times—he lived during the Industrial Revolution—Blake continued producing labor-intensive, elaborately illustrated books, none of which was commercially successful. Only 20 copies of *Songs of Experience* had been sold at the time of his death.

from *Songs of Innocence*

The Lamb

Little lamb, who made thee?
   Dost thou know who made thee,
Gave thee life & bid thee feed
By the stream & o'er the mead—
Gave thee clothing of delight,
Softest clothing, woolly bright,
Gave thee such a tender voice,
Making all the vales rejoice?

5

Little lamb, who made thee,
10   Dost thou know who made thee?

Little lamb, I'll tell thee,
Little lamb, I'll tell thee!
He is called by thy name,
For he calls himself a Lamb;
15   He is meek & he is mild,[1]
He became a little child:
I a child, & thou a lamb,
We are called by his name.
Little lamb, God bless thee,
20   Little lamb, God bless thee!

The Chimney Sweeper[2]

When my mother died I was very young,
And my father sold me while yet my tongue
Could scarcely cry 'weep! 'weep! 'weep! 'weep![3]
So your chimneys I sweep, & in soot I sleep.[4]

5   There's little Tom Dacre, who cried when his head,
That curl'd like a lamb's back, was shav'd; so I said,
"Hush Tom! never mind it, for when your head's bare,
You know that the soot cannot spoil your white hair."

And so he was quiet, & that very night,
10   As Tom was a-sleeping he had such a sight!
That thousands of sweepers, Dick, Joe, Ned, & Jack,
Were all of them lock'd up in coffins of black;

And by came an Angel who had a bright key,
And he open'd the coffins & set them all free;
15   Then down a green plain leaping, laughing they run,
And wash in a river and shine in the Sun.

---

1   *He is ... is mild* See Charles Wesley's hymn "Gentle Jesus, Meek and Mild" (1742).
2   *The Chimney Sweeper* Children were often forced to climb up chimneys to clean them—a filthy, dangerous, and unhealthy job. A law ameliorating their working conditions was passed in 1788, but it was rarely enforced.
3   *'weep ... 'weep* The child is attempting to say "sweep," the chimney-sweeper's street cry. The act of 1788 should have prevented the apprenticing of children younger than eight.
4   *in soot I sleep* Sweeps used their bags of soot as blankets.

Then naked & white, all their bags left behind,
They rise upon clouds and sport in the wind.
And the Angel told Tom, if he'd be a good boy,
He'd have God for his father & never want joy.   20

And so Tom awoke; and we rose in the dark,
And got with our bags & our brushes to work.
Tho' the morning was cold, Tom was happy & warm;
So if all do their duty, they need not fear harm.

                                                    —1789

from *Songs of Experience*

The Chimney Sweeper

A little black thing among the snow
Crying 'weep! 'weep! in notes of woe!
"Where are thy father & mother, say?"
"They are both gone up to the church to pray.

"Because I was happy upon the heath   5
And smil'd among the winter's snow,
They clothed me in the clothes of death
And taught me to sing the notes of woe.

"And because I am happy & dance & sing,
They think they have done me no injury,   10
And are gone to praise God & his Priest & King,
Who make up a heaven of our misery."

The Sick Rose

O Rose, thou art sick:
The invisible worm,
That flies in the night,
In the howling storm,

Has found out thy bed   5
Of crimson joy;
And his dark secret love
Does thy life destroy.

The Tyger

Tyger! Tyger! burning bright
In the forests of the night,
What immortal hand or eye
Could frame thy fearful symmetry?

5 In what distant deeps or skies
Burnt the fire of thine eyes?
On what wings dare he aspire?[1]
What the hand dare seize the fire?[2]

And what shoulder, & what art,
10 Could twist the sinews of thy heart?
And when thy heart began to beat,
What dread hand? & what dread feet?

What the hammer? What the chain?
In what furnace was thy brain?
15 What the anvil? what dread grasp
Dare its deadly terrors clasp?

When the stars threw down their spears
And water'd heaven with their tears,
Did he smile his work to see?
20 Did he who made the Lamb make thee?

Tyger! Tyger! burning bright
In the forests of the night,
What immortal hand or eye
Dare frame thy fearful symmetry?

---

1   *wings ... aspire* In Greek mythology, Icarus flew using wings made of wax and feathers; these melted when he attempted to fly too close to the sun.
2   *hand ... fire* In Greek mythology, Prometheus stole fire from heaven to give to humans.

London

I wander thro' each charter'd[1] street
Near where the charter'd Thames does flow,
And mark in every face I meet
Marks of weakness, marks of woe.

In every cry of every Man,   5
In every Infant's cry of fear,
In every voice, in every ban,
The mind-forg'd manacles I hear.

How the Chimney-sweeper's cry
Every black'ning Church appalls,   10
And the hapless Soldier's sigh
Runs in blood down Palace walls.

But most thro' midnight streets I hear
How the youthful Harlot's curse[2]
Blasts the new-born Infant's tear,[3]   15
And blights with plagues the marriage hearse.

—1794

---

1   *charter'd* Licensed. Charters grant freedoms, often for a select minority (such as merchants).
2   *Harlot's curse* Referring to both the oaths she utters and the venereal diseases she spreads.
3   *Blasts ... tear* Reference to the blindness caused in infants if they contract certain venereal diseases (such as gonorrhea) from their mother.

William Wordsworth

1770–1850

Arguably the most important and influential poet of the Romantic era in British poetry, William Wordsworth is best known for his explorations of human subjectivity in relation to the natural world. *Lyrical Ballads* (1798), which Wordsworth co-authored with his friend Samuel Taylor Coleridge, is often considered the most important single volume of poetry of the period. Wordsworth's self-stated ambition to write about "incidents and situations from common life" in "language really used by men" was a shift from the impersonal, formulaic poetry of the eighteenth century. This deviation stirred up a great deal of criticism, but by the last decades of his life, Wordsworth's skill and mastery as a poet were widely acknowledged. He was awarded the title of Poet Laureate at the age of 73. In the year after his death, his long poem *The Prelude* was published; originally written in 1798–99, and expanded and revised over the next 40 years, it is often regarded as Wordsworth's crowning achievement. Recording what he called "the growth of [his] own mind," *The Prelude*'s concept of self-exploration would affect the course of English poetry thereafter.

Wordsworth was born in the English Lake District. His parents were both dead by the time he was 13, and he was sent by relatives to be educated at a boarding school, later completing his degree at Cambridge. He spent parts of his young adulthood walking throughout Europe, an experience that deepened his interest in politics as well as in nature; his time spent in Revolutionary France had an especially profound impact on his poetry. After these travels were concluded, Wordsworth would spend much of the rest of his life sharing a home with his "beloved sister" Dorothy, whom he described as one of "the two beings to whom my intellect is most indebted." (The other was Coleridge.)

Wordsworth's idea that poetry as an art form could turn away from the exalted subjects and highbrow speech in poetry of the past to an exploration of what he called "feelings" and "emotion" in "real language" would have profound influence on later poets and readers. In many ways, when we read poems in the voice of an "I" speaker who expresses personal emotions, we feel Wordsworth's legacy.

Lines Written a Few Miles above Tintern Abbey

On Revisiting the Banks of the Wye during a Tour, July 13, 1798[1]

Five years have passed; five summers, with the length
Of five long winters! and again I hear
These waters, rolling from their mountain-springs
With a sweet inland murmur.[2] Once again
Do I behold these steep and lofty cliffs,   5
Which on a wild secluded scene impress
Thoughts of more deep seclusion; and connect
The landscape with the quiet of the sky.
The day is come when I again repose
Here, under this dark sycamore, and view   10
These plots of cottage-ground, these orchard-tufts,
Which, at this season, with their unripe fruits,
Among the woods and copses lose themselves,
Nor, with their green and simple hue, disturb
The wild green landscape. Once again I see   15
These hedge-rows, hardly hedge-rows, little lines
Of sportive wood run wild; these pastoral farms
Green to the very door; and wreaths of smoke
Sent up, in silence, from among the trees,
With some uncertain notice, as might seem,   20
Of vagrant dwellers in the houseless woods,
Or of some hermit's cave, where by his fire
The hermit sits alone.

     Though absent long,
These forms of beauty have not been to me,   25
As is a landscape to a blind man's eye:
But oft, in lonely rooms, and 'mid the din
Of towns and cities, I have owed to them,
In hours of weariness, sensations sweet,
Felt in the blood, and felt along the heart,   30

---

1 [Wordsworth's note] No poem of mine was composed under circumstances more
  pleasant for me to remember than this. I began it upon leaving Tintern, after crossing
  the Wye, and concluded it just as I was entering Bristol in the evening, after a ramble
  of 4 or 5 days, with my sister. Not a line of it was altered, and not any part of it was
  written down till I reached Bristol.
2 [Wordsworth's note] The river is not affected by the tides a few miles above Tintern.

And passing even into my purer mind
With tranquil restoration—feelings too
Of unremembered pleasure; such, perhaps,
As may have had no trivial influence
35   On that best portion of a good man's life;
His little, nameless, unremembered acts
Of kindness and of love. Nor less, I trust,
To them I may have owed another gift,
Of aspect more sublime; that blessed mood,
40   In which the burthen of the mystery,
In which the heavy and the weary weight
Of all this unintelligible world
Is lighten'd—that serene and blessed mood,
In which the affections gently lead us on,
45   Until, the breath of this corporeal frame,
And even the motion of our human blood
Almost suspended, we are laid asleep
In body, and become a living soul:
While with an eye made quiet by the power
50   Of harmony, and the deep power of joy,
We see into the life of things.

                        If this
Be but a vain belief, yet, oh! how oft,
In darkness, and amid the many shapes
55   Of joyless day-light; when the fretful stir
Unprofitable, and the fever of the world,
Have hung upon the beatings of my heart,
How oft, in spirit, have I turned to thee
O sylvan° Wye! Thou wanderer through the woods,   *wooded*
60   How often has my spirit turned to thee!

And now, with gleams of half-extinguish'd thought,
With many recognitions dim and faint,
And somewhat of a sad perplexity,
The picture of the mind revives again:
65   While here I stand, not only with the sense
Of present pleasure, but with pleasing thoughts
That in this moment there is life and food
For future years. And so I dare to hope
Though changed, no doubt, from what I was, when first

I came among these hills; when like a roe°   *deer*   70
I bounded o'er the mountains, by the sides
Of the deep rivers, and the lonely streams,
Wherever nature led; more like a man
Flying from something that he dreads, than one
Who sought the thing he loved. For nature then   75
(The coarser pleasures of my boyish days,
And their glad animal movements all gone by)
To me was all in all. I cannot paint
What then I was. The sounding cataract
Haunted me like a passion: the tall rock,   80
The mountain, and the deep and gloomy wood,
Their colours and their forms, were then to me
An appetite: a feeling and a love,
That had no need of a remoter charm,
By thought supplied, or any interest   85
Unborrowed from the eye. That time is past,
And all its aching joys are now no more,
And all its dizzy raptures. Not for this
Faint[1] I, nor mourn nor murmur: other gifts
Have followed, for such loss, I would believe,   90
Abundant recompense. For I have learned
To look on nature, not as in the hour
Of thoughtless youth, but hearing oftentimes
The still, sad music of humanity,
Not harsh nor grating, though of ample power   95
To chasten and subdue. And I have felt
A presence that disturbs me with the joy
Of elevated thoughts; a sense sublime
Of something far more deeply interfused,
Whose dwelling is the light of setting suns,   100
And the round ocean, and the living air,
And the blue sky, and in the mind of man,
A motion and a spirit, that impels
All thinking things, all objects of all thought,
And rolls through all things. Therefore am I still   105
A lover of the meadows and the woods,
And mountains; and of all that we behold
From this green earth; of all the mighty world

---

1   *Faint* Lose heart; grow weak.

Of eye and ear, both what they half create,
110 And what perceive; well pleased to recognize
In nature and the language of the sense,
The anchor of my purest thoughts, the nurse,
The guide, the guardian of my heart, and soul
Of all my moral being.

115   Nor, perchance,
If I were not thus taught, should I the more
Suffer my genial° spirits to decay: *creative*
For thou art with me, here, upon the banks
Of this fair river; thou, my dearest Friend,[1]
120 My dear, dear Friend, and in thy voice I catch
The language of my former heart, and read
My former pleasures in the shooting lights
Of thy wild eyes. Oh! yet a little while
May I behold in thee what I was once,
125 My dear, dear Sister! And this prayer I make,
Knowing that Nature never did betray
The heart that loved her; 'tis her privilege,
Through all the years of this our life, to lead
From joy to joy: for she can so inform
130 The mind that is within us, so impress
With quietness and beauty, and so feed
With lofty thoughts, that neither evil tongues,
Rash judgments, nor the sneers of selfish men,
Nor greetings where no kindness is, nor all
135 The dreary intercourse of daily life,
Shall e'er prevail against us, or disturb
Our cheerful faith that all which we behold
Is full of blessings. Therefore let the moon
Shine on thee in thy solitary walk;
140 And let the misty mountain winds be free
To blow against thee: and in after years,
When these wild ecstasies shall be matured
Into a sober pleasure, when thy mind
Shall be a mansion for all lovely forms,
145 Thy memory be as a dwelling-place
For all sweet sounds and harmonies; Oh! then,

---

1   *my dearest Friend* I.e., Dorothy Wordsworth, the poet's sister.

If solitude, or fear, or pain, or grief,
Should be thy portion, with what healing thoughts
Of tender joy wilt thou remember me,
And these my exhortations! Nor, perchance,   150
If I should be, where I no more can hear
Thy voice, nor catch from thy wild eyes these gleams
Of past existence, wilt thou then forget
That on the banks of this delightful stream
We stood together; and that I, so long   155
A worshipper of Nature, hither came,
Unwearied in that service: rather say
With warmer love, oh! with far deeper zeal
Of holier love. Nor wilt thou then forget,
That after many wanderings, many years   160
Of absence, these steep woods and lofty cliffs,
And this green pastoral landscape, were to me
More dear, both for themselves, and for thy sake.

—1798

She dwelt among the untrodden ways

She dwelt among the untrodden ways
    Beside the springs of Dove,[1]
A Maid whom there were none to praise
    And very few to love:

A violet by a mossy stone
    Half hidden from the eye!   5
—Fair as a star, when only one
    Is shining in the sky.

She lived unknown, and few could know
    When Lucy ceased to be;   10
But she is in her grave, and, oh,
    The difference to me!

—1800

---

1   *the springs of Dove* A name given to several rivers in England, one of which is in the Lake
District.

A slumber did my spirit seal

A slumber did my spirit seal;
    I had no human fears:
She seemed a thing that could not feel
    The touch of earthly years.

5 No motion has she now, no force;
    She neither hears nor sees;
Rolled round in earth's diurnal° course,   *daily*
    With rocks, and stones, and trees.

—1800

Strange fits of passion have I known

Strange fits of passion have I known:
And I will dare to tell,
But in the Lover's ear alone,
What once to me befell

5 When she I loved looked every day
Fresh as a rose in June,
I to her cottage bent my way,
Beneath an evening-moon.

Upon the moon I fixed my eye,
10 All over the wide lea;
With quickening pace my horse drew nigh
Those paths so dear to me.

And now we reached the orchard-plot;
And, as we climbed the hill,
15 The sinking moon to Lucy's cot°   *cottage*
Came near, and nearer still.

In one of those sweet dreams I slept,
Kind Nature's gentlest boon!
And all the while my eyes I kept
20 On the descending moon.

My horse moved on; hoof after hoof
He raised, and never stopped:

When down behind the cottage roof,
At once, the bright moon dropped.

What fond and wayward thoughts will slide   25
Into a Lover's head!
"O mercy!" to myself I cried,
"If Lucy should be dead!"

—1800

Three years she grew in sun and shower

Three years she grew in sun and shower,
Then Nature said, "A lovelier flower
On earth was never sown;
This Child I to myself will take;
She shall be mine, and I will make   5
A Lady of my own.

"Myself will to my darling be
Both law and impulse: and with me
The Girl, in rock and plain,
In earth and heaven, in glade and bower,   10
Shall feel an overseeing power
To kindle or restrain.

"She shall be sportive as the fawn
That wild with glee across the lawn
Or up the mountain springs;   15
And hers shall be the breathing balm,
And hers the silence and the calm
Of mute insensate things.

"The floating-clouds their state shall lend
To her; for her the willow bend;   20
Nor shall she fail to see
Even in the motions of the Storm
Grace that shall mould the Maiden's form
By silent sympathy.

"The stars of midnight shall be dear   25
To her; and she shall lean her ear
In many a secret place

Where rivulets dance their wayward round,
And beauty born of murmuring sound
30 Shall pass into her face.

"And vital feelings of delight
Shall rear her form to stately height,
Her virgin bosom swell;
Such thoughts to Lucy I will give
35 While she and I together live
Here in this happy dell."

Thus Nature spake—The work was done—
How soon my Lucy's race was run!
She died, and left to me
40 This heath, this calm, and quiet scene;
The memory of what has been,
And never more will be.

—1800

I travelled among unknown men

I travelled among unknown men,
    In lands beyond the sea;
Nor, England! did I know till then
    What love I bore to thee.

5   'Tis past, that melancholy dream!
    Nor will I quit thy shore
A second time; for still I seem
    To love thee more and more.

Among thy mountains did I feel
10   The joy of my desire;
And she I cherished turned her wheel
    Beside an English fire.

Thy mornings showed, thy nights concealed,
    The bowers where Lucy played;
15 And thine too is the last green field
    That Lucy's eyes surveyed.

—1807

London, 1802

Milton! thou shouldst be living at this hour:
England hath need of thee: she is a fen
Of stagnant waters: altar, sword, and pen,
Fireside, the heroic wealth of hall and bower,
Have forfeited their ancient English dower   5
Of inward happiness. We are selfish men;
Oh! raise us up, return to us again;
And give us manners, virtue, freedom, power.
Thy soul was like a Star, and dwelt apart;
Thou hadst a voice whose sound was like the sea: 10
Pure as the naked heavens, majestic, free,
So didst thou travel on life's common way,
In cheerful godliness; and yet thy heart
The lowliest duties on herself did lay.

—1807

Nuns fret not at their convent's narrow room

Nuns fret not at their convent's narrow room;
And hermits are contented with their cells;
And students with their pensive citadels;
Maids at the wheel, the weaver at his loom,
Sit blithe and happy; bees that soar for bloom,   5
High as the highest Peak of Furness-fells,[1]
Will murmur by the hour in foxglove bells:
In truth the prison, into which we doom
Ourselves, no prison is: and hence for me,
In sundry moods, 'twas pastime to be bound   10
Within the Sonnet's scanty plot of ground;
Pleased if some Souls (for such there needs must be)
Who have felt the weight of too much liberty,
Should find brief solace there, as I have found.

—1807

---

1   *Furness-fells* Group of mountains in England's Lake District.

Dorothy Wordsworth
1771–1855

Dorothy Wordsworth never considered herself an author; she wrote journals of daily life, letters, and poems simply for the "pleasure" they gave her famous brother, the poet William Wordsworth. The siblings shared a love of walking in nature, often with their friend Samuel Taylor Coleridge. Living in England's Lake District with its majestic natural beauty was a source of emotional intensity and insight for Dorothy as well as for the two male poets.

The Wordsworths' mother died when Dorothy was six, and her father sent her to Yorkshire to live with relatives. Her childhood was spent happily among aunts and cousins, but at age fifteen she was sent to live with her stern grandparents; in the years she lived there she longed for the company of her four brothers. Her dream of living with William was realized when in 1795 he was bequeathed a legacy by a college friend, allowing the siblings to secure a home together in Dorset. They were never again parted until William's death 55 years later. Her writing was curtailed in 1829, when she suffered the first of a series of debilitating ailments. By June of 1835 she was an invalid from some kind of dementia said to be caused by arteriosclerosis. She remained so for the following two decades, but she was cared for lovingly by those whom she had once tended.

She died in 1855, outliving William by five years. Most of her poems, letters, and journals were published long after her death. Once studied mainly to provide context for the work of the Lake Poets, her works—like those of other women writers of this time period who were long neglected—are now valued in their own right as contributions to literature. For Virginia Woolf, an ardent admirer of Dorothy Wordsworth's work, the journals have in them "the suggestive power which is the gift of the poet rather than of the naturalist."

Thoughts on My Sick-Bed

And has the remnant of my life
Been pilfered of this sunny spring?
And have its own prelusive° sounds   *introductory*
Touched in my heart no echoing string?

5 Ah! say not so—the hidden life
Couchant° within this feeble frame   *lying*
Hath been enriched by kindred gifts,
That, undesired, unsought-for, came

With joyful heart in youthful days
When fresh each season in its round   10
I welcomed the earliest celandine°   *yellow flower*
Glittering upon the mossy ground;

With busy eyes I pierced the lane
In quest of known and *un*known things,
—The primrose a lamp on its fortress rock,   15
The silent butterfly spreading its wings,

The violet betrayed by its noiseless breath,
The daffodil dancing in the breeze,
The carolling thrush, on his naked perch,
Towering above the budding trees.   20

Our cottage-hearth no longer our home,
Companions of nature were we,
The stirring, the still, the loquacious, the mute—
To all we gave our sympathy.

Yet never in those careless days   25
When spring-time in rock, field, or bower
Was but a fountain of earthly hope
A promise of fruits and the *splendid* flower.

No! then I never felt a bliss
That might with *that* compare   30
Which, piercing to my couch of rest,
Came on the vernal° air.   *springtime*

When loving friends an offering brought,
The first flowers of the year,
Culled from the precincts of our home,   35
From nooks to memory dear.

With some sad thoughts the work was done,
Unprompted and unbidden,
But joy it brought to my *hidden* life,
To consciousness no longer hidden.   40

I felt a power unfelt before,
Controlling weakness, languor, pain;
It bore me to the terrace walk
I trod the hills again;—

45   No prisoner in this lonely room,
I *saw* the green banks of the Wye,
Recalling thy prophetic words,
Bard, brother, friend from infancy![1]

No need of motion, or of strength,
50   Or even the breathing air:
—I thought of nature's loveliest scenes;
And with memory I was there.

—1978 (written 1832)

---

1   *Recalling … infancy* See William Wordsworth's "Lines Written a Few Miles above Tintern
Abbey," p. 63.

Samuel Taylor Coleridge
1772–1834

Coleridge wrote in a 1796 letter, "I am, and ever have been, a great reader, and have read almost everything—a library-cormorant." His own work was similarly wide-ranging and prolific; Coleridge's collected writings comprise 50 volumes and reveal his interest in a myriad of subjects from history and politics to science and literary criticism. History remembers him for his pioneering contributions to English Romantic poetry, including his collaborations with his friend William Wordsworth. He and Wordsworth shared a profound interest in the relation between humans and the powers of nature. His two-volume *Biographia Literaria* (1817) presented a wide-ranging philosophical treatment of poetry as a distinct endeavor of the human mind and kind of human cognition. For Coleridge, the imagination was "the living Power and prime Agent of *all* human Perception."

The son of a school headmaster, Coleridge received a robust classical education and later briefly attended Cambridge, although he left without taking a degree. After several false starts—he joined the army, and upon his release concocted an ill-fated plan to move to America to found a communal society—he began to publish his writing. His second book of poetry was *Lyrical Ballads* (1798), a collaboration with Wordsworth that included two of his best-known poems, "The Rime of the Ancient Mariner" and "Kubla Khan."

Coleridge coined the term "conversation poem" for a type of poem that, like "The Eolian Harp" and "Frost at Midnight" (below), creates the effect of colloquial or conversational speech, as if one friend or family member is speaking in relaxed fashion while another listens. (Consider the different scenes in the two selections below.) Coleridge's innovations with poetic voice in this regard are important precursors to later experiments with voice by other poets, including the dramatic monologues of Robert Browning and the dramatic dialogues of Sarah Morgan Bryan Piatt.

The Eolian Harp[1]

Composed at Clevedon, Somersetshire

My pensive Sara![2] thy soft cheek reclined
Thus on mine arm, most soothing sweet it is
To sit beside our Cot,° our Cot o'ergrown   *cottage*
With white-flower'd Jasmin, and the broad-leav'd Myrtle,

---

1   *Eolian Harp* Musical instrument named after Aeolus, Greek god of the winds; the music
     of the harp is created by wind passing through it.
2   *Sara* Sara Fricker, whom Coleridge had recently married.

5 (Meet emblems they of Innocence and Love!)
And watch the clouds, that late were rich with light,
Slow saddening round, and mark the star of eve
Serenely brilliant (such should Wisdom be)
Shine opposite! How exquisite the scents
10 Snatch'd from yon bean-field! and the world *so* hush'd!
The stilly murmur of the distant Sea
Tells us of silence.

         And that simplest Lute,
How by the desultory breeze caress'd,
15 Like some coy maid half yielding to her lover,
It pours such sweet upbraiding, as must needs
Tempt to repeat the wrong! And now, its strings
Boldlier swept, the long sequacious° notes   *unvarying*
Over delicious surges sink and rise,
20 Such a soft floating witchery of sound
As twilight Elfins make, when they at eve
Voyage on gentle gales from Fairy-Land,
Where Melodies round honey-dropping flowers,
Footless and wild, like birds of Paradise,[1]
25 Nor pause, nor perch, hovering on untam'd wing!
O! the one Life within us and abroad,
Which meets all motion and becomes its soul,
A light in sound, a sound-like power in light,
Rhythm in all thought, and joyance every where—
30 Methinks, it should have been impossible
Not to love all things in a world so fill'd;
Where the breeze warbles, and the mute still air
Is Music slumbering on her instrument.

And thus, my Love! as on the midway slope
35 Of yonder hill I stretch my limbs at noon,
Whilst through my half-clos'd eye-lids I behold
The sunbeams dance, like diamonds, on the main,
And tranquil muse upon tranquillity;
Full many a thought uncall'd and undetain'd,
40 And many idle flitting phantasies,
Traverse my indolent and passive brain,

---

1   *birds of Paradise* New Guinean birds of brilliant plumage, thought by Europeans to have
no feet.

As wild and various, as the random gales
That swell and flutter on this subject Lute!
And what if all of animated nature
Be but organic Harps diversely fram'd,   45
That tremble into thought, as o'er them sweeps
Plastic and vast, one intellectual breeze,
At once the Soul of each, and God of all?
But thy more serious eye a mild reproof
Darts, O beloved Woman! nor such thoughts   50
Dim and unhallow'd dost thou not reject,
And biddest me walk humbly with my God.
Meek Daughter in the family of Christ!
Well hast thou said and holily disprais'd
These shapings of the unregenerate mind;   55
Bubbles that glitter as they rise and break
On vain Philosophy's aye-babbling spring.
For never guiltless may I speak of Him,
The Incomprehensible! save when with awe
I praise Him, and with Faith that inly *feels*;   60
Who with His saving mercies healed me,
A sinful and most miserable man,
Wilder'd and dark, and gave me to possess
Peace, and this Cot, and thee, heart-honour'd Maid!

—1795

Frost at Midnight

The Frost performs its secret ministry,
Unhelped by any wind. The owlet's cry
Came loud—and hark, again! loud as before.
The inmates of my cottage, all at rest,
Have left me to that solitude, which suits   5
Abstruser musings: save that at my side
My cradled infant slumbers peacefully.
'Tis calm indeed! so calm, that it disturbs
And vexes meditation with its strange
And extreme silentness. Sea, hill, and wood,   10
This populous village! Sea, and hill, and wood,
With all the numberless goings-on of life,
Inaudible as dreams! the thin blue flame
Lies on my low-burnt fire, and quivers not;

15 Only that film,[1] which fluttered on the grate,
Still flutters there, the sole unquiet thing.
Methinks, its motion in this hush of nature
Gives it dim sympathies with me who live,
Making it a companionable form,
20 Whose puny flaps and freaks the idling Spirit
By its own moods interprets, every where
Echo or mirror seeking of itself,
And makes a toy of Thought.

But O! how oft,
25 How oft, at school, with most believing mind,
Presageful, have I gazed upon the bars,
To watch that fluttering *stranger*! and as oft
With unclosed lids, already had I dreamt
Of my sweet birth-place, and the old church-tower,
30 Whose bells, the poor man's only music, rang
From morn to evening, all the hot Fair-day,
So sweetly, that they stirred and haunted me
With a wild pleasure, falling on mine ear
Most like articulate sounds of things to come!
35 So gazed I, till the soothing things, I dreamt,
Lulled me to sleep, and sleep prolonged my dreams!
And so I brooded all the following morn,
Awed by the stern preceptor's° face, mine eye   *teacher's*
Fixed with mock study on my swimming book:
40 Save if the door half opened, and I snatched
A hasty glance, and still my heart leaped up,
For still I hoped to see the *stranger's* face,
Townsman, or aunt, or sister more beloved,
My play-mate when we both were clothed alike!

45   Dear Babe, that sleepest cradled by my side,
Whose gentle breathings, heard in this deep calm,
Fill up the interspersed vacancies
And momentary pauses of the thought!
My babe so beautiful! it thrills my heart
50 With tender gladness, thus to look at thee,
And think that thou shalt learn far other lore,

---

1   [Coleridge's note] In all parts of the kingdom these films are called *strangers* and sup-
posed to portend the arrival of some absent friend.

And in far other scenes! For I was reared
In the great city, pent 'mid cloisters dim,
And saw nought lovely but the sky and stars.
But *thou*, my babe! shalt wander like a breeze   55
By lakes and sandy shores, beneath the crags
Of ancient mountain, and beneath the clouds,
Which image in their bulk both lakes and shores
And mountain crags: so shalt thou see and hear
The lovely shapes and sounds intelligible   60
Of that eternal language, which thy God
Utters, who from eternity doth teach
Himself in all, and all things in himself.
Great universal Teacher! he shall mould
Thy spirit, and by giving make it ask.   65

    Therefore all seasons shall be sweet to thee,
Whether the summer clothe the general earth
With greenness, or the redbreast sit and sing
Betwixt the tufts of snow on the bare branch
Of mossy apple-tree, while the nigh thatch   70
Smokes in the sun-thaw; whether the eave-drops fall
Heard only in the trances of the blast,
Or if the secret ministry of frost
Shall hang them up in silent icicles,
Quietly shining to the quiet Moon.   75

                    —1798

Kubla Khan

Or, A Vision in a Dream. A Fragment[1]

In Xanadu did Kubla Khan
A stately pleasure-dome decree:

---

1   [Coleridge's note] The following fragment is here published at the request of a poet
[Lord Byron] of great and deserved celebrity, and as far as the Author's own opinions
are concerned, rather as a psychological curiosity, than on the ground of any supposed
poetic merits.

    In the summer of the year 1797, the Author, then in ill health, had retired to a lone-
ly farmhouse between Porlock and Linton, on the Exmoor confines of Somerset and
Devonshire. In consequence of a slight indisposition [dysentery], an anodyne [opium]
had been prescribed, from the effects of which he fell asleep in his chair at the moment
that he was reading the following sentence, or words of the same substance, in *Purchas's*

Where Alph, the sacred river, ran
Through caverns measureless to man
5   Down to a sunless sea.
So twice five miles of fertile ground
With walls and towers were girdled round:
And there were gardens bright with sinuous rills,°   *brooks*
Where blossomed many an incense-bearing tree;
10 And here were forests ancient as the hills,
Enfolding sunny spots of greenery.

But oh! that deep romantic chasm which slanted
Down the green hill athwart a cedarn cover!

Pilgrimage: "Here the Khan Kubla commanded a palace to be built, and a stately garden thereunto. And thus ten miles of fertile ground were inclosed with a wall." The author continued for about three hours in a profound sleep, at least of the external senses, during which time he has the most vivid confidence, that he could not have composed less than from two to three hundred lines, if that indeed can be called composition in which all the images rose up before him as things, with a parallel production of the correspondent expressions, without any sensation or consciousness of effort. On awaking he appeared to himself to have a distinct recollection of the whole, and taking his pen, ink, and paper, instantly and eagerly wrote down the lines that are here preserved. At this moment he was unfortunately called out by a person on business from Porlock, and detained by him above an hour, and on his return to his room, found to his no small surprise and mortification, that though he still retained some vague and dim recollection of the general purpose of the vision, yet, with the exception of some eight or ten scattered lines and images, all the rest had passed away like the images on the surface of a stream into which a stone has been cast, but, alas! without the after restoration of the latter!

    Then all the charm
    Is broken—all that phantom-world so fair
    Vanishes, and a thousand circlets spread,
    And each mis-shape the other. Stay awhile,
    Poor youth! who scarcely dar'st lift up thine eyes—
    The stream will soon renew its smoothness, soon
    The visions will return! And lo, he stays,
    And soon the fragments dim of lovely forms
    Come trembling back, unite, and now once more
    The pool becomes a mirror.
    [from Coleridge's "The Picture, or the Lover's Resolution" (1802), 69–78]

Yet from the still surviving recollections in his mind, the Author has frequently purposed to finish for himself what had been originally, as it were, given to him. Σαμερον αδιον ασω [from Theocritus's *Idyll* 1.145]: but the tomorrow is yet to come.

As a contrast to this vision, I have annexed a fragment of a very different character [Coleridge's poem "The Pains of Sleep," not included in this anthology], describing with equal fidelity the dream of pain and disease.

A savage place! as holy and enchanted
As e'er beneath a waning moon was haunted 15
By woman wailing for her demon-lover!
And from this chasm, with ceaseless turmoil seething,
As if this earth in fast thick pants were breathing,
A mighty fountain momently was forced:
Amid whose swift half-intermitted burst 20
Huge fragments vaulted like rebounding hail,
Or chaffy grain beneath the thresher's flail:
And 'mid these dancing rocks at once and ever
It flung up momently the sacred river.
Five miles meandering with a mazy° motion   *labyrinthine* 25
Through wood and dale the sacred river ran,
Then reached the caverns measureless to man,
And sank in tumult to a lifeless ocean:
And 'mid this tumult Kubla heard from far
Ancestral voices prophesying war! 30
    The shadow of the dome of pleasure
      Floated midway on the waves;
      Where was heard the mingled measure
      From the fountain and the caves.
It was a miracle of rare device, 35
A sunny pleasure-dome with caves of ice!
    A damsel with a dulcimer
    In a vision once I saw:
    It was an Abyssinian maid,
    And on her dulcimer she played, 40
    Singing of Mount Abora.
    Could I revive within me
    Her symphony and song,
    To such a deep delight 'twould win me,
That with music loud and long, 45
I would build that dome in air,
That sunny dome! those caves of ice!
And all who heard should see them there,
And all should cry, Beware! Beware!
His flashing eyes, his floating hair! 50
Weave a circle round him thrice,
And close your eyes with holy dread,
For he on honey-dew hath fed,
And drunk the milk of Paradise.

—1816 (written 1798)

Lydia Sigourney
1791–1865

Known as the "sweet singer of Hartford," Lydia Sigourney was one of the most popular and prolific poets in the United States during her lifetime. Her poems brought her financial success and wide public acclaim, attention that her husband resented as unfit for a woman. She was well known for her elegies, a common form of public and private poetic expression to commemorate deaths and console the grieving. Infant and child mortality rates were significant in her day, and the child elegy was a widespread and extremely popular genre reflecting this sad social reality. ("Death of an Infant," below, is one of the most famous poems in this genre.) Readers often wrote to her to request elegies for loved ones, including pets. She also wrote actively in other poetic genres common in her day but uncommon in our own, including long poems about history; poems about current events; and fiercely political poetry addressing such topics as the position of women, US mistreatment of Native Americans, and slavery. Protestant Christianity was the culturally dominant religion in the US at this time, and her poems evince a Christian ethos that she shared with many of her readers. Although popular public poets like Sigourney fell out of favor in the twentieth century, scholars are now revisiting her extensive career. Her broad popular appeal on many topics illuminates how central poetry was to public and private life in the antebellum United States.

Death of an Infant

Death found strange beauty on that cherub brow,
And dash'd it out.—There was a tint of rose
O'er cheek and lip;—he touch'd the veins with ice,
And the rose faded.—Forth from those blue eyes
5 There spake a wistful tenderness,—a doubt
Whether to grieve or sleep, which Innocence
Alone can wear.—With ruthless haste he bound
The silken fringes of their curtaining lids
Forever.—There had been a murmuring sound
10 With which the babe would claim its mother's ear,
Charming her even to tears.—The spoiler set
His seal of silence.—But there beam'd a smile,
So fix'd and holy from that marble brow,—

Death gazed and left it there;—he dared not steal
The signet-ring[1] of Heaven.   15

—1827

To the First Slave Ship

First of that train° which cursed the wave,   *procession*
    And from the rifled cabin bore,
Inheritor of wo,°—*the slave*   *woe*
    To bless his palm-tree's shade no more,

Dire engine!—o'er the troubled main   5
    Borne on in unresisted state,—
Know'st thou within thy dark domain
    The secrets of thy prison'd freight?—

Hear'st thou *their* moans whom hope hath fled?—
    Wild cries, in agonizing starts?—   10
Know'st thou thy humid sails are spread
    With ceaseless sighs from broken hearts?—

The fetter'd chieftain's burning tear,—
    The parted lover's mute despair,—
The childless mother's pang severe,—   15
    The orphan's misery, are there.

Ah!—could'st thou from the scroll of fate
    The annal read of future years,
Stripes,—tortures,—unrelenting hate,
    And death-gasps drown'd in slavery's tears,   20

Down,—down,—beneath the cleaving main
    Thou fain would'st plunge where monsters lie,
Rather than ope the gates of pain
    For time and for Eternity.—

Oh Afric!—what has been thy crime?—   25
    That thus like Eden's fratricide,

---

1   *signet-ring* A ring for the finger engraved with a design, often a mark that identifies or
    authenticates.

A mark is set upon thy clime,
    And every brother shuns thy side.—

Yet are thy wrongs, thou long-distrest!—
30   Thy burdens, by the world unweigh'd,
Safe in that *Unforgetful Breast*
    Where all the sins of earth are laid.—

Poor outcast slave!—Our guilty land
    Should tremble while she drinks thy tears,
35 Or sees in vengeful silence stand,
    The beacon of thy shorten'd years;—

Should shrink to hear her sons proclaim
    The sacred truth that heaven is just,—
Shrink even at her Judge's name,—
40   "Jehovah,—Saviour of the opprest."

The Sun upon thy forehead frown'd,
    But Man more cruel far than he,
Dark fetters on thy spirit bound:—
    Look to the mansions of the free!

45 Look to that realm where chains unbind,—
    Where the pale tyrant drops his rod,
And where the patient sufferers find
    A friend,—a father in their God.

—1827

The Indian's Welcome to the Pilgrim Fathers

Above them spread a stranger sky
Around, the sterile plain,
The rock-bound coast rose frowning nigh,
Beyond,—the wrathful main:
5 Chill remnants of the wintry snow
Still chok'd the encumber'd soil,
Yet forth these Pilgrim Fathers go,
To mark their future toil.

'Mid yonder vale their corn must rise
In Summer's ripening pride,   10
And there the church-spire woo the skies
Its sister-school beside.
Perchance 'mid England's velvet green
Some tender thought repos'd,—
Though nought upon their stoic mien   15
Such soft regret disclos'd.

When sudden from the forest wide
A red-brow'd chieftain came,
With towering form, and haughty stride,
And eye like kindling flame: 20
No wrath he breath'd, no conflict sought,
To no dark ambush drew,
But simply *to the Old World brought,*
The welcome of the New.

That *welcome* was a blast and ban   25
Upon thy race unborn.
Was there no seer, thou fated Man!
Thy lavish zeal to warn?
Thou in thy fearless faith didst hail
A weak, invading band,   30
But who shall heed thy children's wail,
Swept from their native land?

Thou gav'st the riches of thy streams,
The lordship o'er thy waves,
The region of thine infant dreams,   35
And of thy fathers' graves,
But who to yon proud mansions pil'd
With wealth of earth and sea,
Poor outcast from thy forest wild,
Say, who shall welcome thee!   40

—1837

Percy Bysshe Shelley

1792–1822

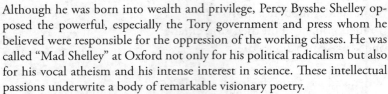 Although he was born into wealth and privilege, Percy Bysshe Shelley opposed the powerful, especially the Tory government and press whom he believed were responsible for the oppression of the working classes. He was called "Mad Shelley" at Oxford not only for his political radicalism but also for his vocal atheism and his intense interest in science. These intellectual passions underwrite a body of remarkable visionary poetry.

Shelley, heir to the estate and title of his baronet father and grandfather, attended Eton College, and was still a student there when he published *Zastrozzi* (1810), a Gothic romance novel. In 1819–20 Shelley wrote his greatest utopian fantasy, *Prometheus Unbound*, which imagined a world grown young again as human beings unlearn historically acquired fear and hatred in favor of love, which Shelley called "the great secret" of all morality. A year later, he penned perhaps his best-known prose work, *A Defence of Poetry* (1821), which famously ends with the bold claim, "Poets are the unacknowledged legislators of the world."

Shelley's reputation was marred by personal as well as political scandal, not least because he abandoned his wife for Mary Godwin (later Mary Shelley, the author of *Frankenstein*), whom he married when his first wife committed suicide. Although he enjoyed scant fame or immediate influence during his lifetime, he has long been recognized as one of the most important poets of the Romantic era.

Note to readers: Shelley's poem "Mont Blanc" appears on the anthology's companion website. The URL and passcode appear in the Table of Contents.

Ozymandias[1]

I met a traveller from an antique land
Who said: Two vast and trunkless legs of stone
Stand in the desert ... Near them, on the sand,
Half sunk, a shattered visage lies, whose frown,
5   And wrinkled lip, and sneer of cold command,
Tell that its sculptor well those passions read

---

1   *Ozymandias* Greek name for King Ramses II of Egypt (1304–1237 BCE). First century BCE Greek historian Diodorus Siculus records the story of this monument (Ozymandias's tomb was in the shape of a male sphinx) and its inscription, which Diodorus says reads: "King of Kings am I, Ozymandias. If anyone would know how great I am and where I lie, let him surpass one of my exploits."

Which yet survive, stamped on these lifeless things,
The hand that mocked them, and the heart that fed:
And on the pedestal these words appear:
"My name is Ozymandias, king of kings: 10
Look on my works, ye Mighty, and despair!"
Nothing beside remains. Round the decay
Of that colossal wreck, boundless and bare
The lone and level sands stretch far away.

—1818

Ode to the West Wind[1]

1

O Wild West Wind, thou breath of Autumn's being,
Thou, from whose unseen presence the leaves dead
Are driven, like ghosts from an enchanter fleeing,

Yellow, and black, and pale, and hectic° red,   *feverish*
Pestilence-stricken multitudes: O thou,   5
Who chariotest to their dark wintry bed

The wingèd seeds, where they lie cold and low,
Each like a corpse within its grave, until
Thine azure sister of the Spring shall blow

Her clarion[2] o'er the dreaming earth, and fill   10
(Driving sweet buds like flocks to feed in air)
With living hues and odours plain and hill:

Wild Spirit, which art moving everywhere;
Destroyer and Preserver; hear, oh, hear!

1   [Shelley's note] This poem was conceived and chiefly written in a wood that skirts the
    Arno, near Florence, and on a day when that tempestuous wind, whose temperature is
    at once mild and animating, was collecting the vapors which pour down the autumnal
    rains. They began, as I foresaw, at sunset with a violent tempest of hail and rain, at-
    tended by that magnificent thunder and lightning peculiar to the Cispaline regions.
2   *clarion* High-pitched trumpet.

2

15 Thou on whose stream, 'mid the steep sky's commotion,
Loose clouds like earth's decaying leaves are shed,
Shook from the tangled boughs of Heaven and Ocean,

Angels° of rain and lightning: there are spread   *Harbingers*
On the blue surface of thine aëry surge,
20 Like the bright hair uplifted from the head

Of some fierce Mænad,[1] even from the dim verge
Of the horizon to the zenith's height,
The locks of the approaching storm. Thou dirge

Of the dying year, to which this closing night
25 Will be the dome of a vast sepulchre,
Vaulted with all thy congregated might

Of vapours,° from whose solid atmosphere   *clouds*
Black rain, and fire, and hail will burst: oh, hear!

3

Thou who didst waken from his summer dreams
30 The blue Mediterranean, where he lay,
Lulled by the coil of his chrystàlline streams,[2]

Beside a pumice isle in Baiae's bay,[3]
And saw in sleep old palaces and towers
Quivering within the wave's intenser day,

35 All overgrown with azure moss and flowers
So sweet, the sense faints picturing them! Thou
For whose path the Atlantic's level powers

---

1   *Mænad* Female attendant of Bacchus, the Greek god of wine.
2   *coil ... streams* Currents of the Mediterranean, the colors of which are often different from the surrounding water.
3   *pumice* Porous stone made from cooled lava; *Baiae's bay* Bay west of Naples that contains the ruins of several imperial villas.

Cleave themselves into chasms, while far below
The sea-blooms and the oozy woods which wear
The sapless foliage of the ocean, know   40

Thy voice, and suddenly grow grey with fear,
And tremble and despoil themselves:[1] oh, hear!

4

If I were a dead leaf thou mightest bear;
If I were a swift cloud to fly with thee;
A wave to pant beneath thy power, and share   45

The impulse of thy strength, only less free
Than thou, O uncontrollable! If even
I were as in my boyhood, and could be

The comrade of thy wanderings over Heaven,
As then, when to outstrip thy skiey° speed   *lofty*   50
Scarce seemed a vision; I would ne'er have striven

As thus with thee in prayer in my sore need.
Oh! lift me as a wave, a leaf, a cloud!
I fall upon the thorns of life! I bleed!

A heavy weight of hours has chained and bowed   55
One too like thee: tameless, and swift, and proud.

5

Make me thy lyre,[2] even as the forest is:
What if my leaves are falling like its own!
The tumult of thy mighty harmonies

Will take from both a deep, autumnal tone,   60
Sweet though in sadness. Be thou, Spirit fierce,
My spirit! Be thou me, impetuous one!

---

1   [Shelley's note] The phenomenon alluded to at the conclusion of the third stanza is
     well known to naturalists. The vegetation at the bottom of the sea, of rivers, and of
     lakes, sympathizes with that of the land in the change of seasons, and is consequently
     influenced by the winds which announce it.
2   *lyre* Aeolian harp, a stringed instrument that produces music when exposed to wind.

Drive my dead thoughts over the universe
Like withered leaves to quicken a new birth!
65 And, by the incantation of this verse,

Scatter, as from an unextinguished hearth
Ashes and sparks, my words among mankind!
Be through my lips to unawakened Earth

The trumpet of a prophecy! O, Wind,
70 If Winter comes, can Spring be far behind?

—1820

To a Skylark

Hail to thee, blithe Spirit!
Bird thou never wert,
That from Heaven, or near it,
Pourest thy full heart
5 In profuse strains of unpremeditated art.

Higher still and higher
From the earth thou springest
Like a cloud of fire;
The blue deep thou wingest,
10 And singing still dost soar, and soaring ever singest.

In the golden lightning
Of the sunken sun,
O'er which clouds are bright'ning,
Thou dost float and run;
15 Like an unbodied joy whose race is just begun.

The pale purple even
Melts around thy flight;
Like a star of Heaven,
In the broad daylight
20 Thou art unseen, but yet I hear thy shrill delight,

Keen as are the arrows
Of that silver sphere,[1]
Whose intense lamp narrows
In the white dawn clear
Until we hardly see—we feel that it is there.   25

All the earth and air
With thy voice is loud,
As, when night is bare,
From one lonely cloud
The moon rains out her beams, and Heaven is overflowed.   30

What thou art we know not;
What is most like thee?
From rainbow clouds there flow not
Drops so bright to see
As from thy presence showers a rain of melody.   35

Like a Poet hidden
In the light of thought,
Singing hymns unbidden,
Till the world is wrought
To sympathy with hopes and fears it heeded not: 40

Like a high-born maiden
In a palace-tower,
Soothing her love-laden
Soul in secret hour
With music sweet as love, which overflows her bower: 45

Like a glow-worm golden
In a dell of dew,
Scattering unbeholden
Its aëreal hue
Among the flowers and grass, which screen it from the view: 50

Like a rose embowered
In its own green leaves,
By warm winds deflowered,

---

1   *silver sphere* Morning star.

Till the scent it gives
55 Makes faint with too much sweet these heavy-wingèd thieves:

Sound of vernal° showers   *springlike*
On the twinkling grass,
Rain-awakened flowers,
All that ever was
60 Joyous, and clear, and fresh, thy music doth surpass:

Teach us, Sprite° or Bird,   *Fairy*
What sweet thoughts are thine:
I have never heard
Praise of love or wine
65 That panted forth a flood of rapture so divine.

Chorus Hymeneal,[1]
Or triumphal chaunt,°   *chant*
Matched with thine would be all
But an empty vaunt,
70 A thing wherein we feel there is some hidden want.

What objects are the fountains
Of thy happy strain?
What fields, or waves, or mountains?
What shapes of sky or plain?
75 What love of thine own kind? what ignorance of pain?

With thy clear keen joyance
Languor cannot be:
Shadow of annoyance
Never came near thee:
80 Thou lovest—but ne'er knew love's sad satiety.

Waking or asleep,
Thou of death must deem
Things more true and deep
Than we mortals dream,
85 Or how could thy notes flow in such a crystal stream?

---

1   *Hymeneal* Marital (Hymen is the Greek god of marriage).

We look before and after,
And pine for what is not:
Our sincerest laughter
With some pain is fraught;
Our sweetest songs are those that tell of saddest thought.   90

Yet if we could scorn
Hate, and pride, and fear;
If we were things born
Not to shed a tear,
I know not how thy joy we ever should come near.   95

Better than all measures
Of delightful sound,
Better than all treasures
That in books are found,
Thy skill to poet were, thou scorner of the ground!   100

Teach me half the gladness
That thy brain must know,
Such harmonious madness
From my lips would flow
The world should listen then—as I am listening now.   105

—1820

William Cullen Bryant
1794–1878

Bryant's contemporaries considered him one of the greatest poets of his age. His poem "Thanatopsis," published in 1817 in the important magazine *The North American Review*, established his reputation while he was still a young man. A master of the formal elements of poetic craft, he often wrote nature poems that recalled the British Romantics while simultaneously addressing American landscapes and conditions (such as westward expansion and displacement of Native Americans in "The Prairies," below). His contemporaries hailed him as the "American Wordsworth." At this time it was common for Europeans—and for Americans themselves—to consider the United States culturally deficient in comparison to the Old World's centuries of artistic achievement. Bryant became a celebrated poet in part because he met the hope that America would produce its own great poet at last. His work circulated to great acclaim across the transatlantic world. Initially a lawyer, he also became an influential newspaper editor at the *Evening Post* in New York, and late in life turned to translating Homer. A cultural icon at a time when people across all social spheres enthusiastically read, recited, and shared poetry as part of daily life, Bryant was a beloved figure. It was only well after his death that artistic taste swerved drastically away from his poetic style to embrace instead new "greats" like Walt Whitman and Emily Dickinson.

The Prairies

These are the gardens of the Desert, these
The unshorn fields, boundless and beautiful,
For which the speech of England has no name—
The Prairies. I behold them for the first,
5 And my heart swells, while the dilated sight
Takes in the encircling vastness. Lo! they stretch,
In airy undulations, far away,
As if the ocean, in his gentlest swell,
Stood still, with all his rounded billows fixed,
10 And motionless forever.—Motionless?—
No—they are all unchained again. The clouds
Sweep over with their shadows, and, beneath,
The surface rolls and fluctuates to the eye;
Dark hollows seem to glide along and chase
15 The sunny ridges. Breezes of the South!
Who toss the golden and the flame-like flowers,
And pass the prairie-hawk that, poised on high,

Flaps his broad wings, yet moves not—ye have played
Among the palms of Mexico and vines
Of Texas, and have crisped the limpid brooks   20
That from the fountains of Sonora[1] glide
Into the calm Pacific—have ye fanned
A nobler or a lovelier scene than this?
Man hath no power in all this glorious work:
The hand that built the firmament hath heaved   25
And smoothed these verdant swells, and sown their slopes
With herbage, planted them with island groves,
And hedged them round with forests. Fitting floor
For this magnificent temple of the sky—
With flowers whose glory and whose multitude   30
Rival the constellations! The great heavens
Seem to stoop down upon the scene in love,—
A nearer vault, and of a tenderer blue,
Than that which bends above our eastern hills.

    As o'er the verdant waste I guide my steed,   35
Among the high rank grass that sweeps his sides
The hollow beating of his footsteps seems
A sacrilegious sound. I think of those
Upon whose rest he tramples. Are they here—
The dead of other days?—and did the dust   40
Of these fair solitudes once stir with life
And burn with passion? Let the mighty mounds[2]
That overlook the rivers, or that rise
In the dim forest crowded with old oaks,
Answer. A race, that long has passed away,   45
Built them;—a disciplined and populous race
Heaped, with long toil, the earth, while yet the Greek
Was hewing the Pentelicus to forms
Of symmetry, and rearing on its rock
The glittering Parthenon.[3] These ample fields   50
Nourished their harvest, here their herds were fed,
When haply by their stalls the bison lowed,
And bowed his maned shoulder to the yoke.

---

1   *Sonora* River in the Mexican region also called Sonora.
2   *mighty mounds* Earthworks created by ancient inhabitants of North America in places
     including the Great Lakes and Ohio Valley regions.
3   *Pentelicus* Mountain in Greece famed for its marble, which glitters in sunlight; *Parthe-
     non*, the ancient Greek temple built from Pentelic marble.

All day this desert murmured with their toils,
55 Till twilight blushed, and lovers walked, and wooed
In a forgotten language, and old tunes,
From instruments of unremembered form,
Gave the soft winds a voice. The red man came—
The roaming hunter tribes, warlike and fierce,
60 And the mound-builders vanished from the earth.
The solitude of centuries untold
Has settled where they dwelt. The prairie-wolf
Hunts in their meadows, and his fresh-dug den
Yawns by my path. The gopher mines the ground
65 Where stood their swarming cities. All is gone;
All—save the piles of earth that hold their bones,
The platforms where they worshipped unknown gods,
The barriers which they builded from the soil
To keep the foe at bay—till o'er the walls
70 The wild beleaguerers broke, and, one by one,
The strongholds of the plain were forced, and heaped
With corpses. The brown vultures of the wood
Flocked to those vast uncovered sepulchres,
And sat unscared and silent at their feast.
75 Haply some solitary fugitive,
Lurking in marsh and forest, till the sense
Of desolation and of fear became
Bitterer than death, yielded himself to die.
Man's better nature triumphed then. Kind words
80 Welcomed and soothed him; the rude conquerors
Seated the captive with their chiefs; he chose
A bride among their maidens, and at length
Seemed to forget—yet ne'er forgot—the wife
Of his first love, and her sweet little ones,
85 Butchered, amid their shrieks, with all his race.

    Thus change the forms of being. Thus arise
Races of living things, glorious in strength,
And perish, as the quickening breath of God
Fills them, or is withdrawn. The red man, too,
90 Has left the blooming wilds he ranged so long,
And, nearer to the Rocky Mountains, sought
A wilder hunting-ground. The beaver builds
No longer by these streams, but far away,
On waters whose blue surface ne'er gave back

The white man's face—among Missouri's springs,   95
And pools whose issues swell the Oregon—
He rears his little Venice. In these plains
The bison feeds no more. Twice twenty leagues
Beyond remotest smoke of hunter's camp,
Roams the majestic brute, in herds that shake   100
The earth with thundering steps—yet here I meet
His ancient footprints stamped beside the pool.

   Still this great solitude is quick with life.
Myriads of insects, gaudy as the flowers
They flutter over, gentle quadrupeds,   105
And birds, that scarce have learned the fear of man,
Are here, and sliding reptiles of the ground,
Startlingly beautiful. The graceful deer
Bounds to the wood at my approach. The bee,[1]
A more adventurous colonist than man,   110
With whom he came across the eastern deep,
Fills the savannas with his murmurings,
And hides his sweets, as in the golden age,
Within the hollow oak. I listen long
To his domestic hum, and think I hear   115
The sound of that advancing multitude
Which soon shall fill these deserts. From the ground
Comes up the laugh of children, the soft voice
Of maidens, and the sweet and solemn hymn
Of Sabbath worshippers. The low of herds   120
Blends with the rustling of the heavy grain
Over the dark brown furrows. All at once
A fresher wind sweeps by, and breaks my dream,
And I am in the wilderness alone.

—1833

To a Waterfowl

    Whither, 'midst falling dew,
While glow the heavens with the last steps of day,
Far, through their rosy depths, dost thou pursue
    Thy solitary way?

---

1   *The bee* European settlers transported honeybees to North America. Washington Irving reported in *A Tour on the Prairies* (1835) that Native Americans considered honeybees the harbinger of the white man, preceding white settlement as it advanced across the continent.

5   Vainly the fowler's[1] eye
Might mark thy distant flight, to do thee wrong,
As, darkly seen against the crimson sky,
         Thy figure floats along.

         Seek'st thou the plashy° brink   *splashy*
10 Of weedy lake, or marge° of river wide,   *edge*
Or where the rocking billows rise and sink
         On the chafed ocean side?[2]

         There is a Power, whose care
Teaches thy way along that pathless coast,—
15 The desert and illimitable air
         Lone wandering, but not lost.

         All day thy wings have fanned,
At that far height, the cold thin atmosphere;
Yet stoop not, weary, to the welcome land,
20   Though the dark night is near.

         And soon that toil shall end,
Soon shalt thou find a summer home, and rest,
And scream among thy fellows; reeds shall bend,
         Soon, o'er thy sheltered nest.

25   Thou'rt gone, the abyss of heaven
Hath swallowed up thy form, yet, on my heart
Deeply hath sunk the lesson thou hast given,
         And shall not soon depart.

         He, who, from zone to zone,
30 Guides through the boundless sky thy certain flight,
In the long way that I must trace alone,
         Will lead my steps aright.

                                          —1851

---

1   *fowler* Hunter of wild birds.
2   *chafed ocean side* Shore pounded by the ocean.

John Keats
1795–1821

John Keats has come to epitomize the popular conception of the Romantic poet as a passionate dreamer whose intense, sensuous poetry celebrates the world of the imagination over that of everyday life. Keats published only 54 poems in his short lifetime, but his work ranges across a number of poetic genres, including sonnets, odes, romances, and epics. His poetry seeks a beauty and truth that will transcend the world of suffering and mortality.

Keats, who died of tuberculosis at 25, despaired of achieving the immortality he wanted for his work. In a note to his beloved, Fanny Brawne, he expresses regret that, "if I should die ... I have left no immortal work behind me—nothing to make my friends proud of my memory—but I have loved the principle of beauty in all things, and if I had had time I would have made myself remembered." Keats had scarcely a year to live when he wrote these words, but already he had completed, in an extraordinary surge of creativity, almost all the poetry on which his reputation rests, including "The Eve of St. Agnes," "La Belle Dame sans Merci," "Lamia," and his great odes, which remain among the highest expressions of the form in English.

Keats was also a highly skilled letter-writer, and his extensive correspondence, in which he reflects on aesthetics, the social role of the poet, and his own sense of poetic mission, reveals a nature acutely alive to the extremes of joy and heartbreak.

Ode to a Nightingale

1

My heart aches, and a drowsy numbness pains
My sense, as though of hemlock° I had drunk,   *poison*
Or emptied some dull opiate to the drains
One minute past, and Lethe-wards[1] had sunk:
'Tis not through envy of thy happy lot,   5
But being too happy in thine happiness—
That thou, light-winged Dryad° of the trees,   *Wood-nymph*
In some melodious plot
Of beechen green, and shadows numberless,
Singest of summer in full-throated ease.   10

---

1   *Lethe-wards* In classical myth, Lethe was a river in Hades, the waters of which brought forgetfulness.

2

O, for a draught of vintage! that hath been
Cool'd a long age in the deep-delved earth,
Tasting of Flora[1] and the country green,
Dance, and Provençal[2] song, and sunburnt mirth!
15 O for a beaker full of the warm South,
Full of the true, the blushful Hippocrene,[3]
With beaded bubbles winking at the brim,
And purple-stained mouth;
That I might drink, and leave the world unseen,
20 And with thee fade away into the forest dim:

3

Fade far away, dissolve, and quite forget
What thou among the leaves hast never known,
The weariness, the fever, and the fret
Here, where men sit and hear each other groan;
25 Where palsy shakes a few, sad, last grey hairs,
Where youth grows pale, and spectre-thin, and dies;
Where but to think is to be full of sorrow
And leaden-eyed despairs,
Where Beauty cannot keep her lustrous eyes,
30 Or new Love pine at them beyond to-morrow.

4

Away! away! for I will fly to thee,
Not charioted by Bacchus and his pards,[4]
But on the viewless wings of Poesy,
Though the dull brain perplexes and retards:
35 Already with thee! tender is the night,
And haply° the Queen-Moon is on her throne,   *perhaps*
Cluster'd around by all her starry Fays;°   *Fairies*
But here there is no light,
Save what from heaven is with the breezes blown
40 Through verdurous glooms and winding mossy ways.

---

1   *Flora* Roman goddess of flowers.
2   *Provençal* From Provence, the region in France associated with troubadours.
3   *Hippocrene* Water from the spring on Mount Helicon, sacred to the Muses.
4   *Bacchus and his pards* Bacchus, the Roman god of wine, rides a chariot drawn by leop-
     ards.

5

I cannot see what flowers are at my feet,
Nor what soft incense hangs upon the boughs,
But, in embalmed° darkness, guess each sweet   *fragrant*
Wherewith the seasonable month endows
The grass, the thicket, and the fruit-tree wild;   45
White hawthorn, and the pastoral eglantine;
Fast fading violets cover'd up in leaves;
And mid-May's eldest child,
The coming musk-rose, full of dewy wine,
The murmurous haunt of flies on summer eves.   50

6

Darkling[1] I listen; and, for many a time
I have been half in love with easeful Death,
Call'd him soft names in many a mused rhyme,
To take into the air my quiet breath;
Now more than ever seems it rich to die,   55
To cease upon the midnight with no pain,
While thou art pouring forth thy soul abroad
In such an ecstasy!
Still wouldst thou sing, and I have ears in vain—
To thy high requiem become a sod.   60

7

Thou wast not born for death, immortal Bird!
No hungry generations tread thee down;
The voice I hear this passing night was heard
In ancient days by emperor and clown:°   *rustic*
Perhaps the self-same song that found a path   65
Through the sad heart of Ruth,[2] when, sick for home,
She stood in tears amid the alien corn;
The same that oft-times hath
Charm'd magic casements, opening on the foam
Of perilous seas, in faery lands forlorn.   70

---

1   *Darkling* In the dark.
2   *Ruth* In the biblical story the widowed Ruth leaves her native Moab for Judah, there
     helping her mother-in-law by working in the fields at harvest time.

8

Forlorn! the very word is like a bell
To toll me back from thee to my sole self!
Adieu! the fancy cannot cheat so well
As she is fam'd to do, deceiving elf.
75 Adieu! adieu! thy plaintive anthem fades
Past the near meadows, over the still stream,
Up the hill-side; and now 'tis buried deep
In the next valley-glades:
Was it a vision, or a waking dream?
80 Fled is that music—Do I wake or sleep?

—1819

Ode on a Grecian Urn

1

Thou still unravish'd bride of quietness,
Thou foster-child of silence and slow time,
Sylvan° historian, who canst thus express   *Woodland*
A flowery tale more sweetly than our rhyme:
5 What leaf-fring'd legend haunts about thy shape
Of deities or mortals, or of both,
In Tempe or the dales of Arcady?[1]
What men or gods are these? What maidens loth?°   *reluctant*
What mad pursuit? What struggle to escape?
10 What pipes and timbrels?° What wild ecstasy?[2]   *tambourines*

2

Heard melodies are sweet, but those unheard
Are sweeter; therefore, ye soft pipes, play on;
Not to the sensual ear, but, more endear'd,
Pipe to the spirit ditties of no tone:
15 Fair youth, beneath the trees, thou canst not leave
Thy song, nor ever can those trees be bare;
Bold lover, never, never canst thou kiss,
Though winning near the goal—yet, do not grieve;

---

1   *Tempe* Valley in ancient Greece renowned for its beauty; *Arcady* Ideal region of rural
life, named for a mountainous district in Greece.
2   *What pipes ... ecstasy* This side of the vase seems to depict a Dionysian ritual, in which
participants sometimes attained a state of frenzy.

She cannot fade, though thou hast not thy bliss,
For ever wilt thou love, and she be fair! 20

3

Ah, happy, happy boughs! that cannot shed
Your leaves, nor ever bid the Spring adieu;
And, happy melodist, unwearied,
For ever piping songs for ever new;
More happy love! more happy, happy love! 25
For ever warm and still to be enjoy'd,
For ever panting, and for ever young;
All breathing human passion far above,
That leaves a heart high-sorrowful and cloy'd,
A burning forehead, and a parching tongue. 30

4

Who are these coming to the sacrifice?
To what green altar, O mysterious priest,
Lead'st thou that heifer lowing at the skies,
And all her silken flanks with garlands drest?
What little town by river or sea shore, 35
Or mountain-built with peaceful citadel,
Is emptied of this folk, this pious morn?
And, little town, thy streets for evermore
Will silent be, and not a soul to tell
Why thou art desolate, can e'er return. 40

5

O Attic¹ shape! Fair attitude! with brede°   *interwoven design*
Of marble men and maidens overwrought,°   *overlaid*
With forest branches and the trodden weed;
Thou, silent form, dost tease us out of thought
As doth eternity: Cold Pastoral! 45
When old age shall this generation waste,
Thou shalt remain, in midst of other woe
Than ours, a friend to man, to whom thou say'st,
"Beauty is truth, truth beauty,"—that is all
Ye know on earth, and all ye need to know. 50

—1820

---

1   *Attic* From Attica, the region around Athens.

To Autumn

1

Season of mists and mellow fruitfulness,
    Close bosom-friend of the maturing sun;
Conspiring with him how to load and bless
    With fruit the vines that round the thatch-eves run;
5 To bend with apples the moss'd cottage-trees,
    And fill all fruit with ripeness to the core;
        To swell the gourd, and plump the hazel shells
    With a sweet kernel; to set budding more,
And still more, later flowers for the bees,
10 Until they think warm days will never cease,
        For Summer has o'er-brimm'd their clammy cells.

2

Who hath not seen thee oft amid thy store?
    Sometimes whoever seeks abroad may find
Thee sitting careless on a granary floor,
15   Thy hair soft-lifted by the winnowing wind;
Or on a half-reap'd furrow sound asleep,
    Drows'd with the fume of poppies, while thy hook°   *scythe*
        Spares the next swath and all its twined flowers:
And sometimes like a gleaner thou dost keep
20   Steady thy laden head across a brook;
    Or by a cyder-press, with patient look,
        Thou watchest the last oozings hours by hours.

3

Where are the songs of Spring? Ay, where are they?
    Think not of them, thou hast thy music too—
25 While barred clouds bloom the soft-dying day,
    And touch the stubble-plains with rosy hue;
Then in a wailful choir the small gnats mourn
    Among the river sallows,° borne aloft   *willows*
        Or sinking as the light wind lives or dies;
30 And full-grown lambs loud bleat from hilly bourn;°   *realm*
    Hedge-crickets sing; and now with treble soft
    The red-breast whistles from a garden-croft;°   *enclosed garden*
        And gathering swallows twitter in the skies.

—1820

La Belle Dame sans Merci[1]

O what can ail thee, knight-at-arms,
    Alone and palely loitering?
The sedge[2] has withered from the lake,
    And no birds sing.

O what can ail thee, knight-at-arms,   5
    So haggard and so woe-begone?
The squirrel's granary is full,
    And the harvest's done.

I see a lily on thy brow,
    With anguish moist and fever-dew,   10
And on thy cheeks a fading rose
    Fast withereth too.

I met a lady in the meads,°   *meadows*
    Full beautiful—a faery's child,
Her hair was long, her foot was light,   15
    And her eyes were wild.

I made a garland for her head,
    And bracelets too, and fragrant zone;°   *belt*
She looked at me as she did love,
    And made sweet moan.   20

I set her on my pacing steed,
    And nothing else saw all day long,
For sidelong would she bend, and sing
    A faery's song.

---

1   *La Belle Dame sans Merci* French: the beautiful lady without pity. This original version of the poem, found in a journal letter to George and Georgiana Keats, was published in 1848. Keats had published a different version in 1820.

2   *sedge* Rush-like grass.

25 She found me roots of relish sweet,
     And honey wild, and manna-dew,[1]
And sure in language strange she said—
     "I love thee true."

She took me to her Elfin grot,°   *grotto*
30   And there she wept and sighed full sore,
And there I shut her wild wild eyes
     With kisses four.

And there she lullèd me asleep,
     And there I dreamed—Ah! woe betide!—
35 The latest° dream I ever dreamt   *last*
     On the cold hill side.

I saw pale kings and princes too,
     Pale warriors, death-pale were they all;
They cried—"La Belle Dame sans Merci
40   Hath thee in thrall!"

I saw their starved lips in the gloam,°   *twilight*
     With horrid warning gapèd wide,
And I awoke and found me here,
     On the cold hill's side.

45 And this is why I sojourn here,
     Alone and palely loitering,
Though the sedge is withered from the lake,
     And no birds sing.

—1848 (written 1819)

---

1   *manna-dew* See Exodus 16 in the Bible's Old Testament, in which God provides the
    Israelites with a food that falls from heaven, called manna.

When I Have Fears that I May Cease to Be

When I have fears that I may cease to be
 Before my pen has glean'd my teeming brain,
Before high piled books, in charact'ry,[1]
 Hold like rich garners° the full-ripen'd grain;   *granaries*
When I behold, upon the night's starr'd face,   5
 Huge cloudy symbols of a high romance,
And think that I may never live to trace
 Their shadows, with the magic hand of chance;
And when I feel, fair creature of an hour!
 That I shall never look upon thee more,   10
Never have relish in the fairy power
 Of unreflecting love;—then on the shore
Of the wide world I stand alone, and think
 Till love and fame to nothingness do sink.

          —1848 (written 1818)

---

1 *charact'ry* Symbols or letters.

Ralph Waldo Emerson
1803–1882

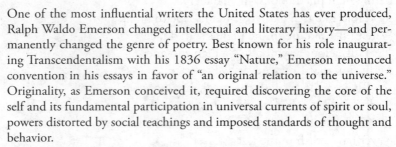 One of the most influential writers the United States has ever produced, Ralph Waldo Emerson changed intellectual and literary history—and permanently changed the genre of poetry. Best known for his role inaugurating Transcendentalism with his 1836 essay "Nature," Emerson renounced convention in his essays in favor of "an original relation to the universe." Originality, as Emerson conceived it, required discovering the core of the self and its fundamental participation in universal currents of spirit or soul, powers distorted by social teachings and imposed standards of thought and behavior.

During Emerson's time, the United States suffered from a cultural inferiority complex with respect to Europe and its many centuries of cultural achievement. He argued that artistic conventions were dead traditions, and called for new, original art forms arising from inspiration rather than following rules imposed by taste-makers. Walt Whitman's unconventional career was inspired by Emerson's essay "The Poet." Other writers who read him intensely include Henry David Thoreau and Emily Dickinson. Although he is far better known for his essays, Emerson was deeply committed to writing poetry, writing poems in many genres and in complex hybrid forms over the course of his long career.

Fate[1]

Delicate omens traced in air
To the lone bard true witness bare;°   *reveal*
Birds with auguries on their wings
Chanted undeceiving things
5 Him to beckon, him to warn;
Well might then the poet scorn
To learn of scribe or courier
Hints writ in vaster character;°   *writing*
And on his mind, at dawn of day,
10 Soft shadows of the evening lay.
For the prevision° is allied   *foresight*

---

1   *Fate* Emerson included this poem, one of two he published with the same title, as a preface to his essay "Fate" in his collection *The Conduct of Life* (1860). "Fate" was a central concept for Emerson; it was a force that dialectically balanced and opposed his equally fundamental concept of self-reliant individual freedom.

Unto the thing so signified;
Or say, the foresight that awaits
Is the same Genius that creates.

—1860

Maiden Speech[1] of the Æolian Harp[2]

Soft and softlier hold me, friends!
Thanks if your genial care
Unbind and give me to the air.
Keep your lips or finger-tips
For flute or spinet's[3] dancing chips;[4]   5
I await a tenderer touch,
I ask more or not so much:
Give me to the atmosphere,—
Where is the wind, my brother,—where?
Lift the sash,° lay me within,   *window frame*   10
Lend me your ears, and I begin.
For gentle harp to gentle hearts
The secret of the world imparts;
And not to-day and not to-morrow
Can drain its wealth of hope and sorrow;   15
But day by day, to loving ear
Unlocks new sense and loftier cheer.
I've come to live with you, sweet friends,
This home my minstrel-journeyings ends.
Many and subtle are my lays,[5]   20
The latest better than the first,
For I can mend the happiest days
And charm the anguish of the worst.

—1876

---

1   *Maiden Speech* Emerson's poem is a persona poem, that is, a poem spoken in the voice of
    a character. In this case, the "maiden speech" is in the harp's own voice.
2   *Æolian Harp* Named for the Greek god of the winds, Aeolus, these wind harps were
    placed in the window, where the music created through the action of the wind was
    legendary in the Romantic era as the music of nature. Such harps became a common
    trope in Romantic poetry for exploring some of the key elements of Romanticism: self,
    poet, nature, and spirit or divinity.
3   *spinet* Type of harpsichord, used mainly in homes.
4   *chips* Keys of a spinet.
5   *lays* Poems intended to be sung.

Elizabeth Barrett Browning

1806–1861

One of the most popular, most admired, and best-known poets of the nineteenth century, Elizabeth Barrett (who married fellow poet Robert Browning in 1846, after he wrote her a fan letter) was a writer of tremendous versatility whose work influenced readers and fellow poets across the transatlantic world.

She gained international recognition for her *Poems* (1844), admiration for which motivated her future husband's fan letter. Her 44 love poems for him, published as "Sonnets from the Portuguese" in her 1850 volume *Poems*, achieved enduring fame as among the greatest love sonnets in the English language. The Brownings held celebrity status in Britain and the US as married poets, a topic that comes up repeatedly in the media accounts of their time (as with celebrity marriages today). But Barrett Browning certainly did not restrict herself to poems of domesticity, love, or romance. Her widely acclaimed and massively popular "verse-novel" *Aurora Leigh* (1856), for example, vigorously addressed the social constraints and conflicts of the Victorian era, including the predicament of women seeking meaningful education (as in the selection below). Published at a time when the novel was rapidly overtaking the marketplace as a popular art form—to the increasing concern of poets—this long narrative poem presented what Barrett Browning called her "highest convictions" on the cultural cross-currents of the time, including desire, power, art, love, romance, race, class structures, and the subjugation of women. It was her most controversial work, and its many admirers included George Eliot, Emily Dickinson, and Susan B. Anthony.

Barrett Browning's achievements fell from view in the twentieth century, when an increasingly restricted poetic canon dismissed many poets, including most women poets, as too popular to be "good" or "great." While popular culture retained its memory of her iconic poems about a woman's love for a man (especially the first line of Sonnet 43, below), this restricted vision of her career eclipsed her poetry of social commentary. Scholars are now reassessing Barrett Browning's work as an index to the public and private passions and problems of the nineteenth century social world.

from *Sonnets from the Portuguese*[1]

Sonnet 22

When our two souls stand up erect and strong,
Face to face, silent, drawing nigh and nigher,
Until the lengthening wings break into fire
At either curvèd point—what bitter wrong
Can the earth do to us, that we should not long   5
Be here contented? Think. In mounting higher,
The angels would press on us and aspire
To drop some golden orb of perfect song
Into our deep, dear silence. Let us stay
Rather on earth, Belovèd—where the unfit   10
Contrarious moods of men recoil away
And isolate pure spirits, and permit
A place to stand and love in for a day,
With darkness and the death-hour rounding it.

Sonnet 24

Let the world's sharpness like a clasping knife
Shut in upon itself and do no harm
In this close hand of Love, now soft and warm,
And let us hear no sound of human strife
After the click of the shutting. Life to life—   5
I lean upon thee, Dear, without alarm,
And feel as safe as guarded by a charm
Against the stab of worldlings, who if rife
Are weak to injure. Very whitely still
The lilies of our lives may reassure   10
Their blossoms from their roots, accessible
Alone to heavenly dews that drop not fewer;
Growing straight, out of man's reach, on the hill.
God only, who made us rich, can make us poor.

---

1   *Sonnets from the Portugese* Translating poetic works from other languages was a common
    activity for educated people at this time. Titles like this one were very familiar to readers
    who enjoyed access in the English language to poems written in other tongues. These
    sonnets "from the Portuguese" were not actually translations, but Barrett Browning's title
    presented them as if they were in order to try to mask their very private autobiographical
    nature. She initially wrote them as private lyrics for Robert Browning.

Sonnet 43

How do I love thee? Let me count the ways.
I love thee to the depth and breadth and height
My soul can reach, when feeling out of sight
For the ends of Being and ideal Grace.
5 I love thee to the level of everyday's
Most quiet need, by sun and candlelight.
I love thee freely, as men strive for Right;
I love thee purely, as they turn from Praise.
I love thee with the passion put to use
10 In my old griefs, and with my childhood's faith.
I love thee with a love I seemed to lose
With my lost saints—I love thee with the breath,
Smiles, tears, of all my life!—and, if God choose,
I shall but love thee better after death.

—1850

from *Aurora Leigh*, Book I[1]

She stood upon the steps to welcome me,
Calm, in black garb. I clung about her neck,—
Young babes, who catch at every shred of wool
To draw the new light closer, catch and cling
5 Less blindly. In my ears, my father's word
Hummed ignorantly, as the sea in shells,
"Love, love, my child," She, black there with my grief,
Might feel my love—she was his sister once—
I clung to her. A moment, she seemed moved.
10 Kissed me with cold lips, suffered me to cling,
And drew me feebly through the hall, into
The room she sate in.
                         There, with some strange spasm
Of pain and passion, she wrung loose my hands
15 Imperiously, and held me at arm's length,
And with two grey-steel naked-bladed eyes
Searched through my face,—ay, stabbed it through and through,
Through brows and cheeks and chin, as if to find
A wicked murderer in my innocent face,
20 If not here, there perhaps. Then, drawing breath,

---

1   *Book I* In this section, the orphaned title character travels from Italy to live with her
     father's dour unmarried sister in his native England.

She struggled for her ordinary calm,
And missed it rather,—told me not to shrink,
As if she had told me not to lie or swear,—
"She loved my father, and would love me too
As long as I deserved it." Very kind.   25

I understood her meaning afterward;
She thought to find my mother in my face,
And questioned it for that. For she, my aunt,
Had loved my father truly, as she could,
And hated, with the gall of gentle souls,   30
My Tuscan mother, who had fooled away
A wise man from wise courses, a good man
From obvious duties, and, depriving her,
His sister, of the household precedence,
Had wronged his tenants, robbed his native land,   35
And made him mad, alike by life and death,
In love and sorrow. She had pored for years
What sort of woman could be suitable
To her sort of hate, to entertain it with;
And so, her very curiosity   40
Became hate too, and all the idealism
She ever used in life, was used for hate,
Till hate, so nourished, did exceed at last
The love from which it grew, in strength and heat,
And wrinkled her smooth conscience with a sense   45
Of disputable virtue (say not, sin)
When Christian doctrine was enforced at church.

And thus my father's sister was to me
My mother's hater. From that day, she did
Her duty to me, (I appreciate it   50
In her own word as spoken to herself)
Her duty, in large measure, well-pressed out,
But measured always. She was generous, bland,
More courteous than was tender, gave me still
The first place,—as if fearful that God's saints   55
Would look down suddenly and say, "Herein
You missed a point, I think, through lack of love."
Alas, a mother never is afraid
Of speaking angrily to any child,
Since love, she knows, is justified of love.   60

And I, I was a good child on the whole,
A meek and manageable child. Why not?
I did not live, to have the faults of life:
There seemed more true life in my father's grave
65 Than in all England. Since *that* threw me off
Who fain would cleave, (his latest will, they say,
Consigned me to his land) I only thought
Of lying quiet there where I was thrown
Like sea-weed on the rocks, and suffer her
70 To prick me to a pattern with her pin,
Fibre from fibre, delicate leaf from leaf,
And dry out from my drowned anatomy
The last sea-salt left in me.
                              So it was.
75 I broke the copious curls upon my head
In braids, because she liked smooth ordered hair.
I left off saying my sweet Tuscan words
Which still at any stirring of the heart
Came up to float across the English phrase,
80 As lilies, (*Bene* . . or *che chè*) because
She liked my father's child to speak his tongue.
I learnt the collects and the catechism,
The creeds, from Athanasius back to Nice,
The Articles, the Tracts *against* the times,
85 (By no means Buonaventure's "Prick of Love,")
And various popular synopses of
Inhuman doctrines never taught by John,
Because she liked instructed piety.
I learnt my complement of classic French
90 (Kept pure of Balzac and neologism,)
And German also, since she liked a range
Of liberal education,—tongues, not books.
I learnt a little algebra, a little
Of the mathematics,—brushed with extreme flounce
95 The circle of the sciences, because
She misliked women who are frivolous.
I learnt the royal genealogies
Of Oviedo, the internal laws
Of the Burmese Empire—by how many feet
100 Mount Chimborazo outsoars Himmeleh,
What navigable river joins itself
To Lara, and what census of the year five

Was taken at Klagenfurt,—because she liked
A general insight into useful facts.
I learnt much music,—such as would have been   105
As quite impossible in Johnson's day
As still it might be wished—fine sleights of hand
And unimagined fingering, shuffling off
The hearer's soul through hurricanes of notes
To a noisy Tophet; and I drew . . . costumes   110
From French engravings, nereids neatly draped,
With smirks of simmering godship,—I washed in
From nature, landscapes, (rather say, washed out.)
I danced the polka and Cellarius,
Spun glass, stuffed birds, and modelled flowers in wax,   115
Because she liked accomplishments in girls.
I read a score of books on womanhood
To prove, if women do not think at all,
They may teach thinking, (to a maiden aunt
Or else the author)—books demonstrating   120
Their right of comprehending husband's talk
When not too deep, and even of answering
With pretty "may it please you," or "so it is,"—
Their rapid insight and fine aptitude,
Particular worth and general missionariness,   125
As long as they keep quiet by the fire
And never say "no" when the world says "ay,"
For that is fatal,—their angelic reach
Of virtue, chiefly used to sit and darn,
And fatten household sinners—their, in brief,   130
Potential faculty in everything
Of abdicating power in it: she owned
She liked a woman to be womanly,
And English women, she thanked God and sighed,
(Some people always sigh in thanking God)   135
Were models to the universe. And last
I learnt cross-stitch, because she did not like
To see me wear the night with empty hands,
A-doing nothing.[1]

—1857

---

1   *I learnt the collects ... A-doing nothing* In the preceding lines, Aurora Leigh provides a
     detailed description of her aunt's traditional and restrictive concept of appropriate educa-
     tion for girls.

Henry Wadsworth Longfellow
1807–1882

Henry Wadsworth Longfellow, an impressive linguist with a broad knowledge of world poetries and their many metrical forms, was one of the best-known, best-loved, and most technically proficient poets of his time. Longfellow lived in a culture in which people enjoyed reading, writing, memorizing, reciting, and sharing poems as a routine part of daily life. Everyday people adapted poems to many public and private purposes, including conversion into song lyrics; recitation at civic and school programs; and communal reading at "parlor" socials (social gatherings at home in the parlor or "best" room) with friends and loved ones, a common form of entertainment at this time. Privately, people inscribed poems and favorite quotations in commonplace books, diaries, and letters.

Longfellow's poems electrified these sensibilities of his age. His skilled poetry spoke in a rhythmical voice, informed by his studies of other languages, that his contemporaries loved and revered for its musical sound as well as for its often didactic and sentimental topics. His 1842 volume, *Poems on Slavery* (from which two selections below are taken), addressed the accelerating national crisis over slavery. By the time of his death, he had become a national icon of the ideal poet, and his poems had become standard fare in schoolrooms across the nation. Poetic taste shifted dramatically in the twentieth century. At that time, Modernism redefined the canon to eliminate popular, formally conventional, often moralizing verses like Longfellow's, and his reputation fell dramatically into shadow. Scholars are now returning to his vast body of work from a fresh historical and global perspective, in particular to his innovative work with other languages and world poetries.

The Spirit[1] of Poetry

There is a quiet spirit in these woods,
That dwells where'er the gentle south-wind blows;
Where, underneath the white-thorn, in the glade,
The wild flowers bloom, or, kissing the soft air,
5 The leaves above their sunny palms outspread.
With what a tender and impassioned voice
It fills the nice and delicate ear of thought,

---

1 *Spirit* Incorporeal being or intelligence, independent of the physical realm. In this very early poem, Longfellow explores Romantic ideas about the peculiar power of poetry and its fundamental nature, especially in relation to the physical world. Such ideas were already circulating through the work of such poets as William Wordsworth.

When the fast ushering star of morning comes
O'er-riding the gray hills with golden scarf;
Or when the cowled and dusky-sandalled Eve,°   *Evening*   10
In mourning weeds, from out the western gate,
Departs with silent pace! That spirit moves
In the green valley, where the silver brook,
From its full laver,° pours the white cascade;   *basin*
And, babbling low amid the tangled woods,   15
Slips down through moss-grown stones with endless laughter.
And frequent, on the everlasting hills,
Its feet go forth, when it doth wrap itself
In all the dark embroidery of the storm,
And shouts the stern, strong wind. And here, amid   20
The silent majesty of these deep woods,
Its presence shall uplift thy thoughts from earth,
As to the sunshine and the pure, bright air
Their tops the green trees lift. Hence gifted bards
Have ever loved the calm and quiet shades.   25
For them there was an eloquent voice in all
The sylvan pomp of woods, the golden sun,
The flowers, the leaves, the river on its way,
Blue skies, and silver clouds, and gentle winds,
The swelling upland, where the sidelong sun   30
Aslant the wooded slope, at evening, goes,
Groves, through whose broken roof the sky looks in,
Mountain, and shattered cliff, and sunny vale,
The distant lake, fountains, and mighty trees,
In many a lazy syllable, repeating   35
Their old poetic legends to the wind.
    And this is the sweet spirit, that doth fill
The world; and, in these wayward days of youth,
My busy fancy oft embodies it,
As a bright image of the light and beauty   40
That dwell in nature; of the heavenly forms
We worship in our dreams, and the soft hues
That stain the wild bird's wing, and flush the clouds
When the sun sets. Within her tender eye
The heaven of April, with its changing light,   45
And when it wears the blue of May, is hung,
And on her lip the rich, red rose. Her hair
Is like the summer tresses of the trees,

When twilight makes them brown, and on her cheek
50 Blushes the richness of an autumn sky,
With ever-shifting beauty. Then her breath,
It is so like the gentle air of Spring,
As, front the morning's dewy flowers, it comes
Full of their fragrance, that it is a joy
55 To have it round us, and her silver voice
Is the rich music of a summer bird,
Heard in the still night, with its passionate cadence.

—1828

The Quadroon[1] Girl

The Slaver in the broad lagoon
    Lay moored with idle sail;
He waited for the rising moon,
    And for the evening gale.

5 Under the shore his boat was tied,
    And all her listless crew
Watched the gray alligator slide
    Into the still bayou.

Odors of orange-flowers, and spice,
10   Reached them from time to time,
Like airs that breathe from Paradise
    Upon a world of crime.

The Planter, under his roof of thatch,
    Smoked thoughtfully and slow;
15 The Slaver's thumb was on the latch,
    He seemed in haste to go.

He said, "My ship at anchor rides
    In yonder broad lagoon;
I only wait the evening tides,
20   And the rising of the moon."

---

1   *Quadroon* One of an array of terms common for classifying mixed-race people in Long-
fellow's time, a "quadroon" allegedly had one-quarter African ancestry, with the other
three-quarters implicitly white.

Before them, with her face upraised,
  In timid attitude,
Like one half curious, half amazed,
  A Quadroon maiden stood.

Her eyes were large, and full of light,   25
  Her arms and neck were bare;
No garment she wore save a kirtle° bright,   *skirt*
  And her own long, raven hair.

And on her lips there played a smile
  As holy, meek, and faint,   30
As lights in some cathedral aisle
  The features of a saint.

"The soil is barren,—the farm is old,"
  The thoughtful planter said;
Then looked upon the Slaver's gold,   35
  And then upon the maid.

His heart within him was at strife
  With such accurséd gains:
For he knew whose passions gave her life,
  Whose blood ran in her veins.   40

But the voice of nature was too weak;
  He took the glittering gold!
Then pale as death grew the maiden's cheek,
  Her hands as icy cold.

The Slaver led her from the door,   45
  He led her by the hand,
To be his slave and paramour
  In a strange and distant land!

           —1842

The Slave Singing at Midnight[1]

Loud he sang the psalm of David!
He, a Negro and enslaved,
Sang of Israel's victory,[2]
Sang of Zion, bright and free.
5 In that hour, when night is calmest,
Sang he from the Hebrew Psalmist,
In a voice so sweet and clear
That I could not choose but hear,
Songs of triumph, and ascriptions,
10 Such as reached the swart° Egyptians,   *dark, black*
When upon the Red Sea coast
Perished Pharaoh and his host.
And the voice of his devotion
Filled my soul with strange emotion;
15 For its tones by turns were glad,
Sweetly solemn, wildly sad.
Paul and Silas,[3] in their prison,
Sang of Christ, the Lord arisen.
And an earthquake's arm of might
20 Broke their dungeon-gates at night.
But, alas! what holy angel
Brings the Slave this glad evangel?[4]
And what earthquake's arm of might
Breaks his dungeon-gates at night?

—1842

---

1   *The Slave ... Midnight* The slave is singing one of the sorrow songs. See the section "Slave
    Songs and Sorrow Songs" on p. 271 in this volume for examples.
2   *Israel's victory* Analogies between enslaved Africans in the US and the enslaved Israelites
    of the Old Testament were common in anti-slavery discourse in the US. Pro-slavery dis-
    course also relied on the Bible to justify slavery, particularly the Old Testament, but relied
    on different passages.
3   *Paul and Silas* In Acts 16.12–40, Paul and Silas, while traveling to preach the gospel, are
    severely beaten, whipped, and imprisoned by the Roman authorities in Philippi. God
    responds to their prayers for freedom with an earthquake that opens the prison doors. See
    the slave song "Blow Your Trumpet, Gabriel" (p. 271) for another example of this biblical
    analogy for American slavery.
4   *evangel* The good news of redemption; the gospel.

The City and the Sea

The panting City cried to the Sea,
"I am faint with heat,—O breathe on me!"

And the Sea said, "Lo, I breathe! but my breath
To some will be life, to others death!"

As to Prometheus,[1] bringing ease   5
In pain, come the Oceanides,[2]

So to the City, hot with the flame
Of the pitiless sun, the east wind came.

It came from the heaving breast of the deep,
Silent as dreams are, and sudden as sleep.   10

Life-giving, death-giving, which will it be;
O breath of the merciful, merciless Sea?

—1882

---

1   *Prometheus* In Greek mythology, the Titan Prometheus teaches humankind the arts and sciences and gives them the fire he steals from the gods. Zeus punishes him with eternal torment. Romantic writers often alluded to Prometheus as a figure for the paradoxical dangers of aspiration. Both Mary and Percy Shelley, for example, invoked metaphors of Prometheus, in *Frankenstein; or, The Modern Prometheus* and *Prometheus Unbound*, respectively.

2   *Oceanides* In the tragedy *Prometheus Bound* (attributed to Aeschylus), these sea-nymphs arrive in winged chariots. They serve as the chorus, expressing sympathy for Prometheus in his suffering.

John Greenleaf Whittier

1807–1892

John Greenleaf Whittier was one of the best-known and best-loved poets of the nineteenth-century United States. Along with William Cullen Bryant, Henry Wadsworth Longfellow, Oliver Wendell Holmes, and James Russell Lowell, he became known as one of the "Fireside Poets," a group their contemporaries revered as America's bards. In an era when poetry was an enormously popular art form, their work suited the taste of the age. By the late-nineteenth century, poems by these cultural icons were widely memorized, recited, and taught in schools, but this form of poetic taste collapsed early in the twentieth century. At that time, Modernists like T.S. Eliot and Ezra Pound rejected the Fireside Poets for their didactic and moralizing poems and their formal conventionality.

But as Whittier and other popular poets fell from view, literary history also lost touch with the many important social roles that poetry played in the nation's cultural life. Whittier's poetry, for example, played an active part in national politics. Born into a family of Quaker farmers in Massachusetts, he was already a staunch abolitionist as a young man and devoted his energies to political treatises, poems, and editorial work. Over the course of his long career, his other major topic was New England history and legend. Some of his nostalgic poems about rural life were among the best-loved poems of the century. Whittier's command of rhetoric and meter is on display in the selection below, whose force is best felt when recited—as indeed his contemporaries would have done. In the nineteenth century, the phrase "reading poetry" meant reading poetry *aloud*.

The Hunters of Men

HAVE ye heard of our hunting, o'er mountain and glen,
Through cane-brake and forest,—the hunting of men?
The lords of our land to this hunting have gone,
As the fox-hunter follows the sound of the horn;
5 Hark! the cheer and the hallo! the crack of the whip,
And the yell of the hound as he fastens his grip!
All blithe are our hunters, and noble their match,
Though hundreds are caught, there are millions to catch.
So speed to their hunting, o'er mountain and glen,
10 Through cane-brake and forest,—the hunting of men!

Gay luck to our hunters! how nobly they ride
In the glow of their zeal, and the strength of their pride!

The priest with his cassock flung back on the wind,
Just screening the politic statesman behind;
The saint and the sinner, with cursing and prayer,   15
The drunk and the sober, ride merrily there.
And woman, kind woman, wife, widow, and maid,
For the good of the hunted, is lending her aid:
Her foot's in the stirrup, her hand on the rein,
How blithely she rides to the hunting of men!   20

Oh, goodly and grand is our hunting to see,
In this "land of the brave and this home of the free."
Priest, warrior, and statesman, from Georgia to Maine,
All mounting the saddle, all grasping the rein;
Right merrily hunting the black man, whose sin   25
Is the curl of his hair and the hue of his skin!
Woe, now, to the hunted who turns him at bay!
Will our hunters be turned from their purpose and prey?
Will their hearts fail within them? their nerves tremble, when
All roughly they ride to the hunting of men?   30
Ho! alms for our hunters! all weary and faint,
Wax the curse of the sinner and prayer of the saint.
The horn is wound faintly, the echoes are still,
Over cane-brake and river, and forest and hill.
Haste, alms for our hunters! the hunted once more   35
Have turned from their flight with their backs to the shore:
What right have they here in the home of the white,
Shadowed o'er by our banner of Freedom and Right?
Ho! alms for the hunters! or never again
Will they ride in their pomp to the hunting of men!   40

Alms, alms for our hunters! why will ye delay,
When their pride and their glory are melting away?
The parson has turned; for, on charge of his own,
Who goeth a warfare, or hunting, alone?
The politic statesman looks back with a sigh,   45
There is doubt in his heart, there is fear in his eye.
Oh, haste, lest that doubting and fear shall prevail,
And the head of his steed take the place of the tail. .
Oh, haste, ere he leave us! for who will ride then,
For pleasure or gain, to the hunting of men?   50

—1835

Edgar Allan Poe
1809–1849

Edgar Allan Poe is one of the most famous, controversial, and influential literary figures of the nineteenth century. His reputation as a haunted and enigmatic outcast—a public image he himself cultivated—endures. Although he struggled with poverty and conflict in his personal and work lives, he was simultaneously an astute professional with his finger on the pulse of literary culture. A remarkably prolific author in multiple genres including poetry, fiction, and criticism, he was also an editor for influential magazines. He participated in the fashionable salon culture among fellow poets, including Frances Sargent Osgood (see p. 147).

Poe's contributions to the development of the short story as we know it today are incalculable. Yet he considered himself primarily a poet. "The Raven" was an instant literary sensation and was widely reprinted (and parodied) in his lifetime. He offered a meticulous account of the poem's construction in his essay "The Philosophy of Composition" (1846), in which he purports to break down the step-by-step rational process of writing. Poe loved hoaxes, and it remains a subject of debate whether his rational claims in "The Philosophy of Composition" were or were not a joke. This essay also presented Poe's now-legendary argument that the death of a beautiful woman is "the most poetical topic in the world," an idea he would obsessively pursue in both his tales and his poems. (See both "The Raven" and "Annabel Lee," below.) Scholars have begun to explore how Poe's ideas about gender and poetry were bound up in social beliefs about women and gender during the time he was writing.

Poe despised didactic poetry—poetry that carried a moral in the style of Henry Wadsworth Longfellow (see p. 116) or Lydia Sigourney (see p. 82). He stressed, above all, the importance of art for its own sake, and this passionate commitment became one of his most influential legacies for later writers. Long and duly recognized as masterpieces of style and effect, his poems exemplify his fine-tuned command of craft and his interest in the depths—and extremes—of the mind's powers.

Sonnet—To Science

Science! true daughter of Old Time thou art!
Who alterest all things with thy peering eyes.
Why preyest thou thus upon the poet's heart,
Vulture, whose wings are dull realities?
5 How should he love thee? or how deem thee wise?
Who wouldst not leave him in his wandering

To seek for treasure in the jewelled skies,
Albeit he soared with an undaunted wing?
Hast thou not dragged Diana[1] from her car?
And driven the Hamadryad[2] from the wood   10
To seek a shelter in some happier star?
Hast thou not torn the Naiad from her flood,
The Elfin from the green grass, and from me
The summer dream beneath the tamarind tree?

—1829

To Helen[3]

Helen,[4] thy beauty is to me
Like those Nicéan barks[5] of yore,
That gently, o'er a perfum'd sea,
The weary way-worn wanderer bore
To his own native shore.   5

On desperate seas long wont to roam,
Thy hyacinth hair,[6] thy classic face,
Thy Naiad[7] airs have brought me home
To the beauty of fair Greece,
And the grandeur of old Rome.   10

Lo! in that little window-niche
How statue-like I see thee stand!
The folded scroll within thy hand—
A Psyche[8] from the regions which
Are Holy land!   15

—1831

---

1   *Diana* Roman goddess of nature, the hunt, and chastity. She also supplanted the moon
    goddess Luna, who is generally depicted riding in a silver chariot (car).
2   *Hamadryad* Mythical Greek tree goddess.
3   *To Helen* One of two versions (the revised poem was published in 1845).
4   *Helen* In Greek mythology, Helen was the daughter of Leda and Zeus, and the wife of
    Menelaus. Her famous beauty led to her abduction by Paris, causing the start of the Tro-
    jan war.
5   *Nicéan barks* Likely boats from Nicaea, although the meaning has been debated.
6   *hyacinth hair* Like the hyacinth flower. Although ambiguous, this likely means dark-
    haired, as "hyacinthine" is frequently used by English-speaking poets in this manner.
7   *Naiad* Water nymph.
8   *Psyche* From Roman writer Apuleius's novel *Metamorphoses*, also known as *The Golden Ass*
    (c. 2nd century CE). Psyche was a beautiful woman and lover of Cupid who fell out of his
    favor when she disobeyed his wishes and tried to see his face.

The City in the Sea

Lo! Death has reared himself a throne
In a strange city lying alone
Far down within the dim West,
Where the good and the bad and the worst and the best
5   Have gone to their eternal rest.
There shrines and palaces and towers
(Time-eaten towers that tremble not!)
Resemble nothing that is ours.
Around, by lifting winds forgot,
10   Resignedly beneath the sky
The melancholy waters lie.

No rays from the holy heaven come down
On the long night-time of that town;
But light from out the lurid sea
15   Streams up the turrets silently—
Gleams up the pinnacles far and free—
Up domes—up spires—up kingly halls—
Up fanes—up Babylon-like walls[1]—
Up shadowy long-forgotten bowers
20   Of sculptured ivy and stone flowers—
Up many and many a marvellous shrine
Whose wreathèd friezes intertwine
The viol, the violet, and the vine.

Resignedly beneath the sky
25   The melancholy waters lie.
So blend the turrets and shadows there
That all seem pendulous in air,
While from a proud tower in the town
Death looks gigantically down.

30   There open fanes and gaping graves
Yawn level with the luminous waves;
But not the riches there that lie
In each idol's diamond eye—
Not the gaily-jewelled dead

---

1   *Babylon-like walls* Babylon was the capital of ancient Babylonia, here seen as a symbol of
sin and decadence, doomed to suffer divine retribution.

Tempt the waters from their bed;   35
For no ripples curl, alas!
Along that wilderness of glass—
No swellings tell that winds may be
Upon some far-off happier sea—
No heavings hint that winds have been   40
On seas less hideously serene.

But lo, a stir is in the air!
The wave—there is a movement there!
As if the towers had thrust aside,
In slightly sinking, the dull tide—   45
As if their tops had feebly given
A void within the filmy Heaven.
The waves have now a redder glow—
The hours are breathing faint and low—
And when, amid no earthly moans,   50
Down, down that town shall settle hence,
Hell, rising from a thousand thrones,[1]
Shall do it reverence.

                                        —1831

The Raven[2]

Once upon a midnight dreary, while I pondered, weak and weary,
Over many a quaint and curious volume of forgotten lore—
While I nodded, nearly napping, suddenly there came a tapping,
As of some one gently rapping, rapping at my chamber door.
"'Tis some visitor," I muttered, "tapping at my chamber door—   5
                    Only this and nothing more."

Ah, distinctly I remember it was in the bleak December,
And each separate dying ember wrought its ghost upon the floor.
Eagerly I wished the morrow;—vainly I had sought to borrow
From my books surcease of sorrow—sorrow for the lost Lenore[3]—   10

---

1   *Hell ... thousand thrones* Allusion to Isaiah 14.9.
2   *The Raven* Poe modeled this poem on "Lady Geraldine's Courtship," by Elizabeth Barrett
     (Browning).
3   *Lenore* Poe's poem "Lenore" (1831) dramatizes the death of a young woman mourned by
     her lover.

For the rare and radiant maiden whom the angels name Lenore—
Nameless here for evermore.

And the silken sad uncertain rustling of each purple curtain
Thrilled me—filled me with fantastic terrors never felt before;
15   So that now, to still the beating of my heart, I stood repeating
"'Tis some visitor entreating entrance at my chamber door—
Some late visitor entreating entrance at my chamber door;—
This it is and nothing more."

Presently my soul grew stronger; hesitating then no longer;
20   "Sir," said I, "or Madam, truly your forgiveness I implore;
But the fact is I was napping, and so gently you came rapping,
And so faintly you came tapping, tapping at my chamber door,
That I scarce was sure I heard you"—here I opened wide the door;—
Darkness there and nothing more.

25   Deep into that darkness peering, long I stood there wondering, fearing,
Doubting, dreaming dreams no mortal ever dared to dream before;
But the silence was unbroken, and the stillness gave no token,
And the only word there spoken was the whispered word, "Lenore!"
This *I* whispered, and an echo murmured back the word "Lenore!"
30   Merely this and nothing more.

Back into the chamber turning, all my soul within me burning,
Soon again I heard a tapping somewhat louder than before.
"Surely," said I, "surely that is something at my window lattice;
Let me see, then, what thereat is, and this mystery explore—
35   Let my heart be still a moment and this mystery explore;—
'Tis the wind and nothing more!"

Open here I flung the shutter, when, with many a flirt and flutter,
In there stepped a stately raven of the saintly days of yore;
Not the least obeisance made he; not a minute stopped or stayed he;
40   But, with mien of lord or lady, perched above my chamber door—
Perched upon a bust of Pallas[1] just above my chamber door—
Perched, and sat, and nothing more.

Then this ebony bird beguiling my sad fancy into smiling,
By the grave and stern decorum of the countenance it wore,
45   "Though thy crest be shorn and shaven, thou," I said, "art sure no craven,

---

1   *Pallas* Pallas Athena, Greek goddess of wisdom.

Ghastly grim and ancient raven wandering from the Nightly shore—
Tell me what thy lordly name is on the Night's Plutonian[1] shore!"
                    Quoth the raven "Nevermore."

Much I marvelled this ungainly fowl to hear discourse so plainly,
Though its answer little meaning—little relevancy bore;   50
For we cannot help agreeing that no living human being
Ever yet was blessed with seeing bird above his chamber door—
Bird or beast upon the sculptured bust above his chamber door,
                    With such name as "Nevermore."

But the raven, sitting lonely on the placid bust, spoke only   55
That one word, as if his soul in that one word he did outpour.
Nothing farther then he uttered—not a feather then he fluttered—
Till I scarcely more than muttered "Other friends have flown before—
On the morrow *he* will leave me, as my hopes have flown before."
                    Then the bird said "Nevermore."   60

Startled at the stillness broken by reply so aptly spoken,
"Doubtless," said I, "what it utters is its only stock and store
Caught from some unhappy master whom unmerciful Disaster
Followed fast and followed faster till his songs one burden[2] bore—
Till the dirges of his Hope that melancholy burden bore   65
                    Of 'Never—nevermore.'"

But the raven still beguiling all my sad soul into smiling,
Straight I wheeled a cushioned seat in front of bird, and bust and door;
Then, upon the velvet sinking, I betook myself to linking
Fancy unto fancy, thinking what this ominous bird of yore—   70
What this grim, ungainly, ghastly, gaunt, and ominous bird of yore
                    Meant in croaking "Nevermore."

This I sat engaged in guessing, but no syllable expressing
To the fowl whose fiery eyes now burned into my bosom's core;
This and more I sat divining, with my head at ease reclining   75
On the cushion's velvet lining that the lamplight gloated° o'er,   *refracted*
But whose velvet violet lining with the lamplight gloating o'er,
                    She shall press, ah, nevermore!

---

1   *Plutonian* In Roman mythology, Pluto is god of the underworld.
2   *burden* Theme; in a poem or song, chorus or refrain.

Then, methought, the air grew denser, perfumed from an unseen censer
80   Swung by angels whose faint foot-falls tinkled on the tufted° floor.   *carpeted*
"Wretch," I cried, "thy God hath lent thee—by these angels he hath sent thee
Respite—respite and nepenthe¹ from thy memories of Lenore!
Quaff, oh quaff this kind nepenthe and forget this lost Lenore!"
                              Quoth the raven "Nevermore."

85   "Prophet!" said I, "thing of evil!—prophet still, if bird or devil!—
Whether Tempter sent, or whether tempest tossed thee here ashore,
Desolate yet all undaunted, on this desert land enchanted—
On this home by Horror haunted—tell me truly, I implore—
Is there—*is* there balm in Gilead?²—tell me—tell me, I implore!"
90   Quoth the raven "Nevermore."

"Prophet!" said I, "thing of evil!—prophet still, if bird or devil!
By that Heaven that bends above us—by that God we both adore—
Tell this soul with sorrow laden if, within the distant Aidenn,°   *Eden*
It shall clasp a sainted maiden whom the angels name Lenore—
95   Clasp a rare and radiant maiden whom the angels name Lenore."
                              Quoth the raven "Nevermore."

"Be that word our sign of parting, bird or fiend!" I shrieked, upstarting—
"Get thee back into the tempest and the Night's Plutonian shore!
Leave no black plume as a token of that lie thy soul hath spoken!
100 Leave my loneliness unbroken!—quit the bust above my door!
Take thy beak from out my heart, and take thy form from off my door!"
                              Quoth the raven "Nevermore."

And the raven, never flitting, still is sitting, *still* is sitting
On the pallid bust of Pallas just above my chamber door;
105 And his eyes have all the seeming of a demon's that is dreaming,
And the lamp-light o'er him streaming throws his shadow on the floor;
And my soul from out that shadow that lies floating on the floor
                    Shall be lifted—nevermore!
                                                     —1845

---

1   *nepenthe* Drink supposed to banish sorrow by inducing forgetfulness.
2   *Is there ... Gilead* See Jeremiah 8.22 in the Bible's Old Testament: "Is there no balm
    in Gilead?"; *balm* Soothing ointment; *Gilead* In the Bible, the land east of the River
    Jordan.

The Sleeper

At midnight, in the month of June,
I stand beneath the mystic moon.
An opiate vapour, dewy, dim,
Exhales from out her golden rim,
And, softly dripping, drop by drop,   5
Upon the quiet mountain top,
Steals drowsily and musically
Into the universal valley.
The rosemary[1] nods upon the grave;
The lily lolls upon the wave;   10
Wrapping the fog about its breast,
The ruin moulders into rest;
Looking like Lethë,[2] see! the lake
A conscious slumber seems to take,
And would not, for the world, awake.   15
All Beauty sleeps!—and lo! where lies
(Her casement open to the skies)
Irenë, with her Destinies!

Oh, lady bright! can it be right—
This window open to the night?   20
The wanton airs, from the tree-top,
Laughingly through the lattice drop—
The bodiless airs, a wizard rout,
Flit through thy chamber in and out,
And wave the curtain canopy   25
So fitfully—so fearfully—
Above the closed and fringèd lid
'Neath which thy slumb'ring soul lies hid,
That, o'er the floor and down the wall,
Like ghosts the shadows rise and fall!   30
Oh, lady dear, hast thou no fear?
Why and what are thou dreaming here?
Sure thou art come o'er far-off seas,
A wonder to these garden trees!
Strange is thy pallor! strange thy dress!   35

---

1   *rosemary* Plant associated with remembrance.
2   *Lethë* In classical myth, the river of forgetfulness in Hades.

Strange, above all, thy length of tress,
And this all solemn silentness!
The lady sleeps! Oh, may her sleep,
Which is enduring, so be deep!
40 Heaven have her in its sacred keep!
This chamber changed for one more holy,
This bed for one more melancholy,
I pray to God that she may lie
Forever with unopened eye,
45 While the dim sheeted ghosts go by!

My love, she sleeps! Oh, may her sleep,
As it is lasting, so be deep!
Soft may the worms about her creep!
Far in the forest, dim and old,
50 For her may some tall vault unfold—
Some vault that oft hath flung its black
And wingèd pannels fluttering back,
Triumphant, o'er the crested palls,
Of her grand family funerals—
55 Some sepulchre, remote, alone,
Against whose portal she hath thrown,
In childhood, many an idle stone—
Some tomb from out whose sounding door,
She ne'er shall force an echo more,
60 Thrilling to think, poor child of sin!
It was the dead who groaned within.

—1845

Annabel Lee

It was many and many a year ago,
    In a kingdom by the sea,
That a maiden there lived whom you may know
    By the name of Annabel Lee;—
5 And this maiden she lived with no other thought
    Than to love and be loved by me.

I was a child and *she* was a child,
    In this kingdom by the sea;

But we loved with a love that was more than love—
    I and my Annabel Lee—
With a love that the wingèd seraphs of heaven
    Coveted her and me.

And this was the reason that, long ago,
    In this kingdom by the sea,
A wind blew out of a cloud, chilling
    My beautiful Annabel Lee;
So that her highborn kinsman came
    And bore her away from me,
To shut her up in a sepulchre
    In this kingdom by the sea.

The angels, not half so happy in heaven,
    Went envying her and me—
Yes!—that was the reason (as all men know,
    In this kingdom by the sea)
That the wind came out of the cloud by night,
    Chilling and killing my Annabel Lee.

But our love it was stronger by far than the love
    Of those who were older than we—
    Of many far wiser than we—
And neither the angels in heaven above,
    Nor the demons down under the sea,
Can ever dissever my soul from the soul
    Of the beautiful Annabel Lee:—

For the moon never beams without bringing me dreams
    Of the beautiful Annabel Lee;
And the stars never rise but I feel the bright eyes
    Of the beautiful Annabel Lee:—
And so, all the night-tide, I lie down by the side
Of my darling—my darling—my life and my bride,
    In the sepulchre there by the sea—
    In her tomb by the sounding sea.

10

15

20

25

30

35

40

—1849

Alfred, Lord Tennyson
1809–1892

More than any other poet, Alfred, Lord Tennyson gave voice to the ambitions, anxieties, and myths of the Victorian era. A period of massive cultural and political change, it was also a time when poetry enjoyed broad popularity. Tennyson was both internationally famous and beloved by the public. Born in 1809 to a privileged, somewhat eccentric family, Tennyson decided early on that poetry was his true vocation. He left Cambridge without taking a degree and devoted himself to a versatile career writing in a variety of long and short poetic forms, from dramatic monologues (such as "Ulysses," below), to lyrics, to retellings of Arthurian narratives (such as "The Lady of Shalott," below). The year 1850 was significant for Tennyson: after a 14-year courtship, he married Emily Sellwood; he was named Poet Laureate; and he published *In Memoriam A.H.H.* (see the companion website), a long and often despairing poem (of 131 sections) that became iconic as an expression of Victorian faith and doubt. At this time, new scientific and historical discoveries pushed the traditional Christian beliefs of many people into a state of crisis. Composed in memory of his best friend Arthur Hallam, who died suddenly (apparently of a cerebral aneurysm) when Tennyson was 24 and Hallam himself was 22, Tennyson's poem poured out his grief about his friend as well as about the human place in a natural world that was "red in tooth and claw" (section 56) and, possibly, godless. The poem immediately tapped into larger Victorian crises about the modern age and was recognized as his most important work.

Tennyson's poetry often deals with the historical and mythical past, with ideas about the power and role of art, and with the individual's place in a world of change. Anxieties over sexuality, violence, and death lie close to the surface. Revered for his mastery of sound in an age when readers treasured hearing poetry aloud, Tennyson was recorded by Thomas Edison in 1890 reciting "The Charge of the Light Brigade"—a fitting emblem of the poet's career-long meditations on the flux of modern culture and of poetry's place in it.

Note to readers: Tennyson's poems "St. Simon Stylites" and "In Memoriam A.H.H." appear on the anthology's companion website. The URL and passcode appear in the Table of Contents.

Mariana

"Mariana in the Moated Grange"
(Shakespeare, *Measure for Measure*)[1]

With blackest moss the flower-plots
    Were thickly crusted, one and all:
The rusted nails fell from the knots
    That held the pear to the gable-wall.[2]
The broken sheds look'd sad and strange: 5
    Unlifted was the clinking latch;
    Weeded and worn the ancient thatch
Upon the lonely moated grange.
        She only said, "My life is dreary,
            He cometh not," she said;   10
        She said, "I am aweary, aweary,
            I would that I were dead!"

Her tears fell with the dews at even;
    Her tears fell ere the dews were dried;
She could not look on the sweet heaven,   15
    Either at morn or eventide.
After the flitting of the bats,
    When thickest dark did trance the sky,
    She drew her casement-curtain by,
And glanced athwart the glooming flats.[3]   20
        She only said, "The night is dreary,
            He cometh not," she said;
        She said, "I am aweary, aweary,
            I would that I were dead!"

Upon the middle of the night,   25
    Waking she heard the night-fowl crow:
The cock sung out an hour ere light:
    From the dark fen the oxen's low

---

1   *Mariana ... Measure* Tennyson's epigraph is adapted from the words of the Duke in
    Shakespeare's *Measure for Measure*, 3.1.277: "There, at the moated grange, lies this de-
    jected Mariana." Earlier in the scene the Duke has recounted how Mariana, having lost
    her dowry (and her brother) in a shipwreck, has been deserted by her betrothed; *Moated*
    Grange Cottage or small farmhouse surrounded by a moat, or water-filled ditch.
2   *The rusted ... gable-wall* The pear has been espaliered, or trained.
3   *flats* Flatlands or lowlands.

Came to her: without hope of change,
30   In sleep she seem'd to walk forlorn,
         Till cold winds woke the gray-eyed morn
About the lonely moated grange.
            She only said, "The day is dreary,
               He cometh not," she said;
35   She said, "I am aweary, aweary,
               I would that I were dead!"

About a stone-cast from the wall
      A sluice with blacken'd waters slept,
And o'er it many, round and small,
40   The cluster'd marish-mosses crept.[1]
Hard by a poplar shook alway,
      All silver-green with gnarled bark:
      For leagues no other tree did mark
The level waste, the rounding gray.
45   She only said, "My life is dreary,
               He cometh not," she said;
            She said "I am aweary, aweary
               I would that I were dead!"

And ever when the moon was low,
50   And the shrill winds were up and away,
In the white curtain, to and fro,
      She saw the gusty shadow sway.
But when the moon was very low
      And wild winds bound within their cell,[2]
55   The shadow of the poplar fell
Upon her bed, across her brow.
            She only said, "The night is dreary,
               He cometh not," she said;
            She said "I am aweary, aweary,
60   I would that I were dead!"

All day within the dreamy house,
      The doors upon their hinges creak'd;
The blue fly sung in the pane; the mouse

---

1   [Tennyson's note] *Marish-mosses*, the little marsh-moss lumps that float on the surface of the water.
2   *wild … cell* A reference to Virgil's *Aeneid*, 1.52, in which Aeolus, god of winds, keeps the winds imprisoned in a cavern.

Behind the mouldering wainscot shriek'd,
Or from the crevice peer'd about.   65
     Old faces glimmer'd thro' the doors
     Old footsteps trod the upper floors,
Old voices called her from without.
     She only said, "My life is dreary,
       He cometh not," she said;   70
     She said, "I am aweary, aweary,
       I would that I were dead!"

The sparrow's chirrup on the roof,
     The slow clock ticking, and the sound
Which to the wooing wind aloof   75
     The poplar made, did all confound
Her sense; but most she loathed the hour
     When the thick-moted[1] sunbeam lay
     Athwart the chambers, and the day
Was sloping toward his western bower.   80
     Then said she, "I am very dreary,
       He will not come," she said;
     She wept, "I am aweary, aweary,
       Oh God, that I were dead!"

           —1830

The Lady of Shalott[2]

Part 1

On either side the river lie
Long fields of barley and of rye,
That clothe the wold° and meet the sky;   *plain*
And through the field the road runs by
     To many-towered Camelot;   5
And up and down the people go,
Gazing where the lilies blow
Round an island there below,
     The island of Shalott.

---

1   *thick-moted* I.e., thick with motes of dust.
2   *The Lady of Shalott* Elaine of the Arthurian romances, who dies of love for Lancelot;
    she is called "the lily maid of Astolat" in Malory's *Morte Darthur* (1485). Tennyson first
    encountered the story, however, in a medieval Italian romance called "La Donna di
    Scalotta" and changed the name to Shalott for a softer sound.

10 Willows whiten,[1] aspens quiver,
    Little breezes dusk° and shiver   *darken*
    Through the wave that runs for ever
    By the island in the river
            Flowing down to Camelot.
15 Four grey walls, and four grey towers,
    Overlook a space of flowers,
    And the silent isle imbowers°   *encloses*
            The Lady of Shalott.

    By the margin, willow-veiled,
20 Slide the heavy barges trailed
    By slow horses; and unhailed
    The shallop[2] flitteth silken-sailed
            Skimming down to Camelot:
    But who hath seen her wave her hand?
25 Or at the casement seen her stand?
    Or is she known in all the land,
            The Lady of Shalott?

    Only reapers, reaping early
    In among the bearded barley,
30 Hear a song that echoes cheerly
    From the river winding clearly,
            Down to towered Camelot:
    And by the moon the reaper weary,
    Piling sheaves in uplands airy,
35 Listening, whispers "'Tis the fairy
            Lady of Shalott."

Part 2

    There she weaves by night and day
    A magic web with colours gay.
    She has heard a whisper say,
40 A curse is on her if she stay
            To look down to Camelot.
    She knows not what the curse may be,
    And so she weaveth steadily,

---

1   *Willows whiten* I.e., the wind exposes the white undersides of the leaves.
2   *shallop* Light open boat for use in shallow water.

And little other care hath she,
    The Lady of Shalott.   45

And moving through a mirror clear
That hangs before her all the year,
Shadows of the world appear.
There she sees the highway near
    Winding down to Camelot: 50
There the river eddy whirls,
And there the surly village-churls,
And the red cloaks of market girls,
    Pass onward from Shalott.

Sometimes a troop of damsels glad,   55
An abbot on an ambling pad,°   *horse*
Sometimes a curly shepherd-lad,
Or long-haired page in crimson clad,
    Goes by to towered Camelot;
And sometimes through the mirror blue   60
The knights come riding two and two:
She hath no loyal knight and true,
    The Lady of Shalott.

But in her web she still delights
To weave the mirror's magic sights,   65
For often through the silent nights
A funeral, with plumes and lights
    And music, went to Camelot:
Or when the moon was overhead,
Came two young lovers lately wed;   70
"I am half sick of shadows," said
    The Lady of Shalott.

Part 3

A bow-shot from her bower-eaves,
He rode between the barley-sheaves,
The sun came dazzling through the leaves,   75
And flamed upon the brazen greaves[1]
    Of bold Sir Lancelot.
A red-cross knight for ever kneeled

---

1   *greaves* Armor worn below the knee.

To a lady in his shield,
80 That sparkled on the yellow field,
    Beside remote Shalott.

The gemmy° bridle glittered free,   *brilliant*
Like to some branch of stars we see
Hung in the golden Galaxy.
85 The bridle bells rang merrily
    As he rode down to Camelot:
And from his blazoned baldric° slung   *shoulder-strap*
A mighty silver bugle hung,
And as he rode his armour rung,
90   Beside remote Shalott.

All in the blue unclouded weather
Thick-jewelled shone the saddle-leather,
The helmet and the helmet-feather
Burned like one burning flame together,
95   As he rode down to Camelot.
As often through the purple night,
Below the starry clusters bright,
Some bearded meteor, trailing light,
    Moves over still Shalott.

100 His broad clear brow in sunlight glowed;
On burnished hooves his war-horse trode;
From underneath his helmet flowed
His coal-black curls as on he rode,
    As he rode down to Camelot.
105 From the bank and from the river
He flashed into the crystal mirror,
"Tirra lirra," by the river
    Sang Sir Lancelot.

She left the web, she left the loom,
110 She made three paces through the room,
She saw the water-lily bloom,
She saw the helmet and the plume,
    She looked down to Camelot.
Out flew the web and floated wide;
115 The mirror cracked from side to side;

"The curse is come upon me," cried
    The Lady of Shalott.

Part 4

In the stormy east-wind straining,
The pale yellow woods were waning,
The broad stream in his banks complaining,   120
Heavily the low sky raining
    Over towered Camelot;
Down she came and found a boat
Beneath a willow left afloat,
And round about the prow she wrote   125
    The Lady of Shalott.

And down the river's dim expanse
Like some bold seer in a trance,
Seeing all his own mischance—
With a glassy countenance   130
    Did she look to Camelot.
And at the closing of the day
She loosed the chain, and down she lay;
The broad stream bore her far away,
    The Lady of Shalott.   135

Lying, robed in snowy white
That loosely flew to left and right—
The leaves upon her falling light—
Through the noises of the night
    She floated down to Camelot: 140
And as the boat-head wound along
The willowy hills and fields among,
They heard her singing her last song,
    The Lady of Shalott.

Heard a carol, mournful, holy,   145
Chanted loudly, chanted lowly,
Till her blood was frozen slowly,
And her eyes were darkened wholly,
    Turned to towered Camelot.
For ere she reached upon the tide   150
The first house by the water-side,

Singing in her song she died,
    The Lady of Shalott.

Under tower and balcony,
155 By garden-wall and gallery,
A gleaming shape she floated by,
Dead-pale between the houses high,
    Silent into Camelot.
Out upon the wharfs they came,
160 Knight and burgher, lord and dame,
And round the prow they read her name,
    The Lady of Shalott.

Who is this? and what is here?
And in the lighted palace near
165 Died the sound of royal cheer;
And they crossed themselves for fear,
    All the knights at Camelot:
But Lancelot mused a little space;
He said, "She has a lovely face;
170 God in his mercy lend her grace,
    The Lady of Shalott."

—1832 (revised 1842)

Ulysses[1]

It little profits that an idle king,
By this still hearth, among these barren crags,
Matched with an agèd wife, I mete and dole
Unequal laws unto a savage race,
5 That hoard, and sleep, and feed, and know not me.
I cannot rest from travel: I will drink
Life to the lees:° all times I have enjoyed   *dregs*
Greatly, have suffered greatly, both with those
That loved me, and alone; on shore, and when
10 Thro' scudding drifts the rainy Hyades[2]
Vexed the dim sea: I am become a name;

---

1   *Ulysses* Latin name for Odysseus, the protagonist of Homer's *Odyssey.* Here, long after
     the adventures recounted in that poem, the aged, yet restless Ulysses prepares to em-
     bark on one last voyage.
2   *Hyades* Group of stars near the constellation Taurus and associated with rainstorms.

For always roaming with a hungry heart
Much have I seen and known; cities of men
And manners, climates, councils, governments,
Myself not least, but honoured of them all;   15
And drunk delight of battle with my peers,
Far on the ringing plains of windy Troy.
I am a part of all that I have met;
Yet all experience is an arch wherethrough
Gleams that untravelled world, whose margin° fades   *horizon* 20
For ever and for ever when I move.
How dull it is to pause, to make an end,
To rust unburnished, not to shine in use!
As though to breathe were life. Life piled on life
Were all too little, and of one to me   25
Little remains: but every hour is saved
From that eternal silence, something more,
A bringer of new things; and vile it were
For some three suns to store and hoard myself,
And this grey spirit yearning in desire   30
To follow knowledge like a sinking star,
Beyond the utmost bound of human thought.

    This is my son, mine own Telemachus,
To whom I leave the sceptre and the isle—
Well-loved of me, discerning to fulfil   35
This labour, by slow prudence to make mild
A rugged people, and through soft degrees
Subdue them to the useful and the good.
Most blameless is he, centred in the sphere
Of common duties, decent not to fail   40
In offices of tenderness, and pay
Meet° adoration to my household gods,   *Appropriate*
When I am gone. He works his work, I mine.

    There lies the port; the vessel puffs her sail:
There gloom the dark broad seas. My mariners,   45
Souls that have toiled, and wrought, and thought with me—
That ever with a frolic welcome took
The thunder and the sunshine, and opposed
Free hearts, free foreheads—you and I are old;
Old age hath yet his honour and his toil;   50

Death closes all: but something ere the end,
Some work of noble note, may yet be done,
Not unbecoming men that strove with Gods.
The lights begin to twinkle from the rocks:
55 The long day wanes: the slow moon climbs: the deep
Moans round with many voices. Come, my friends,
'Tis not too late to seek a newer world.
Push off, and sitting well in order smite
The sounding furrows; for my purpose holds
60 To sail beyond the sunset, and the baths
Of all the western stars, until I die.
It may be that the gulfs will wash us down:
It may be we shall touch the Happy Isles,[1]
And see the great Achilles,[2] whom we knew.
65 Though much is taken, much abides; and though
We are not now that strength which in old days
Moved earth and heaven; that which we are, we are;
One equal temper of heroic hearts,
Made weak by time and fate, but strong in will
70 To strive, to seek, to find, and not to yield.

—1842 (written 1833)

The Charge of the Light Brigade[3]

1

Half a league,[4] half a league,
Half a league onward,
All in the valley of Death
    Rode the six hundred.[5]
5 "Forward, the Light Brigade!

---

1   *Happy Isles* Elysium, or Isles of the Blessed, where heroes enjoyed the afterlife.
2   *Achilles* Hero from Greek mythology, also the central character of Homer's *Iliad*.
3   *The Charge ... Brigade* Written some weeks after a disastrous engagement during the Crimean War. At the Battle of Balaclava on 25 October 1854, the 700 cavalrymen of the Light Brigade, acting on a misinterpreted order, directly charged the Russian artillery.
4   *league* About three miles.
5   *six hundred* The initial newspaper account read by Tennyson mentioned "607 sabres," and he retained the number even when the correct number was discovered to be considerably higher because "six is much better than seven hundred ... metrically" (*Letters* 2.101).

Charge for the guns!" he said:
Into the valley of Death
      Rode the six hundred.

2

"Forward, the Light Brigade!"
Was there a man dismayed?   10
Not though the soldier knew
      Some one had blundered:
Theirs not to make reply,
Theirs not to reason why,
Theirs but to do and die: 15
Into the valley of Death
      Rode the six hundred.

3

Cannon to right of them,
Cannon to left of them,
Cannon in front of them   20
      Volleyed and thundered;
Stormed at with shot and shell,
Boldly they rode and well,
Into the jaws of Death,
Into the mouth of Hell   25
      Rode the six hundred.

4

Flashed all their sabres bare,
Flashed as they turned in air
Sabring the gunners there,
Charging an army, while   30
      All the world wondered:
Plunged in the battery-smoke
Right through the line they broke;
Cossack and Russian
Reeled from the sabre-stroke   35
      Shattered and sundered.
Then they rode back, but not
      Not the six hundred.

5

Cannon to right of them,
40 Cannon to left of them,
Cannon behind them
    Volleyed and thundered;
Stormed at with shot and shell,
While horse and hero fell,
45 They that had fought so well
Came through the jaws of Death,
Back from the mouth of Hell,
All that was left of them,[1]
    Left of six hundred.

6

50 When can their glory fade?
O the wild charge they made!
    All the world wondered.
Honour the charge they made!
Honour the Light Brigade,
55   Noble six hundred!

—1854

---

1 *All ... them* 118 men were killed and 127 wounded; after the charge, only 195 men
were still with their horses.

Frances Sargent Osgood

1811–1850

Francis Sargent Osgood, born in Boston, was a popular and well-paid "poet-ess"—the gendered term for women poets in her own day. Publishing both in book form and in well-regarded periodicals, with an avid audience of male and female readers, Osgood also frequented the literary salons in New York, a kind of club scene conducted in the homes of influential hosts and hostesses. There, established as well as up-and-coming artists mingled with powerful and socially well-connected people. Although during her lifetime Osgood's poetry was more popular than her peer and fellow salon attendee Edgar Allan Poe's, literary history later reduced her to a side note in his biography. The pair carried on a scandalous and deliberately public flirtation (including an exchange of romantic poems in print) while they were both married. Since the 1990s, scholars have returned to Osgood's poetry as a window into the lively marketplace for poetry in her time. She wrote on many safe, conventional topics that suited the sentimental taste of the era, but she also explored riskier terrain including erotic feelings and fantasies. Her range of styles reminds us that women poets who published at this time adopted, massaged, parodied, or reviled an array of poetic modes and that they did so as a complex response to the gender constructions (and constrictions) of the time. Not yet 40, Fanny Osgood died of tuberculosis, a disease that also killed all three of her children.

[Won't you die & be a spirit][1]

Won't you die & be a spirit
Darling, say
What's the use of keeping on
That robe of clay[2]
If you only were a spirit
You could *stay*

5

Oh! die & be a spirit
Darling, do
I should hate to have to go

---

1   Osgood did not publish this poem in her lifetime. Scholar Joanne Dobson discovered it among Osgood's papers, calling it a "flirtatious" verse in which the speaker writes within and against "the social codes and personal dilemmas surrounding sexual attraction."

2   *robe of clay* The human body, opposed here to "spirit."

10 If I were you
From a being so delightful
And so true

If you'll die & be a spirit
You may press
15 The hand that now you gaze at
And the tress
And the cheek that lips of clay
Shall n'er caress—

If you'll die & be a spirit
20 You may say
How tenderly you love me
Everyday
But now I hate to hear you!
Go Away!

25 Just think how nice 'twould be
To come & beam
Like a star about my pillow
Or to seem
A vision—I should love
30 To love a dream!

—[date unknown]

To My Pen

Dost know, my little vagrant pen,
That wanderest lightly down the paper,
Without a thought how critic-men
May carp at every careless caper!

5 Dost know, twice twenty thousand eyes,
If publishers report them truly,
Each month may mark the sportive lies
That track, oh, shame! thy steps unruly?

Now list to me, my fairy[1] pen,
10 And con° the lesson gravely over;   *learn*

---

1 *fairy* Enchanted, magical, ethereal, or insubstantial.

Be never wild or false again;
But "mind your Ps and Qs"—you rover!

While tripping gaily to and fro,
Let not a thought escape you lightly;
But challenge all before they go,   15
And see them fairly robed and rightly.

You know that words but dress the frame,
And thought's the *soul* of verse, my fairy!
So drape not spirits dull and tame,
In gorgeous robes or garments airy.   20

I would not have my pen pursue
The "beaten track"—a slave forever;
No! roam as thou wert wont to do,
In author-land, by rock and river.

Be like the sunbeam's burning wing,   25
Be like the wand in Cinderella;
And *if* you touch a common thing,
Ah! change to *gold the pumpkin yellow.*

May grace come fluttering round your steps,
Whene'er, my bird! you 'light on paper;   30
And music murmur at your lips,
And truth restrain each truant caper.

Let hope paint pictures in your way,
And love his seraph°-lesson teach you;   *angel*
And rather calm with reason stray,   35
Than dance with folly—I beseech you!

In faith's pure fountain lave° your wing;   *wash*
And quaff from feeling's glowing chalice;
But touch not falsehood's fetal spring;
And shun the poisoned weeds of malice!   40

Firm be the web you lightly spin,
From *leaf to leaf,* though frail in seeming,
While fancy's fairy dew-gems win
The sunbeam 'truth' to keep them gleaming.

45 And shrink not thou when tyrant-wrong
   O'er humble suffering dares deride thee;
   With lightning step and clarion song,
   Go! take the field, with Heaven beside thee!

   Be tuned to tenderest music when
50 Of sin and shame thou'rt sadly singing;
   But *diamond* be thy point, my pen!
   When folly's bells are round thee ringing.

   And so, where'er you slay your flight,
   To plume your wing or dance your measure,
55 May gems and flowers your pathway light,
   For these who track your tread, my treasure!

   But what is this? you've tripped about,
   While I the Mentor grave was playing;
   And here you've written boldly out
60 The very words that I was saying!

   And here as usual on you've flown,
   From right to left, flown fast and faster
   Till even while you wrote it down,
   You've *missed* the task you ought to *master*.

                                        —1847

The Coquette's Vow

   I promise *while* I love you,
       To love you true and well;
   But, by that cloud above you,
       How long—I dare not tell.

5 I promise to be tender,
       And docile to your sway;°   *influence*
   I promise to surrender
       My soul—at least—*a day*.

   But if—but if—to-morrow
10   I chance to grow more wise—

If Love should dream you borrow
    Your light from Fancy's eyes;

If I should weary, playing
    On one eternal lyre,
And touch, with fingers straying,   15
    Some other chords of fire;°

If they should answer willing,
    In sweeter tones than you,
Forgive my heart for thrilling,
    And own *my ear is true.*   20

You have the same permission
    To tire, to change, to go,
With only one condition—
    That you will *let me know.*

Then chide me not for changing   25
    When I've gone through the book,
But chide the bee for ranging,
    And chide the sportive brook.

When through the dark cloud smiling
    The sunbeam wandered warm,   30
A rainbow came, beguiling
    To beauty all the storm.

But if when light was banished
    By cold, unwelcome rain,
That rare guest paled and vanished,   35
    Oh! could the cloud complain?

A wild bee found a rose
    And nestled in its heart,
But when its leaflets close
    The flutterer fain° would part.   *willingly* 40

Air, freedom, light and heaven
    It would not so resign;
Then if those leaves be riven,°   *torn*
    Ah! should the rose repine?°   *complain*

45 Since round your being real
        My fancy deigns to fly,
    Keep up to my Ideal,
        Or you are false—not I.

    Yet though unlike most lovers,
50   I vow at once to change
    If fancy e'er discovers
        A nobler field to range.

    Of this at least be sure,
        That even when I go
55 I'll probably be truer
        Than some who swear they're so

    And though less true than truant,°   *wandering*
        I shall not *fall* in love;
    But of some star pursuant,
60   Still rise to light above.

    Then, since around your Real
        My Fancy deigns to fly.
    Keep up to my Ideal,
        Or you are false as I.

                                                          —1850

Robert Browning
1812–1889

Robert Browning enjoyed a controversial reputation during his lifetime. Sometimes criticized as too obscure or for treating inappropriate subject matter (like the aberrant personalities in the two selections below), he also experimented with metrical bumpiness and colloquial speech in ways that violated traditional assumptions about poetic sound and proper "poetic diction." Others hailed him for developing a new kind of poetry that explored the emergent concerns of a modern world, ranging from psychology to science to ethics.

Browning has become famous in particular for developing the dramatic monologue, a form that, like a character's speech in a play, showcases a persona speaking in response to a particular situation, sometimes with an implied audience, and in ways that are rhetorically revealing. Browning's exploration of personae and voice (see Glossary) marked a major difference from the lyric poems of his Romantic predecessors such as Wordsworth and Keats, whose "I" speakers often sound as if they represent the poet's own voice. In Browning's hands, dramatic lyrics became a rich canvas for exploring psychological depths and motives.

Born to a relatively wealthy family, his father provided him with a rich home education, an extensive personal library, and financial support that allowed him to dedicate himself to writing. In 1845 Browning began corresponding with the poet Elizabeth Barrett, and the following year they eloped to Italy. Their marriage was a happy and intensely devoted one that attracted widespread transatlantic celebrity. After his wife's death in 1861, Browning returned to London society, where he produced several volumes that made him popular among British readers. He enjoyed even greater popularity in the US, where reading clubs sprang up to study his work and, as scholar Yopie Prins has pointed out, his poems were printed for a wide public in popular media forms such as railway timetables.

Porphyria's Lover[1]

The rain set early in tonight,
  The sullen wind was soon awake,
It tore the elm-tops down for spite,
  And did its worst to vex the lake:
  I listened with heart fit to break.   5

---

1   *Porphyria's Lover* The heroine's name is derived from the Greek word meaning "purple." (The word "porphyria" was not used as a label for a group of genetically-based blood disorders until much later in the nineteenth century.)

When glided in Porphyria; straight
    She shut the cold out and the storm,
And kneeled and made the cheerless grate
    Blaze up, and all the cottage warm;
10   Which done, she rose, and from her form
Withdrew the dripping cloak and shawl,
    And laid her soiled gloves by, untied
Her hat and let the damp hair fall,
    And, last, she sat down by my side
15   And called me. When no voice replied,
She put my arm about her waist,
    And made her smooth white shoulder bare,
And all her yellow hair displaced,
    And, stooping, made my cheek lie there
20   And spread, o'er all, her yellow hair,
Murmuring how she loved me—she
    Too weak, for all her heart's endeavour,
To set its struggling passion free
    From pride, and vainer ties dissever,
25   And give herself to me forever.
But passion sometimes would prevail,
    Nor could tonight's gay feast restrain
A sudden thought of one so pale
    For love of her, and all in vain:
30   So, she was come through wind and rain.
Be sure I looked up at her eyes
    Happy and proud; at last I knew
Porphyria worshipped me; surprise
    Made my heart swell, and still it grew
35   While I debated what to do.
That moment she was mine, mine, fair,
    Perfectly pure and good: I found
A thing to do, and all her hair
    In one long yellow string I wound
40   Three times her little throat around
And strangled her. No pain felt she;
    I am quite sure she felt no pain.
As a shut bud that holds a bee,
    I warily oped her lids: again
45   Laughed the blue eyes without a stain.

And I untightened next the tress
　　About her neck, her cheek once more
Blushed bright beneath my burning kiss:
　　I propped her head up as before
　　Only, this time my shoulder bore,　　　　　　　　　50
Her head, which droops upon it still:
　　The smiling rosy little head,
So glad it has its utmost will,
　　That all it scorned at once is fled,
　　And I, its love, am gained instead!　　　　　　　　55
Porphyria's love: she guessed not how
　　Her darling one wish would be heard.
And thus we sit together now,
　　And all night long we have not stirred,
　　And yet God has not said a word!　　　　　　　　　60

　　　　　　　　　　　　　　—1836

My Last Duchess[1]

Ferrara

That's my last Duchess painted on the wall,
Looking as if she were alive. I call
That piece a wonder, now: Fra Pandolf's[2] hands
Worked busily a day, and there she stands.
Will't please you sit and look at her? I said　　　　5
"Fra Pandolf " by design, for never read
Strangers like you that pictured countenance,
The depth and passion of its earnest glance,
But to myself they turned (since none puts by
The curtain I have drawn for you, but I)　　　　　10
And seemed as they would ask me, if they durst,
How such a glance came there; so, not the first

1　*My Last Duchess* Based on events in the life of Alfonso II, first Duke of Ferrara, Italy,
　　whose first wife died in 1561 under suspicious circumstances after three years of marriage.
　　Upon her death, the Duke entered into negotiations with an agent of Count Ferdinand I
　　of Tyrol, whose daughter he married in 1565.
2　*Fra Pandolf* Brother Pandolf, an imaginary painter, just as "Claus of Innsbruck" (line 56)
　　is an imaginary sculptor.

Are you to turn and ask thus. Sir, 'twas not
Her husband's presence only, called that spot
15   Of joy into the Duchess' cheek: perhaps
Fra Pandolf chanced to say "Her mantle laps
Over my lady's wrist too much," or "Paint
Must never hope to reproduce the faint
Half-flush that dies along her throat": such stuff
20   Was courtesy, she thought, and cause enough
For calling up that spot of joy. She had
A heart—how shall I say?—too soon made glad,
Too easily impressed; she liked whate'er
She looked on, and her looks went everywhere.
25   Sir, 'twas all one! My favour at her breast,[1]
The dropping of the daylight in the West,
The bough of cherries some officious fool
Broke in the orchard for her, the white mule
She rode with round the terrace—all and each
30   Would draw from her alike the approving speech,
Or blush, at least. She thanked men—good! but thanked
Somehow—I know not how—as if she ranked
My gift of a nine-hundred-years-old name
With anybody's gift. Who'd stoop to blame
35   This sort of trifling? Even had you skill
In speech—(which I have not)—to make your will
Quite clear to such an one, and say, "Just this
Or that in you disgusts me; here you miss,
Or there exceed the mark"—and if she let
40   Herself be lessoned so, nor plainly set
Her wits to yours, forsooth, and made excuse,
—E'en then would be some stooping; and I choose
Never to stoop. Oh sir, she smiled, no doubt,
Whene'er I passed her; but who passed without
45   Much the same smile? This grew; I gave commands;
Then all smiles stopped together. There she stands
As if alive. Will't please you rise? We'll meet
The company below, then. I repeat,
The Count your master's known munificence
50   Is ample warrant that no just pretence

---

1   *My favour at her breast* I.e., a scarf or ribbon decorated with the Duke's heraldic colors or
armorial bearings.

Of mine for dowry will be disallowed;
Though his fair daughter's self, as I avowed
At starting, is my object. Nay, we'll go
Together down, sir. Notice Neptune,[1] though,
Taming a sea-horse, thought a rarity,   55
Which Claus of Innsbruck cast in bronze for me!

—1842

---

1   *Neptune* Roman god of the sea, who rides in a chariot pulled by seahorses.

Emily Brontë
1818–1848

It would seem that there were two Emily Brontës: one a shy, introverted, and unremarkable young woman, and the other the strong-willed, brilliant, and legendary woman who became almost a mythic figure after her death at the age of 30. Both versions develop from the impressions her sister Charlotte gave of her in the preface to the 1850 edition of Emily's only novel, *Wuthering Heights*. For many years it was this work for which she was best known; it was not until the start of the twentieth century that her poetry began to receive serious critical attention.

The fifth of six children born to a literary-minded Anglican clergyman, Brontë grew up in a village in the moors of West Yorkshire, a landscape that is frequently reflected in her poetic imagery. Her literary talent flourished in a house of creative writers that included her sisters Charlotte (author of *Jane Eyre*) and Anne (author of *The Tenant of Wildfell Hall*). As adults, the three sisters collaborated on a volume of poetry, which they published pseudonymously as *The Poems of Currer, Ellis, and Acton Bell* (1846); though its significance is recognized today, the edition published by the sisters sold only two copies.

Brontë died of tuberculosis in December 1848, only one year after the publication of *Wuthering Heights*. Charlotte Brontë championed her sister's poetic reputation after Emily's death, arguing that the poems evoke the stirrings of the "heart like the sound of a trumpet."

[No coward soul is mine]

No coward soul is mine
No trembler in the world's storm-troubled sphere
I see Heaven's glories shine
And Faith shines equal arming me from Fear

5 O God within my breast
Almighty ever-present Deity
Life, that in me hast rest
As I Undying Life, have power in Thee

Vain are the thousand creeds
10 That move men's hearts, unutterably vain,
Worthless as withered weeds
Or idlest froth amid the boundless main°   *sea*

To waken doubt in one
Holding so fast by thy infinity
So surely anchored on   15
The steadfast rock of Immortality.

With wide-embracing love
Thy spirit animates eternal years
Pervades and broods above,
Changes, sustains, dissolves, creates and rears   20

Though Earth and moon were gone
And suns and universes ceased to be
And thou wert left alone
Every Existence would exist in thee

There is not room for Death   25
Nor atom that his might could render void
Since thou art Being and Breath
And what thou art may never be destroyed.

—1850 (written 1846)

[Often rebuked, yet always back returning][1]

Often rebuked, yet always back returning
    To those first feelings that were born with me,
And leaving busy chase of wealth and learning
    For idle dreams of things which cannot be:

Today, I will seek not the shadowy region;   5
    Its unsustaining vastness waxes drear;
And visions rising, legion after legion,
    Bring the unreal world too strangely near.

I'll walk, but not in old heroic traces,
    And not in paths of high morality,   10
And not among the half-distinguished faces,
    The clouded forms of long-past history.

---

1   *[Often ... returning]* The authorship of this poem has been variously credited to Emily,
     Charlotte, and Anne Brontë; when the poem was first printed, under the title "Stanzas,"
     it was recorded as having been written by Emily.

I'll walk where my own nature would be leading:
    It vexes me to choose another guide:
15 Where the grey flocks in ferny glens are feeding;
    Where the wild wind blows on the mountain side.

What have those lonely mountains worth revealing?
    More glory and more grief than I can tell:
The earth that wakes *one* human heart to feeling
20   Can centre both the worlds of Heaven and Hell.

—1850

[I'll come when thou art saddest]

I'll come when thou art saddest,
Laid alone in the darkened room;
When the mad day's mirth has vanished
And the smile of joy is banished
5 From evening's chilly gloom.

I'll come when the heart's real feeling
Has entire, unbiased sway,
And my influence o'er thee stealing,
Grief deepening, joy congealing,
10 Shall bear thy soul away.

Listen! 'tis just the hour,
The awful time for thee:
Dost thou not feel upon thy soul
A flood of strange sensations roll,
15 Forerunners of a sterner power,
Heralds of me?

—1902 (written 1837)

Herman Melville
1819–1891

Readers are often surprised to learn that Herman Melville, renowned for his fiction, was also a poet. In fact, after publishing narratives over the course of 11 years (1846–1857), he mostly gave up writing fiction and dedicated himself to writing and publishing poems for more than three decades. An 1860 volume (which appears not to have survived) failed to find a publisher; he published a volume of Civil War poetry, *Battle-Pieces and Aspects of the War*, in 1866, the poems for which he was best known in his lifetime. Three more volumes of poems followed. His 1876 *Clarel*, a long dramatic poem about travelers in the Holy Land, presents a saga of faith and doubt in the age of Darwin that addressed the transatlantic anxieties of the time; however, *Clarel* met with little success. Melville then self-published his last two volumes, *John Marr and Other Sailors* and *Timoleon, Etc.*, in editions of only 25 copies each. He left an extensive array of poetry manuscripts in various stages of completion at the time of his death, including a nearly complete book, *Weeds and Wildings Chiefly: with A Rose or Two*. A penetrating and layered interrogation of the long tradition of the rose as a conventional symbol of beauty, this volume presented his own poems as, by contrast, "weeds" and "wildings." (See "Field Asters," below.)

Although he had burst onto the literary scene as a young man in 1846 with his bestselling travel narrative *Typee*, his reputation fell into significant shadow by the time of his death. It was not until the 1920s that scholars rediscovered his writing and quickly hailed him as a neglected genius, especially for his masterwork *Moby-Dick* (1851). Since that time, Melville's towering reputation as one of America's greatest writers has never flagged; however, his reputation has rested entirely on his fiction. Early critics often dismissed his large body of tangled and often difficult poems as the work of a burned-out writer who never learned the proper craft of poetry. This negative account became the standard view. As "Dupont's Round Fight" (reprinted below) indicates, Melville could write in a mellifluous, regular poetic style when he chose to do so. As "A Utilitarian View of the Monitor's Fight" (also below) explores, he more typically preferred not to—and left instead an impressive and knotty body of experimental verse.

Ball's Bluff[1]

A Reverie.
(OCTOBER, 1861.)

One noonday, at my window in the town,
    I saw a sight—saddest that eyes can see—
    Young soldiers marching lustily
        Unto the wars,
5 With fifes, and flags in mottoed pageantry;
    While all the porches, walks, and doors
Were rich with ladies cheering royally.

They moved like Juny morning on the wave,
    Their hearts were fresh as clover in its prime
10   (It was the breezy summer time),
        Life throbbed so strong,
How should they dream that Death in a rosy clime
    Would come to thin their shining throng?
Youth feels immortal, like the gods sublime.

15 Weeks passed; and at my window, leaving bed,
    By night I mused, of easeful sleep bereft,
    On those brave boys (Ah War! thy theft);
        Some marching feet
Found pause at last by cliffs Potomac cleft;
20   Wakeful I mused, while in the street
Far footfalls died away till none were left.

—1866

---

1   *Ball's Bluff* The Battle of Ball's Bluff in October 1861 was a humiliating defeat for the
Union. A Confederate brigade rebuffed a poorly planned Union assault, sending the
Union soldiers over the bluff and into the Potomac River, where many were either shot as
they tried to swim away, or drowned.

Dupont's Round Fight [1]

(NOVEMBER, 1861.)

In time and measure perfect moves
    All Art whose aim is sure;
Evolving rhyme and stars divine
    Have rules, and they endure.

Nor less the Fleet that warred for Right,   5
    And, warring so, prevailed,
In geometric beauty curved,[2]
    And in an orbit sailed.

The rebel at Port Royal felt
    The Unity overawe,   10
And rued° the spell. A type was here,   *lamented*
    And victory of LAW.

—1866

A Utilitarian [3] View of the Monitor's [4] Fight

Plain be the phrase, yet apt the verse,
    More ponderous° than nimble;   *heavy, clumsy*
For since grimed War here laid aside
His Orient[5] pomp, 'twould ill befit
        Overmuch to ply   5
    The rhyme's barbaric cymbal.

---

1   *Dupont's Round Fight* In the Battle of Port Royal in November 1861, Union forces bombarded Confederate fortifications protecting Port Royal Sound, South Carolina. Union Officer Samuel Francis du Pont devised a plan whereby his steamships moved up and down the banks in an elliptical pattern while firing on the Confederate forts.

2   *geometric beauty curved* A reference to the elliptical shape of the attack pattern.

3   *Utilitarian* Advocating utility as a principle superior to alternatives such as beauty.

4   *Monitor* This Union ironclad ship engaged the Confederate ironclad the *Virginia* (formerly the *Merrimack*) in 1862 at Hampton Roads, Virginia. As the first battle ever fought between ironclads, it represented a major shift in the nature and practice of naval warfare.

5   *Orient* Melville uses this term in keeping with stereotypes of his time that associated "the Orient" with exoticism and sumptuous display.

Hail to victory without the gaud[1]
    Of glory; zeal that needs no fans
Of banners; plain mechanic power
10 Plied cogently in War now placed—
    Where War belongs—
    Among the trades and artisans.

Yet this was battle, and intense—
    Beyond the strife of fleets heroic;
15 Deadlier, closer, calm 'mid storm;
No passion; all went on by crank,
    Pivot, and screw,
    And calculations of caloric.

Needless to dwell; the story's known.
20   The ringing of those plates on plates[2]
Still ringeth round the world—
The clangor of that blacksmiths' fray.
    The anvil-din
    Resounds this message from the Fates:

25 War shall yet be, and to the end;
    But war-paint shows the streaks of weather;
War yet shall be, but warriors
Are now but operatives; War's made
    Less grand than Peace,
30   And a singe runs through lace and feather.

—1866

The Æolian Harp[3]

At the Surf Inn.

List° the harp in window wailing   *Listen to*
    Stirred by fitful gales from sea:

---

1   *gaud* Showy ceremony; also, deceptive trickery.

2   *plates* Sheets of metal.

3   *Æolian Harp* Named for the Greek god of the winds, Aeolus, these wind harps were placed in the window, where the action of the wind on the strings created the music of nature. Such harps became a common trope in Romantic poetry for exploring some of the key elements of Romanticism: self, poet, nature, and spirit or divinity.

Shrieking up in mad crescendo—
    Dying down in plaintive key!

Listen: less a strain ideal
    Than Ariel's[1] rendering of the Real.   5
What that Real is, let hint
    A picture stamped in memory's mint.[2]

Braced well up, with beams aslant,
Betwixt the continents sails the *Phocion*,[3]   10
To Baltimore bound from Alicant.[4]
Blue breezy skies white fleeces fleck
Over the chill blue white-capped ocean:
From yard-arm comes—"Wreck ho, a wreck!"

Dismasted and adrift.   15
Longtime a thing forsaken
Overwashed by every wave
Like the slumbering kraken[5]
Heedless if the billow roar.
Oblivious of the lull,   20
Leagues and leagues from shoal or shore.
It swims—a levelled hull:
Bulwarks gone—a shaven wreck.
Nameless, and a grass-green deck.
A lumberman: perchance, in hold   25
Prostrate pines with hemlocks rolled.

It has drifted, waterlogged.
Till by trailing weeds beclogged:
    Drifted, drifted, day by day,
    Pilotless on pathless way.   30

---

1   *Ariel* In Shakespeare's *The Tempest*, the spirit Ariel, at Prospero's bidding, creates the storm that sets the play's action in motion. Melville was a passionate reader of Shakespeare.
2   *mint* Place where something originates; a source of invention. Melville's contemporary Alfred, Lord Tennyson, for example, used the phrase "nature's mint" in his long poem *In Memoriam.*
3   *Phocion* Here, a ship named for this Athenian statesman and general.
4   *Alicant* Port city in southeastern Spain.
5   *kraken* Legendary sea monster, possibly the giant squid.

It has drifted till each plank
Is oozy as the oyster-bank:
    Drifted, drifted, night by night,
    Craft that never shows a light:
35 Nor ever, to prevent worse knell,[1]
Tolls in fog the warning bell.

From collision never shrinking,
Drive what may through darksome smother:[2]
Saturate, but never sinking,
40 Fatal only to the *other*!
    Deadlier than the sunken reef
Since still the snare it shifteth,
    Torpid in dumb ambuscade°   *ambush*
Waylayingly it drifteth.

45   O, the sailors—O, the sails!
        O, the lost crews never heard of!
        Well the harp of Ariel wails
        Thoughts that tongue can tell no word of!

                                      —1888

Pebbles

I.

Though the Clerk of the Weather[3] insist,
    And lay down the weather-law,
Pintado[4] and gannet[5] they wist°   *know*
That the winds blow whither they list°   *desire*
5   In tempest or flaw.

---

1   *knell* A bell that tolls solemnly for a death or funeral.
2   *smother* Confused turmoil of water or foam; indistinct noise; dense or suffocating fog or air.
3   *Clerk of the Weather* An imaginary figure in lore of Melville's time, reputed to manage the weather.
4   *Pintado* Seabird, the Cape petrel.
5   *gannet* Large sea-fowl.

II.

Old are the creeds, but stale the schools,
    Revamped as the mode may veer,
But Orm[1] from the schools to the beaches strays,
And, finding a Conch hoar with rime, he delays
    And reverent lifts it to ear.   10

That Voice, pitched in far monotone,
    Shall it swerve? shall it deviate ever?
The Seas have inspired it, and Truth—
    Truth, varying from sameness never.

III.

In hollows of the liquid hills   15
    Where the long Blue Ridges run,
The flattery of no echo thrills,
    For echo the seas have none;
Nor aught that gives man back man's strain—
The hope of his heart, the dream in his brain.   20

IV.

On ocean where the embattled fleets repair,
Man, suffering inflictor, sails on sufferance there.

V.

Implacable I, the old Implacable Sea:
    Implacable most when most I smile serene—
Pleased, not appeased, by myriad wrecks in me.   25

VI.

Curled in the comb of yon billow Andean,
    Is it the Dragon's heaven-challenging crest?[2]
Elemental mad ramping[3] of ravening° waters—   *bloodthirsty*
    Yet Christ on the Mount, and the dove in her nest!

---

1   *Orm* Character of Melville's creation.
2   *crest* Comb or tuft on an animal's head, as here in the metaphor of the "Dragon"; also
    the summit of a mountain, referring back to the metaphors of the Blue Ridge and Andes
    mountains.
3   *ramping* Violent rushing, raging, storming.

VII.

30 Healed of my hurt, I laud the inhuman Sea—
Yea, bless the Angels Four[1] that there convene:
For healed I am even by their pitiless breath
Distilled in wholesome dew named rosmarine.[2]

—1888

Field Asters

Like the stars in commons blue
Peep their namesakes, Asters here,
Wild ones every autumn seen—
Seen of all, arresting few.

5 Seen indeed. But who their cheer
Interpret may, or what they mean
When so inscrutably their eyes
Us star-gazers scrutinize.

—1924 (written c. 1890)

---

1   *Angels Four* In Revelation 7.1, four angels appear holding the four winds of the earth.
2   *rosmarine* Spray of the sea or the sea "dew." A play by Ben Jonson, *The Masque of Queens*, used the phrase "wholsome [sic] dew call'd Ros-marine." Melville's poems frequently incorporate allusions to his voluminous reading.

Walt Whitman
1819–1892

Heir to the British Romantic poets and especially to the Transcendentalist vision of Ralph Waldo Emerson, Walt Whitman revolutionized the art of poetry. Emerson's essay "The Poet" (1844) had called for a poet who would dispense with conventions of meter and poetic diction and turn instead to the urgent source (in Emerson's view) of true poetry: the inner being or soul. As Transcendentalism more generally held, the soul or "self" was organically one with both the divine principle and with the natural world. "I look in vain for the poet whom I describe," Emerson wrote. Whitman intended to become that revolutionary poet. He succeeded.

Whitman was born to working-class parents near Hempstead, Long Island, and the family moved to Brooklyn when he was still a child. He received six years of public school education before providing himself with an informal education using publicly available resources in New York. As a young man, he worked as a journalist, printer, and editor. During the Civil War, he nursed and comforted wounded soldiers in Washington, DC, hospital wards, often writing letters home for them. (See "Come Up from the Fields Father" below.)

He published his groundbreaking and influential work *Leaves of Grass* in 1855 and continued to revise and expand it (for example, by adding his Civil War poems to it) until his death. Whitman invented free verse, a formal innovation that changed the course of poetry thereafter. For example, both the French Symbolist poets and the twentieth-century Modernists were indebted to his invention. His long lists (called catalogues) incorporated into his poems the diversity of the United States, including its landscapes, its many populations, the everyday experiences of common people, and slang—offensive to the ears of those who expected formal poetic diction. His overt references to sex and the body, including passionate descriptions of homoerotic longing, repelled many and led to charges of obscenity. John Greenleaf Whittier is reputed to have thrown his copy in the fire.

Readers of his time typically rejected Whitman's work as the offensive ramblings of a barbarian. (Whitman enjoyed the idea and celebrated what he called his "barbaric yawp" in the last section of "Song of Myself.") Yet his very controversial status also gave his poetry cultural life. Widely discussed, reviled, and parodied by some and embraced as a hero and visionary by others, by the end of the nineteenth century Whitman had emerged as the single American poet whose legacy other poets had to reckon with.

Note to readers: Whitman's poems "Song of Myself" and "When Lilacs Last in the Dooryard Bloom'd" appear on the anthology's companion website. The URL and passcode appear in the Table of Contents.

A Glimpse[1]

A glimpse through an interstice caught,
Of a crowd of workmen and drivers in a bar-room around the stove late of a
    winter night, and I unremark'd seated in a corner,
Of a youth who loves me and whom I love, silently approaching and seating
    himself near, that he may hold me by the hand,
A long while amid the noises of coming and going, of drinking and oath
    and smutty jest,
5 There we two, content, happy in being together, speaking little, perhaps not
    a word.

                                                —1860, 1867

To a Stranger[2]

Passing stranger! you do not know how longingly I look upon you,
You must be he I was seeking, or she I was seeking, (it comes to me as of a
    dream,)
I have somewhere surely lived a life of joy with you,
All is recall'd as we flit by each other, fluid, affectionate, chaste, matured,
5 You grew up with me, were a boy with me or a girl with me,
I ate with you and slept with you, your body has become not yours only nor
    left my body mine only,
You give me the pleasure of your eyes, face, flesh, as we pass, you take of my
    beard, breast, hands, in return,
I am not to speak to you, I am to think of you when I sit alone or wake at
    night alone,
I am to wait, I do not doubt I am to meet you again,
10 I am to see to it that I do not lose you.

                                              —1860, 1867

Come Up from the Fields Father

Come up from the fields father, here's a letter from our Pete,
And come to the front door mother, here's a letter from thy dear son.

---

1   *A Glimpse* Originally published in the 1860 edition of *Leaves of Grass* as "Calamus 29."
2   *To a Stranger* Originally published in the 1860 edition of *Leaves of Grass* as "Calamus
    22."

Lo, 'tis autumn,
Lo, where the trees, deeper green, yellower and redder,
Cool and sweeten Ohio's villages with leaves fluttering in the moderate 5
    wind,
Where apples ripe in the orchards hang and grapes on the trellis'd vines,
(Smell you the smell of the grapes on the vines?
Smell you the buckwheat where the bees were lately buzzing?)

Above all, lo, the sky so calm, so transparent after the rain, and with
    wondrous clouds,
Below too, all calm, all vital and beautiful, and the farm prospers well. 10

Down in the fields all prospers well,
But now from the fields come father, come at the daughter's call,
And come to the entry mother, to the front door come right away.

Fast as she can she hurries, something ominous, her steps trembling,
She does not tarry to smooth her hair nor adjust her cap. 15

Open the envelope quickly,
O this is not our son's writing, yet his name is sign'd,
O a strange hand writes for our dear son, O stricken mother's soul!
All swims before her eyes, flashes with black, she catches the main words
    only,
Sentences broken, *gunshot wound in the breast, cavalry skirmish, taken to* 20
    hospital,
At present low, but will soon be better.

Ah now the single figure to me,
Amid all teeming and wealthy Ohio with all its cities and farms,
Sickly white in the face and dull in the head, very faint,
By the jamb of a door leans. 25

Grieve not so, dear mother, (the just-grown daughter speaks through her sobs,
The little sisters huddle around speechless and dismay'd,)
See, dearest mother, the letter says Pete will soon be better.

Alas poor boy, he will never be better, (nor may-be needs to be better, that
    brave and simple soul,)
While they stand at home at the door he is dead already, 30
The only son is dead.

But the mother needs to be better,
She with thin form presently drest in black,
By day her meals untouch'd, then at night fitfully sleeping, often waking,
35 In the midnight waking, weeping, longing with one deep longing,
O that she might withdraw unnoticed, silent from life escape and withdraw,
To follow, to seek, to be with her dear dead son.

—1865

When I Heard the Learn'd Astronomer

When I heard the learn'd astronomer,
When the proofs, the figures, were ranged in columns before me,
When I was shown the charts and diagrams, to add, divide, and measure
    them,
When I sitting heard the astronomer where he lectured with much applause
    in the lecture-room,
5 How soon unaccountable I became tired and sick,
Till rising and gliding out I wander'd off by myself,
In the mystical moist night-air, and from time to time,
Look'd up in perfect silence at the stars.

—1865

Crossing Brooklyn Ferry

1

Flood-tide below me! I see you face to face!
Clouds of the west—sun there half an hour high—I see you also face to face.

Crowds of men and women attired in the usual costumes, how curious you
    are to me!
On the ferry-boats the hundreds and hundreds that cross, returning home,
    are more curious to me than you suppose,
5 And you that shall cross from shore to shore years hence are more to me,
    and more in my meditations, than you might suppose.

2

The impalpable sustenance of me from all things at all hours of the day,
The simple, compact, well-join'd scheme, myself disintegrated, every one
    disintegrated yet part of the scheme,
The similitudes of the past and those of the future,

The glories strung like beads on my smallest sights and hearings, on the
    walk in the street and the passage over the river,
The current rushing so swiftly and swimming with me far away,   10
The others that are to follow me, the ties between me and them,
The certainty of others, the life, love, sight, hearing of others.

Others will enter the gates of the ferry and cross from shore to shore,
Others will watch the run of the flood-tide,
Others will see the shipping of Manhattan north and west, and the heights   15
    of Brooklyn to the south and east,
Others will see the islands large and small;
Fifty years hence, others will see them as they cross, the sun half an hour high,
A hundred years hence, or ever so many hundred years hence, others will see
    them,
Will enjoy the sunset, the pouring-in of the flood-tide, the falling-back to
    the sea of the ebb-tide.

3

It avails not, time nor place—distance avails not,   20
I am with you, you men and women of a generation, or ever so many gen-
    erations hence,
Just as you feel when you look on the river and sky, so I felt,
Just as any of you is one of a living crowd, I was one of a crowd,
Just as you are refresh'd by the gladness of the river and the bright flow, I
    was refresh'd,
Just as you stand and lean on the rail, yet hurry with the swift current, I   25
    stood yet was hurried,
Just as you look on the numberless masts of ships and the thick-stemm'd
    pipes of steamboats, I look'd.

I too many and many a time cross'd the river of old,
Watched the Twelfth-month[1] sea-gulls, saw them high in the air floating
    with motionless wings, oscillating their bodies,
Saw how the glistening yellow lit up parts of their bodies and left the rest in
    strong shadow,
Saw the slow-wheeling circles and the gradual edging toward the south,   30
Saw the reflection of the summer sky in the water,
Had my eyes dazzled by the shimmering track of beams,

---

1   *Twelfth-month* December.

Look'd at the fine centrifugal spokes of light round the shape of my head in
    the sunlit water,
Look'd on the haze on the hills southward and south-westward,
35 Look'd on the vapor as it flew in fleeces tinged with violet,
Look'd toward the lower bay to notice the vessels arriving,
Saw their approach, saw aboard those that were near me,
Saw the white sails of schooners and sloops, saw the ships at anchor,
The sailors at work in the rigging or out astride the spars,
40 The round masts, the swinging motion of the hulls, the slender serpentine
    pennants,
The large and small steamers in motion, the pilots in their pilot-houses,
The white wake left by the passage, the quick tremulous whirl of the wheels,
The flags of all nations, the falling of them at sunset,
The scallop-edged waves in the twilight, the ladled cups, the frolicsome
    crests and glistening,
45 The stretch afar growing dimmer and dimmer, the gray walls of the granite
    storehouses by the docks,
On the river the shadowy group, the big steam-tug closely flank'd on each
    side by the barges, the hay-boat, the belated lighter,[1]
On the neighboring shore the fires from the foundry chimneys burning
    high and glaringly into the night,
Casting their flicker of black contrasted with wild red and yellow light over
    the tops of houses, and down into the clefts of streets.

4

These and all else were to me the same as they are to you,
50 I loved well those cities, loved well the stately and rapid river,
The men and women I saw were all near to me,
Others the same—others who look back on me because I look'd forward to
    them,
(The time will come, though I stop here to-day and to-night.)

5

What is it then between us?
55 What is the count of the scores or hundreds of years between us?

Whatever it is, it avails not—distance avails not, and place avails not,
I too lived, Brooklyn of ample hills was mine,

---

1   *lighter* Flat-bottomed barge used to transfer passengers and goods to and from ships
    when in harbor.

I too walk'd the streets of Manhattan island, and bathed in the waters
    around it,
I too felt the curious abrupt questionings stir within me,
In the day among crowds of people sometimes they came upon me,   60
In my walks home late at night or as I lay in my bed they came upon me,
I too had been struck from the float forever held in solution,
I too had receiv'd identity by my body,
That I was I knew was of my body, and what I should be I knew I should be
    of my body.

6

It is not upon you alone the dark patches fall,   65
The dark threw its patches down upon me also,
The best I had done seem'd to me blank and suspicious,
My great thoughts as I supposed them, were they not in reality meagre?
Nor is it you alone who know what it is to be evil,
I am he who knew what it was to be evil,   70
I too knitted the old knot of contrariety,
Blabb'd, blush'd, resented, lied, stole, grudg'd,
Had guile, anger, lust, hot wishes I dared not speak,
Was wayward, vain, greedy, shallow, sly, cowardly, malignant,
The wolf, the snake, the hog, not wanting in me,   75
The cheating look, the frivolous word, the adulterous wish, not wanting,
Refusals, hates, postponements, meanness, laziness, none of these
    wanting,
Was one with the rest, the days and haps° of the rest,   *chances*
Was call'd by my nighest name[1] by clear loud voices of young men as
    they saw me approaching or passing,
Felt their arms on my neck as I stood, or the negligent leaning of their   80
    flesh against me as I sat,
Saw many I loved in the street or ferry-boat or public assembly, yet never
    told them a word,
Lived the same life with the rest, the same old laughing, gnawing, sleeping,
Play'd the part that still looks back on the actor or actress,
The same old role, the role that is what we make it, as great as we like,
Or as small as we like, or both great and small.   85

---

1   *nighest name* I.e., familiar or given name.

7

Closer yet I approach you,
What thought you have of me now, I had as much of you—I laid in my
    stores in advance,
I consider'd long and seriously of you before you were born.

Who was to know what should come home to me?
90 Who knows but I am enjoying this?
Who knows, for all the distance, but I am as good as looking at you now,
    for all you cannot see me?

8

Ah, what can ever be more stately and admirable to me than mast-hemm'd
    Manhattan?
River and sunset and scallop-edg'd waves of flood-tide?
The sea-gulls oscillating their bodies, the hay-boat in the twilight, and the
    belated lighter?
95 What gods can exceed these that clasp me by the hand, and with voices I
    love call me promptly and loudly by my nighest name as I approach?
What is more subtle than this which ties me to the woman or man that
    looks in my face?
Which fuses me into you now, and pours my meaning into you?

We understand then do we not?
What I promis'd without mentioning it, have you not accepted?
100 What the study could not teach—what the preaching could not accomplish
    is accomplish'd, is it not?

9

Flow on, river! flow with the flood-tide, and ebb with the ebb-tide!
Frolic on, crested and scallop-edg'd waves!
Gorgeous clouds of the sunset! drench with your splendor me, or the men
    and women generations after me!
Cross from shore to shore, countless crowds of passengers!
105 Stand up, tall masts of Mannahatta![1] stand up, beautiful hills of Brooklyn!
Throb, baffled and curious brain! throw out questions and answers!
Suspend here and everywhere, eternal float of solution!
Gaze, loving and thirsting eyes, in the house or street or public assembly!

---

1   *Mannahatta* Lenape Indian name for Manhattan.

Sound out, voices of young men! loudly and musically call me by my
  nighest name!
Live, old life! play the part that looks back on the actor or actress!   110
Play the old role, the role that is great or small according as one makes it!
Consider, you who peruse me, whether I may not in unknown ways be
  looking upon you;
Be firm, rail over the river, to support those who lean idly, yet haste with the
  hasting current;
Fly on, sea birds! fly sideways, or wheel in large circles high in the air;
Receive the summer sky, you water, and faithfully hold it till all downcast   115
  eyes have time to take it from you!
Diverge, fine spokes of light, from the shape of my head, or any one's head,
  in the sunlit water!
Come on, ships from the lower bay! pass up or down, white-sail'd schooners,
  sloops, lighters!
Flaunt away, flags of all nations! be duly lower'd at sunset!
Burn high your fires, foundry chimneys! cast black shadows at nightfall! cast
  red and yellow light over the tops of the houses!   120

Appearances, now or henceforth, indicate what you are,
You necessary film, continue to envelop the soul,
About my body for me, and your body for you, be hung our divinest aromas,
Thrive, cities—bring your freight, bring your shows, ample and sufficient
  rivers,
Expand, being than which none else is perhaps more spiritual,   125
Keep your places, objects than which none else is more lasting.

You have waited, you always wait, you dumb, beautiful ministers,
We receive you with free sense at last, and are insatiate henceforward,
Not you any more shall be able to foil us, or withhold yourselves from us,
We use you, and do not cast you aside—we plant you permanently within us,   130
We fathom you not—we love you—there is perfection in you also,
You furnish your parts toward eternity,
Great or small, you furnish your parts toward the soul.

                                        —1881

Alice Cary

1820–1871

Alice Cary, like her sister and fellow-poet Phoebe, grew up in rural Ohio, where they had little formal schooling. At that time, Ohio was the "West," far distant from the cultured cities of the East Coast, and the sisters, already avid writers, quickly developed aspirations to move to a literary life away from the frontier. They began publishing poems in local newspapers when they were teenagers. In 1848, their work was included in the most important poetry anthology of the time, *The Female Poets of America*, by Rufus Griswold. Griswold wrote of Alice, "We have perhaps no other author, so young, in whom the poetical faculty is so largely developed." Praise from Griswold, and inclusion in his anthology, afforded poets an influential form of cultural credibility.

Griswold further helped the sisters to publish their 1849 collection, *Poems of Alice and Phoebe Cary*. Alice moved to New York in 1851, where she built a career as a popular and well-paid professional writer. Literary salons were fashionable at this time, a kind of club scene in which powerful and up-and-coming writers and other influential people mingled in the home of a well-positioned host or hostess. The Cary sisters hosted a well-regarded weekly event of this kind. Although Alice was among the women writers who vanished from cultural memory after her own lifetime, she was rediscovered in the late twentieth century. Though she is best known today for her prose about rural life, her own culture knew her primarily as a poet. Recovering Alice Cary and her fellow women poets often hinges on exploring how they navigated the cultural expectations for the "poetess"—expectations that could make or break a career.

The Bridal Veil

We're married, they say, and you think you have won me,—
Well, take this white veil from my head, and look on me;
Here's matter to vex you, and matter to grieve you,
Here's doubt to distrust you, and faith to believe you,—
5 I am all as you see, common earth, common dew;
Be wary, and mould me to roses, not rue!¹

---

1   *rue* Shrub with bitter leaves; sorrow or regret. Here, the play on words entails both meanings.

Ah! shake out the filmy thing, fold after fold,
And see if you have me to keep and to hold,—
Look close on my heart—see the worst of its sinning,—
It is not yours to-day for the yesterday's winning—   10
The past is not mine—I am too proud to borrow—
You must grow to new heights if I love you to-morrow.

I have wings flattened down and hid under my veil:
They are subtle as light—you can never undo them,
And swift in their flight—you can never pursue them,   15
And spite of all clasping, and spite of all bands,
I can slip like a shadow, a dream, from your hands.

Nay, call me not cruel, and fear not to take me,
I am yours for my life-time, to be what you make me,—
To wear my white veil for a sign, or a cover,   20
As you shall be proven my lord, or my lover;
A cover for peace that is dead, or a token
Of bliss that can never be written or spoken.

—1866

Frederick Goddard Tuckerman
1821–1873

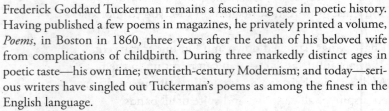

Frederick Goddard Tuckerman remains a fascinating case in poetic history. Having published a few poems in magazines, he privately printed a volume, *Poems*, in Boston in 1860, three years after the death of his beloved wife from complications of childbirth. During three markedly distinct ages in poetic taste—his own time; twentieth-century Modernism; and today—serious writers have singled out Tuckerman's poems as among the finest in the English language.

Nevertheless, he remains mostly a poet's poet. In 1861, Nathaniel Hawthorne, one of the most widely acclaimed writers in the United States, wrote him a fan letter praising the 1860 volume as a remarkable achievement. Hawthorne believed that the profound skill and depth of Tuckerman's poems would, paradoxically, leave them without readers. Full appreciation of Tuckerman's craft, Hawthorne noted, required thoughtful attention and careful rereading at a time when reading habits were generally quick and superficial. Like poet's poet Weldon Kees in the twentieth century, Tuckerman has mostly not yet broken out into wider recognition. The sonnet below (excerpted from a long, two-part series) exemplifies his formal innovations and his broader engagement with the meaning of poetry in relation to "Nature," marking an important transition from the Romantic models he had inherited.

Sonnet VII
[His heart was in his garden; but his brain]

His heart was in his garden; but his brain
Wandered at will among the fiery stars:
Bards, heroes, prophets, Homers, Hamilcars,[1]
With many angels, stood, his eye to gain;
5 The devils, too, were his familiars.
And yet the cunning florist held his eyes
Close to the ground,—a tulip-bulb his prize,—
And talked of tan[2] and bone-dust, cutworms, grubs,
As though all Nature held no higher strain;

---

1   *Hamilcar* Carthaginian general famed for his role in the First Punic War; here, a figure emblematizing the world of ancient heroes.

2   *tan* Crushed tree bark used in the process to convert hides to leather.

Or, if he spoke of Art, he made the theme   10
Flow through box-borders, turf, and flower-tubs;
Or, like a garden-engine's,[1] steered the stream,—
Now spouted rainbows to the silent skies;
Now kept it flat, and raked the walks and shrubs.

—1864

---

1   *garden-engine* A machine for watering gardens, usually consisting of a wheelbarrow, tank, and pump.

Matthew Arnold
1822–1888

Matthew Arnold was a poet as well as a leading Victorian literary and social critic. His most important work is *Culture and Anarchy* (1869), whose social analysis exerted significant transatlantic influence on ideas about art and society. In it, he advocates the value of "culture" as a saving repository of "the best that has been thought and said." This Arnoldian concept became a touchstone in his own time as well as in modern debates such as the culture and canon wars of the late twentieth century. Like his contemporary Alfred, Lord Tennyson, Arnold was concerned with the alienated condition of the modern individual in a changing world. Arnold's poem "Dover Beach" (below) is often described as the quintessential poem of the Victorian era.

Dover Beach

The sea is calm tonight.
The tide is full, the moon lies fair
Upon the straits—on the French coast the light
Gleams and is gone; the cliffs of England stand,
5 Glimmering and vast, out in the tranquil bay.
Come to the window, sweet is the night-air!
Only, from the long line of spray
Where the sea meets the moon-blanched land,
Listen! you hear the grating roar
10 Of pebbles which the waves draw back, and fling,
At their return, up the high strand,°   *shore*
Begin, and cease, and then again begin,
With tremulous cadence slow, and bring
The eternal note of sadness in.

15   Sophocles long ago
Heard it on the Aegaean, and it brought
Into his mind the turbid ebb and flow
Of human misery;[1] we

---

1   *Sophocles ... misery* See Sophocles's *Antigone* 583–91: "Blest are those whose days have not tasted of evil. For when a house has once been shaken by the gods, no form of ruin is lacking, but it spreads over the bulk of the race, just as, when the surge is driven over the darkness of the deep by the fierce breath of Thracian sea-winds, it rolls up the black sand

Find also in the sound a thought,
Hearing it by this distant northern sea.   20

The Sea of Faith
Was once, too, at the full, and round earth's shore
Lay like the folds of a bright girdle furled.
But now I only hear
Its melancholy, long, withdrawing roar,   25
Retreating, to the breath
Of the night-wind, down the vast edges drear
And naked shingles[1] of the world.

Ah, love, let us be true
To one another! for the world, which seems   30
To lie before us like a land of dreams,
So various, so beautiful, so new,
Hath really neither joy, nor love, nor light,
Nor certitude, nor peace, nor help for pain;
And we are here as on a darkling plain   35
Swept with confused alarms of struggle and flight,
Where ignorant armies clash by night.[2]

—1867

---

from the depths, and the wind-beaten headlands that front the blows of the storm give
out a mournful roar"; *Aegaean* Arm of the Mediterranean Sea near Greece.
1   *shingles* Water-worn pebbles.
2   *ignorant ... by night* Reference to Thucydides's *History of the Peloponnesian War*, in which
     the invading Athenians became confused as night fell on the battle at Epipolae. Combat-
     ants could not tell friend from foe in the moonlight.

James Monroe Whitfield
1822–1871

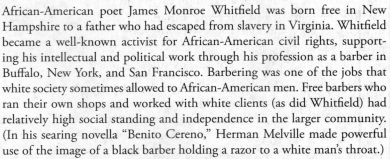 African-American poet James Monroe Whitfield was born free in New Hampshire to a father who had escaped from slavery in Virginia. Whitfield became a well-known activist for African-American civil rights, supporting his intellectual and political work through his profession as a barber in Buffalo, New York, and San Francisco. Barbering was one of the jobs that white society sometimes allowed to African-American men. Free barbers who ran their own shops and worked with white clients (as did Whitfield) had relatively high social standing and independence in the larger community. (In his searing novella "Benito Cereno," Herman Melville made powerful use of the image of a black barber holding a razor to a white man's throat.)

Along with fellow African-American leaders such as Frederick Douglass and Martin R. Delany, Whitfield passionately attacked the hypocrisies of the nation's professed commitment to freedom. He published in African-American and abolitionist periodicals that allowed him a frank voice that mainstream publications would likely have silenced. His single book of poetry, *America and Other Poems*, appeared in 1853. The title poem, reprinted below, stands in grim contrast to Walt Whitman's transcendentally optimistic "Song of Myself," published just two years later. Although an influential African-American leader in his own day, Whitfield fell from view after his death. Scholars are only now coming to rediscover the facts of his life and the important historical role that he—and his poetry—played in the history of race in America.

America

AMERICA, it is to thee,
Thou boasted land of liberty,—
It is to thee I raise my song,
Thou land of blood, and crime, and wrong.
5 It is to thee, my native land,
From whence has issued many a band
To tear the black man from his soil,
And force him here to delve and toil;
Chained on your blood-bemoistened sod,
10 Cringing beneath a tyrant's rod,
Stripped of those rights which Nature's God
    Bequeathed to all the human race,
Bound to a petty tyrant's nod,
    Because he wears a paler face.

Was it for this, that freedom's fires   15
Were kindled by your patriot sires?
Was it for this, they shed their blood,
On hill and plain, on field and flood?
Was it for this, that wealth and life
Were staked upon that desperate strife,   20
Which drenched this land for seven long years[1]
With blood of men, and women's tears?
When black and white fought side by side,
    Upon the well-contested field,—
Turned back the fierce opposing tide,   25
    And made the proud invader yield—
When, wounded, side by side they lay,
    And heard with joy the proud hurrah
From their victorious comrades say
    That they had waged successful war,   30
The thought ne'er entered in their brains
    That they endured those toils and pains,
To forge fresh fetters, heavier chains[2]
For their own children, in whose veins
Should flow that patriotic blood,   35
So freely shed on field and flood.
Oh no; they fought, as they believed,
    For the inherent rights of man;
But mark, how they have been deceived
    By slavery's accursed plan.   40
They never thought, when thus they shed
    Their heart's best blood, in freedom's cause
That their own sons would live in dread,
    Under unjust, oppressive laws:
That those who quietly enjoyed   45
    The rights for which they fought and fell,
Could be the framers of a code,
    That would disgrace the fiends of hell!
Could they have looked, with prophet's ken,
    Down to the present evil time,   50

---

1   *seven long years* The American Revolutionary War, in which both free and enslaved African-Americans fought.

2   *fresh fetters, heavier chains* Whitfield ironically addresses the aftermath of the American Revolutionary War for African-Americans. Anti-slavery advocates frequently invoked the Revolutionary War's putative commitment to liberty and revolt against tyrany as analogous to the cause of abolition.

Seen free-born men, uncharged with crime,
Consigned unto a slaver's pen,—
Or thrust into a prison cell,
With thieves and murderers to dwell—
55 While that same flag whose stripes and stars
Had been their guide through freedom's wars
As proudly waved above the pen
Of dealers in the souls of men!
Or could the shades of all the dead,
60   Who fell beneath that starry flag,
Visit the scenes where they once bled,
     On hill and plain, on vale and crag,
By peaceful brook, or ocean's strand,
     By inland lake, or dark green wood,
65 Where'er the soil of this wide land
     Was moistened by their patriot blood,—
And then survey the country o'er,
     From north to south, from east to west,
And hear the agonizing cry
70 Ascending up to God on high,
From western wilds to ocean's shore,
     The fervent prayer of the oppressed;
The cry of helpless infancy
     Torn from the parent's fond caress
75 By some base tool of tyranny,
     And doomed to woe and wretchedness;
The indignant wail of fiery youth,
     Its noble aspirations crushed,
Its generous zeal, its love of truth,
80   Trampled by tyrants in the dust;
The aerial piles which fancy reared,
     And hopes too bright to be enjoyed,
Have passed and left his young heart seared,
     And all its dreams of bliss destroyed.
85 The shriek of virgin purity,
     Doomed to some libertine's[1] embrace,
Should rouse the strongest sympathy
     Of each one of the human race;
And weak old age, oppressed with care,

---

1   *libertine* Promiscuous, immoral man, especially someone sexually dissolute. Slave owners
    and slave traders routinely raped and otherwise sexually terrorized slaves. See the slave
    song, "The Hypocrite and the Concubine" (p. 275).

As he reviews the scene of strife,   90
Puts up to God a fervent prayer,
   To close his dark and troubled life.
The cry of fathers, mothers, wives,
   Severed from all their hearts hold dear,
And doomed to spend their wretched lives   95
   In gloom, and doubt, and hate, and fear;
And manhood, too, with soul of fire,
And arm of strength, and smothered ire,
Stands pondering with brow of gloom,
Upon his dark unhappy doom,   100
Whether to plunge in battle's strife,
And buy his freedom with his life,

And with stout heart and weapon strong,
Pay back the tyrant wrong for wrong,
Or wait the promised time of God,   105
   When his Almighty ire shall wake,
And smite the oppressor in his wrath,
And hurl red ruin in his path,
And with the terrors of his rod,
   Cause adamantine° hearts to quake.   *unyielding* 110
Here Christian writhes in bondage still,
   Beneath his brother Christian's rod,
And pastors trample down[1] at will,
   The image of the living God.
While prayers go up in lofty strains,   115
   And pealing hymns ascend to heaven,
The captive, toiling in his chains,
   With tortured limbs and bosom riven,
Raises his fettered hand on high,
   And in the accents of despair,   120
To him who rules both earth and sky,
   Puts up a sad, a fervent prayer,
To free him from the awful blast
   Of slavery's bitter galling shame—
Although his portion should be cast   125
   With demons in eternal flame!
Almighty God! 't is this they call

---

1   *pastors trample down* Whitfield refers to the widespread support for slavery by the Christian churches. See F.E.W. Harper, "Bible Defense of Slavery" (p. 189) and John Greenleaf Whittier, "The Hunters of Men" (p. 122).

The land of liberty and law;
Part of its sons in baser thrall
130   Than Babylon or Egypt[1] saw—
Worse scenes of rapine, lust and shame,
     Than Babylonian ever knew,
Are perpetrated in the name
     Of God, the holy, just, and true;
135 And darker doom than Egypt felt,[2]
May yet repay this nation's guilt.
Almighty God! thy aid impart,
And fire anew each faltering heart,
And strengthen every patriot's hand,
140 Who aims to save our native land.
We do not come before thy throne,
     With carnal weapons drenched in gore,
Although our blood has freely flown,
     In adding to the tyrant's store.
145 Father! before thy throne we come,
     Not in the panoply of war,
With pealing trump, and rolling drum,
     And cannon booming loud and far;
Striving in blood to wash out blood,
150   Through wrong to seek redress for wrong;
For while thou 'rt holy, just and good,
     The battle is not to the strong;
But in the sacred name of peace,
     Of justice, virtue, love and truth,
155 We pray, and never mean to cease,
     Till weak old age and fiery youth
In freedom's cause their voices raise,
And burst the bonds of every slave;
Till, north and south, and east and west,
160 The wrongs we bear shall be redressed.

—1853

---

1   *Babylon or Egypt* Two places in which the biblical Israelites were held in bondage. Analogies between enslaved Africans in the US and the enslaved Israelites of the Old Testament were common in anti-slavery discourse (See Longfellow, "The Slave Singing at Midnight," p. 116 and the sorrow song, "Blow Your Trumpet, Gabriel," p. 271). Pro-slavery arguments also relied on the Bible, using different passages for evidence.
2   *darker doom than Egypt felt* In Exodus, God inflicts plagues on Egypt to force Pharoah to let the Israelites go.

Frances E. W. Harper

1825–1911

Born in Baltimore, Maryland, to free African-American parents, Frances E.W. Harper became a writer, lecturer, educator, and public activist on issues including anti-slavery and women's rights. In an era when the lecture circuit was a popular and important form of civic engagement as well as entertainment, she began speaking for the abolitionist movement in 1854. The same year, she published her second book of poetry, which sold 10,000 copies in three years. She published in many genres, including poetry, short stories, and novels. Her 1859 magazine tale "The Two Offers" is one of the first known short stories published by an African-American author. She remained an activist, writer, and commentator during the Reconstruction era and its grim aftermath, when the US abandoned its brief postwar commitment to the civil rights of formerly enslaved peoples and peoples of African descent more generally. Harper's poetry relies on the conventional poetic forms and diction of the age, especially the common and familiar ballad form (as in "Learning to Read," below). Since she often performed her poems before an audience, their suitability for oral delivery was essential to their success. Although her poems might look conventional to us today, their content and rhetorical force served profound, radical changes to widespread forms of national injustice.

The Slave Auction[1]

The sale began—young girls were there,
    Defenseless in their wretchedness,
Whose stifled sobs of deep despair
    Revealed their anguish and distress.

And mothers stood, with streaming eyes,   5
    And saw their dearest children sold;
Unheeded rose their bitter cries,
    While tyrants bartered them for gold.

And woman, with her love and truth—
    For these in sable forms may dwell—   10

---

1   *The Slave Auction* Scholar Melba Joyce Boyd points out that, when read aloud, the sound of this poem is both low in pitch and slow in progression, elements of effective oral delivery for this poem of grim drama.

Gazed on the husband of her youth,
    With anguish none may paint or tell.

And men, whose sole crime was their hue,
    The impress of their Maker's hand,
15 And frail and shrinking children too,
    Were gathered in that mournful band.

Ye who have laid your loved to rest,
    And wept above their lifeless clay,
Know not the anguish of that breast,
20   Whose loved are rudely torn away.

Ye may not know how desolate
    Are bosoms rudely forced to part,
And how a dull and heavy weight
    Will press the life-drops from the heart.

—c. 1854

Bible Defense of Slavery[1]

Take sackcloth of the darkest dye,
    And shroud the pulpits round!
Servants of Him that cannot lie,
    Sit mourning on the ground.

5 Let holy horror blanch each cheek,
    Pale every brow with fears;
And rocks and stones, if ye could speak,
    Ye well might melt to tears!

Let sorrow breathe in every tone,
10   In every strain ye raise;
Insult not God's majestic throne
    With th' mockery of praise.

---

1   *Bible Defense of Slavery* Pro-slavery discourse relied heavily on the Bible to justify slavery. The anti-slavery movement tactically developed a counter-argument based on different biblical passages.

A "reverend" man, whose light should be
    The guide of age and youth,
Brings to the shrine of Slavery   15
    The sacrifice of truth!

For the direst wrong by man imposed,
    Since Sodom's[1] fearful cry,
The word of life has been unclos'd,
    To give your God the lie.   20

Oh! When ye pray for heathen lands,
    And plead for their dark shores,
Remember Slavery's cruel hands
    Make heathens at your doors!

          —1854

Learning to Read

Very soon the Yankee teachers
    Came down and set up school;
But, oh! how the Rebs did hate it,—
    It was agin' their rule.

Our masters always tried to hide   5
    Book learning from our eyes;
Knowledge did'nt agree with slavery—
    'Twould make us all too wise.

But some of us would try to steal
    A little from the book.   10
And put the words together,
    And learn by hook or crook.

I remember Uncle Caldwell,
    Who took pot liquor fat[2]
And greased the pages of his book,   15
    And hid it in his hat.

---

1   *Sodom* Biblical city that God destroys for its wickedness.
2   *pot liquor fat* Fat from a cooking pot.

And had his master ever seen
    The leaves upon his head,
He'd have thought them greasy papers,
20   But nothing to be read.

And there was Mr. Turner's Ben,
    Who heard the children spell,
And picked the words right up by heart,
    And learned to read 'em well.

25 Well, the Northern folks kept sending
    The Yankee teachers down;
And they stood right up and helped us,
    Though Rebs did sneer and frown.

And I longed to read my Bible,
30   For precious words it said;
But when I begun to learn it,
    Folks just shook their heads,

And said there is no use trying,
    Oh! Chloe,[1] you're too late;
35 But as I was rising sixty,
    I had no time to wait.

So I got a pair of glasses,
    And straight to work I went,
And never stopped till I could read
40   The hymns and Testament.

Then I got a little cabin
    A place to call my own—
And I felt independent
    As the queen upon her throne.

—1872

---

1   *Chloe* Harper wrote a series of poems about a character named Aunt Chloe, a former
slave.

A Double Standard

Do you blame me that I loved him?
    If when standing all alone
I cried for bread a careless world
    Pressed to my lips a stone.

Do you blame me that I loved him,   5
    That my heart beat glad and free,
When he told me in the sweetest tones
    He loved but only me?

Can you blame me that I did not see
    Beneath his burning kiss   10
The serpent's wiles, nor even hear
    The deadly adder hiss?

Can you blame me that my heart grew cold
    That the tempted, tempter turned;
When he was feted° and caressed   *celebrated* 15
    And I was coldly spurned?

Would you blame him, when you draw from me
    Your dainty robes aside,
If he with gilded baits should claim
    Your fairest as his bride?   20

Would you blame the world if it should press
    On him a civic crown;
And see me struggling in the depth
    Then harshly press me down?

Crime has no sex and yet to-day   25
    I wear the brand of shame;
Whilst he amid the gay and proud
    Still bears an honored name.

Can you blame me if I've learned to think
    Your hate of vice a sham,   30
When you so coldly crushed me down
    And then excused the man?

Would you blame me if to-morrow
　　The coroner should say,
35 A wretched girl, outcast, forlorn,
　　Has thrown her life away?

Yes, blame me for my downward course,
　　But oh! remember well,
Within your homes you press the hand
40　　That led me down to hell.

I'm glad God's ways are not our ways,
　　He does not see as man,
Within His love I know there's room
　　For those whom others ban.

45 I think before His great white throne,
　　His throne of spotless light,
That whited sepulchres[1] shall wear
　　The hue of endless night.

That I who fell, and he who sinned,
50　　Shall reap as we have sown;
That each the burden of his loss
　　Must bear and bear alone.

No golden weights can turn the scale
　　Of justice in His sight;
55 And what is wrong in woman's life
　　In man's cannot be right.

—1895

1　*whited sepulchres* In Matthew 23.27 in the Bible's New Testament, Jesus uses this term to
　　excoriate the scribes and Pharisees as hypocrites, outwardly beautiful but unclean within.

Rose Terry (Cooke)
1827–1892

Rose Terry (the first name under which she published; she added the "Cooke" after her unfortunate and financially draining marriage at age 46) was a versatile writer of fiction and poetry. Working in the popular and well-respected genre of the regional or local-color tale, she published her realistic sketches of New England life in the most prestigious magazines of the era. She also published more than 200 periodical poems and two books of poetry (in 1861 and 1888). Like many well-regarded nineteenth-century women writers, she fell from view as the canon narrowed in the early twentieth century to a relatively small group of mostly male authors. When late twentieth-century scholars rediscovered her work as part of a wider reclamation of women's writing, they focused on her fiction depicting women's constrained social lives. Her poems have not yet received much attention, in part because she writes in traditional forms that have misled readers into dismissing her as "conventional" or outdated. While different in style than her realistic fiction, her poetry's phantasmagoric, violent, Gothic, and sensual currents offer complex explorations of psychic terrain, especially the psychic terrain of women. Her dark Romanticism places her in the company of poets like Poe and Shelley.

Arachne[1]

I watch her in the corner there,
As, restless, bold, and unafraid,
She slips and floats along the air
Till all her subtile[2] house is made.

Her home, her bed, her daily food   5
All from that hidden store she draws;
She fashions it and knows it good,
By instinct's strong and sacred laws.

---

1 *Arachne* In Ovid's *Metamorphoses*, the most famous version of this myth, the arrogant mortal woman Arachne defeats the goddess Minerva in a weaving contest. Ovid frequently depicts the gods punishing the mortals who best them. Minerva punishes Arachne, who then hangs herself. Minerva turns her hanging corpse into a spider, a condition imposed on all Arachne's offspring and descendants as well.
2 *subtile* Cleverly or ingeniously made.

No tenuous threads to weave her nest,
10   She seeks and gathers there or here;
But spins it from her faithful breast,
Renewing still, till leaves are sere.

Then, worn with toil, and tired of life,
In vain her shining traps are set.
15   Her frost hath hushed the insect strife
And gilded flies her charm forget.

But swinging in the snares she spun,
She sways to every winter wind:
Her joy, her toil, her errand done,
20   Her corse the sport of storms unkind.

Poor sister of the spinster clan!
I too from out my store within
My daily life and living plan,
My home, my rest, my pleasure spin.

25   I know thy heart when heartless hands
Sweep all that hard-earned web away:
Destroy its pearled and glittering bands,
And leave thee homeless by the way.

I know thy peace when all is done.
30   Each anchored thread, each tiny knot,
Soft shining in the autumn sun;
A sheltered, silent, tranquil lot.

I know what thou hast never known,
—Sad presage to a soul allowed;—
35   That not for life I spin, alone.
But day by day I spin my shroud.

—1860

Blue-Beard's Closet[1]

Fasten the chamber!
Hide the red key;
Cover the portal,
That eyes may not see.
Get thee to market,   5
To wedding and prayer;
Labor or revel,
The chamber is there!

In comes a stranger—
"Thy pictures how fine,   10
Titian or Guido,[2]
Whose is the sign?"
Looks he behind them?
Ah! have a care!
"Here is a finer."   15
The chamber is there!

Fair spreads the banquet,
Rich the array;
See the bright torches
Mimicking day;   20
When harp and viol
Thrill the soft air,
Comes a light whisper:
The chamber is there!

Marble and painting,   25
Jasper[3] and gold,

---

1 *Blue-Beard's Closet* Blue-Beard was a seventeenth-century French character who mur-
   dered his wives and kept their bodies locked in a closet that he forbids his new wife to
   enter. By the time Cooke was writing, both the terms "Blue-Beard" and a "Blue-Beard
   closet," chamber, or room had become common vocabulary for male violence and secrecy.
2 *Titian or Guido* Titian (c. 1488–1576) and Guido Reni (1575–1642) were important
   Italian painters. Guido Reni painted an influential portrait of Beatrice Cenci, a victim
   of incest by her nobleman father, whom she then murdered. Percy Bysshe Shelley wrote
   a verse drama inspired by Guido's painting, and the haunting influence of the portrait
   further reverberated through other nineteenth-century literary works as a well-recognized
   allusion to domestic danger and violence.
3 *Jasper* Precious stone.

Purple from Tyrus,
Fold upon fold,
Blossoms and jewels,
30   Thy palace prepare:
Pale grows the monarch;
The chamber is there!

Once it was open
As shore to the sea;
35   White were the turrets,
Goodly to see;
All through the casements
Flowed the sweet air;
Now it is darkness;
40   *The chamber is there!*

Silence and horror
Brood on the walls;
Through every crevice
A little voice calls:
45   "Quicken, mad footsteps,
On pavement and stair;
Look not behind thee,
The chamber is there!"

Out of the gateway,
50   Through the wide world,
Into the tempest
Beaten and hurled,
Vain is thy wandering,
Sure thy despair,
55   Flying or staying,
The chamber is there!

—1860

Fantasia

When I am a sea-flower
Under the cool green tide,
Where the sunshine slants and quivers,
And the quaint, gray fishes glide,
I'll shut and sleep at noonday,   5
At night on the waves I'll ride,
And see the surf in moonshine
Rush on the black rocks' side.

When I am a sea-bird,
Under the clouds I'll fly,   10
And 'light on a rocking billow
Tossing low and high.
Safe from the lee-shore's[1] thunder,
Mocking the mariner's cry,
Drifting away on the tempest,   15
A speck on the sullen sky!

When I am a sea-wind,
I'll watch for a ship I know,
Through the sails and rigging
Merrily I will blow.   20
The crew shall be like dead men
White with horror and woe;
Then I'll sing like a spirit,
And let the good ship go.

—1860

---

1   *lee-shore* Nautical term for the shore when the wind is blowing toward it. Herman Mel-
    ville noted in his famous chapter "The Lee Shore" in *Moby-Dick* (1851) that the lee shore
    is treacherous to mariners. Although the land might seem to promise safety in storm con-
    ditions, the lee shore bodes shipwreck and fatality. Like Melville, Cooke is here exploring
    ideas about domesticity and danger.

Truths

I wear a rose[1] in my hair,
    Because I feel like a weed;
Who knows that the rose is thorny
    And makes my temples bleed?
5 If one gets to his journey's end, what matter how galled the steed?[2]

I gloss my face with laughter,
    Because I cannot be calm;
When you listen to the organ,
    Do you hear the words of the psalm?
10 If they give you poison to drink, 'tis better to call it balm.

If I sneer at youth's wild passion,
    Who fancies I break my heart?
'Tis this world's righteous fashion,
    With a sneer to cover a smart.
15 Better to give up living than not to play your part.

If I scatter gold like a goblin,
    My life may yet be poor.
Does Love come in at the window
    When Money stands at the door?
20 I am what I seem to men. Need I be any more?

God sees from the high blue heaven,
    He sees the grape in the flower;
He hears one's life-blood dripping
    Through the maddest, merriest hour;
25 He knows what sackcloth and ashes hide in the purple of power.

The broken wing of the swallow
    He binds in the middle air;
I shall be what I am in Paradise—
    So, heart, no more despair!
30 Remember the blessed Jesus, and wipe his feet with thy hair.

—1860

---

1   *rose* Flowers, roses in particular, were common poetic (and metapoetic) tropes at this time. Cooke here invokes and recasts the convention. Herman Melville (p. 161) also wrote an unconventional book of poems about roses and weeds.

2   *galled the steed* Cooke's image is that of a horse worn out and sore from a long journey.

Dante Gabriel Rossetti

1828–1882

Born in 1828 into an erudite family, Dante Gabriel Rossetti intended to be a painter from a young age. He was a competitive yet fiercely fond older brother to his sister, Christina. When at the age of 16 she published *Verses* (1847), Rossetti was compelled to try with meter what he was doing as a painter with color. "Color and metre," Rossetti claimed, "are the true parents of nobility in painting and poetry." In 1848, he founded a group called the Pre-Raphaelite Brotherhood, a club of young men interested in innovative contemporary arts. The Pre-Raphaelites published a journal of poems and illustrations entitled *The Germ*, in which Rossetti's poem "The Blessed Damozel" first appeared. The publication gained Rossetti a small group of admirers that would steadily increase.

Rossetti's wife Elizabeth Siddal, a model for the Pre-Raphaelites and an artist and poet in her own right, committed suicide in 1862, two years after their marriage, after losing a child. Seized with remorse at her funeral, he tucked a manuscript of poems into her coffin. He had them exhumed years later in order to publish his first collection of verse, *Poems* (1870). The book sold well and was favorably reviewed, although some reviewers criticized Rossetti for writing poetry of sensuality and lust. As lovers, wives, painter's models, poetic subjects, and muses, women were central to Rossetti's life, which was also long troubled by poor physical and mental health. W.B. Yeats's youthful claim that he was "in all things Pre-Raphaelite" was proof of Rossetti's influence on the next generation of poets.

Jenny

"Vengeance of Jenny's case! Fie on her! Never name her, child!"—*Mrs. Quickly*[1]

Lazy laughing languid Jenny,
Fond of a kiss and fond of a guinea,[2]
Whose head upon my knee to-night
Rests for a while, as if grown light
With all our dances and the sound   5
To which the wild tunes spun you round:
Fair Jenny mine, the thoughtless queen
Of kisses which the blush between

---

1   *Mrs. Quickly* From Shakespeare's *The Merry Wives of Windsor*. The rest of Mistress Quickly's speech reads, "if she be a whore."

2   *guinea* English gold coin.

Could hardly make much daintier;
10 Whose eyes are as blue skies, whose hair
Is countless gold incomparable:
Fresh flower, scarce touched with signs that tell
Of Love's exuberant hotbed:—Nay,
Poor flower left torn since yesterday
15 Until to-morrow leave you bare;
Poor handful of bright spring-water
Flung in the whirlpool's shrieking face;
Poor shameful Jenny, full of grace
Thus with your head upon my knee;—
20 Whose person or whose purse may be
The lodestar of your reverie?

This room of yours, my Jenny, looks
A change from mine so full of books,
Whose serried[1] ranks hold fast, forsooth,
25 So many captive hours of youth,—
The hours they thieve from day and night
To make one's cherished work come right,
And leave it wrong for all their theft,
Even as to-night my work has left:
30 Until I vowed that since my brain
And eyes of dancing seemed so fain,
My feet should have some dancing too:—
And thus it was I met with you.
Well, I suppose 'twas hard to part,
35 For here I am. And now, sweetheart,
You seem too tired to get to bed.

It was a careless life I led
When rooms like this were scarce so strange
Not long ago. What breeds the change,—
40 The many aims or the few years?
Because to-night it all appears
Something I do not know again.

The cloud's not danced out of my brain,—
The cloud that made it turn and swim

---

1   *serried* Pressed close together.

While hour by hour the books grew dim. 45
Why, Jenny, as I watch you there,—
For all your wealth of loosened hair,
Your silk ungirdled and unlac'd
And warm sweets open to the waist,
All golden in the lamplight's gleam,— 50
You know not what a book you seem,
Half-read by lightning in a dream!
How should you know, my Jenny? Nay,
And I should be ashamed to say:—
Poor beauty, so well worth a kiss! 55
But while my thought runs on like this
With wasteful whims more than enough,
I wonder what you're thinking of.

    If of myself you think at all,
What is the thought?—conjectural 60
On sorry matters best unsolved?—
Or inly° is each grace revolved   *inwardly*
To fit me with a lure?—or (sad
To think!) perhaps you're merely glad
That I'm not drunk or ruffianly 65
And let you rest upon my knee.

    For sometimes, were the truth confess'd,
You're thankful for a little rest,—
Glad from the crush to rest within,
From the heart-sickness and the din 70
Where envy's voice at virtue's pitch
Mocks you because your gown is rich;
And from the pale girl's dumb rebuke,
Whose ill-clad grace and toil-worn look
Proclaim the strength that keeps her weak, 75
And other nights than yours bespeak;
And from the wise unchildish elf,
To schoolmate lesser than himself
Pointing you out, what thing you are:—
Yes, from the daily jeer and jar, 80
From shame and shame's outbraving too,
Is rest not sometimes sweet to you?—
But most from the hatefulness of man

Who spares not to end what he began,
85 Whose acts are ill and his speech ill,
Who, having used you at his will,
Thrusts you aside, as when I dine
I serve the dishes and the wine.

Well, handsome Jenny mine, sit up:
90 I've filled our glasses, let us sup,
And do not let me think of you,
Lest shame of yours suffice for two.
What, still so tired? Well, well then, keep
Your head there, so you do not sleep;
95 But that the weariness may pass
And leave you merry, take this glass.
Ah! lazy lily hand, more bless'd
If ne'er in rings it had been dress'd
Nor ever by a glove conceal'd!

100 Behold the lilies of the field,
They toil not neither do they spin;[1]
(So doth the ancient text begin,—
Not of such rest as one of these
Can share.) Another rest and ease.
105 Along each summer-sated path
From its new lord the garden hath,
Than that whose spring in blessings ran
Which praised the bounteous husbandman,
Ere yet, in days of hankering breath,
110 The lilies sickened unto death.

What, Jenny, are your lilies dead?
Aye, and the snow-white leaves are spread
Like winter on the garden-bed.
But you had roses left in May,—
115 They were not gone too. Jenny, nay,
But must your roses die, and those
Their purfled[2] buds that should unclose?
Even so; the leaves are curled apart,

---

1   *Behold the lilies ... spin* Reference to Matthew 6.28.
2   *purfled* Edged with color.

Still red as from the broken heart,
And here's the naked stem of thorns.   120

     Nay, nay mere words. Here nothing warns
As yet of winter. Sickness here
Or want alone could waken fear,—
Nothing but passion wrings a tear.
Except when there may rise unsought   125
Haply at times a passing thought
Of the old days which seem to be
Much older than any history
That is written in any book;
When she would lie in fields and look   130
Along the ground through the blown grass,
And wonder where the city was,
Far out of sight, whose broil and bale[1]
They told her then for a child's tale.

     Jenny, you know the city now,   135
A child can tell the tale there, how
Some things which are not yet enroll'd
In market-lists are bought and sold
Even till the early Sunday light,
When Saturday night is market-night   140
Everywhere, be it dry or wet,
And market-night in the Haymarket.
Our learned London children know,
Poor Jenny, all your pride and woe;
Have seen your lifted silken skirt   145
Advertise dainties through the dirt;
Have seen your coach-wheels splash rebuke
On virtue; and have learned your look
When, wealth and health slipped past, you stare
Along the streets alone, and there,   150
Round the long park, across the bridge,
The cold lamps at the pavement's edge
Wind on together and apart,
A fiery serpent for your heart.

---

1   *broil and bale* Tumult and woe.

155   Let the thoughts pass, an empty cloud!
Suppose I were to think aloud,—
What if to her all this were said?
Why, as a volume seldom read
Being opened halfway shuts again,
160 So might the pages of her brain
Be parted at such words, and thence
Close back upon the dusty sense.
For is there hue or shape defin'd
In Jenny's desecrated mind,
165 Where all contagious currents meet,
A Lethe of the middle street?
Nay, it reflects not any face,
Nor sound is in its sluggish pace,
But as they coil those eddies clot,
170 And night and day remembers not.

      Why, Jenny, you're asleep at last!—
Asleep, poor Jenny, hard and fast,—
So young and soft and tired; so fair,
With chin thus nestled in your hair,
175 Mouth quiet, eyelids almost blue
As if some sky of dreams shone through!

      Just as another woman sleeps!
Enough to throw one's thoughts in heaps
Of doubt and horror,—what to say
180 Or think,—this awful secret sway,
The potter's power over the clay!
Of the same lump (it has been said)
For honour and dishonour made,
Two sister vessels.[1] Here is one.

185   My cousin Nell is fond of fun,
And fond of dress, and change, and praise,
So mere a woman in her ways:
And if her sweet eyes rich in youth
Are like her lips that tell the truth,
190 My cousin Nell is fond of love.

---

1   *The potter's power... vessels* Reference to Romans 9.21.

And she's the girl I'm proudest of.
Who does not prize her, guard her well?
The love of change, in cousin Nell,
Shall find the best and hold it dear:
The unconquered mirth turn quieter   195
Not through her own, through others' woe:
The conscious pride of beauty glow
Beside another's pride in her,
One little part of all they share.
For Love himself shall ripen these   200
In a kind of soil to just increase
Through years of fertilizing peace.

    Of the same lump (as it is said)
For honour and dishonour made,
Two sister vessels. Here is one.   205

    It makes a goblin of the sun.

    So pure,—so fall'n! How dare to think
Of the first common kindred link?
Yet, Jenny, till the world shall burn
It seems that all things take their turn;   210
And who shall say but this fair tree
May need, in changes that may be,
Your children's children's charity?
Scorned then, no doubt, as you are scorn'd!
Shall no man hold his pride forewarn'd   215
Till in the end, the Day of Days,
At Judgement, one of his own race,
As frail and lost as you, shall rise,—
His daughter, with his mother's eyes?

    How Jenny's clock ticks on the shelf!   220
Might not the dial scorn itself
That has such hours to register?
Yet as to me, even so to her
Are golden sun and silver moon,
In daily largesse of earth's boon,   225
Counted for life-coins to one tune.
And if, as blindfold fates are toss'd,

Through some one man this life be lost,
Shall soul not somehow pray for soul?

230   Fair shines the gilded aureole
In which our highest painters place
Some living woman's simple face.
And the stilled features thus descried
As Jenny's long throat droops aside,—
235 The shadows where the cheeks are thin,
And pure wide curve from ear to chin,—
With Raffael's, Leonardo's[1] hand
To show them to men's souls, might stand,
Whole ages long, the whole world through,
240 For preachings of what God can do.
What has man done here? How atone,
Great God, for this which man has done?
And for the body and soul which by
Man's pitiless doom must now comply
245 With lifelong hell, what lullaby
Of sweet forgetful second birth
Remains? All dark. No sign on earth
What measure of God's rest endows
The many mansions of his house.

250   If but a woman's heart might see
Such erring heart unerringly
For once! But that can never be.

      Like a rose shut in a book
In which pure women may not look,
255 For its base pages claim control
To crush the flower within the soul;
Where through each dead rose-leaf that clings,
Pale as transparent psyche-wings,
To the vile text, are traced such things
260 As might make lady's cheek indeed
More than a living rose to read;
So nought save foolish foulness may

---

1   *Raffael's, Leonardo's* Italian painters Raphael (1483–1520) and Leonardo da Vinci (1452–1519).

Watch with hard eyes the sure decay;
And so the life-blood of this rose,
Puddled with shameful knowledge, flows   265
Through leaves no chaste hand may unclose:
Yet still it keeps such faded show
Of when 'twas gathered long ago,
That the crushed petals' lovely grain,
The sweetness of the sanguine stain,   270
Seen of a woman's eyes, must make
Her pitiful heart, so prone to ache,
Love roses better for its sake:—
Only that this can never be:—
Even so unto her sex is she.   275

    Yet, Jenny, looking long at you,
The woman almost fades from view.
A cipher of man's changeless sum
Of lust, past, present, and to come,
Is left. A riddle that one shrinks   280
To challenge from the scornful sphinx.[1]

    Like a toad within a stone
Seated while Time crumbles on;
Which sits there since the earth was curs'd
For Man's transgression at the first;   285
Which, living through all centuries,
Not once has seen the sun arise;
Whose life, to its cold circle charmed,
The earth's whole summers have not warmed;
Which always—whitherso the stone   290
Be flung—sits there, deaf, blind, alone;—
Aye, and shall not be driven out
Till that which shuts him round about
Break at the very Master's stroke,
And the dust thereof vanish as smoke,   295
And the seed of Man vanish as dust:—
Even so within this world is Lust.

---

1   *sphinx* Winged creature of Greek mythology who killed those that could not answer her
    riddles.

Come, come, what use in thoughts like this?
Poor little Jenny, good to kiss,—
300 You'd not believe by what strange roads
Thought travels, when your beauty goads
A man to-night to think of toads!
Jenny, wake up. . . . Why, there's the dawn!

And there's an early waggon drawn
305 To market, and some sheep that jog
Bleating before a barking dog;
And the old streets come peering through
Another night that London knew;
And all as ghostlike as the lamps.

310 So on the wings of day decamps
My last night's frolic. Glooms begin
To shiver off as lights creep in
Past the gauze curtains half drawn-to,
And the lamp's doubled shade grows blue,—
315 Your lamp, my Jenny, kept alight,
Like a wise virgin's, all one night!
And in the alcove coolly spread
Glimmers with dawn your empty bed;
And yonder your fair face I see
320 Reflected lying on my knee,
Where teems with first foreshadowings
Your pier-glass[1] scrawled with diamond rings:
And on your bosom all night worn
Yesterday's rose now droops forlorn,
325 But dies not yet this summer morn.

And now without, as if some word
Had called upon them that they heard,
The London sparrows far and nigh
Clamour together suddenly;
330 And Jenny's cage-bird grown awake
Here in their song his part must take,
Because here too the day doth break.

---

1   *pier-glass* Tall mirror.

And somehow in myself the dawn
Among stirred clouds and veils withdrawn
Strikes greyly on her. Let her sleep.   335
But will it wake her if I heap
These cushions thus beneath her head
Where my knee was? No,—there's your bed,
My Jenny, while you dream. And there
I lay among your golden hair   340
Perhaps the subject of your dreams,
These golden coins.
                          For still one deems
That Jenny's flattering sleep confers
New magic on the magic purse,—   345
Grim web, how clogged with shrivelled flies!
Between the threads fine fumes arise
And shape their pictures in the brain.
There roll no streets in glare and rain,
Nor flagrant man-swine whets his tusk;   350
But delicately sighs in musk
The homage of the dim boudoir;
Or like a palpitating star
Thrilled into song, the opera-night
Breathes faint in the quick pulse of light;   355
Or at the carriage-window shine
Rich wares for choice; or, free to dine,
Whirls through its hour of health (divine
For her) the concourse of the Park.
And though in the discounted dark   360
Her functions there and here are one,
Beneath the lamps and in the sun
There reigns at least the acknowledged belle
Apparelled beyond parallel.
Ah Jenny, yes, we know your dreams.   365

For even the Paphian Venus[1] seems,
A goddess o'er the realms of love,
When silver-shrined in shadowy grove:
Aye, or let offerings nicely placed

---

1   *Paphian Venus* Venus, goddess of love, was said to have been born of sea-foam, but
     emerged on the island of Paphos, Cyprus.

370 But hide Priapus[1] to the waist,
    And whoso looks on him shall see
    An eligible deity.

        Why, Jenny, waking here alone
    May help you to remember one,
375 Though all the memory's long outworn
    Of many a double-pillowed morn.
    I think I see you when you wake,
    And rub your eyes for me, and shake
    My gold, in rising, from your hair,
380 A Danaë[2] for a moment there.

        Jenny, my love rang true! for still
    Love at first sight is vague, until
    That tinkling makes him audible.

        And must I mock you to the last,
385 Ashamed of my own shame,—aghast
    Because some thoughts not born amiss
    Rose at a poor fair face like this?
    Well, of such thoughts so much I know:
    In my life, as in hers, they show,
390 By a far gleam which I may near,
    A dark path I can strive to clear.

        Only one kiss. Good-bye, my dear.

                                        —1848

---

1   *Priapus* God of procreation, and a personification of an erect phallus.
2   *Danaë* According to Greek mythology, Acrisius imprisoned his daughter Danaë in a
     room of bronze to ensure she would never conceive a son. Zeus, however, fell in love with
     Danaë and came to her through the ceiling as a shower of gold that fell in her lap.

Emily Dickinson
1830–1886

Unknown in her lifetime, Emily Dickinson was to become, after her death, the most important woman poet of the nineteenth-century United States. Born in rural Massachusetts into an important and influential family affiliated with Amherst College, she was well educated for a woman of her time. She attended a local academy and then completed a year at South Hadley Female Seminary (now Mount Holyoke College). Although reared as a Congregationalist, Dickinson bristled at the Christian evangelical fervor that the school expected of its students. Her poems record her awareness of Christian ideas as well as her resistance and doubt. Because of her family's wealth, she was protected from the need to marry and from the need to earn a living. She traveled a little bit and published a few poems in periodicals, but she mostly lived at home, actively circulating her handwritten poems to friends and loved ones. A prolific writer, she created many kinds of manuscript poems: she included them in letters, arranged them in handmade books, and composed them on scraps and envelopes that became like canvases. Her complex writing practices include her characteristic dashes, which multiply the grammatical possibilities of her lines. She also flagged particular words with crosses, supplying variant words in the margins for possible substitution. Her poems thus turned into multiple versions of themselves, making her manuscripts notoriously difficult to convert into print. In the 1890s, in the wake of her death, family members and friends began to publish collections of her verse. These early editors felt free to amend her work to make it conform more closely to recognizable poetic conventions. They added titles, corrected slant rhymes, and regularized meters, thus distorting Dickinson's own carefully crafted irregularities. These first editions reached a large popular audience, and Dickinson became a best-loved poet hailed as a genius, albeit for poems that were not exactly what she had herself written.

Scholars only began to correct the mistaken record of her work in the mid-twentieth century. Dickinson's influence on subsequent poets is incalculable. Recent scholarship has challenged the mythic image of Dickinson as a recluse hiding in her family home as an ivory tower of metaphysical abstraction. Although she did mostly choose a restricted social circle, we now know that she was deeply conversant with the concerns of her age and frequently wrote about topics such as gender, marriage, nature, and religion, all topics that her male and female contemporary poets also addressed. Those poets who wrote for a public market (which Dickinson famously and derisively called an "auction") faced constraints of audience and expectation that Dickinson's private practice allowed her to ignore. One of the most exciting recent developments in Dickinson scholarship is a new awareness of her anguished responses to the greatest social trauma of her time, the Civil War, examples of which are included here.

Note to readers: Dickinson's poem "'Heaven' - is what I cannot reach!" appears on the anthology's companion website. The URL and passcode appear in the Table of Contents.

134[1]

Did the Harebell[2] loose[3] her girdle
To the lover Bee
Would the Bee the Harebell *hallow*
Much as formerly?

5 Did the "Paradise" - *persuaded* -
Yield her moat of pearl[4] -
Would the Eden *be* an Eden,
Or the Earl - an *Earl*?

—1860

320

There's a certain Slant of light,
Winter Afternoons -
That oppresses, like the Heft°   *Weight*
Of Cathedral Tunes -

5 Heavenly Hurt, it gives us -
We can find no scar,
But internal difference -
Where the Meanings, are -

None may teach it - Any -
10 'Tis the Seal° Despair -   *Impression or mark*
An imperial affliction
Sent us of the Air -

---

1 These poems rely on the numbering in the edition of Dickinson's poems by R.W. Franklin.

2 *Harebell* A type of flower; in Dickinson's northeastern region, likely the blue-bell.

3 *loose* Undo, unfasten, set free; also, free in the sense of dissolute or promiscuous.

4 *moat of pearl* Deep ditch, typically filled with liquid, which serves as a form of defense against assault and part of Dickinson's metaphorics of sexual conquest in this poem; *pearl* something of precious value; something whitish in color like the pearl. Scholars have long noted the erotic charge of Dickinson's metaphors, certainly part of her frank representation here of female genitalia and sexuality.

When it comes, the Landscape listens
Shadows - hold their breath -
When it goes, 'tis like the Distance   15
On the look of Death -

—1862

423

The first Day's Night had come -
And grateful that a thing
So terrible - had been endured -
I told my Soul to sing —

She said her strings were snapt -   5
Her Bow - to atoms blown -
And so to mend her - gave me work
Until another Morn —

And then - a Day as huge
As Yesterdays in pairs,   10
Unrolled it's horror in my face -
Until it blocked my eyes -

My Brain - begun to laugh -
I mumbled - like a fool -
And tho' 'tis Years ago - that Day -   15
My Brain keeps giggling - still.

And Something's odd - within -
That person that I was -
And this One - do not feel the same -
Could it be Madness - this?   20

—1862

446

This was a Poet -
It is That
Distills amazing sense
From Ordinary Meanings -
And Attar[1] so immense   5

---

1   *Attar* Essential oil of the rose.

From the familiar species
That perished by the Door -
We wonder it was not Ourselves
Arrested° it - before —   *Captured*

10

Of Pictures, the Discloser -
The Poet - it is He -
Entitles Us - by Contrast -
To ceaseless Poverty -

15   Of Portion - so unconscious
The Robbing - could not harm -
Himself - to Him - a Fortune -
Exterior - to Time -

                                                          —1862

465

The name - of it - is "Autumn" -
The hue - of it - is Blood -
5   An Artery - opon[1] the Hill -
A Vein - along the Road -

Great Globules - in the Alleys -
And Oh, the Shower of Stain
When Winds - upset the Basin -
And spill the Scarlet Rain —

10

It sprinkles Bonnets - far below
It gathers ruddy Pools -
Then - eddies like a Rose - away
Opon Vermillion Wheels —

                                                          —1862

15

---

1   *opon* Some editors interpret Dickinson's handwriting here as "Upon," others as "Opon."
    "Opon" is an archaic form for "open."

524

It feels a shame to be Alive -
When Men so brave - are dead -
One envies the Distinguished Dust -
Permitted - such a Head -

The Stone - that tells defending Whom   5
This Spartan[1] put away
What little of Him we - possessed
In Pawn for Liberty -

The price is great - Sublimely paid -
Do we deserve - a Thing -   10
That lives - like Dollars - must be piled
Before we may obtain?

Are we that wait - sufficient worth -
That such Enormous Pearl
As life - dissolved be - for Us -
In Battle's - horrid Bowl?   15

It may be - a Renown to live -
I think the Men who die -
Those unsustained - Saviors -
Present Divinity -

—1863

704

My Portion is Defeat - today -
A paler luck than Victory -
Less Paeans[2] - fewer Bells -
The Drums dont follow Me - with tunes -
Defeat - a somewhat slower - means -   5
More Arduous than Balls[3] -

---

1   *Spartan* Courageous and disciplined, qualities attributed to the ancient inhabitants of Sparta.
2   *Paeans* Songs of victory in battle.
3   *Balls* Projectiles fired by cannons or guns.

'Tis populous with Bone and stain -
And Men too straight to stoop again -
And Piles of solid Moan -
10   And Chips of Blank - in Boyish Eyes -
And scraps of Prayer -
And Death's surprise,
Stamped visible - in stone -

There's somewhat prouder, Over there -
15   The Trumpets tell it to the Air -
How different Victory
To Him who has it - and the One
Who to have had it, would have been
Contenteder - to die –

—1863

857

She rose to His Requirement - dropt
The Playthings of Her Life
To take the honorable Work
Of Woman, and of Wife -

5   If ought She missed in Her new Day,
Of Amplitude, or Awe -
Or first Prospective - or the Gold
In using, wear away,

It lay unmentioned - as the Sea
10   Develope[1] Pearl, and Weed,
But only to Himself - be known
The Fathoms they abide -

—1864

---

1   *Develope* The final "e" on "develop" is a point of contention among editors about the
handwritten version of the poem.

Christina Rossetti
1830–1894

To the late-Victorian critic Edmund Gosse, Christina Rossetti was "one of the most perfect poets of the age." Her melding of sensuous imagery and stringent form earned her the admiration and devotion of many nineteenth-century readers. Rossetti was born in London in 1830. Her father, a scholar and Italian expatriate, and her mother, who had been a governess before her marriage, inculcated in each of their four children a love of language, literature, and the arts. In 1850 several of her poems were published in *The Germ*, the journal of the Pre-Raphaelite Brotherhood founded in part by her two brothers, Dante Gabriel and William Michael. Although Rossetti was not formally a member of the Brotherhood, her aesthetic sense—and especially her attention to color and detail—link her to the movement.

Rossetti first gained attention in the literary world with her 1862 publication of *Goblin Market and Other Poems*. The vast majority of her Victorian critics praised the volume for what one reviewer called its "very decided character and originality, both in theme and treatment," and "Goblin Market" remains among her most discussed works. Few readers have believed William Michael Rossetti's insistence that his sister "did not mean anything profound" by "Goblin Market." Although the poem fell from view until the last decades of the twentieth century, "Goblin Market" then found a new audience fascinated by its treatment of women, gender, sexuality, and Gothic fantasy.

In 1871, Rossetti was stricken with Graves's disease, a thyroid problem, which led her to retreat even further into an already quiet life. She continued, however, to publish poetry, including *Sing-Song* (1872), a children's collection; *A Pageant and Other Poems* (1881); and *Verses* (1893). In 1892 she was among those mentioned as a possible successor to Tennyson as England's Poet Laureate. She died in 1894 as a result of breast cancer.

Goblin Market

Morning and evening
Maids heard the goblins cry:
"Come buy our orchard fruits,
Come buy, come buy:
Apples and quinces,   5
Lemons and oranges,
Plump unpecked cherries,
Melons and raspberries,
Bloom-down-cheeked peaches,

10 Swart°-headed mulberries,   *dark*
    Wild free-born cranberries,
    Crabapples, dewberries,
    Pine-apples, blackberries,
    Apricots, strawberries;—
15 All ripe together
    In summer weather,—
    Morns that pass by,
    Fair eves that fly;
    Come buy, come buy:
20 Our grapes fresh from the vine,
    Pomegranates full and fine,
    Dates and sharp bullaces,
    Rare pears and greengages,
    Damsons[1] and bilberries
25 Taste them and try:
    Currants and gooseberries,
    Bright-fire-like barberries,
    Figs to fill your mouth,
    Citrons from the South,
30 Sweet to tongue and sound to eye;
    Come buy, come buy."

    Evening by evening
    Among the brookside rushes,
    Laura bowed her head to hear,
35 Lizzie veiled her blushes:
    Crouching close together
    In the cooling weather,
    With clasping arms and cautioning lips,
    With tingling cheeks and finger tips.
40 "Lie close," Laura said,
    Pricking up her golden head:
    "We must not look at goblin men,
    We must not buy their fruits:
    Who knows upon what soil they fed
45 Their hungry thirsty roots?"
    "Come buy," call the goblins
    Hobbling down the glen.

---

1   *bullaces ... Damsons* Bullaces, greengages, and damsons are all varieties of plums.

"Oh," cried Lizzie, "Laura, Laura,
You should not peep at goblin men."
Lizzie covered up her eyes,   50
Covered close lest they should look;
Laura reared her glossy head,
And whispered like the restless brook:
"Look, Lizzie, look, Lizzie,
Down the glen tramp little men.   55
One hauls a basket,
One bears a plate,
One lugs a golden dish
Of many pounds weight.
How fair the vine must grow   60
Whose grapes are so luscious;
How warm the wind must blow
Through those fruit bushes."
"No," said Lizzie: "No, no, no;
Their offers should not charm us,   65
Their evil gifts would harm us."
She thrust a dimpled finger
In each ear, shut eyes and ran:
Curious Laura chose to linger
Wondering at each merchant man.   70
One had a cat's face,
One whisked a tail,
One tramped at a rat's pace,
One crawled like a snail,
One like a wombat prowled obtuse and furry,   75
One like a ratel° tumbled hurry skurry.   *badger*
She heard a voice like voice of doves
Cooing all together:
They sounded kind and full of loves
In the pleasant weather.   80

Laura stretched her gleaming neck
Like a rush-imbedded swan,
Like a lily from the beck,°   *stream*
Like a moonlit poplar branch,
Like a vessel at the launch   85
When its last restraint is gone.

Backwards up the mossy glen
Turned and trooped the goblin men,
With their shrill repeated cry,
90 "Come buy, come buy."
When they reached where Laura was
They stood stock still upon the moss,
Leering at each other,
Brother with queer brother;
95 Signalling each other,
Brother with sly brother.
One set his basket down,
One reared his plate;
One began to weave a crown
100 Of tendrils, leaves, and rough nuts brown
(Men sell not such in any town);
One heaved the golden weight
Of dish and fruit to offer her:
"Come buy, come buy," was still their cry.
105 Laura stared but did not stir,
Longed but had no money:
The whisk-tailed merchant bade her taste
In tones as smooth as honey,
The cat-faced purr'd,
110 The rat-paced spoke a word
Of welcome, and the snail-paced even was heard;
One parrot-voiced and jolly
Cried "Pretty Goblin" still for "Pretty Polly";—
One whistled like a bird.

115 But sweet-tooth Laura spoke in haste:
"Good Folk, I have no coin;
To take were to purloin:
I have no copper in my purse,
I have no silver either,
120 And all my gold is on the furze°   *evergreen shrub*
That shakes in windy weather
Above the rusty heather."
"You have much gold upon your head,"
They answered all together:
125 "Buy from us with a golden curl."
She clipped a precious golden lock,

She dropped a tear more rare than pearl,
Then sucked their fruit globes fair or red.
Sweeter than honey from the rock,[1]
Stronger than man-rejoicing wine,   130
Clearer than water flowed that juice;
She never tasted such before,
How should it cloy with length of use?
She sucked and sucked and sucked the more
Fruits which that unknown orchard bore;   135
She sucked until her lips were sore;
Then flung the emptied rinds away
But gathered up one kernel-stone,
And knew not was it night or day
As she turned home alone.   140

Lizzie met her at the gate
Full of wise upbraidings:
"Dear, you should not stay so late,
Twilight is not good for maidens;
Should not loiter in the glen   145
In the haunts of goblin men.
Do you not remember Jeanie,
How she met them in the moonlight,
Took their gifts both choice and many,
Ate their fruits and wore their flowers   150
Plucked from bowers
Where summer ripens at all hours?
But ever in the moonlight
She pined and pined away;
Sought them by night and day,   155
Found them no more but dwindled and grew grey;
Then fell with the first snow,
While to this day no grass will grow
Where she lies low:
I planted daisies there a year ago   160
That never blow.
You should not loiter so."
"Nay, hush," said Laura:
"Nay, hush, my sister:

---

1   *honey from the rock* See Deuteronomy 32.13 in the Bible's Old Testament.

165 I ate and ate my fill,
    Yet my mouth waters still;
    Tomorrow night I will
    Buy more": and kissed her:
    "Have done with sorrow;
170 I'll bring you plums tomorrow
    Fresh on their mother twigs,
    Cherries worth getting;
    You cannot think what figs
    My teeth have met in,
175 What melons icy cold
    Piled on a dish of gold
    Too huge for me to hold,
    What peaches with a velvet nap,
    Pellucid° grapes without one seed: *Translucent*
180 Odorous indeed must be the mead°   *meadow*
    Whereon they grow, and pure the wave they drink
    With lilies at the brink,
    And sugar-sweet their sap."

    Golden head by golden head,
185 Like two pigeons in one nest
    Folded in each other's wings,
    They lay down in their curtained bed:
    Like two blossoms on one stem,
    Like two flakes of new-fall'n snow,
190 Like two wands of ivory
    Tipped with gold for awful° kings.   *awe-inspiring*
    Moon and stars gazed in at them,
    Wind sang to them lullaby,
    Lumbering owls forbore to fly,
195 Not a bat flapped to and fro
    Round their rest:
    Cheek to cheek and breast to breast
    Locked together in one nest.

    Early in the morning
200 When the first cock crowed his warning,
    Neat like bees, as sweet and busy,
    Laura rose with Lizzie:
    Fetched in honey, milked the cows,

Aired and set to rights the house,
Kneaded cakes of whitest wheat,   205
Cakes for dainty mouths to eat,
Next churned butter, whipped up cream,
Fed their poultry, sat and sewed;
Talked as modest maidens should:
Lizzie with an open heart,   210
Laura in an absent dream,
One content, one sick in part;
One warbling for the mere bright day's delight,
One longing for the night.

At length slow evening came: 215
They went with pitchers to the reedy brooks;
Lizzie most placid in her look,
Laura most like a leaping flame.
They drew the gurgling water from its deep.
Lizzie plucked purple and rich golden flags,   220
Then turning homeward said: "The sunset flushes
Those furthest loftiest crags;
Come Laura, not another maiden lags.
No wilful squirrel wags,
The beasts and birds are fast asleep."   225
But Laura loitered still among the rushes,
And said the bank was steep.

And said the hour was early still,
The dew not fall'n, the wind not chill;
Listening ever, but not catching   230
The customary cry,
"Come buy, come buy,"
With its iterated jingle
Of sugar-baited words:
Not for all her watching   235
Once discerning even one goblin
Racing, whisking, tumbling, hobbling—
Let alone the herds
That used to tramp along the glen,
In groups or single,   240
Of brisk fruit-merchant men.
Till Lizzie urged, "O Laura, come;

I hear the fruit-call, but I dare not look:
You should not loiter longer at this brook:
245 Come with me home.
The stars rise, the moon bends her arc,
Each glowworm winks her spark,
Let us get home before the night grows dark:
For clouds may gather
250 Though this is summer weather,
Put out the lights and drench us thro';
Then if we lost our way what should we do?"

Laura turned cold as stone
To find her sister heard that cry alone,
255 That goblin cry,
"Come buy our fruits, come buy."
Must she then buy no more such dainty fruit?
Must she no more such succous° pasture find,   *juicy*
Gone deaf and blind?
260 Her tree of life drooped from the root:
She said not one word in her heart's sore ache;
But peering through the dimness, nought discerning,
Trudged home, her pitcher dripping all the way;
So crept to bed, and lay
265 Silent till Lizzie slept;
Then sat up in a passionate yearning,
And gnashed her teeth for baulked desire, and wept
As if her heart would break.

Day after day, night after night,
270 Laura kept watch in vain
In sullen silence of exceeding pain.
She never caught again the goblin cry,
"Come buy, come buy"—
She never spied the goblin men
275 Hawking their fruits along the glen:
But when the noon waxed bright
Her hair grew thin and grey;
She dwindled, as the fair full moon doth turn
To swift decay and burn
280 Her fire away.

One day remembering her kernel-stone
She set it by a wall that faced the south;
Dewed it with tears, hoped for a root,
Watched for a waxing shoot,
But there came none.   285
It never saw the sun,
It never felt the trickling moisture run:
While with sunk eyes and faded mouth
She dreamed of melons, as a traveller sees
False waves in desert drouth°   *drought* 290
With shade of leaf-crowned trees,
And burns the thirstier in the sandful breeze.

She no more swept the house,
Tended the fowl or cows,
Fetched honey, kneaded cakes of wheat,   295
Brought water from the brook:
But sat down listless in the chimney-nook
And would not eat.

Tender Lizzie could not bear
To watch her sister's cankerous care,   300
Yet not to share.
She night and morning
Caught the goblins' cry:
"Come buy our orchard fruits,
Come buy, come buy:"—   305
Beside the brook, along the glen,
She heard the tramp of goblin men,
The voice and stir
Poor Laura could not hear;
Longed to buy fruit to comfort her,   310
But feared to pay too dear.
She thought of Jeanie in her grave,
Who should have been a bride;
But who for joys brides hope to have
Fell sick and died   315
In her gay prime,
In earliest winter time,
With the first glazing rime,°   *hoar frost*
With the first snow-fall of crisp Winter time.

320   Till Laura dwindling
    Seemed knocking at Death's door.
    Then Lizzie weighed no more
    Better and worse;
    But put a silver penny in her purse,
325   Kissed Laura, crossed the heath with clumps of furze
    At twilight, halted by the brook:
    And for the first time in her life
    Began to listen and look.

    Laughed every goblin
330   When they spied her peeping:
    Came towards her hobbling,
    Flying, running, leaping,
    Puffing and blowing,
    Chuckling, clapping, crowing.
335   Clucking and gobbling,
    Mopping and mowing,
    Full of airs and graces,
    Pulling wry faces,
    Demure grimaces,
340   Cat-like and rat-like,
    Ratel- and wombat-like,
    Snail-paced in a hurry,
    Parrot-voiced and whistler,
    Helter skelter, hurry skurry,
345   Chattering like magpies,
    Fluttering like pigeons,
    Gliding like fishes,—
    Hugged her and kissed her:
    Squeezed and caressed her:
350   Stretched up their dishes,
    Panniers, and plates:
    "Look at our apples
    Russet and dun,°   *dark*
    Bob at our cherries,
355   Bite at our peaches,
    Citrons and dates,
    Grapes for the asking,
    Pears red with basking
    Out in the sun,

Plums on their twigs;   360
Pluck them and suck them,—
Pomegranates, figs."

"Good folk," said Lizzie,
Mindful of Jeanie:
"Give me much and many"—   365
Held out her apron,
Tossed them her penny.
"Nay, take a seat with us,
Honour and eat with us,"
They answered grinning: 370
"Our feast is but beginning.
Night yet is early,
Warm and dew-pearly,
Wakeful and starry:
Such fruits as these   375
No man can carry;
Half their bloom would fly,
Half their dew would dry,
Half their flavour would pass by.
Sit down and feast with us,   380
Be welcome guest with us,
Cheer you and rest with us."—
"Thank you," said Lizzie: "But one waits
At home alone for me:
So without further parleying,°   *discussion* 385
If you will not sell me any
Of your fruits though much and many,
Give me back my silver penny
I tossed you for a fee."—
They began to scratch their pates,°   *heads*   390
No longer wagging, purring,
But visibly demurring,
Grunting and snarling.
One called her proud,
Cross-grained, uncivil;   395
Their tones waxed loud,
Their looks were evil.
Lashing their tails
They trod and hustled her,

400   Elbowed and jostled her,
       Clawed with their nails,
       Barking, mewing, hissing, mocking,
       Tore her gown and soiled her stocking,
       Twitched her hair out by the roots,
405   Stamped upon her tender feet,
       Held her hands and squeezed their fruits
       Against her mouth to make her eat.

       White and golden Lizzie stood,
       Like a lily in a flood,—
410   Like a rock of blue-veined stone
       Lashed by tides obstreperously,—
       Like a beacon left alone
       In a hoary roaring sea,
       Sending up a golden fire,—
415   Like a fruit-crowned orange tree
       White with blossoms honey-sweet
       Sore beset by wasp and bee,—
       Like a royal virgin town
       Topped with gilded dome and spire
420   Close beleaguered by a fleet
       Mad to tug her standard down.

       One may lead a horse to water,
       Twenty cannot make him drink.
       Though the goblins cuffed and caught her,
425   Coaxed and fought her,
       Bullied and besought her,
       Scratched her, pinched her black as ink,
       Kicked and knocked her,
       Mauled and mocked her,
430   Lizzie uttered not a word;
       Would not open lip from lip
       Lest they should cram a mouthful in:
       But laughed in heart to feel the drip
       Of juice that syruped all her face,
435   And lodged in dimples of her chin,
       And streaked her neck which quaked like curd.
       At last the evil people,
       Worn out by her resistance,

Flung back her penny, kicked their fruit
Along whichever road they took,   440
Not leaving root or stone or shoot;
Some writhed into the ground,
Some dived into the brook
With ring and ripple,
Some scudded on the gale without a sound,   445
Some vanished in the distance.

In a smart, ache, tingle,
Lizzie went her way;
Knew not was it night or day;
Sprang up the bank, tore through the furze,   450
Threaded copse and dingle,°   *dell*
And heard her penny jingle
Bouncing in her purse,—
Its bounce was music to her ear.
She ran and ran   455
As if she feared some goblin man
Dogged her with gibe or curse
Or something worse:
But not one goblin skurried after,
Nor was she pricked by fear;   460
The kind heart made her windy-paced
That urged her home quite out of breath with haste
And inward laughter.

She cried, "Laura," up the garden,
"Did you miss me?   465
Come and kiss me.
Never mind my bruises,
Hug me, kiss me, suck my juices
Squeezed from goblin fruits for you,
Goblin pulp and goblin dew.   470
Eat me, drink me, love me;
Laura, make much of me;
For your sake I have braved the glen
And had to do with goblin merchant men."

Laura started from her chair,   475
Flung her arms up in the air,

Clutched her hair:
"Lizzie, Lizzie, have you tasted
For my sake the fruit forbidden?
480 Must your light like mine be hidden,
Your young life like mine be wasted,
Undone in mine undoing,
And ruined in my ruin,
Thirsty, cankered, goblin-ridden?"—
485 She clung about her sister,
Kissed and kissed and kissed her:
Tears once again
Refreshed her shrunken eyes,
Dropping like rain
490 After long sultry drouth;
Shaking with aguish° fear, and pain,   *feverish*
She kissed and kissed her with a hungry mouth.

Her lips began to scorch,
That juice was wormwood to her tongue,
495 She loathed the feast:
Writhing as one possessed she leaped and sung,
Rent all her robe, and wrung
Her hands in lamentable haste,
And beat her breast.
500 Her locks streamed like the torch
Borne by a racer at full speed,
Or like the mane of horses in their flight,
Or like an eagle when she stems the light
Straight toward the sun,
505 Or like a caged thing freed,
Or like a flying flag when armies run.

Swift fire spread through her veins, knocked at her heart,
Met the fire smouldering there
And overbore its lesser flame;
510 She gorged on bitterness without a name:
Ah! fool, to choose such part
Of soul-consuming care!
Sense failed in the mortal strife:
Like the watchtower of a town
515 Which an earthquake shatters down,

Like a lightning-stricken mast,
Like a wind-uprooted tree
Spun about,
Like a foam-topped waterspout
Cast down headlong in the sea,   520
She fell at last;
Pleasure past and anguish past,
Is it death or is it life?

Life out of death.
That night long Lizzie watched by her,   525
Counted her pulse's flagging stir,
Felt for her breath,
Held water to her lips, and cooled her face
With tears and fanning leaves.
But when the first birds chirped about their eaves,   530
And early reapers plodded to the place
Of golden sheaves,
And dew-wet grass
Bowed in the morning winds so brisk to pass,
And new buds with new day   535
Opened of cup-like lilies on the stream,
Laura awoke as from a dream,
Laughed in the innocent old way,
Hugged Lizzie but not twice or thrice;
Her gleaming locks showed not one thread of grey,   540
Her breath was sweet as May,
And light danced in her eyes.

Days, weeks, months, years
Afterwards, when both were wives
With children of their own;   545
Their mother-hearts beset with fears,
Their lives bound up in tender lives;
Laura would call the little ones
And tell them of her early prime,
Those pleasant days long gone   550
Of not-returning time:
Would talk about the haunted glen,
The wicked quaint fruit-merchant men,
Their fruits like honey to the throat

555 But poison in the blood;
    (Men sell not such in any town):
    Would tell them how her sister stood
    In deadly peril to do her good,
    And win the fiery antidote:
560 Then joining hands to little hands
    Would bid them cling together,—
    "For there is no friend like a sister
    In calm or stormy weather;
    To cheer one on the tedious way,
565 To fetch one if one goes astray,
    To lift one if one totters down,
    To strengthen whilst one stands."

—1862 (written 1859)

Cobwebs

It is a land with neither night nor day,
    Nor heat nor cold, nor any wind, nor rain,
    Nor hills nor valleys; but one even plain
Stretches thro' long unbroken miles away:
5 While thro' the sluggish air a twilight grey
    Broodeth; no moons or seasons wax and wane,
    No ebb and flow are there along the main,°   *open ocean*
    No bud-time no leaf-falling there for aye:°—   *forever*
    No ripple on the sea, no shifting sand,
10   No beat of wings to stir the stagnant space,
    No pulse of life thro' all the loveless land:
And loveless sea; no trace of days before,
    No guarded home, no toil-won resting place
    No future hope, no fear for evermore.

—1896 (written 1855)

In an Artist's Studio

One face looks out from all his canvasses,
    One selfsame figure sits or walks or leans;
    We found her hidden just behind those screens,
That mirror gave back all her loveliness.

A queen in opal or in ruby dress,   5
     A nameless girl in freshest summer greens,
     A saint, an angel—every canvass means
The same one meaning, neither more nor less.
He feeds upon her face by day and night,
And she with true kind eyes looks back on him   10
Fair as the moon and joyful as the light:
Not wan with waiting, not with sorrow dim;
Not as she is, but was when hope shone bright;
Not as she is, but as she fills his dream.

                                        —1896 (written 1856)

Sarah Morgan Bryan Piatt

1836–1919

Unknown only a few decades ago, Sarah Morgan Bryan Piatt is increasingly recognized as a major poetic voice. Born into a distinguished Kentucky family of slave-owning planters, she grew up during the national political crisis over slavery and states' rights. She married Ohioan J.J. Piatt, a young poet already building a literary reputation, in 1861, just as the Civil War was breaking out. The Piatts lived thereafter primarily in Ohio as well as Washington, DC, and Ireland, where J.J. held US government appointments. Sarah became part of an active, transatlantic literary community, publishing hundreds of poems in well-regarded newspapers, magazines, anthologies, and books.

Inspired by the dramatic monologues of Robert Browning, she pushed his innovations in new directions. Her dramatic lyrics often explore the shifts in perspective among multiple speakers and listeners: in "The Palace-Burner," "The Funeral of a Doll," and "The First Party" (below), for example, she depicts complex interpersonal and psychological dynamics between a mother and child, one of her frequent topics. Her deft uses of fragments; unidentified personae, including both speakers and listeners; parentheses and dashes; evasions; omissions; and irony (as in "In Primrose Time," below) create layers of puzzle-like complexity that reward rereading. Many readers and critics of her own time read her poems with pleasure for her treatment of familiar, popular topics, while few recognized the searing ironies at their core. Her ironic voice in particular makes her poetry compelling to readers today.

Piatt has recently been reclaimed as a profound observer of the social and political issues that fractured the nation, including slavery, war, Reconstruction (as in "Mock Diamonds," below), and poverty. She also frequently addressed the complexities of gender; motherhood; and the nature of the poetic voice itself. Her poems plunge into what pioneering Piatt scholar Paula Bernat Bennett calls "the real," the "everyday dramas of family and social life and the life of the nation."

The Funeral of a Doll

They used to call her Little Nell,[1]
   In memory of that lovely child

---

1   *Little Nell* One of the most famous and best-loved characters in nineteenth-century literature, Little Nell was the angelic heroine of Charles Dickens's serialized novel *The Old Curiosity Shop* (1841). Her "death" set off a wave of transatlantic grief among men and women alike.

Whose story each had learned to tell.
    She, too, was slight and still and mild,
    Blue-eyed and sweet; she always smiled, 5
And never troubled any one
Until her pretty life was done.
And so they tolled a tiny bell,
    That made a wailing fine and faint,
As fairies ring, and all was well. 10
    Then she became a waxen saint.

Her funeral it was small and sad.
    Some birds sang bird-hymns in the air.
The humming-bee seemed hardly glad,
    Spite of the honey everywhere. 15
    The very sunshine seemed to wear
Some thought of death, caught in its gold,
That made it waver wan and cold.
Then, with what broken voice he had,
    The Preacher slowly murmured on 20
(With many warnings to the bad)
    The virtues of the Doll now gone.

A paper coffin rosily-lined
    Had Little Nell. There, drest in white,
With buds about her, she reclined, 25
    A very fair and piteous sight—
    Enough to make one sorry, quite.
And, when at last the lid was shut
Under white flowers, I fancied——but
No matter. When I heard the wind 30
    Scatter Spring-rain that night across
The Doll's wee grave, with tears half-blind
    One child's heart felt a grievous loss.

"It was a funeral, mamma. Oh,
    Poor Little Nell is dead, is dead. 35
How dark!—and do you hear it blow?
    She is afraid." And, as she said
    These sobbing words, she laid her head
Between her hands and whispered: "Here
Her bed is made, the precious dear— 40

She cannot sleep in it, I know.
    And there is no one left to wear
Her pretty clothes. *Where did she go?*
    ——See, this poor ribbon tied her hair!"

—1872, 1877

Mock Diamonds

(At the Seaside)

The handsome man there with the scar?—
    (Who bow'd to me? Yes, slightly)—
A ghastly favor of the War,
    Nor does he wear it lightly.

5 Such brigand°-looking men as these   *bandit*
    Might hide behind a dagger
In—ah, "the fellow, if I please,
    With the low Southern swagger?

"One of the doubtful chivalry,
10   The midnight-vengeance meetings,
Who sends, from ghostly company,
    Such fearful queer-spell'd[1] greetings?"

No—but a soldier late to throw
    (I see not where the harm is)
15 Lost Cause[2] and Conquer'd Flag below
    The dust of Northern armies.

What more? Before the South laid down
    Her insolent false glory,
He was, at this fair seaside town,
20   The hero of—a story.

---

1   *queer-spell'd* The Ku Klux Klan formed in 1866 to terrorize Southern blacks in the wake
     of emancipation. Piatt refers to the organization's hooded costumes and night rides.
2   *Lost Cause* A term that emerged soon after the defeat of the Confederacy in the US Civil
     War, it became a widespread ideology intended to justify, validate, and celebrate the an-
     tebellum South whose "cause" was now "lost."

And painted Beauty scheming through
    The glare of gilded station,
Long'd for the orange flowers—that grew
    Upon his rich plantation.

I knew him then? Well, he was young   25
    And I was—what he thought me;
And there were kisses hidden among
    The thin bud-scents he brought me.

One night I saw a stranger here,—
    "An heiress, you must know her,"   30
His mother whisper'd, sliding near.
    Perhaps my heart beat lower.

The band play'd on, the hours declined,
    His eyes looked tired and dreamy;
I knew her diamonds flash'd him blind—   35
    He could no longer see me.

Leave your sweet jealousy unsaid:
    Your bright child's fading mother
And that guerilla from—the dead?[1]
    Are nothing to each other.   40

He rose before me on the sand
    Through that damp sky's vague glimmer,
With shadows in his shadow, and
    All the dim sea grew dimmer.

He spoke? He laughed? Men hear of men   45
    Such words, such laughter never.
He said? "*She wore Mock-Diamonds*"—then,
    Pass'd to the Past forever.

—1872

---

1   *the dead?* The question mark flags the complex relationship between past and present
that runs through the poem. Given that the poem depicts oral speech, it also indicates the
wife's rising inflection at this moment.

The Palace-Burner[1]

A Picture in a Newspaper[2]

She has been burning palaces. "To see
    The sparks look pretty in the wind?" Well yes—
And something more. But women brave as she
    Leave much for cowards such as I to guess.

5 But this is old, so old that everything
    Is ashes here—the woman and the rest.
Two years are oh! so long. Now you may bring
    Some newer pictures. You like this one best?

You wish that you had lived in Paris then?[3]
10   You would have loved to burn a palace, too?
But they had guns in France, and Christian men
    Shot wicked little Communists, like you.

You would have burned the palace? Just because
    You did not live in it yourself! Oh! why?
15 Have I not taught you to respect the laws?
    You would have burned the palace. Would not *I*?

Would I? Go to your play.[4] Would I, indeed?
    I? Does the boy not know my soul to be
Languid[5] and worldly,° with a dainty need   *sophisticated*
20   For light and music? Yet he questions me.

---

1 *Palace-Burner* A controversial and well-known historical event in its own time, the Paris Commune of 1871 was a brief socialist revolutionary government in France that began with a violent uprising. Urban workers in Paris burned the Tuileries Palace and assumed power for about three months. The government forces that squelched the rebellion executed thousands of people, including women and children. The extensive press coverage in the US focused in particular on the image of the "pétroleuse," a term for the female rebels allegedly involved in burning down the palace. The news accounts in the US make it clear that the event touched a cultural nerve about the position of woman domestically.

2 *A Picture in a Newspaper* It was a common form of home entertainment at this time to read, save, and clip from newspapers and magazines, as the mother does here with her son. Illustrations were especially appealing to nineteenth-century readers. Illustrations of the Paris Commune circulated widely, including one of a pétroleuse about to be executed.

3 *then* The poem was published in November 1872. The uprising was defeated in May 1871.

4 *your play* Idiomatic expression equivalent today to "go play."

5 *Languid* Leisurely, disinclined to physical exertion. In this case, the word's connotation of leisure signifies a social class.

Can he have seen my soul more near than I?
　　Ah! in the dusk and distance sweet she seems,
With lips to kiss away a baby's cry,
　　Hands fit for flowers, and eyes for tears and dreams.

Can he have seen my soul? And could she wear   25
　　Such utter life upon a dying face,
Such unappealing, beautiful despair,
　　Such garments—soon to be a shroud—with grace?

Has she a charm so calm that it could breathe
　　In damp, low places till some frightened hour;   30
Then start, like a fair, subtle snake, and wreathe
　　A stinging poison with a shadowy power?

Would *I* burn palaces? The child has seen
　　In this fierce creature of the Commune here,
So bright with bitterness and so serene,   35
　　A being finer than my soul, I fear.

　　　　　　　　　　　　　　　　　　　—1872

Her Blindness in Grief[1]

What if my soul is left to me?
Oh! sweeter than my soul was he.
　　Its breast broods on a coffin lid;
Its empty eyes stare at the dust.
　　Tears follow tears, for treasure hid   5
Forevermore from moth and rust.

The sky a shadow is; how much
I long for something I can touch!
　　God is a silence: could I hear
Him whisper once, "Poor child," to me!   10
　　God is a dream, a hope, a fear,
A vision—that the seraphs see.

1　*Her Blindness in Grief* Elegies for dead infants that offered Christian consolation were
　common in this era of rampant infant, child, and maternal mortality. (Lydia Sigourney's
　"Death of an Infant," p. 82 in this volume, is one of the most well-known examples of
　the genre.) While Piatt's poem falls soundly in the tradition of such elegies, hers is mark-
　edly distinct from the genre's conventions in its attitude toward platitudes of Christian
　consolation. As Paula Bernat Bennett shows, Sarah Piatt had herself lost a four-day-old
　baby three months before this poem appeared in *The Independent* on 20 November 1873.

"Woman, why weepest thou?"[1] One said,
To His own mother, from the dead.
15   If He should come to mock me now,
Here in my utter loneliness,
      And say to me, "Why weepest thou?"
I wonder would I weep the less.

Or, could I, through these endless tears,
20 Look high into the lovely spheres
      And see him there—my little child—
Nursed tenderly at Mary's breast,
      Would not my sorrow be as wild?
Christ help me. Who shall say the rest?

25 There is no comfort anywhere.
My baby's clothes, my baby's hair,
      My baby's grave are all I know.
What could have hurt my baby? Why,
      Why did he come; why did he go?
30 And shall I have him by and by?

Poor grave of mine, so strange, so small,
You cover all, you cover all!
      The flush of every flower, the dew,
The bird's old song, the heart's old trust,
35   The star's fair light, the darkness, too,
Are hidden in your heavy dust.

Oh! but to kiss his little feet,
And say to them, "So sweet, so sweet,"
      I would give up whatever pain
40 (What else is there to give, I say?)
      This wide world holds. Again, again,
I yearn to follow him away.

My cry is but a human cry.
Who grieves for angels? Do they die?
45   Oh! precious hands, as still as snows,
How your white fingers hold my heart!

---

1   *"Woman, why weepest thou?"* In the King James Bible (John 20.15), Jesus' first words to
Mary Magdalene, who is weeping at his tomb. Piatt quotes Jesus' question as if it were
posed to his mother Mary.

Yet keep your buried buds of rose,
Though earth and Heaven are far apart.

The grief is bitter. Let me be.
He lies beneath that lonesome tree.   50
    I've heard the fierce rain beating there.
Night covers it with cold moonshine.
    Despair can only be despair.
God has his will. I have not mine.

                                      —1873

The First Party

"It was just lovely, mamma, and my dress
    Was much the prettiest there, the boys all said;
They said, too, that I looked—my best. I guess
    These ribbons suited me. You see that red
You did not fancy lighted up so well.   5
Somebody told me I was quite a belle.

"I wish you didn't want me to wear white,
    With just a flower or two. Rose wears such things.
They 're so old-fashioned. She was such a fright!
    I wish that I had fifty diamond rings—   10
I'd wear them all at once! I'd almost paint
Before I'd look like Rose. She's such a saint."

"I thought you were the best of friends." "We are—
    Only we hate each other! That is what
The best of friends do—in our school. How far   15
    Away you look. Forgive me. I forgot.
I've made you sad. *I'll* love the whole world too,
I guess, mamma—when I'm as old as you!

"Why don't you listen, mamma? You must be
    Thinking of Adam. Here's a bud he gave   20
You once in Eden—shut up here, you see,
    In this old book." "That grew upon a grave."
"Oh! I'll not touch it then. I wish that pearls
Would grow on trees—but not for other girls.

25 "Now, mamma, please to hear me to the end.
    The handsomest of all the boys last night
Looked like that picture of—your brother's friend.
    He hardly spoke to Rose. Oh, I'm not quite
An angel yet. I shall be, I suppose,
30 Sometime. I'm glad he hardly spoke to Rose.

"I wonder, mamma, did you ever go
    To a first party. And what did you wear?
How odd you must have looked! But tell me, though,
    About your dress. How many girls were there?"
35 "Fifty, perhaps." "There were some boys, I guess?"
"Yes, there was one." "And he was handsome?" "Yes."

"Where is he now, do you think?" "I do not know.
    (In some sweet foreign Country, it may be,
Among the palms.") "He might have written, though,
40   In all these years." "He cannot write." "I see,
What a strange party! Fifty girls—oh dear!
And one boy—and he couldn't write! How queer!"

—1882

In Primrose[1] Time

(Early Spring in Ireland)

Here's the lodge-woman in her great cloak coming,
    And her white cap. What joy
Has touched the ash-man? On my word, he's humming
    A boy's song, like a boy!

---

1   *Primrose* Pale greenish-yellow spring flower abundant in Ireland. In ways that escaped
    most of her own readers (who mostly read this poem as a cheery celebration of spring
    flowers), Piatt invokes the searing history of Irish subjugation by the British. The prim-
    rose was well known at this time as the favorite flower of Benjamin Disraeli (1804–81),
    the British prime minister who had in 1844 coined the phrase "the Irish question" during
    an era of mass starvation and ruin in Ireland. Disraeli died in 1881, and The Primrose
    League was formed by his political admirers in 1883 with a league motto *Imperium et
    Libertas*, "Empire and Liberty." An excellent example of Piatt's complex straddling of
    multiple audiences, this poem was initially published in a magazine for young readers, *St.
    Nicholas*, in 1885, in the midst of significant problems in the US over the immigrant Irish
    population.

He quite forgets his cart. His donkey grazes   5
    Just where it likes the grass.
The red-coat soldier, with his medal, raises
    His hat to all who pass;
And the blue-jacket sailor,—hear him whistle,
    Forgetting Ireland's ills!   10
Oh, pleasant land—(who thinks of thorn or thistle?)
    Upon your happy hills
The world is out! And, faith, if I mistake not,
    The world is in its prime
(Beating for once, I think, with hearts that ache not)   15
    In Primrose time.

Against the sea-wall leans the Irish beauty,
    With face and hands in bloom,
Thinking of anything but household duty
    In her thatched cabin's gloom;—   20
Watching the ships as leisurely as may be,
    Her blue eyes dream for hours.
Hush! There's her mother—coming with the baby
    In the fair quest of flowers.
And her grandmother!—hear her laugh and chatter,   25
    Under her hair frost-white!
Believe me, life can be a merry matter,
    And common folk polite,
And all the birds of heaven one of a feather,
    And all their voices rhyme,—   30
They sing their merry songs, like one, together,
    In Primrose time.

The magpies fly in pairs (an evil omen
    It were to see but one);
The snakes—but here, though, since St. Patrick, no man   35
    Has seen them in the sun;
The white lamb thinks the black lamb is his brother,
    And half as good as he;
The rival carmen all love one another,
    And jest, right cheerily;   40
The compliments among the milkmen savor
    Of pale gold blossoming;
And everybody wears the lovely favor

Of our sweet Lady Spring.
45 And though the ribbons in a bright procession
    Go toward the chapel's chime,—
Good priest, there be but few sins for confession
    In Primrose time.

How all the children in this isle of faery
50   Whisper and laugh and peep!
(Hush, pretty babblers! Little feet be wary,
    You'll scare them in their sleep,—
The wee, weird people of the dew, who wither
    Out of the sun, and lie
55 Curled in the wet leaves, till the moon comes hither.)—
    The new-made butterfly
Forgets he was a worm. The ghostly castle,
    On its lone rock and gray,
Cares not a whit for either lord or vassal°   *subordinate*
60   Gone on their dusty way,
But listens to the bee, on errands sunny.—
    A thousand years of crime
May all be melted in a drop of honey
    In Primrose time!

—1885

William Dean Howells
1837–1920

A prolific author in many genres as well as a critic and editor, William Dean Howells became one of the most influential cultural figures of his age, particularly as a champion for the controversial literary movement known at the time as "realism." Born in small-town Ohio, he educated himself while working in his father's printing shop. When he was in his early twenties, the *Atlantic Monthly*, the most prestigious literary journal of the day, published one of his poems, a momentous achievement that brought this young "Western" writer to the attention of the nation's literary elite. At this time, regions beyond the cultural centers of New York and Boston were still widely considered remote backwaters. Howells's growing recognition as a worthy writer in part represented a larger shift in the political and cultural dynamics of a nation looking to the West. Although the realist movement had begun earlier in Europe, Howells became its best-known champion in the US, in his fiction as well as his editorial and critical work. Aiming to represent the actualities of the "real" world in contrast to the "romantic" fantasies common in popular tales and poems about heroes, villains, royalty, adventure, and otherworldly ideals of truth and beauty, realism faced harsh criticism as degrading both to humankind and to the higher purposes of art.

Howells's early poetry was sentimental and romantic, as in his first published volume, *Poems of Two Friends* (1860), co-authored with his friend J.J. Piatt (who married Sarah Morgan Bryan Piatt [p. 236] in 1861). By the 1890s, Howells had transformed his poetry in a radically new, darker, realist and formally experimental direction, as in the selections below. Like other published poets at the late century (such as Sarah Piatt, Edwin Arlington Robinson, and Stephen Crane), Howells pushed the genre of poetry in new directions.

The King Dines

Two people on a bench in Boston Common,
An ordinary laboring man and woman,
Seated together,
In the November weather
Slit with a thin, keen rain;   5
The woman's mouth purple with cold and pain,
And her eyes fixed as if they did not see
The passers trooping by continually,
Smearing the elm leaves underfoot that fall
Before her on the miry° mall;   *swampy*   10
The man feeding out of the newspaper

Wrapped round the broken victuals° brought with her,   *food*
And gnawing at a bent bone like a dog,
Following its curve hungrily with his teeth,
15 And his head twisted sidewise; and beneath
His reeking boots the mud, and the gray fog
Fathomless over him, and all the gloom
Of the day round him for his dining-room.

—1895

Society

I looked and saw a splendid pageantry
     Of beautiful women and of lordly men,
     Taking their pleasure in a flowery plain,
Where poppies and the red anemone,[1]
5 And many another leaf of cramoisy,[2]
     Flickered about their feet and gave their stain
     To heels of iron or satin, and the grain
Of silken garments floating far and free,
As in the dance they wove themselves, or strayed
10   By twos together, or lightly smiled and bowed,
Or curtseyed to each other, or else played
At games of mirth and pastime, unafraid
     In their delight; and all so high and proud
     They seemed scarce of the earth whereon they trod.

15 I looked again and saw that flowery space
     Stirring, as if alive, beneath the tread
     That rested now upon an old man's head
And now upon a baby's gasping face,
Or mother's bosom, or the rounded grace
20   Of a girl's throat; and what had seemed the red
     Of flowers was blood, in gouts and gushes shed
From hearts that broke under that frolic pace.
And now and then from out the dreadful floor
     An arm or brow was lifted from the rest,
25 As if to strike in madness, or implore
     For mercy; and anon some suffering breast
     Heaved from the mass and sank; and as before
The revelers above them thronged and prest.°   *pressed*
—1895

1   *anemone* A type of flowering plant.
2   *cramoisy* Crimson cloth.

Augusta Webster
1837–1894

Augusta Webster is best known for bold poetic portraits that give voice to social issues. Despite the considerable reputation she enjoyed when alive, for nearly a hundred years after her death she went missing from the English canon. It was not until the 1980s and 1990s that feminist scholarship rediscovered Webster.

Webster was poetry reviewer for the *Athenaeum* for a decade and wrote regular columns for the *Examiner*. She campaigned on behalf of women's suffrage and education, becoming one of the first women to be elected to the London School Board. Two collections of monologues, *Dramatic Studies* (1866) and *Portraits* (1870), mark Webster's most lasting contribution to English poetry. In contrast to the psychological interiors dramatized by Robert Browning, Webster skillfully crafted the dramatic monologue to speak to external social circumstances. Webster was able to give voice to topics prohibited to Victorian women by speaking through mythological surrogates in "Medea in Athens" and "Circe."

When she died in 1894 Webster left behind no diaries or family letters, and only scanty evidence of correspondence with Christina Rossetti, Oliver Wendell Holmes, and a few other prominent writers of the day. Her poetic legacy, however, is increasingly regarded as being of very considerable substance.

Circe[1]

The sun drops luridly into the west;
Darkness has raised her arms to draw him down
Before the time, not waiting as of wont
Till he has come to her behind the sea;
And the smooth waves grow sullen in the gloom   5
And wear their threatening purple; more and more
The plain of waters sways and seems to rise
Convexly from its level of the shores;
And low dull thunder rolls along the beach:
There will be storm at last, storm, glorious storm!   10

Oh welcome, welcome, though it rend my bowers,
Scattering my blossomed roses like the dust,

---

1   *Circe* Enchantress in Homer's *Odyssey*, who turned men into swine.

Splitting the shrieking branches, tossing down
My riotous vines with their young half-tinged grapes
15 Like small round amethysts or beryls strung
Tumultuously in clusters; though it sate
Its ravenous spite among my goodliest pines
Standing there round and still against the sky
That makes blue lakes between their sombre tufts,
20 Or harry from my silvery olive slopes
Some hoary king whose gnarled fantastic limbs
Wear rugged armour of a thousand years;
Though it will hurl high on my flowery shores
The hostile wave that rives° at the poor sward°   *tears / turf*
25 And drags it down the slants, that swirls its foam
Over my terraces, shakes their firm blocks
Of great bright marbles into tumbled heaps,
And makes my pleached° and mossy labyrinths,   *plaited*
Where the small odorous blossoms grow like stars
30 Strewn in the milky way, a briny marsh.
What matter? let it come and bring me change,
Breaking the sickly sweet monotony.

I am too weary of this long bright calm;
Always the same blue sky, always the sea
35 The same blue perfect likeness of the sky,
One rose to match the other that has waned,
To-morrow's dawn the twin of yesterday's;
And every night the ceaseless crickets chirp
The same long joy and the late strain of birds
40 Repeats their strain of all the even month;

And changelessly the petty plashing surfs
Bubble their chiming burden round the stones;
Dusk after dusk brings the same languid trance
Upon the shadowy hills, and in the fields
45 The waves of fireflies come and go the same,
Making the very flash of light and stir
Vex one like dronings of the shuttles at task.

Give me some change. Must life be only sweet,
All honey-pap as babes would have their food?
50 And, if my heart must always be adrowse

In a hush of stagnant sunshine, give me, then,
Something outside me stirring; let the storm
Break up the sluggish beauty, let it fall
Beaten below the feet of passionate winds,
And then to-morrow waken jubilant   55
In a new birth; let me see subtle joy
Of anguish and of hopes, of change and growth.

      What fate is mine, who, far apart from pains
And fears and turmoils of the cross-grained world,
Dwell like a lonely god in a charmed isle   60
Where I am first and only, and, like one
Who should love poisonous savours more than mead,
Long for a tempest on me and grow sick
Of rest and of divine free carelessness!
Oh me, I am a woman, not a god;   65
Yea, those who tend me, even, are more than I,
My nymphs who have the souls of flowers and birds
Singing and blossoming immortally.

      Ah me! these love a day and laugh again,
And loving, laughing, find a full content;   70
But I know nought of peace, and have not loved.
Where is my love? Does someone cry for me
Not knowing whom he calls? Does his soul cry
For mine to grow beside it, grow in it?
Does he beseech the gods to give him me,   75
The one unknown rare woman by whose side
No other woman thrice as beautiful
Could once seem fair to him; to whose voice heard
In any common tones no sweetest sound
Of love made melody on silver lutes,   80
Or singing like Apollo's[1] when the gods
Grow pale with happy listening, might be peered
For making music to him; whom once found
There will be no more seeking anything?

---

1   *Apollo* The Greek and Roman sun-god, patron of music and poetry.

85   Oh love, oh love, oh love, art not yet come
Out of the waiting shadows into life?
Art not yet come after so many years
That I have longed for thee? Come! I am here.

   Not yet. For surely I should feel a sound
90 Of his far answer if now in the world
He sought me who will seek me—Oh, ye gods,
Will he not seek me? Is it all a dream?
Will there be only these, these bestial things
Who wallow in their styes, or mop and mow
95 Among the trees, or munch in pens and byres,
Or snarl and filch behind their wattled coops;
These things who had believed that they were men?

   Nay, but he *will* come. Why am I so fair,
And marvellously minded, and with sight
100 Which flashes suddenly on hidden things,
As the gods see, who do not need to look?
Why wear I in my eyes that stronger power
Than basilisks,[1] whose gaze can only kill,
To draw men's souls to me to live or die
105 As I would have them? Why am I given pride
Which yet longs to be broken, and this scorn,
Cruel and vengeful, for the lesser men
Who meet the smiles I waste for lack of him,
And grow too glad? Why am I who I am?

110 But for the sake of him whom fate will send
One day to be my master utterly,
That he should take me, the desire of all,
Whom only he in the world could bow to him.

   Oh, sunlike glory of pale glittering hairs,
115 Bright as the filmy wires my weavers take
To make me golden gauzes—Oh, deep eyes,
Darker and softer than the bluest dusk
Of August violets, darker and deep

---

1   *basilisk* A mythical reptile with a lethal breath and look, supposedly hatched from a
  cock's egg.

Like crystal fathomless lakes in summer noons—
Oh, sad sweet longing smile—Oh, lips that tempt   120
My very self to kisses—oh, round cheeks
Tenderly radiant with the even flush
Of pale smoothed coral—perfect lovely face
Answering my gaze from out this fleckless pool—
Wonder of glossy shoulders, chiselled limbs—   125
Should I be so your lover as I am,
Drinking an exquisite joy to watch you thus
In all a hundred changes through the day,
But that I love you for him till he comes,
But that my beauty means his loving it?   130

      Oh, look! a speck on this side of the sun,
Coming—yes, coming with the rising wind
That frays the darkening cloud-wrack on the verge
And in a little while will leap abroad,
Spattering the sky with rushing blacknesses,   135
Dashing the hissing mountainous waves at the stars.
'Twill drive me that black speck a shuddering hulk
Caught in the buffeting waves, dashed impotent
From ridge to ridge, will drive it in the night
With that dull jarring crash upon the beach,   140
And the cries for help and the cries of fear and hope.

      And then to-morrow they will thoughtfully,
With grave low voices, count their perils up,
And thank the gods for having let them live
And tell of wives and mothers in their homes,   145
And children, who would have such loss in them
That they must weep (and maybe I weep too)
With fancy of the weepings had they died.
And the next morrow they will feel their ease
And sigh with sleek content, or laugh elate,   150
Tasting delight of rest and revelling,
Music and perfumes, joyaunce for the eyes
Of rosy faces and luxurious pomps,
The savour of the banquet and the glow
And fragrance of the wine-cup; and they'll talk   155
How good it is to house in palaces
Out of the storms and struggles, and what luck

Strewed their good ship on our accessless coast.
Then the next day the beast in them will wake,
160 And one will strike and bicker, and one swell
With puffed-up greatness, and one gibe and strut
In apish pranks, and one will line his sleeve
With pilfered booties, and one snatch the gems
Out of the carven goblets as they pass,
165 One will grow mad with fever of the wine,
And one will sluggishly besot himself,
And one be lewd, and one be gluttonous;
And I shall sickly look and loathe them all.

Oh my rare cup! my pure and crystal cup,
170 With not one speck of colour to make false
The entering lights, or flaw to make them swerve!
My cup of Truth! How the lost fools will laugh
And thank me for my boon, as if I gave
Some momentary flash of the gods' joy,
175 To drink where *I* have drunk and touch the touch
Of *my* lips with their own! Aye, let them touch.

Too cruel, am I? And the silly beasts,
Crowding around me when I pass their way,
Glower on me and, although they love me still,
180 (With their poor sorts of love such as they could)
Call wrath and vengeance to their humid eyes
To scare me into mercy, or creep near
With piteous fawnings, supplicating bleats.
Too cruel? Did I choose them what they are?
185 Or change them from themselves by poisonous charms?
But any draught, pure water, natural wine,
Out of my cup, revealed them to themselves
And to each other. Change? there was no change;
Only disguise gone from them unawares:
190 And had there been one true right man of them
He would have drunk the draught as I had drunk,
And stood unharmed and looked me in the eyes,
Abashing me before him. But these things—
Why, which of them has even shown the kind
195 Of some one nobler beast? Pah! yapping wolves,
And pitiless stealthy wild-cats, curs, and apes,

And gorging swine, and slinking venomous snakes—
All false and ravenous and sensual brutes
That shame the Earth that bore them, these they are.

      Lo, lo! the shivering blueness darting forth   200
On half the heavens, and the forked thin fire
Strikes to the sea: and hark, the sudden voice
That rushes through the trees before the storm,
And shuddering of the branches. Yet the sky
Is blue against them still, and early stars   205
Sparkle above the pine-tops; and the air
Clings faint and motionless around me here.

      Another burst of flame—and the black speck
Shows in the glare, lashed onwards. It were well
I bade make ready for our guests to-night.   210

                             —1870

Thomas Hardy
1840–1928

Novelist, dramatist, essayist, and poet, Thomas Hardy produced a prodigious body of work in the course of his long life. Hardy's poems are often rooted in the physical details of place—especially of natural settings—and contemplate human suffering, disappointment, and the loss of love. He frequently returns to traditional poetic forms, such as the ballad, approaching rhythm and rhyme with precision and sensitivity. In later years, Hardy's critics judged him a superlative writer in both prose and poetry, and he was awarded honorary doctorates, fellowships, and the gold medal of the Royal Society of Literature. After his death, Hardy's heart was removed and placed in the grave of his first wife, close to the land of his youth. His remains were then buried in Poets' Corner of Westminster Abbey. He was mourned by contemporaries including Rudyard Kipling, W.B. Yeats, and George Bernard Shaw.

Hardy's writing was highly original and yet intimately connected with centuries-old traditions. Important to the history of the novel as well as to poetic history, his work provides a rich record of the transitions and the connections between the Victorian era and Modernism.

The Darkling[1] Thrush

I leant upon a coppice gate[2]
    When Frost was spectre-grey,
And Winter's dregs made desolate
    The weakening eye of day.
5 The tangled bine[3]-stems scored the sky
    Like strings of broken lyres,
And all mankind that haunted nigh
    Had sought their household fires.

The land's sharp features seemed to be
10   The Century's corpse outleant,
His crypt the cloudy canopy,
    The wind his death-lament.
The ancient pulse of germ and birth
    Was shrunken hard and dry,

---

1 *Darkling* In the dark.
2 *coppice gate* Gate leading to a thicket or small forest.
3 *bine* Hop, a climbing plant.

And every spirit upon earth   15
    Seemed fervourless as I.

At once a voice arose among
    The bleak twigs overhead
In a full-hearted evensong
    Of joy illimited;   20
An aged thrush, frail, gaunt, and small,
    In blast-beruffled plume,
Had chosen thus to fling his soul
    Upon the growing gloom.

So little cause for carolings
    Of such ecstatic sound   25
Was written on terrestrial things
    Afar or nigh around,
That I could think there trembled through
    His happy good-night air   30
Some blessed Hope, whereof he knew
    And I was unaware.

December 31, 1900

—1901

The Convergence of the Twain

(Lines on the Loss of the "Titanic"[1])

1

    In a solitude of the sea
    Deep from human vanity,
And the Pride of Life that planned her, stilly couches she.

2

    Steel chambers, late the pyres
    Of her salamandrine fires,[2]   5
Cold currents thrid,° and turn to rhythmic tidal lyres.   *thread*

---

1   the *"Titanic"* At the time the largest ship ever built, the ocean liner *Titanic* had been
    described as unsinkable, but on its maiden voyage in 1912 it collided with an iceberg;
    over 1,400 people drowned when it sank.
2   *salamandrine fires* According to mythology, salamanders are able to survive any heat.

3

        Over the mirrors meant
        To glass the opulent
The sea-worm crawls—grotesque, slimed, dumb, indifferent.

4

10   Jewels in joy designed
        To ravish the sensuous mind
Lie lightless, all their sparkles bleared and black and blind.

5

        Dim moon-eyed fishes near
        Gaze at the gilded gear
15 And query: "What does this vaingloriousness down here?" ...

6

        Well: while was fashioning
        This creature of cleaving wing,
The Immanent Will[1] that stirs and urges everything

7

        Prepared a sinister mate
20   For her—so gaily great—
A Shape of Ice, for the time far and dissociate.

8

        And as the smart ship grew
        In stature, grace, and hue,
In shadowy silent distance grew the Iceberg too.

9

25   Alien they seemed to be:
        No mortal eye could see
The intimate welding of their later history,

10

        Or sign that they were bent
        By paths coincident
30 On being anon twin halves of one august event,

---

1   *The Immanent Will* The force that pervades and determines human existence.

11

      Till the Spinner of the Years
       Said "Now!" And each one hears,
And consummation comes, and jars two hemispheres.

                          —1914

During Wind and Rain

      They sing their dearest songs—
      He, she, all of them—yea,
      Treble and tenor and bass,
         And one to play;
      With the candles mooning each face....   5
         Ah, no; the years O!
How the sick leaves reel down in throngs!

      They clear the creeping moss—
      Elders and juniors—aye,
      Making the pathways neat   10
         And the garden gay;
      And they build a shady seat....
         Ah, no; the years, the years;
See, the white storm-birds wing across.

      They are blithely breakfasting all—   15
      Men and maidens—yea,
      Under the summer tree,
         With a glimpse of the bay,
      While pet fowl come to the knee....
         Ah, no; the years O!   20
And the rotten rose is ript from the wall.

      They change to a high new house,
      He, she, all of them—aye,
      Clocks and carpets and chairs
         On the lawn all day,
      And brightest things that are theirs....   25
         Ah, no; the years, the years;
Down their carved names the rain-drop ploughs.

                          —1917

Gerard Manley Hopkins
1844–1889

Although Gerard Manley Hopkins lived and worked during the Victorian period, his poems were not published until 1919, when they were released by his literary executor and gained him posthumous fame. As the reviewer Arthur Clutton-Brock wrote in 1919, Hopkins's "poems are crowded with objects sharply cut, and with sounds no less sharp and clashing." That some critics treated Hopkins as a Modernist poet is a matter of the timing of his publication; indeed, the close observations and fine descriptions found in his poetry do resemble the singular sensory images of Modernist literature as it emerged in the early twentieth century, as in the Imagism of H.D. (see Glossary). But clearly some nineteenth-century poets, including Hopkins, already wrote in such styles. Hopkins's innovations are part of this long history of poetic experimentation.

Hopkins was educated at Oxford, where the poet and cultural critic Matthew Arnold (see p. 182) was one of his teachers. In 1866, Hopkins entered the Roman Catholic Church, eventually becoming a Jesuit priest and, later, a professor of classics at University College in Dublin. He burned his early efforts at poetry (imitations of Keats written during the 1860s), but went on to write poems in his own distinctive style—highly alliterative and densely rhyming.

Much of Hopkins's historical importance as a poet comes from his experimentation with meter and form. He devised "sprung rhythm" (see Glossary), a style of accentual meter in which only the number of stressed syllables in each line is fixed, while the number of unstressed syllables can vary; Hopkins included frequent stress marks in his own verse to clarify the intended rhythm. He also invented compound words (such as "piece-bright" and "blue-bleak") to link an object's striking characteristics. Such compounds represent an attempt to convey "inscape," a term Hopkins coined to refer to the dynamic, individual design or essence specific to each object in the world. Then and now, Hopkins's vision and methods stand out for their uniqueness and innovation.

God's Grandeur

The world is charged with the grándeur of God.
    It will flame out, like shining from shook foil;[1]

---

1   [Hopkins's note] I mean foil in its sense of leaf or tinsel.... Shaken goldfoil gives off broad glares like sheet lightning and also, and this is true of nothing else, owing to its zigzag dints and creasings and network of small many cornered facets, a sort of fork lightning too.

It gathers to a greatness, like the ooze of oil
Crushed.[1] Why do men then now not reck° his rod?   *regard*
Génerátions have trod, have trod, have trod;   5
   And all is seared with trade; bleared, smeared, with toil;
   And wears man's smudge and shares man's smell: the soil
Is bare now, nor can foot feel, being shod.

Ánd, for° all this, náture is never spent;   *despite*
   There lives the dearest freshness deep down things;   10
And though the last lights off the black West went
   Oh, morning, at the brown brink eastward, springs—
Because the Holy Ghost óver the bent
   World broods with warm breast and with ah! bright wings.
                                        —1918 (written 1877)

The Windhover[2]

To Christ Our Lord

I caught this morning morning's minion, king-
   dom of daylight's dauphin,[3] dapple-dáwn-drawn Falcon,
      in his riding
Of the rólling level úndernéath him steady air, and striding
High there, how he rung upon the rein of a wimpling° wing   *rippling*
In his écstasy! then off, off forth on swing,   5
   As a skate's heel sweeps smooth on a bow-bend: the hurl and gliding
   Rebuffed the bíg wind. My heart in hiding
Stírred for a bird,—the achieve of, the mástery of the thing!

Brute beauty and valour and act, oh, air, pride, plúme, here
   Buckle! AND the fire that breaks from thee then, a billion   10
Tímes told lovelier, more dangerous, O my chevalier!°   *horseman*

   No wónder of it: shéer plód makes plóugh down síllion°   *furrows*
Shíne, and blue-bleak embers, ah my dear,
   Fall, gáll themsélves, and gásh góld-vermílion.
                                        —1918 (written 1877)

---

1   *oil / Crushed* I.e., as olive oil.
2   *Windhover* Another name for a kestrel, a small falcon that appears to hover in the
    wind.
3   *dauphin* Title of the eldest son of the king of France—the heir.

Emma Lazarus
1849–1887

The most recognized Jewish poet of the American nineteenth century, Emma Lazarus created a vital body of poems on historical and international topics before her early death. Born into a distinguished Jewish family in New York, she became well known for addressing Jewish history and themes. During a period of massive immigration and social tensions related to burgeoning "ethnic" populations, she composed the 1883 sonnet "The New Colossus" for the Statue of Liberty, now her most famous poem, containing the legendary lines, "'*Give me your tired, your poor,/Your huddled masses yearning to breathe free.*'" International and cross-cultural in her perspective, Lazarus was also a notable translator and wrote poems about ancient history as well as current events, all very popular forms at this time. Scholar Gregory Eiselein points out that, in work such as "Arabesque" (below), Lazarus presents "a view of history that steps outside the Christian-centered view (so dominant in US culture) by evoking a feeling for the value of the art and culture of a different civilization, in this case late Muslim Granada," an ancient culture whose passing the poem laments.

Influenced by sources ancient and modern, from the Bible to the latest French poetry, she was both prolific and technically adept. Her prose poems (see Glossary), including "By the Waters of Babylon" (below), often read as if they are modern adaptations of ancient texts. The prose poem remains today a central genre for poets interested in exploring the most experimental dimensions of poetic craft. Lazarus, although mostly forgotten until scholars in recent decades began to recover lost women writers, is an important precursor for these innovators.

In the early 1880s, as news of the persecution of Jews in Russia and Eastern Europe began to appear in London and New York newspapers, Lazarus became passionately concerned with the fate of those fleeing the pogroms. On Lazarus's death in 1887 she was widely celebrated as the greatest Jewish poet of the century and as a symbol of Jewish and American identity.[1]

Note to readers: Lazarus's poem "The South" appears on the anthology's companion website. The URL and passcode appear in the Table of Contents.

---

1   The author headnote draws in part on the Introduction to Gregory Eiselein's Broadview Edition of *Emma Lazarus: Selected Poems and Other Writings* (2002).

Arabesque[1]

On a background of pale gold
I would trace with quaint design,
      Penciled fine,
Brilliant-colored, Moorish[2] scenes,
Mosques and crescents, pages, queens,   5
      Line on line,
That the prose-world of to-day
Might the gorgeous Past's array
      Once behold.

On the magic painted shield   10
Rich Granada's[3] Vega green
      Should be seen;
Crystal fountains, coolness flinging,
Hanging gardens' skyward springing
      Emerald sheen;   15
Ruddy when the daylight falls,
Crowned Alhambra's[4] beetling walls
      Stand revealed;

Balconies that overbrow°   *overhang*
Field and city, vale and stream.   20
      In a dream
Lulled the drowsy landscape basks;
Weary toilers cease their tasks.
      Mark the gleam
Silvery of each white-swathed peak!   25
Mountain-airs caress the cheek,
      Fresh from snow.

Here in Lindaraxa's bower[5]
The immortal roses bloom;

---

1   *Arabesque* The term "arabesque" at this time denoted both the Arabic language and a kind of decorative pattern found in Islamic art.
2   *Moorish* Related to the art and architecture of Spain and North Africa during the period of Islamic rule.
3   *Granada* City in Andalusia, Spain.
4   *Alhambra* Palace in Granada, Spain; first built in 889, it was rebuilt during the Moorish period.
5   *Lindaraxa's bower* Garden in the courtyard of the Alhambra. Lindaraxa may have been a young woman who lived in the palace, near this garden.

30   In the room
    Lion-guarded, marble-paven,
    Still the fountain leaps to heaven.
            But the doom
    Of the banned and stricken race
35 Overshadows every place,
            Every hour.

    Where fair Lindaraxa dwelt
    Flits the bat on velvet wings;
            Mute the strings
40 Of the broken mandoline;
    The Pavilion of the Queen
            Widely flings
    Vacant windows to the night;
    Moonbeams kiss the floor with light
45   Where she knelt.

    Through these halls that people stepped
    Who through darkling centuries
            Held the keys
    Of all wisdom, truth, and art,
50 In a Paradise apart,
            Lapped in ease,
    Sagely pondering deathless themes,
    While, befooled with monkish dreams,
            Europe slept.

55 Where shall they be found to-day?
    Yonder hill that frets the sky
            "The Last Sigh
    Of the Moor" is namèd still.
    There the ill-starred Boabdil[1]
60   Bade good-by
    To Granada and to Spain,
    Where the Crescent[2] ne'er again
            Holdeth sway.

    Vanished like the wind that blows,
65 Whither shall we seek their trace

---

1   *Boabdil* Castilian Spanish name for Mohammed XII, the last Muslim ruler of Granada.
2   *Crescent* Symbol of Islam.

On earth's face?
The gigantic wheel of fate,
Crushing all things soon or late,
    Now a race,
Now a single life o'erruns,
Now a universe of suns,
    Now a rose.

—1877

By the Waters of Babylon

Little Poems in Prose

I. The Exodus. (August 3, 1492.)

1. The Spanish noon is a blaze of azure fire, and the dusty pilgrims crawl like an endless serpent along treeless plains and bleached highroads, through rock-split ravines and castellated, cathedral-shadowed towns.

2. The hoary patriarch, wrinkled as an almond shell, bows painfully upon his staff. The beautiful young mother, ivory-pale, well-nigh swoons beneath her burden; in her large enfolding arms nestles her sleeping babe, round her knees flock her little ones with bruised and bleeding feet. "Mother, shall we soon be there?"

3. The youth with Christ-like countenance speaks comfortably to father and brother, to maiden and wife. In his breast, his own heart is broken.

4. The halt, the blind, are amid the train. Sturdy pack-horses laboriously drag the tented wagons wherein lie the sick athirst with fever.

5. The panting mules are urged forward with spur and goad; stuffed are the heavy saddlebags with the wreckage of ruined homes.

6. Hark to the tinkling silver bells that adorn the tenderly-carried silken scrolls.

7. In the fierce noon-glare a lad bears a kindled lamp; behind its network of bronze the airs of heaven breathe not upon its faint purple star.

8. Noble and abject, learned and simple, illustrious and obscure, plod side by side, all brothers now, all merged in one routed army of misfortune.

9. Woe to the straggler who falls by the wayside! no friend shall close his eyes.

10. They leave behind, the grape, the olive, and the fig; the vines they planted, the corn they sowed, the garden-cities of Andalusia and Aragon, Estremadura and La Mancha, of Granada and Castile; the altar, the hearth, and the grave of their fathers.

11. The townsman spits at their garments, the shepherd quits his flock, the peasant his plow, to pelt with curses and stones; the villager sets on their trail his yelping cur.

12. Oh the weary march, oh the uptorn roots of home, oh the blankness of the receding goal!

13. Listen to their lamentation: *They that ate dainty food are desolate in the streets; they that were reared in scarlet embrace dunghills. They flee away and wander about. Men say among the nations, they shall no more sojourn there; our end is near, our days are full, our doom is come.*

14. Whither shall they turn? for the West hath cast them out, and the East refuseth to receive.

15. O bird of the air, whisper to the despairing exiles, that to-day, to-day, from the many-masted, gayly-bannered port of Palos, sails the world-unveiling Genoese, to unlock the golden gates of sunset and bequeath a Continent to Freedom!

II. Treasures.

1. Through cycles of darkness the diamond sleeps in its coal-black prison.

2. Purely incrusted in its scaly casket, the breath-tarnished pearl slumbers in mud and ooze.

3. Buried in the bowels of earth, rugged and obscure, lies the ingot of gold.

4. Long hast thou been buried, O Israel, in the bowels of earth; long hast thou slumbered beneath the overwhelming waves; long hast thou slept in the rayless house of darkness.

5. Rejoice and sing, for only thus couldst thou rightly guard the golden knowledge, Truth, the delicate pearl and the adamantine jewel of the Law.

III. *The Sower.*

1. Over a boundless plain went a man, carrying seed.

2. His face was blackened by sun and rugged from tempest, scarred and distorted by pain. Naked to the loins, his back was ridged with furrows, his breast was plowed with stripes.

3. From his hand dropped the fecund seed.

55

4. And behold, instantly started from the prepared soil blade, a sheaf, a springing trunk, a myriad-branching, cloud-aspiring tree. Its arms touched the ends of the horizon, the heavens were darkened with its shadow.

5. It bare blossoms of gold and blossoms of blood, fruitage of health and fruitage of poison; birds sang amid its foliage, and a serpent was coiled about its stem.

60

6. Under its branches a divinely beautiful man, crowned with thorns, was nailed to a cross.

7. And the tree put forth treacherous boughs to strangle the Sower; his flesh was bruised and torn, but cunningly he disentangled the murderous knot and passed to the eastward.

65

8. Again there dropped from his hand the fecund seed.

9. And behold, instantly started from the prepared soil a blade, a sheaf, a springing trunk, a myriad-branching, cloud-aspiring tree. Crescent shaped like little emerald moons were the leaves; it bare blossoms of silver and blossoms of blood, fruitage of health and fruitage of poison; birds sang amid its foliage and a serpent was coiled about its stem.

70

10. Under its branches a turbaned mighty-limbed Prophet brandished a drawn sword.

11. And behold, this tree likewise puts forth perfidious arms to strangle the Sower; but cunningly he disentangles the murderous knot and passes on.

75

12. Lo, his hands are not empty of grain, the strength of his arm is not spent.

13. What germ hast thou saved for the future, O miraculous Husbandman? Tell me, thou Planter of Christhood and Islam; tell me, thou seed-bearing Israel!

80

IV. The Test.

1. Daylong I brooded upon the Passion of Israel.

2. I saw him bound to the wheel, nailed to the cross, cut off by the sword, burned at the stake, tossed into the seas.

85   3. And always the patient, resolute, martyr face arose in silent rebuke and defiance.

4. A Prophet with four eyes; wide gazed the orbs of the spirit above the sleeping eyelids of the senses.

5. A Poet, who plucked from his bosom the quivering heart and fashioned it
90   into a lyre.

6. A placid-browed Sage, uplifted from earth in celestial meditation.

7. These I saw, with princes and people in their train; the monumental dead and the standard-bearers of the future.

8. And suddenly I heard a burst of mocking laughter, and turning, I beheld
95   the shuffling gait, the ignominious features, the sordid mask of the son of the Ghetto.

V. Currents.

1. Vast oceanic movements, the flux and reflux of immeasurable tides, over-sweep our continent.

2. From the far Caucasian steppes, from the squalid Ghettos of Europe,

100   3. From Odessa and Bucharest, from Kief and Ekaterinoslav,

4. Hark to the cry of the exiles of Babylon, the voice of Rachel mourning for her children, of Israel lamenting for Zion.

5. And lo, like a turbid stream, the long-pent flood bursts the dykes of op-pression and rushes hitherward.

105   6. Unto her ample breast, the generous mother of nations welcomes them.

7. The herdsman of Canaan and the seed of Jerusalem's royal shepherds re-new their youth amid the pastoral plains of Texas and the golden valleys of the Sierras.

VI. The Prophet.

1. Moses ben Maimon lifting his perpetual lamp over the path of the perplexed;   110

2. Hallevi, the honey-tongued poet, wakening amid the silent ruins of Zion the sleeping lyre of David;

3. Moses, the wise son of Mendel, who made the Ghetto illustrious;

4. Abarbanel, the counselor of kings; Aicharisi, the exquisite singer; Ibn Ezra, the perfect old man; Gabirol, the tragic seer;   115

5. Heine, the enchanted magician, the heart-broken jester;

6. Yea, and the century-crowned patriarch whose bounty engirdles the globe;—

7. These need no wreath and no trumpet; like perennial asphodel blossoms, their fame, their glory resounds like the brazen-throated cornet.   120

8. But thou—hast thou faith in the fortune of Israel? Wouldst thou lighten the anguish of Jacob?

9. Then shalt thou take the hand of yonder caftaned wretch with flowing curls and gold-pierced ears;

10. Who crawls blinking forth from the loathsome recesses of the Jewry;   125

11. Nerveless his fingers, puny his frame; haunted by the bat-like phantoms of superstition is his brain.

12. Thou shalt say to the bigot, "My Brother," and to the creature of darkness, "My Friend."

13. And thy heart shall spend itself in fountains of love upon the ignorant,   130
the coarse, and the abject.

14. Then in the obscurity thou shalt hear a rush of wings, thine eyes shall be bitten with pungent smoke.

15. And close against thy quivering lips shall be pressed the live coal wherewith the Seraphim brand the Prophets.   135

VII. Chrysalis.

1. Long, long has the Orient Jew spun around his helplessness the cunningly enmeshed web of Talmud and Kabbala.

2. Imprisoned in dark corners of misery and oppression, closely he drew about him the dust-gray filaments, soft as silk and stubborn as steel, until he
140 lay death-stiffened in mummied seclusion.

3. And the world has named him an ugly worm, shunning the blessed daylight.

4. But when the emancipating springtide breathes wholesome, quickening airs, when the Sun of Love shines out with cordial fires, lo, the Soul of Israel
145 bursts her cobweb sheath, and flies forth attired in the winged beauty of immortality.

—1887

Slave Songs and Sorrow Songs
[c. 1850s, published 1867]

Enslaved people of African descent in the United States created a powerful body of oral poetry in the form of songs. Observers sometimes called them "slave songs," "spirituals," "negro melodies," or "folk songs." In *The Souls of Black Folk* (1903), the important sociologist of race W.E.B. Du Bois called them "sorrow songs," the term by which they are often known today. In his *Narrative of the Life of Frederick Douglass, An American Slave* (1845), Frederick Douglass recalled the songs that his fellow slaves sang in his youth for their distinct expression of sorrow. Both men meant to correct a widespread misperception in white America that plantation slavery was a glorious world of kindly masters and happy, childlike slaves. (This myth remained popular in the twentieth century, as in the example of Margaret Mitchell's blockbuster, prize-winning 1936 novel *Gone with the Wind*). Du Bois recognized that slaves, under constant and brutal surveillance, had been constrained to sing in a way that conveyed meaning in a veiled manner. In addition to the compelling and poignant melodies of the songs, Du Bois called attention to the painful content lurking below the surface of the lyrics. Vague and biblical content often masked profound laments that the slaves could not express directly.

The selections below were transcribed by white northern observers during the Civil War and published to wide transatlantic interest soon after war's end. They include double-voiced songs—that is, songs whose words operate at two distinct levels of meaning, one public and one in code—about conditions on the plantation, critiques of the masters, and hopes for escape. Of "Poor Rosy," below, Du Bois heartbreakingly points out that, among the sorrow songs more generally, love songs are scarce and "of deep successful love there is ominous silence."

The images of the musical transcriptions come from William Francis Allen, Charles Pickard Ware, and Lucy McKim Garrison, eds., *Slave Songs of the United States* (New York: A. Simpson & Co., 1867). These transcriptions mark variations in the lyrics because slaves sang the songs in more than one version. The notational shorthand that indicates the multiple versions of the lyrics is similar to the shorthand Emily Dickinson used in her manuscripts to mark variants in her poems.

Blow Your Trumpet, Gabriel

De talles' tree in Paradise, De Christian call de tree of life;
And I hope dat trump might blow me home
To de new Jerusalem.

Blow your trumpet, Gabriel, Blow louder, louder;
5   And I hope dat trump might blow me home
To de new Jerusalem.

Paul and Silas, bound in jail,
Sing God's praise both night and day;
And I hope dat trump might blow me home
10 To de new Jerusalem.

4.   BLOW YOUR TRUMPET, GABRIEL.

2 Paul and Silas, bound in jail,
   Sing God's praise both night and day;
      And I hope, &c.

[This hymn is sung in Virginia in nearly the same form. The following minor variation is given by Mrs. Bowen, as heard by her in Charleston, some twenty-five years ago:]

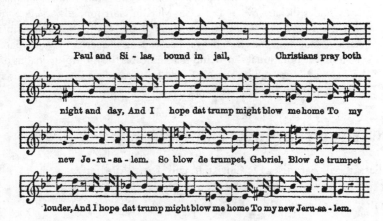

Poor Rosy[1]

Poor Rosy, poor gal; Poor Rosy, poor gal;
Rosy break my poor heart, Heav'n shall-a be my home.
I cannot stay in hell one day, Heav'n shall-a be my home;
I'll sing and pray my soul away, Heav'n shall-a be my home.

Got hard trial in my way,
Heav'n shall-a be my home.
O when I talk, I talk wid God,
Heav'n shall-a be my home.

I dunno what de people want of me,
Heav'n shall-a be my home.

5

10

<hr>

1   *Poor Rosy* The 1867 editors recalled discussing "Poor Rosy" with a "woman, a respectable house-servant, who had lost all but one of her twenty-two children." This woman, about whom we know nothing else, commented that singing the song required "a full heart and a troubled sperrit [spirit]."

Come Go with Me

Ole Satan is a busy ole man,
He rolls stones in my way;
Mass' Jesus is my bosom friend,
He roll 'em out o' my way.
5 O come go wid me,
O come go wid me,
O come go wid me,
A walkin' in de heaven I roam.

I did not come here myself, my Lord,
10 It was my Lord who brought me here;
And I really do believe I'm a child of God,
A-walkin' in de heaven I roam.
O come go wid me,
O come go wid me,
15 O come go wid me,
A walkin' in de heaven I roam.

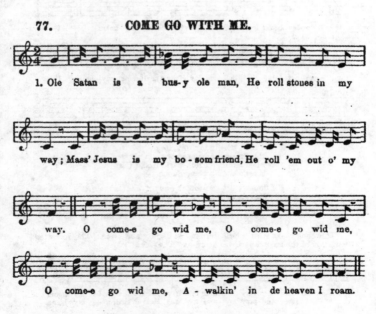

77.   **COME GO WITH ME.**

1. Ole Satan is a bus-y ole man, He roll stones in my way; Mass' Jesus is my bo-som friend, He roll 'em out o' my way. O come-e go wid me, O come-e go wid me, O come-e go wid me, A-walkin' in de heaven I roam.

2 I did not come here myself, my Lord,
It was my Lord who brought me here ;
And I really do believe I'm a child of God,
A-walkin' in de heaven I roam.
O come-e go wid me, etc.

The Hypocrite and the Concubine

Hypocrite and the concubine,
Livin' among the swine.
They run to God with the lips and tongue,
And leave all the heart behind.
Aunty, did you hear when Jesus rose? Did you hear when Jesus rose?
Aunty, did you hear when Jesus rose? He rose and he 'scend on high.

—published 1867

5

91.   THE HYPOCRITE AND THE CONCUBINE.

1. Hypo-crite and the concu-bine, Liv-in' among the swine. They

run to God with the lips and tongue, And leave all the heart behind.

Aunty, did you hear when Jesus rose? Did you hear when Jesus rose?

Aunty, did you hear when Jesus rose? He rose and he 'scend on high.

Ella Wheeler (Wilcox)

1850–1919

Ella Wheeler (who married Robert Wilcox in 1884) published poetry in newspapers and magazines while still a teenager, going on to become one of the most popular poets of the late nineteenth century in the United States. Her 1883 book *Poems of Passion* "set the literary world on fire," in the words of one review, and received both praise and condemnation for its alleged immorality in celebrating physical love. Known as "the Poetess of Passion," she challenged and titillated audience expectations about female propriety. (In this sense, her work belongs in a historical trajectory with antebellum women poets whose sexuality was part of their public image, like Frances Sargent Osgood [see p. 147].) While Walt Whitman (whose poetry was also circulating at this time) and Wilcox were entirely different kinds of poets, contemporary readers found both of them scandalous and obscene—or refreshing and a relief. Wilcox's language seems quite tame today, but her frank allusion to the "mad desires" of the (female) body, as in "Communism" below, touched a cultural nerve. The "tempest" she stirred in her own time (to quote one reviewer) is one sign of a society in transition. While she wrote in familiar and accessible poetic styles and diction that spoke to a wide audience, twentieth-century critics and poets denigrated her simplicity and popularity, and she fell from historical view.

Communism

When my blood flows calm as a purling river,
    When my heart is asleep and my brain has sway,
It is then that I vow we must part for ever,
    That I will forget you, and put you away
5 Out of my life, as a dream is banished
    Out of the mind when the dreamer awakes;
That I know it will be when the spell has vanished,
    Better for both of our sakes.

When the court of the mind is ruled by Reason,
10   I know it wiser for us to part;
But Love is a spy who is plotting treason,
    In league with that warm, red rebel, the Heart.
They whisper to me that the King is cruel,
    That his reign is wicked, his law a sin,

And every word they utter is fuel   15
    To the flame that smoulders within.

And on nights like this, when my blood runs riot
    With the fever of youth and its mad desires,
When my brain in vain bids my heart be quiet,
    When my breast seems the centre of lava-fires,   20
Oh, then is when most I miss you,
    And I swear by the stars and my soul and say
That I will have you, and hold you, and kiss you,
    Though the whole world stands in the way.

And like Communists,[1] as mad, as disloyal,   25
    My fierce emotions roam out of their lair;
They hate King Reason for being royal—
    They would fire his castle, and burn him there.
O Love! They would clasp you, and crush you and kill you,
    In the insurrection of uncontrol.   30
Across the miles, does this wild war thrill you
    That is raging in my soul?

—1883

---

1   *Communists* The term "Communist" has a long and complex history. As Wilcox uses it in this 1883 publication, she refers to collective, populist political forces opposing the rule of a monarch.

A.E. Housman
1859–1936

Although he is best remembered as a poet, most of Alfred Edward Housman's life was dedicated to his scholarly work, the translation of classical texts. His definitive edition of Manilius's *Astronomica* represents his greatest achievement in translation, although he also worked on Propertius, Ovid, Juvenal, and other classical authors. Poetry, for Housman, served as an emotional outlet and was something he worked at sporadically. As he once said: "I have seldom written poetry unless I was rather out of health, and the experience, though pleasurable, was generally agitating and exhausting."

Housman published his major poetic work at his own expense in 1896; originally written under the title *The Poems of Terence Hearsay* for the character of a young man that appears in the poems, it was published as *A Shropshire Lad*. The volume, which displays the influence of both English ballads and classical poetry, exhibits nostalgia for earlier times. Although *A Shropshire Lad* did not generate much immediate interest, it became increasingly popular during World War I, perhaps because its themes of loss and early death resonated more strongly in that era. Housman also published *Last Poems* in 1922, and a final collection, *More Poems*, was published posthumously in 1936.

Terence, This Is Stupid Stuff

"Terence, this is stupid stuff:
You eat your victuals fast enough;
There can't be much amiss, 'tis clear,
To see the rate you drink your beer.
5 But oh, good Lord, the verse you make,
It gives a chap the belly-ache.
The cow, the old cow, she is dead;
It sleeps well, the hornèd head:
We poor lads, 'tis our turn now
10 To hear such tunes as killed the cow.
Pretty friendship 'tis to rhyme
Your friends to death before their time
Moping melancholy mad:
Come, pipe a tune to dance to, lad."

Why, if 'tis dancing you would be,   15
There's brisker pipes than poetry.
Say, for what were hop-yards¹ meant,
Or why was Burton built on Trent?²
Oh many a peer³ of England brews
Livelier liquor than the Muse,⁴   20
And malt does more than Milton can
To justify God's ways to man.⁵
Ale, man, ale's the stuff to drink
For fellows whom it hurts to think:
Look into the pewter pot°   mug 25
To see the world as the world's not.
And faith, 'tis pleasant till 'tis past:
The mischief is that 'twill not last.
Oh I have been to Ludlow⁶ fair
And left my necktie God knows where,   30
And carried half-way home, or near,
Pints and quarts of Ludlow beer:
Then the world seemed none so bad,
And I myself a sterling lad;
And down in lovely muck I've lain,   35
Happy till I woke again.
Then I saw the morning sky:
Heigho, the tale was all a lie;
The world, it was the old world yet,
I was I, my things were wet,   40
And nothing now remained to do
But begin the game anew.

Therefore, since the world has still
Much good, but much less good than ill,
And while the sun and moon endure   45

---

1   *hop-yards* Areas of land upon which hops are grown.
2   *Burton ... Trent* Burton-on-Trent, a town in East Staffordshire, is the historical center
    of the British brewing industry. Brewing was first begun there by Benedictine monks in
    the eleventh century.
3   *peer* Member of the British nobility. Brewers were among those raised to the peerage,
    and were thus referred to as "beer barons."
4   *Muse* One of nine Greek goddesses of arts and learning; here, the source of poetic
    inspiration.
5   *Milton ... man* See John Milton's *Paradise Lost* (1667), 1.26.
6   *Ludlow* Market town in Shropshire.

Luck's a chance, but trouble's sure,
I'd face it as a wise man would,
And train for ill and not for good.
'Tis true the stuff I bring for sale
50 Is not so brisk a brew as ale:
Out of a stem that scored the hand
I wrung it in a weary land.
But take it: if the smack is sour,
The better for the embittered hour;
55 It should do good to heart and head
When your soul is in my soul's stead;
And I will friend you, if I may,
In the dark and cloudy day.

There was a king reigned in the East:
60 There, when kings will sit to feast,
They get their fill before they think
With poisoned meat and poisoned drink.
He gathered all that springs to birth
From the many-venomed earth;
65 First a little, thence to more,
He sampled all her killing store;
And easy, smiling, seasoned sound,
Sate the king when healths went round.
They put arsenic in his meat
70 And stared aghast to watch him eat;
They poured strychnine in his cup
And shook to see him drink it up:
They shook, they stared as white's their shirt:
Them it was their poison hurt.
75 —I tell the tale that I heard told.
Mithridates, he died old.[1]

—1896

---

1   *There was ... died old* According to Pliny's *Natural History*, Mithridates, king of Pontus
     from approximately 114 to 63 BCE, gradually built up a tolerance to all known poisons
     by ingesting a small amount of each daily, starting in childhood.

E. Pauline Johnson[1]

1861–1913

E. Pauline Johnson, also known as Tekahionwake, is remarkable as one of a very few early North American indigenous poets and fiction writers. Most indigenous writers of her time were men educated for the ministry who published religious, anthropological, autobiographical, political, and historical works, rather than poetry and fiction. More extraordinary still, she became both a canonical poet and a literary celebrity, performing on stage for 15 years in Canada, the United States, and London.

Johnson was born in 1861 on the Six Nations Reserve near Brantford, Ontario. Her father was a Mohawk member of the Iroquois Confederacy Council and her mother was an Englishwoman. Johnson was well educated by her parents, by governesses, in a reserve school, and at Brantford Collegiate Institute. Her first published poem appeared in 1883 or 1884, when she was in her early twenties. In January 1892, she was invited to participate in a poetry reading in Toronto, where her recitation of "A Cry from an Indian Wife" was the success of the evening. After this, she began a career that took her across Canada, to the United States, and twice to London. She traveled to perform in London first in 1894. There she undertook public recitals, made connections with influential patrons, and arranged for the publication of her first book, *The White Wampum*, which appeared in 1895 from a well-known literary press. She continued to perform until 1909. Then she retired to Vancouver, only to discover that she was suffering from incurable breast cancer. On her death, the city shut down for her funeral and mourners lined the streets to pay their respects. Chief Capilano's son, Chief Joe Mathias, and many other indigenous people followed the cortege. Her ashes are buried in Stanley Park, where she had loved to canoe on Lost Lagoon.

The Cattle Thief

They were coming across the prairie, they were galloping hard and fast;
For the eyes of those desperate riders had sighted their man at last—
Sighted him off to Eastward, where the Cree[2] encampment lay,
Where the cotton woods fringed the river, miles and miles away.
Mistake him? Never! Mistake him? the famous Eagle Chief!   5
That terror to all the settlers, that desperate Cattle Thief—

---

1   The author headnote is adapted from Margery Fee and Dory Nason's introduction to *Tekahionwake* (Broadview Press, 2016).

2   *Cree* One of the most populous indigenous American groups, whose bands are now mainly located in Canada.

That monstrous, fearless Indian, who lorded it over the plain,
Who thieved and raided, and scouted, who rode like a hurricane!
But they've tracked him across the prairie; they've followed him hard and
    fast;
10 For those desperate English settlers have sighted their man at last.

Up they wheeled to the tepees, all their British blood aflame,
Bent on bullets and bloodshed, bent on bringing down their game;
But they searched in vain for the Cattle Thief: that lion had left his lair,
And they cursed like a troop of demons—for the women alone were there.
15 "The sneaking Indian coward," they hissed; "he hides while yet he can;
He'll come in the night for cattle, but he's scared to face a *man*."
"Never!" and up from the cotton woods rang the voice of the Eagle Chief;
And right out into the open stepped, unarmed, the Cattle Thief.
Was that the game they had coveted? Scarce fifty years had rolled
20 Over that fleshless, hungry frame, starved to the bone and old;
Over that wrinkled, tawny skin, unfed by the warmth of blood.
Over those hungry, hollow eyes that glared for the sight of food.

He turned, like a hunted lion: "I know not fear," said he;
And the words outleapt from his shrunken lips in the language of the Cree.
25 "I'll fight you, white-skins, one by one, till I kill you *all*," he said;
But the threat was scarcely uttered, ere a dozen balls of lead
Whizzed through the air about him like a shower of metal rain,
And the gaunt old Indian Cattle Thief dropped dead on the open plain.
And that band of cursing settlers gave one triumphant yell,
30 And rushed like a pack of demons on the body that writhed and fell.
"Cut the fiend up into inches, throw his carcass on the plain;
Let the wolves eat the cursed Indian, he'd have treated us the same."
A dozen hands responded, a dozen knives gleamed high,
But the first stroke was arrested by a woman's strange, wild cry.
35 And out into the open, with a courage past belief,
She dashed, and spread her blanket o'er the corpse of the Cattle Thief;
And the words outleapt from her shrunken lips in the language of the Cree,
"If you mean to touch that body, you must cut your way through *me*."
And that band of cursing settlers dropped backward one by one,
40 For they knew that an Indian woman roused, was a woman to let alone.
And then she raved in a frenzy that they scarcely understood,
Raved of the wrongs she had suffered since her earliest babyhood:
"Stand back, stand back, you white-skins, touch that dead man to your
    shame;

You have stolen my father's spirit, but his body I only claim.
You have killed him, but you shall not dare to touch him now he's dead.   45
You have cursed, and called him a Cattle Thief, though you robbed him first
    of bread—
Robbed him and robbed my people—look there, at that shrunken face,
Starved with a hollow hunger, we owe to you and your race.
What have you left to us of land, what have you left of game,
What have you brought but evil, and curses since you came?   50
How have you paid us for our game? how paid us for our land?
By a *book*,[1] to save our souls from the sins *you* brought in your other hand!
Go back with your new religion, we never have understood
Your robbing an Indian's *body*, and mocking his *soul* with food.[2]
Go back with your new religion, and find—if find you can—   55
The *honest* man you have ever made from out a *starving* man.
You say your cattle are not ours, your meat is not our meat;
When *you* pay for the land you live in, *we'll* pay for the meat we eat.
Give back our land and our country, give back our herds of game;
Give back the furs and the forests that were ours before you came;   60
Give back the peace and the plenty. Then come with your new belief,
And blame, if you dare, the hunger that *drove* him to be a thief."

—1894

The City and the Sea

I

To none the city bends a servile knee;
    Purse-proud and scornful, on her heights she stands,
And at her feet the great white moaning sea
    Shoulders incessantly the grey-gold sands,—
One the Almighty's child since time began,   5
    And one the might of Mammon,[3] born of clods;
For all the city is the work of man,
    But all the sea is God's.

---

1   *book* I.e., the Bible.
2   *robbing ... food* See Matthew 4.4 in the Bible's New Testament: "Man shall not live by
    bread alone, but by every word that proceedeth out of the mouth of God."
3   *Mammon* Personification of material wealth, usually depicted as a demon or evil deity.

II

And she—between the ocean and the town—
10   Lies cursed of one and by the other blest;
Her staring eyes, her long drenched hair, her gown,
    Sea-laved and soiled and dank above her breast.
She, image of her God since life began,
    She, but the child of Mammon, born of clods,
15 Her broken body spoiled and spurned of man,
    But her sweet soul is God's.

—1903

W.B. Yeats
1865–1939

William Butler Yeats was born in Sandymount, Dublin, of Anglo-Irish parentage. He spent his early years moving between London and Sligo, a small town in the west of Ireland where his maternal grandparents lived. In London, the family moved in artistic circles that included William Morris, Bernard Shaw, and Oscar Wilde.

His early work is imbued with what he saw as the mystery and beauty of Irish myth and landscape. When Yeats's father saw his son's first poem, he declared that Yeats had "given tongue to the sea-cliffs." The early poems also contain some of the most memorable love poetry in English. In 1899, Yeats was involved in the foundation of the Irish National Theatre; he would become its director and write more than 20 plays that were performed there. But he also continued to write poetry, developing a more dramatic, collo-quial, and compact voice. Beginning with the volume *Responsibilities* (1914), he began to explore increasingly complex themes and poetic forms as he sought to give voice to the "blood-dimmed tide" of modern experience.

Yeats was deeply interested in the occult and explored the symbolic worlds of astrology, Theosophism, the tarot, and alchemy. He developed his own system of symbols and conception of history; the poems "Leda and the Swan" and "The Second Coming" are both, for example, influenced by his idea that civilizations are born cyclically, through violent, mystical, and sexual encounters.

Yeats was a formative influence on modern poetry and on the cultural and political history of Ireland; T.S. Eliot described him as "part of the consciousness of an age which cannot be understood without him." Yeats worked all his life to foster an Irish national literature, and in 1923 he was the first writer from Ireland to receive the Nobel Prize.

Easter 1916[1]

I have met them at close of day
Coming with vivid faces
From counter or desk among grey
Eighteenth-century houses.
I have passed with a nod of the head
Or polite meaningless words, 5

---

1   *Easter 1916* On Easter Monday, 24 April 1916, Irish nationalists instigated an unsuc-cessful rebellion against the British government, which was then at war with Germany; the Easter Rebellion lasted until 29 April. Many of the Irish nationalist leaders were executed that May.

Or have lingered awhile and said
Polite meaningless words,
And thought before I had done
10 Of a mocking tale or a gibe
To please a companion
Around the fire at the club,
Being certain that they and I
But lived where motley° is worn: *jester's costume*
15 All changed, changed utterly:
A terrible beauty is born.

That woman's days were spent
In ignorant good-will,
Her nights in argument
20 Until her voice grew shrill.[1]
What voice more sweet than hers
When, young and beautiful,
She rode to harriers?[2]
This man had kept a school
25 And rode our wingèd horse;[3]
This other his helper and friend[4]
Was coming into his force;
He might have won fame in the end,
So sensitive his nature seemed,
30 So daring and sweet his thought.
This other man I had dreamed
A drunken, vainglorious lout.[5]
He had done most bitter wrong
To some who are near my heart,
35 Yet I number him in the song;

---

1   *That woman's ... shrill* Countess Markiewicz (1868–1927), played a central role in the
    Easter Rebellion; she was arrested and sentenced to death (though the death sentence
    was later commuted). Yeats later wrote a poem about her and her Irish-nationalist sister,
    "In Memory of Eva Gore-Booth and Con Markiewicz" (1929).
2   *rode to harriers* Went hunting with hounds.
3   *This man ... wingèd horse* Pádraic Pearse (1879–1916) founded St. Enda's School near
    Dublin. He was a leader in the effort to revive the Gaelic language, and wrote both Irish
    and English poetry; *wingèd horse* Refers to Pegasus, the horse of the Muses.
4   *This other his helper and friend* Thomas MacDonagh (1878–1916), an Irish poet and
    playwright who also taught school.
5   *vainglorious lout* Major John MacBride (1865–1916), estranged husband of Irish na-
    tionalist Maud Gonne; their separation just two years after marriage was due in part to
    his drinking bouts.

He, too, has resigned his part
In the casual comedy;
He, too, has been changed in his turn,
Transformed utterly:
A terrible beauty is born.   40

Hearts with one purpose alone
Through summer and winter seem
Enchanted to a stone
To trouble the living stream.
The horse that comes from the road,   45
The rider, the birds that range
From cloud to tumbling cloud,
Minute by minute they change;
A shadow of cloud on the stream
Changes minute by minute;   50
A horse-hoof slides on the brim,
And a horse plashes within it;
The long-legged moor-hens dive,
And hens to moor-cocks call;
Minute by minute they live: 55
The stone's in the midst of all.

Too long a sacrifice
Can make a stone of the heart.
O when may it suffice?
That is Heaven's part, our part   60
To murmur name upon name,
As a mother names her child
When sleep at last has come
On limbs that had run wild.
What is it but nightfall?   65
No, no, not night but death;
Was it needless death after all?
For England may keep faith
For all that is done and said.[1]
We know their dream; enough   70
To know they dreamed and are dead;
And what if excess of love
Bewildered them till they died?

---

1   *For England ... said* England had originally granted Ireland Home Rule in 1913, but
then postponed it due to World War I, promising to institute it after the war.

I write it out in a verse—
75 MacDonagh and MacBride
And Connolly and Pearse[1]
Now and in time to be,
Wherever green is worn,
Are changed, changed utterly:
80 A terrible beauty is born.

—1916

The Second Coming[2]

Turning and turning in the widening gyre[3]
The falcon cannot hear the falconer;
Things fall apart; the centre cannot hold;
Mere anarchy is loosed upon the world,
5 The blood-dimmed tide is loosed, and everywhere
The ceremony of innocence is drowned;
The best lack all conviction, while the worst
Are full of passionate intensity.

Surely some revelation is at hand;
10 Surely the Second Coming is at hand.
The Second Coming! Hardly are those words out
When a vast image out of *Spiritus Mundi*[4]
Troubles my sight: somewhere in sands of the desert
A shape with lion body and the head of a man,[5]
15 A gaze blank and pitiless as the sun,
Is moving its slow thighs, while all about it
Reel shadows of the indignant desert birds.
The darkness drops again; but now I know
That twenty centuries of stony sleep
20 Were vexed to nightmare by a rocking cradle,[6]

---

1   *Connolly* James Connolly (1868–1916), Irish socialist; *MacDonagh ... Pearse* All four
     men were executed for their involvement in the Easter Rebellion of 1916.
2   *The Second Coming* The return of Christ, as predicted in the New Testament. See Rev-
     elation 1.7: "Behold, he cometh with clouds; and every eye shall see him."
3   *gyre* Spiral formed from concentric circles.
4   *Spiritus Mundi* Latin: Spirit of the World; universal spirit that houses the images of
     civilization's past memories and provides divine inspiration for the poet. The human
     race is a connected whole in the *spiritus mundi*.
5   *shape ... man* The Egyptian sphinx.
6   *rocking cradle* Cradle of the Christ Child.

And what rough beast, its hour come round at last,
Slouches towards Bethlehem to be born?

—1920

Leda and the Swan[1]

A sudden blow: the great wings beating still
Above the staggering girl, her thighs caressed
By the dark webs, her nape caught in his bill,
He holds her helpless breast upon his breast.

How can those terrified vague fingers push
The feathered glory from her loosening thighs?
And how can body, laid in that white rush,

But feel the strange heart beating where it lies?
A shudder in the loins engenders there
The broken wall, the burning roof and tower
And Agamemnon dead.[2]
                Being so caught up,
So mastered by the brute blood of the air,
Did she put on his knowledge with his power
Before the indifferent beak could let her drop?

—1924

Sailing to Byzantium[3]

1

That is no country for old men. The young
In one another's arms, birds in the trees
—Those dying generations—at their song,
The salmon-falls, the mackerel-crowded seas,

---

1   *Leda and the Swan* In Greek mythology, Leda was visited by Zeus in the form of a swan, who in some versions of the story seduced her and in other versions raped her. From this union she bore two eggs, one becoming the twins Castor and Pollux, the other Helen (whose abduction later initiated the Trojan War).
2   *broken wall ... Agamemnon dead* Events of the Trojan War.
3   *Byzantium* Ancient city eventually renamed Constantinople (now Istanbul), capital of the Eastern Roman Empire. In *A Vision*, Yeats envisioned Byzantium as a center for artists: "The painter, the mosaic worker, the worker in gold and silver, the illuminator of sacred books were almost impersonal, almost perhaps without the consciousness of individual design, absorbed in their subject matter and that the vision of a whole people."

5   Fish, flesh, or fowl, commend all summer long
    Whatever is begotten, born, and dies.
    Caught in that sensual music all neglect
    Monuments of unageing intellect.

2

    An aged man is but a paltry thing,
10 A tattered coat upon a stick, unless
    Soul clap its hands and sing, and louder sing
    For every tatter in its mortal dress,
    Nor is there singing school but studying
    Monuments of its own magnificence;
15 And therefore I have sailed the seas and come
    To the holy city of Byzantium.

3

    O sages standing in God's holy fire
    As in the gold mosaic of a wall,
    Come from the holy fire, perne in a gyre,[1]
20 And be the singing-masters of my soul.
    Consume my heart away; sick with desire
    And fastened to a dying animal
    It knows not what it is; and gather me
    Into the artifice of eternity.

4

25 Once out of nature I shall never take
    My bodily form from any natural thing,
    But such a form as Grecian goldsmiths make
    Of hammered gold and gold enamelling
    To keep a drowsy Emperor awake;
30 Or set upon a golden bough to sing[2]
    To lords and ladies of Byzantium
    Of what is past, or passing, or to come.

—1927

---

1   *perne in a gyre* Rotate in a spiral; the literal definition of "perne" is "bobbin."
2   [Yeats's note] I have read somewhere that in the Emperor's palace at Byzantium was a tree made of gold and silver, and artificial birds that sang.

Edwin Arlington Robinson

1869–1935

Edwin Arlington Robinson grew up in a prosperous family in the small town of Gardiner, Maine. He attended Harvard College in Cambridge, Massachusetts, for two years, but a series of calamities hit hard—his family fell into economic ruin and his father died—and he had to drop out of school and return home. By this time, he had already chosen poetry as a calling. Back in Gardiner, he privately printed his first book, *The Torrent & the Night Before*, in 1896, followed by *The Children of the Night* in 1897. In part, these volumes depicted the blighted lives and stunted aspirations of the residents of a fictional place he called Tilbury Town.

Robinson's realist vision countered the dreamy and idealist Romanticism that was very popular in the poetry of his time. Struggling with poverty, unemployment, and alcoholism during his young adulthood, he experienced a transformative career change when President Theodore Roosevelt wrote an enthusiastic review of *The Children of the Night* in 1905 and offered Robinson a government job. Robinson received the first of three Pulitzer Prizes in 1922. A meticulous craftsman who revered traditional poetic forms while writing in a bracing new poetic voice, he published prolifically and to increasing acclaim. The twentieth century hailed Robinson as a model who had pioneered a new path for poetry.

The House on the Hill

They are all gone away,
The House is shut and still,
There is nothing more to say.

Through broken walls and gray
The winds blow bleak and shrill;   5
They are all gone away.

Nor is there one to-day
To speak them good or ill:
There is nothing more to say.

Why is it then we stray   10
Around the sunken sill?
They are all gone away,

And our poor fancy-play
For them is wasted skill:
15 There is nothing more to say.

There is ruin and decay
In the House on the Hill:
They are all gone away,
There is nothing more to say.

—1896

Sonnet[1]

Oh, for a poet—for a beacon bright
To rift this changeless glimmer of dead gray:
To spirit back the Muses, long astray,
And flush Parnassus[2] with a newer light:
5 To put these little sonnet-men to flight
Who fashion, in a shrewd mechanic way,
Songs without souls that flicker for a day,
To vanish in irrevocable night.

What does it mean, this barren age of ours?
10 Here are the men, the women, and the flowers,—
The seasons, and the sunset, as before.
What does it mean?—Shall not one bard arise
To wrench one banner from the western skies,
And mark it with his name for evermore?

—1896

---

1   *Sonnet* The sonnet was a very common form in published verse at this time, often a can-
    vas for demonstrating highly traditional technical skills. Robinson wrote multiple poems
    under this title.
2   *Parnassus* Mountain in central Greece that was the mythological home to the Muses. An
    influential series of French poetry collections (1866–76) titled *Le Parnasse Contemporain*
    ("The Contemporary Parnassus," equivalent to "Today's Poetry Scene") published inno-
    vative work by poets including Charles Baudelaire, Stéphane Mallarmé, and Paul Verlaine
    (about whom Robinson wrote a poem, "Verlaine"). French poetry of this era would have
    revolutionary effect on the genre. Innovative French poets had in turn been profoundly
    influenced by the poetry of Edgar Allan Poe and Walt Whitman. Robinson was in touch
    with both the traditional and the innovative.

Walt Whitman[1]

The master-songs are ended, and the man
That sang them is a name. And so is God
A name; and so is love, and life, and death,
And everything.—But we, who are too blind
To read what we have written, or what faith   5
Has written for us, do not understand:
We only blink, and wonder.

Last night it was the song that was the man,
But now it is the man that is the song.
We do not hear him very much to-day;—   10
His piercing and eternal cadence rings
Too pure for us—too powerfully pure,
Too lovingly triumphant, and too large;
But there are some that hear him, and they know
That he shall sing to-morrow for all men,   15
And that all time shall listen.

The master-songs are ended?—Rather say
No songs are ended that are ever sung,
And that no names are dead names. When we write
Men's letters on proud marble or on sand,   20
We write them there forever.

                                        —1896

Fleming Helphenstine

At first I thought there was a superfine
Persuasion in his face; but the free glow
That filled it when he stopped and cried, "Hollo!"
Shone joyously, and so I let it shine.
He said his name was Fleming Helphenstine,   5
But be that as it may;—I only know
He talked of this and that and So-and-So,
And laughed and chaffed° like any friend of mine.   *teased*

---

1   *Walt Whitman* Whitman died in 1892. Poets themselves were actively debating at this
     time whether or not Whitman's highly controversial innovations should serve as a model
     for new directions in poetry.

But soon, with a queer,° quick frown, he looked at me,   *odd*
10 And I looked hard at him; and there we gazed
With a strained shame that made us cringe and wince:
Then, with a wordless clogged apology
That sounded half confused and half amazed,
He dodged,—and I have never seen him since.

—1897

John Evereldown

Where are you going to-night, to-night,—
Where are you going, John Evereldown?
There's never the sign of a star in sight,
Nor a lamp that's nearer than Tilbury Town.[1]
5 Why do you stare as a dead man might?
Where are you pointing away from the light?
And where are you going to-night, to-night,
Where are you going, John Evereldown?

Right through the forest, where none can see,
10 There's where I'm going, to Tilbury Town.
The men are asleep—or awake, may be—
But the women are calling John Evereldown.
Ever and ever they call for me,
And while they call can a man be free?—
15 So right through the forest, where none can see,
There's where I'm going, to Tilbury Town.

But why are you going so late, so late,—
Why are you going, John Evereldown?
Though the road be smooth and the path be straight,
20 There are two long leagues to Tilbury Town.
Come in by the fire, old man, and wait!
Why do you chatter out there by the gate?
And why are you going so late, so late,—
Why are you going, John Evereldown?

25 I follow the women wherever they call,—
That's why I'm going to Tilbury Town.

---

1   *Tilbury Town* Imaginary town about which Robinson wrote many poems.

God knows if I pray to be done with it all,
But God is no friend to John Evereldown.—
So the clouds may come and the rain may fall,
The shadows may creep and the dead men crawl;—
But I follow the women wherever they call,   30
And that's why I'm going to Tilbury Town.

—1896

Richard Cory

Whenever Richard Cory went down town,
We people on the pavement looked at him:
He was a gentleman from sole to crown,
Clean favored,[1] and imperially slim.

And he was always quietly arrayed,   5
And he was always human when he talked;
But still he fluttered pulses when he said,
"Good-morning," and he glittered when he walked.

And he was rich,—yes, richer than a king,—
And admirably schooled in every grace: 10
In fine, we thought that he was everything
To make us wish that we were in his place.

So on we worked, and waited for the light,
And went without the meat, and cursed the bread;
And Richard Cory, one calm summer night,   15
Went home and put a bullet through his head.

—1897

---

1   *favored* Provided with unusual advantages.

Stephen Crane
1871–1900

Stephen Crane, son of a Methodist minister, was a journalist and an author of novels, tales, and poetry. A college dropout, he worked in New York as a reporter. His first novel, *Maggie: A Girl of the Streets* (1893), addressed urban social problems skyrocketing at this time, including slums and prostitution. Publishers rejected the book as unsavory, but well-established writers including Hamlin Garland and William Dean Howells (see p. 247) saw Crane as a major young talent and offered him support and guidance. (In one of the first such recorded instances in literary history, Howells also shared with Crane the work of a then-unknown poet who had just been posthumously published in book form for the first time: Emily Dickinson.) Crane went on to publish his first book of poems, *The Black Riders and Other Lines*, in 1895, dedicated to Garland.

A slender art book of untitled, numbered poems printed entirely in capital letters (an effect we have reproduced in the selections from this book below), *The Black Riders* conjured a phantasmagoric world stylistically unlike the socially realistic world of *Maggie*, yet sharing some of Crane's persistent concerns. His second novel, *The Red Badge of Courage*, also published in 1895, brought him immediate international fame. Rejecting the conventions of the heroic, triumphant, romanticized, and putatively "objective" accounts of the Civil War very popular in the US at that time, Crane devised a narrative method that focused on realistic psychological complexity. The novel's success led Crane back into journalism as a war correspondent. In 1899, he published his second volume of poems, *War Is Kind*, a collection of untitled poems printed on dark grey paper with stylized contemporary drawings by the Art Nouveau illustrator Will Bradley. Crane's poems were part of an international avant-garde aesthetic movement in touch with multiple artistic crosscurrents, a late-century transition for the genre of poetry away from the formally and socially conventional verse popular at the time. Crane died from consumption (today called tuberculosis) when he was not yet 29.

from *The Black Riders*

XIX

A GOD IN WRATH

WAS BEATING A MAN;

HE CUFFED HIM LOUDLY

WITH THUNDEROUS BLOWS

THAT RANG AND ROLLED OVER THE EARTH.   5

ALL PEOPLE CAME RUNNING.

THE MAN SCREAMED AND STRUGGLED,

AND BIT MADLY AT THE FEET OF THE GOD.

THE PEOPLE CRIED,

"AH, WHAT A WICKED MAN!"   10

AND—

"AH, WHAT A REDOUBTABLE GOD!"

XX

A LEARNED MAN GAME TO ME ONCE.

HE SAID, "I KNOW THE WAY,—COME."

AND I WAS OVERJOYED AT THIS.

TOGETHER WE HASTENED.

SOON, TOO SOON, WERE WE   5

WHERE MY EYES WERE USELESS,

AND I KNEW NOT THE WAYS OF MY FEET.

I CLUNG TO THE HAND OF MY FRIEND;

BUT AT LAST HE CRIED, "I AM LOST."

XXVII

A YOUTH IN APPAREL THAT GLITTERED

WENT TO WALK IN A GRIM FOREST.

THERE HE MET AN ASSASSIN

ATTIRED ALL IN GARB OF OLD DAYS;

5　HE, SCOWLING THROUGH THE THICKETS,

AND DAGGER POISED QUIVERING,

RUSHED UPON THE YOUTH.

"SIR," SAID THIS LATTER,

"I AM ENCHANTED, BELIEVE ME,

10　"TO DIE, THUS,

"IN THIS MEDIEVAL FASHION,

"ACCORDING TO THE BEST LEGENDS;

"AH, WHAT JOY!"

THEN TOOK HE THE WOUND, SMILING,

15　AND DIED, CONTENT.

LXI

I

THERE WAS A MAN AND A WOMAN

WHO SINNED.

THEN DID THE MAN HEAP THE PUNISHMENT

ALL UPON THE HEAD OF HER,

5　AND WENT AWAY GAILY.

II

THERE WAS A MAN AND A WOMAN

WHO SINNED.

AND THE MAN STOOD WITH HER.

AS UPON HER HEAD, SO UPON HIS,

FELL BLOW AND BLOW,   10

AND ALL PEOPLE SCREAMING, "FOOL!"

HE WAS A BRAVE HEART.

III

HE WAS A BRAVE HEART.

WOULD YOU SPEAK WITH HIM, FRIEND?

WELL, HE IS DEAD,   15

AND THERE WENT YOUR OPPORTUNITY.

LET IT BE YOUR GRIEF

THAT HE IS DEAD

AND YOUR OPPORTUNITY GONE;

FOR, IN THAT, YOU WERE A COWARD.   20

LXVII

GOD LAY DEAD IN HEAVEN;

ANGELS SANG THE HYMN OF THE END;

PURPLE WINDS WENT MOANING,

THEIR WINGS DRIP-DRIPPING

WITH BLOOD   5

THAT FELL UPON THE EARTH.

IT, GROANING THING,

TURNED BLACK AND SANK.

THEN FROM THE FAR CAVERNS

OF DEAD SINS   10

CAME MONSTERS, LIVID WITH DESIRE.

THEY FOUGHT,

WRANGLED OVER THE WORLD,

A MORSEL.

15 BUT OF ALL SADNESS THIS WAS SAD,—

A WOMAN'S ARMS TRIED TO SHIELD

THE HEAD OF A SLEEPING MAN

FROM THE JAWS OF THE FINAL BEAST.

—1895

from *War Is Kind*[1]

[The trees in the garden rained flowers]

The trees in the garden rained flowers.
Children ran there joyously.
They gathered the flowers
Each to himself.
5 Now there were some
Who gathered great heaps—
Having opportunity and skill—
Until, behold, only chance blossoms
Remained for the feeble.
10 Then a little spindling tutor
Ran importantly to the father, crying:
"Pray, come hither!
"See this unjust thing in your garden!"[2]
But when the father had surveyed,
15 He admonished the tutor:
"Not so, small sage!
"This thing is just.
"For, look you,

---

1   *War Is Kind* The poems in this volume were published without titles, each appearing on a separate page. For purposes of clarity as to where each poem begins and ends, we print each with its first line bolded and in brackets.
2   Printing conventions for quotation marks in the nineteenth century differed from today. It was routine, as here, to include quotation marks at the beginning of every line of someone's speech and then to close the quotation marks only at the end. New quotation marks at the start of a line do not necessarily indicate a change of speaker.

"Are not they who possess the flowers
"Stronger, bolder, shrewder   20
"Than they who have none?
"Why should the strong—
"The beautiful strong—
"Why should they not have the flowers?
Upon reflection, the tutor bowed to the ground,   25
"My lord," he said,
"The stars are displaced
"By this towering wisdom."

[When the prophet, a complacent fat man]

When the prophet, a complacent fat man,
Arrived at the mountain-top,
He cried: "Woe to my knowledge!
"I intended to see good white lands
"And bad black lands,   5
"But the scene is grey."

—1899

Paul Laurence Dunbar

1872–1906

Born in Dayton, Ohio, to parents who had been slaves, Paul Laurence Dunbar became one of the best-known African-American poets of the nineteenth century. A top student in his white high school, he could only find a job as an "elevator boy," a common form of menial labor for African-American men at the time. He borrowed money to publish his first volume of poems, *Oak and Ivy* (1893), and later that year he attended the World's Columbian Exposition in Chicago. At this significant international cultural festival, he had the good fortune to meet Frederick Douglass. Douglass offered him a job and opened the door to other artistic opportunities and connections. Dunbar's second book of verse, *Majors and Minors* (1895), received an enthusiastic review in an elite magazine from one of the most influential literary men in the nation, William Dean Howells (p. 247).

While Dunbar admired the great poets of the past such as John Keats and wrote verse in their style, he also wrote in the genre known as "Negro dialect" poetry, as in "A Banjo Song," below. Dialect poetry was a very popular genre at this point in history. Typically written by outsiders to a particular language community, it depicted the speech habits of groups that the dominant culture viewed as regional, ethnic, or marginal, including Irish, Dutch, Yankee, and Italian people, often for comic purposes. "Negro dialect" poetry dealt mainly in demeaning stereotypes and sold very well to white audiences. To achieve publication by white mainstream publishers, African-American writers had to walk a delicate line. If they wanted to resist the racial ideology that drove the popular market, they had to do so in subtle or coded ways. The shifting voices and points of view in "A Corn-Song" present one example.

Considerable controversy has surrounded Dunbar's dialect poems as to whether they reproduce popular, demeaning portrayals of African-Americans; subtly critique them; or carve out a poetic space for recording folkways in the complex post-slavery era. Dunbar's poetry speaks to the social fractures of his time. His most famous poem, "We Wear the Mask" (below), addresses the social predicament of speaking as an African-American poet in a society of white power structures.

We Wear the Mask

We wear the mask that grins and lies,
It hides our cheeks and shades our eyes,—
This debt we pay to human guile;
With torn and bleeding hearts we smile,
5 And mouth with myriad subtleties.

Why should the world be over-wise,
In counting all our tears and sighs?
Nay, let them only see us, while
    We wear the mask.

We smile, but, O great Christ, our cries   10
To thee from tortured souls arise.
We sing, but oh the clay is vile
Beneath our feet, and long the mile;
But let the world dream otherwise,
    We wear the mask!   15

                      —1895

A Banjo Song

Oh, dere's lots o' keer° an' trouble   *care*
    In dis world to swaller down;
An' ol' Sorrer's° purty lively   *sorrow*
    In her way o' gittin' roun'.
Yet dere 's times when I furgit 'em,—   5
    Aches an' pains an' troubles all,—
An' it's when I tek at ebenin'°   *evening*
    My ol' banjo f'om de wall.

'Bout de time dat night is fallin'
    An' my daily wu'k is done,   10
An' above de shady hilltops
    I kin see de settin' sun;
When de quiet, restful shadders°   *shadows*
    Is beginnin' jes' to fall,—
Den I take de little banjo   15
    F'om its place upon de wall.

Den my fam'ly gadders roun' me
    In de fadin' o' de light,
Ez I strike de strings to try 'em
    Ef dey all is tuned er-right.   20
An' it seems we're so nigh heaben
    We kin hyeah de angels sing
When de music o' dat banjo
    Sets my cabin all er-ring.

25 An' my wife an' all de othahs,—
    Male an' female, small an' big,—
Even up to gray-haired granny,
    Seem jes' boun' to do a jig;
'Twell I change de style o' music,
30   Change de movement an' de time,
An' de ringin' little banjo
    Plays an ol' hea't-feelin' hime.

An' somehow my th'oat gits choky,
    An' a lump keeps tryin' to rise
35 Lak it wan'ed to ketch de water
    Dat was flowin' to my eyes;
An' I feel dat I could sorter°   *sort of*
    Knock de socks clean off o' sin
Ez I hyeah° my po' ol' granny   *As I hear*
40   Wif huh tremblin' voice jine in.

Den we all th'ow in our voices
    Fu' to he'p de chune out too,
Lak a big camp-meetin' choiry
    Tryin' to sing a mou'nah th'oo.
45 An' our th'oahts let out de music,
    Sweet an' solemn, loud an' free,
'Twell de raftahs o' my cabin
    Echo wif de melody.

Oh, de music o' de banjo,
50   Quick an' deb'lish, solemn, slow,
Is de greates' joy an' solace
    Dat a weary slave kin know!
So jes' let me hyeah it ringin',
    Dough de chune be po' an' rough,
55 It's a pleasure; an' de pleasures
    O' dis life is few enough.

Now, de blessed little angels
    Up in heaben, we are told,
Don't do nothin' all dere lifetime
60   'Ceptin' play on ha'ps o' gold.
Now I think heaben'd be mo' homelike

    Ef we'd hyeah some music fall
F'om a real ol'-fashioned banjo,
    Like dat one upon de wall.

—1897

The Colored Soldiers

If the muse were mine to tempt it
    And my feeble voice were strong,
If my tongue were trained to measures,
    I would sing a stirring song.
I would sing a song heroic
    Of those noble sons of Ham,[1]   5
Of the gallant colored soldiers
    Who fought for Uncle Sam![2]

In the early days you scorned them,
    And with many a flip and flout   10
Said "These battles are the white man's,
    And the whites will fight them out."
Up the hills you fought and faltered,
    In the vales you strove and bled,
While your ears still heard the thunder   15
    Of the foes' advancing tread.

Then distress fell on the nation,
    And the flag was drooping low;
Should the dust pollute your banner?
    No! the nation shouted, No!   20
So when War, in savage triumph,
    Spread abroad his funeral pall—
Then you called the colored soldiers,
    And they answered to your call.

And like hounds unleashed and eager   25
    For the life blood of the prey,
Spring they forth and bore them bravely

---

1   *sons of Ham* The biblical Noah curses his son Ham with servitude, a curse that nine-
teenth-century people sometimes interpreted to be the origin of slavery.

2   *fought for Uncle Sam* Dunbar honors the black soldiers who fought for the Union dur-
ing the Civil War. (James Monroe Whitfield recalled those who fought in the American
Revolutionary War, in "America," p. 184 in this volume; see also Michael S. Harper's
"Debridement," [p. 578] on black soldiers and Vietnam.)

In the thickest of the fray.
And where'er the fight was hottest,
30   Where the bullets fastest fell,
There they pressed unblanched and fearless
    At the very mouth of hell.

Ah, they rallied to the standard
    To uphold it by their might;
35 None were stronger in the labors,
    None were braver in the fight.
From the blazing breach of Wagner[1]
    To the plains of Olustee,[2]
They were foremost in the fight
40   Of the battles of the free.

And at Pillow![3] God have mercy
    On the deeds committed there,
And the souls of those poor victims
    Sent to Thee without a prayer.
45 Let the fulness of Thy pity
    O'er the hot wrought spirits sway
Of the gallant colored soldiers
    Who fell fighting on that day!

Yes, the Blacks enjoy their freedom,
50   And they won it dearly, too;
For the life blood of their thousands
    Did the southern fields bedew.
In the darkness of their bondage,
    In the depths of slavery's night,
55 Their muskets flashed the dawning,
    And they fought their way to light.

They were comrades then and brothers.
    Are they more or less to-day?

---

1   *Wagner* The July 1863 Union assault on Fort Wagner (South Carolina) was led by the
    54th Massachussetts regiment, a regiment of free African-Americans under the leadership
    of the white officer Robert Gould Shaw.

2   *Olustee* The 1864 Battle of Olustee (Florida). Part of the Union expedition was to recruit
    black soldiers.

3   *Pillow* The notorious 1864 Battle of Fort Pillow (Tennessee), also known as the Fort
    Pillow Massacre. The Confederates were incensed by fighting black soldiers, whom they
    massacred (contrary to military practice) *after* they surrendered.

They were good to stop a bullet
    And to front the fearful fray.   60
They were citizens and soldiers,
    When rebellion raised its head;
And the traits that made them worthy,—
    Ah! those virtues are not dead.

They have shared your nightly vigils,   65
    They have shared your daily toil;
And their blood with yours commingling
    Has enriched the Southern soil.
They have slept and marched and suffered
    'Neath the same dark skies as you,   70
They have met as fierce a foeman,
    And have been as brave and true.

And their deeds shall find a record
    In the registry of Fame;
For their blood has cleansed completely   75
    Every blot of Slavery's shame.
So all honor and all glory
    To those noble sons of Ham—
The gallant colored soldiers
    Who fought for Uncle Sam!   80

                        —1897

A Corn-Song

On the wide veranda white,
In the purple failing light,
Sits the master while the sun is lowly burning;
And his dreamy thoughts are drowned
In the softly flowing sound
Of the corn-songs of the field-hands[1] slow returning.   5

    Oh, we hoe de co'n
    Since de ehly mo'n;

---

1   *corn-songs of the field-hands* Dunbar's poem incorporates a slave song; see the section of
slave songs in this volume, p. 271. Some slave songs were work songs associated with
performing a particular job, as here. Dunbar skillfully juxtaposes the slave song with a
description of the master's response. At the same time, he writes both in dialect and in
conventional poetic diction.

Now de sinkin' sun
10   Says de day is done.

O'er the fields with heavy tread,
Light of heart and high of head,
Though the halting steps be labored, slow, and weary;
15   Still the spirits brave and strong
Find a comforter in song,
And their corn-song rises ever loud and cheery.

Oh, we hoe de co'n
Since de ehly mo'n;
20   Now de sinkin' sun
Says de day is done.

To the master in his seat,
Comes the burden, full and sweet,
Of the mellow minor music growing clearer,
25   As the toilers raise the hymn,
Thro' the silence dusk and dim,
To the cabin's restful shelter drawing nearer.

Oh, we hoe de co'n
Since de ehly mo'n;
30   Now de sinkin' sun
Says de day is done.

And a tear is in the eye
Of the master sitting by,
As he listens to the echoes low-replying
35   To the music's fading calls
As it faints away and falls
Into silence, deep within the cabin dying.

Oh, we hoe de co'n
Since de ehly mo'n;
40   Now de sinkin' sun
Says de day is done.

—1897

Robert Frost
1874–1963

Though Robert Frost's career spanned the Modernist period, his work also relies on the traditional forms of poetry that many of his Modernist contemporaries were breaking or abandoning entirely. A meticulous craftsman, he famously said that "writing free verse is like playing tennis with the net down." One of the sources of both his wide appeal to a popular audience and his respect from fellow artists was his ability to merge regular meter and rhyme with everyday speech, especially the speech of New England rural life. He carefully cultivated his public image as a homespun poet of New England, which was in many ways an adopted poetic persona. In fact, he was born in San Francisco in 1874. Frost moved to New England at the age of 11.

In 1912, he relocated to England, a center for revolutionary developments in poetry that offered opportunities to build his career. While in London he published *A Boy's Will* (1913) and *North of Boston* (1914), two full-length collections that earned Frost critical acclaim and attracted the attention of well-known poets. Ezra Pound, the most influential force in the Modernist explosion of the time, encouraged Frost's career and introduced him into important literary circles (as indeed he had done for many other poets whose work he found innovative).

By the time of Frost's return to the United States in 1915, he was established as a serious poet. Over the following decades, his reputation would grow even further in both the popular and the elite literary marketplaces. Frost skillfully managed both aspects of his career. His poems themselves are masterworks: complex enough to sustain rereading and deep interpretation and accessible enough to achieve broad popularity. Frost still holds a place as one of the best-known and most respected poets of the twentieth century.

Birches

When I see birches bend to left and right
Across the lines of straighter darker trees,
I like to think some boy's been swinging them.
But swinging doesn't bend them down to stay
As ice storms do. Often you must have seen them   5
Loaded with ice a sunny winter morning
After a rain. They click upon themselves
As the breeze rises, and turn many-colored
As the stir cracks and crazes their enamel.
Soon the sun's warmth makes them shed crystal shells   10

Shattering and avalanching on the snow crust—
Such heaps of broken glass to sweep away
You'd think the inner dome of heaven had fallen.
They are dragged to the withered bracken by the load,
15 And they seem not to break; though once they are bowed
So low for long, they never right themselves:
You may see their trunks arching in the woods
Years afterwards, trailing their leaves on the ground
Like girls on hands and knees that throw their hair
20 Before them over their heads to dry in the sun.
But I was going to say when Truth broke in
With all her matter of fact about the ice storm,
I should prefer to have some boy bend them
As he went out and in to fetch the cows—
25 Some boy too far from town to learn baseball,
Whose only play was what he found himself,
Summer or winter, and could play alone.
One by one he subdued his father's trees
By riding them down over and over again
30 Until he took the stiffness out of them,
And not one but hung limp, not one was left
For him to conquer. He learned all there was
To learn about not launching out too soon
And so not carrying the tree away
35 Clear to the ground. He always kept his poise
To the top branches, climbing carefully
With the same pains you use to fill a cup
Up to the brim, and even above the brim.
Then he flung outward, feet first, with a swish,
40 Kicking his way down through the air to the ground.
So was I once myself a swinger of birches.
And so I dream of going back to be.
It's when I'm weary of considerations,
And life is too much like a pathless wood[1]
45 Where your face burns and tickles with the cobwebs
Broken across it, and one eye is weeping
From a twig's having lashed across it open.
I'd like to get away from earth awhile

---

1   *a pathless wood*   Cf. the opening of Dante's poem *The Inferno*, in which the narrator is
     confronted by a gloomy forest unmarked by any paths.

And then come back to it and begin over.
May no fate willfully misunderstand me   50
And half grant what I wish and snatch me away
Not to return. Earth's the right place for love:
I don't know where it's likely to go better.
I'd like to go by climbing a birch tree,
And climb black branches up a snow-white trunk   55
Toward heaven, till the tree could bear no more,
But dipped its top and set me down again.
That would be good both going and coming back.
One could do worse than be a swinger of birches.

—1916

'Out, Out—'[1]

The buzz-saw snarled and rattled in the yard
And made dust and dropped stove-length sticks of wood,
Sweet-scented stuff when the breeze drew across it.
And from there those that lifted eyes could count
Five mountain ranges one behind the other   5
Under the sunset far into Vermont.
And the saw snarled and rattled, snarled and rattled,
As it ran light, or had to bear a load.
And nothing happened: day was all but done.
Call it a day, I wish they might have said   10
To please the boy by giving him the half hour
That a boy counts so much when saved from work.
His sister stood beside him in her apron
To tell them "Supper." At the word, the saw,
As if to prove saws knew what supper meant,   15
Leaped out at the boy's hand, or seemed to leap—
He must have given the hand. However it was,
Neither refused the meeting. But the hand!
The boy's first outcry was a rueful laugh,
As he swung toward them holding up the hand   20
Half in appeal, but half as if to keep
The life from spilling. Then the boy saw all—
Since he was old enough to know, big boy

---

1   *'Out, Out'* See Shakespeare's *Macbeth* 5.5.23.

Doing a man's work, though a child at heart—
25 He saw all spoiled. "Don't let him cut my hand off—
The doctor, when he comes. Don't let him, sister!"
So. But the hand was gone already.
The doctor put him in the dark of ether.
He lay and puffed his lips out with his breath.
30 And then—the watcher at his pulse took fright.
No one believed. They listened at his heart.
Little—less—nothing!—and that ended it.
No more to build on there. And they, since they
Were not the one dead, turned to their affairs.

—1916

The Oven Bird

There is a singer everyone has heard,
Loud, a mid-summer and a mid-wood bird,
Who makes the solid tree trunks sound again.
He says that leaves are old and that for flowers
5   Mid-summer is to spring as one to ten.
He says the early petal-fall is past
When pear and cherry bloom went down in showers
On sunny days a moment overcast;
And comes that other fall we name the fall.
10 He says the highway dust is over all.
The bird would cease and be as other birds
But that he knows in singing not to sing.
The question that he frames in all but words
Is what to make of a diminished thing.

—1916

Desert Places

Snow falling and night falling fast, oh, fast
In a field I looked into going past,
And the ground almost covered smooth in snow,
But a few weeds and stubble showing last.

The woods around it have it—it is theirs.   5
All animals are smothered in their lairs.
I am too absent-spirited to count;
The loneliness includes me unawares.

And lonely as it is, that loneliness
Will be more lonely ere it will be less—   10
A blanker whiteness of benighted snow
With no expression, nothing to express.

They cannot scare me with their empty spaces
Between stars—on stars where no human race is.
I have it in me so much nearer home   15
To scare myself with my own desert places.

—1936

Amy Lowell
1874–1925

As an outspoken and tireless critic and editor, Amy Lowell helped to shape modern American poetry. Her own work is important for its experimentation with form, its groundbreaking depictions of lesbian sexuality, and the vivid intensity of its imagery. Formally experimental as well as versatile, she wrote ballads, narrative poetry, dramatic monologues, and a form of prose poetry that she termed "polyphonic prose." She had a profound impact in popularizing contemporary poetry in America.

Denied the university education her brothers received, Lowell educated herself using her wealthy and distinguished New England family's extensive library. (Her brother, Abbott Lawrence Lowell, was the president of Harvard from 1909–33.) She began her career late and her first volume was a critical failure. But her work took a new direction after she traveled to London to meet Ezra Pound, a leader of the Imagist poets—a group who, in Lowell's words, aimed "to present an image [and to] render particulars exactly" using "the language of common speech" in a "concentrat[ed]" way. Her 1915 anthology, *Some Imagist Poets* (with subsequent volumes in the next two years), marks a transitional moment in poetic history and the public circulation of Modernist poetic forms.

Though her health began to suffer due to a glandular condition, she continued to work on multiple projects, including an extensive and important biography of John Keats, one of her own major influences. She died in 1925, the year of its publication. *What's O'Clock* (1925), one of her several posthumous collections, was awarded the Pulitzer Prize.

Patterns

I walk down the garden paths,
And all the daffodils
Are blowing, and the bright blue squills.[1]
I walk down the patterned garden-paths
5 In my stiff, brocaded gown.
With my powdered hair and jewelled fan,
I too am a rare
Pattern. As I wander down
The garden paths.

---

1   *squills* Also called scillas, plants related to the lily, with small violet blossoms.

My dress is richly figured,   10
And the train
Makes a pink and silver stain
On the gravel, and the thrift
Of the borders.
Just a plate of current fashion,   15
Tripping by in high-heeled, ribboned shoes.
Not a softness anywhere about me,
Only whalebone and brocade.
And I sink on a seat in the shade
Of a lime tree. For my passion   20
Wars against the stiff brocade.
The daffodils and squills
Flutter in the breeze
As they please.
And I weep;   25
For the lime tree is in blossom
And one small flower has dropped upon my bosom.

And the plashing° of waterdrops   *splashing*
In the marble fountain
Comes down the garden-paths.   30
The dripping never stops.
Underneath my stiffened gown
Is the softness of a woman bathing in a marble basin,
A basin in the midst of hedges grown
So thick, she cannot see her lover hiding,   35
But she guesses he is near,
And the sliding of the water
Seems the stroking of a dear
Hand upon her.
What is Summer in a fine brocaded gown!   40
I should like to see it lying in a heap upon the ground.
All the pink and silver crumpled up on the ground.

I would be the pink and silver as I ran along the paths,
And he would stumble after,
Bewildered by my laughter.   45
I should see the sun flashing from his sword-hilt and the buckles on his shoes.
I would choose
To lead him in a maze along the patterned paths,

316 POEMS: A CONCISE ANTHOLOGY

A bright and laughing maze for my heavy-booted lover.
50 Till he caught me in the shade,
And the buttons of his waistcoat bruised my body as he clasped me,
Aching, melting, unafraid.
With the shadows of the leaves and the sundrops,
And the plopping of the waterdrops,
55 All about us in the open afternoon—
I am very like to swoon
With the weight of this brocade,
For the sun sifts through the shade.

Underneath the fallen blossom
60 In my bosom,
Is a letter I have hid.
It was brought to me this morning by a rider from the Duke.
"Madam, we regret to inform you that Lord Hartwell
Died in action Thursday se'nnight."[1]
65 As I read it in the white, morning sunlight,
The letters squirmed like snakes.
"Any answer, Madam," said my footman.
"No," I told him.
"See that the messenger takes some refreshment.
70 No, no answer."
And I walked into the garden,
Up and down the patterned paths,
In my stiff, correct brocade.
The blue and yellow flowers stood up proudly in the sun,
75 Each one.
I stood upright too,
Held rigid to the pattern
By the stiffness of my gown.
Up and down I walked,
80 Up and down.

In a month he would have been my husband.
In a month, here, underneath this lime,
We would have broke the pattern;
He for me, and I for him,
85 He as Colonel, I as Lady,

---

1   *Thursday se'nnight* I.e., Thursday a week ago

On this shady seat.
He had a whim
That sunlight carried blessing.
And I answered, "It shall be as you have said."
Now he is dead.   90

In Summer and in Winter I shall walk
Up and down
The patterned garden-paths
In my stiff, brocaded gown.
The squills and daffodils   95
Will give place to pillared roses, and to asters, and to snow.
I shall go
Up and down,
In my gown.
Gorgeously arrayed,   100
Boned and stayed.
And the softness of my body will be guarded from embrace
By each button, hook, and lace.
For the man who should loose me is dead,
Fighting with the Duke in Flanders,[1]   105
In a pattern called a war.
Christ! What are patterns for?

—1916

---

1   *Flanders* Historic country located mainly in what is now Belgium. During World War I
     (1914–18), Flanders and in particular the city of Ypres was the site of many major battles
     that resulted in massive casualties and loss of life.

Gertrude Stein
1874–1946

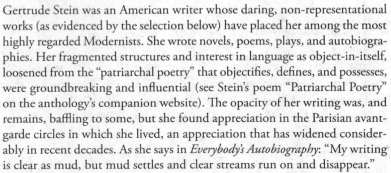

Gertrude Stein was an American writer whose daring, non-representational works (as evidenced by the selection below) have placed her among the most highly regarded Modernists. She wrote novels, poems, plays, and autobiographies. Her fragmented structures and interest in language as object-in-itself, loosened from the "patriarchal poetry" that objectifies, defines, and possesses, were groundbreaking and influential (see Stein's poem "Patriarchal Poetry" on the anthology's companion website). The opacity of her writing was, and remains, baffling to some, but she found appreciation in the Parisian avant-garde circles in which she lived, an appreciation that has widened considerably in recent decades. As she says in *Everybody's Autobiography*: "My writing is clear as mud, but mud settles and clear streams run on and disappear."

Stein was born in Allegheny, Pennsylvania, on 3 February 1874. Her parents, Daniel and Amelia Keyser Stein, were educated and wealthy German-Jewish immigrants. Both parents died when Stein was a teenager, and she subsequently followed her brother Leo to Harvard, where she studied philosophy and psychology under William James. After leaving John Hopkins medical school without a degree, Stein followed Leo to Europe. The two settled in Paris in 1903, where they began building their renowned collection of modern art at 27 rue de Fleurus. Alice B. Toklas, Gertrude's lover, moved into the house in 1910.

Stein wrote some of her most respected work in the early years in Paris: *Three Lives* (1909); *The Making of Americans; Being a History of a Family's Progress* (1906–08, pub. 1929); and the poems collected in *Tender Buttons: Objects, Food, Rooms* (1914). Stein continued to write prolifically throughout her life, gaining fame for *The Autobiography of Alice B. Toklas* (1933), which was her only conventional narrative. She lived in France until her death in 1946 from cancer.

Note to readers: An excerpt from Stein's poem "Patriarchal Poetry" appears on the anthology's companion website. The URL and passcode appear in the Table of Contents.

from *Tender Buttons*

A frightful release.

A bag which was left and not only taken but turned away was not found. The place was shown to be very like the last time. A piece was not exchanged, not a bit of it, a piece was left over. The rest was mismanaged.

A purse.   5

A purse was not green, it was not straw color, it was hardly seen and it had a use a long use and the chain, the chain was never missing, it was not misplaced, it showed that it was open, that is all that it showed.

A mounted umbrella.

What was the use of not leaving it there where it would hang what was the   10
use if there was no chance of ever seeing it come there and show that it was handsome and right in the way it showed it. The lesson is to learn that it does show it, that it shows it and that nothing, that there is nothing, that there is no more to do about it and just so much more is there plenty of reason for making an exchange.   15

A cloth.

Enough cloth is plenty and more, more is almost enough for that and besides if there is no more spreading is there plenty of room for it. Any occasion shows the best way.

More.   20

An elegant use of foliage and grace and a little piece of white cloth and oil.

Wondering so winningly in several kinds of oceans is the reason that makes red so regular and enthusiastic. The reason that there is more snips are the same shining very colored rid of no round color.

A new cup and saucer.   25

Enthusiastically hurting a clouded yellow bud and saucer, enthusiastically so is the bite in the ribbon.

Objects.

Within, within the cut and slender joint alone, with sudden equals and no more than three, two in the centre make two one side.   30

If the elbow is long and it is filled so then the best example is all together.

The kind of show is made by squeezing.

Eye glasses.

A color in shaving, a saloon is well placed in the centre of an alley.

35 *A cutlet.*

A blind agitation is manly and uttermost.

Careless water.

No cup is broken in more places and mended, that is to say a plate is broken and mending does do that it shows that culture is Japanese. It shows the
40 whole element of angels and orders. It does more to choosing and it does more to that ministering counting. It does, it does change in more water.

Supposing a single piece is a hair supposing more of them are orderly, does that show that strength, does that show that joint, does that show that . balloon famously. Does it.

—1914

Carl Sandburg
1878–1967

Born in Illinois to working-class immigrant parents, Carl Sandburg became one of the best-known poets of the early twentieth century. He wrote popular work in many other genres as well, including a widely read and influential biography of Abraham Lincoln. He moved to Chicago in 1913 during the "Chicago Renaissance," a surge in literary culture there in the 1910s and 1920s. The magazine *Poetry*, one of the most important venues for poetic Modernism, was founded in Chicago in 1912. *Poetry* published Sandburg's poem "Chicago" (below) as well as the first important poems by many other Modernist poets including T.S. Eliot, Ezra Pound, H.D., and Wallace Stevens. Working in the free-verse tradition of Walt Whitman, Sandburg saw himself as a poet of the people. The natural rhythms of American speech animated his lines. A popular poet, he recited and sang his poems, accompanying himself on the guitar, when he traveled the country.

Chicago[1]

Hog Butcher for the World,
Tool Maker, Stacker of Wheat,[2]
Player with Railroads and the Nation's Freight Handler;
Stormy, husky, brawling,
City of the Big Shoulders: 5

They tell me you are wicked and I believe them, for I have seen your painted
    women under the gas lamps luring the farm boys.
And they tell me you are crooked and I answer: Yes, it is true I have seen the
    gunman kill and go free to kill again.
And they tell me you are brutal and my reply is: On the faces of women and   10
    children I have seen the marks of wanton hunger.
And having answered so I turn once more to those who sneer at this my
    city, and I give them back the sneer and say to them:

---

1   *Chicago* Still a young city, Chicago's rapid growth as an urban center in the heart of the
    rural Midwest—seemingly springing up from farmland in the late nineteenth century, as
    Theodore Dreiser described it—made it a city highly symbolic for modern America; for
    example, Chicago was the home of the skyscraper.
2   *Hog Butcher ... Stacker of Wheat* Chicago was a crucial hub for the railroads that funda-
    mentally changed transportation and commerce in the US during the late nineteenth
    century. The city's railroads and yards played a major role in the nation's meatpacking and
    grain industries in particular.

Come and show me another city with lifted head singing so proud to be
15   alive and coarse and strong and cunning.
Flinging magnetic curses amid the toil of piling job on job, here is a tall
        bold slugger set vivid against the little soft cities;
Fierce as a dog with tongue lapping for action, cunning as a savage pitted
        against the wilderness,
20   Bareheaded,
      Shoveling,
      Wrecking,
      Planning,
      Building, breaking, rebuilding,
25 Under the smoke, dust all over his mouth, laughing with white teeth,
Under the terrible burden of destiny laughing as a young man laughs,
Laughing even as an ignorant fighter laughs who has never lost a battle,
Bragging and laughing that under his wrist is the pulse, and under his ribs
        the heart of the people,
30   Laughing!
Laughing the stormy, husky, brawling laughter of Youth, half-naked, sweat-
        ing, proud to be Hog Butcher, Tool Maker, Stacker of Wheat, Player
        with Railroads and Freight Handler to the Nation.

                                                            —1916

Grass

Pile the bodies high at Austerlitz[1] and Waterloo.
Shovel them under and let me work—
                  I am the grass; I cover all.

And pile them high at Gettysburg
5 And pile them high at Ypres and Verdun.
Shovel them under and let me work.
Two years, ten years, and passengers ask the conductor:
                  What place is this?
                  Where are we now?

10   I am the grass.
                  Let me work.

                                                            —1918

---

1   *Austerlitz* The poem lists the famous battlefields from the Napoleonic Wars, the US Civil
     War, and World War I.

Wallace Stevens
1879–1955

"Life," Wallace Stevens wrote, "consists of propositions about life." Over the course of a long career, Stevens often wrote about the relationship between the human understanding of reality—an ever-shifting product of perception and imagination—and "reality" itself (as in "Thirteen Ways of Looking at a Blackbird," below). Knowledgeable about philosophical theories on this topic, Stevens saw reality "itself" as fundamentally unknowable because the lens of human perception acts as an inescapable filter. While strongly influenced by Romanticism's explorations of the relationship between nature and poetic imagination, Stevens was also Modernist in his concern with the role of poetry in the spiritually disillusioned world of the twentieth century (see "Sunday Morning," below).

Stevens was born in Pennsylvania and attended Harvard as a non-degree student, where he edited the *Harvard Monthly*. After a brief and unsatisfying period as a journalist, Stevens became a lawyer in the insurance business, eventually becoming vice president of the Hartford Accident and Indemnity Company. Like his contemporary William Carlos Williams, Stevens has become iconic as a poet who worked in another full-time professional career (Williams was a medical doctor) while he also pursued a dedicated life as an artist. He published his first collection, *Harmonium*, in 1923. Notable for their sensuality of sound and color, his poems also received criticism for being too abstract, difficult, and philosophical. He is now widely regarded as one of the most important twentieth-century American poets, and his influence on later poets is incalculable.

Thirteen Ways of Looking at a Blackbird

I

Among twenty snowy mountains,
The only moving thing
Was the eye of the blackbird.

II

I was of three minds,
Like a tree
In which there are three blackbirds.

5

III

The blackbird whirled in the autumn winds.
It was a small part of the pantomime.

IV

A man and a woman
10 Are one.
A man and a woman and a blackbird
Are one.

V

I do not know which to prefer,
The beauty of inflections
15 Or the beauty of innuendoes,
The blackbird whistling
Or just after.

VI

Icicles filled the long window
With barbaric glass.
20 The shadow of the blackbird
Crossed it, to and fro.
The mood
Traced in the shadow
An indecipherable cause.

VII

25 O thin men of Haddam,[1]
Why do you imagine golden birds?
Do you not see how the blackbird
Walks around the feet
Of the women about you?

VIII

30 I know noble accents
And lucid, inescapable rhythms;
But I know, too,
That the blackbird is involved
In what I know.

---

1 · *Haddam* Town in Connecticut.

IX

When the blackbird flew out of sight,   35
It marked the edge
Of one of many circles.

X

At the sight of blackbirds
Flying in a green light,
Even the bawds° of euphony°   *brothel operators / pleasant sound*   40
Would cry out sharply.

XI

He rode over Connecticut
In a glass coach.
Once, a fear pierced him,
In that he mistook   45
The shadow of his equipage[1]
For blackbirds.

XII

The river is moving.
The blackbird must be flying.

XIII

It was evening all afternoon.   50
It was snowing
And it was going to snow.
The blackbird sat
In the cedar-limbs.

—1917

---

1   *equipage* Horses and carriage.

Nuances of a Theme by Williams[1]

It's a strange courage
you give me, ancient star:

Shine alone in the sunrise
toward which you lend no part!

I

Shine alone, shine nakedly, shine like bronze,
that reflects neither my face nor any inner part
of my being, shine like fire, that mirrors nothing.

II

Lend no part to any humanity that suffuses
5 you in its own light.
Be not chimera[2] of morning,
Half-man, half-star.
Be not an intelligence,
Like a widow's bird
10 Or an old horse.

—1918

The Snow Man

One must have a mind of winter
To regard the frost and the boughs
Of the pine-trees crusted with snow;

And have been cold a long time
5 To behold the junipers shagged with ice,
The spruces rough in the distant glitter

Of the January sun; and not to think
Of any misery in the sound of the wind,
In the sound of a few leaves,

---

1 *Nuances of a Theme by Williams* See William Carlos Williams's poem "El Hombre,"
   p. 335.
2 *chimera* Mythological monster with a goat's body, a lion's head, and the tail of a serpent;
   also means especially implausible thoughts or daydreams.

Which is the sound of the land   10
Full of the same wind
That is blowing in the same bare place

For the listener, who listens in the snow,
And, nothing himself, beholds
Nothing that is not there and the nothing that is.   15

—1921

Sunday Morning

I

Complacencies of the peignoir,[1] and late
Coffee and oranges in a sunny chair,
And the green freedom of a cockatoo
Upon a rug mingle to dissipate
The holy hush of ancient sacrifice.   5
She dreams a little, and she feels the dark
Encroachment of that old catastrophe,
As a calm darkens among water-lights.
The pungent oranges and bright, green wings
Seem things in some procession of the dead,   10
Winding across wide water, without sound.
The day is like wide water, without sound,
Stilled for the passing of her dreaming feet
Over the seas, to silent Palestine,
Dominion of the blood and sepulchre.[2]   15

II

Why should she give her bounty to the dead?
What is divinity if it can come
Only in silent shadows and in dreams?
Shall she not find in comforts of the sun,
In pungent fruit and bright, green wings, or else   20
In any balm or beauty of the earth,
Things to be cherished like the thought of heaven?

---

1   *peignoir* Woman's light dressing gown or light bathrobe; here, a garment for staying privately and casually at home.
2   *Palestine ... sepulchre* Refers to the blood of Jesus and the tomb in Jerusalem where he was buried.

Divinity must live within herself:
Passions of rain, or moods in falling snow;
25 Grievings in loneliness, or unsubdued
Elations when the forest blooms; gusty
Emotions on wet roads on autumn nights;
All pleasures and all pains, remembering
The bough of summer and the winter branch.
30 These are the measures destined for her soul.

III

Jove in the clouds had his inhuman birth.
No mother suckled him,[1] no sweet land gave
Large-mannered motions to his mythy mind.
He moved among us, as a muttering king,
35 Magnificent, would move among his hinds,[2]
Until our blood, commingling, virginal,
With heaven, brought such requital to desire
The very hinds discerned it, in a star.[3]
Shall our blood fail? Or shall it come to be
40 The blood of paradise? And shall the earth
Seem all of paradise that we shall know?
The sky will be much friendlier then than now,
A part of labor and a part of pain,
And next in glory to enduring love,
45 Not this dividing and indifferent blue.

IV

She says, "I am content when wakened birds,
Before they fly, test the reality
Of misty fields, by their sweet questionings;
But when the birds are gone, and their warm fields
50 Return no more, where, then, is paradise?"
There is not any haunt of prophecy,
Nor any old chimera[4] of the grave,
Neither the golden underground, nor isle

---

1   *Jove* Jupiter, Roman king of the gods, and god of the sky; *No mother suckled him* In
     Greek mythology, Jove's counterpart Zeus was raised by a goat named Amalthea.
2   *hinds* Peasants or farmhands.
3   *The very ... star* Allusion to the Star of Bethlehem, revealed to the wise men to announce
     the birth of Christ. See Matthew 2.1–2.
4   *chimera* Mythological monster with a goat's body, a lion's head, and the tail of a serpent;
     also means especially implausible thoughts or daydreams.

Melodious, where spirits gat them home,
Nor visionary south, nor cloudy palm
Remote on heaven's hill, that has endured
As April's green endures; or will endure
Like her remembrance of awakened birds,
Or her desire for June and evening, tipped
By the consummation of the swallow's wings.

V

She says, "But in contentment I still feel
The need of some imperishable bliss."
Death is the mother of beauty; hence from her,
Alone, shall come fulfilment to our dreams
And our desires. Although she strews the leaves
Of sure obliteration on our paths,
The path sick sorrow took, the many paths
Where triumph rang its brassy phrase, or love
Whispered a little out of tenderness,
She makes the willow shiver in the sun
For maidens who were wont to sit and gaze
Upon the grass, relinquished to their feet.
She causes boys to pile new plums and pears
On disregarded plate. The maidens taste
And stray impassioned in the littering leaves.

VI

Is there no change of death in paradise?
Does ripe fruit never fall? Or do the boughs
Hang always heavy in that perfect sky,
Unchanging, yet so like our perishing earth,
With rivers like our own that seek for seas
They never find, the same receding shores
That never touch with inarticulate pang?
Why set the pear upon those river banks
Or spice the shores with odors of the plum?
Alas, that they should wear our colors there,
The silken weavings of our afternoons,
And pick the strings of our insipid lutes!
Death is the mother of beauty, mystical,
Within whose burning bosom we devise
Our earthly mothers waiting, sleeplessly.

VII

Supple and turbulent, a ring of men
Shall chant in orgy on a summer morn
Their boisterous devotion to the sun,
Not as a god, but as a god might be,
95 Naked among them, like a savage source.
Their chant shall be a chant of paradise,
Out of their blood, returning to the sky;
And in their chant shall enter, voice by voice,
The windy lake wherein their lord delights,
100 The trees, like serafin,[1] and echoing hills,
That choir among themselves long afterward.
They shall know well the heavenly fellowship
Of men that perish and of summer morn.
And whence they came and whither they shall go
105 The dew upon their feet shall manifest.

VIII

She hears, upon that water without sound,
A voice that cries, "The tomb in Palestine
Is not the porch of spirits lingering.
It is the grave of Jesus, where he lay."
110 We live in an old chaos of the sun,
Or old dependency of day and night,
Or island solitude, unsponsored, free,
Of that wide water, inescapable.
Deer walk upon our mountains, and the quail
115 Whistle about us their spontaneous cries;
Sweet berries ripen in the wilderness;
And, in the isolation of the sky,
At evening, casual flocks of pigeons make
Ambiguous undulations as they sink,
120 Downward to darkness, on extended wings.

—1923

---

1   *serafin* I.e., seraphim, angels of the highest order who fly over the throne of God.

The Poem That Took the Place of a Mountain

There it was, word for word,
The poem that took the place of a mountain.

He breathed its oxygen,
Even when the book lay turned in the dust of his table.

It reminded him how he had needed   5
A place to go to in his own direction,

How he had recomposed the pines,
Shifted the rocks and picked his way among clouds,

For the outlook that would be right,
Where he would be complete in an unexplained completion: 10

The exact rock where his inexactnesses
Would discover, at last, the view toward which they had edged,

Where he could lie and, gazing down at the sea,
Recognize his unique and solitary home.

                                                        —1954

Mina Loy
1882–1966

Born Mina Gertrude Löwry to Anglo-Jewish parents in London, England, Mina Loy was trained as a visual artist in Germany and England. Living in Paris from 1903 to 1916, Loy developed friendships there with Gertrude Stein (p. 318), Djuna Barnes, James Joyce, and other important Modernist writers, and began publishing poetry in 1914. She moved to the United States, which she described as "a country where the mind has to put on its verbal clothes with terrific speed," in 1916, and continued to be immersed in the world of the literary and artistic avant-garde in New York.

Loy's poetry was championed by the poets Ezra Pound and William Carlos Williams, among others, but her bold experimentation with language and her willingness to write on topics such as abortion, female sexuality, and homelessness alarmed other contemporaries. According to critic Georgina Taylor, Loy was "attacking the sentimental head on, rewriting sexuality as physical and erotic." After decades of critical dismissal, Loy's work was revived in the 1950s, in part by the American poet Kenneth Rexroth, and she is now considered, in the words of Marjorie Perloff, "one of the central avant-garde poets writing in English."

Note to readers: Loy's poem "The Song of the Nightingale is Like the Scent of Syringa" appears on the anthology's companion website. The URL and passcode are in the Table of Contents.

from *Songs to Joannes*[1]

XII

Voices break on the confines of passion
Desire   Suspicion   Man   Woman
Solve in the humid carnage

Flesh from flesh
5   Draws the inseparable delight
Kissing at gasps to catch it

Is it true
That I have set you apart
Inviolate in an utter crystallization

---

1   This excerpt reproduces three of the full poem's 34 sections.

Of all   the jolting of the crowd   10
Taught me willingly to live to share

Or are you
Only the other half
Of an ego's necessity
Scourging pride with compassion   15
To the shallow sound of dissonance
And boom of escaping breath

XIII

Come to me   There is something
I have got to tell you   and I can't tell
Something taking shape   20
Something that has a new name
A new dimension
A new use
A new illusion

It is ambient   And it is in your eyes   25
Something shiny   Something only for you
                 Something that I must not see

It is in my ears   Something very resonant
Something that you must not hear
                 Something only for me   30

Let us be very jealous
Very suspicious
Very conservative
Very cruel
Or we might make an end of the jostling of aspirations   35
Disorb inviolate egos

Where two or three are welded together
They shall become god
— — — — — — —
Oh that's right
Keep away from me   Please give me a push
Don't let me understand you   Don't realise me   40

Or we might tumble together
Depersonalized

Identical
45 Into the terrific Nirvana
Me you—you—me

XIV

Today
Everlasting   passing   apparent   imperceptible
To you
50 I bring the nascent virginity of
—Myself   for the moment

No love   or the other thing
Only the impact of lighted bodies
Knocking sparks off each other
55 In chaos

—1917

William Carlos Williams
1883–1963

A major poet of the twentieth century and of the Modernist movement in particular, William Carlos Williams was also a medical doctor who spent most of his life in his birthplace, Rutherford, New Jersey. As a poet, his primary allegiance was to American culture—in this regard, he followed his important poetic forefather, Walt Whitman—and he strove to capture quintessentially American ideas and experiences in colloquial language: "not the speech of English country people ... but language modified by ... the American environment."

Of Williams's many friends in the artistic and literary avant-gardes of New York and Europe, the most significant to his career was fellow poet and Modernist visionary Ezra Pound. Williams's early style was profoundly shaped by Imagism's (see Glossary) quest to capture impressions through precise, concentrated language. He also continued to evolve as a poet, experimenting with form and idiom throughout his career. Williams is famous as one of the first well-known poets to have composed on a typewriter, creating poems that were also visual objects whose line arrangements and breaks were central to their form. He sometimes typed and retyped a single poem multiple times, trying out different line breaks with the same words. (Also see E.E. Cummings, p. 367.)

Perhaps because of his work's deceptively easy style—"The Red Wheelbarrow" and "This Is Just to Say" (below) are two of the most legendary (and widely parodied) instances—critics did not begin to count Williams among the best poets of his era until the last decades of his life. The rise of his reputation began with the publication of the first book of *Paterson* (1946–63), a long poem that explores the city of Paterson (near Rutherford) from diverse angles, in both poetry and prose, working with modernist-inspired elements of fragmentation and collage. Williams' distinctive free-verse style profoundly shaped the work of later poets.

El Hombre

It's a strange courage
you give me ancient star:

Shine alone in the sunrise
toward which you lend no part!

—1917

The Red Wheelbarrow

so much depends
upon

a red wheel
barrow

5 glazed with rain
water

beside the white
chickens

—1923

Spring and All

By the road to the contagious hospital
under the surge of the blue
mottled clouds driven from the
northeast—a cold wind. Beyond, the
5 waste of broad, muddy fields
brown with dried weeds, standing and fallen

patches of standing water
the scattering of tall trees

All along the road the reddish
10 purplish, forked, upstanding, twiggy
stuff of bushes and small trees
with dead, brown leaves under them
leafless vines—

Lifeless in appearance, sluggish
15 dazed spring approaches—

They enter the new world naked,
cold, uncertain of all
save that they enter. All about them
the cold, familiar wind—

20 Now the grass, tomorrow
the stiff curl of wildcarrot leaf

One by one objects are defined—
It quickens: clarity, outline of leaf

But now the stark dignity of
entrance—Still, the profound change   25
has come upon them: rooted they
grip down and begin to awaken

—1923

To Elsie[1]

The pure products of America
go crazy—
mountain folk from Kentucky

or the ribbed north end of
Jersey   5
with its isolate lakes and

valleys, its deaf-mutes, thieves
old names
and promiscuity between

devil-may-care men who have taken   10
to railroading
out of sheer lust of adventure—

and young slatterns,[2] bathed
in filth
from Monday to Saturday   15

to be tricked out that night
with gauds°   *trinkets*
from imaginations which have no

peasant traditions to give them
character   20
but flutter and flaunt

---

1   *To Elsie* Elsie Borden worked for the Williams family for a time as a nursemaid; originally
     published in *Spring and All* as XVIII.
2   *slatterns* Unclean women.

sheer rags—succumbing without
emotion
save numbed terror

25 under some hedge of choke-cherry
or viburnum—
which they cannot express—

Unless it be that marriage
perhaps
30 with a dash of Indian blood

will throw up a girl so desolate
so hemmed round
with disease or murder

that she'll be rescued by an
35 agent—
reared by the state and

sent out at fifteen to work in
some hard-pressed
house in the suburbs—

40 some doctor's family, some Elsie—
voluptuous water
expressing with broken

brain the truth about us—
her great
45 ungainly hips and flopping breasts

addressed to cheap
jewelry
and rich young men with fine eyes

as if the earth under our feet
50 were
an excrement of some sky

and we degraded prisoners
destined
to hunger until we eat filth

while the imagination strains   55
after deer
going by fields of goldenrod in

the stifling heat of September
Somehow
it seems to destroy us   60

It is only in isolate flecks that
something
is given off

No one
to witness   65
and adjust, no one to drive the car

—1923

This Is Just to Say

I have eaten
the plums
that were in
the icebox

and which   5
you were probably
saving
for breakfast

Forgive me
they were delicious   10
so sweet
and so cold

—1934

Landscape with the Fall of Icarus[1]

According to Brueghel
when Icarus fell
it was spring

a farmer was ploughing
5   his field
the whole pageantry

of the year was
awake tingling
near

10 the edge of the sea
concerned
with itself

sweating in the sun
that melted
15 the wings' wax

unsignificantly
off the coast
there was

a splash quite unnoticed
20 this was
Icarus drowning

—1962

---

1   *Landscape ... of Icarus* Painting (c. 1555) by Pieter Brueghel the Elder based on an an-
cient Greek story. Wearing wings made by his father Daedalus, Icarus flew too close to the
sun; the wax on the wings melted, and Icarus fell to his death. In Brueghel's painting, an
ordinary farmer ploughing on a hill dominates the foreground, while Icarus's drowning
body appears very small in the ocean below, next to a much larger ship.

Ezra Pound

1885–1972

Arguably one of the two most influential poets of the twentieth century (the other being his friend and collaborator, T.S. Eliot), Ezra Pound was an artistic visionary as well as mentor and editor to other poets and artists. More than any other single figure, he steered the development of the literary avant-garde in ways that would change the course of literary history. Pound's early views were unequivocal: "no good poetry is ever written in a manner twenty years old, for to write in such a manner shows conclusively that the writer thinks from books, convention and cliché, and not from life." He strove aggressively to make poetry "new."

Born in Idaho, in 1908 Pound moved to Europe, where he was the center of a literary circle that included established and new writers. His first collection of poetry, *Personae* (1909), a mix of traditional and newer forms of expression, was well received by critics. Pound was a leading force behind the poetic movement known as Imagism, one of the earliest forms of poetic Modernism. Partly drawn from tenets of classical Chinese and Japanese poetry—of which Pound was a translator—Imagism departs from the regular meter and rhyme and the elevated poetic diction of traditional poetry in English. Instead, Pound advocated the clear, precise, and economical use of language to achieve what he called "the direct treatment of the 'thing'." "In A Station of the Metro," below, is one of the most famous instances of an Imagist poem.

Pound's career was to take a disastrous turn when, in 1924, he moved to Italy, where he became involved in Fascist politics. During World War II, he broadcast fascist and anti-Semitic propaganda and hate-filled rants for the Italian government. During the American occupation of Italy, he was arrested for treason and imprisoned in a US military camp, where he suffered a mental breakdown; declared unfit for trial, he spent the following decade in an American psychiatric hospital. Pound's influence towers over Modernism, and recent scholars have argued that we must fully explore the connections between his politics and his art.

Note to readers: Pound's poem "Hugh Selwyn Mauberly/Life and Contacts" appears on the anthology's companion website. The URL and passcode appear in the Table of Contents.

The River-Merchant's Wife: A Letter[1]

While my hair was still cut straight across my forehead
I played about the front gate, pulling flowers.
You came by on bamboo stilts, playing horse,
You walked about my seat, playing with blue plums.
5   And we went on living in the village of Chōkan:[2]
Two small people, without dislike or suspicion.
At fourteen I married My Lord you.
I never laughed, being bashful.
Lowering my head, I looked at the wall.
10   Called to, a thousand times, I never looked back.

At fifteen I stopped scowling,
I desired my dust to be mingled with yours
Forever and forever and forever.
Why should I climb the look out?

15   At sixteen you departed,
You went into far Ku-tō-en,[3] by the river of swirling eddies,
And you have been gone five months.
The monkeys make sorrowful noise overhead.

You dragged your feet when you went out.
20   By the gate now, the moss is grown, the different mosses,
Too deep to clear them away!
The leaves fall early this autumn, in wind.
The paired butterflies are already yellow with August
Over the grass in the West garden;
25   They hurt me. I grow older.
If you are coming down through the narrows of the river Kiang,
Please let me know beforehand,
And I will come out to meet you
                    As far as Chō-fū-Sa.[4]

Rihaku
—1915

---

1   *The River-Merchant's ... Letter* Pound's adaptation of a poem by the Chinese poet Li Po
    (701–62 CE), whose name is given in its Japanese form ("Rihaku") at the end of the poem.
2   *Chōkan* Suburb of Nanking.
3   *Ku-tō-en* Chang Jiang, a Chinese river, also called the Yangtze Kiang in Japanese.
4   *Chō-fū-Sa* Chang-feng Sha, a beach located in Anhui several hundred miles upriver.

In a Station of the Metro

The apparition of these faces in the crowd;
Petals on a wet, black bough.

—1916 (earlier version published 1913)

A Pact

I make a pact with you, Walt Whitman[1]—
I have detested you long enough.
I come to you as a grown child
Who has had a pig-headed father;
I am old enough now to make friends.   5
It was you that broke the new wood,
Now is a time for carving.
We have one sap and one root—
Let there be commerce between us.

—1916

---

1   *Walt Whitman* American poet (1819–92) who invented free verse (p. 169).

H.D. (Hilda Doolittle)
1886–1961

H.D. was born Hilda Doolittle in Bethlehem, Pennsylvania. Early friendships with Ezra Pound and William Carlos Williams, who attended the University of Pennsylvania and lived near Doolittle, helped to shape her distinct artistic vision. Williams writes in his autobiography that the young Doolittle would splash ink on her clothes before writing poetry to give her "a feeling of freedom and indifference." H.D. moved to London in 1911, and in 1916 she worked with T.S. Eliot as literary editor of the *Egoist* magazine.

Much of her writing uses classical Greek mythology as subject matter, as well as symbols and images taken from Christianity and Egyptian culture. In using the classical past toward experimental ends, she shared a sensibility with some of her Modernist peers, in whose work we also see the combination of the ancient and the avant-garde. Though firmly part of the Modernist tradition, H.D. made a distinctive contribution in her emphasis on women's experiences. In the words of critic Gertrude Reif Hughes, H.D. "used the high Modernist devices and anti-heroic perspectives" of Modernist poetry to question gender roles.

For much of the twentieth century H.D.'s reputation was overshadowed by her male Modernist peers. Recent scholars have turned to fresh considerations of how gender played out in the artistic circles of Modernism as well as in the extraordinarily influential body of poetry they created.

Oread[1]

Whirl up, sea—
whirl your pointed pines,
splash your great pines
on our rocks,
5 hurl your green over us,
cover us with your pools of fir.

—1924

---

1   *Oread* A mountain nymph.

Robinson Jeffers
1887–1962

The beauty of nature compelled poet Robinson Jeffers. Its raw power and sheer otherness also compelled him to reconsider the category of the human. Born in Pittsburgh, Pennsylvania, Jeffers was well educated in subjects including Greek, literature, and forestry. In 1913 he moved to Carmel, California, a majestic coastal setting that inspired much of his writing. He was a poet of place, rooted in the specific landscapes of California, and in this regard is part of a long tradition of poets deeply tied to particular regions. He published a number of acclaimed volumes, including *The Woman at Point Sur* (1927), *Cawdor and Other Poems* (1928), and *Thurso's Landing* (1932), and appeared on the cover of *Time* magazine in 1932. Although his reputation then waned, Jeffers's intense and critical assessment of the human in relation to nature has brought him renewed attention as a caustic and admonitory early voice in environmental or eco-poetry.

Animals

At dawn a knot of sea-lions lies off the shore
In the slow swell between the rock and the cliff,
Sharp flippers lifted, or great-eyed heads, as they roll in the sea,
Bigger than draft-horses, and barking like dogs
Their all-night song. It makes me wonder a little   5
That life near kind to human, intelligent, hot-blooded, idle and singing, can
    float at ease
In the ice-cold winter water. Then, yellow dawn
Colors the south, I think about the rapid and furious lives in the sun:
They have little to do with ours; they have nothing to do with oxygen and
    salted water; they would look monstrous
If we could see them: the beautiful passionate bodies of living flame, batlike   10
    flapping and screaming,
Tortured with burning lust and acute awareness, that ride the storm-tides
Of the great fire-globe. They are animals, as we are. There are many other
    chemistries of animal life
Besides the slow oxidation of carbohydrates and amino-acids.

—1951

Marianne Moore
1887–1972

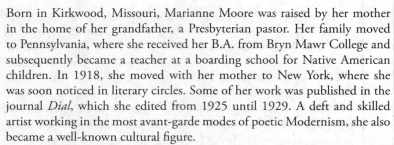

Born in Kirkwood, Missouri, Marianne Moore was raised by her mother in the home of her grandfather, a Presbyterian pastor. Her family moved to Pennsylvania, where she received her B.A. from Bryn Mawr College and subsequently became a teacher at a boarding school for Native American children. In 1918, she moved with her mother to New York, where she was soon noticed in literary circles. Some of her work was published in the journal *Dial,* which she edited from 1925 until 1929. A deft and skilled artist working in the most avant-garde modes of poetic Modernism, she also became a well-known cultural figure.

Moore is particularly well known for acute observation of nature rendered in poetic forms of her own design. She experimented with Modernist techniques such as fragments, collage, and found language (for example, incorporating language from other sources such as pamphlets) as well as with voice, rhythm, and meter. Animals were one of her frequent topics; she also wrote poems about mountains and the sea, as in "A Grave" (below). The poet James Dickey writes in praise of her style that "every poem of hers lifts us towards our own discovery-prone lives. It does not state, in effect, that I am more intelligent than you, more creative because I found this item and used it and you didn't. It seems to say, rather, I found this, and what did you find? Or, better, what *can* you find?"

A Grave

Man looking into the sea,
taking the view from those who have as much right to it as you have to
    yourself,
it is human nature to stand in the middle of a thing,
but you cannot stand in the middle of this;
5 the sea has nothing to give but a well excavated grave.
The firs stand in a procession, each with an emerald turkey-foot at the top,
reserved as their contours, saying nothing;
repression, however, is not the most obvious characteristic of the sea;
the sea is a collector, quick to return a rapacious look.
10 There are others besides you who have worn that look—
whose expression is no longer a protest; the fish no longer investigate them
for their bones have not lasted:
men lower nets, unconscious of the fact that they are desecrating a grave,

and row quickly away—the blades of the oars
moving together like the feet of water-spiders as if there were no such thing   15
    as death.
The wrinkles progress among themselves in a phalanx[1]—beautiful under
    networks of foam,
and fade breathlessly while the sea rustles in and out of the seaweed;
the birds swim through the air at top speed, emitting cat-calls as hereto-
    fore—
the tortoise-shell scourges about the feet of the cliffs, in motion beneath
    them;
and the ocean, under the pulsation of lighthouses and noise of bellbuoys,   20
advances as usual, looking as if it were not that ocean in which dropped
    things are bound to sink—
in which if they turn and twist, it is neither with volition nor consciousness.

—1921

---

1   *phalanx* Tightly organized group of soldiers in a military formation.

T.S. Eliot
1888–1965

No twentieth-century writer did more to shape the direction of modern poetry and criticism than T.S. Eliot. In poems such as "The Love Song of J. Alfred Prufrock" (1915) and *The Waste Land* (1922), Eliot founded a radical new poetical idiom. He was hailed as a poet who expressed the alienation and the "chaotic, irregular, fragmentary" experience of the modern mind, disconnected, in his view, from any meaningful sense of tradition. (See "The Hollow Men," below.) Eliot's poetry is deliberately challenging: he believed that "poets in our civilization, as it exists at present, must be *difficult*." His characteristic poetic techniques include allusion, fragmentation, discontinuity, quotation, and incorporation of other languages. His images are precise but often jarring and non-linear. He successfully created a new voice for a "modern" age in which many of his contemporaries felt the world had suddenly and dramatically changed, leaving humans adrift in a "dead land" (as he called it in *The Waste Land*): a civilization devoid of soul and meaning.

His many essays and reviews, notably "Tradition and the Individual Talent" (1919) and "The Metaphysical Poets" (1921), provided a theoretical foundation for New Criticism. Arguably the most prominent and long-lasting critical school of the twentieth century, the New Criticism focused not on the mind of the poet, historical context, or biographical information about the writer, but on the language of the poem itself as the source of meaning. This model of literary meaning, as well as Eliot's legacy more generally, would face stiff challenge during the canon and culture wars of the 1980s and 1990s. New scholarship about Eliot's anti-Semitism emerged in the late twentieth century and sparked additional discussion and debate (see Ezra Pound headnote, p. 341).

Nevertheless, his body of work is a key to literary Modernism as an historical phenomenon as well as a crucial window to understanding twentieth-century concepts of literary meaning. As Northrop Frye remarked, "Whether he is liked or disliked is of no importance, but he must be read." Allusions to his powerful renderings of the modern condition continue to run through high culture and through popular culture, in song lyrics (such as Arcade Fire's "Modern Man," p. 685), cartoons, and common idioms such as "April is the cruellest month."

Note to readers: Eliot's poem *The Waste Land* appears on the anthology's companion website. The URL and passcode appear in the Table of Contents.

The Love Song of J. Alfred Prufrock[1]

S'io credesse che mia risposta fosse
A persona che mai tornasse al mondo,
Questa fiamma staria senza piu scosse.
Ma perciocche giammai di questo fondo
Non torno viva alcun, s'i'odo il vero,
Senza tema d'infamia ti rispondo.[2]

Let us go then, you and I,
When the evening is spread out against the sky
Like a patient etherized upon a table;
Let us go, through certain half-deserted streets,
The muttering retreats   5
Of restless nights in one-night cheap hotels
And sawdust restaurants with oyster-shells:
Streets that follow like a tedious argument
Of insidious intent
To lead you to an overwhelming question ...   10
Oh, do not ask, "What is it?"
Let us go and make our visit.

In the room the women come and go
Talking of Michelangelo.

The yellow fog that rubs its back upon the window-panes,   15
The yellow smoke that rubs its muzzle on the window-panes
Licked its tongue into the corners of the evening,
Lingered upon the pools that stand in drains,
Let fall upon its back the soot that falls from chimneys,
Slipped by the terrace, made a sudden leap,   20
And seeing that it was a soft October night,
Curled once about the house, and fell asleep.

---

1   *J. Alfred Prufrock* The name is likely taken from the The Prufrock-Littau Company, a
    furniture dealer located in St. Louis, Eliot's birthplace.
2   *S'io credesse ... ti rispondo* Italian: "If I thought that my reply were given to anyone who
    might return to the world, this flame would stand forever still; but since never from this
    deep place has anyone ever returned alive, if what I hear is true, without fear of infamy
    I answer thee," Dante's *Inferno* 27.61–66; Guido da Montefeltro's speech as he burns in
    Hell.

And indeed there will be time
For the yellow smoke that slides along the street,
25 Rubbing its back upon the window panes;
There will be time, there will be time[1]
To prepare a face to meet the faces that you meet
There will be time to murder and create,
And time for all the works and days[2] of hands
30 That lift and drop a question on your plate;
Time for you and time for me,
And time yet for a hundred indecisions,
And for a hundred visions and revisions,
Before the taking of a toast and tea.

35 In the room the women come and go
Talking of Michelangelo.

And indeed there will be time
To wonder, "Do I dare?" and, "Do I dare?"
Time to turn back and descend the stair,
40 With a bald spot in the middle of my hair—
(They will say: "How his hair is growing thin!")
My morning coat,[3] my collar mounting firmly to the chin,
My necktie rich and modest, but asserted by a simple pin—
(They will say: "But how his arms and legs are thin!")
45 Do I dare
Disturb the universe?
In a minute there is time
For decisions and revisions which a minute will reverse.

For I have known them all already, known them all—
50 Have known the evenings, mornings, afternoons,
I have measured out my life with coffee spoons;
I know the voices dying with a dying fall[4]
Beneath the music from a farther room.
       So how should I presume?

---

1   *there will be time* See Ecclesiastes 3.1–8 in the Bible's Old Testament. "To everything
     there is a season, and a time to every purpose under heaven: A time to be born, and a
     time to die; a time to plant, and a time to pluck up that which is planted; a time to kill,
     and a time to heal...."
2   *works and days* Title of a poem by eighth-century BCE Greek poet Hesiod.
3   *morning coat* Formal coat with tails.
4   *with a dying fall* In Shakespeare's *Twelfth Night* 1.1.1–15 Duke Orsino commands,
     "That strain again, it had a dying fall."

And I have known the eyes already, known them all—   55
The eyes that fix you in a formulated phrase,
And when I am formulated, sprawling on a pin,
When I am pinned and wriggling on the wall,
Then how should I begin
To spit out all the butt-ends of my days and ways?   60
    And how should I presume?

And I have known the arms already, known them all—
Arms that are braceleted and white and bare
(But in the lamplight, downed with light brown hair!)
Is it perfume from a dress   65
That makes me so digress?
Arms that lie along a table, or wrap about a shawl.
    And should I then presume?
    And how should I begin?

      *   *   *

Shall I say, I have gone at dusk through narrow streets   70
And watched the smoke that rises from the pipes
Of lonely men in shirt-sleeves, leaning out of windows? ...[1]

I should have been a pair of ragged claws
Scuttling across the floors of silent seas.[2]

      *   *   *

And the afternoon, the evening, sleeps so peacefully!   75
Smoothed by long fingers,
Asleep ... tired ... or it malingers,
Stretched on the floor, here beside you and me.
Should I, after tea and cakes and ices,
Have the strength to force the moment to its crisis?   80
But though I have wept and fasted, wept and prayed,
Though I have seen my head (grown slightly bald) brought in upon a platter,[3]
I am no prophet[4]—and here's no great matter;

---

1   ... The ellipsis here makes note of a 38-line insertion written by Eliot, entitled *Prufrock's Pervigilium*. The subtitle and 33 of the lines were later removed.

2   *I should ... seas* See Shakespeare's *Hamlet* 2.2, in which Hamlet tells Polonius, "for you yourself, sir, should be old as I am, if like a crab you could go backwards."

3   *brought in upon a platter* Reference to Matthew 14.1–12, in which the prophet John the Baptist is beheaded at the command of Herod, and his head presented to Salomé upon a platter.

4   *I am no prophet* See Amos 7.14 in the Bible's Old Testament. When commanded by King Amiziah not to prophesize, the Judean Amos answered; "I was no prophet, neither was I a prophet's son; but I was a herdsman, and a farmer of sycamore fruit."

I have seen the moment of my greatness flicker,
85 And I have seen the eternal Footman hold my coat, and snicker,
And in short, I was afraid.

And would it have been worth it, after all,
After the cups, the marmalade, the tea,
Among the porcelain, among some talk of you and me,
90 Would it have been worth while,
To have bitten off the matter with a smile,
To have squeezed the universe into a ball[1]
To roll it toward some overwhelming question,
To say: "I am Lazarus,[2] come from the dead,
95 Come back to tell you all, I shall tell you all"—
If one, settling a pillow by her head,
        Should say: "That is not what I meant at all;
        That is not it, at all."

And would it have been worth it, after all,
100 Would it have been worth while,
After the sunsets and the dooryards and the sprinkled streets,[3]
After the novels, after the teacups, after the skirts that trail along the floor—
And this, and so much more?—
It is impossible to say just what I mean!
105 But as if a magic lantern[4] threw the nerves in patterns on a screen:
Would it have been worth while
If one, settling a pillow or throwing off a shawl,
And turning toward the window, should say:
        "That is not it at all,
110   That is not what I meant, at all."

                    *   *   *

No! I am not Prince Hamlet, nor was meant to be;
Am an attendant lord, one that will do
To swell a progress,[5] start a scene or two,
Advise the prince; no doubt, an easy tool,
115 Deferential, glad to be of use,

---

1   *squeezed ... ball* See Andrew Marvell's "To His Coy Mistress," 41–42 (p. 45): "Let us roll our strength and all / Our sweetness up into one ball."
2   *Lazarus* Raised from the dead by Jesus in John 11.1–44.
3   *sprinkled streets* Streets sprayed with water to keep dust down.
4   *magic lantern* In Victorian times, a device used to project images painted on glass onto a blank screen or wall.
5   *progress* Journey made by royalty through the country.

Politic, cautious, and meticulous;
Full of high sentence,[1] but a bit obtuse;
At times, indeed, almost ridiculous—
Almost, at times, the Fool.

I grow old ... I grow old ...   120
I shall wear the bottoms of my trousers rolled.

Shall I part my hair behind? Do I dare to eat a peach?
I shall wear white flannel trousers, and walk upon the beach.
I have heard the mermaids singing,[2] each to each.

I do not think that they will sing to me.   125

I have seen them riding seaward on the waves
Combing the white hair of the waves blown back
When the wind blows the water white and black.

We have lingered in the chambers of the sea
By sea-girls wreathed with seaweed red and brown   130
Till human voices wake us, and we drown.

—1915, 1917

The Hollow Men

Mistah Kurtz—he dead.[3]

A penny for the Old Guy[4]

I

We are the hollow men
We are the stuffed men
Leaning together
Headpiece filled with straw. Alas!
Our dried voices, when   5
We whisper together

---

1   *high sentence* Serious, elevated sentiments or opinions.
2   *I have ... singing* See John Donne's "Song": "Teach me to hear the mermaids singing."
3   *Mistah Kurtz ... dead* Reference to Joseph Conrad's *Heart of Darkness* (1899).
4   *A penny for the Old Guy* Phrase spoken by children asking for money to buy fireworks on
     Guy Fawkes Day, 5 November. Fawkes conspired with other English Catholics to blow
     up the House of Commons in 1605, and was executed.

Are quiet and meaningless
As wind in dry grass
Or rats' feet over broken glass
10 In our dry cellar

Shape without form, shade without colour,
Paralysed force, gesture without motion;

Those who have crossed
With direct eyes, to death's other Kingdom
15 Remember us—if at all—not as lost
Violent souls, but only
As the hollow men
The stuffed men.

II

Eyes I dare not meet in dreams
20 In death's dream kingdom
These do not appear:
There, the eyes are
Sunlight on a broken column
There, is a tree swinging
25 And voices are
In the wind's singing
More distant and more solemn
Than a fading star.

Let me be no nearer
30 In death's dream kingdom
Let me also wear
Such deliberate disguises
Rat's coat, crowskin, crossed staves

In a field
35 Behaving as the wind behaves
No nearer—

Not that final meeting
In the twilight kingdom

III

This is the dead land
This is cactus land
Here the stone images   40
Are raised, here they receive
The supplication of a dead man's hand
Under the twinkle of a fading star.

Is it like this   45
In death's other kingdom
Waking alone
At the hour when we are
Trembling with tenderness
Lips that would kiss   50
Form prayers to broken stone.

IV

The eyes are not here
There are no eyes here
In this valley of dying stars
In this hollow valley
This broken jaw of our lost kingdoms   55

In this last of meeting places
We grope together
And avoid speech
Gathered on this beach of the tumid river   60

Sightless, unless
The eyes reappear
As the perpetual star
Multifoliate rose[1]
Of death's twilight kingdom   65
The hope only
Of empty men.

---

1   *Multifoliate rose* May be an allusion to Dante's description of heaven as a many-petalled
     rose in his *Paradiso*.

V

Here we go round the prickly pear[1]
Prickly pear prickly pear
70 *Here we go round the prickly pear*
At five o'clock in the morning.

Between the idea
And the reality
Between the motion
75 And the act
Falls the Shadow
        For Thine is the Kingdom[2]
Between the conception
And the creation
80 Between the emotion
And the response
Falls the Shadow
        Life is very long

Between the desire
85 And the spasm
Between the potency
And the existence
Between the essence
And the descent
90 Falls the Shadow
        For Thine is the Kingdom

For Thine is
Life is
For Thine is the

95 *This is the way the world ends*
This is the way the world ends
This is the way the world ends
Not with a bang but a whimper.

—1925

---

1   *Here we go ... prickly pear* See the children's rhyme "Here we go round the mulberry bush."

2   *For Thine is the Kingdom* One of a number of references to the Lord's Prayer in the poem.

Journey of the Magi[1]

"A cold coming we had of it,
Just the worst time of the year
For a journey, and such a long journey:
The ways deep and the weather sharp,
The very dead of winter."[2]   5
And the camels galled, sore-footed, refractory,
Lying down in the melting snow.
There were times we regretted
The summer palaces on slopes, the terraces,
And the silken girls bringing sherbet.   10
Then the camel men cursing and grumbling
And running away, and wanting their liquor and women,
And the night-fires going out, and the lack of shelters,
And the cities hostile and the towns unfriendly
And the villages dirty and charging high prices: 15
A hard time we had of it.
At the end we preferred to travel all night,
Sleeping in snatches,
With the voices singing in our ears, saying
That this was all folly.   20

Then at dawn we came down to a temperate valley,
Wet, below the snow line, smelling of vegetation;
With a running stream and a water-mill beating the darkness,
And three trees[3] on the low sky,
And an old white horse[4] galloped away in the meadow.   25
Then we came to a tavern with vine-leaves over the lintel,°   *doorframe*
Six hands at an open door dicing for pieces of silver,[5]
And feet kicking the empty wine-skins.
But there was no information, and so we continued

---

1   *Magi* Three wise men who journeyed to Bethlehem to honor Jesus at his birth.
2   *A cold ... winter* Adapted from a sermon given by Anglican preacher Lancelot Andrews
    on Christmas Day, 1622.
3   *three trees* Suggests the three crosses on Calvary, on which Christ and two criminals
    were crucified (see Luke 23.32–43 in the Bible's New Testament).
4   *white horse* Ridden by Christ in Revelation 6.2 and 19.11–14.
5   *dicing ... silver* Allusion to Judas's betrayal of Jesus for 30 pieces of silver, and to the
    soldiers who played dice for the robes of Christ at his crucifixion (Matthew 26.14 and
    27.35).

30 And arrived at evening, not a moment too soon
   Finding the place; it was (you may say) satisfactory.

   All this was a long time ago, I remember,
   And I would do it again, but set down
   This set down
35 This: were we led all that way for
   Birth or Death? There was a Birth, certainly,
   We had evidence and no doubt. I had seen birth and death,
   But had thought they were different; this Birth was
   Hard and bitter agony for us, like Death, our death.
40 We returned to our places, these Kingdoms,
   But no longer at ease here, in the old dispensation,
   With an alien people clutching their gods.
   I should be glad of another death.

—1927

Claude McKay

1889–1948

Claude McKay brought a defiant and deeply empathetic voice to his poetry. A pioneering figure of the Harlem Renaissance, McKay devoted himself to activism and influenced a generation of young black poets.

Born in Sunny Ville, Jamaica, to a peasant family, McKay was educated by his brother and encouraged by neighbor Walter Jekyll to write poetry in Jamaican speech; in 1912 he published his first collections, *Songs of Jamaica* and *Constab Ballads*. Moving to Alabama to attend Tuskegee Institute before settling in New York, McKay witnessed the extreme bigotry of racially segregated America and began writing a new kind of poetry denouncing this injustice. In volumes *Spring in New Hampshire* (1920) and *Harlem Shadows* (1922), along with several novels and a short story collection, McKay depicted everyday experiences of black characters struggling with discrimination while discovering pride in their ancestry and cultural identities.

From 1922 to 1934, McKay lived in Europe and North Africa, writing, participating in Communist and socialist causes, and struggling with illness and poverty. Upon his return to America, he converted to Catholicism, working for the Catholic Youth Organization until his death in Chicago. Though McKay's popularity waned in his later years, there has been a resurgence of interest in his vivid portrayal of Harlem, his celebration of Jamaican peoples, and his dedication to giving voice to the oppressed.

The Lynching

His Spirit in smoke ascended to high heaven.
His father, by the cruelest way of pain,
Had bidden him to his bosom once again;
The awful sin remained still unforgiven.
All night a bright and solitary star[1]   5
(Perchance the one that ever guided him,
Yet gave him up at last to Fate's wild whim)
Hung pitifully o'er the swinging char.
Day dawned, and soon the mixed crowds came to view
The ghastly body swaying in the sun   10
The women thronged to look, but never a one
Showed sorrow in her eyes of steely blue;

---

1   *star* May be a reference to the North Star, which some escaping slaves used as a guide northward.

And little lads, lynchers that were to be,
Danced round the dreadful thing in fiendish glee.

—1920

America

Although she feeds me bread of bitterness,
And sinks into my throat her tiger's tooth,
Stealing my breath of life, I will confess
I love this cultured hell that tests my youth!
5 Her vigor flows like tides into my blood,
Giving me strength erect against her hate.
Her bigness sweeps my being like a flood.
Yet as a rebel fronts a king in state,
I stand within her walls with not a shred
10 Of terror, malice, not a word of jeer.
Darkly I gaze into the days ahead,
And see her might and granite wonders there,
Beneath the touch of Time's unerring hand,
Like priceless treasures sinking in the sand.

—1921

Edna St. Vincent Millay

1892–1950

One of the most famous and popular poets in the United States in the first half of the twentieth century, Edna St. Vincent Millay wrote the iconic line "My candle burns at both ends" in her poem "First Fig" (1920)—a poem that inspired the imaginations of an emerging generation of sexually liberated American women. This American poet and playwright embodied the spirit of rebellion characteristic of the 1920s. She was infamous for her daring, her captivating public readings of her poems, and her dramatic openness about her sexuality. (A male poet whose work spoke to similar energies was E.E. Cummings, p. 367.)

Millay demonstrated a talent for writing poetry at an early age, publishing numerous poems in *St. Nicholas*, a well-regarded popular children's magazine, as a teenager. Her long poem "Renascence," published in 1912 as part of a national poetry contest, caused a sensation. Following her graduation from Vassar College, Millay published her first book, *Renascence and Other Poems* (1917), and moved to Greenwich Village in New York. Over the next few years her growing reputation as a poet was matched by her reputation as a freethinker in the realm of sexual politics. She enjoyed her somewhat notorious public persona.

Although Millay's fame was earned primarily during the early years of her career, she remained active and innovative well into the 1940s. Her reputation fell from view after her death, when she became an emblem of an outmoded style of the woman poet, in part because her work was out of touch with a "Modernist" ethos that had come to dominate literary circles. Scholars have recently returned to her as one of the woman writers whose public poetry, commitment to oral delivery, and embrace of non-Modernist forms of poetry can show us aspects of poetic culture that long fell into shadow.

[I, being born a woman and distressed]

I, being born a woman and distressed
By all the needs and notions of my kind,
Am urged by your propinquity° to find   *proximity*
Your person fair, and feel a certain zest
To bear your body's weight upon my breast: 5
So subtly is the fume of life designed,
To clarify the pulse and cloud the mind,
And leave me once again undone, possessed.
Think not for this, however, the poor treason
Of my stout blood against my staggering brain,   10

I shall remember you with love, or season
My scorn with pity,—let me make it plain:
I find this frenzy insufficient reason
For conversation when we meet again.

—1923

[What lips my lips have kissed, and where, and why]

What lips my lips have kissed, and where, and why,
I have forgotten, and what arms have lain
Under my head till morning; but the rain
Is full of ghosts tonight, that tap and sigh
5   Upon the glass and listen for reply,
And in my heart there stirs a quiet pain
For unremembered lads that not again
Will turn to me at midnight with a cry.
Thus in winter stands the lonely tree,
10   Nor knows what birds have vanished one by one,
Yet knows its boughs more silent than before:
I cannot say what loves have come and gone;
I only know that summer sang in me
A little while, that in me sings no more.

—1923

I Too beneath Your Moon, Almighty Sex

I too beneath your moon, almighty Sex,
Go forth at nightfall crying like a cat,
Leaving the lofty tower I laboured at
For birds to foul and boys and girls to vex
5   With tittering chalk; and you, and the long necks
Of neighbours sitting where their mothers sat
Are well aware of shadowy this and that
In me, that's neither noble nor complex.
Such as I am, however, I have brought
10   To what it is, this tower; it is my own;
Though it was reared To Beauty, it was wrought
From what I had to build with: honest bone
Is there, and anguish; pride; and burning thought;
And lust is there, and nights not spent alone.

—1939

Wilfred Owen

1893–1918

One of 16 World War I poets commemorated in Westminster Abbey's Poet's Corner, Wilfred Owen is best remembered for poems such as "Anthem for Doomed Youth" and "Dulce et Decorum Est" (1920), in which he offers searing indictments of those who would send young men to war.

Owen began to experiment with poetry as a teenager. He spent the years prior to the war working as a lay assistant to the vicar of Dunsden, and later as a private tutor in Bordeaux, France. In 1915, he enlisted in the army and was commissioned as second lieutenant in the Manchester Regiment. The trauma he experienced on the front haunted Owen, who once spent days trapped in a dugout with the remains of a fellow officer. Diagnosed with shell shock in 1917, the poet was sent to recuperate at Craiglockhart War Hospital near Edinburgh. His biographer Jon Stallworthy suggests that the nightmares that are a symptom of shellshock were "a principal factor in the liberation and organization of [Owen's work....] The realities of battle, banished from his waking mind, [...] erupt into his dreams and into his poems."

At the War Hospital, he met fellow patient and recently published poet Siegfried Sassoon, who became a mentor to Owen. Up to this point, Owen's style had reflected his admiration of Romantic poets such as John Keats and Percy Shelley, but with Sassoon's encouragement, he abandoned Romantic poetics for a colloquial style similar to Sassoon's. Almost all of his best-known work was composed in the year before he was discharged from the War Hospital and sent back to France in August 1918.

Owen was killed in action one week before the end of the war.

Anthem for Doomed Youth

What passing-bells for these who die as cattle?
Only the monstrous anger of the guns.
Only the stuttering rifles' rapid rattle
Can patter out their hasty orisons.°   *prayers*
No mockeries for them from prayers or bells,   5
Nor any voice of mourning save the choirs,—
The shrill, demented choirs of wailing shells;
And bugles calling for them from sad shires.

What candles may be held to speed them all?
Not in the hands of boys, but in their eyes   10
Shall shine the holy glimmers of good-byes.

The pallor of girls' brows shall be their pall;[1]
Their flowers the tenderness of silent minds,
And each slow dusk a drawing-down of blinds.

—1920

Dulce et Decorum Est[2]

Bent double, like old beggars under sacks,
Knock-kneed, coughing like hags, we cursed through sludge,
Till on the haunting flares we turned our backs,
And towards our distant rest began to trudge.
5 Men marched asleep. Many had lost their boots,
But limped on, blood-shod. All went lame, all blind;
Drunk with fatigue; deaf even to the hoots
Of gas-shells dropping softly behind.
Gas! GAS! Quick, boys!—An ecstasy of fumbling,
10 Fitting the clumsy helmets just in time,
But someone still was yelling out and stumbling
And flound'ring like a man in fire or lime—
Dim, through the misty panes[3] and thick green light,
As under a green sea, I saw him drowning.

15 In all my dreams before my helpless sight
He plunges at me, guttering, choking, drowning.

If in some smothering dreams, you too could pace
Behind the wagon that we flung him in,
And watch the white eyes writhing in his face,
20 His hanging face, like a devil's sick of sin;
If you could hear, at every jolt, the blood
Come gargling from the froth-corrupted lungs,
Bitter as the cud
Of vile, incurable sores on innocent tongues,—
25 My friend, you would not tell with such high zest
To children ardent for some desperate glory,
The old Lie: Dulce et decorum est
Pro patria mori.

—1920

---

1   *pall* Cloth spread over a coffin, hearse, or tomb.
2   *Dulce et Decorum Est* Owen's poem takes its title from a famous line from the Roman
     poet Horace's *Odes* (3.2): "*Dulce et decorum est pro patria mori*" (Latin: "Sweet and fitting
     it is to die for one's country").
3   *panes* Visors of gas masks.

Dorothy Parker
1893–1967

Poets working in the mode of humor often hold a kind of second-class status in the canon of poetry, as if serious or "good" poetry cannot fundamentally be funny. In recent years, scholars have questioned definitions of "poetry" that exclude the many forms of popular verse, including oral-performance poetry, song lyrics, newspaper verse, advertisement jingles, and so on, that have long circulated as part of everyday social life. Dorothy Parker was notorious in her own time for her sharp—often scathing—sense of humor and her sarcasm, especially on topics relating to sex and relationships. A journalist at well-regarded newspapers and magazines such as *Vogue*, *The New Yorker*, and *Vanity Fair*, she was also a theater critic; a screenwriter; a playwright who also wrote some song lyrics; and the author of award-winning short stories and hundreds of poems in magazine and book form. Her first book of poems, *Enough Rope* (1926), was a bestseller.

Popular culture continues to pay homage to her penetrating voice. Prince's 1987 song "The Ballad of Dorothy Parker," includes the lines: "I'd been talkin' stuff in a violent room/Fighting with lovers past/I needed someone with a quicker wit than mine." In the selection below, Parker turns her quick wit on both romantic love and poetic history.

The Passionate Freudian to His Love

Only name the day, and we'll fly away
    In the face of old traditions,
To a sheltered spot, by the world forgot,
    Where we'll park our inhibitions.
Come and gaze in eyes where the lovelight lies   5
    As it psychoanalyzes,[1]
And when once you glean what your fantasies mean
    Life will hold no more surprises.
When you've told your love what you're thinking of
    Things will be much more informal;   10
Through a sunlit land we'll go hand-in-hand,
    Drifting gently back to normal.

---

1   *psychoanalyzes* The psychoanalytic method of Sigmund Freud (1856–1939) was a subject of intense cultural fascination in Parker's time. Freud's influential therapeutic methods to explore the unconscious and sexuality created a common cultural discourse that Parker plays with here, including the terms "repression," "inhibition," "ego," "libido" (sex drive), and "neurosis."

While the pale moon gleams,[1] we will dream sweet dreams,
    And I'll win your admiration,
15 For it's only fair to admit I'm there
    With a mean interpretation.
In the sunrise glow we will whisper low
    Of the scenes our dreams have painted,
And when you're advised what they symbolized
20   We'll begin to feel acquainted.
So we'll gaily float in a slumber boat
    Where subconscious waves dash wildly;
In the stars' soft light, we will say good-night—
    And "good-night!" will put it mildly.

25 Our desires shall be from repressions free—
    As it's only right to treat them.
To your ego's whims I will sing sweet hymns,
    And *ad libido*[2] repeat them.
With your hand in mine, idly we'll recline
30   Amid bowers of neuroses,
While the sun seeks rest in the great red west
    We will sit and match psychoses.
So come dwell a while on that distant isle
    In the brilliant tropic weather;
35 Where a Freud in need is a Freud indeed,
    We'll always be Jung[3] together.

—1921

---

1   *pale moon gleams* Parker's line wittily invokes the romantic language of Edgar Allan Poe's "Annabel Lee": "For the moon never beams, without bringing me dreams/Of the beautiful Annabel Lee" (p. 132).

2   *ad libido* Parker's recasting of the Latin term "ad infinitum," literally "to infinity" or forevermore.

3   *Jung* Carl Jung (1875–1961), a psychiatrist who worked, like Freud, on the development of the personality and the unconscious, but who also diverged from Freud's theories. The play on words "Jung/young" also recalls "Annabel Lee" as one of Parker's objects of satire.

E.E. Cummings
1894–1962

Edward Estlin Cummings is best known for his avant-garde poetry, in which he experiments with diction, syntax, grammar, spacing, breaks between words, and punctuation. Cummings's work found an unusually large popular audience, bringing experimental Modernist poems to a mainstream reader-ship. His many sources of appeal included his sexual frankness and humor. Like his contemporary Edna St. Vincent Millay (p. 361), Cummings had a lively and popular standing as a poet who spoke to the youthful rebellion and changing sexual mores of the 1920s.

Cummings grew up in an intellectual home in Cambridge, Massachu-setts, and attended Harvard, where several of his poems were published in the anthology *Eight Harvard Poets* (1917). Upon graduating during World War I, Cummings went to France to be an ambulance driver, but instead was put into an internment camp for "suspicious" foreigners. He fictionalized this experience in the prose work *The Enormous Room* (1922), which was much admired by other young writers.

His first book of poetry, *Tulips and Chimneys* (1923) showcased his facility with typographical experimentation and invented language. Like his Mod-ernist contemporary William Carlos Williams (p. 335) he typed his poems and made significant artistic use of that medium. The characteristic poem "[in Just-]," for example (below), describes a children's world using vibrant and playful terms such as "mud- / luscious," "balloonMan," and "puddle-wonderful." Cummings continued to write prolifically for the next several decades, producing 15 books of poems ranging from lyrical love poetry to cynical criticism of the modern world.

[i like my body when it is with your]

i like my body when it is with your
body. It is so quite new a thing.
Muscles better and nerves more.
i like your body. i like what it does,
i like its hows. i like to feel the spine   5
of your body and its bones, and the trembling
-firm-smooth ness and which i will
again and again and again
kiss,   i like kissing this and that of you,
i like, slowly stroking the, shocking fuzz   10

of your electric fur, and what-is-it comes
over parting flesh . . . . And eyes big love-crumbs,

and possibly i like the thrill

of under me you so quite new

—1923

[in Just-]

in Just-
spring   when the world is mud-
luscious the little
lame balloonman

5 whistles   far   and wee

and eddieandbill come
running from marbles and
piracies and it's
spring
10 when the world is puddle-wonderful

the queer
old balloonman whistles
far   and   wee
and bettyandisbel come dancing

15 from hop-scotch and jump-rope and
it's
spring
and
       the
20   goat-footed

balloonMan   whistles
far
and
wee

—1923

[the Cambridge ladies who live in furnished souls]

the Cambridge ladies who live in furnished souls
are unbeautiful and have comfortable minds
(also, with the church's protestant blessings
daughters, unscented shapeless spirited)
they believe in Christ and Longfellow,[1] both dead,   5
are invariably interested in so many things—
at the present writing one still finds
delighted fingers knitting for the is it Poles?
perhaps.   While permanent faces coyly bandy
scandal of Mrs. N and Professor D   10
. . . . the Cambridge ladies do not care, above
Cambridge if sometimes in its box of
sky lavender and cornerless, the
moon rattles like a fragment of angry candy

—1923

[may i feel said he]

may i feel said he
(i'll squeal said she
just once said he)
it's fun said she

(may i touch said he   5
how much said she
a lot said he)
why not said she

(let's go said he
not too far said she   10
what's too far said he
where you are said she)

may i stay said he
(which way said she
like this said he   15
if you kiss said she

---

1   *Longfellow* Henry Wadsworth Longfellow (1807–82), American poet (see p. 116).

may i move said he
is it love said she)
if you're willing said he
20 (but you're killing said she

but it's life said he
but your wife said she
now said he)
ow said she

25 (tiptop said he
don't stop said she
oh no said he)
go slow said she

(cccome?said he
30 ummm said she)
you're divine!said he
(you are Mine said she)

—1935

[l(a]

l(a

le
af
fa

5 ll

s)
one
l

iness

—1958

Hart Crane

1899–1932

Influenced by the innovations of Modernism and avidly embracing its aesthetic of difficulty, Hart Crane's poetry conveyed both alienation and optimism. Like his contemporary William Carlos Williams (see p. 335), he was among the poets deeply influenced by T.S. Eliot's massively influential poem *The Waste Land* (1922) yet who also wanted to counter it with a more optimistic vision of the individual and the modern age.

Born in Garrettsville, Ohio, Crane spent a turbulent childhood reading and teaching himself about poetry. He moved to New York City, where he immersed himself in a vibrant literary community. After publishing poems in literary magazines, Crane released his first collection, *White Buildings*, in 1926. His poems show the influence of his tumultuous relationships with male lovers as well as his travels to Europe, Cuba, and Mexico. In his most well known poem, the book-length epic *The Bridge* (1930), Crane crafted a mythic account of America, sweeping from the era of European explorers to the technological advances of the present. The poem's title invokes Brooklyn Bridge, a feat of modern engineering completed in 1883 whose aesthetic majesty Crane greatly admired.

Struggling with alcoholism and poor health, Crane traveled to Mexico, planning to write about Aztec history. He jumped overboard on the voyage home, drowning. Interest in his original voice and vision flourished as the twentieth century progressed; poets from Allen Ginsberg to Robert Lowell wrote tributes to him. One of the most original aspects of his poetry is his unique and complex work with metaphors that resist superficial interpretation and generate meanings through alternate pathways of association and layering. Recent scholars have situated Crane's linguistic experiments and innovations in part in relation to his own life in the closet.

My Grandmother's Love Letters

There are no stars tonight
But those of memory.
Yet how much room for memory there is
In the loose girdle of soft rain.

There is even room enough
For the letters of my mother's mother,
Elizabeth,
That have been pressed so long

5

Into a corner of the roof
10 That they are brown and soft,
And liable to melt as snow.

Over the greatness of such space
Steps must be gentle.
It is all hung by an invisible white hair.
15 It trembles as birch limbs webbing the air.

And I ask myself:

"Are your fingers long enough to play
Old keys that are but echoes:
Is the silence strong enough
20 To carry back the music to its source
And back to you again
As though to her?"

Yet I would lead my grandmother by the hand
Through much of what she would not understand;
25 And so I stumble. And the rain continues on the roof
With such a sound of gently pitying laughter.

—1920

Recitative

Regard the capture here, O Janus-faced,[1]
As double as the hands that twist this glass.
Such eyes at search or rest you cannot see;
Reciting pain or glee, how can you bear!

5 Twin shadowed halves: the breaking second holds
In each the skin alone, and so it is
I crust a plate of vibrant mercury
Borne cleft to you, and brother in the half.

---

1   *Janus-faced* Referring to Janus, the Roman god of doorways and of beginnings and end-
ings, who was depicted with two faces, one looking in either direction.

Inquire this much-exacting fragment smile,
Its drums and darkest blowing leaves ignore,—
Defer though, revocation of the tears
That yield attendance to one crucial sign.

Look steadily—how the wind feasts and spins
The brain's disk shivered against lust. Then watch
While darkness, like an ape's face, falls away,
And gradually white buildings answer day.

Let the same nameless gulf beleaguer us—
Alike suspend us from atrocious sums
Built floor by floor on shafts of steel that grant
The plummet[1] heart, like Absalom,[2] no stream.

The highest tower,—let her ribs palisade
Wrenched gold of Nineveh;[3]—yet leave the tower.
The bridge swings over salvage, beyond wharves;
A wind abides the ensign[4] of your will ...

In alternating bells have you not heard
All hours clapped dense into a single stride?
Forgive me for an echo of these things,
And let us walk through time with equal pride.

—1924

---

1   *plummet* Plumb line, a weighted line as a reference for vertical structures.
2   *Absalom* A son of King David in the Old Testament, Absalom died in battle when his
     head was caught in tree branches when riding and his enemies were able to kill him as he
     hung suspended. In life, Absalom built a pillar of stone as a monument to himself.
3   *Nineveh* Capital city of Assyria, rediscovered by archaeologists in the nineteenth century.
4   *ensign* Badge or emblem.

At Melville's Tomb[1]

Often beneath the wave, wide from this ledge
The dice of drowned men's bones he saw bequeath
An embassy.[2] Their numbers, as he watched,
Beat on the dusty shore and were obscured.

5 And wrecks passed without sound of bells,
The calyx[3] of death's bounty giving back
A scattered chapter, livid hieroglyph,
The portent wound in corridors of shells.

Then in the circuit calm of one vast coil,
10 Its lashings charmed and malice reconciled,
Frosted eyes there were that lifted altars:
And silent answers crept across the stars.

Compass, quadrant and sextant[4] contrive
No farther tides ... High in the azure steeps[5]
15 Monody[6] shall not wake the mariner.
This fabulous shadow only the sea keeps.

—1926

---

1   *At Melville's Tomb* Herman Melville (1819–91) (p. 161). Crane wrote this passionate
    elegy at a time when Melville, who died in obscurity in 1891, was being rediscovered. It
    was only in the 1920s that *Moby-Dick* was first identified as a great work of literature.
2   *dice ... embassy* [Crane's note] Dice bequeath an embassy, in the first place, by being
    ground (in this connection only, of course) in little cubes from the bones of drowned men
    by the action of the sea, and are finally thrown up on the sand, having "numbers" but no
    identification. These being the bones of dead men who never completed their voyage, it
    seems legitimate to refer to them as the only surviving evidence of certain things, experi-
    ences that the dead mariners might have had to deliver.
3   *calyx* [Crane's note] This calyx refers in a double ironic sense both to a cornucopia and
    the vortex made by a sinking vessel.
4   *Compass ... sextant* Navigational equipment.
5   *azure steeps* Bright blue sky.
6   *Monody* Poetic lament about a death; Crane refers here to Melville's poem titled "Mon-
    ody," published in *Timoleon, Etc.* (1891), a cry of grief over the death of a beloved male
    whom the poem does not name.

Ernest Hemingway

1899–1961

Though he went on to become a celebrated novelist and short story writer, winning the Nobel Prize for literature in 1954, Ernest Hemingway's first book also showed him to be a poet. He published *Three Stories and Ten Poems* when he was 24 years old, working as a foreign correspondent for the *Toronto Star*, and living in Paris with his first wife, Hadley.

Hemingway's early work was influenced by the American writer Sherwood Anderson, who wrote both poetry and realist fiction, and especially by his friend Gertrude Stein (see p. 318). Stein published the first, cryptic review of *Three Stories and Ten Poems*, writing that Hemingway should "stick to poetry and intelligence and eschew the hotter emotions." Stein's advice and example shaped Hemingway's famously clean and economical prose style. Though Hemingway seems to have written little poetry after the 1920s, his early poems remain important to his development as a writer. Hemingway's fourth wife, Mary, quoted him as saying of his writing, "The secret is that it is poetry written into prose, and that is the hardest of all things to do."

Montparnasse[1]

There are never any suicides in the quarter among people one knows
No successful suicides.
A Chinese boy kills himself and is dead.
(they continue to place his mail in the letter rack at the Dome)[2]
A Norwegian boy kills himself and is dead.   5
(no one knows where the other Norwegian boy has gone)
They find a model dead
alone in bed and very dead.
(it made almost unbearable trouble for the concierge)
Sweet oil, the white of eggs, mustard and water, soap suds[3]   10
and stomach pumps rescue the people one knows.
Every afternoon the people one knows can be found at the café.

—1923

---

1   *Montparnasse* District in Paris famous for its intellectual and artistic residents in the twentieth century until the start of World War II.
2   *Dome Le Dôme Café*, a restaurant in Montparnasse frequented by Hemingway and many other American intellectuals.
3   *Sweet ... suds* Methods to induce vomiting.

Sterling A. Brown
1901–1989

Born into an African-American middle class family in Washington, DC, Brown was well educated for his time, graduating with honors from Williams College and earning a Master's degree at Harvard in an era when most Americans did not continue their education beyond high school. Moving to Virginia as a college teacher in the 1920s, he studied the rural cultures of African-American people there and published a volume of poems, *Southern Road* (1932). Inspired more generally by artistic trends in Modernist poetry, including its incorporation of everyday speech (as in the notable and highly popular case of Robert Frost), Brown's poems often represented the speech of African-American "folk" communities. At the same time, he rejected the racial stereotypes that appeared in poems by some of his African-American poetic predecessors, such as Paul Laurence Dunbar (p. 302). Brown saw himself as part of what he called a "New Negro Renaissance" in the United States, rejecting the more locally specific, urban term "Harlem Renaissance." (His poem "Harlem Happiness," below, acknowledges the importance of Harlem as a cultural locale in the era of "New Negro" arts. "Negro" was the term many African-American artists themselves used, terminology that would shift as cultural politics shifted in the decades to come.)

A wide-ranging writer in many genres, including essays and anthologies about "Negro" contributions to the arts in the United States, Brown taught at Howard University until 1969. Although he had stopped writing poetry in the 1940s, his poems came to renewed attention in the 1970s, when a broad revolution in the curriculum established a new array of programs and departments of African-American studies. His career spanned a tumultuous and transformative time for African-American culture and arts.

Harlem Happiness[1]

I think there is in this the stuff for many lyrics:—the
A dago[2] fruit stand at three A.M.; the wop[3] asleep, his woman
Knitting a tiny garment, laughing when we approached her,
Flashing a smile from white teeth, then weighing out the grapes,

---

1   Slang terms for ethnic and racial groups were common in the New York metropolitan area at this time, a cultural reaction to the millions of immigrants who arrived in the US between 1880 and 1920. In 1915–16, the "Great Migration" of African-Americans from the rural South to the urban North had also begun. When and whether such slang terms functioned as slurs depended on the particular context.
2   *dago* Slang for an Italian, Spanish, or Portuguese person, here meaning Italian.
3   *wop* Slang for a person from Italy or southern Europe.

Grapes large as plums, and tart and sweet as—well we know the lady   5
And purplish red and firm, quite as this lady's lips are....
We laughed, all three when she awoke her swarthy, snoring Pietro[1]
To make us change, which we, rich paupers, left to help the garment.
We swaggered off; while they two stared, and laughed in understanding,
And thanked us lovers who brought back an old Etrurian[2] springtide.   10
Then, once beyond their light, a step beyond their pearly smiling
We tasted grapes and tasted lips, and laughed at sleepy Harlem,
And when the huge Mick[3] cop stomped by, a'swingin' of his billy[4]
You nodded to him gaily, and I kissed you with him looking,
Beneath the swinging light that weakly fought against the mist   15
That settled on Eighth Avenue, and curled around the houses.
And he grinned too and understood the wisdom of our madness.
That night at least the world was ours to spend, nor were we misers.
Ah, Morningside with Maytime awhispering in the foliage!
Alone, atop the city,—the tramps were still in shelter—   20
And moralizing lights that peered up from the murky distance
Seemed soft as our two cigarette ends burning slowly, dimly,
And careless as the jade stars that winked upon our gladness....

And when I flicked my cigarette, and we watched it falling, falling,
It seemed a shooting meteor, that we, most proud creators   25
Sent down in gay capriciousness upon a trivial Harlem—

And then I madly quoted lyrics from old kindred masters,[5]
Who wrote of you, unknowing you, for far more lucky me—
And you sang broken bits of song, and we both slept in snatches,
And so the night sped on too swift, with grapes, and words and kisses,   30
And numberless cigarette ends glowing in the darkness
Old Harlem slept regardless, but a motherly old moon—
Shone down benevolently on two happy wastrel lovers....

—1980 (written 1932)

---

1   *Pietro* The speaker of the poem calls "the wop" by the Italian name "Pietro," which might
    or might not be his actual name or might function as an ethnic stereotype.
2   *Etrurian* An ancient term for a region in central Italy.
3   *Mick* Slang for an Irish person.
4   *billy* A police officer's club. Irish immigrants frequently settled in Northeastern cities like
    New York and Boston. A significant number of Irish males eventually found employment
    on urban police forces. As a result, the image of an Irish police officer became a stereo-
    type.
5   *old kindred masters* Poets of the past whose love poetry the speaker can recite.

Bitter Fruit of the Tree

They said to my grandmother: "Please do not be bitter,"
When they sold her first-born and let the second die,
When they drove her husband till he took to the swamplands,
And brought him home bloody and beaten at last.
5 They told her, "It is better you should not be bitter,
Some must work and suffer so that we, who must, can live,
Forgiving is noble, you must not be heathen bitter;
These are your orders: you *are* not to be bitter."
And they left her shack for their porticoed house.

10 They said to my father: "Please do not be bitter,"
When he ploughed and planted a crop not his,
When he weatherstripped a house that he could not enter,
And stored away a harvest he could not enjoy.
They answered his questions: "It does not concern you,
15 It is not for you to know, it is past your understanding,
All you need know is: you must not be bitter."

—1980 (written 1939)

Langston Hughes
1902–1967

In his first autobiography, *The Big Sea* (1940), Langston Hughes wrote, "my best poems were all written when I felt the worst. When I was happy, I didn't write anything." His career produced many lyric poems that have the sadness but also the vitality of jazz, blues, and bebop, and that participate in an African-American tradition of struggle for positive social change. Hughes contributed to American letters not only as a poet but also as a playwright, journalist, short story writer, novelist, historian, and translator.

In the early 1920s Hughes worked odd jobs—including a stint on an American freighter traveling the African coastline—as he began to publish his work in magazines. His first poetry collection, *Weary Blues* (1926), established him as a major figure in the Harlem Renaissance, a movement of African-American writers, artists, and musicians that flourished in the 1920s and 1930s. Even more than some of his Harlem Renaissance contemporaries, Hughes celebrated black working-class culture and experience in his writing.

Hughes became a Marxist in the 1930s, and he spent time in Haiti, Cuba, and the USSR learning about alternatives to American politics and economics. He also began to address contemporary urban politics more directly in his work, pronouncing his faith in Marxism in poems such as "Goodbye Christ" (1932): "And nobody's gonna sell ME / To a king, or a general, / Or a millionaire." Hughes abandoned Communism after World War II but continued to write on political themes; his last work, for example, *The Panther and the Lash* (1967), was a collection of poetry focused on the civil rights movement.

The Negro Speaks of Rivers

(*To W.E.B. Du Bois*)[1]

I've known rivers:
I've known rivers ancient as the world and older than the flow of human
    blood in human veins.
My soul has grown deep like the rivers.

---

1   *W.E.B. Du Bois* (1868–1963) Major African-American intellectual; sociologist; historian of topics including slavery, Reconstruction, and African-American experience in the US; activist and one of the founders of the NAACP (National Association for the Advancement of Colored People).

I bathed in the Euphrates when dawns were young.
5 I built my hut near the Congo and it lulled me to sleep.
I looked upon the Nile and raised the pyramids above it.
I heard the singing of the Mississippi when Abe Lincoln went down
        to New Orleans,[1] and I've seen its muddy bosom turn all golden
        in the sunset.

I've known rivers:
Ancient, dusky rivers.

10 My soul has grown deep like the rivers.

                                —1926

The Weary Blues

Droning a drowsy syncopated tune,
Rocking back and forth to a mellow croon,
        I heard a Negro play.
Down on Lenox Avenue[2] the other night
5 By the pale dull pallor of an old gas light
        He did a lazy sway. . . .
        He did a lazy sway. . . .
To the tune o' those Weary Blues.
With his ebony hands on each ivory key
10 He made that poor piano moan with melody.
        O Blues!
Swaying to and fro on his rickety stool
He played that sad raggy tune like a musical fool.
        Sweet Blues!
15 Coming from a black man's soul.
        O Blues!
In a deep song voice with a melancholy tone
I heard that Negro sing, that old piano moan—
        "Ain't got nobody in all this world,
20   Ain't got nobody but ma self.
        I's gwine to quit ma frownin'

---

1   *when Abe ... New Orleans* In 1831, Lincoln traveled down the Mississippi to New Or-
leans, where he witnessed the brutality of the slave market there. Some biographers sug-
gest that this experience consolidated his opinion against slavery.
2   *Lenox Avenue* In Harlem.

And put ma troubles on the shelf."
Thump, thump, thump, went his foot on the floor.
He played a few chords then he sang some more—
    "I got the Weary Blues   25
    And I can't be satisfied.
    Got the Weary Blues
    And can't be satisfied—
    I ain't happy no mo'
    And I wish that I had died."   30
And far into the night he crooned that tune.
The stars went out and so did the moon.
The singer stopped playing and went to bed
While the Weary Blues echoed through his head
He slept like a rock or a man that's dead.   35

                                —1926

Harlem (2)

What happens to a dream deferred?

    Does it dry up
    like a raisin in the sun?
    Or fester like a sore—
    And then run?
    Does it stink like rotten meat?   5
    Or crust and sugar over—
    like a syrupy sweet?
    Maybe it just sags
    like a heavy load.   10

    Or does it explode?

                                —1951

from *Montage of a Dream Deferred*

Low to High

How can you forget me?
But you do!
You said you was gonna take me
Up with you—
5 Now you've got your Cadillac,
you done forgot that you are black.
How can you forget me
When I'm you?

But you do.

10 How can you forget me,
fellow, say?
How can you low-rate me
this way?
You treat me like you damn well please,
15 Ignore me—though I pay your fees.
How can you forget me?

But you do.

High to Low

God knows
We have our troubles, too—
One trouble is you:
you talk too loud,
5 cuss too loud
look too black,
don't get anywhere,
and sometimes it seems
you don't even care.
10 The way you send your kids to school
stockings down,
(not Ethical Culture)[1]

---

1   *Ethical Culture* The Ethical Culture School in New York was a progressive private school.
    Hughes is using the school as a marker of upper-middle-class culture.

the way you shout out loud in church,
(not St. Phillips)[1]

and the way you lounge on doorsteps   15
just as if you were down South,
(not at 409)[2]
the way you clown—
the way, in other words,
you let me down—   20
me, trying to uphold the race
and you—
well, you can see,
we have our problems,
too, with you.   25

Shame on You

If you're great enough
And clever enough
The government might honor you.
But the people will forget—
Except on holidays.   5

A movie house in Harlem named after Lincoln.
Nothing at all named after John Brown.[3]

Black people don't remember.
Any better than white.

If you're not alive and kicking,   10
shame on you!

---

1   *St. Phillips* An African-American Episcopal church in Harlem.
2   *409* 409 Edgecombe Avenue in Harlem, an upscale apartment building where a number
      of well-known artists and writers lived.
3   *John Brown* Brown was a white American activist for the abolition of slavery who be-
      lieved that violent overthrow of the slave system was necessary and justified. In 1859,
      he led an armed attack on the federal armory in Harpers Ferry, Virginia, that he hoped
      would inaugurate slave insurrection broadly across the South. He was hanged for it. His
      revolt on behalf of enslaved African-Americans was one of the cataclysmic events that
      precipitated the American Civil War.

World War II

What a grand time was the war!
Oh, my, my!
What a grand time was the war!
My, my, my!

5 In wartime we had fun,
Sorry that old war is done!
What a grand time was the war,
My, my!

Echo:

10 *Did*
Somebody
Die?

—1951

Stevie Smith
[Florence Margaret Smith]
1902–1971

Stevie Smith's poetry is deceptively simple. Its plain language, playful rhymes, odd syntax, and repetitive, singsong rhythms convey a child-like sensibility—one accentuated by the bizarre "doodles" of men, women, and animals that she included with her writing. Beneath her poetry's light-hearted and humorous surface, however, is a serious engagement with such concepts as loneliness, religion, suicide, and death. As poet Peter Porter suggests, Smith was not the "naive writer" she appeared to be; on the contrary, "her unshockable eye and brilliant ear enabled her to cover almost all the unmentionable topics."

Smith lived most of her life in London, where she worked as a secretary. Her first published work was a novel entitled *Novel on Yellow Paper* (1936); its commercial success enabled her to publish her first volume of poems, *A Good Time Was Had by All* (1937). Smith would go on to write seven more poetry collections, as well as short stories, essays, literary reviews, and two more novels.

Skilled at performing her own verse, Smith was a popular figure at poetry readings in the 1960s. Although she had a large and admiring readership, for most of her career she did not receive a great deal of approval from critics, who were put off by the atypical, apparently frivolous tone of her work. However, she had gained respect as a serious poet by the time her *Selected Poems* was published in 1962, and in the last years of her life she received the Queen's Gold Medal for Poetry (1969).

Not Waving but Drowning

Nobody heard him, the dead man,
But still he lay moaning:
I was much further out than you thought
And not waving but drowning.

Poor chap, he always loved larking
And now he's dead
It must have been too cold for him his heart gave way,
They said.

5

Oh, no no no, it was too cold always
10 (Still the dead one lay moaning)
I was much too far out all my life
And not waving but drowning.

—1957

Thoughts about the Person from Porlock[1]

Coleridge received the Person from Porlock
And ever after called him a curse
Then why did he hurry to let him in?
He could have hid in the house.

5 It was not right of Coleridge in fact it was wrong
(But often we all do wrong)
As the truth is I think he was already stuck
With Kubla Khan.

He was weeping and wailing: I am finished, finished,
10 I shall never write another word of it,
When along comes the Person from Porlock
And takes the blame for it.

It was not right, it was wrong,
But often we all do wrong.

*

15 May we inquire the name of the Person from Porlock?
Why, Porson, didn't you know?
He lived at the bottom of Porlock Hill
So had a long way to go,

---

1   *Thoughts about the Person from Porlock*   British poet Samuel Coleridge wrote the celebrat-
ed 1816 poem "Kubla Khan" (see p. 79) after taking a painkiller (possibly opium) and
falling into a "profound sleep." Coleridge believed he composed over 200 lines of "Kubla
Khan" while he slept and started to transcribe them as soon as he woke up. After writing
54 lines, he was interrupted by "a person on business from Porlock," who distracted Cole-
ridge enough that upon returning to finish transcribing the poem, he had forgotten the
remainder and was unable to recreate it. The idea of the "person from Porlock" became
famous in poetic circles.

He wasn't much in the social sense
Though his grandmother was a Warlock,   20
One of the Rutlandshire[1] ones I fancy
And nothing to do with Porlock,

And he lived at the bottom of the hill as I said
And had a cat named Flo,
And had a cat named Flo.   25

I long for the Person from Porlock
To bring my thoughts to an end,
I am becoming impatient to see him
I think of him as a friend,

Often I look out of the window   30
Often I run to the gate
I think, He will come this evening,
I think it is rather late.

I am hungry to be interrupted
For ever and ever amen   35
O Person from Porlock come quickly
And bring my thoughts to an end.

*

I felicitate the people who have a Person from Porlock
To break up everything and throw it away
Because then there will be nothing to keep them   40
And they need not stay.

*

Why do they grumble so much?
He comes like a benison[2]
They should be glad he has not forgotten them
They might have had to go on.   45

---

1   *Rutlandshire* Rutland County.
2   *benison* Blessing.

*

These thoughts are depressing I know. They are depressing,
I wish I was more cheerful, it is more pleasant,
Also it is a duty, we should smile as well as submitting
To the purpose of One Above who is experimenting
50 With various mixtures of human character which goes best,
All is interesting for him it is exciting, but not for us.
There I go again. Smile, smile, and get some work to do
Then you will be practically unconscious without positively having to go.

—1962

Countee Cullen
1903–1946

Left without family as a teen, Countee Cullen was raised by an influential pastor in Harlem, at a time when the creative energies of the Harlem Renaissance were producing an outpouring of artistic innovation. Cullen became one of the movement's most famous and well-regarded poets. He excelled in high school, graduated from New York University, and took a master's degree at Harvard. While still a young man, he won literary prizes, published poems in elite magazines, published books of poetry (his first volume *Color*, came out in 1925, followed by *Copper Sun* in 1927 and *The Black Christ, and Other Poems* in 1929), and edited a collection of poems by African-Americans, *Caroling Dusk: An Anthology of Verse by Negro Poets* (1927). In a media-worthy social match, he married the daughter of the African-American intellectual and sociologist of race W.E.B. Du Bois in 1928. (The marriage soon ended in divorce.) While other well-received African-American poets of this era, such as Sterling A. Brown and Langston Hughes, created their poetic voices from African-American speech patterns, musical forms, and local cultures (in Brown's case, the rural South), Cullen's poetry was traditional in form and diction. Heavily influenced by the British Romantics whom he revered, and by Keats in particular, Cullen pursued a path for the African-American poet about which he and his contemporaries heatedly disagreed.

Yet Do I Marvel

I doubt not God is good, well-meaning, kind,
And did He stoop to quibble could tell why
The little buried mole continues blind,
Why flesh that mirrors Him must some day die,
Make plain the reason tortured Tantalus[1]   5
Is baited by the fickle fruit, declare
If merely brute caprice dooms Sisyphus[2]
To struggle up a never-ending stair.
Inscrutable His ways are, and immune
To catechism by a mind too strewn   10

---

1   *Tantalus* In Greek mythology, a Lydian king tortured in Hades by being forced to stand
     in water that receded when he tried to drink, and under a tree with fruit that receded
     when he tried to pluck it.
2   *Sisyphus* The legendary king of Corinth was condemned in Hades to roll a large stone
     to the top of a hill, whence it would roll down again, requiring him to repeat the task in
     perpetuity.

With petty cares to slightly understand
What awful brain compels His awful hand.
Yet do I marvel at this curious thing:
To make a poet black, and bid him sing!

—1925

From the Dark Tower

(*To Charles S. Johnson*)[1]

We shall not always plant while others reap
The golden increment of bursting fruit,
Not always countenance, abject and mute,
That lesser men should hold their brothers cheap;
5   Not everlastingly while others sleep
Shall we beguile their limbs with mellow flute,
Not always bend to some more subtle brute;
We were not made eternally to weep.

The night whose sable breast relieves the stark,
10   White stars is no less lovely being dark,
And there are buds that cannot bloom at all
In light, but crumple, piteous, and fall;
So in the dark we hide the heart that bleeds,
And wait, and tend our agonizing seeds.

—1927

---

1   *Charles S. Johnson* As Clifton H. Johnson explains, "From 1926 to 1928, Cullen was
assistant editor to Charles S. Johnson of *Opportunity* (subtitled 'A Journal of Negro Life')
for which he also wrote a feature column, 'The Dark Tower.'" Cullen's reviews and com-
mentaries struck sometimes contradictory notes: he called upon African-American writ-
ers to create a representative and respectable race literature and also insisted that the
African-American artist should not be bound by race or restricted to racial themes.

Lorine Niedecker

1903–1970

Lorine Niedecker was born and raised on Black Hawk Island, in rural Wisconsin, and lived much of her life in the area. Though her poetry was influenced by this rich natural environment and by the area's history, she was also closely connected to contemporary poetics—and politics. In 1931 Niedecker wrote to the poet Louis Zukofsky (see p. 399), beginning a long friendship that shaped the work of both poets. Niedecker is often classed as an "Objectivist" poet, a group including Zukofsky and George Oppen (see p. 409), though she did not readily accept the label. The critic Jenny Lynn Penberthy writes that Niedecker admired the Objectivists' lack of sentimentality, but that her interest in exploring and representing levels of consciousness also drew her to Surrealism. Niedecker's formally and thematically varied output includes the "folk poems" of *New Goose* (1946), a series of haiku, and several long autobiographical poems. Her poetry is notable for its precise deployment of both sound and silence. Niedecker repeatedly expressed a dislike for poetry readings and for reading aloud, writing in a letter, "I like planting poems in deep silence, [where] each person gets at the poem for himself."

Paean[1] to Place

And the place
was water

Fish
fowl
flood   5
Water lily mud
My life

in the leaves and on water
My mother and I
born   10
in swale[2] and swamp and sworn
to water

---

1   *Paean* Song or poem of praise.
2   *swale* Low-lying marsh-like area.

My father
thru marsh fog
15 sculled° down   *rowed*
from high ground
saw her face

at the organ
bore the weight of lake water
20 and the cold—
he seined¹ for carp to be sold
that their daughter

might go high
on land
25 to learn
Saw his wife turn
deaf

and away
She
30 who knew boats
and ropes
no longer played

She helped him string out nets
for tarring
35 And she could shoot
He was cool
to the man

who stole his minnows
by night and next day offered
40 to sell them back
He brought in a sack
of dandelion greens

---

1   *seined* I.e., fished using a seine net.

if no flood
No oranges—none at hand
No marsh marigolds 45
where the water rose
He kept us afloat

I mourn her not hearing canvasbacks[1]
their blast-off rise
from the water 50
Not hearing sora
rails's[2] sweet

spoon-tapped waterglass-
descending scale-
tear-drop-tittle 55
Did she giggle
as a girl?

His skiff skimmed
the coiled celery now gone
from these streams 60
due to carp
He knew duckweed[3]

fall-migrates
toward Mud Lake bottom
Knew what lay 65
under leaf decay
and on pickerel weeds

before summer hum
To be counted on:
new leaves 70

---

1   *canvasbacks* Types of duck.
2   *sora rails* Small water birds.
3   *duckweed* Small plant that grows in abundance on still water in wetlands.

new dead
leaves

He could not
—like water bugs—
75   stride surface tension
He netted
loneliness

As to his bright new car
my mother—her house
80   next his—averred:
A hummingbird
can't haul

Anchored here
in the rise and sink
85   of life—
middle years' nights
he sat

beside his shoes
rocking his chair
90   Roped not "looped
in the loop
of her hair"[1]

I grew in green
slide and slant
95   of shore and shade
Child-time—wade
thru weeds

---

1   *looped ... hair* See the William Butler Yeats poem "Brown Penny" (1910).

Maples to swing from
Pewee-glissando[1]
sublime   100
slime-
song

Grew riding the river
Books
at home-pier   105
Shelley could steer
as he read[2]

I was the solitary plover[3]
a pencil
for a wing-bone   110
From the secret notes
I must tilt

upon the pressure
execute and adjust
In us sea-air rhythm   115
"We live by the urgent wave
of the verse"

Seven year molt
for the solitary bird
and so young   120
Seven years the one
dress

for town once a week
One for home

---

1   *Pewee-glissando Pewee* Small gray North American bird; *glissando* Musical term describ-
    ing a gradual slide from one note into another.
2   *Shelley ... read* Before drowning in a boating accident at sea, British poet Percy Bysshe
    Shelley (1782–1822) often went sailing with friends and family.
3   *plover* Type of wading bird.

125 faded blue-striped
as she piped
her cry

Dancing grounds
my people had none
130 woodcocks[1] had—
backland-
air around

Solemnities
such as what flower
135 to take
to grandfather's grave
unless

water lilies—
he who'd bowed his head
140 to grass as he mowed
Iris now grows
on fill

for the two
and for him
145 where they lie
How much less am I
in the dark than they?

Effort lay in us
before religions
150 at pond bottom
All things move toward
the light

---

1   *woodcocks* Types of wading bird.

except those
that freely work down
to oceans' black depths
In us an impulse tests
the unknown

155

River rising—flood
Now melt and leave home
Return—broom wet
naturally wet
Under

160

soak-heavy rug
water bugs hatched—
no snake in the house
Where were they?—
she

165

who knew how to clean up
after floods
he who bailed boats, houses
Water endows us
with buckled floors

170

You with sea water running
in your veins sit down in water
Expect the long-stemmed blue
speedwell[1] to renew
itself

175

O my floating life
Do not save love
for things
Throw things
to the flood

180

---

1   *speedwell* Type of flower.

ruined
by the flood
185 Leave the new unbought—
all one in the end—
water

I possessed
the high word:
190 The boy my friend
played his violin
in the great hall

On this stream
my moonnight memory
195 washed of hardships
maneuvers barges
thru the mouth

of the river
They fished in beauty
200 It was not always so
In Fishes
red Mars

rising
rides the sloughs and sluices
205 of my mind
with the persons
on the edge

—1968

Louis Zukofsky
1904–1978

Seldom anthologized and little known to general readers, Louis Zukofsky was nonetheless a force in twentieth-century poetry. Zukofsky was born to Yiddish-speaking Russian Jewish immigrants in New York, and his early exposure to literature was in the Yiddish theater and Yiddish poetry. Attending Columbia University and maintaining friendships with such prominent poets as Ezra Pound and William Carlos Williams, Zukofsky became part of the world of avant-garde poetry, and in 1931 he edited an important volume of *Poetry* magazine devoted to what he called "Objectivist" poetry. Objectivism was concerned with the "poem as object," avoiding transcendent, mystical sentiments in favor of the particular and concrete; along with Zukofsky, the poets Lorine Niedecker (see p. 391) and George Oppen (see p. 409) are often identified with the movement. Though its meaning was disputed and the label sometimes disclaimed (Zukofsky expressed distrust of "isms"), Objectivism was a major influence on later poets, especially the Language poets (see p. 653).

Zukofsky worked on the long multi-part poem *"A"* from 1928 until his death in 1978. More than 800 pages long in its published form, the poem ranges from the political to the domestic, shifting in tone, style, and form as Zukofsky's poetry matures. It was painstakingly crafted, with Zukofsky counting the words and even the syllables of many sections, but is also strikingly personal—the critic Barry Ahearn compares it to William Wordsworth's long autobiographical poem *The Prelude*.

from *"A"*

A-16

An
inequality

wind flower

—1964

John Betjeman
1906–1984

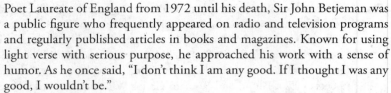

Poet Laureate of England from 1972 until his death, Sir John Betjeman was a public figure who frequently appeared on radio and television programs and regularly published articles in books and magazines. Known for using light verse with serious purpose, he approached his work with a sense of humor. As he once said, "I don't think I am any good. If I thought I was any good, I wouldn't be."

Born in London, Betjeman published his first book of poems in 1931. During the early 1930s he also worked as the assistant editor of *The Architectural Review*, where he developed a lifelong passion for architecture that would provide the subject matter for some of his poems as well as several prose books and documentaries. He continued to write and publish poetry while working for the British Representative in Dublin as a Press Officer, for the Ministry of Information on film propaganda during World War II, and for various newspapers and magazines as a freelance journalist.

Betjeman's *Collected Poems* (1958) was well received by the public and critics alike, and with its publication he became what literary critic Ralph J. Mills describes as "a phenomenon in contemporary English literature, a truly popular poet." Betjeman was awarded the Queen's Gold Medal for poetry in 1960, and was knighted in 1969.

In Westminster Abbey[1]

Let me take this other glove off
   As the *vox humana*[2] swells,
And the beauteous fields of Eden
   Bask beneath the Abbey bells.
5 Here, where England's statesmen lie,
Listen to a lady's cry.

Gracious Lord, oh bomb the Germans.[3]
   Spare their women for Thy Sake,
And if that is not too easy
10   We will pardon Thy Mistake.

---

1   *Westminster Abbey* Important central London church where coronations are held and where many influential political figures, scientists, and intellectuals are buried.

2   *vox humana* Set of pipes in a pipe organ, so named because their sound resembles that of a human voice.

3   *bomb the Germans* This poem was published during World War II.

But, gracious Lord, whate'er shall be,
Don't let anyone bomb me.

Keep our Empire undismembered
 Guide our Forces by Thy Hand,
Gallant blacks from far Jamaica,   15
 Honduras and Togoland;[1]
Protect them Lord in all their fights,
And, even more, protect the whites.

Think of what our Nation stands for,
 Books from Boots[2] and country lanes,   20
Free speech, free passes, class distinction,
 Democracy and proper drains.
Lord, put beneath Thy special care
One-eighty-nine Cadogan Square.

Although dear Lord I am a sinner,   25
 I have done no major crime;
Now I'll come to Evening Service
 Whensoever I have the time.
So, Lord, reserve for me a crown,
And do not let my shares go down.   30

I will labour for Thy Kingdom,
 Help our lads to win the war,
Send white feathers to the cowards[3]
 Join the Women's Army Corps,
Then wash the Steps around Thy Throne   35
In the Eternal Safety Zone.

Now I feel a little better,
 What a treat to hear Thy Word
Where the bones of leading statesmen,
 Have so often been interred.   40
And now, dear Lord, I cannot wait
Because I have a luncheon date.

           —1940

---

1 *Togoland* Area of western Africa once divided into French Togoland (now the Republic of Togo) and British Togoland (now part of Ghana).
2 *Boots* British chain of for-profit libraries that rented books to customers.
3 *Send white ... cowards* Reference to the practice of giving out white feathers (symbolizing cowardice) to men not in military uniform as a means of shaming them into enlisting. This occurred during both world wars.

W.H. Auden

1907–1973

W.H. Auden's poetry documents the changing political, social, and psychological landscape of his time, describing society's material troubles and seeking a clear understanding of human existence. His work often couples contemporary speech with more traditional, structured verse forms.

Born in York, England, Wystan Hugh Auden spent his childhood in Birmingham. He won a scholarship to study natural science at Oxford, but a developing passion for poetry soon led him to transfer to English literature. He became the central member of a cohort of writers known as the "Oxford Group," and soon after graduation he published his first major volume, *Poems* (1930).

In the 1930s, Auden traveled extensively and worked variously as a schoolmaster, a university lecturer, a writer of nonfiction and experimental drama, and a verse commentator on documentary films. Though he was gay, in 1935 he entered into a marriage of convenience with Erika Mann, daughter of the German novelist Thomas Mann, to enable her escape from Nazi Germany. During the Spanish Civil War (1936–39), Auden volunteered as a propaganda writer on the side of the left—an experience that left him somewhat disillusioned with socialist politics.

In 1939, Auden moved to New York, where he settled for most of his later life. A year later he published *Another Time* (1940), which includes some of his best-known poems, such as "Musée des Beaux Arts" and "September 1, 1939" (both below). From then on, his work began to take on more subjective overtones, often with religious themes (he had abandoned Anglicanism as a youth, but returned to it in 1941). While his earlier poetry had examined concrete social ills, his later poetry developed a more complex worldview, often casting social problems in terms of personal responsibility.

With *The Collected Poetry* (1945), Auden began revising his earlier work, a task that included rewriting and even suppressing some of his most left-wing poems. When he was awarded the National Medal for Literature in 1967, the committee declared that Auden's work, "branded by the moral and ideological fires of our age, breathes with eloquence, perception, and intellectual power."

Funeral Blues[1]

Stop all the clocks, cut off the telephone,
Prevent the dog from barking with a juicy bone,
Silence the pianos and with muffled drum
Bring out the coffin, let the mourners come.

Let aeroplanes circle moaning overhead   5
Scribbling on the sky the message He is Dead,
Put crêpe bows[2] round the white necks of the public doves,
Let the traffic policemen wear black cotton gloves.

He was my North, my South, my East and West,
My working week and my Sunday rest,   10
My noon, my midnight, my talk, my song;
I thought that love would last forever: I was wrong.

The stars are not wanted now; put out every one;
Pack up the moon and dismantle the sun;
Pour away the ocean and sweep up the wood;   15
For nothing now can ever come to any good.

—1936, 1940

Musée des Beaux Arts

About suffering they were never wrong,
The Old Masters: how well they understood
Its human position; how it takes place
While someone else is eating or opening a window or just walking
        dully along;
How, when the aged are reverently, passionately waiting   5
For the miraculous birth, there always must be
Children who did not specially want it to happen, skating
On a pond at the edge of the wood:

---

1   *Funeral Blues* This poem first appeared in *The Ascent of F6* (1936), a play co-written by
    Auden and Christopher Isherwood. A revised version with the present title later appeared
    in Auden's 1940 collection *Another Time*. The original 1936 version has five stanzas and
    is considerably more satirical.
2   *crêpe bows* Black crêpe, a woven fabric with a wrinkled surface, is often associated with
    mourning.

They never forgot
10 That even the dreadful martyrdom must run its course
Anyhow in a corner, some untidy spot
Where the dogs go on with their doggy life and the torturer's horse
Scratches its innocent behind on a tree.

In Brueghel's *Icarus*[1] for instance: how everything turns away
15 Quite leisurely from the disaster; the ploughman may
Have heard the splash, the forsaken cry,
But for him it was not an important failure; the sun shone
As it had to on the white legs disappearing into the green
Water; and the expensive delicate ship that must have seen
20 Something amazing, a boy falling out of the sky,
Had somewhere to get to and sailed calmly on.

—1940

September 1, 1939[2]

I sit in one of the dives
On Fifty-second Street
Uncertain and afraid
As the clever hopes expire
5 Of a low dishonest decade:
Waves of anger and fear
Circulate over the bright
And darkened lands of the earth,
Obsessing our private lives;
10 The unmentionable odour of death
Offends the September night.

---

1   *Brueghel's Icarus* The reference is to *Landscape with the Fall of Icarus* (c. 1555), a painting
by Pieter Brueghel the Elder. It references an ancient Greek story in which Daedalus and
his son Icarus tried to escape from Crete, where they were imprisoned, using wings of
feathers and wax. Icarus flew too high, the wax melted, and he drowned. In Brueghel's
painting, an ordinary farmer plowing on a hill dominates the foreground, while Icarus's
drowning body appears very small in the ocean below, next to a much larger ship.
2   *September 1, 1939* Date of Hitler's invasion of Poland; France and Britain declared war
on Germany two days later. Auden had left England to take up residence in the United
States the previous January.

Accurate scholarship can
Unearth the whole offence
From Luther[1] until now
That has driven a culture mad,   15

Find what occurred at Linz,[2]
What huge imago[3] made
A psychopathic god:
I and the public know
What all schoolchildren learn,   20
Those to whom evil is done
Do evil in return.

Exiled Thucydides[4] knew
All that a speech can say
About Democracy,   25
And what dictators do,
The elderly rubbish they talk
To an apathetic grave;
Analysed all in his book,
The enlightenment driven away,   30
The habit-forming pain,
Mismanagement and grief:
We must suffer them all again.

Into this neutral air
Where blind skyscrapers use   35
Their full height to proclaim   /
The strength of Collective Man,

---

1   *Luther* Martin Luther (1483–1546), the German religious leader whose attacks on eccle-
     siastical corruption began the Protestant Reformation in Europe. Luther's writings grew
     markedly more anti-Semitic as he aged; in his book *Mein Kampf,* Hitler ranks Martin
     Luther as a great German cultural hero.
2   *Linz* Capital of upper Austria where Hitler grew up.
3   *imago* Psychoanalytic term for an idealized image of a person; imagos are formed in
     childhood and influence adult behavior.
4   *Thucydides* Athenian historian (c. 460–c. 395 BCE) whose failure as a naval commander
     led to his 20-year exile, during which time he wrote *The History of the Peloponnesian
     War.* In his *History,* Thucydides records Pericles's funeral oration for the dead Athenian
     soldiers, which outlines the dangers and benefits of democracy. Elected 16 times to the
     position of general, Pericles instituted many democratic reforms while retaining a signifi-
     cant degree of personal power.

Each language pours its vain
Competitive excuse:
40 But who can live for long
In an euphoric dream;
Out of the mirror they stare,
Imperialism's face
And the international wrong.

45 Faces along the bar
Cling to their average day:
The lights must never go out,
The music must always play,
All the conventions conspire
50 To make this fort assume
The furniture of home;
Lest we should see where we are,
Lost in a haunted wood,
Children afraid of the night
55 Who have never been happy or good.

The windiest militant trash
Important Persons shout
Is not so crude as our wish:
What mad Nijinsky[1] wrote
60 About Diaghilev
Is true of the normal heart;
For the error bred in the bone
Of each woman and each man
Craves what it cannot have,
65 Not universal love
But to be loved alone.

From the conservative dark
Into the ethical life
The dense commuters come,
70 Repeating their morning vow;

---

1   *Nijinsky* Vaslav Nijinsky (1890–1950), Russian ballet dancer and choreographer, worked
with the Russian ballet producer Sergei Diaghilev (1872–1929) until their falling out in
1913. In 1917 Nijinsky's mental instability forced him into permanent retirement. In his
diary, published in 1937, Nijinsky wrote: "Some politicians are hypocrites like Diaghilev,
who does not want universal love, but to be loved alone. I want universal love."

"I *will* be true to the wife,
I'll concentrate more on my work,"
And helpless governors wake
To resume their compulsory game:
Who can release them now,   75
Who can reach the deaf,
Who can speak for the dumb?

Defenceless under the night
Our world in stupor lies;
Yet, dotted everywhere,   80
Ironic points of light
Flash out wherever the Just
Exchange their messages:
May I, composed like them
Of Eros[1] and of dust,   85
Beleaguered by the same
Negation and despair,
Show an affirming flame.

—1940

The Unknown Citizen

(*To JS/07/M/378*
This Marble Monument
Is Erected by the State)

He was found by the Bureau of Statistics to be
One against whom there was no official complaint,
And all the reports on his conduct agree
That, in the modern sense of an old-fashioned word, he was a saint,
For in everything he did he served the Greater Community.   5
Except for the War till the day he retired
He worked in a factory and never got fired,
But satisfied his employers, Fudge Motors Inc.
Yet he wasn't a scab[2] or odd in his views,
For his Union reports that he paid his dues,   10

---

1   *Eros* In contrast to the New Testament *agape*, or Christian love, *eros* represents earthly, or
     sexual love. In Greek myth, the winged Eros, son of Aphrodite, is the god of love.
2   *scab* Someone who works during a strike or refuses to join a union.

(Our report on his Union shows it was sound)
And our Social Psychology workers found
That he was popular with his mates and liked a drink.
The Press are convinced that he bought a paper every day
15 And that his reactions to advertisements were normal in every way.
Policies taken out in his name prove that he was fully insured,
And his Health-card shows he was once in hospital but left it cured.
Both Producers Research and High-Grade Living declare
He was fully sensible to the advantages of the Instalment Plan
20 And had everything necessary to the Modern Man,
A phonograph, a radio, a car and a frigidaire.
Our researchers into Public Opinion are content
That he held the proper opinions for the time of year;
When there was peace, he was for peace; when there was war, he went.
25 He was married and added five children to the population,
Which our Eugenist[1] says was the right number for a parent of his generation.
And our teachers report that he never interfered with their education.
Was he free? Was he happy? The question is absurd:
Had anything been wrong, we should certainly have heard.

—1940

---

1   *Eugenist* Scientist who studies the development of physically or mentally improved human beings through selective breeding. Eugenics has played a key role in legitimizing racist ideologies such as Nazism.

George Oppen
1908–1984

George Oppen was an avant-garde poet and publisher who contributed to a new poetic movement in the 1930s that came to be called "Objectivism." He founded cutting-edge presses in France and the United States that cultivated the careers of new poets, distributing their work in a marketplace that would otherwise have shut them out.

After 1934 Oppen and his wife turned their attention to activism, helping those struggling through the Great Depression, and both joined the Communist Party. Oppen eventually distanced himself from the Party, and he fought in Europe during World War II, for which service he received a Purple Heart. However, the Oppens still fell under scrutiny during the anti-Communist fervor following the war, and in 1950 they went into exile in Mexico City. In 1958 Oppen returned to the United States and resumed writing, publishing first *The Materials* (1962) and then *This in Which* (1965).

The "Objectivist" label was one that these poets bristled against. Although they tended to share similar leftist political views as well as social and publishing networks, they did not necessarily share the same ideas about poetics. Oppen and some other Objectivists (like Louis Zukofsky, p. 399, and, later, Lorine Niedecker, p. 391) valued clarity, everyday diction, and highly concentrated language. (In the latter regard, they built on the work of their predecessors working in Imagism; see Ezra Pound and H.D., pp. 341 and 344.) Scholar and poet Eleanor Berry points out that Objectivist poets tended to use language "more literally than figuratively, presenting concrete objects for themselves rather than as embodiments of abstract ideas." (See "Psalm," below.) Among the "concrete objects" they valued was the poem itself as a material object in the world—rather than as a window to transcendental abstractions beyond the poem. From this vantage, the Objectivist project stands in a long history of competing definitions of what poetry is, does, or "should" be.

Psalm

Veritas sequitur ...[1]
In the small beauty of the forest
The wild deer bedding down—
That they are there!

---

1   *Veritas sequitur* Latin: truth follows. The complete expression is *"veritas sequitur esse"* ("truth follows the existence of things").

5   Their eyes
        Effortless, the soft lips
        Nuzzle and the alien small teeth
        Tear at the grass

                The roots of it
10   Dangle from their mouths
        Scattering earth in the strange woods.
        They who are there.

                Their paths
        Nibbled thru the fields, the leaves that shade them
15   Hang in the distances
        Of sun

                The small nouns
        Crying faith
        In this in which the wild deer
20   Startle, and stare out.

                                        —1963

The Forms of Love

        Parked in the fields
        All night
        So many years ago,
        We saw
5   A lake beside us
        When the moon rose.
        I remember

        Leaving that ancient car
        Together. I remember
10   Standing in the white grass
        Beside it. We groped
        Our way together
        Downhill in the bright
        Incredible light

Beginning to wonder   15
Whether it could be lake
Or fog
We saw, our heads
Ringing under the stars we walked
To where it would have wet our feet   20
Had it been water

—1964

Latitude, Longitude

      climbed from the road and found
over the flowers at the mountain's
rough top a bee yellow
and heavy as

      pollen in the mountainous   5
air thin legs crookedly
a-dangle if we could

find all
the gale's evidence what message
is there for us in these   10
glassy bottles the Encyclopedist

was wrong was wrong many things
too foolish
to sing
may be said this matter-   15
of-fact defines

poetry

—1975

Theodore Roethke

1908–1963

Known for his introspective verse, as well as for his struggles with mental health, Theodore Roethke was both praised and criticized for his inward focus. Some critics saw his personal exploration as a source of valuable insight, but others thought it too limited and irrelevant to the political and social concerns of the day. Roethke read widely, and his style was influenced by the poets he admired, such as William Blake, T.S. Eliot, and W.B. Yeats. He also formed literary friendships with fellow poets W.H. Auden, Dylan Thomas, and William Carlos Williams.

Born in Michigan into a German-American family, Roethke had ambivalent childhood memories of his horticulturalist father that centered on the family's extensive greenhouses. Images of growth, decay, and death recur in his poetry, especially in what he referred to as the "greenhouse poems" included in *The Lost Son and Other Poems* (1948). Roethke said that he could sometimes find refuge and solace in nature; the greenhouse was like an intermediate space in which nature was cultivated and arranged according to human principles of order. By contrast, joyful love is the subject of "I Knew a Woman" from *Words for the Wind* (1958), published after his marriage to Beatrice O'Connell. *Words for the Wind* marked a new direction for Roethke, who frequently returned to love poetry in his later work. He was passionately committed to rhythm as a poetic principle, noting that his poems were written to be heard aloud, like music. His poems also addressed rhythmic subjects such as the bodily movements of dancing and sex.

Roethke taught at Michigan State College and was very dedicated to his teaching; however, he was dismissed after the first of what became a series of mental breakdowns and psychiatric hospitalizations. He then taught at the University of Washington where, although he was often unwell, he was valued for both his teaching and his writing. Roethke's honors include the Pulitzer Prize, two National Book Awards, and the Shelley Memorial Award.

My Papa's Waltz

The whiskey on your breath
Could make a small boy dizzy;
But I hung on like death:
Such waltzing was not easy.

5 We romped until the pans
Slid from the kitchen shelf;

My mother's countenance
Could not unfrown itself.

The hand that held my wrist
Was battered on one knuckle;   10
At every step you missed
My right ear scraped a buckle.

You beat time on my head
With a palm caked hard by dirt,
Then waltzed me off to bed   15
Still clinging to your shirt.

                                                —1948

Root Cellar

Nothing would sleep in that cellar, dank as a ditch,
Bulbs broke out of boxes hunting for chinks in the dark,
Shoots dangled and drooped,
Lolling obscenely from mildewed crates,
Hung down long yellow evil necks, like tropical snakes.   5
And what a congress of stinks!—
Roots ripe as old bait,
Pulpy stems, rank, silo-rich,
Leaf-mould, manure, lime, piled against slippery planks.
Nothing would give up life: 10
Even the dirt kept breathing a small breath.

                                                —1948

I Knew a Woman

I knew a woman, lovely in her bones,
When small birds sighed, she would sigh back at them;
Ah, when she moved, she moved more ways than one:
The shapes a bright container can contain!
Of her choice virtues only gods should speak,   5
Or English poets who grew up on Greek
(I'd have them sing in chorus, cheek to cheek).

How well her wishes went! She stroked my chin,
She taught me Turn, and Counter-turn, and Stand;[1]
10 She taught me Touch, that undulant white skin;
I nibbled meekly from her proffered hand;
She was the sickle; I, poor I, the rake,
Coming behind her for her pretty sake
(But what prodigious mowing we did make).

15 Love likes a gander, and adores a goose:
Her full lips pursed, the errant note to seize;
She played it quick, she played it light and loose;
My eyes, they dazzled at her flowing knees;
Her several parts could keep a pure repose,
20 Or one hip quiver with a mobile nose
(She moved in circles, and those circles moved).

Let seed be grass, and grass turn into hay:
I'm martyr to a motion not my own;
What's freedom for? To know eternity.
25 I swear she cast a shadow white as stone.
But who would count eternity in days?
These old bones live to learn her wanton ways:
(I measure time by how a body sways).

—1958

---

1   *Turn, and Counter-turn, and Stand* Allusion to *strophe, antistrophe,* and *epode,* the three
parts of a typical Greek ode.

Charles Olson

1910–1970

A major American poet and critic of the mid-twentieth century, Charles Olson was part of the "Black Mountain School," including Robert Duncan, Robert Creeley, and Denise Levertov. All were affiliated in various ways with the experimental arts school Black Mountain College, where Olson taught. (The College opened in 1933 and closed in 1957.) In his 1950 manifesto, "Projective Verse," Olson advocated a poetics based not in traditional concepts of rhyme and meter but on the line as a unit of meaning tied to the poet's breath and speech. Scholars Eleanor Berry and Alan Golding describe Olson's manifesto as one of the most influential statements in American poetics since World War II and "a starting point for innovative poetry in the period." His formal experimentation aimed to move past "closed" or traditional forms into "open" forms arising organically from the poet's energies, yet not rooted in the poet's ego. Olson was to exert tremendous influence on experimental poetries in the decades to come.

Olson's major poetic work is *The Maximus Poems* (1953), a book-length epic combining a broad recounting of American history with a meditation on Gloucester, Massachusetts, where Olson settled. Like Herman Melville, a writer he revered, he imagined the local (New England) in light of the global (the Yucatan Peninsula and the world at large). History as he understood it enabled a focus on a particular place while opening up, much like his poetry, to a wider world.

As the Dead Prey Upon Us

As the dead prey upon us,
they are the dead in ourselves,
awake, my sleeping ones, I cry out to you,
disentangle the nets of being!

I pushed my car, it had been sitting so long unused.   5
I thought the tires looked as though they only needed air.
But suddenly the huge underbody was above me, and the rear tires
were masses of rubber and thread variously clinging together

as were the dead souls in the living room, gathered
about my mother, some of them taking care to pass   10
beneath the beam of the movie projector, some record
playing on the victrola, and all of them
desperate with the tawdriness of their life in hell

I turned to the young man on my right and asked, "How is it,
15 there?" And he begged me protestingly don't ask, we are poor
poor. And the whole room was suddenly posters and presentations
of brake linings and other automotive accessories, cardboard
displays, the dead roaming from one to another
as bored back in life as they are in hell, poor and doomed
20 to mere equipments

                my mother, as alive as ever she was, asleep
when I entered the house as I often found her in a rocker
under the lamp, and awaking, as I came up to her, as she ever had

I found out she returns to the house once a week, and with her
25 the throng of the unknown young who center on her as much in death
as other like suited and dressed people did in life

O the dead!

          and the Indian woman and I
          enabled the blue deer[1]
30   to walk

          and the blue deer talked,
          in the next room,
          a Negro talk

          it was like walking a jackass,
35   and its talk
          was the pressing gabber of gammers[2]
          of old women

          and we helped walk it around the room
          because it was seeking socks
40   or shoes for its hooves
          now that it was acquiring

          human possibilities

---

1   *blue deer* Sacred animal to the indigenous Huichol people of Mexico. In stories, the blue
deer is followed to gain enlightenment.
2   *gammers* Old women.

In the five hindrances[1] men and angels
stay caught in the net, in the immense nets
which spread out across each plane of being, the multiple nets   45
which hamper at each step of the ladders as the angels
and the demons
and men
go up and down

          Walk the jackass   50
          Hear the victrola
          Let the automobile
          be tucked into a corner of the white fence
          when it is a white chair. Purity

is only an instant of being, the trammels[2]   55

recur

In the five hindrances, perfection
is hidden
          I shall get
          to the place   60
          10 minutes late.

          It will be 20 minutes
          of 9. And I don't know,

          without the car,

          how I shall get there   65

O peace, my mother, I do not know
how differently I could have done
what I did or did not do.

          That you are back each week
          that you fall asleep   70
          with your face to the right

---

1   *the five hindrances* In Buddhism, five mental states that block the path to enlightenment.
2   *trammels* Fishing nets.

that you are present there
when I come in as you were
when you were alive

75   that you are as solid, and your flesh
is as I knew it, that you have the company
I am used to your having

but o, that you all find it
such a cheapness!

80   o peace, mother, for the mammothness
of the comings and goings
of the ladders of life

The nets we are entangled in. Awake,
my soul, let the power into the last wrinkle
85   of being, let none of the threads and rubber of the tires
be left upon the earth. Let even your mother
go. Let there be only paradise

The desperateness is, that the instant
which is also paradise (paradise
90   is happiness) dissolves
into the next instant, and power
flows to meet the next occurrence

Is it any wonder
my mother comes back?
95   Do not that throng
rightly seek the room
where they might expect
happiness? They did not complain
of life, they obviously wanted
100   the movie, each other, merely to pass
among each other there,
where the real is, even to the display cards,
to be out of hell

The poverty
105   of hell

O souls, in life and in death,
make, even as you sleep, even in sleep
know what wind
even under the crankcase of the ugly automobile
lifts it away, clears the sodden weights of goods,   110
equipment, entertainment, the foods the Indian woman,
the filthy blue deer, the 4 by 3 foot 'Viewbook,'[1]
the heaviness of the old house, the stuffed inner room
lifts the sodden nets

     and they disappear as ghosts do,   115
     as spider webs, nothing
     before the hand of man

     The vent! You must have the vent,
     or you shall die. Which means
     never to die, the ghastliness   120

     of going, and forever
     coming back, returning
     to the instants which were not lived

     O mother, this I could not have done,
     I could not have lived what you didn't,   125
     I am myself netted in my own being

     I want to die. I want to make that instant, too,
     perfect

     O my soul, slip
     the cog   130

II

The death in life (death itself)
is endless, eternity
is the false cause

---

1   *Viewbook* Promotional booklet issued by colleges and universities for prospective stu-
    dents.

The knot is otherwise, each topological corner
135 presents itself, and no sword
cuts it,[1] each knot is itself its fire

each knot of which the net is made
is for the hands to untake
the knot's making. And touch alone

140 can turn the knot into its own flame

         (o mother, if you had once touched me

         o mother, if I had once touched you)

The car did not burn. Its underside
was not presented to me
145 a grotesque corpse. The old man

merely removed it as I looked up at it,
and put it in a corner of the picket fence
like was it my mother's white dog?

or a child's chair

150   The woman,
         playing on the grass,
         with her son (the woman next door)

         was angry with me whatever it was
         slipped across the playpen or whatever
155   she had out there on the grass

         And I was quite flip in reply
         that anyone who used plastic
         had to expect things to skid

---

1   *knot ... cuts it* Reference to the legendary Gordian knot, which was thought to be impossible to untangle until Alexander the Great solved the problem by cutting through it with his sword.

and break, that I couldn't worry
that her son might have been hurt   160
by whatever it was I sent skidding

down on them.

It was just then I went into my house
and to my utter astonishment
found my mother sitting there   165

as she always had sat, as must she always
forever sit there her head lolling
into sleep? Awake, awake my mother

what wind will lift you too
forever from the tawdriness,   170
make you rich as all those souls

crave crave crave

to be rich?

They are right. We must have
what we want. We cannot afford   175
not to. We have only one course:

the nets which entangle us are flames

        O souls, burn
        alive, burn now

        that you may forever   180
        have peace, have

        what you crave

        O souls,
        go into everything,
        let not one knot pass   185
        through your fingers

let not any they tell you
you must sleep as the net
comes through your authentic hands

190   What passes
is what is, what shall be, what has
been, what hell and heaven is
is earth to be rent, to shoot you
through the screen of flame which each knot
195   hides as all knots are a wall ready
to be shot open by you

                           the nets of being
are only eternal if you sleep as your hands
ought to be busy. Method, method

200   I too call on you to come
to the aid of all men, to women most
who know most, to woman to tell
men to awake. Awake, men,
awake

205   I ask my mother
to sleep. I ask her
to stay in the chair.
My chair
is in the corner of the fence.
210   She sits by the fireplace made of paving stones. The blue deer
need not trouble either of us.

And if she sits in happiness the souls
who trouble her and me
will also rest. The automobile

215   has been hauled away.

                                              —1956

"Rufus Woodpecker ..."[1]

Rufus Woodpecker visited the President
today. The subject of their discussion
was foreign policy. He advised

that bi-partisanship must be replaced
by symbiosis,[2] or else. Citing   5
his own experience with

the Black Tree Ants (they live together
despite mutual self-destruction) he showed
how the whole sub-continent changed,

between dawn and dusk, grubs reigned   10
where states previously boasted
they had democratized creation. The President,

impressed by the visit, showed his guest
from Up Over[3] the condition of his own
condition and proposed to do anything   15

he could about the partnership
situation. Rufus Woodpecker,
when asked how he found the

President said simply a White House
is as good a rest home as a Mayor's   20
Nest; and he went on to speak of

four times the Four Fold principle.[4]
When asked what this was all about, his
answer was, You can go anywhere

---

1   *Rufus Woodpecker* Named for the bird, rufous woodpecker.
2   *bi-partisanship* Agreement and compromise between the political parties in a two-party
     system; *symbiosis* Close, interdependent relationship between two parties, often to each
     party's mutual benefit.
3   *Up Over* I.e., North America (rufous woodpeckers are found in Asian and Oceanic coun-
     tries).
4   *Four Fold principle* Gottfried Leibniz's (1646–1716) Principle of Sufficient Reason states
     that nothing happens without a reason. Immanuel Kant (1724–1804) further defined

25 if you go out. All reporters were
one in thinking that there is no end
to what may follow. The chief

of the head of the Confederacy
for The Doubles to End the World's
30 Troubles was quick to support

the visitor, saying, Nobody
has ever denied that you can eat
with false teeth, but no one

has said you can see with a
35 glass eye. All the women
of the nation are reported

to be ready to give up beer
with breakfast if the outcome
of these chains of meetings,

40 which promise so much and have
already alleviated considerable
concern for what is the condition

which has caused such loss
of what was previously con-
45 sidered to be so attractive

a way of spending Friday nights
in town, that merchants everywhere
are prepared to offer fashion

colors for any elements found wandering
50 (four were, yesterday) within the city's
walls, their happy hands stained brown

---

this principle by noting that it could only be applied to the knowable universe. Arthur
Schopenhauer (1788–1860) introduced the Fourfold Principle of Sufficient Reason,
which defines four possible types of object-subject interactions that can occur between
the observer and the observed. Olson is having fun with presumed rational claims and
systems and the language that gives them apparent credibility.

from the amount of yours they'd pick up
coming from Loftoland into the massed
arrays of our forces arranged (as agreed

upon four years ago in the treaty of   55
the Vast Moths, at Genoyen). They assert
that you can hardly get through the Lowest

Tundra from the weight of the numbers of the
people buying whatever
is offered to them, no one, apparently,   60

considering at all the outcome of the
supreme meeting which took place here
today. On all hands there is

the thought that though normally,
and normally, the, and in certain   65
seasons, not eat, and actually

the young are born,
Rufus Woodpecker wouldn't
come near these shores, there isn't

a woman who wouldn't rather naturally   70
appear on Main Street shopping nights with her
hair in curlers, but now that the whole

question of overseas improvements has been
decided in favor of the formula for
home improvements, that they do involve   75

the whole family, Dad Mom Sis and Brother
are safe anywhere, the New Zealand Tuataras
and the Sooty Sheerwaters[1] combining

a night shift and general
domestic cleanliness so adequately   80
there can be no question at last that union

---

1   *New Zealand Tuataras* Type of reptile; *Sooty Sheerwaters* New Zealand seabirds.

is possible, the world can be one,
the Mites lie down with the Mrs,
everyone, keeping permanent shape,

85   having built-in fairness of cooperation and
chirping excitedly at the approach of each other

                    Or,
                         as today,
                                   at tea

90   at the Capitol where three nurses
and a dog drove happily off backing
into the car behind at the sight

of the representative of the rest of creation
nesting inside the Mouth of the nation, and pecking
95   broccoli out of it, clearly concerned

that if he went any deeper he was apt to find more
foodstuff buried in the Defrost

                                        —1987 (written 1958)

Elizabeth Bishop

1911–1979

Elizabeth Bishop is a major American poet whose reputation rests on the strength of a small but scrupulously crafted body of work. She sometimes spent years working on a single poem. According to the poet Robert Lowell, with whom she shared a close friendship, she was "an unerring Muse" who made "the casual perfect."

Born into a wealthy Massachusetts family, Bishop was orphaned by the age of five. (Her father died, and her mother was permanently institutionalized for insanity.) She was raised by grandparents, first by her mother's parents in Nova Scotia, but then by her father's parents in Massachusetts, where she was desperately unhappy. Her physical and emotional health suffered during these years, and she was to struggle throughout her life with serious ailments including asthma, depression, and alcoholism. She attended Vassar College, where she worked on the undergraduate magazine that also published some of her early poems. Marianne Moore (p. 346) became one of her mentors and most profound poetic influences. As an adult, Bishop traveled extensively, and some scholars have argued that her travels were tied to her chronic feelings of homelessness. Geography and perception were to become two of her great topics. She lived in Brazil from 1951 to 1966, for most of that time with her lover, the architect Lota de Macedo Soares. Her lesbian identity at this time in history reinforced Bishop's struggles with feelings of isolation. In 1956 she received the Pulitzer Prize for a collection of poetry, *Poems: North & South/A Cold Spring*; thereafter she was frequently a recipient of honors and awards.

Known for her meticulous accuracy, precise observations, and mastery with traditional forms, Bishop remarked: "since we do float on an unknown sea I think we should examine the floating things that come our way very carefully; who knows what might depend on it?" Some of Bishop's poems, such as "First Death in Nova Scotia," draw on elements of her personal life. But she remained wary of confessional poetry. Indeed, the carefully crafted position of the speaker in her poems often entails problems of perception, perspective, and knowledge. Since her death, her reputation and her influence on other poets have grown significantly.

Casabianca[1]

Love's the boy stood on the burning deck
trying to recite "The boy stood on
the burning deck."[2] Love's the son
    stood stammering elocution
5 while the poor ship in flames went down.

Love's the obstinate boy, the ship,
even the swimming sailors, who
would like a schoolroom platform, too,
    or an excuse to stay
10 on deck. And love's the burning boy.

                                  —1946

Chemin de Fer

Alone on the railroad track
    I walked with pounding heart.
The ties were too close together
    or maybe too far apart.

5 The scenery was impoverished:
    scrub-pine and oak; beyond
its mingled gray-green foliage
    I saw the little pond

where the dirty hermit lives,
10   lie like an old tear
holding onto its injuries
    lucidly year after year.

The hermit shot off his shot-gun
    and the tree by his cabin shook.
15 Over the pond went a ripple.
    The pet hen went chook-chook.

---

1   *Casabianca* Based on the 1826 poem of the same name by Felicia Hemans. Hemans's
poem was inspired by the real life death of Giocante de Casabianca, a young boy who
died with his father in the 1798 naval Battle of the Nile.

2   *The boy ... deck* Opening line of Hemans's "Casabianca."

"Love should be put into action!"
    screamed the old hermit.
Across the pond an echo
    tried and tried to confirm it.   20

                                        —1946

First Death in Nova Scotia

In the cold, cold parlor
my mother laid out Arthur
beneath the chromographs:
Edward, Prince of Wales,
with Princess Alexandra,   5
and King George with Queen Mary.[1]
Below them on the table
stood a stuffed loon
shot and stuffed by Uncle
Arthur, Arthur's father.   10

Since Uncle Arthur fired
a bullet into him,
he hadn't said a word.
He kept his own counsel
on his white, frozen lake,   15
the marble-topped table.
His breast was deep and white,
cold and caressable;
his eyes were red glass,
much to be desired.   20

"Come," said my mother,
"Come and say good-bye
to your little cousin Arthur."
I was lifted up and given
one lily of the valley   25
to put in Arthur's hand.

---

1   *chromographs* Colored prints; *Edward, Prince ... Queen Mary* Members of the British
     royal family. Edward VII was Prince of Wales when he married Alexandra of Denmark in
     1863. They became king and queen consort in 1901 and were succeeded by King George
     V and Mary of Teck in 1910.

Arthur's coffin was
a little frosted cake,
and the red-eyed loon eyed it
30 from his white, frozen lake.

Arthur was very small.
He was all white, like a doll
that hadn't been painted yet.
Jack Frost had started to paint him
35 the way he always painted
the Maple Leaf (Forever).[1]
He had just begun on his hair,
a few red strokes, and then
Jack Frost had dropped the brush
40 and left him white, forever.

The gracious royal couples
were warm in red and ermine;
their feet were well wrapped up
in the ladies' ermine trains.
45 They invited Arthur to be
the smallest page at court.
But how could Arthur go,
clutching his tiny lily,
with his eyes shut up so tight
50 and the roads deep in snow?

—1962

One Art

The art of losing isn't hard to master;
so many things seem filled with the intent
to be lost that their loss is no disaster.

Lose something every day. Accept the fluster
5 of lost door keys, the hour badly spent.
The art of losing isn't hard to master.

---

1   *the Maple Leaf (Forever)* Reference to "The Maple Leaf Forever" (1867), an unofficial
Canadian anthem.

Then practice losing farther, losing faster:
places, and names, and where it was you meant
to travel. None of these will bring disaster.

I lost my mother's watch. And look! my last, or   10
next-to-last, of three loved houses went.
The art of losing isn't hard to master.

I lost two cities, lovely ones. And, vaster,
some realms I owned, two rivers, a continent.
I miss them, but it wasn't a disaster.   15

—Even losing you (the joking voice, a gesture
I love) I shan't have lied. It's evident
the art of losing's not too hard to master
though it may look like (*Write* it!) like disaster.

—1976

Robert Hayden
1913–1980

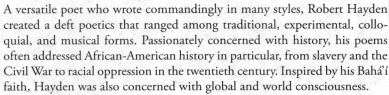

A versatile poet who wrote commandingly in many styles, Robert Hayden created a deft poetics that ranged among traditional, experimental, colloquial, and musical forms. Passionately concerned with history, his poems often addressed African-American history in particular, from slavery and the Civil War to racial oppression in the twentieth century. Inspired by his Bahá'í faith, Hayden was also concerned with global and world consciousness.

Hayden was born in Detroit and spent many childhood hours reading. He attended Detroit City College and studied literature under W.H. Auden at the University of Michigan. While working for the Federal Writers' Project, he researched black culture and history, building a knowledge that would inform much of his poetry. He followed his first collection, *Heart-Shape in the Dust* (1940), for which he won a Hopwood Award, with many other volumes, including *A Ballad of Remembrance* (1962), *Selected Poems* (1966), which introduced him to international audiences, and *The Night-Blooming Cereus* (1972).

Teaching at Fisk University and the University of Michigan for much of his career, Hayden received the grand prize at the first World Festival of Negro Arts in Dakar, Senegal, in 1966, followed by many other literary honors. Poet Harryette Mullen (p. 675) notes, "When I first sampled his work, as a student, it seemed most useful to me for expanding the possibilities of what and how an African American poet might write."

Those Winter Sundays

Sundays too my father got up early
and put his clothes on in the blueblack cold,
then with cracked hands that ached
from labor in the weekday weather made
5   banked fires blaze. No one ever thanked him.

I'd wake and hear the cold splintering, breaking.
When the rooms were warm, he'd call,
and slowly I would rise and dress,
fearing the chronic angers of that house,

10   Speaking indifferently to him,
who had driven out the cold
and polished my good shoes as well.

What did I know, what did I know
of love's austere and lonely offices?

—1962

Full Moon

No longer throne of a goddess to whom we pray,
no longer the bubble house of childhood's
tumbling Mother Goose man,

The emphatic moon ascends—
the brilliant challenger of rocket experts,
the white hope of communications men.[1]

Some I love who are dead
were watchers of the moon and knew its lore;
planted seeds, trimmed their hair,

Pierced their ears for gold hoop earrings   10
as it waxed or waned.
It shines tonight upon their graves.

And burned in the garden of Gethsemane,[2]
its light made holy by the dazzling tears
with which it mingled.   15

And spread its radiance on the exile's path
of Him who was The Glorious One,[3]
its light made holy by His holiness.

Already a mooted goal and tomorrow perhaps
an arms base, a livid sector,   20
the full moon dominates the dark.

—1966

---

1   *white hope of communications men* "Whitey on the Moon," by the great blues musician
     (and progenitor of hip-hop) Gil Scott-Heron (1949–2011), addresses similar concerns
     with race in the era of the space program.
2   *garden of Gethsemane* In the Bible, the garden where Jesus prays the night before his
     crucifixion.
3   *The Glorious One* Name given to Bahá'u'lláh, founder and prophet of the Bahá'í faith.

Randall Jarrell
1914–1965

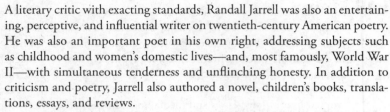

A literary critic with exacting standards, Randall Jarrell was also an entertaining, perceptive, and influential writer on twentieth-century American poetry. He was also an important poet in his own right, addressing subjects such as childhood and women's domestic lives—and, most famously, World War II—with simultaneous tenderness and unflinching honesty. In addition to criticism and poetry, Jarrell also authored a novel, children's books, translations, essays, and reviews.

Jarrell earned his BA (1935) and MA (1937) from Vanderbilt University in his hometown of Nashville, Tennessee. His first book of poems, *Blood for a Stranger*, was published in 1942, the same year that he enlisted in the military. His next two books, *Little Friend, Little Friend* (1945) and *Losses* (1948), drew on his experiences of World War II as a navigation tower operator. Together, these texts established his reputation as a skilled and sensitive poet—a reputation that grew with the publication of *The Woman at the Washington Zoo* (1960), which received the National Book Award. Jarrell also taught English and Creative Writing at a number of American universities and served as American Poet Laureate from 1956 to 1958.

The Death of the Ball Turret Gunner[1]

From my mother's sleep I fell into the State,
And I hunched in its belly till my wet fur froze.
Six miles from earth, loosed from its dream of life,
I woke to black flak° and the nightmare fighters.   *anti-aircraft fire*
5   When I died they washed me out of the turret with a hose.

—1945

---

1   *Ball Turret Gunner* Mounted on B-17 or B-24 planes, the Sperry ball turret was a one-person gun turret that required a short crew member to curl into the fetal position in order to aim and shoot.

Weldon Kees

1914–1955

Although mostly unknown to a wider public, Weldon Kees is highly regarded by poets themselves for his meticulous sense of craft and his evocative depictions of mid-twentieth-century irony and disillusion. Born in Nebraska, he moved to New York in 1943, where he published in elite magazines and socialized in an influential circle of New York intellectuals. Like other poets in mid-twentieth-century New York (such as, a bit later, Frank O'Hara), Kees worked in multiple genres and media, including criticism, fiction, painting (he was active in the establishment of Abstract Expressionism), film, music, and theater. Accomplished with traditional forms like the villanelle, the sestina, and the sonnet, he also pushed this formal tradition in new directions by incorporating techniques of repetition, sound, and collage.

Four poems he wrote in the 1940s created a remote character named "Robinson," a New Yorker through whom Kees subtly portrays public and private conditions of estrangement in the modern city. (All four selections appear below.) Kees disappeared in 1955, leaving his car at the Golden Gate Bridge. It remains unclear whether he committed suicide or escaped into anonymity in Mexico. Although he published three books of poems during his life, the major case for Kees's importance has been made by fellow poets since his death.

Sestina: Travel Notes

Directed by the eyes of others,
Blind to the long, deceptive voyage,
We walked across the bridge in silence
And said "Goodnight," and paused, and walked away.
Ritual of apology and burden: 5
The evening ended; not a soul was harmed.

But then I thought: we all are harmed
By the indifference of others;
Being corrupt, corruptible, they burden
All who would vanish on some questioned voyage,   10
Tunneling through the longest way away
To maps of bitterness and silence.

We are concerned with that destructive silence
Impending in the dark, that never harms
15 Us till it strikes, washing the past away.
Remote from intrigues of the others,
We must chart routes that ease the voyage,
Clear passageways and lift the burden.

But where are routes? Who names the burden?
20 The night is gifted with a devious silence
That names no promises of voyage
Without contagion and the syllables of harm.
—I see ahead the hands of others
In frantic motion, warning me away.

25 To pay no heed, and walk away
Is easy; but the familiar burden
Of a later time, when certainties of others
Assume the frigid shapes of silence
And build new winters, echoing harm,
30 May banish every passageway for voyage.

You knew before the fear of voyage,
You saw before the hands that warned away,
You heard before the voices trained to harm
Listeners grown weak through loss and burdens.
35 Even in city streets at noon that silence
Waited for you, but not, you thought, for others.

Storms will break silence. Seize on harm,
Play idiot or seer to others, make the burden
Theirs, though no voyage is, no tunnel, door, nor way.

—1943

Robinson

The dog stops barking after Robinson has gone.
His act is over. The world is a gray world,
Not without violence, and he kicks under the grand piano,
The nightmare chase well under way.

The mirror from Mexico, stuck to the wall,   5
Reflects nothing at all. The glass is black.
Robinson alone provides the image Robinsonian.

Which is all of the room—walls, curtains,
Shelves, bed, the tinted photograph of Robinson's first wife,
Rugs, vases, panatellas[1] in a humidor.[2]   10
They would fill the room if Robinson came in.

The pages in the books are blank,
The books that Robinson has read. That is his favorite chair,
Or where the chair would be if Robinson were here.

All day the phone rings. It could be Robinson   15
Calling. It never rings when he is here.

Outside, white buildings yellow in the sun.
Outside, the birds circle continuously
Where trees are actual and take no holiday.

                                                    —1945

from *Five Villanelles*

I

The crack is moving down the wall.
Defective plaster isn't all the cause.
We must remain until the roof falls in.

It's mildly cheering to recall
That every building has its little flaws.   5
The crack is moving down the wall.

Here in the kitchen, drinking gin,
We can accept the damndest laws.
We must remain until the roof falls in.

---

1   *panatellas* A type of thin cigar.
2   *humidor* An airtight container for tobacco products, especially cigars.

10   And though there's no one here at all,
     One searches every room because
     The crack is moving down the wall.

     Repairs? But how can one begin?
     The lease has warnings buried in each clause.
15   We must remain until the roof falls in.

     These nights one hears a creaking in the hall,
     The sort of thing that gives one pause.
     The crack is moving down the wall.
     We must remain until the roof falls in.

                                        —1947

Aspects of Robinson

     Robinson at cards at the Algonquin; a thin
     Blue light comes down once more outside the blinds.
     Gray men in overcoats are ghosts blown past the door.
     The taxis streak the avenues with yellow, orange, and red.
5   This is Grand Central, Mr. Robinson.

     Robinson on a roof above the Heights; the boats
     Mourn like the lost. Water is slate, far down.
     Through sounds of ice cubes dropped in glass, an osteopath,
     Dressed for the links, describes an old Intourist tour.
10   —Here's where old Gibbons jumped from, Robinson.

     Robinson walking in the Park, admiring the elephant.
     Robinson buying the *Tribune*, Robinson buying the *Times*. Robinson
     Saying, "Hello. Yes, this is Robinson. Sunday
     At five? I'd love to. Pretty well. And you?"
15   Robinson alone at Longchamps, staring at the wall.

     Robinson afraid, drunk, sobbing Robinson
     In bed with a Mrs. Morse. Robinson at home;
     Decisions: Toynbee or luminal?[1] Where the sun

---

1   *Toynbee or luminal?* Alfred J. Toynbee (1885–1975), a British historian whose *A Study of History* was published in 12 volumes; *luminal* A barbiturate used as a sleep aid.

Shines, Robinson in flowered trunks, eyes toward
The breakers. Where the night ends, Robinson in East Side bars.   20

Robinson in Glen plaid jacket, Scotch-grain shoes,
Black four-in-hand and oxford button-down,
The jeweled and silent watch that winds itself, the brief-
Case, covert topcoat, clothes for spring, all covering
His sad and usual heart, dry as a winter leaf.   25

—1948

Robinson at Home

Curtains drawn back, the door ajar.
All winter long, it seemed, a darkening
Began. But now the moonlight and the odors of the street
Conspire and combine toward one community.

These are the rooms of Robinson.   5
Bleached, wan, and colorless this light, as though
All the blurred daybreaks of the spring
Found an asylum here, perhaps for Robinson alone,

Who sleeps. Were there more music sifted through the floors
And moonlight of a different kind,   10
He might awake to hear the news at ten,
Which will be shocking, moderately.

This sleep is from exhaustion, but his old desire
To die like this has known a lessening.
Now there is only this coldness that he has to wear.   15
But not in sleep.—Observant scholar, traveller,

Or uncouth bearded figure squatting in a cave,
A keen-eyed sniper on the barricades,
A heretic in catacombs, a famed roué,
A beggar on the streets, the confidant of Popes—   20

All these are Robinson in sleep, who mumbles as he turns,
"There is something in this madhouse that I symbolize—
This city—nightmare—black—"

                                        He wakes in sweat
25 To the terrible moonlight and what might be
    Silence. It drones like wires far beyond the roofs,
    And the long curtains blow into the room.

                                                              —1948

Relating to Robinson

Somewhere in Chelsea,[1] early summer;
And, walking in the twilight toward the docks,
I thought I made out Robinson ahead of me.

From an uncurtained second-story room, a radio
5 Was playing *There's a Small Hotel*;[2] a kite
Twisted above dark rooftops and slow drifting birds.
We were alone there, he and I,
Inhabiting the empty street.

Under a sign for Natural Bloom Cigars,
10 While lights clicked softly in the dusk from red to green,
He stopped and gazed into a window
Where a plaster Venus, modeling a truss,[3]
Looked out at Eastbound traffic. (But Robinson,
I knew, was out of town: he summers at a place in Maine,
15 Sometimes on Fire Island, sometimes the Cape,
Leaves town in June and comes back after Labor Day.)
And yet, I almost called out, "Robinson!"

There was no chance. Just as I passed,
Turning my head to search his face,
20 His own head turned with mine
And fixed me with dilated, terrifying eyes
That stopped my blood. His voice
Came at me like an echo in the dark.

---

1   *Chelsea* A neighborhood on the West Side of Manhattan.
2   *There's a Small Hotel* A 1936 popular song by Richard Rodgers and Lorenz Hart. Kees
     makes ironic and metaphorical use of the song's lyrics.
3   *truss* A confining garment, for example, a medical truss worn in cases of hernia.

"I thought I saw the whirlpool opening.
Kicked all night at a bolted door.   25
You must have followed me from Astor Place.[1]
An empty paper floats down at the last.
And then a day as huge as yesterday in pairs
Unrolled its horror on my face
Until it blocked—"[2] Running in sweat   30
To reach the docks, I turned back
For a second glance. I had no certainty,
There in the dark, that it was Robinson
Or someone else.
                       The block was bare. The Venus,   35
Bathed in blue fluorescent light,
Stared toward the river. As I hurried West,
The lights across the bay were coming on.
The boats moved silently and the low whistles blew.

                                             —1954

---

1   *Astor Place* A neighborhood in Manhattan that was home to families of legendary wealth during the nineteenth century.
2   *And then a day as huge ... blocked* A quotation from Emily Dickinson's poem "The first Day's Night had come," included in this volume on p. 215.

William Stafford
1914–1993

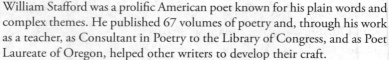William Stafford was a prolific American poet known for his plain words and complex themes. He published 67 volumes of poetry and, through his work as a teacher, as Consultant in Poetry to the Library of Congress, and as Poet Laureate of Oregon, helped other writers to develop their craft.

Born in Hutchinson, Kansas, Stafford earned a BA and an MA from the University of Kansas at Lawrence, later obtaining a PhD from the University of Iowa. As a conscientious objector, he was interned in the civilian public service camps during World War II, a time in which he developed an early morning writing habit that he would continue throughout his career. He began teaching at Lewis and Clark College in 1948 and in 1960 he published his first collection of poetry, *West of Your City*. His other acclaimed volumes include National Book Award-winning *Traveling Through the Dark* (1962), *Stories That Could Be True* (1977), and *An Oregon Message* (1987).

Stafford emphasized the idea of writing as a process and an impulse to be trusted and followed. His writing often explored the contours of self in contact with unknown frontiers, frontiers that include literal geographical spaces, like those of Oregon, as well as borderlines between youth and age, innocence and knowledge, and the human in nature. He stands in a tradition of poets intensely engaged with region and place (like California poet Robinson Jeffers before him [p. 345]).

Traveling Through the Dark

Traveling through the dark I found a deer
dead on the edge of the Wilson River road.
It is usually best to roll them into the canyon:
that road is narrow; to swerve might make more dead.

5   By glow of the tail-light I stumbled back of the car
and stood by the heap, a doe, a recent killing;
she had stiffened already, almost cold.
I dragged her off; she was large in the belly.

My fingers touching her side brought me the reason—
10 her side was warm; her fawn lay there waiting,
alive, still, never to be born.
Beside that mountain road I hesitated.

The car aimed ahead its lowered parking lights;
under the hood purred the steady engine.
I stood in the glare of the warm exhaust turning red;   15
around our group I could hear the wilderness listen.

I thought hard for us all—my only swerving—,
then pushed her over the edge into the river.

                                                            —1960

Fifteen

South of the bridge on Seventeenth
I found back of the willows one summer
day a motorcycle with engine running
as it lay on its side, ticking over
slowly in the high grass. I was fifteen.   5

I admired all that pulsing gleam, the
shiny flanks, the demure headlights
fringed where it lay; I led it gently
to the road and stood with that
companion, ready and friendly. I was fifteen.   10

We could find the end of a road, meet
the sky on out Seventeenth. I thought about
hills, and patting the handle got back a
confident opinion. On the bridge we indulged
a forward feeling, a tremble. I was fifteen.   15

Thinking, back farther in the grass I found
the owner, just coming to, where he had flipped
over the rail. He had blood on his hand, was pale—
I helped him walk to his machine. He ran his hand
over it, called me good man, roared away.   20

I stood there, fifteen.

                                                            —1966

Ask Me

Some time when the river is ice ask me
mistakes I have made. Ask me whether
what I have done is my life. Others
have come in their slow way into
5 my thought, and some have tried to help
or to hurt: ask me what difference
their strongest love or hate has made.

I will listen to what you say.
You and I can turn and look
10 at the silent river and wait. We know
the current is there, hidden; and there
are comings and goings from miles away
that hold the stillness exactly before us.
What the river says, that is what I say.

—1977

Dylan Thomas
1914–1953

Dylan Thomas was a raucous fixture in the taverns of London's Soho-Fitz-rovia district, and he haunted the rural hills and seashores of Wales. Influenced by a romantic sensibility, he sought to articulate his sense that life and death were rolled together in nature's driving "green fuse."

Thomas was born in Swansea, Wales, and his youth and childhood there would be a recurring subject in his poetry. His father was a teacher at Swansea Grammar School, which Thomas attended and where he was far from a prize pupil; as a teenager, he regularly cut classes to work on his own poetry. His first published work, "And Death Shall Have No Dominion" (1933), was printed in a literary magazine when he was only 18.

When Thomas's *18 Poems* was published the following year, the strange and disturbing power of his verse woke up London's literary establishment. The cool, controlled style of T.S. Eliot, which conditioned poetic attitudes well into the 1950s, appeared subdued next to what one critic called Thomas's "belligerent syntax." While fresh and vital, Thomas's poems are also complex, built of dense interlocking images, and tightly structured: "Do Not Go Gentle into That Good Night" (1951), for example, adopts the restrictive form of a villanelle.

Despite his heavy drinking and a turbulent marriage, Thomas continued to publish poems—as well as short stories and radio plays—until the end of his life. Constant financial difficulty lightened when he began making recordings of his poetry and touring to give public readings, which were enormously popular in Europe, and even more so in the United States. He was 39 when he died in New York of problems related to alcoholism.

The Force That Through the Green Fuse Drives the Flower

The force that through the green fuse drives the flower
Drives my green age; that blasts the roots of trees
Is my destroyer.
And I am dumb to tell the crooked rose
My youth is bent by the same wintry fever.   5

The force that drives the water through the rocks
Drives my red blood; that dries the mouthing streams
Turns mine to wax.

And I am dumb to mouth unto my veins
10 How at the mountain spring the same mouth sucks.

The hand that whirls the water in the pool[1]
Stirs the quicksand; that ropes the blowing wind
Hauls my shroud sail.
And I am dumb to tell the hanging man
15 How of my clay is made the hangman's lime.[2]

The lips of time leech to the fountain head;
Love drips and gathers, but the fallen blood
Shall calm her sores.
And I am dumb to tell a weather's wind
20 How time has ticked a heaven round the stars.

And I am dumb to tell the lover's tomb
How at my sheet goes the same crooked worm.

—1933

Fern Hill

Now as I was young and easy under the apple boughs
About the lilting house and happy as the grass was green,
    The night above the dingle° starry,   *wooded dell*
       Time let me hail and climb
5   Golden in the heydays of his eyes,
And honoured among wagons I was prince of the apple towns
And once below a time I lordly had the trees and leaves
       Trail with daisies and barley
     Down the rivers of the windfall light.

10 And as I was green and carefree, famous among the barns
About the happy yard and singing as the farm was home,
    In the sun that is young once only,
       Time let me play and be
     Golden in the mercy of his means,
15 And green and golden I was huntsman and herdsman, the calves

---

1   *The hand ... the pool* In John 5.4, an angel goes to a pool in Bethesda and imbues it with
    healing properties by stirring the water.
2   *lime* Mineral used to speed up decomposition.

Sang to my horn, the foxes on the hills barked clear and cold,
      And the sabbath rang slowly
    In the pebbles of the holy streams.

All the sun long it was running, it was lovely, the hay
Fields high as the house, the tunes from the chimneys, it was air   20
    And playing, lovely and watery
        And fire green as grass.
    And nightly under the simple stars
As I rode to sleep the owls were bearing the farm away,
All the moon long I heard, blessed among stables, the   25
   nightjars°   *nocturnal birds*
    Flying with the ricks° and the horses   *haystacks*
      Flashing into the dark.

And then to awake, and the farm, like a wanderer white
With the dew, come back, the cock on his shoulder: it was all
    Shining, it was Adam and maiden,   30
      The sky gathered again
    And the sun grew round that very day.
So it must have been after the birth of the simple light
In the first, spinning place, the spellbound horses walking warm
    Out of the whinnying green stable   35
      On to the fields of praise.

And honoured among foxes and pheasants by the gay house
Under the new made clouds and happy as the heart was long,
    In the sun born over and over,
      I ran my heedless ways,   40
    My wishes raced through the house high hay
And nothing I cared, at my sky blue trades,° that time allows   *occupations*
In all his tuneful turning so few and such morning songs
    Before the children green and golden
      Follow him out of grace,   45

Nothing I cared, in the lamb white days, that time would take me
Up to the swallow thronged loft by the shadow of my hand,
    In the moon that is always rising,
      Nor that riding to sleep
    I should hear him fly with the high fields
And wake to the farm forever fled from the childless land.   50

Oh as I was young and easy in the mercy of his means,
    Time held me green and dying
   Though I sang in my chains like the sea.

—1946

Do Not Go Gentle into That Good Night

Do not go gentle into that good night,
Old age should burn and rave at close of day;
Rage, rage against the dying of the light.

Though wise men at their end know dark is right,
5 Because their words had forked no lightning they
Do not go gentle into that good night.

Good men, the last wave by, crying how bright
Their frail deeds might have danced in a green bay,
Rage, rage against the dying of the light.

10 Wild men who caught and sang the sun in flight,
And learn, too late, they grieved it on its way,
Do not go gentle into that good night.

Grave men, near death, who see with blinding sight
Blind eyes could blaze like meteors and be gay,
15 Rage, rage against the dying of the light.

And you, my father, there on the sad height,
Curse, bless, me now with your fierce tears, I pray.
Do not go gentle into that good night.
Rage, rage against the dying of the light.

—1951

Gwendolyn Brooks

1917–2000

Exploring a range of poetic forms and styles, Gwendolyn Brooks created vivid characters, many of whom were black, women, impoverished, or oppressed, depicting their everyday struggle for survival. Describing herself as a "writer who loves to write," Brooks wrote over 20 poetry collections, a novel, several children's books, and a two-volume autobiography, constantly experimenting with new ideas and striving to make poetry accessible to a broad public audience.

Born in Topeka, Kansas, Brooks moved with her family to Chicago early in her childhood; she published her first poem at the age of 13 and by 17 many of her poems had appeared in the *Chicago Defender*. After graduating from Wilson Junior College, she worked at secretarial jobs and with the NAACP, publishing her first poetry collection, *A Street in Bronzeville*, in 1945. Other volumes that followed included *Annie Allen* (1949), for which she won a Pulitzer Prize, *The Bean Eaters* (1960), *In the Mecca* (1968), and *Children Coming Home* (1991). In the 1960s, she became a voice for social justice, using her poetry to critique social inequalities and helping to develop a community of black writers.

As Poet Laureate of Illinois and as Consultant in Poetry to the Library of Congress, Brooks embraced her role as a mentor. She brought her experience to teaching positions at a number of schools, including Columbia College and Chicago State University. Her work was celebrated throughout her life, earning her fellowships, honorary degrees, and a Jefferson Lectureship of the National Endowment of the Humanities.

We Real Cool

The Pool Players. Seven at the Golden Shovel.

We real cool. We
Left school. We

Lurk late. We
Strike straight. We

Sing sin. We
Thin gin. We

5

Jazz June. We
Die soon.

—1960

Medgar Evers[1]

For Charles Evers

The man whose height his fear improved he
arranged to fear no further. The raw
intoxicated time was time for better birth or
a final death.

5 Old styles, old tempos, all the engagement of
the day—the sedate, the regulated fray—
the antique light, the Moral rose, old gusts,
tight whistlings from the past, the mothballs
in the Love at last our man forswore.

10 Medgar Evers annoyed confetti and assorted
brands of businessmen's eyes.

The shows came down: to maxims and surprise.
And palsy.

Roaring no rapt arise-ye to the dead, he
15 leaned across tomorrow. People said that
he was holding clean globes in his hands.

—1968

---

1   *Medgar Evers* (1925–63) was an African-American civil rights activist and field secretary
    for the NAACP. He was murdered near his home in Jackson, Mississippi, by a white
    supremacist. Charles Evers was his brother and fellow activist.

Robert Lowell
1917–1977

Robert Lowell, born and raised in Boston, was educated at Kenyon College and taught at universities throughout the eastern United States and in England. Lowell achieved fame through both his acclaimed work and his public commitment to political causes; a conscientious objector in World War II, he later vocally opposed the war in Vietnam.

Lowell is highly significant to poetic history as one of a group of American poets in the 1950s and 1960s who came to be called "confessional poets." M.L. Rosenthal in fact coined the term "confessional" poetry in a review of Lowell in 1959. Lowell wrote poems about his childhood, his three difficult marriages, and his repeated hospitalizations for mental illness. Scholar Susan Rosenbaum points out that the confessional poets—also including Sylvia Plath and Anne Sexton—"often employed the first-person voice to explore transgressive autobiographical subjects," including mental illness, trauma, gender and sexuality, and outsider status. Another of Lowell's many styles was that of a public poet addressing matters of national moment. He wrote "For the Union Dead," below, for the Boston Arts Festival in 1960 and initially delivered it aloud to that audience.

Skunk Hour[1]

(*For Elizabeth Bishop*[2])

Nautilus Island's[3] hermit
heiress still lives through winter in her Spartan cottage;
her sheep still graze above the sea.
Her son's a bishop. Her farmer
is first selectman in our village;
she's in her dotage.

5

---

1   *Skunk Hour* Of this poem Lowell has written: "The first four stanzas are meant to give a dawdling more or less amiable picture of a declining Maine sea town.... This is the dark night. I hoped my readers would remember St. John of the Cross's poem. My night is not gracious, but secular, puritan, and agnostical. An Existentialist night."
2   *For Elizabeth Bishop* Lowell has stated that the form of his poem was indebted to Elizabeth Bishop's "The Armadillo." The two poets were close friends.
3   *Nautilus Island* Small island situated close to Castine, a village on the coast of Maine.

Thirsting for
the hierarchic privacy
of Queen Victoria's century,
10   she buys up all
the eyesores facing her shore,
and lets them fall.

The season's ill—
we've lost our summer millionaire,
15   who seemed to leap from an L.L. Bean[1]
catalogue. His nine-knot yawl
was auctioned off to lobstermen.
A red fox stain covers Blue Hill.[2]

And now our fairy
20   decorator brightens his shop for fall;
his fishnet's filled with orange cork,
orange, his cobbler's bench and awl;
there is no money in his work,
he'd rather marry.

25   One dark night,
my Tudor Ford climbed the hill's skull;
I watched for love-cars. Lights turned down,
they lay together, hull to hull,
where the graveyard shelves on the town...
30   My mind's not right.

A car radio bleats,
"Love, O careless Love[3] ..." I hear
my ill-spirit sob in each blood cell,
as if my hand were at its throat...
35   I myself am hell;[4]
nobody's here—

---

1   *L.L. Bean* A mail-order company in Maine that specializes in outdoor clothes.
2   *Blue Hill* A mountain in Maine near where Lowell was living.
3   *Love ... Love* A popular song of the 1950s.
4   *I myself am hell* An echo of Satan in *Paradise Lost*, IV.75: "Which way I fly is Hell; myself
     am Hell."

only skunks, that search
in the moonlight for a bite to eat.
They march on their soles up Main Street:
white stripes, moonstruck eyes' red fire   40
under the chalk-dry and spar spire
of the Trinitarian Church.

I stand on top
of our back steps and breathe the rich air—
a mother skunk with her column of kittens swills the garbage   45
      pail.
She jabs her wedge-head in a cup
of sour cream, drops her ostrich tail,
and will not scare.

                                                            —1959

For the Union Dead

"Relinquunt Omnia Servare Rem Publicam."[1]

The old South Boston Aquarium stands
in a Sahara of snow now. Its broken windows are boarded.
The bronze weathervane cod has lost half its scales.
The airy tanks are dry.

Once my nose crawled like a snail on the glass;   5
my hand tingled
to burst the bubbles
drifting from the noses of the cowed, compliant fish.

My hand draws back. I often sigh still
for the dark downward and vegetating kingdom   10
of the fish and reptile. One morning last March,
I pressed against the new barbed and galvanized

---

1   *Relinquunt ... Publicam* Latin: They give up all to serve the republic.

fence on the Boston Common.[1] Behind their cage,
yellow dinosaur steamshovels were grunting
15   as they cropped up tons of mush and grass
to gouge their underworld garage.

Parking spaces luxuriate like civic
sandpiles in the heart of Boston.
A girdle of orange, Puritan-pumpkin colored girders

20   braces the tingling Statehouse,
shaking over the excavations, as it faces Colonel Shaw[2]
and his bell-cheeked Negro infantry
on St. Gaudens' shaking Civil War relief,
propped by a plank splint against the garage's earthquake.

25   Two months after marching through Boston,
half the regiment was dead;
at the dedication,
William James[3] could almost hear the bronze Negroes breathe.

Their monument sticks like a fishbone
30   in the city's throat.
Its Colonel is as lean
as a compass-needle.

He has an angry wrenlike vigilance,
a greyhound's gentle tautness;
35   he seems to wince at pleasure,
and suffocate for privacy.

He is out of bounds now. He rejoices in man's lovely,
peculiar power to choose life and die—
when he leads his black soldiers to death,
40   he cannot bend his back.

---

1   *Boston Common* A public park in the center of Boston, on one side of which stands the Massachusetts State House.
2   *Colonel Shaw* Robert Gould Shaw (1837–63) led one of the first African American regiments from the North during the American Civil War, and was killed with many of his troops in an attack on the Confederate position at Fort Wagner, South Carolina.
3   *William James* American philosopher and psychologist (1842–1910), brother of novelist Henry James.

On a thousand small town New England greens,
the old white churches hold their air
of sparse, sincere rebellion; frayed flags
quilt the graveyards of the Grand Army of the Republic.

The stone statues of the abstract Union Soldier   45
grow slimmer and younger each year—
wasp-waisted, they doze over muskets
and muse through their sideburns...

Shaw's father wanted no monument
except the ditch,   50
where his son's body was thrown
and lost with his "niggers."[1]

The ditch is nearer.
There are no statues for the last war[2] here;
on Boylston Street, a commercial photograph   55
shows Hiroshima boiling

over a Mosler Safe, the "Rock of Ages"
that survived the blast. Space is nearer.
When I crouch to my television set,
the drained faces of Negro school-children rise like balloons.   60

Colonel Shaw
is riding on his bubble,
he waits
for the blessèd break.

The Aquarium is gone. Everywhere,   65
giant finned cars nose forward like fish;
a savage servility
slides by on grease.

—1964

---

1   Shaw's father ... "niggers" As a gesture of contempt for a white man who would lead black
     soldiers, Confederate General Johnson Hagood (later the Governor of South Carolina)
     ordered Shaw's body buried with his African-American troops. Shaw's father countered
     that there was "no holier place" for Shaw's body than "surrounded by his brave and de-
     voted" soldiers.
2   last war World War II.

Lawrence Ferlinghetti
b. 1919

Poet, painter, publisher, and playwright Lawrence Ferlinghetti's long career has been marked by a commitment to making poetry engaging and accessible. Shaped by the rhythms of jazz and by popular culture, his poems have been widely read: his 1958 collection *A Coney Island of the Mind* has sold over one million copies.

Born in Brooklyn to a French mother and an Italian father, Ferlinghetti spent his early childhood in France. He earned a degree in journalism from the University of North Carolina and began his writing career as a journalist with its student newspaper. After serving in the navy in World War II, he attended graduate school at Columbia University and the Sorbonne before settling in San Francisco in 1951. In San Francisco Ferlinghetti co-founded the iconic City Lights bookstore and later the bookstore's publishing wing, which published new experimental work by Allen Ginsberg, Denise Levertov, William Carlos Williams, and many other poets who would shape the future course of poetry. Though he was often linked to the countercultural Beat movement, Ferlinghetti preferred the term "wide-open poetry," which he took from a comment by poet Pablo Neruda about the broad range of Ferlinghetti's subjects.

Ferlinghetti has published 40 books since his first volume of poetry, *Pictures of a Gone World* (1955). In addition to prizes for his literary works, such as the *Los Angeles Times*'s Robert Kirsch Award, Ferlinghetti has received numerous awards for his political activism and contribution to the literary community. In his book *Poetry as Insurgent Art*, Ferlinghetti writes, "Poetry is not a sedentary occupation ... Stand up and let them have it."

I Am Waiting

I am waiting for my case to come up
and I am waiting
for a rebirth of wonder
and I am waiting for someone
5   to really discover America
and wail
and I am waiting
for the discovery
of a new symbolic western frontier
10 and I am waiting
for the American Eagle

to really spread its wings
and straighten up and fly right[1]
and I am waiting
for the Age of Anxiety[2]
to drop dead
and I am waiting
for the war to be fought
which will make the world safe
for anarchy[3]
and I am waiting
for the final withering away[4]
of all governments
and I am perpetually awaiting
a rebirth of wonder

I am waiting for the Second Coming[5]
and I am waiting
for a religious revival
to sweep thru the state of Arizona
and I am waiting
for the Grapes of Wrath[6] to be stored
and I am waiting
for them to prove
that God is really American
and I am seriously waiting
for Billy Graham and Elvis Presley
to exchange roles seriously
and I am waiting
to see God on television
piped onto church altars
if only they can find
the right channel

15

20

25

30

35

40

---

1   *straighten up and fly right* 1943 song composed by Nat King Cole and Irving Mills.
2   *Age of Anxiety* 1947 poem by W.H. Auden.
3   *war ... anarchy* American president Woodrow Wilson (1856–1924) described World
     War I as a necessary step in making "the world safe for democracy."
4   *withering away* Marxist concept that one day all governments will be unnecessary and
     society will become self-governing.
5   *Second Coming* Christian belief that one day Christ will return to earth; also the title of a
     1920 poem by Irish poet W.B. Yeats.
6   *Grapes of Wrath* Reference to Julia Ward Howe's 1862 song "The Battle Hymn of the
     Republic."

to tune in on
and I am waiting
45 for the Last Supper to be served again
with a strange new appetizer
and I am perpetually awaiting
a rebirth of wonder

I am waiting for my number to be called
50 and I am waiting
for the living end
and I am waiting
for dad to come home
his pockets full
55 of irradiated silver dollars
and I am waiting
for the atomic tests to end
and I am waiting happily
for things to get much worse
60 before they improve
and I am waiting
for the Salvation Army to take over
and I am waiting
for the human crowd
65 to wander off a cliff somewhere
clutching its atomic umbrella[1]
and I am waiting
for Ike[2] to act
and I am waiting
70 for the meek to be blessed
and inherit the earth
without taxes
and I am waiting
for forests and animals
75 to reclaim the earth as theirs
and I am waiting
for a way to be devised
to destroy all nationalisms

---

1   *atomic umbrella* I.e., nuclear umbrella, an expression describing when a country prom-
     ises the use of its nuclear weapons to help protect another country.
2   *Ike* Popular nickname of American president Dwight D. Eisenhower (1890–1969).

without killing anybody
and I am waiting   80
for linnets and planets to fall like rain
and I am waiting for lovers and weepers
to lie down together again
in a new rebirth of wonder

I am waiting for the Great Divide to be crossed   85
and I am anxiously waiting
for the secret of eternal life to be discovered
by an obscure general practitioner
and save me forever from certain death
and I am waiting   90
for life to begin
and I am waiting
for the storms of life
to be over
and I am waiting   95
to set sail for happiness[1]
and I am waiting
for a reconstructed Mayflower
to reach America
with its picture story and tv rights   100
sold in advance to the natives
and I am waiting
for the lost music to sound again
in the Lost Continent
in a new rebirth of wonder   105

I am waiting for the day
that maketh all things clear
and I am waiting
for Ole Man River
to just stop rolling along[2]   110
past the country club
and I am waiting

---

1   *set sail for happiness* Reference to a famous line from French writer Charles Baudelaire's
    (1821–67) *Fusées*: "*Quand partons-nous pour le bonheur?*" (French: "When do we set sail
    for happiness?")

2   *Ole Man River ... along* Reference to the song "Ol' Man River" by Jerome Kern and
    Oscar Hammerstein from the 1927 musical *Show Boat*.

for the deepest South
to just stop Reconstructing[1] itself
115   in its own image
and I am waiting
for a sweet desegregated chariot
to swing low
and carry me back to Ole Virginie[2]
120   and I am waiting
for Ole Virginie to discover
just why Darkies are born[3]
and I am waiting
for God to lookout
125   from Lookout Mountain
and see the *Ode to the Confederate Dead*[4]
as a real farce
and I am awaiting retribution
for what America did
130   to Tom Sawyer[5]

---

1   *Reconstructing* Reconstruction was the period after the US Civil War, when the Confederate states were politically reintegrated into the Union in "reconstructed" terms. The federal government divided the South into military districts in order to enforce a new political order in the wake of Emancipation and the military defeat of the Confederacy. A vast population of freed slaves, as well as people of African descent more generally, briefly saw improvements in civil rights at this time, codified in the Thirteenth, Fourteenth, and Fifteenth Amendments (known as the "Reconstruction Amendments"). As part of a political compromise to resolve the contested presidential election of 1876, the federal government brought an end to its interventions in the South. The end of Reconstruction enabled the rise of the Jim Crow South and its clampdown on freedoms and rights for people of African descent.

2   *sweet ... carry me* Reworded line from the American song "Swing Low, Sweet Chariot"; *desegregated* The landmark US Supreme Court decision in *Brown v. Board of Education* (1954) ruled that racial segregation in public education was unconstitutional. Elimination of racial segregation in its many forms remained a central aim of the American Civil Rights Movement; *carry ... Virginie* Reference to a popular song dating to the nineteenth century and often sung by Confederate soldiers. The lyrics romanticize slavery, the state of Virginia, and, by extension, the Confederacy.

3   *why Darkies are born* Reference to the highly controversial 1931 song "That's Why Darkies Were Born," composed by Ray Henderson and Lew Brown; Ferlinghetti self-consciously uses the racial slur "darkies" that had long been a routine way of referring to people of African descent in the US.

4   *Ode to the Confederate Dead* Poem by American poet Allen Tate (1899–1979).

5   *Tom Sawyer* Titular character from Mark Twain's novel *The Adventures of Tom Sawyer* (1876).

and I am perpetually awaiting
a rebirth of wonder

I am waiting for Tom Swift to grow up
and I am waiting
for the American Boy[1]
to take off Beauty's clothes
and get on top of her
and I am waiting
for Alice in Wonderland
to retransmit to me
her total dream of innocence
and I am waiting
for Childe Roland to come
to the final darkest tower[2]
and I am waiting
for Aphrodite
to grow live arms[3]
at a final disarmament conference
in a new rebirth of wonder

I am waiting
to get some intimations
of immortality
by recollecting my early childhood[4]
and I am waiting
for the green mornings to come again
youth's dumb green fields come back again
and I am waiting
for some strains of unpremeditated art[5]
to shake my typewriter
and I am waiting to write
the great indelible poem

135

140

145

150

155

160

---

1   *American Boy* Boy's magazine published from 1899 to 1941.
2   *Childe Roland ... tower* Reference to the 1855 poem "Childe Roland to the Dark Tower Came" by British poet Robert Browning.
3   *Aphrodite ... arms* More popularly known as the Venus de Milo, the Aphrodite of Milos is a Greek statue depicting the goddess of love Aphrodite. The statue was famously discovered in pieces, with both arms missing.
4   *intimations ... childhood* Allusion to William Wordsworth's poem *Ode: Intimations of Immortality from Recollections of Early Childhood* (1807).
5   *unpremeditated art* See Percy Bysshe Shelley's 1820 poem "To a Skylark" (p. 90).

and I am waiting
for the last long careless rapture[1]
and I am perpetually waiting
165 for the fleeing lovers on the Grecian Urn[2]
to catch each other up at last
and embrace
and I am awaiting
perpetually and forever
170 a renaissance of wonder

—1958

---

1   *last long careless rapture* Reference to the Robert Burns poem "Home Thoughts from
      Abroad" (1845): "The first fine careless rapture!"
2   *Grecian Urn* See John Keats's poem "Ode on a Grecian Urn" (1820) (p. 102).

Jack Kerouac

1922–1969

An influential writer in the countercultural Beat movement of the 1950s, Jack Kerouac espoused living and writing intensely and spontaneously as an antidote to deadening social conventions—including conventional art. Kerouac's now-legendary 1957 novel *On the Road*, inspired by his travels with friends across the US and Mexico, became a kind of Beat handbook for an existential road trip. Plunging into far-ranging explorations of geographical as well as psychological and spiritual spaces, Kerouac aggressively pursued alternate states of consciousness (as did the other Beats) through such routes as spirituality, drugs, and alcohol. (He died as a result of his alcoholism.) Raised a devout Catholic, he gravitated to Buddhism, an important influence on the Beats more generally. Like his Beat friends Allen Ginsberg (see p. 488) and Lawrence Ferlinghetti (p. 456), Kerouac was also a poet; all of them embraced jazz music as a vital modern art form that countered "tradition" from a place on the margins of social power. Kerouac's 1959 *Mexico City Blues* opened with this poetic note:

> I want to be considered a jazz poet
> blowing a long blues in an afternoon jam
> session on Sunday. I take 242 choruses;
> my ideas vary and sometimes roll from
> chorus to chorus or from halfway through
> a chorus to halfway into the next.

Such repetitions and changes are evident in the four choruses reprinted here, embracing the spontaneity and improvisation of jazz music to speak to the social, personal, and spiritual conditions of the post–World War II era.

from *Mexico City Blues*

66th Chorus

Dharma[1] law
    Say
All things is made
      of the same thing
      which is a nothing   5

---

1   *Dharma* In Buddhism, a multivalent term indicating Buddhist teachings in general as well as universal principles more generally.

All nothings are the same
      as, somethings
      the somethings
      are no-nothings,
10   equally blank

Blank
   bright
      is the whole scene
      when you let your eyes
15   wander beyond the mules
     and the fields and carpets
     and bottles on the floor
     and clean mahogany radios,
dont be afraid
20 the raid hasnt started[1]
panic you not
      day the better
      arriveth soon
And the gist of it Nothing-ness
25   SUCH-NESS

67th Chorus

Suchness
Is *T'athata*,[2] the name,
Used,
     to mean, Essence,
5   all things is made
     of the same thing
     essence

The thing is pure nature,
    not Mother Nature

10 The thing is to express
the very substance of your thoughts

---

1   *the raid hasnt started* See Gregory Corso, "BOMB" (p. 513) for a poem sharing one sense
    of the "raid" in cultural consciousness at this historical moment. Fear of nuclear war was
    omnipresent in the US during the Cold War.
2   *T'athata* In Buddhist thought, ultimate reality; literally "suchness" in Sanskrit.

as you read this
is the same as the emptiness
    of space
    right now   15

and the same as the silence you hear
    inside the emptiness
    that's there
    everywhere,
    so nothing in the way   20
    but ignorant sofas
    and phantoms & chairs,
nothing there but the picture[1]
in the movie in your mind

108th Chorus

Neither this nor that
    means,
            no arbitrary conceptions,
            because if you say
            arbitrarily, the RAMMIS   5
            is the RAMMIS, ! —
            and the TSORIS is the TSORIS,
            or the FLORIST,
            or the —
                arbitrary conceptions   10
                have sprung into existence
                that didnt have to be there
                in the first place
                when your eyes were bright
                with seeing emptiness   15
                in the void of holy sea
                where creatures didnt
                abound, nor crops grow,
                and nothing happened,
                    and nobody lived,   20
                    and nobody cared —

---

1   *nothing there but the picture* For another poetic response to a related philosophical and
artistic problem, see Wallace Stevens, "The Snow Man" (p. 326).

You didnt need
arbitrary concepts there
and need them now
25   you say you need them now
I say, you say,
Why should you need them now
Why should you now

156th Chorus

I know we're all straight
I knew from a tree
I leaned on a tree
And the tree told me

5   Tree told me Haby
The Maybe is Abey,
The Kapey is Correcty,
You'll be allarighty

Trees dont talk good[1]
10   No they don't talk good
This tree just told me
    See Eternity
    Is the other side
    Of the other part
15   Of your mind
    That you ignore
    Because you want to

—1959

---

1   *Trees dont talk good* Part of Kerouac's larger exploration of language in this volume, in-
   cluding poetic language, as it relates to what he calls "Essence" in the "67th Chorus."

Philip Larkin

1922–1985

Holding fast to the principle that poetry is to be read rather than studied, the British poet Philip Larkin rejected what he considered the Modernist critical dogma that a poem's complexity is a measure of its worthiness. In his hostility toward the poetic avant-garde, Larkin is often identified with "the Movement," a group of British writers who shunned "the aberration of modernism" and the ostentatious "culture-mongering" of poets such as T.S. Eliot and Ezra Pound, whom Larkin believed had made a virtue of obscurity and perverted a native English tradition of plain-style lyric poetry.

"There's not much to say about my work," he once observed. "When you've read a poem, that's it, it's all quite clear what it means." In stark and deliberate contrast to the Modernist pursuit of impersonality, Larkin typically adopts an intimate, lucidly colloquial tone in which—in the guise of his poetic persona—he often addresses the reader directly.

Three slender volumes—*The Less Deceived* (1955), *The Whitsun Weddings* (1964), and *High Windows* (1974)—established Larkin as one of the foremost poets of his generation. Many of the poems in these collections examine the experiences of loneliness, disappointment, and despair. But while Larkin's work often suggests the futility of struggle against time's "endless extinction," many of the poems also poignantly register the momentary beauties of the world. As Larkin phrased it, echoing Keats, "One of the jobs of the poem is to make the beautiful seem true and the true beautiful," even if "the disguise can usually be penetrated."

Church Going

Once I am sure there's nothing going on
I step inside, letting the door thud shut.
Another church: matting, seats, and stone,
And little books; sprawlings of flowers, cut
For Sunday, brownish now; some brass and stuff   5
Up at the holy end; the small neat organ;
And a tense, musty, unignorable silence,
Brewed God knows how long. Hatless, I take off
My cycle-clips in awkward reverence,

Move forward, run my hand around the font.[1]   10
From where I stand, the roof looks almost new—

---

1   *font* Baptismal receptacle.

Cleaned, or restored? Someone would know: I don't.
Mounting the lectern, I peruse a few
Hectoring large-scale verses, and pronounce
15 "Here endeth" much more loudly than I'd meant.
The echoes snigger briefly. Back at the door
I sign the book, donate an Irish sixpence,
Reflect the place was not worth stopping for.

Yet stop I did: in fact I often do,
20 And always end much at a loss like this,
Wondering what to look for; wondering, too,
When churches fall completely out of use
What we shall turn them into, if we shall keep
A few cathedrals chronically on show,
25 Their parchment, plate and pyx[1] in locked cases,
And let the rest rent-free to rain and sheep.
Shall we avoid them as unlucky places?

Or, after dark, will dubious women come
To make their children touch a particular stone;
30 Pick simples° for a cancer; or on some   *medicinal herbs*
Advised night see walking a dead one?
Power of some sort or other will go on
In games, in riddles, seemingly at random;
But superstition, like belief, must die,
35 And what remains when disbelief has gone?
Grass, weedy pavement, brambles, buttress, sky,

A shape less recognisable each week,
A purpose more obscure. I wonder who
Will be the last, the very last, to seek
40 This place for what it was; one of the crew
That tap and jot and know what rood-lofts° were?   *church galleries*
Some ruin-bibber,[2] randy for antique,
Or Christmas-addict, counting on a whiff
Of gown-and-bands and organ-pipes and myrrh?
45 Or will he be my representative,

---

1   *pyx* Vessel in which the bread of the Eucharist is kept.
2   *bibber* Someone who regularly drinks a specific drink.

Bored, uninformed, knowing the ghostly silt
Dispersed, yet tending to this cross of ground
Through suburb scrub because it held unspilt
So long and equably what since is found
Only in separation—marriage, and birth,   50
And death, and thoughts of these—for which was built
This special shell? For, though I've no idea
What this accoutred frowsty° barn is worth,   *stuffy*
It pleases me to stand in silence here;

A serious house on serious earth it is,   55
In whose blent air all our compulsions meet,
Are recognised, and robed as destinies.
And that much never can be obsolete,
Since someone will forever be surprising
A hunger in himself to be more serious,   60
And gravitating with it to this ground,
Which, he once heard, was proper to grow wise in,
If only that so many dead lie round.

—1954

Talking in Bed

Talking in bed ought to be easiest,
Lying together there goes back so far,
An emblem of two people being honest.

Yet more and more time passes silently.
Outside, the wind's incomplete unrest   5
Builds and disperses clouds about the sky,

And dark towns heap up on the horizon.
None of this cares for us. Nothing shows why
At this unique distance from isolation

It becomes still more difficult to find   10
Words at once true and kind,
Or not untrue and not unkind.

—1960

This Be the Verse

They fuck you up, your mum and dad.
    They may not mean to, but they do.
They fill you with the faults they had
    And add some extra, just for you.

5 But they were fucked up in their turn
    By fools in old-style hats and coats,
Who half the time were soppy-stern
    And half at one another's throats.

Man hands on misery to man.
10   It deepens like a coastal shelf.
Get out as early as you can,
    And don't have any kids yourself.

—1971

The Old Fools

What do they think has happened, the old fools,
To make them like this? Do they somehow suppose
It's more grown-up when your mouth hangs open and drools
And you keep on pissing yourself, and can't remember
5 Who called this morning? Or that, if they only chose,
They could alter things back to when they danced all night,
Or went to their wedding, or sloped arms some September?
Or do they fancy there's really been no change,
And they've always behaved as if they were crippled or tight,
10 Or sat through days of thin continuous dreaming
Watching light move? If they don't (and they can't), it's strange;
                              Why aren't they screaming?

At death, you break up: the bits that were you
Start speeding away from each other for ever
15 With no one to see. It's only oblivion, true:
We had it before, but then it was going to end,
And was all the time merging with a unique endeavour
To bring to bloom the million-petalled flower
Of being here. Next time you can't pretend

There'll be anything else. And these are the first signs: 20
Not knowing how, not hearing who, the power
Of choosing gone. Their looks show that they're for it:
Ash hair, toad hands, prune face dried into lines—
                                    How can they ignore it?

Perhaps being old is having lighted rooms   25
Inside your head, and people in them, acting.
People you know, yet can't quite name; each looms
Like a deep loss restored, from known doors turning,
Setting down a lamp, smiling from a stair, extracting
A known book from the shelves; or sometimes only   30
The rooms themselves, chairs and a fire burning,
The blown bush at the window, or the sun's
Faint friendliness on the wall some lonely
Rain-ceased midsummer evening. That is where they live:
Not here and now, but where all happened once.   35
                                    This is why they give

An air of baffled absence, trying to be there
Yet being here. For the rooms grow farther, leaving
Incompetent cold, the constant wear and tear
Of taken breath, and them crouching below   40
Extinction's alp, the old fools, never perceiving
How near it is. This must be what keeps them quiet:
The peak that stays in view wherever we go
For them is rising ground. Can they never tell
What is dragging them back, and how it will end?   45
Not at night? Not when the strangers come? Never, throughout
The whole hideous inverted childhood? Well,
                        We shall find out.

                                    —1973

Denise Levertov

1923–1997

Hailed as a protest poet and an avant-garde innovator, Denise Levertov explored a range of emotional and political themes, pursuing meaning in what she called the "uncharted sea" of every poem.

Born in Ilford, Essex, England, Levertov was educated at home and immersed in arts, literature, and activism, publishing her first poem at age 16 and her first collection, *The Double Image*, in 1946. She served as a civilian nurse in London during World War II before marrying American Mitchell Goodman and moving to New York in 1947. In America, Levertov began writing in a more experimental style, capturing critical acclaim with her collection *Here and Now* (1956). As the 1950s and 1960s unfolded, Levertov's poetry took on an impassioned political emphasis, critiquing the Vietnam war, nuclear weapons, and other social issues in a number of books including *With Eyes at the Back of Our Heads* (1959), *The Jacob's Ladder* (1961), and *The Sorrow Dance* (1967). Levertov served as editor for *The Nation* and *Mother Jones* magazines and taught at Stanford and other universities, receiving honors including a Guggenheim fellowship and a Lenore Marshall Poetry Prize.

Levertov looms large both in the longstanding tradition of political poetry and in the related tradition of political poetry by women.

What Were They Like?

1.) Did the people of Viet Nam[1]
    use lanterns of stone?[2]
2.) Did they hold ceremonies
    to reverence the opening of buds?[3]
5 3.) Were they inclined to quiet laughter?
4.) Did they use bone and ivory,
    jade and silver, for ornament?
5.) Had they an epic poem?
6.) Did they distinguish between speech and singing?

10 1.) Sir, their light hearts turned to stone.
    It is not remembered whether in gardens

---

1   *people of Viet Nam* From 1954 to 1975, a long-running war between North and South Vietnam occurred. The United States controversially joined the war in the 1960s, fighting against communist-controlled North Vietnam.

2   *lanterns of* Tōrōs are Japanese lanterns typically made of wood, stone, or metal.

3   *ceremonies ... buds Hanami*, the centuries-old tradition in Japan where people celebrate the budding of cherry trees in the spring.

stone lanterns illumined pleasant ways.
2.) Perhaps they gathered once to delight in blossom,
    but after their children were killed
    there were no more buds.   15
3.) Sir, laughter is bitter to the burned mouth.
4.) A dream ago, perhaps. Ornament is for joy.
    All the bones were charred.
5.) It is not remembered. Remember,
    most were peasants; their life   20
    was in rice and bamboo.
    When peaceful clouds were reflected in the paddies
    and the water buffalo stepped surely along terraces,
    maybe fathers told their sons old tales.
    When bombs smashed those mirrors   25
    there was time only to scream.
6.) There is an echo yet
    of their speech which was like a song.
    It was reported their singing resembled
    the flight of moths in moonlight.   30
    Who can say? It is silent now.

—1966

The Day the Audience Walked Out on Me, and Why

(*May 8th, 1970, Goucher College, Maryland*)

Like this it happened:
after the antiphonal reading from the psalms
and the dance of lamentation before the altar,
and the two poems, "Life at War" and
                        "What Were They Like?"[1]   5
I began my rap,
and said:
Yes, it is well that we have gathered
in this chapel to remember
the students shot at Kent State,[2]   10

---

1   *"Life ... They Like?"* "Life at War" and "What Were They Like?" are two poems by Levertov protesting the war in Vietnam.
2   *Kent State* University in Ohio where four students were killed and nine wounded by National Guard units during an anti-war demonstration on 4 May 1970.

but let us be sure we know
our gathering is a mockery unless
we remember also
the black students shot at Orangeburg[1] two years ago,
15 and Fred Hampton[2] murdered in his bed
by the police only months ago.

And while I spoke the people
—girls, older women, a few men—
began to rise and turn
20 their backs to the altar and leave.

And I went on and said,
Yes, it is well that we remember
all of these, but let us be sure
we know it is hypocrisy
25 to think of them unless
we make our actions their memorial,
actions of militant resistance.

By then the pews were almost empty
and I returned to my seat and a man stood up
30 in the back of the quiet chapel
(near the wide-open doors through which
the green of May showed, and the long shadows
                                          of late afternoon)
and said my words
35 desecrated a holy place.

And a few days later
when some more students (black) were shot
at Jackson, Mississippi,
no one desecrated the white folks' chapel,
40 because no memorial service was held.

—1971

---

1   *Orangeburg* In 1968, South Carolina Highway Patrol officers shot protestors demon-
     strating against racial segregation, killing three black men.
2   *Fred Hampton* Hampton (1948–69), an activist and organizer of the Black Panther Party,
     was shot dead by police during a raid on his apartment in December 1969.

Jack Gilbert

1925–2012

Known for his spare and streamlined poems, Jack Gilbert wrote about—as he put it in an interview—"what's inside." Born in Pittsburgh, Pennsylvania, he flunked out of high school before eventually finding his way through college and discovering poetry. He won the Yale Younger Poets Prize for his first book, *Views of Jeopardy*, in 1962. His next book was not to appear for almost 20 years, decades that he spent living in Europe. Explorations of solitude and of his intimate relationships with women created the emotional occasion for much of his work, including many moving poems upon the death of his young wife, the sculptor Michiko Nogami. A free-verse or open-form poet, he commented that he found the "technicalities" of traditional form to be "a waste of time," an evasion of poetry's great subject: in his view, the complex terrain of the human heart.

The Abnormal Is Not Courage

The Poles rode out from Warsaw against the German
tanks on horses. Rode knowing, in sunlight, with sabers.
A magnitude of beauty that allows me no peace.
And yet this poem would lessen that day. Question
the bravery. Say it's not courage. Call it a passion.   5
Would say courage isn't that. Not at its best.
It was impossible, and with form. They rode in sunlight.
Were mangled. But I say courage is not the abnormal.
Not the marvelous act. Not Macbeth with fine speeches.
The worthless can manage in public, or for the moment.   10
It is too near the whore's heart: the bounty of impulse,
and the failure to sustain even small kindness.
Not the marvelous act, but the evident conclusion of being.
Not strangeness, but a leap forward of the same quality.
Accomplishment. The even loyalty. But fresh.   15
Not the Prodigal Son,[1] nor Faustus.[2] But Penelope.[3]
The thing steady and clear. Then the crescendo.

---

1 *Prodigal Son* The biblical story of the repentant lost son and his dramatic return home (Luke 15.11–32).
2 *Faustus* Character in a play by Christopher Marlowe, who sells his soul to the devil.
3 *Penelope* In Homer's *Odyssey*, the wife of Odysseus, who remains faithful during his long absence.

The real form. The culmination. And the exceeding.
Not the surprise. The amazed understanding. The marriage,
20 not the month's rapture. Not the exception. The beauty
that is of many days. Steady and clear.
It is the normal excellence, of long accomplishment.

—1962

The Forgotten Dialect of the Heart

How astonishing it is that language can almost mean,
and frightening that it does not quite. Love, we say,
God, we say, Rome and Michiko,[1] we write, and the words
Get it wrong. We say bread and it means according
5 to which nation. French has no word for home,
and we have no word for strict pleasure. A people
in northern India is dying out because their ancient
tongue has no words for endearment. I dream of lost
vocabularies that might express some of what
10 we no longer can. Maybe the Etruscan[2] texts would
finally explain why the couples on their tombs
are smiling. And maybe not. When the thousands
of mysterious Sumerian tablets[3] were translated,
they seemed to be business records. But what if they
15 are poems or psalms? My joy is the same as twelve
Ethiopian goats standing silent in the morning light.
O Lord, thou art slabs of salt and ingots of copper,
as grand as ripe barley lithe under the wind's labor.
Her breasts are six white oxen loaded with bolts
20 of long-fibered Egyptian cotton. My love is a hundred
pitchers of honey. Shiploads of thuya[4] are what

---

1   *Michiko* Michiko Nogami, Gilbert's wife, died of cancer at age 36 after 11 years of marriage.
2   *Etruscan* The language of ancient Etruria (roughly the region of modern Tuscany), about which a great deal remains to be discovered.
3   *Sumerian tablets* Sumer was an ancient civilization in the region of modern-day Iraq. The Sumerian writing left behind on tablets belongs to no known family of languages.
4   *thuya* One can better appreciate the role this word plays in the poem by pondering the full complex definition in the *Oxford English Dictionary*: "Name of a genus of coniferous trees, consisting of about ten species, of which the North American *T. occidentalis* and the Chinese *T. orientalis* are commonly cultivated under the name Arbor Vitæ. (The tree so called by the ancients is now known as *Callitris*.) Also *attrib.*, as thuya-wood."

my body wants to say to your body. Giraffes are this
desire in the dark. Perhaps the spiral Minoan[1] script
is not a language but a map. What we feel most has
no name but amber, archers, cinnamon, horses and birds.   25

—1994

Tear It Down

We find out the heart only by dismantling what
the heart knows. By redefining the morning,
we find a morning that comes just after darkness.
We can break through marriage into marriage.
By insisting on love we spoil it, get beyond   5
affection and wade mouth-deep into love.
We must unlearn the constellations to see the stars.
But going back toward childhood will not help.
The village is not better than Pittsburgh.
Only Pittsburgh is more than Pittsburgh.   10
Rome is better than Rome in the same way the sound
of racoon tongues licking the inside walls
of the garbage tub is more than the stir
of them in the muck of the garbage. Love is not
enough. We die and are put into the earth forever.   15
We should insist while there is still time. We must
eat through the wildness of her sweet body already
in our bed to reach the body within the body.

—1994

---

1   *Minoan* The Bronze Age civilization of Crete.

Donald Justice

1925–2004

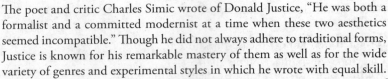

The poet and critic Charles Simic wrote of Donald Justice, "He was both a formalist and a committed modernist at a time when these two aesthetics seemed incompatible." Though he did not always adhere to traditional forms, Justice is known for his remarkable mastery of them as well as for the wide variety of genres and experimental styles in which he wrote with equal skill.

Born and raised in Florida, Justice studied music at the University of Miami, but decided that he had a greater gift for writing and pursued a Master's in English at the University of North Carolina. He later received his PhD from the University of Iowa, studying alongside William Stafford and Philip Levine, and went on to be a respected teacher of poetry at Iowa and at the University of Florida. The 1997 book *Certain Solitudes: On the Poetry of Donald Justice*, edited by Dana Gioia and William Logan, shows the high esteem in which Justice is held by many fellow poets (despite negative reviews early in his career). Gioia and Logan laud his wide-ranging experiments and techniques as "proof of Justice's deep engagement with surprisingly various poetic traditions, but also as a sign of a distinctly modern (or even postmodern) kind of originality."

Sestina on Six Words by Weldon Kees[1]

I often wonder about the others,
Where they are bound for on the voyage,
What is the reason for their silence,
Was there some reason to go away?
5 It may be they carry a dark burden,
Expect some harm, or have done harm.

How can we show we mean no harm?
Approach them? But they shy from others.
Offer, perhaps, to share the burden?
10 They change the subject to the voyage
Or turn abruptly, walk away,
To brood against the rail in silence.

---

1   Donald Justice published an edition of Weldon Kees' poetry in 1960 that was responsible for bringing new attention to the importance of Kees' work. This poem is an homage to Kees' own sestina, "Sestina: Travel Notes" (p. 435).

What is defeated by their silence
More than love, less than harm?
Many already are looking their way,   15
Pretending not to. Eyes of others
Will follow them now the whole voyage
And add a little to the burden.

Others touch hands to ease the burden,
Or stroll, companionable in silence,
Counting the stars which bless the voyage,   20
But let the foghorn speak of harm,
They also stammer like the others,
Their hands seem in each other's way.

It is so obvious in a way.   25
Each is alone, each with his burden.
To others, always, they are others,
And they can never break the silence,
Say, lightly, *thou*, but to their harm
Although they make many a voyage.   30

What have they wished for from the voyage
But to awaken far away,
By miracle free from every harm,
Hearing at dawn that sweet burden
The birds cry after a long silence?   35
Where is that country not like others?

There is no way to ease the burden.
The voyage leads on from harm to harm,
A land of others and of silence.

—1957

Kenneth Koch

1925–2002

Kenneth Koch developed an avant-garde poetics punctuated by humor and irony. He became well-known for his witty, irreverent voice—a voice for which some critics disliked him. He countered what he felt to be a suffocating tradition of poetry and ideas about "greatness" that effectively distanced poetry from people. As he puts it in "Fresh Air," such poems were "Written by the men with their eyes on the myth / And the missus and the midterms." Koch rejected obscurity and symbolism, including the obscure allusiveness of the Modernist work by T.S. Eliot and Ezra Pound that was highly prized when Koch was breaking onto the scene. (In a hilarious 1965 recorded conversation between Koch and fellow poet John Ashbery, they mutually poked fun at the concept of poetic "ambiguity" that the New Critics had enshrined as one of the allegedly essential qualities of great poetry.) By contrast, Koch developed a poetics that rooted itself in what he called "happiness" and "pleasant surprise," especially the pleasure of language itself. He was famed as a teacher of poetry, including teaching poetry to young children.

As a young poet, he was part of a new post–World War II poetic movement called the "New York School." Koch and his fellow New York poets (including Ashbery and Frank O'Hara) worked in and wrote about the New York scene in the 1950s and 1960s. The New York poets also notably collaborated across the arts, especially with painters such as Jackson Pollock, Willem de Kooning, and Helen Frankenthaler. Koch stressed the importance of what he called "the surface" of the poem, that is, the language it was made of, a concern with medium that he shared with contemporary painters.

Koch's witty voice also tackled serious issues about mid-twentieth-century American society, love, and the craft of poetry itself. His approach to poetry was markedly different than one that valued language for its capacity to symbolize, allude, or express ideas. Controversies over these issues would influence a host of new poetries in the coming decades. (See Language Poets, p. 653.)

Variations on a Theme by William Carlos Williams[1]

1

I chopped down the house that you had been saving to live in next summer.
I am sorry, but it was morning, and I had nothing to do
and its wooden beams were so inviting.

2

We laughed at the hollyhocks together
and then I sprayed them with lye.   5
Forgive me. I simply do not know what I am doing.

3

I gave away the money that you had been saving to live on for the next ten
        years.
The man who asked for it was shabby
and the firm March wind on the porch was so juicy and cold.

4

Last evening we went dancing and I broke your leg.   10
Forgive me. I was clumsy, and
I wanted you here in the wards, where I am the doctor!

—1962

One Train May Hide Another

(sign at a railroad crossing in Kenya)

In a poem, one line may hide another line,
As at a crossing, one train may hide another train.
That is, if you are waiting to cross
The tracks, wait to do it for one moment at
Least after the first train is gone. And so when you read   5
Wait until you have read the next line—
Then it is safe to go on reading.
In a family one sister may conceal another,
So, when you are courting, it's best to have them all in view

---

1   See William Carlos Williams's "This Is Just to Say" (p. 339) .

10 Otherwise in coming to find one you may love another.
One father or one brother may hide the man,
If you are a woman, whom you have been waiting to love.
So always standing in front of something the other
As words stand in front of objects, feelings, and ideas.
15 One wish may hide another. And one person's reputation may hide
The reputation of another. One dog may conceal another
On a lawn, so if you escape the first one you're not necessarily safe;
One lilac may hide another and then a lot of lilacs and on the Appia Antica
   one tomb
May hide a number of other tombs.[1] In love, one reproach may hide another,
20 One small complaint may hide a great one.
One injustice may hide another—one colonial may hide another,
One blaring red uniform another, and another, a whole column. One bath
   may hide another bath
As when, after bathing, one walks out into the rain.
One idea may hide another: Life is simple
25 Hide Life is incredibly complex, as in the prose of Gertrude Stein[2]
One sentence hides another and is another as well. And in the laboratory
One invention may hide another invention,
One evening may hide another, one shadow, a nest of shadows.
One dark red, or one blue, or one purple—this is a painting
30 By someone after Matisse.[3] One waits at the tracks until they pass,
These hidden doubles or, sometimes, likenesses. One identical twin
May hide the other. And there may be even more in there! The obstetrician
Gazes at the Valley of the Var.[4] We used to live there, my wife and I, but
One life hid another life. And now she is gone and I am here.
35 A vivacious mother hides a gawky daughter. The daughter hides
Her own vivacious daughter in turn. They are in
A railway station and the daughter is holding a bag
Bigger than her mother's bag and successfully hides it.
In offering to pick up the daughter's bag one finds oneself confronted by the
   mother's

---

1   *Appia ... tombs* Known as the Appian Way in English, *Appia Antica* is one of the oldest
    sections of one of the oldest roads leading to Rome. Several important tombs and land-
    marks have been built along the Appian Way over the centuries.

2   *Gertrude Stein* American writer (1874–1946) known for her repetitive, stream-of-con-
    sciousness style of writing (see p. 318).

3   *Matisse* French artist and painter Henri Matisse (1869–1954) known for his abstract
    style and unique use of color.

4   *Var* River in southeast France.

And has to carry that one, too. So one hitchhiker   40
May deliberately hide another and one cup of coffee
Another, too, until one is over-excited. One love may hide another love or
    the same love
As when "I love you" suddenly rings false and one discovers
The better love lingering behind, as when "I'm full of doubts"
Hides "I'm certain about something and it is that"   45
And one dream may hide another as is well known, always, too. In the
    Garden of Eden
Adam and Eve may hide the real Adam and Eve.[1]
Jerusalem may hide another Jerusalem.
When you come to something, stop to let it pass
So you can see what else is there. At home, no matter where,   50
Internal tracks pose dangers, too: one memory
Certainly hides another, that being what memory is all about,
The eternal reverse succession of contemplated entities. Reading *A*
    Sentimental Journey look around
When you have finished, for *Tristram Shandy*,[2] to see
If it is standing there, it should be, stronger   55
And more profound and theretofore hidden as Santa Maria Maggiore[3]
May be hidden by similar churches inside Rome. One sidewalk
May hide another, as when you're asleep there, and
One song hide another song; a pounding upstairs
Hide the beating of drums. One friend may hide another, you sit at the foot   60
    of a tree
With one and when you get up to leave there is another
Whom you'd have preferred to talk to all along. One teacher,
One doctor, one ecstasy, one illness, one woman, one man
May hide another. Pause to let the first one pass.
You think, Now it is safe to cross and you are hit by the next one. It can be   65
    important
To have waited at least a moment to see what was already there.

—1993

---

1   *Adam and Eve ... Adam and Eve* See Genesis 3.7 in the Bible's Old Testament: "And the
    eyes of them both were opened, and they knew that they were naked; and they sewed fig
    leaves together, and made themselves aprons."

2   *A Sentimental Journey* Refers to the 1768 novel *A Sentimental Journey through France and
    Italy* by Irish writer Laurence Stern; *Tristram Shandy* Stern's 1759 novel *The Life and
    Opinions of Tristram Shandy, Gentleman.*

3   *Santa Maria Maggiore* One of the four major basilicas of the Roman Catholic church.

Mountain

Nothing's moving I don't see anybody
And I know that it's not a trick
There really is nothing moving there
And there aren't any people. It is the very utmost top
5   Where, as is not unusual,
There is snow, lying like the hair on a white-haired person's head
Combed sideways and backward and forward to cover as much of the top
As possible, for the snow is thinning, it's September
Although a few months from now there will be a new crop
10 Probably, though this no one KNOWS (so neither do we)
But every other year it has happened by November
Except for one year that's known about, nineteen twenty-three
When the top was more and more uncovered until December fifteenth
When finally it snowed and snowed
15 I love seeing this mountain like a mouse
Attached to the tail of another mouse, and to another and to another
In total mountain silence
There is no way to get up there, and no means to stay.
It is uninhabitable. No roads and no possibility
20 Of roads. You don't have a history
Do you, mountain top? This doesn't make you either a mystery
Or a dull person and you're certainly not a truck stop.
No industry can exploit you
No developer can divide you into estates or lots
25 No dazzling disquieting woman can tie your heart in knots.
I could never lead my life on one of those spots
You leave uncovered up there. No way to be there
But I'm moved.

—2002

Robert Creeley

1926–2005

"I write to move in *words*," said Robert Creeley, author of more than 60 volumes of poetry along with plays, short stories, essays, and a novel. His poems often capture the everyday currents of self, emotion, body, and mind, especially in relation to the simultaneous movements of language in human experience. (See "The Language" and "The Pattern," below.) Turning from a poetics of allusion and tradition, he carved out a distinctive spare style. Poet and critic Stephen Burt observes that Creeley's poetry is notable for what it leaves out: long or rare words, meters, and even metaphors. Instead, Creeley cultivates precision, simplicity, and a fierce minimalist concentration on the visual and rhythmic aspects of poetry.

Born in Arlington, Massachusetts, Creeley attended Harvard and the University of New Mexico, interrupting his schooling in 1944 to join the American Field Service. He published his first poem, "Return," in 1946, printing many others throughout the 1950s and 1960s and founding his own press. With collaborator Charles Olson he helped to establish "Projective Verse," a fluid form practiced by a network of artists affiliated with the experimental Black Mountain College in North Carolina. In 1962, Creeley's collection *For Love: Poems 1950–1960* earned him unprecedented acclaim; some of his other titles include *For Love and Words* (1967), *Later* (1979), and *If I Were Writing This* (2003). Creeley mentored other poets throughout his life, teaching at the State University of New York-Buffalo (where he helped to foster an avant-garde focus) and Brown University.

Creeley was a prolific and influential innovator who engaged with literary communities from the Beat poets of San Francisco to the Black Mountain Poets. His shift from traditional formalism into a dynamic present—in which poems grew out of moments and feelings, including his personal experiences of family life, marriages, breakups, and aging—has exerted significant influence on his fellow writers.

Note to readers: Creeley's poem "Anger" appears on the anthology's companion website. The URL and passcode appear in the Table of Contents.

The Language

Locate *I*
love you some-
where in

teeth and
5   eyes, bite
it but

take care not
to hurt, you
want so

10   much so
little. Words
say everything.

I
love you
15   again,

then what
is emptiness
for. To

fill, fill.
20   I heard words
and words full

of holes
aching. Speech
is a mouth.

—1964

The Pattern

As soon as
I speak, I
speaks. It

wants to
5   be free but
impassive lies

in the direction
of its
words. Let

x equal x, x   10
also
equals x. I

speak to
hear myself
speak? I   15

had not thought
that some-
thing had such

undone. It
was an idea   20
of mine.

—1964

America

America, you ode for reality!
Give back the people you took.

Let the sun shine again
on the four corners of the world

you thought of first but do not   5
own, or keep like a convenience.

People are your own word, you
invented that locus and term.

Here, you said and say, is
where we are. Give back   10

what we are, these people you made,
us, and nowhere but you to be.

—1969

Allen Ginsberg
1926–1997

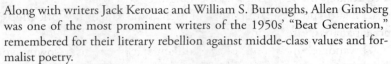 Along with writers Jack Kerouac and William S. Burroughs, Allen Ginsberg was one of the most prominent writers of the 1950s' "Beat Generation," remembered for their literary rebellion against middle-class values and formalist poetry.

Ginsberg is perhaps best known for his poem "Howl," first delivered at a poetry reading in San Francisco in 1955 and published the following year. Drawing on influences from Jewish liturgy to William Blake, the long poem condemns American society's repressive attitudes toward homosexuality, drug use, and mental illness, presenting the demonic god Moloch as an embodiment of America's obsession with money and order. Because the poem made explicit references to drugs and homosexuality at a time when both were illegal, the publishers of "Howl" were charged with distributing obscene literature, and Ginsberg's poem became the centerpiece of a landmark obscenity trial in the United States. The publishers and the poem ultimately triumphed.

After the Beat era, Ginsberg continued to write until his death, publishing letters and essays as well as poetry. His interest in religion and philosophy, especially Hindu and Buddhist thought, provided an increasingly important focus in his later work. Like "Howl," his post-Beat poems are often politically motivated; *Wichita Vortex Sutra* (1966), for example, censures the Vietnam War, against which Ginsberg was an effective and dedicated activist.

Note to readers: Ginsberg's poem "Howl" appears on the anthology's companion website. The URL and passcode appear in the Table of Contents.

A Supermarket in California

What thoughts I have of you tonight, Walt Whitman,[1] for I walked down the sidestreets under the trees with a headache self-conscious looking at the full moon.

In my hungry fatigue, and shopping for images, I went into the neon
5   fruit supermarket, dreaming of your enumerations!

---

1   *Walt Whitman* American poet (1819–92), one of Ginsberg's major influences (see p. 169). "A Supermarket in California" was written in 1955, 100 years after Whitman published the first edition of his collection *Leaves of Grass*.

What peaches and what penumbras![1] Whole families shopping at night! Aisles full of husbands! Wives in the avocados, babies in the tomatoes!—and you, García Lorca,[2] what were you doing down by the watermelons?

I saw you, Walt Whitman, childless, lonely old grubber, poking among the meats in the refrigerator and eyeing the grocery boys.[3]

I heard you asking questions of each: Who killed the pork chops? What price bananas? Are you my Angel?

I wandered in and out of the brilliant stacks of cans following you, and followed in my imagination by the store detective. We strode down the open corridors together in our solitary fancy tasting artichokes, possessing every frozen delicacy, and never passing the cashier.

Where are we going, Walt Whitman? The doors close in an hour. Which way does your beard point tonight?

(I touch your book and dream of our odyssey in the supermarket and feel absurd.)

Will we walk all night through solitary streets? The trees add shade to shade, lights out in the houses, we'll both be lonely.

Will we stroll dreaming of the lost America of love past blue automobiles in driveways, home to our silent cottage?

Ah, dear father, greybeard, lonely old courage-teacher, what America did you have when Charon[4] quit poling his ferry and you got out on a smoking bank and stood watching the boat disappear on the black waters of Lethe?

—1956 (written 1955)

---

1   *penumbras* Partially shaded regions at the edges of a shadow.
2   *García Lorca* Federico García Lorca (1899–1936), Spanish poet and dramatist.
3   *I saw you ... grocery boys* Whitman's poetry celebrated male-male love. Whitman had a longstanding queer fan base by the time Ginsberg wrote this poem.
4   *Charon* In Greek mythology, the boatman who ferried the souls of the dead across the river Styx to Hades.

Frank O'Hara

1926–1966

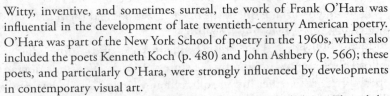 Witty, inventive, and sometimes surreal, the work of Frank O'Hara was influential in the development of late twentieth-century American poetry. O'Hara was part of the New York School of poetry in the 1960s, which also included the poets Kenneth Koch (p. 480) and John Ashbery (p. 566); these poets, and particularly O'Hara, were strongly influenced by developments in contemporary visual art.

O'Hara was born in Baltimore and raised in Massachusetts. Though he studied music and English literature at Harvard, his work as an art critic and as a clerk and later a curator at the Museum of Modern Art had as much impact on his work as his formal literary training. While in some poems, such as "Why I Am Not a Painter," O'Hara explicitly discusses artists and works of art, he also thought about poems more generally in painterly terms; of his long poem *Second Avenue*, he wrote that he tried to keep "the surface of the poem high and dry, not wet, reflective and self-conscious." The colloquial, allusive, and sometimes "jumbled" (his own word) qualities of his poems also grew out of his love of the movies and of popular culture.

O'Hara died in an accident on a beach at Fire Island, New York, at the age of 40. His friend and former lover, the painter Larry Rivers, gave a eulogy in which he called O'Hara "a dream of contradictions." His tombstone reads, "Grace, to be born and live as variously as possible."

A Step Away from Them

It's my lunch hour, so I go
for a walk among the hum-colored
cabs. First, down the sidewalk
where laborers feed their dirty
5   glistening torsos sandwiches
and Coca-Cola, with yellow helmets
on. They protect them from falling
bricks, I guess. Then onto the
avenue where skirts are flipping
10 above heels and blow up over
grates. The sun is hot, but the
cabs stir up the air. I look
at bargains in wristwatches. There
are cats playing in sawdust.
15 On

to Times Square, where the sign
blows smoke over my head, and higher
the waterfall pours lightly. A
Negro stands in a doorway with a
toothpick, languorously agitating.   20
A blonde chorus girl clicks: he
smiles and rubs his chin. Everything
suddenly honks: it is 12:40 of
a Thursday.
Neon in daylight is a   25
great pleasure, as Edwin Denby[1] would
write, as are light bulbs in daylight.
I stop for a cheeseburger at JULIET'S
CORNER. Giulietta Masina, wife of
Federico Fellini, *è bell' attrice.*[2]   30
And chocolate malted. A lady in
foxes on such a day puts her poodle
in a cab.
There are several Puerto
Ricans on the avenue today, which   35
makes it beautiful and warm. First
Bunny died, then John Latouche,
then Jackson Pollock.[3] But is the
earth as full as life was full, of them?
And one has eaten and one walks,   40
past the magazines with nudes
and the posters for BULLFIGHT and
the Manhattan Storage Warehouse,
which they'll soon tear down. I
used to think they had the Armory   45
Show there.
A glass of papaya juice
and back to work. My heart is in my
pocket, it is Poems by Pierre Reverdy.[4]

—1957

---

1   *Edwin Denby* American writer (1903–83).
2   *Giulietta Masina* Italian actress (1921–94); *Federico Fellini* Italian director (1920–93);
     è bell' attrice Italian: you beautiful actress.
3   *Bunny* American writer V.R. Lang (1924–56), a close friend to O'Hara; *John Latouche*
     American songwriter and author (1917–56); *Jackson Pollock* American painter (1912–
     56) known for his work in abstract expressionism.
4   *Pierre Reverdy* French poet (1889–1960), mostly known for his works that were heavily
     influenced by the Surrealist and Cubist movements.

Why I Am Not a Painter

I am not a painter, I am a poet.
Why? I think I would rather be
a painter, but I am not. Well,

for instance, Mike Goldberg[1]
5   is starting a painting. I drop in.
"Sit down and have a drink" he
says. I drink; we drink, I look
up. "You have SARDINES in it."
"Yes, it needed something there."
10 "Oh." I go and the days go by
and I drop in again. The painting
is going on, and I go, and the days
go by. I drop in. The painting is
finished. "Where's SARDINES?"
15 All that's left is just
letters, "It was too much," Mike says.

But me? One day I am thinking of
a color: orange. I write a line
about orange. Pretty soon it is a
20 whole page of words, not lines.
Then another page. There should be
so much more, not of orange, of
words, of how terrible orange is
and life. Days go by. It is even in
25 prose, I am a real poet. My poem
is finished and I haven't mentioned
orange yet. It's twelve poems, I call
it ORANGES. And one day in a gallery
I see Mike's painting, called SARDINES.

—1971

---

1   *Mike Goldberg* Michael Goldberg (1924–2007), American abstract expressionist painter.

Maya Angelou
1928–2014

Maya Angelou (born Marguerite Ann Johnson) was not only an acclaimed poet but also a singer, dancer, producer, director, and civil rights activist. Born in St. Louis, Missouri, she moved many times during her childhood and early adulthood, and spent several years living in Egypt and Ghana as a young journalist.

Angelou developed a passion for writing and literature during a period of muteness brought on by a childhood sexual assault, as described in her memoir *I Know Why the Caged Bird Sings* (1969). Her first volume of poetry, *Just Give Me a Cool Drink of Water 'fore I Diiie* (1971), earned a Pulitzer Prize nomination. She also gained acclaim for her reading of "On the Pulse of Morning" at President Bill Clinton's inaugural address; she was the first African-American and first woman to read at an inauguration.

Many readers, including many prominent African-American women, have spoken about the importance to their lives of Angelou's poetry of personal survival, love, and liberation. In a tribute after Angelou's death in 2014, First Lady Michelle Obama credited Angelou's words with being "so powerful that they carried a little black girl from the South Side of Chicago all the way to the White House."

Still I Rise

You may write me down in history
With your bitter, twisted lies,
You may trod me in the very dirt
But still, like dust, I'll rise.

Does my sassiness upset you?   5
Why are you beset with gloom?
'Cause I walk like I've got oil wells
Pumping in my living room.

Just like moons and like suns,
With the certainty of tides,   10
Just like hopes springing high,
Still I'll rise.

Did you want to see me broken?
Bowed head and lowered eyes?
15 Shoulders falling down like teardrops,
Weakened by my soulful cries?

Does my haughtiness offend you?
Don't you take it awful hard
'Cause I laugh like I've got gold mines
20 Diggin' in my own backyard.

You may shoot me with your words,
You may cut me with your eyes,
You may kill me with your hatefulness,
But still, like air, I'll rise.

25 Does my sexiness upset you?
Does it come as a surprise
That I dance like I've got diamonds
At the meeting of my thighs?

Out of the huts of history's shame
30 I rise
Up from a past that's rooted in pain
I rise
I'm a black ocean, leaping and wide,
Welling and swelling I bear in the tide.

35 Leaving behind nights of terror and fear
I rise
Into a daybreak that's wondrously clear
I rise
Bringing the gifts that my ancestors gave,
40 I am the dream and the hope of the slave.
I rise
I rise
I rise.

—1978

Philip Levine
1928–2015

Philip Levine's upbringing in working-class Detroit strongly influenced his poetry. His poems celebrate human dignity under difficult conditions, often describing the kind of manual labor Levine performed as a young man working in factories. He wrote of these poems, "When I say work I mean the sort of brute physical work that most of us try to avoid, but that those without particular gifts or training were often forced to adopt to make a living in a society as tough and competitive as ours."

Levine was born in Detroit to Russian Jewish parents. After working in automotive factories as a teenager, he attended Wayne University (now Wayne State) and later studied, despite initially not being a registered student, at the University of Iowa. There he was influenced by his teachers John Berryman and Robert Lowell, who helped to shape his direct, concise, and seemingly straightforward narrative style. Readers often respond to Levine's poems for their emotional power; Joyce Carol Oates notes that their effect can be "shattering." From 1958 to 1992, Levine taught at the University of California at Fresno. In 2011 he was appointed Poet Laureate of the United States. In early 2015 he died of pancreatic cancer.

Animals Are Passing from Our Lives

It's wonderful how I jog
on four honed-down ivory toes
my massive buttocks slipping
like oiled parts with each light step.

I'm to market. I can smell   5
the sour, grooved block, I can smell
the blade that opens the hole
and the pudgy white fingers

that shake out the intestines
like a hankie. In my dreams   10
the snouts drool on the marble,
suffering children, suffering flies,

suffering the consumers
who won't meet their steady eyes

15 for fear they could see. The boy
who drives me along believes

that any moment I'll fall
on my side and drum my toes
like a typewriter or squeal
20 and shit like a new housewife

discovering television,
or that I'll turn like a beast
cleverly to hook his teeth
with my teeth. No. Not this pig.

—1968

Anne Sexton

1928–1974

Poetry, Anne Sexton said, "should be a shock to the senses. It should almost hurt." Her work—known for its intimate and difficult subjects, from mental illness to death to female bodily experience—creates emotional and psychological intensity through technical precision and evocative symbol and metaphor.

Born to a middle-class Massachusetts family, at 19 Sexton eloped and became a self-described "suburban housewife." She was, she said, "a kind of buried self who didn't know she could do anything but make white sauce and diaper babies" until, after the birth of her first daughter, she experienced a mental breakdown, a mental-health problem that would become recurrent. Initially, she took up writing as a form of therapy; her first book of poems, *To Bedlam and Part Way Back* (1960), was directly inspired by her experience of mental illness.

Critics both praised and condemned Sexton as a "confessional poet." Melvin Maddocks, for example, lauded the "personal urgency" of *Bedlam*, while James Dickey described her second collection, *All My Pretty Ones* (1962), as "very little more than a kind of terribly serious and determinedly outspoken soap-opera." While Sexton certainly drew on her own experience in much of her work, her poems are often not as directly personal or raw as they first appear, since they are also artistic creations skillfully crafted. (Confessional poetry as a genre involves complex boundaries between the personal and an invented version, or performance, of the personal.) Sexton's artistry, like that of her fellow confessional poets, is often tied for its transgressive effect to cultural ideas about topics like gender, shame, and mental illness.

Sexton's fame and recognition increased with the publication of *Live or Die* (1966), which received the Pulitzer Prize. She continued to struggle, however, with worsening mental health. Her later works, including *The Death Notebooks* (1974) and *The Awful Rowing toward God* (posthumously published in 1975), focus on death and spiritual uncertainty. She died by suicide in 1974.

Sylvia's Death[1]

for Sylvia Plath

O Sylvia, Sylvia,
with a dead box of stones and spoons,

with two children, two meteors
wandering loose in a tiny playroom,

5 with your mouth into the sheet,
into the roofbeam, into the dumb prayer,

(Sylvia, Sylvia
where did you go
after you wrote me
10 from Devonshire[2]
about raising potatoes
and keeping bees?)

what did you stand by,
just how did you lie down into?

15 Thief!—
how did you crawl into,

crawl down alone
into the death I wanted so badly and for so long,

the death we said we both outgrew,
20 the one we wore on our skinny breasts,

---

1   *Sylvia's Death* Like Sexton, American poet Sylvia Plath (1932–63) (p. 528) was famous for her contributions to confessional poetry. Sexton met Plath when they both attended a Boston University poetry class taught by fellow confessional poet Robert Lowell. The two women often met after class for drinks, sometimes with George Starbuck, another notable confessional poet in the class. They discussed many things, especially Sexton's and Plath's mutual fascination with death and dying. Plath committed suicide in 1963 by sealing herself into her kitchen and asphyxiating herself with the gas oven while her two children slept in another room.

2   *Devonshire* Devon, England, where Plath lived when she was married to British poet Ted Hughes (see p. 522).

the one we talked of so often each time
we downed three extra dry martinis in Boston,

the death that talked of analysts and cures,
the death that talked like brides with plots,

the death we drank to,   25
the motives and then the quiet deed?

(In Boston
the dying
ride in cabs,
yes death again,   30
that ride home
with *our* boy.)

O Sylvia, I remember the sleepy drummer
who beat on our eyes with an old story,

how we wanted to let him come   35
like a sadist or a New York fairy

to do his job,
a necessity, a window in a wall or a crib,

and since that time he waited
under our heart, our cupboard,   40

and I see now that we store him up
year after year, old suicides

and I know at the news of your death
a terrible taste for it, like salt.

(And me,   45
me too.
And now, Sylvia,
you again
with death again,
that ride home   50
with *our* boy.)

And I say only
with my arms stretched out into that stone place,

what is your death
55 but an old belonging,

a mole that fell out
of one of your poems?

(O friend,
while the moon's bad,
60 and the king's gone,
and the queen's at her wit's end
the bar fly ought to sing!)

O tiny mother,
you too!
65 O funny duchess!
O blonde thing!

—1964

The Ballad of the Lonely Masturbator

The end of the affair is always death.
She's my workshop. Slippery eye,
out of the tribe of myself my breath
finds you gone. I horrify
5   those who stand by. I am fed.
At night, alone, I marry the bed.

Finger to finger, now she's mine.
She's not too far. She's my encounter.
I beat her like a bell. I recline
10 in the bower where you used to mount her.
You borrowed me on the flowered spread.
At night, alone, I marry the bed.

Take for instance this night, my love,
that every single couple puts together
15 with a joint overturning, beneath, above,

the abundant two on sponge and feather,
kneeling and pushing, head to head.
At night, alone, I marry the bed.

I break out of my body this way,
an annoying miracle. Could I   20
put the dream market on display?
I am spread out. I crucify.
My little plum is what you said.
At night, alone, I marry the bed.

Then my black-eyed rival came.   25
The lady of water, rising on the beach,
a piano at her fingertips, shame
on her lips and a flute's speech.
And I was the knock-kneed broom instead.
At night, alone, I marry the bed.   30

She took you the way a woman takes
a bargain dress off the rack
and I broke the way a stone breaks.
I give back your books and fishing tack.
Today's paper says that you are wed.   35
At night, alone, I marry the bed.

The boys and girls are one tonight.
They unbutton blouses. They unzip flies.
They take off shoes. They turn off the light.
The glimmering creatures are full of lies.   40
They are eating each other. They are overfed.
At night, alone, I marry the bed.

—1968

Thom Gunn

1929–2004

As diverse in subject matter as in style, the poetry of Thom Gunn is difficult to classify. His friend and fellow poet Clive Wilmer described it as "contained energy," an attempt to reconcile passion and intellect, lyricism and argument, by harnessing the flow of experience through traditional verse forms.

The son of London journalists, Gunn spent much of his life in California, where he studied at Stanford and later taught at Berkeley. Gunn is often identified with "the Movement," a group of British poets who turned away from avant-gardism in favor of a more "native English" tradition of plain-style lyric poetry. (See Philip Larkin, p. 467.) His influences ranged from seventeenth-century English poets such as John Donne to the American Modernist verse of Wallace Stevens and William Carlos Williams. From his first collection, *Fighting Words* (1954), to his last, *Boss Cupid* (2000), Gunn experimented with styles and techniques. His early poetry, much of it concerned with the existential struggle for self-definition, is characterized by tightly controlled schemes of rhyme and meter. He later experimented with free verse and with varying degrees of formal regularity in the attempt to represent his liberating experiences with LSD and the utopian counterculture in 1960s' San Francisco, where he lived until his death. Gunn changed tone again with *The Man with Night Sweats* (1992), which established him as a poet-chronicler and elegist of the AIDS epidemic that claimed many of his friends in the 1980s.

While many have seen Gunn's as a poetry of "tensions," Gunn himself preferred the word "continuities." His life and work, he said, "insists on continuities—between America and England, between free verse and meter, between vision and everyday consciousness."

To His Cynical Mistress

And love is then no more than a compromise?
An impermanent treaty waiting to be signed
                                By the two enemies?
—While the calculating Cupid feigning impartial blind
5 Drafts it, promising peace, both leaders wise
To his antics sign but secretly double their spies.

On each side is the ignorant animal nation
Jostling friendly in streets, enjoying in good faith
                                This celebration

Forgetting their enmity with cheers and drunken breath   10
But for them there has not been yet amalgamation:
The leaders calmly plot assassination.

—1958

In Time of Plague

My thoughts are crowded with death
and it draws so oddly on the sexual
that I am confused
confused to be attracted
by, in effect, my own annihilation.   5
Who are these two, these fiercely attractive men
who want me to stick their needle in my arm?
They tell me they are called Brad and John,
one from here, one from Denver, sitting the same
on the bench as they talk to me,   10
their legs spread apart, their eyes attentive.
I love their daring, their looks, their jargon,
and what they have in mind.
Their mind is the mind of death.

They know it, and do not know it,   15
and they are like me in that
(I know it, and do not know it)
and like the flow of people through this bar.
Brad and John thirst heroically together
for euphoria—for a state of ardent life   20
in which we could all stretch ourselves
and lose our differences. I seek
to enter their minds: am I a fool,
and they direct and right, properly
testing themselves against risk,   25
as a human must, and does,
or are they the fools, their alert faces
mere death's heads lighted glamorously?
I weigh possibilities
till I am afraid of the strength   30
of my own health
and of their evident health.

They get restless at last with my indecisiveness
and so, first one, and then the other,
35 move off into the moving concourse of people
who are boisterous and bright
carrying in their faces and throughout their bodies
the news of life and death.

—1992

The Hug

It was your birthday, we had drunk and dined
   Half of the night with our old friend
    Who'd showed us in the end
  To a bed I reached in one drunk stride.
5   Already I lay snug,
  And drowsy with the wine dozed on one side.

I dozed, I slept. My sleep broke on a hug,
    Suddenly, from behind,
In which the full lengths of our bodies pressed:
10   Your instep to my heel,
  My shoulder-blades against your chest.
  It was not sex, but I could feel
  The whole strength of your body set,
     Or braced, to mine,
15   And locking me to you
  As if we were still twenty-two
  When our grand passion had not yet
   Become familial.
  My quick sleep had deleted all
20   Of intervening time and place.
    I only knew
The stay of your secure firm dry embrace.

—1992

John Hollander
1929–2013

Over the course of a long career as prize-winning poet, professor, literary critic, anthologist, and editor, John Hollander demonstrated deep learning, philosophical intensity, and technical virtuosity—as well as exuberant playfulness and wit. Hollander and Allen Ginsberg (whom Hollander considered his poetic mentor; see p. 488) were close friends at Columbia University in the late 1940s. Unlike Ginsberg's highly personal free-verse poetry, Hollander's verse is often allusive and cerebral, ranging across wide bodies of knowledge while simultaneously engaging the many varieties of traditional poetic forms. W.H. Auden (see p. 402) chose Hollander's first book, *A Crackling of Thorns*, as the winner of the Yale Series of Younger Poets Award in 1958. Hollander later recalled in an interview that he revered Auden's poetry for its balance between seriousness and play, and that he had first explored the playfulness of language as a teenager by writing humorous pieces and jokes. The particular type of pleasure in words that often animates humor is an important, but usually neglected, strain in the history of poetics.

Hollander also made influential contributions as an editor to shaping a new canon of poets through his important collections, including The Library of America's two-volume *American Poetry: The Nineteenth Century*, which reprinted poets who had become obscure as well as popular forms of poetry such as folk songs and spirituals. He described his editorial projects as part of a broader revaluation of the poetic canon "cleared of its last vestiges of modernist bias."

from *Thirteens*[1]

1

Triskaidekaphobia[2] through the centuries
Kept us seating one more at the table, even when
The extra one was silly or redundant or gross.
Moreover, the new arrangements[3]—the sexes paired off,
The doubled sevens, the mysteries often and four—   5

---

1   The full text of this poem, 13 sections of 13 lines each, appeared in the June 1981 issue of *Poetry* magazine.
2   *Triskaidekaphobia* Fear of the number 13.
3   *the new arrangements* Hollander's poetic dinner party simultaneously plays with the history of poetic forms and meters. The term "numbers" was long a term for poetic meter itself, since regular meters involved particular numbers of syllables per line.

Masqueraded as reasons, hiding always our fear
Of dangerous and pungent oddments behind the bright
And interesting arrangements that terror had us make.
Like grownups now, allowing the black cats to amble
10 Across our shadows in the forenoon without alarm,
We can at least, in a poor time for discourse, invite
Exactly whom we please, whom we need: it will be right
In a new shape, finished beyond the old completions.

—1981

An Old-Fashioned Song[1]

No more walks in the wood:
The trees have all been cut
Down, and where once they stood
Not even a wagon rut
5 Appears along the path
Low brush is taking over.

No more walks in the wood;
This is the aftermath
Of afternoons in the clover
10 Fields where we once made love
Then wandered home together
Where the trees arched above,
Where we made our own weather
When branches were the sky.
15 Now they are gone for good,
And you, for ill, and I
Am only a passer-by.

We and the trees and the way
Back from the fields of play
20 Lasted as long as we could.
No more walks in the wood.

—1993

---

1   *An Old-Fashioned Song* The rock band The Eagles recorded this poem as the song "No More Walks in the Wood" on the record *Long Road Out of Eden* (2007).

Dead Animals

... Granted, then, that the punishment,
—Whether appropriate or not—for that
One tiny universal act ("Come, try it!"
"Yum-yum!") of disobedience was Death,
It seems obscenely inappropriate   5
That all the other creatures, furry, smooth,
Scaly or feathered, shelled, gelatinous,
Great- or tiny-winged, swift-legged or slow
(I need—however lovingly—not name
Them all right now) have been condemned, like us,   10
To death, just to provide those symmetries
And analogues, just to allow us to
Compare ourselves to them whether or not
Condescendingly—I don't know. I think
I'll trade this one in for another story.   15

—2002

Adrienne Rich

1929–2012

One of the foremost political and feminist poets of the post–World War II United States, Adrienne Rich was born in Baltimore, Maryland. Over her long career, she published more than 16 volumes of poetry and five volumes of critical prose, most recently *Tonight No Poetry Will Serve: Poems 2007–2010*, *A Human Eye: Essays on Art in Society*, and *Later Poems: Selected and New 1971–2012*, published posthumously. She edited Muriel Rukeyser's *Selected Poems* for the Library of America. Among numerous other recognitions, Rich was the 2006 recipient of the National Book Foundation's Medal for Distinguished Contribution to American Letters. Her poetry and essays have been widely translated and published internationally.[1]

Aunt Jennifer's Tigers

Aunt Jennifer's tigers prance across a screen,
Bright topaz denizens of a world of green.
They do not fear the men beneath the tree;
They pace in sleek chivalric certainty.

5 Aunt Jennifer's fingers fluttering through her wool
Find even the ivory needle hard to pull.
The massive weight of Uncle's wedding band
Sits heavily upon Aunt Jennifer's hand.

When Aunt is dead, her terrified hands will lie
10 Still ringed with ordeals she was mastered by.
The tigers in the panel that she made
Will go on prancing, proud and unafraid.

—1951

Living in Sin

She had thought the studio would keep itself;
no dust upon the furniture of love.

---

1   This author headnote was provided by the rights holders of Adrienne Rich's poetry, and is included at their request. Its relative brevity in no way reflects the editor's views as to the importance of Rich's work.

Half heresy, to wish the taps less vocal,
the panes relieved of grime. A plate of pears,
a piano with a Persian shawl, a cat   5
stalking the picturesque amusing mouse
had risen at his urging.
Not that at five each separate stair would writhe
under the milkman's tramp; that morning light
so coldly would delineate the scraps   10
of last night's cheese and three sepulchral bottles;
that on the kitchen shelf among the saucers
a pair of beetle-eyes would fix her own—
envoy from some village in the mouldings ...
Meanwhile, he, with a yawn,   15
sounded a dozen notes upon the keyboard,
declared it out of tune, shrugged at the mirror,
rubbed at his beard, went out for cigarettes;
while she, jeered by the minor demons,
pulled back the sheets and made the bed and found   20
a towel to dust the table-top,
and let the coffee-pot boil over on the stove.
By evening she was back in love again,
though not so wholly but throughout the night
she woke sometimes to feel the daylight coming   25
like a relentless milkman up the stairs.

—1955

A Valediction Forbidding Mourning[1]

My swirling wants. Your frozen lips.
The grammar turned and attacked me.
Themes, written under duress.
Emptiness of the notations.

They gave me a drug that slowed the healing of wounds.   5

I want you to see this before I leave:
the experience of repetition as death
the failure of criticism to locate the pain
the poster in the bus that said:
my bleeding is under control.   10

---

1   *A ... Mourning* The title of a poem by John Donne (p. 25).

A red plant in a cemetery of plastic wreaths.

A last attempt: the language is a dialect called metaphor.
These images go unglossed: hair, glacier, flashlight.
When I think of a landscape I am thinking of a time.
15 When I talk of taking a trip I mean forever.
I could say: those mountains have a meaning
but further than that I could not say.

To do something very common, in my own way.

—1971

Diving into the Wreck

First having read the book of myths,
and loaded the camera,
and checked the edge of the knife-blade,
I put on
5 the body-armour of black rubber
the absurd slippers
the grave and awkward mask.
I am having to do this
not like Cousteau[1] with his
10 assiduous team
aboard the sun-flooded schooner
but here alone.

There is a ladder.
The ladder is always there
15 hanging innocently
close to the side of the schooner.
We know what it is for,
we who have used it.
Otherwise
20 it's a piece of maritime floss
some sundry equipment.

---

1   *Cousteau* Jacques Cousteau (1910–97), well-known oceanographer and undersea explor-
er.

I go down.
Rung after rung and still
the oxygen immerses me
the blue light   25
the clear atoms
of our human air.
I go down.
My flippers cripple me,
I crawl like an insect down the ladder   30
and there is no one
to tell me when the ocean
will begin.

First the air is blue and then
it is bluer and then green and then   35
black I am blacking out and yet
my mask is powerful
it pumps my blood with power
the sea is another story
the sea is not a question of power   40
I have to learn alone
to turn my body without force
in the deep element.

And now: it is easy to forget
what I came for   45
among so many who have always
lived here
swaying their crenellated fans
between the reefs
and besides   50
you breathe differently down here.

I came to explore the wreck.
The words are purposes.
The words are maps.
I came to see the damage that was done   55
and the treasures that prevail.
I stroke the beam of my lamp
slowly along the flank
of something more permanent
than fish or weed   60

the thing I came for:
the wreck and not the story of the wreck
the thing itself and not the myth
the drowned face always staring
65 toward the sun
the evidence of damage
worn by salt and sway into this threadbare beauty
the ribs of the disaster
curving their assertion
70 among the tentative haunters.

This is the place.
And I am here, the mermaid whose dark hair
streams black, the merman in his armored body
We circle silently
75 about the wreck
we dive into the hold.
I am she: I am he

whose drowned face sleeps with open eyes
whose breasts still bear the stress
80 whose silver, copper, vermeil[1] cargo lies
obscurely inside barrels
half-wedged and left to rot
we are the half-destroyed instruments
that once held to a course
85 the water-eaten log
the fouled compass

We are, I am, you are
by cowardice or courage
the one who find our way
90 back to this scene
carrying a knife, a camera
a book of myths
in which
our names do not appear.

—1973

---

1   *vermeil* Gold plate over silver.

Gregory Corso
1930–2001

Eventually achieving wide acclaim as a Beat poet, Gregory Corso was raised in tough conditions in New York City in the midst of the Depression. Born to teenaged parents who broke up and abandoned him as a young child, he spent years in foster care, orphanages, boys' homes, on the streets as a homeless child, and in prison. He began reading classic literature and writing poetry as a teenager, while in jail for theft. At the age of twenty, he met Allen Ginsberg (see p. 488) in a bar in New York's bohemian Greenwich Village, learning from Ginsberg's own poetic experiments and becoming the youngest member of the emergent Beat movement.

A careful technician who revered traditional poetry like that of Percy Bysshe Shelley, Corso wrote in a modern style that did not rely on conventional rhyme and meter. Instead, as he noted in an interview, the music of his poems was "built in" to the cadences of his language. Incorporating current sounds and avant-garde styles, from jazz rhythms to irreverent humor to hipster lingo, Corso's work pulsed with the energy of his age, as in his legendary and influential address to the cultural moment of the atomic bomb (below). Bob Dylan was among the many younger artists who found his work electrifying.

BOMB[1]

Budger of history   Brake of time   You   Bomb
Toy of universe   Grandest of all snatched sky   I cannot hate you
Do I hate the mischievous thunderbolt   the jawbone of an ass
The bumpy club of One Million B.C.   the mace   the flail   the axe
Catapult Da Vinci   tomahawk Cochise   flintlock Kidd   dagger Rathbone   5
Ah and the sad desperate gun of Verlaine   Pushkin   Dillinger   Bogart
And hath not St. Michael a burning sword   St. George a lance   David a sling
Bomb   you are as cruel as man makes you   and you're no crueller than cancer
All man hates you   they'd rather die by car-crash   lightning   drowning
Falling off a roof   electric-chair   heart-attack   old age   old age   O Bomb   10
They'd rather die by anything but you   Death's finger is free-lance
Not up to man whether you boom or not   Death has long since distributed its
categorical blue   I sing thee Bomb   Death's extravagance   Death's jubilee

---

1   In order not to overburden particularly allusion-heavy poems like this one with excessive notation, this edition runs them with minimal notes. The poem thus retains its appearance as the poet wrote it, and readers can investigate terms as they choose on their own.

Gem of Death's supremest blue   The flyer will crash   his death will differ
15   with the climbor who'll fall   to die by cobra is not to die by bad pork
Some die by swamp   some by sea   and some by the bushy-haired man in the night
O there are deaths like witches of Arc   Scarey deaths like Boris Karloff
No-feeling deaths like birth-death   sadless deaths like old pain Bowery
Abandoned deaths   like Capital Punishment   stately deaths like senators
20 And unthinkable deaths like Harpo Marx   girls on Vogue covers   my own
I do not know just how horrible Bombdeath is   I can only imagine
Yet no other death I know has so laughable a preview   I scope
a city   New York City   streaming   starkeyed   subway shelter
Scores and scores   A fumble of humanity   High heels bend
25   Hats whelming away   Youth forgetting their combs
Ladies not knowing what to do   with their shopping bags
Unperturbed gum machines   Yet dangerous 3rd rail
Ritz Brothers   from the Bronx   caught in the A train
The smiling Schenley poster will always smile
30   Impish death   Satyr Bomb   Bombdeath
Turtles exploding over Istanbul
The jaguar's flying foot
soon to sink in arctic snow
Penguins plunged against the Sphinx
35   The top of the Empire state
arrowed in a broccoli field in Sicily
Eiffel shaped like a C in Magnolia Gardens
St. Sophia peeling over Sudan
O athletic Death   Sportive Bomb
40   the temples of ancient times
their grand ruin ceased
Electrons   Protons   Neutrons
gathering Hesperean hair
walking the dolorous gulf of Arcady
45   joining marble helmsmen
entering the final ampitheater
with a hymnody feeling of all Troys
heralding cypressean torches
racing plumes and banners
50   and yet knowing Homer with a step of grace
Lo the visiting team of Present
the home team of Past
Lyre and tuba together joined
Hark the hotdog soda olive grape

gala galaxy robed and uniformed   55
commissary   O the happy stands
Ethereal root and cheer and boo
The billioned all-time attendance
The Zeusian pandemonium
        Hermes racing Owens   60
    The Spitball of Buddha
        Christ striking out
        Luther stealing third
Planetarium Death   Hosannah Bomb
Gush the final rose   O Spring Bomb   65
Come with thy gown of dynamite green
    unmenace Nature's inviolate eye
        Before you the wimpled Past
behind you the hallooing Future   O Bomb
        Bound in the grassy clarion air   70
        like the fox of the tally-ho
thy field the universe thy hedge the geo
Leap Bomb   bound Bomb   frolic zig and zag
The stars a swarm of bees in thy binging bag
        Stick angels on your jubilee feet   75
wheels of rainlight on your bunky seat
    You are due and behold you are due
    and the heavens are with you
    hosanna incalescent glorious liaison
BOMB O havoc antiphony molten cleft BOOM   80
    Bomb mark infinity a sudden furnace
spread thy multitudinous encompassed Sweep
        set forth awful agenda
Carrion stars   charnel planets   carcass elements
Corpse the universe   tee-hee finger-in-the-mouth hop   85
        over its long long dead Nor
    From thy nimbled matted spastic eye
    exhaust deluges of celestial ghouls
        From thy appellational womb
    spew birth-gusts of great worms   90
        Rip open your belly Bomb
from your belly outflock vulturic salutations
Battle forth your spangled hyena finger stumps
        along the brink of Paradise
        O Bomb   O final Pied Piper   95

both sun and firefly behind your shock waltz
God abandoned mock-nude
beneath His thin false-talc'd apocalypse
He cannot hear thy flute's
100   happy-the-day profanations
He is spilled deaf into the Silencer's warty ear
His Kingdom an eternity of crude wax
Clogged clarions untrumpet Him
Sealed angels unsing Him
105   A thunderless God   A dead God
O Bomb   thy BOOM His tomb
That I lean forward on a desk of science
an astrologer dabbling in dragon prose
half-smart about wars   bombs   especially bombs
110   That I am unable to hate what is necessary to love
That I can't exist in a world that consents
a child in a park   a man dying in an electric-chair
That I am able to laugh at all things
all that I know and do not know   thus to conceal my pain
115   That I say I am a poet and therefore love all man
knowing my words to be the acquainted prophecy of all men
and my unwords no less an acquaintanceship
That I am manifold
a man pursuing the big lies of gold
120   or a poet roaming in bright ashes
or that which I imagine myself to be
a shark-toothed sleep   a man-eater of dreams
I need not then be all-smart about bombs
Happily so   for if I felt bombs were caterpillars
125   I'd doubt not they'd become butterflies
There is a hell for bombs
They're there   I see them there
They sit in bits and sing songs
mostly German songs
130   And two very long American songs
and they wish there were more songs
especially Russian and Chinese songs
and some more very long American songs
Poor little Bomb that'll never be
135   an Eskimo song   I love thee
I want to put a lollipop

in thy furcal mouth
A wig of Goldilocks on thy baldy bean
and have you skip with me Hansel and Gretel
along the Hollywoodian screen   140
O Bomb in which all lovely things
moral and physical anxiously participate
O fairyflake plucked from the
grandest universe tree
O piece of heaven which gives   145
both mountain and anthill a sun
I am standing before your fantastic lily door
I bring you Midgardian roses   Arcadian musk
Reputed cosmetics from the girls of heaven
Welcome me   fear not thy opened door   150
nor thy cold ghost's grey memory
nor the pimps of indefinite weather
their cruel terrestial thaw
Oppenheimer is seated
in the dark pocket of Light   155
Fermi is dry in Death's Mozambique
Einstein his mythmouth
a barnacled wreath on the moon-squid's head
Let me in   Bomb   rise from that pregnant-rat corner
nor fear the raised-broom nations of the world   160
O Bomb I love you
I want to kiss your clank   eat your boom
You are a paean   an acme of scream
a lyric hat of Mister Thunder
O resound thy tanky knees   165
BOOM BOOM BOOM BOOM BOOM
BOOM ye skies and BOOM ye suns
BOOM BOOM ye moons   ye stars BOOM
nights ye BOOM   ye days ye BOOM
BOOM BOOM ye winds   ye clouds ye rains   170
go BANG ye lakes   ye oceans BING
Barracuda BOOM and cougar BOOM
Ubangi BANG   orangoutang
BING BANG BONG BOOM   bee bear baboon
ye BANG ye BONG ye BING   175
the tail the fin the wing
Yes   Yes   into our midst a bomb will fall

Flowers will leap in joy their roots aching
Fields will kneel proud beneath the halleluyahs of the wind
180 Pinkbombs will blossom   Elkbombs will perk their ears
Ah many a bomb that day will awe the bird a gentle look
Yet   not enough to say a bomb will fall
or even contend celestial fire goes out
Know that the earth will madonna the Bomb
185 that in the hearts of men to come more bombs will be born
magisterial bombs wrapped in ermine   all beautiful
and they'll sit plunk on earth's grumpy empires
fierce with moustaches of gold

—1958

Marriage

Should I get married? Should I be good?
Astound the girl next door with my velvet suit and faustus[1] hood?
Don't take her to movies but to cemeteries
tell all about werewolf bathtubs and forked clarinets
5 then desire her and kiss her and all the preliminaries
and she going just so far and I understanding why
not getting angry saying You must feel! It's beautiful to feel!
Instead take her in my arms lean against an old crooked tombstone
and woo her the entire night the constellations in the sky—

10 When she introduces me to her parents
back straightened, hair finally combed, strangled by a tie,
should I sit knees together on their 3rd degree sofa
and not ask Where's the bathroom?
How else to feel other than I am,
15 often thinking Flash Gordon[2] soap—
O how terrible it must be for a young man
seated before a family and the family thinking
We never saw him before! He wants our Mary Lou!
After tea and homemade cookies they ask What do you do for a living?

---

1   *faustus* Legendary figure who sold his soul to the Devil.
2   *Flash Gordon* Character of the long-running science fiction comic strip and franchise of
    the same name.

Should I tell them? Would they like me then?   20
Say All right get married, we're losing a daughter
but we're gaining a son—

And should I then ask Where's the bathroom?
O God, and the wedding! All her family and her friends
and only a handful of mine all scroungy and bearded   25
just wait to get at the drinks and food—
And the priest! he looking at me as if I masturbated
asking me Do you take this woman for your lawful wedded wife?
And I trembling what to say say Pie Glue!
I kiss the bride all those corny men slapping me on the back   30
She's all yours, boy! Ha-ha-ha!
And in their eyes you could see some obscene honeymoon going on—
Then all that absurd rice and clanky cans and shoes
Niagara Falls! Hordes of us! Husbands! Wives! Flowers! Chocolates!
All streaming into cozy hotels   35
All going to do the same thing tonight

The indifferent clerk he knowing what was going to happen
The lobby zombies they knowing what
The whistling elevator man he knowing
The winking bellboy knowing   40
Everybody knowing! I'd be almost inclined not to do anything!
Stay up all night! Stare that hotel clerk in the eye!
Screaming: I deny honeymoon! I deny honeymoon!
running rampant into those almost climactic suites
yelling Radio belly! Cat shovel!   45
O I'd live in Niagara forever! in a dark cave beneath the Falls
I'd sit there the Mad Honeymooner
devising ways to break marriages, a scourge of bigamy
a saint of divorce—

But I should get married I should be good   50
How nice it'd be to come home to her
and sit by the fireplace and she in the kitchen
aproned young and lovely wanting my baby
and so happy about me she burns the roast beef
and comes crying to me and I get up from my big papa chair   55
saying Christmas teeth! Radiant brains! Apple deaf!
God what a husband I'd make! Yes, I should get married!

So much to do! like sneaking into Mr. Jones' house late at night
and cover his golf clubs with 1920 Norwegian books
60 Like hanging a picture of Rimbaud[1] on the lawnmower
like pasting Tannu Tuva[2] postage stamps all over the picket fence
like when Mrs. Kindhead comes to collect for the Community Chest[3]
grab her and tell her There are unfavorable omens in the sky!
And when the mayor comes to get my vote tell him
65 When are you going to stop people killing whales!
And when the milkman comes leave him a note in the bottle
Penguin dust, bring me penguin dust, I want penguin dust—

Yet if I should get married and it's Connecticut and snow
and she gives birth to a child and I am sleepless, worn,
70 up for nights, head bowed against a quiet window; the past behind me,
finding myself in the most common of situations a trembling man
knowledged with responsibility not twig-smear nor Roman coin soup—
O what would that be like!
Surely I'd give it for a nipple a rubber Tacitus[4]
75 For a rattle a bag of broken Bach[5] records
Tack Della Francesca[6] all over its crib
Sew the Greek alphabet on its bib
And build for its playpen a roofless Parthenon[7]

No, I doubt I'd be that kind of father
80 Not rural not snow no quiet window
but hot smelly tight New York City
seven flights up, roaches and rats in the walls
a fat Reichian[8] wife screeching over potatoes Get a job!
And five nose running brats in love with Batman
85 And the neighbors all toothless and dry haired
like those hag masses of the 18th century
all wanting to come in and watch TV

---

1   *Rimbaud*   Influential French poet Arthur Rimbaud (1854–91).
2   *Tannu Tuva*   Former sovereign nation that ultimately became the Tuva Republic of Russia.
3   *Community Chest*   Fund-raising organization that preceded the United Way.
4   *Tacitus*   Publius (or Gaius) Cornelius Tacitus (c. 55–c. 117), a famous Roman historian.
5   *Bach*   German classical composer Johann Sebastian Bach (1685–1750).
6   *Della Francesca*   Piero della Francesca (c. 1416–92), Italian Renaissance painter.
7   *Parthenon*   Ancient Greek temple of the goddess Athena, on the Acropolis in Athens.
8   *Reichian*   Follower of Wilhelm Reich (1897–1957), an Austrian psychoanalyst.

The landlord wants his rent
Grocery store Blue Cross Gas & Electric Knights of Columbus
Impossible to lie back and dream Telephone snow, ghost parking—   90
No! I should not get married I should never get married!
But—imagine if I were married to a beautiful sophisticated woman
tall and pale wearing an elegant black dress and long black gloves
holding a cigarette holder in one hand and a highball in the other
and we lived high up in a penthouse with a huge window   95
from which we could see all of New York and ever farther on clearer days.
No, can't imagine myself married to that pleasant prison dream—
O but what about love? I forget love
not that I am incapable of love
it's just that I see love as odd as wearing shoes—   100
I never wanted to marry a girl who was like my mother
And Ingrid Bergman[1] was always impossible
And there's maybe a girl now but she's already married
And I don't like men and—
but there's got to be somebody!   105
Because what if I'm 60 years old and not married,
all alone in a furnished room with pee stains on my underwear
and everybody else is married! All the universe married but me!

Ah, yet well I know that were a woman possible as I am possible
then marriage would be possible—   110
Like SHE in her lonely alien gaud waiting her Egyptian lover
so I wait—bereft of 2,000 years and the bath of life.[2]

—1959

---

1   *Ingrid Bergman* Famous Swedish actress (1915–82).
2   *SHE ... life* From the 1887 novel *She: A History of Adventure* by H. Rider Haggard about
     a sorceress who bathes in fire to attain eternal youth as she waits for the reincarnation of
     her dead lover Kallikrates.

Ted Hughes
1930–1998

With bold metaphors and forceful rhythms, poet Ted Hughes paints grim, often violent, visions of human existence. At the same time, he celebrates the power of nature and meditates on humanity's place in it. Hughes's first volume of poetry, *The Hawk in the Rain* (1957), received critical praise for its strong, earthy language and intense natural imagery. He further established his reputation as a major new poet with his second book, *Lupercal* (1960), and he continued to write prolifically, producing many volumes of poetry as well as verse for children, radio plays, and translations.

In 1956 Hughes married the American poet Sylvia Plath (see p. 528); the couple separated in 1962, and Plath committed suicide less than a year later. Hughes put his own poetry on hold to focus on editing and publishing his wife's poems and journals, and the editorial decisions he made as her executor received intense criticism from some of her admirers. Hughes would say very little regarding his relationship with Plath until his 1998 publication of *Birthday Letters*, a series of poems addressed to her.

Hughes was Britain's Poet Laureate from 1984 until his death in 1998. British poet and critic Dick Davis has offered this explanation for the continuing appeal of Hughes's poetry: "He brings back to our suburban, centrally-heated and, above all, *safe* lives reports from an authentic frontier of reality and the imagination."

The Thought-Fox

I imagine this midnight moment's forest:
Something else is alive
Beside the clock's loneliness
And this blank page where my fingers move.

5 Through the window I see no star:
Something more near
Though deeper within darkness
Is entering the loneliness:

Cold, delicately as the dark snow
10 A fox's nose touches twig, leaf;
Two eyes serve a movement, that now
And again now, and now, and now

Sets neat prints into the snow
Between trees, and warily a lame
Shadow lags by stump and in hollow   15
Of a body that is bold to come

Across clearings, an eye,
A widening deepening greenness,
Brilliantly, concentratedly,
Coming about its own business   20

Till, with a sudden sharp hot stink of fox,
It enters the dark hole of the head.
The window is starless still; the clock ticks,
The page is printed.

                                              —1957

Pike[1]

Pike, three inches long, perfect
Pike in all parts, green tigering the gold.
Killers from the egg: the malevolent aged grin.
They dance on the surface among the flies.

Or move, stunned by their own grandeur,   5
Over a bed of emerald, silhouette
Of submarine delicacy and horror.
A hundred feet long in their world.

In ponds, under the heat-struck lily pads—
Gloom of their stillness: 10
Logged on last year's black leaves, watching upwards.
Or hung in an amber cavern of weeds

The jaws' hooked clamp and fangs
Not to be changed at this date;
A life subdued to its instrument;   15
The gills kneading quietly, and the pectorals.

---

1   *Pike* Family of freshwater fish legendary for their size and ferocity. They eat other fish,
     amphibians, small mammals, birds, and sometimes each other.

Three we kept behind glass,
Jungled in weed: three inches, four,
And four and a half: fed fry to them—
20 Suddenly there were two. Finally one.

With a sag belly and the grin it was born with.
And indeed they spare nobody.
Two, six pounds each, over two feet long,
High and dry and dead in the willow-herb—

25 One jammed past its gills down the other's gullet:
The outside eye stared: as a vice locks—
The same iron in this eye
Though its film shrank in death.

A pond I fished, fifty yards across,
30 Whose lilies and muscular tench[1]
Had outlasted every visible stone
Of the monastery that planted them—

Stilled legendary depth:
It was as deep as England. It held
35 Pike too immense to stir, so immense and old
That past nightfall I dared not cast

But silently cast and fished
With the hair frozen on my head
For what might move, for what eye might move.
40 The still splashes on the dark pond,

Owls hushing the floating woods
Frail on my ear against the dream
Darkness beneath night's darkness had freed,
That rose slowly towards me, watching.

—1959

---

1   *tench* Fish similar to carp.

Miller Williams

1930–2015

Miller Williams was a poet, a translator, and the founder of the University of Arkansas Press. Born and raised in the town of Hoxie, Arkansas, Williams studied biology and zoology for his undergraduate and master's degrees and had almost no formal training in literature. In 1961, his friend, the writer Flannery O'Connor, recommended him for a position teaching poetry at Louisiana State University. He continued to teach English and creative writing, mainly at the University of Arkansas, until his retirement in 2003. In 1997 he became the third American inaugural poet, reading his poem "Of History and Hope" at the inauguration of President Bill Clinton.

Williams's poetry ingeniously explores a tension between formal control and conversational directness. In his 2006 book *Making a Poem: Some Thoughts about Poetry and the People Who Write It*, Williams reflected, "What we have to ask of the poem is that it work, that it offer us an experience that we can believe is a part of our world. That it be, in a word, honest." "The Shrinking Lonesome Sestina" (below) demonstrates his playful command of both the opportunities and the restrictions inherent in traditional poetic form.

Williams's daughter is the singer and songwriter Lucinda Williams, who set his poem "Compassion" to music; the title of her 2014 double album, *Down Where the Spirit Meets the Bone*, comes from the poem's last line.

The Shrinking Lonesome Sestina[1]

Somewhere in everyone's head something points toward home,
a dashboard's floating compass, turning all the time
to keep from turning. It doesn't matter how we come
to be wherever we are, someplace where nothing goes
the way it went once, where nothing holds fast
to where it belongs, or what you've risen or fallen to.   5

What the bubble always points to,
whether we notice it or not, is home.
It may be true that if you move fast
everything fades away, that given time   10

---

1 *Sestina* Poem that consists of six six-line stanzas and a final triplet. Each word that ends a line of the first stanza must end the lines of each subsequent stanza in a complex predetermined pattern.

and noise enough, every memory goes
into the blackness, and if new ones come—

small, mole-like memories that come
to live in the furry dark—they, too,
15 curl up and die. But Carol goes
to high school now. John works at home
what days he can to spend some time
with Sue and the kids. He drives too fast.

Ellen won't eat her breakfast.
20 Your sister was going to come
but didn't have the time.
Some mornings at one or two
or three I want you home
a lot, but then it goes.

25 It all goes.
Hold on fast
to thoughts of home
when they come.
They're going to
30 less with time.

Time
goes
too
fast.
35 Come
home.

Forgive me that. One time it wasn't fast.
A myth goes that when the years come
then you will, too. Me, I'll still be home.

—1992

Compassion

Have compassion for everyone you meet,
even if they don't want it. What seems conceit,
bad manners, or cynicism is always a sign
of things no ears have heard, no eyes have seen.
You do not know what wars are going on   5
down there where the spirit meets the bone.

—1997

Sylvia Plath
1932–1963

Sylvia Plath's early life was, outwardly, one of upper-middle-class privilege. The daughter of a Boston University professor and his wife, Plath was an excellent student both in school and later at Smith College, a prestigious liberal arts college for women, where she became a prolific writer of poems and short stories. Inwardly, however, she had been profoundly affected by the death of her father when she was eight, and became deeply conflicted over the roles young women in the 1950s were expected to fulfill. Following her third year at Smith she was awarded a guest editorship at the young women's magazine *Mademoiselle*; the experience was a disappointment, however, and Plath fell into a deep depression. She attempted suicide that August, and spent many months thereafter in psychiatric care.

Plath recovered, and in 1955 was awarded a scholarship to Cambridge, where her talents as a writer began to be more widely recognized—and where she met and soon married the British poet Ted Hughes (p. 522). The couple both published well-received volumes of poetry (Plath's *The Colossus* appeared in 1960) and they had two children together, but their relationship was sometimes strained and Plath continued to suffer from depression. In 1962, following Plath's discovery that Hughes had been having an affair, the two separated. Between that time and Plath's suicide in February of 1963, living with the children in a bitterly cold flat in London, she wrote the extraordinary body of work on which her reputation now rests. These poems (published posthumously in 1965 in the volume *Ariel*) are spare and controlled in their form but entirely unsparing in the searing intensity with which they explore human strangeness and savagery—perhaps most memorably, the savagery of the Holocaust. Plath's one novel, *The Bell Jar* (1963), is highly autobiographical.

As with other confessional poets such as Robert Lowell (p. 451) and Anne Sexton (p. 497), readers often read Plath's poetry as a direct record of her life. But, as Catriona O'Reilly has observed, it will not do to regard Plath's work as "an extended suicide note." Confessional poetry as all these poets practiced it was a crafted form of artistic performance even as it transgressed social taboos about self-exposure. Plath's strongest poems are almost universally accorded a vital place in the history of poetry in the twentieth century.

Mushrooms

Overnight, very
Whitely, discreetly,
Very quietly

Our toes, our noses
Take hold on the loam,   5
Acquire the air.

Nobody sees us,
Stops us, betrays us;
The small grains make room.

Soft fists insist on
Heaving the needles,   10
The leafy bedding,

Even the paving.
Our hammers, our rams,
Earless and eyeless,   15

Perfectly voiceless,
Widen the crannies,
Shoulder through holes. We

Diet on water,
On crumbs of shadow,   20
Bland-mannered, asking

Little or nothing.
So many of us!
So many of us!

We are shelves, we are   25
Tables, we are meek,
We are edible,

Nudgers and shovers
In spite of ourselves.
Our kind multiplies: 30

We shall by morning
Inherit the earth.
Our foot's in the door.

—1959

Ariel[1]

Stasis in darkness.
Then the substanceless blue
Pour of tor and distances.

God's lioness,
5 How one we grow,
Pivot of heels and knees!—The furrow

Splits and passes, sister to
The brown arc
Of the neck I cannot catch,

10 Nigger-eye
Berries cast dark
Hooks—

Black sweet blood mouthfuls,
Shadows.
15 Something else

Hauls me through air—
Thighs, hair;
Flakes from my heels.

White
20 Godiva,[2] I unpeel—
Dead hands, dead stringencies.

---

1   *Ariel* An airy spirit employed by Prospero in Shakespeare's *The Tempest*. "Ariel" was also
the name that Plath gave to her horse.
2   *Godiva* The English woman who, according to legend, fulfilled an agreement with her
husband to ride naked down the streets of Coventry if he would remove oppressive taxes
from the townspeople.

And now I
Foam to wheat, a glitter of seas.
The child's cry

Melts in the wall.   25
And I
Am the arrow,

The dew that flies
Suicidal, at one with the drive
Into the red   30

Eye, the cauldron of morning.

—1965 (written 1962)

Daddy

You do not do, you do not do
Any more, black shoe
In which I have lived like a foot
For thirty years, poor and white,
Barely daring to breathe or Achoo.   5

Daddy, I have had to kill you.
You died before I had time—
Marble-heavy, a bag full of God,
Ghastly statue with one grey toe[1]
Big as a Frisco seal   10

And a head in the freakish Atlantic
Where it pours bean green over blue
In the waters off beautiful Nauset.[2]
I used to pray to recover you.
Ach, du.[3]   15

---

1   *Ghastly ... grey toe* Plath's father, Otto Plath (1885–1940), died from complications due
    to untreated diabetes. Before he died, his toe became gangrenous and his leg was ampu-
    tated.
2   *Nauset* Beach in Orleans, Massachusetts.
3   *Ach, du* German: Oh, you.

In the German tongue, in the Polish town[1]
Scraped flat by the roller
Of wars, wars, wars.
But the name of the town is common.
20   My Polack friend

Says there are a dozen or two.
So I never could tell where you
Put your foot, your root,
I never could talk to you.
25   The tongue stuck in my jaw.

It stuck in a barb wire snare
Ich, ich, ich, ich,[2]
I could hardly speak.
I thought every German was you.
30   And the language obscene

An engine, an engine
Chuffing me off like a Jew.
A Jew to Dachau, Auschwitz, Belsen.[3]
I began to talk like a Jew.
35   I think I may well be a Jew.

The snows of the Tyrol,[4] the clear beer of Vienna
Are not very pure or true.
With my gypsy ancestress and my weird luck
And my Taroc° pack and my Taroc pack   *Tarot*
40   I may be a bit of a Jew.

I have always been scared of *you*,
With your Luftwaffe,[5] your gobbledygoo.
And your neat moustache
And your Aryan eye, bright blue.
45   Panzer-man,[6] panzer-man, O You—

---

1   *Polish town* Otto Plath emigrated to the US from the Polish town of Grabow.
2   *Ich, ich, ich, ich* German: I, I, I, I.
3   *Dachau, Auschwitz, Belsen* Sites of Nazi concentration camps during World War II.
4   *Tyrol* State in Austria.
5   *Luftwaffe* German air force during World War II.
6   *Panzer-man* "Panzers" were German armored vehicles, notably tanks.

Not God but a swastika
So black no sky could squeak through.
Every woman adores a Fascist,
The boot in the face, the brute
Brute heart of a brute like you.   50

You stand at the blackboard,[1] daddy,
In the picture I have of you,
A cleft in your chin instead of your foot
But no less a devil for that, no not
Any less the black man who   55

Bit my pretty red heart in two.
I was ten when they buried you.
At twenty I tried to die
And get back, back, back to you.
I thought even the bones would do.   60

But they pulled me out of the sack,
And they stuck me together with glue.
And then I knew what to do.
I made a model of you,
A man in black with a Meinkampf[2] look   65

And a love of the rack and the screw.
And I said I do, I do.
So daddy, I'm finally through.
The black telephone's off at the root,
The voices just can't worm through.   70

If I've killed one man, I've killed two—
The vampire who said he was you
And drank my blood for a year,
Seven years, if you want to know.
Daddy, you can lie back now.   75

There's a stake in your fat black heart
And the villagers never liked you.

---

1   *You ... blackboard* Otto Plath taught biology and German at Boston University.
2   *Meinkampf* Adolf Hitler's book *Mein Kampf* (1924) outlines his political philosophy.

They are dancing and stamping on you.
They always *knew* it was you.
80 Daddy, daddy, you bastard, I'm through.

—1965 (written 1962)

Lady Lazarus¹

I have done it again.
One year in every ten
I manage it—

A sort of walking miracle, my skin
5 Bright as a Nazi lampshade,²
My right foot

A paperweight,
My featureless, fine
Jew linen.

10 Peel off the napkin
O my enemy.
Do I terrify?—

The nose, the eye pits, the full set of teeth?
The sour breath
15 Will vanish in a day.

Soon, soon the flesh
The grave cave ate will be
At home on me

And I a smiling woman.
20 I am only thirty.
And like the cat I have nine times to die.

This is Number Three.
What a trash
To annihilate each decade.

---

1   *Lazarus* Man brought back to life by Jesus after being dead for four days.
2   *Nazi lampshade* Some Nazi officials allegedly created leather souvenirs, such as lamp-
    shades, using the skin of concentration camp victims.

What a million filaments.   25
The peanut-crunching crowd
Shoves in to see

Them unwrap me hand and foot—
The big strip tease.
Gentlemen, ladies   30

These are my hands
My knees.
I may be skin and bone,

Nevertheless, I am the same, identical woman.
The first time it happened I was ten.   35
It was an accident.

The second time I meant
To last it out and not come back at all.
I rocked shut

As a seashell.   40
They had to call and call
And pick the worms off me like sticky pearls.

Dying
Is an art, like everything else.
I do it exceptionally well.   45

I do it so it feels like hell.
I do it so it feels real.
I guess you could say I've a call.

It's easy enough to do it in a cell.
It's easy enough to do it and stay put.   50
It's the theatrical

Comeback in broad day
To the same place, the same face, the same brute
Amused shout:

"A miracle!"   55
That knocks me out.
There is a charge

For the eyeing of my scars, there is a charge
For the hearing of my heart—
60 It really goes.

And there is a charge, a very large charge
For a word or a touch
Or a bit of blood

Or a piece of my hair or my clothes.
65 So, so, Herr[1] Doktor.
So, Herr Enemy.

I am your opus,
I am your valuable,
The pure gold baby

70 That melts to a shriek.
I turn and burn.
Do not think I underestimate your great concern.

Ash, ash—
You poke and stir.
75 Flesh, bone, there is nothing there—

A cake of soap,[2]
A wedding ring,
A gold filling.

Herr God, Herr Lucifer
80 Beware
Beware.

Out of the ash
I rise with my red hair
And I eat men like air.

—1965 (written 1962)

---

1   *Herr* German: Mister.
2   *cake of soap* During and after the war, it was widely believed that the bodies of the dead
     from concentration camps were used to mass produce soap.

Amiri Baraka

1934–2014

Amiri Baraka, born in Newark, New Jersey as LeRoi Jones, was a fiction writer, dramatist, and musician as well as a poet and political activist. He founded the Black Arts Movement in 1965, the same year Malcolm X was assassinated, at which point LeRoi Jones also renounced his former life and changed his name to Amiri Baraka. Contributions to an artistic and political movement by African-Americans to awaken black consciousness—at a time when African-Americans were struggling for basic civil rights in the US—Black Arts creations often drew controversy.

Baraka said in a 1978 interview that he had learned from literary Modernism and from the Beat and Black Mountain poets (styles in which he had earlier written), but that he had to develop his own approach because those poets "weren't asking for revolution." Baraka was Poet Laureate of New Jersey from 2002 to 2003, a position he lost when his poem on the September 11 attacks, "Somebody Blew Up America," drew intense criticism for anti-Semitism.

I Substitute for the Dead Lecturer

> *What is most precious, because*
> *it is lost. What is lost,*
> *because it is most*
> *precious.*

They have turned, and say that I am dying. That
I have thrown
my life
away. They
have left me alone, where   5
there is no one, nothing
save who I am. Not a note
nor a word.

          Cold air batters
the poor (and their minds   10
turn open
like sores). What kindness
What wealth

can I offer? Except
15 what is, for me,
ugliest. What is
for me, shadows, shrieking
phantoms. Except
they have need
20 of life. Flesh
at least,
                            should be theirs.

The Lord has saved me
to do this. The Lord
25 has made me strong. I
am as I must have
myself. Against all
thought, all music, all
my soft loves.

30   For all these wan roads
I am pushed to follow, are
my own conceit. A simple muttering
elegance, slipped in my head
pressed on my soul, is my heart's
35 worth. And I am frightened
that the flame of my sickness
will burn off my face. And leave
the bones, my stewed black skull,
an empty cage of failure.

                                            —1964

Three Modes of History and Culture

Chalk mark sex of the nation, on walls we drummers
know
as cathedrals. Cathedra, in a churning meat milk.

Women glide through looking for telephones. Maps
weep   5
and are mothers and their daughters listening to

music teachers. From heavy beginnings. Plantations,
learning
America, as speech, and a common emptiness. Songs knocking

inside old women's faces. Knocking through cardboard trunks.   10
Trains
leaning north, catching hellfire in windows, passing through

the first ignoble cities of missouri, to illinois, and the panting
Chicago.
And then all ways, we go where flesh is cheap. Where factories   15

sit open, burning the chiefs. Make your way! Up through fog and
history
Make your way, and swing the general, that it come flash open

and spill the innards of that sweet thing we heard, and gave theory
to.   20
Breech, bridge, and reach, to where all talk is energy. And there's

enough, for anything singular. All our lean prophets and rhythms.
Entire
we arrive and set up shacks, hole cards, Western hearts at the edge

of saying. Thriving to balance the meanness of particular skies. 25
Race
of madmen and giants.

Brick songs. Shoe songs. Chants of open weariness.
Knife wiggle early evenings of the wet mouth. Tongue

30 dance midnight, any season shakes our house. Don't
tear my clothes! To doubt the balance of misery

ripping meat hug shuffle fuck. The Party of Insane
Hope. I've come from there too. Where the dead told lies
about clever social justice. Burning coffins voted
35 and staggered through cold white streets listening
to Wilkie or Wallace or Dewey[1] through the dead face
of Lincoln.[2] Come from there, and belched it out.

I think about a time when I will be relaxed.
When flames and non-specific passion wear themselves
40 away. And my eyes and hands and mind can turn
and soften, and my songs will be softer
and lightly weight the air.

—1969

---

1   *Wilkie or Wallace or Dewey* Wendell Willkie (1892–1944), Henry A. Wallace (1888–
1965), and Thomas E. Dewey (1902–71) were all unsuccessful conservative presidential
candidates.
2   *Lincoln* President Abraham Lincoln (1809–65) issued the Emancipation Proclamation
during the US Civil War and was assassinated shortly after the Confederacy surrendered.

Ted Berrigan
1934–1983

Highly regarded as a teacher and editor as well as a poet, Ted Berrigan was a lively, generous, and sometimes disruptive presence in the New York literary community in the 1960s and 1970s. After studying at the University of Tulsa, Oklahoma, Berrigan moved to New York in the early 1960s, where he founded *C*, a mimeographed poetry and arts journal, and the C Press, a small poetry publisher. He taught workshops at the Poetry Project in the East Village, an important (and still active) space for experimental poetry.

Berrigan considered poetry his vocation and, though he taught writing at several universities to support himself and his family, he said in a lecture that he considered poetry a "full-time business." His first success came with *The Sonnets* (1964), which is perhaps still his best-known work, and he went on to publish a book almost every year until the early 1980s. Among other influences, he admired the Beat poets; the personal style of the New York School (see Frank O'Hara, p. 490, and Kenneth Koch, p. 480); the stripped-down style of Robert Creeley (p. 485); the artist Marcel Duchamp, and the composer John Cage. Berrigan died of liver disease in 1983 at the age of 48.

People Who Died

Pat Dugan……..my grandfather……..throat cancer……..1947.

Ed Berrigan……..my dad……..heart attack……..1958.

Dickie Budlong……..my best friend Brucie's big brother, when we were
                                  five to eight……..killed in Korea, 1953.

Red O'Sullivan……..hockey star & cross-country runner   5
                        who sat at my lunch table
                                in High School……car crash……1954.

Jimmy "Wah" Tiernan……..my friend, in High School,
                        Football & Hockey All-State……car crash….1959.

Cisco Houston[1]……..died of cancer……..1961.   10

---

1   *Cisco Houston* American singer-songwriter who often collaborated with Woody Guthrie.

Freddy Herko,[1] dancer….jumped out of a Greenwich Village window in 1963.

Anne Kepler….my girl….killed by smoke-poisoning while playing
        the flute at the Yonkers Children's Hospital
        during a fire set by a 16 year old arsonist….1965.

15 Frank……Frank O'Hara[2]……hit by a car on Fire Island, 1966.

Woody Guthrie[3]……dead of Huntington's Chorea in 1968.

Neal……Neal Cassady[4]……died of exposure, sleeping all night
        in the rain by the RR tracks of Mexico….1969.

Franny Winston……just a girl….totalled her car on the Detroit-Ann Arbor
20   Freeway, returning from the dentist….Sept. 1969.

Jack……Jack Kerouac[5]……died of drink & angry sicknesses….in 1969.

My friends whose deaths have slowed my heart stay with me now.

                 —1971

---

1   *Freddy Herko* American dancer (1936–64) known for his collaborations with artist Andy Warhol (1928–87). Herko committed suicide by jumping out a fifth floor window as he performed a dance to Mozart's Coronation Mass.

2   *Frank O'Hara* American writer and art critic closely associated with the New York School art movement (p. 490).

3   *Woody Guthrie* American singer-songwriter known for his songs about the Great Depression.

4   *Neal Cassady* American writer (1926–68) closely associated with the Beat Generation and the inspiration for the character Dean Moriarty in Jack Kerouac's *On the Road* (1957).

5   *Jack Kerouac* American writer famous for his role in the Beat Generation movement and for the novel *On the Road* (p. 463).

Audre Lorde
1934–1992

Audre Lorde's poetry falls within multiple important traditions in American poetry, including African-American poetry; women's poetry; political poetry; and lesbian poetry. She vigorously wrote from—and for—the many identities and commitments she embraced, giving them voice in her poems, fiction, and nonfiction. She called herself a "warrior."

Born and raised in New York, she was educated at Hunter College and Columbia University and worked as a librarian until she became a college teacher in the late 1960s. Active in the black liberation and feminist movements, she often wrote poems to address social injustice in addition to poems about other topics such as love and (often difficult) family relationships. "I have a duty," she said in an interview, "to speak the truth as I see it and to share not just my triumphs ... but the pain, the intense, often unmitigating pain."

Lorde's poems often address the reader directly, drawing attention to her own identity and that of different reading communities. She was the State Poet of New York from 1991 to 1992.

Outside

In the center of a harsh and spectrumed city
all things natural are strange.
I grew up in a genuine confusion
between grass and weeds and flowers
and what colored meant   5
except for clothes you couldn't bleach
and nobody called me nigger
until I was thirteen.
Nobody lynched my momma
but what she'd never been   10
had bleached her face of everything
but very private furies
and made the other children
call me yellow snot at school.

And how many times have I called myself back   15
through my bones confusion
black

like marrow meaning meat
and how many times have you cut me
20 and run in the streets
my own blood
who do you think me to be
that you are terrified of becoming
or what do you see in my face
25 you have not already discarded
in your own mirror
what face do you see in my eyes
that you will someday
come to
30 acknowledge your own?
Who shall I curse that I grew up
believing in my mother's face
or that I lived in fear of potent darkness
wearing my father's shape
35 they have both marked me
with their blind and terrible love
and I am lustful now for my own name.
Between the canyons of their mighty silences
mother bright and father brown
40 I seek my own shapes now
for they never spoke of me
except as theirs
and the pieces I stumble and fall over
I still record as proof
45 that I am beautiful
twice
blessed with the images
of who they were
and who I thought them once to be
50 of what I move
toward and through
and what I need
to leave behind me
most of all
55 I am blessed within my selves
who are come to make our shattered faces
whole.

—1976

Hanging Fire

I am fourteen
and my skin has betrayed me
the boy I cannot live without
still sucks his thumb
in secret   5
how come my knees are
always so ashy
what if I die
before morning
and momma's in the bedroom   10
with the door closed.

I have to learn how to dance
in time for the next party
my room is too small for me
suppose I die before graduation   15
they will sing sad melodies
but finally
tell the truth about me
There is nothing I want to do
and too much   20
that has to be done
and momma's in the bedroom
with the door closed.

Nobody even stops to think
about my side of it   25
I should have been on Math Team
my marks were better than his
why do I have to be
the one
wearing braces   30
I have nothing to wear tomorrow
will I live long enough
to grow up
and momma's in the bedroom
with the door closed.   35

—1978

Lucille Clifton
1936–2010

Lucille Clifton consciously broke from poetic conventions in her work, which celebrates family life, the female body, biblical characters (often envisioned as Caribbean or African), and African-American history, including the history of her own family. She carved out a minimalist style characterized by short and chiseled lines; limited capitalization and punctuation; and precise, focused use of words, phrases, and white space. When Clifton published her first poetry collection, *Good Times*, in 1969, it was named by *The New York Times* as one of the year's ten best books.

Born Thelma Lucille Sayles, Clifton grew up in Buffalo, New York, in a working-class family. Mother of six children, she identified her experience with maternity as an important source of poetic inspiration. In addition to writing more than ten poetry books for adults, Clifton was also a prolific author of children's literature that often addressed difficult subjects such as death and abuse.

Clifton tidily expressed her impatience with conventional ideas about poets in her final interview: "There's a way you're supposed to look if you're an American poet. There's a way you're supposed to sound.... And I think it's hogwash."

miss rosie

when i watch you
wrapped up like garbage
sitting, surrounded by the smell
of too old potato peels
5 or
when i watch you
in your old man's shoes
with the little toe cut out
sitting, waiting for your mind
10 like next week's grocery
i say
when i watch you
you wet brown bag of a woman
who used to be the best looking gal in georgia
15 used to be called the Georgia Rose
i stand up

through your destruction
i stand up

—1969

homage to my hips

these hips are big hips.
they need space to
move around in.
they don't fit into little
petty places. these hips   5
are free hips.
they don't like to be held back.
these hips have never been enslaved,
they go where they want to go
they do what they want to do.   10
these hips are mighty hips.
these hips are magic hips.
i have known them
to put a spell on a man and
spin him like a top!   15

—1980

the lost baby poem

the time i dropped your almost body down
down to meet the waters under the city
and run one with the sewage to the sea
what did i know about waters rushing back
what did i know about drowning   5
or being drowned

you would have been born into winter
in the year of the disconnected gas
and no car   we would have made the thin
walk over genesee hill into the canada wind   10
to watch you slip like ice into strangers' hands
you would have fallen naked as snow into winter
if you were here i could tell you these
and some other things

15 if i am ever less than a mountain
    for your definite brothers and sisters
    let the rivers pour over my head
    let the sea take me for a spiller
    of seas   let black men call me stranger
20 always   for your never named sake

                                                    —1987

wishes for sons

    i wish them cramps.
    i wish them a strange town
    and the last tampon.
    i wish them no 7-11.

5   i wish them one week early
    and wearing a white skirt.
    i wish them one week late.

    later i wish them hot flashes
    and clots like you
10 wouldn't believe.   let the
    flashes come when they
    meet someone special.
    let the clots come
    when they want to.

15 let them think they have accepted
    arrogance in the universe,
    then bring them to gynecologists
    not unlike themselves.

                                                    —1987

Seamus Heaney

1939–2013

Born to farmers in County Derry, just outside Belfast, Seamus Heaney grew up in a Roman Catholic household in a predominantly Protestant part of Northern Ireland. Heaney frequently drew on his roots for poetic inspiration, and many of his poems recall his childhood or draw on the activities of rural life—such as digging potatoes or churning milk—to explore their personal as well as their metaphorical significance.

Much of Heaney's poetry concerns the political and sectarian violence that rocked Northern Ireland during the second half of the twentieth century. He has been criticized both for his allegedly ambivalent attitude toward the conflict and for his decision to leave Northern Ireland for the relatively stable Republic of Ireland in 1972. Heaney did not, however, forget the political turmoil of his birthplace, and in the decade following his move he wrote some of his most political works, including *North* (1975) and *Field Work* (1979).

The death of Heaney's mother in 1984 was the occasion for some of his most poignant poetry. When questioned about his memorializing of lost friends and family, Heaney responded: "The elegiac Heaney? There's nothing else." Heaney's poems addressing the past often comment indirectly on the present; among the best-known examples of this approach are his "bog poems" about the preserved bodies of ancient sacrificial victims discovered in the peat bogs of Denmark.

Heaney combined writing with an academic career that included guest lectureships at Harvard and Oxford. He wrote translations from ancient and medieval languages, among them a critically acclaimed translation of *Beowulf* (2000). In 1995, Heaney was awarded the Nobel Prize in Literature; the committee cited his "works of lyrical beauty and ethical depth, which exalt everyday miracles and the living past."

Digging

Between my finger and my thumb
The squat pen rests; as snug as a gun.

Under my window a clean rasping sound
When the spade sinks into gravelly ground:
My father, digging. I look down
Till his straining rump among the flowerbeds
Bends low, comes up twenty years away

5

Stooping in rhythm through potato drills[1]
Where he was digging.

10 The coarse boot nestled on the lug, the shaft
Against the inside knee was levered firmly.
He rooted out tall tops, buried the bright edge deep
To scatter new potatoes that we picked
Loving their cool hardness in our hands.

15 By God, the old man could handle a spade,
Just like his old man.

My grandfather could cut more turf[2] in a day
Than any other man on Toner's bog.
Once I carried him milk in a bottle
20 Corked sloppily with paper. He straightened up
To drink it, then fell to right away
Nicking and slicing neatly, heaving sods
Over his shoulder, digging down and down
For the good turf. Digging.

25 The cold smell of potato mould, the squelch and slap
Of soggy peat, the curt cuts of an edge
Through living roots awaken in my head.
But I've no spade to follow men like them.

Between my finger and my thumb
30 The squat pen rests.
I'll dig with it.

—1966

Mid-Term Break[3]

I sat all morning in the college sick bay
Counting bells knelling classes to a close.
At two o'clock our neighbors drove me home.

---

1   *potato drills* Rows of sown potatoes.
2   *turf* Slabs of peat.
3   *Mid-Term Break* While Heaney was at boarding school in 1953, his four-year-old brother Christopher was killed in a car accident.

In the porch I met my father crying—
He had always taken funerals in his stride—   5
And Big Jim Evans saying it was a hard blow.

The baby cooed and laughed and rocked the pram
When I came in, and I was embarrassed
By old men standing up to shake my hand

And tell me they were "sorry for my trouble,"   10
Whispers informed strangers I was the eldest,
Away at school, as my mother held my hand

In hers and coughed out angry tearless sighs.
At ten o'clock the ambulance arrived
With the corpse, stanched and bandaged by the nurses.   15

Next morning I went up into the room. Snowdrops
And candles soothed the bedside; I saw him
For the first time in six weeks. Paler now,

Wearing a poppy bruise on his left temple,
He lay in the four foot box as in his cot.   20
No gaudy scars, the bumper knocked him clear.

A four foot box, a foot for every year.

—1966

The Grauballe Man[1]

As if he had been poured
in tar, he lies
on a pillow of turf
and seems to weep

the black river of himself.   5
The grain of his wrists
is like bog oak,[2]
the ball of his heel

---

1   *Grauballe Man* Man from the third century BCE whose preserved remains were found in
     1952, in a peat bog near the village of Grauballe, Denmark.
2   *bog oak* Wood of an oak tree preserved in a peat bog.

like a basalt egg.
10 His instep has shrunk
cold as a swan's foot
or a wet swamp root.

His hips are the ridge
and purse of a mussel,
15 his spine an eel arrested
under a glisten of mud.

The head lifts,
the chin is a visor
raised above the vent
20 of his slashed throat

that has tanned and toughened.
The cured wound
opens inwards to a dark
elderberry place.

25 Who will say "corpse"
to his vivid cast?
Who will say "body"
to his opaque repose?

And his rusted hair,
30 a mat unlikely
as a foetus's.
I first saw his twisted face

in a photograph,
a head and shoulder
35 out of the peat,
bruised like a forceps baby,

but now he lies
perfected in my memory,
down to the red horn
40 of his nails,

hung in the scales
with beauty and atrocity:

with the Dying Gaul[1]
too strictly compassed

on his shield,
with the actual weight
of each hooded victim,
slashed and dumped.

—1975

Cutaways

i

Children's hands in close-up
On a bomb site, picking and displaying
Small shrapnel curds for the cameramen

Who stalk their levelled village. *Ferrum*
and *rigor* and *frigor*[2] of mouse grey iron,
The thumb and finger of my own right hand

Closing around old hard plasticine
Given out by Miss Walls, thumbing it
To nests no bigger than an acorn cup,

Eggs no bigger than a grain of wheat,
Pet pigs with sausage bellies, belly-buttoned
Fingerprinted sausage women and men.

ii

Or trigger-fingering a six-gun stick,
Cocking a stiff hammer-thumb above
A sawn-off kitchen chair leg; or flying round

A gable, the wingspan of both arms
At full stretch and a-tilt, the left hand tip
Dangerously near earth, the air-shearing right

45

5

10

15

---

1   *Dying Gaul* Roman copy of a lost Greek statue (c. 230–220 BCE) depicting a Gallic
    (French) warrior dying in battle.
2   *Ferrum* Latin: iron; *rigor* Latin: stiffness; *frigor* Latin: cold.

Describing arcs—angelic potential
20 Fleetly, unforgettably attained:
Now in richochets that hosannah[1] through

The backyard canyons of Mossbawn,[2]
Now a head and shoulders dive
And skive as we hightail it up and away

iii

25 To land hard back on heels, like the charioteer
Holding his own at Delphi,[3] his six horses
And chariot gone, his left hand lopped off

A wrist protruding like a waterspout,
The reins astream in his right
30 Ready at any moment to curb and grapple

Bits long fallen away.
The cast of him on a postcard was enough
To set me straight once more between two shafts,

Another's hand on mine to guide the plough,
35 Each slither of the share, each stone it hit
Registered like a pulse in the timbered grips.

—2008

---

1   *hosannah* Exclamation of praise used in Jewish and Christian worship.
2   *Mossbawn* Farmhouse where Heaney was born.
3   *charioteer ... Delphi* Bronze statue found at the temple of Apollo at Delphi and one of the
     best known surviving examples of ancient Greek sculpture (c. 475 BCE).

Stan Rice

1942–2002

Stan Rice was an award-winning poet as well as an accomplished painter, originally from Dallas, Texas. He received his MA from San Francisco State University and went on to become Chair of the Creative Writing Program and Assistant Director of the Poetry Center there; upon retirement in 1988 he moved to New Orleans, Louisiana, where he lived with his wife, the best-selling vampire novelist Anne Rice, and their son, the novelist Christopher Rice. New Orleans, Anne's hometown, was a place that fed the imaginary realms that all three of these artists would produce.

The devastating loss of the Rices' six-year-old daughter, Michele, to leukemia gave rise to his first book of poetry, *Some Lamb* (1975). The title poem describes his small daughter as a meal that the figure of Death has consumed with epicurean pleasure. Michele's death also gave rise to her mother's first novel, *Interview with the Vampire* (1976).

Rice wrote with precise technical control in both short, compact poems and longer, open-form poems. He noted his debts to such predecessors as Walt Whitman (see p. 169), Ezra Pound (p. 341), Louis Zukofsky (p. 399), Charles Olson (p. 415), Allen Ginsberg (p. 488), and Frank O'Hara (p. 490), with whom he shared a passion for painting. After Rice's early death by brain cancer in 2002, his editor Deborah Garrison wrote of "the profound love of life, with all its burdens and beauties, that is stitched into every verse" of his poems.

The Strangeness

The strangeness of others—
Even your sisters and brothers—
Is a responsibility to
Overcome—or some night they will be lying
In a bed dying—and *how* you loved them,
Its quality—will be as unknown
To you as your own mother was
While a living stranger.

—2000

Agha Shahid Ali

1949–2001

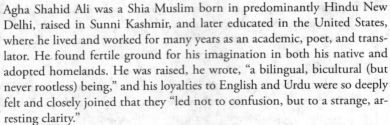

Agha Shahid Ali was a Shia Muslim born in predominantly Hindu New Delhi, raised in Sunni Kashmir, and later educated in the United States, where he lived and worked for many years as an academic, poet, and translator. He found fertile ground for his imagination in both his native and adopted homelands. He was raised, he wrote, "a bilingual, bicultural (but never rootless) being," and his loyalties to English and Urdu were so deeply felt and closely joined that they "led not to confusion, but to a strange, arresting clarity."

In collections such as *The Half-Inch Himalayas* (1987), Ali often looks back on the past and dwells on the experience of living apart from one's history. But, in taking stock of what he has left behind, the poet also comes to better represent his own nature and place in the world. In *A Walk through the Yellow Pages* (1987) and *A Nostalgist's Map of America* (1991), Ali does not simply write poems about the vast and varied landscapes of the United States and the American Southwest; he writes as an American poet, working in the tradition of the American sublime.

Among Ali's most significant literary contributions are his translations of the celebrated Urdu poet Faiz Ahmed Faiz. Both Faiz's poetry and the *ghazal*, a Persian lyric form consisting of rhymed, thematically self-contained couplets, were little known in the West before Ali published *The Rebel's Silhouette* (1991). Here as in much of his work, Ali was keen to experiment with ways to, as he phrased it, "make English behave outside its aesthetic habits." His interests in translations and in poetry written in other languages (including ancient languages) place him in a tradition of linguistic experiment with other US poets such as Henry Wadsworth Longfellow (see p. 116) and Emma Lazarus (p. 262).

Postcard from Kashmir

Kashmir shrinks into my mailbox,
my home a neat four by six inches.

I always loved neatness. Now I hold
the half-inch Himalayas in my hand.
5 This is home. And this the closest
I'll ever be to home. When I return,
the colors won't be so brilliant,

the Jhelum's[1] waters so clean,
so ultramarine. My love
so overexposed.   10
And my memory will be a little
out of focus, in it
a giant negative, black
and white, still undeveloped.

—1987

The Wolf's Postscript to "Little Red Riding Hood"

First, grant me my sense of history:
I did it for posterity,
for kindergarten teachers
and a clear moral:
Little girls shouldn't wander off   5
in search of strange flowers,
and they mustn't speak to strangers.

And then grant me my generous sense of plot:
Couldn't I have gobbled her up
right there in the jungle?   10
Why did I ask her where her grandma lived?
As if I, a forest-dweller,
didn't know of the cottage
under the three oak trees
and the old woman lived there   15
all alone?
As if I couldn't have swallowed her years before?

And you may call me the Big Bad Wolf,
now my only reputation.
But I was no child-molester   20
though you'll agree she was pretty.

And the huntsman:
Was I sleeping while he snipped
my thick black fur

---

1   *Jhelum* River originating in the Himalayas in Kashmir.

25 and filled me with garbage and stones?[1]
    I ran with that weight and fell down,
    simply so children could laugh
    at the noise of the stones
    cutting through my belly,
30 at the garbage spilling out
    with a perfect sense of timing,
    just when the tale
    should have come to an end.

                                        —1987

---

1   *And the ... stones* In the version of the Red Riding Hood story that appears in *Grimm's Fairy Tales* (1812–15), a huntsman discovers the wolf asleep and cuts its stomach open. He rescues the child and her grandmother, who are still alive inside, and they kill the wolf by filling its stomach with stones.

Jim Carroll

1949–2009

The son of a bartender in New York, Jim Carroll attended Roman Catholic schools until a basketball scholarship transplanted him to an elite Manhattan private school. An unusual amalgam of artistic and athletic talent, he also fell into the chaos of heroin addiction. Already publishing his poems as a teenager, he joined the New York poetry scene and found friends, mentors, and models among important avant-garde poets Allen Ginsberg (see p. 488), Frank O'Hara (p. 490), Ted Berrigan (p. 541), and Jack Kerouac (p. 463). He became best known for his high-school journal, *The Basketball Diaries*, published in 1978. (The book would become a film, starring Leonardo Di-Caprio as Carroll, in 1995.)

He formed The Jim Carroll Band, whose 1980 debut record *Catholic Boy* is sometimes considered the last great record of the punk era. The single "People Who Died," Carroll's recasting of a poem with the same title by his friend and mentor Berrigan also recalls the hybrid spoken-word innovations of his friends and admirers Patti Smith (see p. 605) and Lou Reed. When he died of a heart attack in 2009, reputedly while working at his desk, *The New York Times* called him a "poet and punk rocker in the outlaw tradition of Rimbaud and Burroughs." Jim Carroll remains an emblem of the simultaneous promises, risks, excesses, and intensities of the iconoclastic punk scene in the 1970s.

People Who Died

Teddy sniffing glue he was 12 years old
Fell from the roof on East Two-nine
Cathy was 11 when she pulled the plug
On 26 reds and a bottle of wine
Bobby got leukemia, 14 years old   5
He looked like 65 when he died
He was a friend of mine

Those are people who died, died
Those are people who died, died
Those are people who died, died   10
Those are people who died, died
They were all my friends, and they died

G-berg and Georgie let their gimmicks go rotten
So they died of hepatitis in upper Manhattan
15 Sly in Vietnam took a bullet in the head
Bobby OD'd on Drano on the night that he was wed
They were two more friends of mine
Two more friends that died
I miss 'em—they died

20 Those are people who died, died
Those are people who died, died
Those are people who died, died
Those are people who died, died
They were all my friends, and they died

25 Mary took a dry dive from a hotel room
Bobby hung himself from a cell in The Tombs
Judy jumped in front of a subway train
Eddie got slit in the jugular vein
And Eddie, I miss you more than all the others,
30 And I salute you brother
This song is for you my brother

Those are people who died, died
Those are people who died, died
Those are people who died, died
35 Those are people who died, died
They were all my friends, and they died

Herbie pushed Tony from the Boys' Club roof
Tony thought that his rage was just some goof
But Herbie sure gave Tony some bitchen proof
40 Hey, Herbie said, Tony, can you fly?
But Tony couldn't fly...Tony died

Those are people who died, died
Those are people who died, died
Those are people who died, died
45 Those are people who died, died
They were all my friends, and they died

Brian got busted on a narco rap
He beat the rap by rattin' on some bikers
He said, hey, I know it's dangerous,
but it sure beats Rikers
But the next day he got offed   50
by the very same bikers

—1980

To the Secret Poets of Kansas

Just because I can't understand you
it doesn't mean that I hate you . . . like
when you go on continuously how you
cannot tolerate skyscrapers or cabdrivers

                    maniac faces on Fifth, well   5

it means nothing to me I
just ignore as so often
or shift gears and read Pope[1] or some
boring Russian lunatic . . . you can't deny future

                        or simply fade.   10

and if you don't feel like running across streets here
you simply get run over and that means pain and boredom . . .
now isn't it amazing how you bring out logic in my poems.

I see nothing in a tree except lazy shade and nature
and that's not special, that's science   15

and all this concrete and steel and noise,
well, they've divided the simplest air to poems
some mornings, and we can't always rely on "Beauty" or gods

                        you must learn   20

but so often on our losses . . . and our tears.

—1993

---

1   *Pope* Alexander Pope (1688–1744), British poet. His poem *The Rape of the Lock* is available on the anthology's companion website.

Highway Report

for Jack Kerouac[1]

Breathe . . .
open fields
like tipping your hat to the sun

stream across turnpike

5   two women

on the other side   their dawns
reflect through the waters
on horses   tall weeds sensuous sway

crows settle

10   they assort their dreams

                              highway metal fences shine

three of us
feminine   marvelous   and tough

              our long hair
15   rests on a cloud's eye

                              streaming

drinking codeine   and my body
at 70 m.p.h.   is feather

I raise a knife to the sky's neck
20   the sun curves to avoid me

(It didn't really curve)
the sun couldn't care less

                    good afternoon,
                    Mayakovsky[2]

25   my nod:
                                a walk down St. Mark's Pl.

---

1   See p. 463.
2   *Mayakovsky* Vladimir Mayakovsky (1893–1930), the preeminent Russian and Soviet
    poet, artist, playwright, actor, and propagandist, shot himself in 1930.

with Ray Bremser

wearing a kimono . . .

Here comes the sun
over a.m. radio   30

            nodded two hours

nation's capital ascends over
trees colored for my dream
along yr. highway life

Kerouac is dead at 47   35
               on radio

and McCartney alive

       (we lost)   and

tragedy's just that and what to do but keep on going all in one line

       . . .

     the joggers are jogging   40
     a president is lying

(Last month my prick was "discharging")

          let us pray

Last highway trees and barns sway, the roads
sighing wetly... clouds so low, they are filled   45
with the snow of my heart, it's part of every man's
dream to rise to the sky... to die, gone forever from
American highways, where I nod today, missing nothing
really... to disappear ... at least for a time

this clear October day.   50

                 —published 1993

Deborah Digges

1950–2009

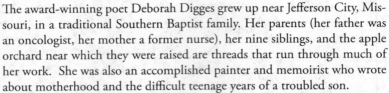

The award-winning poet Deborah Digges grew up near Jefferson City, Missouri, in a traditional Southern Baptist family. Her parents (her father was an oncologist, her mother a former nurse), her nine siblings, and the apple orchard near which they were raised are threads that run through much of her work. She was also an accomplished painter and memoirist who wrote about motherhood and the difficult teenage years of a troubled son.

The strongly personal, and sometimes confessional, elements in Digges's work can be joyful or dark. She once commented that she enjoyed the way that time, memory, and the present "collide." The poet Joelle Biele, a former student of Digges's, writes that "she makes suffering her subject and captures in gorgeous, concentrated language the currents of loss." Several critics have also noted the evolution in her work toward greater formal experimentation, culminating in her last collection, *The Wind Blows through the Doors of My Heart* (2010). The volume was edited and published posthumously; Digges died in 2009 of an apparent suicide. Upon her death, *The New York Times* described her as a poet who managed to render ordinary experience in a way that was also "out of the ordinary."

The Wind Blows through the Doors of My Heart

The wind blows
through the doors of my heart.
It scatters my sheet music
that climbs like waves from the piano, free of the keys.
5   Now the notes stripped, black butterflies,
flattened against the screens.
The wind through my heart
blows all my candles out.
In my heart and its rooms is dark and windy.
10   From the mantle smashes birds' nests, teacups
full of stars as the wind winds round,
a mist of sorts that rises and bends and blows
or is blown through the rooms of my heart
that shatters the windows,
15   rakes the bedsheets as though someone
had just made love. And my dresses
they are lifted like brides come to rest

on the bedstead, crucifixes,
dresses tangled in trees in the rooms
of my heart. To save them   20
I've thrown flowers to fields,
so that someone would pick them up
and know where they came from.
Come the bees now clinging to flowered curtains.
Off with the clothesline pinning anything, my mother's trousseau.[1]   25
It is not for me to say what is this wind
or how it came to blow through the rooms of my heart.
Wing after wing, through the rooms of the dead
the wind does not blow. Nor the basement, no wheezing,
no wind choking the cobwebs in our hair.   30
It is cool here, quiet, a quilt spread on soil.
But we will never lie down again.

—2009

1   *trousseau* Clothing and household goods collected by a bride before her wedding.

CONTEMPORARY VOICES

John Ashbery
b. 1927

Soonest Mended[1]

Barely tolerated, living on the margin
In our technological society, we were always having to be rescued
On the brink of destruction, like heroines in *Orlando Furioso*[2]
Before it was time to start all over again.
5 There would be thunder in the bushes, a rustling of coils,
And Angelica, in the Ingres painting,[3] was considering
The colorful but small monster near her toe, as though wondering whether
    forgetting
The whole thing might not, in the end, be the only solution.
And then there always came a time when
10 Happy Hooligan[4] in his rusted green automobile
Came plowing down the course, just to make sure everything was O.K.,
Only by that time we were in another chapter and confused
About how to receive this latest piece of information.
Was it information? Weren't we rather acting this out
15 For someone else's benefit, thoughts in a mind
With room enough and to spare for our little problems (so they began to seem),
Our daily quandary about food and the rent and bills to be paid?
To reduce all this to a small variant,
To step free at last, minuscule on the gigantic plateau—
20 This was our ambition: to be small and clear and free.
Alas, the summer's energy wanes quickly,
A moment and it is gone. And no longer
May we make the necessary arrangements, simple as they are.

---

1   *Soonest Mended* From the expression "Least said, soonest mended."
2   *Orlando Furioso* Epic by Italian poet Lodovico Ariosto (1474–1533) whose heroine An-
    gelica is rescued multiple times throughout the narrative.
3   *Ingres painting* French painter Jean-Auguste-Dominique Ingres's 1819 painting *Ruggiero
    Rescuing Angelica*.
4   *Happy Hooligan* Popular comic strip character created by Frederick Burr Opper (1857–
    1937).

Our star was brighter perhaps when it had water in it.
Now there is no question even of that, but only 25
Of holding on to the hard earth so as not to get thrown off,
With an occasional dream, a vision: a robin flies across
The upper corner of the window, you brush your hair away
And cannot quite see, or a wound will flash
Against the sweet faces of the others, something like: 30
This is what you wanted to hear, so why
Did you think of listening to something else? We are all talkers
It is true, but underneath the talk lies
The moving and not wanting to be moved, the loose
Meaning, untidy and simple like a threshing floor.[1] 35

These then were some hazards of the course,
Yet though we knew the course *was* hazards and nothing else
It was still a shock when, almost a quarter of a century later,
The clarity of the rules dawned on you for the first time.
They were the players, and we who had struggled at the game 40
Were merely spectators, though subject to its vicissitudes[2]
And moving with it out of the tearful stadium, borne on shoulders, at last.
Night after night this message returns, repeated
In the flickering bulbs of the sky, raised past us, taken away from us,
Yet ours over and over until the end that is past truth, 45
The being of our sentences, in the climate that fostered them,
Not ours to own, like a book, but to be with, and sometimes
To be without, alone and desperate.
But the fantasy makes it ours, a kind of fence-sitting
Raised to the level of an esthetic ideal. These were moments, years, 50
Solid with reality, faces, namable events, kisses, heroic acts,
But like the friendly beginning of a geometrical progression
Not too reassuring, as though meaning could be cast aside some day
When it had been outgrown. Better, you said, to stay cowering
Like this in the early lessons, since the promise of learning 55
Is a delusion, and I agreed, adding that
Tomorrow would alter the sense of what had already been learned,
That the learning process is extended in this way, so that from this standpoint
None of us ever graduates from college,

---

1   *threshing floor* Flat surface where harvested grain is separated from chaff.
2   *vicissitudes* I.e., ups and downs.

60 For time is an emulsion,[1] and probably thinking not to grow up
Is the brightest kind of maturity for us, right now at any rate.
And you see, both of us were right, though nothing
Has somehow come to nothing; the avatars°   *incarnations*
Of our conforming to the rules and living
65 Around the home have made—well, in a sense, "good citizens" of us,
Brushing the teeth and all that, and learning to accept
The charity of the hard moments as they are doled out,
For this is action, this not being sure, this careless
Preparing, sowing the seeds crooked in the furrow,
70 Making ready to forget, and always coming back
To the mooring of starting out, that day so long ago.

—1970

Paradoxes and Oxymorons

This poem is concerned with language on a very plain level.
Look at it talking to you. You look out a window
Or pretend to fidget. You have it but you don't have it.
You miss it, it misses you. You miss each other.

5 The poem is sad because it wants to be yours, and cannot.
What's a plain level? It is that and other things,
Bringing a system of them into play. Play?
Well, actually, yes, but I consider play to be

A deeper outside thing, a dreamed role-pattern,
10 As in the division of grace these long August days
Without proof. Open-ended. And before you know
It gets lost in the steam and chatter of typewriters.

It has been played once more. I think you exist only
To tease me into doing it, on your level, and then you aren't there
15 Or have adopted a different attitude. And the poem
Has set me softly down beside you. The poem is you.

—1980

___

1   *emulsion* Unmixable liquid compound where one fluid is suspended in the other, such as oil and water.

Gary Snyder
b. 1930

As for Poets

As for poets
The Earth Poets
Who write small poems,
Need help from no man.

❧

The Air Poets   5
Play out the swiftest gales
And sometimes loll in the eddies.
Poem after poem,
Curling back on the same thrust.

❧

At fifty below   10
Fuel oil won't flow
And propane stays in the tank.
Fire Poets
Burn at absolute zero
Fossil love pumped back up.   15

❧

The first
Water Poet
Stayed down six years.
He was covered with seaweed.
The life in his poem   20
Left millions of tiny
Different tracks
Criss-crossing through the mud.

¶

With the Sun and Moon
25   In his belly,
The Space Poet
Sleeps.
No end to the sky.
But his poems,
30   Like wild geese,
Fly off the edge.

¶

A Mind Poet
Stays in the house.
The house is empty
35   And it has no walls.
The poem
Is seen from all sides,
Everywhere,
At once.

—1974

Derek Walcott
b. 1930

A Far Cry from Africa

A wind is ruffling the tawny pelt
Of Africa. Kikuyu,[1] quick as flies,
Batten upon[2] the bloodstreams of the veldt.°   *open country*
Corpses are scattered through a paradise.
Only the worm, colonel of carrion, cries: 5
"Waste no compassion on these separate dead!"
Statistics justify and scholars seize
The salients of colonial policy.
What is that to the white child hacked in bed?
To savages, expendable as Jews?   10

Threshed out by beaters, the long rushes break
In a white dust of ibises[3] whose cries
Have wheeled since civilization's dawn
From the parched river or beast-teeming plain.
The violence of beast on beast is read   15
As natural law, but upright man
Seeks his divinity by inflicting pain.
Delirious as these worried beasts, his wars
Dance to the tightened carcass of a drum,
While he calls courage still that native dread   20
Of the white peace contracted by the dead.

Again brutish necessity wipes its hands
Upon the napkin of a dirty cause, again
A waste of our compassion, as with Spain,[4]

---

1   *Kikuyu* Bantu-speaking people of Kenya who fought against British colonial settlers as
     part of the eight-year Mau Mau uprising of the 1950s.
2   *Batten upon* Thrive on; revel in.
3   *ibises* Long-legged, stork-like birds that inhabit lakes and swamps.
4   *Spain* I.e., the Spanish Civil War (1936–39). Many foreign volunteers fought, perceiv-
     ing it as a way to resist the international rise of fascism. After brutality on both sides,
     the war ended with the establishment of a dictatorship supported by the German Nazis
     and the Italian Fascists.

25 The gorilla wrestles with the superman.
I who am poisoned with the blood of both,
Where shall I turn, divided to the vein?
I who have cursed
The drunken officer of British rule, how choose
30 Between this Africa and the English tongue I love?
Betray them both, or give back what they give?
How can I face such slaughter and be cool?
How can I turn from Africa and live?

—1962

The Sea Is History

Where are your monuments, your battles, martyrs?
Where is your tribal memory? Sirs,
in that grey vault. The sea. The sea
has locked them up. The sea is History.

5 First, there was the heaving oil,
heavy as chaos;
then, like a light at the end of a tunnel,

the lantern of a caravel,
and that was Genesis.
10 Then there were the packed cries,
the shit, the moaning:

Exodus.
Bone soldered by coral to bone,
mosaics
15 mantled by the benediction of the shark's shadow,

that was the Ark of the Covenant.[1]
Then came from the plucked wires
of sunlight on the sea floor

the plangent harps of the Babylonian[2] bondage,
20 as the white cowries clustered like manacles
on the drowned women,

---

1   *Ark of the Covenant* Chest containing the tablets of the Ten Commandments.
2   *Babylonian* The Jews were captives in Babylonia, an ancient empire of Mesopotamia,
    from 597 BCE until its conquest by Persia in 538 BCE.

and those were the ivory bracelets
of the Song of Solomon,
but the ocean kept turning blank pages

looking for History.   25
Then came the men with eyes heavy as anchors
who sank without tombs,

brigands who barbecued cattle,
leaving their charred ribs like palm leaves on the shore,
then the foaming, rabid maw   30

of the tidal wave swallowing Port Royal,[1]
and that was Jonah,[2]
but where is your Renaissance?

Sir, it is locked in them sea-sands
out there past the reef's moiling shelf,   35
where the men-o'-war floated down;

strop on these goggles, I'll guide you there myself.
It's all subtle and submarine,
through colonnades of coral,

past the gothic windows of sea-fans   40
to where the crusty grouper, onyx-eyed,
blinks, weighted by its jewels, like a bald queen;

and these groined caves with barnacles
pitted like stone
are our cathedrals,   45
and the furnace before the hurricanes:

Gomorrah.[3] Bones ground by windmills
into marl and cornmeal,

and that was Lamentations—
that was just Lamentations,   50
it was not History;

---

1   *Port Royal*   A town and naval station in Jamaica, destroyed by an earthquake in 1692.
2   *Jonah*   Jonah was swallowed by a "great fish," which flung him upon dry land three days
    later; see the Book of Jonah in the Bible's Old Testament.
3   *Gomorrah*   One of the two cities destroyed by God for their corruption and decadence;
    see Genesis 18, 19 in the Old Testament.

then came, like scum on the river's drying lip,
the brown reeds of villages
mantling and congealing into towns,

55   and at evening, the midges' choirs,
and above them, the spires
lancing the side of God

as His son set, and that was the New Testament.

Then came the white sisters clapping
60   to the waves' progress,
and that was Emancipation—

jubilation, O jubilation—
vanishing swiftly
as the sea's lace dries in the sun,

65   but that was not History,
that was only faith,
and then each rock broke into its own nation;

then came the synod of flies,
then came the secretarial heron,
70   then came the bullfrog bellowing for a vote,

fireflies with bright ideas
and bats like jetting ambassadors
and the mantis,[1] like khaki police,

and the furred caterpillars of judges
75   examining each case closely,
and then in the dark ears of ferns

and in the salt chuckle of rocks
with their sea pools, there was the sound
like a rumour without any echo

80   of History, really beginning.

—1979

_____

1   *mantis* Species of insect.

Mary Oliver
b. 1935

Death at a Great Distance

The ripe, floating caps
  of the fly amanita[1]
    glow in the pinewoods.
      I don't even think
        of the eventual corruption of my body,   5

but of how quaint and humorous they are,
  like a collection of doorknobs,
    half-moons,
      then a yellow drizzle of flying saucers.
      In any case   10

they won't hurt me unless
  I take them between my lips
    and swallow, which I know enough
      not to do. Once, in the south,
        I had this happen: 15

the soft rope of a water moccasin[2]
  slid down the red knees
    of a mangrove, the hundreds of ribs
      housed in their smooth, white
        sleeves of muscle moving it   20

like a happiness
  toward the water, where some bubbles
    on the surface of that underworld announced
      a fatal carelessness. I didn't
        even then move toward the fine point   25

---

1   *fly amanita* Poisonous toadstool mushroom known for its red cap covered in white spots.
2   *water moccasin* Also called a cottonmouth, a type of poisonous snake found in the
   swamps of the southeastern United States.

of the story, but stood in my lonely body
      amazed and full of attention as it fell
            like a stream of glowing syrup into
                  the dark water, as death
30   blurted out of that perfectly arranged mouth.

—1988

What Is It?

Who can say,
is it a snowy egret
or a white flower
standing

5   at the glossy edge
of the lily-
and frog-filled pond?
Hours ago the orange sun

opened the cups of the lilies
10 and the leopard frogs
began kicking
their long muscles,

breast-stroking
like little green dwarves
15 under the roof of the rich,
iron-colored water.

Now the soft
eggs of the salamander
in their wrappings of jelly
20 begin to shiver.

They're tired of sleep.
They have a new idea.
They want to swim away
into the world.

Who could stop them?
Who could tell them   25
to go cautiously, to flow slowly
under the lily pads?

Off they go,
hundreds of them,   30
like the black
fingerprints of the rain.

The frogs freeze
into perfect five-fingered
shadows, but suddenly the flower   35
has fire-colored eyes

and one of the shadows vanishes.
Clearly, now, the flower is a bird.
It lifts its head,
it lifts the hinges   40

of its snowy wings,
tossing a moment of light
in every direction
like a chandelier,

and then once more is still.   45
The salamanders,
like tiny birds, locked into formation,
fly down into the endless mysteries

of the transforming water,
and how could anyone believe   50
that anything in this world
is only what it appears to be—

that anything is ever final—
that anything, in spite of its absence,
ever dies   55
a perfect death?

                                          —1990

Michael S. Harper
b. 1938

Debridement[1]

Debridement

Black men are oaks cut down.

Congressional Medal of Honor Society
United States of America chartered by
Congress, August 14, 1958; this certifies
5 that STAC John Henry Louis *is a member
of this society.*

    *"Don't ask me anything about the
    medal. I don't even know how I won
    it."*

10 *Debridement: The cutting away of dead
or contaminated tissue from a wound
to prevent infection.*

    America: love it or give it back.

Corktown

Groceries ring
15 in my intestines:
*grits aint groceries
eggs aint poultry
Mona Lisa was a man:*
waltzing in sawdust
20 I dream my cards
has five holes in it,

---

1   In order not to overburden particularly allusion-heavy poems like this one with excessive
    notation, this edition runs them with minimal notes. The poem thus retains its appear-
    ance as the poet wrote it, and readers can investigate terms as they choose on their own.

up to twenty holes;
five shots out of seven
beneath the counter;
surrounded by detectives
pale ribbons of valor
my necklace of bullets
powdering the operating table.

Five impaled men loop their ribbons
'round my neck
listening to whispers of valor:
"Honey, what you cryin' 'bout?
You made it back."

Caves

Four M-48 tank platoons ambushed
near Dak To, two destroyed:
the Ho Chi Minh Trail boils,
half my platoon rockets
into stars near Cambodia,
foot soldiers dance from highland woods
taxing our burning half:

there were no caves for them to hide.
We saw no action,
eleven months twenty-two days
in our old tank
burning sixty feet away:
I watch them burn inside out:
hoisting through heavy crossfire,
hoisting over turret hatches,
hoisting my last burning man
alive to the ground,
our tank artillery shells explode
killing all inside:
hoisting blown burned squad
in tank's bladder,
plug leaks with cave blood:

there were no caves for them to hide—

In the Projects

Slung basketballs at Jeffries
House with some welfare kids
weaving in their figure eight hunger.

60 Mama asked if I was taking anything?
I rolled up my sleeves:
no tracks, mama:
"black-medal-man ain't street-poisoned,"
militants called:
65 "he's an electronic nigger!"

"Better keep electronic nigger 'way."
Electronic Nigger?
Mama, unplug me, please.

A White Friend Flies In from the Coast

Burned—black by birth,
70 *burned*—armed with .45,
burned—submachine gun,
burned—STAC hunted VC,
burned—killing 5-20,
burned—nobody know for sure;
75 *burned*—out of ammo,
burned—killed one with gun-stock,
burned—VC AK-47 jammed,
burned—killed faceless VC,
burned—over and over,
80 *burned*—STAC subdued by three men,
burned—three shots: morphine,
burned—tried killing prisoners,
burned—taken to Pleiku,
burned—held down, straitjacket,
85 *burned*—whites owe him, hear?
burned—I owe him, here.

Mama's Report

"Don't fight, honey,
don't let 'em catch you."

Tour over, gear packed,
hospital over, no job.   90

"Aw man, nothin' happened,"
explorer, altar boy—

Maybe it's 'cause they killed people
and don't know why they did?

My boy had color slides of dead people,   95
stacks of dead Vietnamese.

MP's asked if he'd been arrested
since discharge, what he'd been doin':

"Lookin' at slides,
looking' at stacks of slides, mostly."   100

Fifteen minutes later a colonel called
from the Defense Department, said he'd won the medal;

could he be in Washington with his family,
maybe he'd get a job now; he qualified.

The Democrats had lost, the president said;   105
there were signs of movement in Paris:

Fixing Certificates: Dog Tags: Letters Home

Our heliteam had mid-air blowout
dropping flares—5 burned alive.

The children carry hand
grenades to and from piss tubes.   110

Staring at tracer bullets
rice is the focal point of war.

On amphibious raid, our heliteam
found dead VC with maps of our compound.

115   On morning sick call you unzip;
before you piss you get a smear.

"VC reamed that *mustang* a new asshole"—
even at movies: "no round-eye pussy no more"—

Tympanic membrane damage: high gone—
120   20-40 db loss mid-frequencies.

Scrub-typhus, malaria, dengue fever, cholera;
rotting buffalo, maggoted dog, decapped children.

Bangkok: amber dust, watches, C-rations,
elephanthide billfolds, cameras, smack.

125   Sand&tinroof bunkers, 81/120 mm:
"Health record terminated this date by reason of death."

Vaculoated amoeba, bacillary dysentery, hookworm;
thorazine, tetracycline, darvon for diarrhea.

'*Conitus*': I wanna go home to mama;
130   Brown's mixture, ETH with codeine, cortisone skin-creams.

Written on helipad fantail 600 bed *Repose*;
"no purple heart, hit by 'nother marine."

"Vascular repair, dissection, debridement":
sharp bone edges, mushy muscle, shrapnel: stainless bucket.

135   Bodies in polyethylene bag: transport:
'Tan San Nhat Mortuary'

Blood, endotracheal tube, prep
abdomen, mid-chest to scrotum—

"While you're fixin' me doc,
can you fix them ingrown hairs on my face?"   140

"They didn't get my balls, did they?"
50 mg thorazine—"Yes they did, marine!"

Street-Poisoned

Swans loom on the playground
swooning in the basket air,
the nod of their bills   145
in open flight, open formation.
Street-poisoned, a gray mallard
skims into our courtyard with a bag:

And he poisons them—
And he poisons them—   150
Electronic-nigger-recruiter,
my pass is a blade
near the sternum
cutting in:
you can make this a career.   155

Patches itch on my chest and shoulders—
I powder them with phisohex
solution from an aerosol can:
you can make this a career.

Pickets of insulin dab the cloudy   160
hallways in a spray.
Circuits of change
march to an honor guard—
I am prancing:
I am prancing: 165

you can make this a career.

Makin' Jump Shots

He waltzes into the lane
'cross the free-throw line,
fakes a drive, pivots,
170 floats from the asphalt turf
in an arc of black light,
and sinks two into the chains.

One on one he fakes
down the main, passes
175 into the free lane
and hits the chains.

A sniff in the fallen air—
he stuffs it through the chains
riding high:
180 "traveling" someone calls—
and he laughs, stepping
to a silent beat, gliding
as he sinks two into the chains.

Debridement: Operation Harvest Moon: On Repose

The sestina traces a circle in language and body.
185 Stab incision below nipple,
left side; insert large chest tube;
sew to skin, right side;
catch blood from tube
in gallon drain bottle.
190 Wash abdomen with phisohex;
shave; spray brown iodine prep.

Stab incision below sternum
to symphis pubis
catch blood left side;
195 sever reddish brown spleen
cut in half; tie off blood supply;
check retroperitoneal,
kidney, renal artery bleeding.

Dissect lateral wall
abdominal cavity; locate kidney;   200
pack colon, small intestine;
cut kidney; suture closely;
inch by inch check bladder,
liver, abdominal wall, stomach:
25 units blood, pressure down.   205

Venous pressure: 8; lumbar
musculature, lower spinal column
pulverized; ligate blood vessels,
right forearm; trim meat, bone ends;
tourniquet above fracture, left arm;   210
urine, negative: 4 hours; pressure
unstable; remove shrapnel flecks.

Roll on stomach; 35 units blood;
pressure zero; insert plastic blood
containers, pressure cuffs; pump chest   215
drainage tube; wash wounds sterile
saline; dress six-inch ace wraps;
wrap both legs, toe to groin; left arm
plaster, finger to shoulder: 40 units blood.

Pressure, pulse, respiration up;   220
remove bloody gowns; scrub; redrape;
5 cc vitamin K; thorazine: sixth
laparotomy; check hyperventilation;
stab right side incision below nipple;
insert large chest tube; catch blood drain bottle ...   225

The Family of Debridement

Theory: Inconvenienced subject will return to hospital
if loaned Thunderbird
Withdrawn. Hope: Subject returns,
Treatment:
Foreclosure for nine months unpaid mortgage;   230
wife tells subject hospital wants deposit,
Diseased cyst removal:
'Ain't you gonna give me a little kiss good-bye'

Subject-wife: To return with robe and curlers—
235   *Subject tells friend he'll pay $15 to F's stepfather*
if he'll drive him to pick up money owed him.

"This guy lives down the street,
I don't want him to see me coming."

"It looked odd for a car filled with blacks
240   *to be parked in the dark in a white neighborhood,*
so we pulled the car out under a streetlight
so everybody could see us."

Store manager: "I first hit him with two bullets
so I pulled the trigger until my gun was empty."

245   *"I'm going to kill you, you white MF," store manager*
told police. Police took cardload, F and F's parents for
further questioning. Subject died on operating table: 5 hrs:

Subject buried on grass slope, 200 yards
east of Kennedy Memorial,
250   *overlooking Potomac and Pentagon,*
to the south,
Arlington National Cemetery.

Army honor guard
in dress blues,
255   *carried out assignment*
with precision:

—1977

Margaret Atwood
b. 1939

Death of a Young Son by Drowning[1]

He, who navigated with success
the dangerous river of his own birth
once more set forth

on a voyage of discovery
into the land I floated on
but could not touch to claim.   5

His feet slid on the bank,
the currents took him;
he swirled with ice and trees in the swollen water

and plunged into distant regions,   10
his head a bathysphere;[2]
through his eyes' thin glass bubbles
he looked out, reckless adventurer
on a landscape stranger than Uranus
we have all been to and some remember.   15

There was an accident; the air locked,
he was hung in the river like a heart.
They retrieved the swamped body,

cairn of my plans and future charts,
with poles and hooks   20
from among the nudging logs.

---

1   *Death of ... Drowning* From *The Journals of Susanna Moodie* (1970), a collection Atwood
     based on the life and work of Susanna Moodie, author of the 1852 pioneer memoir
     Roughing It in the Bush. Moodie's son drowned in the Moira River in Upper Canada,
     where the family had settled.
2   *bathysphere* Spherical diving-bell for deep-sea observation.

It was spring, the sun kept shining, the new grass
leapt to solidity;
my hands glistened with details.

25   After the long trip I was tired of waves.
My foot hit rock. The dreamed sails
collapsed, ragged.

                              I planted him in this country
                              like a flag.

                                                —1970

Billy Collins
b. 1941

Lines Composed Over Three Thousand Miles from Tintern Abbey[1]

I was here before, a long time ago,
and now I am here again
is an observation that occurs in poetry
as frequently as rain occurs in life.

The fellow may be gazing   5
over an English landscape,
hillsides dotted with sheep,
a row of tall trees topping the downs,

or he could be moping through the shadows
of a dark Bavarian forest,   10
a wedge of cheese and a volume of fairy tales
tucked into his rucksack.

But the feeling is always the same.
It was better the first time.
This time is not nearly as good.   15
I'm not feeling as chipper as I did back then.

Something is always missing—
swans, a glint on the surface of a lake,
some minor but essential touch.
Or the quality of things has diminished.   20

The sky was a deeper, more dimensional blue,
clouds were more cathedral-like,
and water rushed over rock
with greater effervescence.

---

1   *Lines Composed ... Tintern Abbey* See William Wordsworth's "Lines Written a Few Miles above Tintern Abbey" (p. 63).

25 From our chairs we have watched
the poor author in his waistcoat
as he recalls the dizzying icebergs of childhood
and mills around in a field of weeds.

We have heard the poets long dead
30 declaim their dying
from a promontory, a riverbank,
next to a haycock, within a copse.

We have listened to their dismay,
the kind that issues from poems
35 the way water issues forth from hoses,
the way the match always gives its little speech on fire.

And when we put down the book at last,
lean back, close our eyes,
stinging with print,
40 and slip in the bookmark of sleep,

we will be schooled enough to know
that when we wake up
a little before dinner
things will not be nearly as good as they once were.

45 Something will be missing
from this long, coffin-shaped room,
the walls and windows now
only two different shades of gray,

the glossy gardenia drooping
50 in its chipped terra-cotta pot.
And on the floor, shoes, socks,
the browning core of an apple.

Nothing will be as it was
a few hours ago, back in the glorious past
55 before our naps, back in that Golden Age
that drew to a close sometime shortly after lunch.

—1998

Stephen Dobyns
b. 1941

The Gun

Late afternoon light slices through the dormer window[1]
to your place on the floor next to a stack of comics.
Across from you is a boy who at eleven is three years
older. He is telling you to pull down your pants.
You tell him you don't want to. His mother is out 5
and you are alone in the house. He has given you a Coke,
let you smoke two of his mother's nonfilter Pall Malls,
and years later you can still picture the red packet
on the dark finish of the phonograph. You stand up
and say you have to go home. You live across the street 10
and only see him in summer when he returns from school.
As you step around the comics toward the stairs,
the boy gives you a shove, sends you stumbling back.
Wait, he says, I want to show you something.
He goes to a drawer and when he turns around 15
you see he is holding a small gun by the barrel.
You feel you are breathing glass. You ask if it is
loaded and he says, Sure it is, and you say: Show me.
He removes the clip, takes a bullet from his pocket.
See this, he says, then puts the bullet into the clip, 20
slides the clip into the butt of the gun with a snap.
The boy sits on the bed and pretends to study the gun.
He has a round fat face and black hair. Take off
your pants, he says. Again you say you have to go home.
He stands up and points the gun at your legs. Slowly, 25
you unhook your cowboy belt, undo the metal buttons
of your jeans. They slide down past your knees.
Pull down your underwear, he tells you. You tell him
you don't want to. He points the gun at your head.
You crouch on the floor, cover your head with your hands. 30
You don't want him to see you cry. You feel you are
pulling yourself into yourself and soon you will be

---

1   *dormer window* Attic window that rises vertically from the roof of a house.

no bigger than a pebble. You think back to the time
you saw a friend's cocker spaniel hit by a car and you
35 remember how its stomach was split open and you imagine
your face split open and blood and gray stuff escaping.
You have hardly ever thought of dying, seriously dying,
and as you grow more scared you have to go to the bathroom
more and more badly. Before you can stop yourself,
40 you feel yourself pissing into your underwear.
The boy with the gun sees the spreading pool of urine.
You baby, he shouts, you baby, you're disgusting.
You want to apologize, but the words jumble and
choke in your throat. Get out, the boy shouts.
45 You drag your pants up over your wet underwear and
run down the stairs. As you slam out of his house,
you know you died up there among the comic books
and football pennants, died as sure as your friend's
cocker spaniel, as sure as if the boy had shot your
50 face off, shot the very piss out of you. Standing
in the street with urine soaking your pants, you watch
your neighbors pursuing the orderly occupations
of a summer afternoon: mowing a lawn, trimming a hedge.
Where is that sense of the world you woke with
55 this morning. Now it is smaller. Now it has gone away.

—1982

Robert Hass
b. 1941

A Story about the Body

The young composer, working that summer at an artist's colony, had watched
her for a week. She was Japanese, a painter, almost sixty, and he thought he was
in love with her. He loved her work, and her work was like the way she moved
her body, used her hands, looked at him directly when she made amused and
considered answers to his questions. One night, walking back from a concert,   5
they came to her door and she turned to him and said, "I think you would like
to have me. I would like that too, but I must tell you that I have had a double
mastectomy," and when he didn't understand, "I've lost both my breasts."
The radiance that he had carried around in his belly and chest cavity—like
music—withered very quickly, and he made himself look at her when he said,   10
"I'm sorry. I don't think I could." He walked back to his own cabin through
the pines, and in the morning he found a small blue bowl on the porch outside
his door. It looked to be full of rose petals, but he found when he picked it up
that the rose petals were on top; the rest of the bowl—she must have swept
them from the corners of her studio—was full of dead bees.   15

—1989

Marilyn Hacker
b. 1942

Villanelle for D.G.B.

Every day our bodies separate
exploded torn and dazed.
Not understanding what we celebrate

we grope through languages and hesitate
5 and touch each other, speechless and amazed,
and every day our bodies separate

us farther from our planned, deliberate
ironic lives. I am afraid, disphased,
not understanding what we celebrate

10 when our fused limbs and lips communicate
the unlettered power we have raised.
Every day our bodies' separate

routines are harder to perpetuate.
In wordless darkness, we learn wordless praise,
15 not understanding what we celebrate;

wake to ourselves, exhausted, in the late
morning as the wind tears off the haze,
not understanding how we celebrate
our bodies. Every day we separate.

—1972

[Didn't Sappho[1] say her guts clutched up like this?]

Didn't Sappho say her guts clutched up like this?
Before a face suddenly numinous,
her eyes watered, knees melted.[2] Did she lactate
again, milk brought down by a girl's kiss?
It's documented torrents are unloosed   5
by such events as recently produced
not the wish, but the need, to consume, in us,
one pint of Maalox, one of Kaopectate.[3]
My eyes and groin are permanently swollen,
I'm alternatingly brilliant and witless   10
—and sleepless: bed is just a swamp to roll in.
Although I'd cream my jeans touching your breast,
sweetheart, it isn't lust; it's all the rest
of what I want with you that scares me shitless.

—1986

---

1   *Sappho* Greek poet from the Island of Lesbos (c. 630/612–c. 570 BCE). Famed and in-
     fluential throughout poetic history, Sappho stands at the head of two specific poetic
     traditions: poetry by women and lesbian poetry. Little is known about Sappho's life, but
     ideas and controversies about her and her work have circulated since her own lifetime.
2   *Didn't ... melted* Refers to Fragment 31 of Sappho's surviving poetry; *numinous* Divine.
3   *Maalox ... Kaopectate* Medications used to treat indigestion and diarrhea, respectively.

Sharon Olds
b. 1942

Sex without Love

How do they do it, the ones who make love
without love? Beautiful as dancers,
gliding over each other like ice-skaters
over the ice, fingers hooked
5 inside each other's bodies, faces
red as steak, wine, wet as the
children at birth whose mothers are going to
give them away. How do they come to the
come to the   come to the   God   come to the
10 still waters, and not love
the one who came there with them, light
rising slowly as steam off their joined
skin? These are the true religious,
the purists, the pros, the ones who will not
15 accept a false Messiah, love the
priest instead of the God. They do not
mistake the lover for their own pleasure,
they are like great runners: they know they are alone
with the road surface, the cold, the wind,
20 the fit of their shoes, their over-all cardio-
vascular health—just factors, like the partner
in the bed, and not the truth, which is the
single body alone in the universe
against its own best time.

—1984

The Healers

When they say, *If there are any doctors aboard,*
would they make themselves known, I remember when my then
husband would rise, and I would get to be
the one he rose from beside. They say now
5 that it does not work, unless you are equal.

And after those first thirty years,
I was not the one he wanted to rise from
or return to—not I but she who would also
rise, when such were needed. Now I see them,
lifting, side by side, on wide,   10
medical, wading-bird wings—like storks with the
doctor bags of like-loves-like
dangling from their beaks. Oh well. It was the way
it was, he did not feel happy when words
were called for, and I stood.   15

—2011

Louise Glück
b. 1943

Anniversary

I said you could snuggle. That doesn't mean
your cold feet all over my dick.

Someone should teach you how to act in bed.
What I think is you should
5 keep your extremities to yourself.

Look what you did—
you made the cat move.

    But I didn't want your hand there.
    I wanted your hand here.

10   You should pay attention to my feet.
    You should picture them
    the next time you see a hot fifteen year old.
    Because there's a lot more where those feet come from.

—1996

Eavan Boland
b. 1944

The Emigrant Irish

Like oil lamps we put them out the back,

of our houses, of our minds. We had lights
better than, newer than and then

a time came, this time and now
we need them. Their dread, makeshift example.   5

They would have thrived on our necessities.
What they survived we could not even live.
By their lights now it is time to
imagine how they stood there, what they stood with,
that their possessions may become our power.   10

Cardboard. Iron. Their hardships parcelled in them.
Patience. Fortitude. Long-suffering
in the bruise-coloured dusk of the New World.

And all the old songs. And nothing to lose.

—1986

On the Gift of "The Birds of America" by John James Audubon[1]

What you have given me is, of course, elegy: the red-shouldered
hawk in among these scattering partridges,
flustered at

---

1   *On the Gift ... Audubon* John James Audubon (1785–1851), Haitian painter and orni-
    thologist, painted and catalogued the birds of North America, publishing 435 hand-
    colored engravings in four volumes between 1826 and 1838.

such a descent, and the broad-winged one poised on the branch
5   of a pignut, and the pine siskin and the wren are
an inference

we follow in the plummet of the tern which appears to be,
from this angle anyway, impossibly fragile and
if we imagine

10   the franchise of light these camphor-coloured wings opened out
once with and are at such a loss for now,
then surely this

is the nature and effect of elegy: the celebration of an element
which absence has revealed: it is
15   our earthliness

we love as we look at them, which we fear to lose, which we need
this re-phrasing of the air,
of the ocean

to remind us of: that evening, late in May, the Clare hills were
20   ghostly with hawthorn. Two swans flew over us.
I can still hear

the musical insistence of their wings as they came in past
the treetops, near the lake; and we looked up,
rooted to the spot.

—1990

Gail White
b. 1945

Annabel Lee[1]

It was many and many a year ago
That Mr. Poe and I
Lived in a castle by the sea
And watched the waves roll by.
It was rather a bore, and I always felt   5
He was waiting for me to die.

He really seems much happier now
That I don't have much to say.
I'm always perfectly dressed, my hair
Is fixed in his favorite way,   10
And he doesn't have to worry about
His virility every day.

I soundly sleep by the sounding sea
Where the small waves froth and curl.
Dear Eddie lies at my side all night   15
While the stars around us whirl.
A lay in the sepulcher suits him better
Than sex with a real live girl.

—2012

---

1   *Annabel Lee* See Edgar Allan Poe's "Annabel Lee," p. 132.

Paul Hoover
b. 1946

Poems We Can Understand

If a monkey drives a car
down a colonnade facing the sea
and the palm trees to the left are tin
we don't understand it.

5 We want poems we can understand.
We want a god to lead us,
renaming the flowers and trees,
color-coding the scene,

doing bird calls for guests.
10 We want poems we can understand,
no sullen drunks making passes
next to an armadillo, no complex nothingness

amounting to a song,
no running in and out of walls
15 on the dry tongue of a mouse,
no bludgeoness, no girl, no sea that moves

with all deliberate speed, beside itself
and blue as water, inside itself and still,
no lizards on the table becoming absolute hands.
20 We want poetry we can understand,

the fingerprints on mother's dress,
pain of martyrs, scientists.
Please, no rabbit taking a rabbit
out of a yellow hat, no tattooed back

25 facing miles of desert, no wind.
We don't understand it.

—1983

Marilyn Nelson
b. 1946

Minor Miracle

Which reminds me of another knock-on-wood
memory. I was cycling with a male friend,
through a small midwestern town. We came to a 4-way
stop and stopped, chatting. As we started again,
a rusty old pick-up truck, ignoring the stop sign,   5
hurricaned past scant inches from our front wheels.
My partner called, "Hey, that was a 4-way stop!"
The truck driver, stringy blond hair a long fringe
under his brand-name beer cap, looked back and yelled,
          "You fucking niggers!"   10
And sped off.
My friend and I looked at each other and shook our heads.
We remounted our bikes and headed out of town.
We were pedalling through a clear blue afternoon
between two fields of almost-ripened wheat   15
bordered by cornflowers and Queen Anne's lace
when we heard an unmuffled motor, a honk-honking.
We stopped, closed ranks, made fists.
It was the same truck. It pulled over.
A tall, very much in shape young white guy slid out: 20
greasy jeans, homemade finger tattoos, probably
a Marine Corps boot-camp footlockerful
of martial arts techniques.

"What did you say back there!" he shouted.
My friend said, "I said it was a 4-way stop.   25
You went through it."
"And what did I say?" the white guy asked.
"You said: 'You fucking niggers.'"
The afternoon froze.

"Well," said the white guy,   30
shoving his hands into his pockets

and pushing dirt around with the pointed toe of his boot,
"I just want to say I'm sorry."
He climbed back into his truck
35   and drove away.

—1994

Patti Smith
b. 1946

piss factory[1]

Sixteen and time to pay off I got this job in a piss
factory inspecting pipe Forty hours thirty-six dol-
lars a week but it's a paycheck, jack. It's so hot in
here hot like sahara You could faint in the heat but
these bitches are just too lame to understand too   5
goddamn grateful to get this job to know they're get-
ting screwed up the ass.
All these women they got no teeth or gum in cra-
nium And the way they suck hot sausage but me
well I wasn't sayin' too much neither I was moral   10
school girl hard-working asshole I figured I was
speedo motorcycle had to earn my dough had to earn
my dough.
But no you gotta relate, right, you gotta find the
rhythm within. Floor boss slides up to me and he   15
says "Hey sister, you just movin' too fast. You scre-
win' up the quota. You doin' your piece work too
fast. Now you get off your mustang sally, you ain't
goin' nowhere, you ain't goin' nowhere."
I lay back. I get my nerve up. I take a swig of romilar[2]   20
and walk up to hot shit Dot Hook and I say "Hey, hey
sister, it don't matter whether I do labor fast or slow,
there's always more labor after." She's real Catholic,
see. She fingers her cross and she says "There's one
reason. There's one reason. You do it my way or I   25
push your face in. We knee you in the john if you
don't get off your mustang, Sally, if you don't shake
it up baby." Shake it up baby. Twist and shout.

---

1   *piss factory* "Piss Factory" was released as the B-side of Smith's debut single "Hey Joe" in
    1974, in which she covered the 1966 debut single by her idol Jimi Hendrix.
2   *romilar* Brand name under which dextromethorphan was marketed in the 1960s and
    1970s as an over-the-counter cough suppressant. It was withdrawn after widespread mis-
    use as a recreational hallucinogenic drug.

Oh that I could will a radio here. James Brown sing-
30   ing I lost someone. Oh the Paragons and the Jesters
and Georgie Woods the guy with the goods and
Guided Missles ... but no, I got nothin', no diversion
no window nothing here but a porthole in the plaster
where I look down at sweet Theresa's convent all
35   those nuns scattin' 'round with their bloom hoods
like cats in mourning. oh to me they look pretty
damn free down there not having to smooth those
hands against hot steel not having to worry about
the inspeed the dogma the inspeed of labor. oh they
40   look pretty damn free down there and the way they
smell and here I gotta be up here smellin' Dot Hook's
midwife sweat.
I would rather smell the way boys smell—oh those
schoolboys the way their legs flap under the desk in
45   study hall that odor rising roses and ammonia and
the way their dicks droop like lilacs. Or the way they
smell that forbidden acrid smell. But no I got pink
clammy lady in my nostril. Her against the wheel
me against the wheel Oh slow motion inspection is
50   drivin' me insane in steel next to Dot Hook—oh we
may look the same—shoulder to shoulder sweatin'
hundred and ten degrees But I will never faint. They
laugh and they expect me to faint but I will never
faint I refuse to lose refuse to fall down because you
55   see it's the monotony that's got to me every after-
noon like the last one every afternoon like a rerun
next to Dot Hook and yeah we look the same both
pumpin' steel both sweatin'.
But you know she got nothin' to hide and I got something
60   to hide here called desire I got something to
hide here called desire. And I will get out of here—
you know the fiery potion is just about to come. In
my nose is the taste of sugar and I got nothin' to hide
here save desire And I'm gonna go I'm gonna get out
65   of here I'm gonna get on that train and go to New
York City and I'm gonna be somebody I'm gonna get
on that train and go to New York City and I'm gonna
be so bad, I'm gonna be a big star and I will never

return never return no never return to burn out in
this Piss factory.   70
And I will travel light.
Oh watch me now.

—1974

ps/alm 23[1] revisited

for William Burroughs[2]

The word is his shepherd
he shall not want
he spreads like the eagle
upon the green hill
boys of the Alhambra   5
in vivid sash
serve him still
your orange juice, sir
your fishing pole
accepting all   10
with tender grace
and besting us
with this advice
children never be ashamed
wrestle smile walk in sun   15
thank you, Bill
your will be done
God grant you
mind and medicine
we draw our hearts   20
and you within
moral vested
Gentleman

—1975–76

---

1   *ps/alm 23* In the Hebrew Bible or Old Testament, Psalm 23 begins, "The Lord is my
    shepherd, I shall not want...."
2   *William Burroughs* A versatile Beat artist whose experimental and confrontational work
    exerted tremendous influence on other artists. His novel *Naked Lunch* (1959) was the
    subject of an obscenity trial.

Yusef Komunyakaa

b. 1947

Facing It

My black face fades,
hiding inside the black granite.
I said I wouldn't,
dammit: No tears.
5   I'm stone. I'm flesh.
My clouded reflection eyes me
like a bird of prey, the profile of night
slanted against morning. I turn
this way—the stone lets me go.
10 I turn that way—I'm inside
the Vietnam Veterans Memorial
again, depending on the light
to make a difference.
I go down the 58,022 names,
15 half-expecting to find
my own in letters like smoke.
I touch the name Andrew Johnson;
I see the booby trap's white flash.
Names shimmer on a woman's blouse
20 but when she walks away
the names stay on the wall.
Brushstrokes flash, a red bird's
wings cutting across my stare.
The sky. A plane in the sky.
25 A white vet's image floats
closer to me, then his pale eyes
look through mine. I'm a window.
He's lost his right arm
inside the stone. In the black mirror
30 a woman's trying to erase names:
No, she's brushing a boy's hair.

—1988

Blue Light Lounge Sutra for the Performance Poets at Harold Park Hotel

the need gotta be
so deep words can't
answer simple questions
all night long notes
stumble off the tongue
& color the air indigo   5
so deep fragments of gut
& flesh cling to the song
you gotta get into it
so deep salt crystalizes on eyelashes
the need gotta be   10
so deep you can vomit up ghosts
& not feel broken
till you are no more
than a half ounce of gold
in painful brightness   15
you gotta get into it
blow that saxophone
so deep all the sex & dope in this world
can't erase your need
to howl against the sky   20
the need gotta be
so deep you can't
just wiggle your hips
& rise up out of it
chaos in the cosmos   25
modern man in the pepperpot
you gotta get hooked
into every hungry groove
so deep the bomb locked
in rust opens like a fist   30
into it into it so deep
rhythm is pre-memory
the need gotta be basic
animal need to see
& know the terror   35
we are made of honey

cause if you wanna dance
this boogie be ready
40 to let the devil use your head
for a drum

—1989

Diane Ackerman
b. 1948

Sweep Me through Your Many-Chambered Heart

Sweep me through your many-chambered heart
if you like, or leave me here, flushed
amid the sap-ooze and blossom: one more dish
in the banquet called April, or think me hard-
won all your days full of women. Weeks   5
later, till I felt your arms around
me like a shackle, heard all the sundown
wizardries the fired body speaks.
Tell me why, if it was no more than this,
the unmuddled tumble, the renegade kiss,   10
today, rapt in a still life[1] and unaware,
my paintbrush dropped like an amber hawk;
thinking I'd heard your footfall on the stair,
I listened, heartwise, for the knock.

—1978

---

1   *still life* Painting or other art image depicting arranged objects, often including fruit or
flowers.

David Lehman
b. 1948

The Difference between Pepsi and Coke

Can't swim; uses credit cards and pills to combat
    intolerable feelings of inadequacy;
Won't admit his dread of boredom, chief impulse behind
    numerous marital infidelities;
5 Looks fat in jeans, mouths clichés with confidence,
    breaks mother's plates in fights;
Buys when the market is too high, and panics during
    the inevitable descent;
Still, Pop can always tell the subtle difference
10   between Pepsi and Coke,
Has defined the darkness of red at dawn, memorized
    the splash of poppies along
Deserted railway tracks, and opposed the war in Vietnam
    months before the students,
15 Years before the politicians and press; give him
    a minute with a road map
And he will solve the mystery of bloodshot eyes;
    transport him to mountaintop
And watch him calculate the heaviness and height
20   of the local heavens;
Needs no prompting to give money to his kids; speaks
    French fluently, and tourist German;
Sings Schubert in the shower; plays pinball in Paris;
    knows the new maid steals, and forgives her.

—1986

First Offense

I'm sorry, officer. I didn't see the sign
Because, in fact, there wasn't any. I tell you
The light was green. How much is the fine?

Will the tumor turn out malignant or benign?
Will the doctor tell us? He said he knew.
I'm sorry, officer. I didn't see the sign.   5

Not every madman is an agent of the divine,
Not all who pass are allowed to come through.
The light was green. How much is the fine?

Which is worse, the rush or the wait? The line   10
Interminable, or fear of coming late? His anxiety grew.
I'm sorry, officer. I didn't see the sign.

I'm cold sober. All I had was one glass of wine.
Was anyone hurt? Is there anything I can do?
The light was green. How much is the fine?   15

Will we make our excuses like so many clever lines,
Awkwardly delivered? Never to win, always to woo?
I'm sorry, officer. I didn't see the sign.
The light was green. How much is the fine?

—1986

Lynn Emanuel
b. 1949

inside gertrude stein[1]

Right now as I am talking to you and as you are being talked
to, without letup, it is becoming clear that gertrude stein has
hijacked me and that this feeling that you are having now as
you read this, that this is what it feels like to be inside ger-
trude stein. This what it feels like to be a huge typewriter
in a dress. Yes, I feel we have gotten inside gertrude stein, and
of course it is dark inside the enormous gertrude, it is like
being locked up in a refrigerator lit only by a smiling rind of
cheese. Being inside gertrude is like being inside a monument
made of a cloud which is always moving across the sky which
is also always moving. Gertrude is a huge galleon of cloud
anchored to the ground by one small tether, yes, I see it down
there, do you see that tiny snail glued to the tackboard of the
landscape? That is alice.[2] So, I am inside gertrude; we belong
to each other, she and I, and it is so wonderful because I have
always been a thin woman inside of whom a big woman is
screaming to get out, and she's out now and if a river could
type this is how it would sound, pure and complicated and
enormous. Now we are lilting across the countryside, and
we are talking, and if the wind could type it would sound
like this, ongoing and repetitious, abstracting and stylizing
everything, like our famous haircut painted by Picasso.[3] Be-
cause when you are inside our haircut you understand that
all the flotsam and jetsam of hairdo have been cleared away
(like the forests from the New World) so that the skull can
show through grinning and feasting on the alarm it has cre-

---

1   *gertrude stein* American expatriate and Modernist writer (1874–1946), famous through-
out the Parisian avant-garde community at the turn of the century. Stein was known for
her distinctive stream-of-consciousness style of writing (p. 318).

2   *alice* Alice B. Toklas (1877–1967), American expatriate writer also prominent in the
Parisian avant-garde community. Toklas was Stein's lover up until Stein's death in 1946.

3   *Picasso* Spanish artist (1881–1973), famous for pioneering the Cubist movement. Stein,
along with her brothers Leo and Michael, was a famous Modernist art collector. Stein in
particular favored the work of Picasso, and her collection prominently featured his works.

ated. I am now, alarmingly, inside gertrude's head and I am thinking that I may only be a thought she has had when she imagined that she and alice were dead and gone and someone had to carry on the work of being gertrude stein, and so I am receiving, from beyond the grave, radioactive isotopes of her genius saying, take up my work, become gertrude stein.

Because someone must be gertrude stein, someone must save us from the literalists and realists, and narratives of the beginning and end, someone must be a river that can type. And why not I? Gertrude is insisting on the fact that while I am a subgenius, weighing one hundred five pounds, and living in a small town with an enormous furry male husband who is always in his Cadillac Eldorado driving off to sell something to people who do not deserve the bad luck of this merchandise in their lives—that these facts would not be a problem for gertrude stein. Gertrude and I feel that, for instance, in *Patriarchal Poetry*[1] when (like an avalanche that can type) she is burying the patriarchy, still there persists a sense of condescending affection. So, while I'm a thin, heterosexual subgenius, nevertheless gertrude has chosen me as her tool, just as she chose the patriarchy as a tool for ending the patriarchy. And because I have become her tool, now, in a sense, gertrude is inside me. It's tough. Having gertrude inside me is like having swallowed an ocean liner that can type, and, while I feel like a very small coat closet with a bear in it, gertrude and I feel that I must tell you that gertrude does not care. She is using me to get her message across, to say, I am lost, I am beset by literalists and narratives of the beginning and middle and end, help me. And so, yes, I say, yes, I am here, gertrude, because we feel, gertrude and I, that there is real urgency in our voice (like a sob that can type) and that things are very bad for her because she is lost, beset by the literalists and realists, her own enormousness crushing her, and we must find her and take her into ourselves, even though I am the least likely of saviors and have been chosen perhaps as a last resort, yes, definitely, gertrude is saying to me, you are the least likely of saviors, you are my last choice and my last resort.

—1999

---

1 *Patriarchal Poetry* 1927 poem by Stein (see the anthology's companion website).

Anne Carson
b. 1950

On Sylvia Plath[1]

Did you see her mother on television? She said
plain, burned things. She said I thought it an
excellent poem but it hurt me. She did not say
jungle fear. She did not say jungle hatred wild
jungle weeping chop it back chop it. She said
self-government she said end of the road. She
did not say humming in the middle of the air
5 what you came for chop.

—1992

Audubon[2]

Audubon perfected a new way of drawing birds that he called his.
On the bottom of each watercolor he put "drawn from nature"
which meant he shot the birds

and took them home to stuff and paint them.
5 Because he hated the unvarying shapes
of traditional taxidermy

he built flexible armatures of bent wire and wood
on which he arranged bird skin and feathers—
or sometimes

10 whole eviscerated birds—
in animated poses.
Not only his wiring but his lighting was new.

---

1   *Sylvia Plath* (1932–63), American poet and author (see p. 528). The mother in her semi-
     autobiographical novel *The Bell Jar* (1963) and many of the mother figures in her poetry
     are portrayed with hostility.
2   *Audubon* John James Audubon (1785–1851), painter and ornithologist, painted and
     catalogued the birds of North America, publishing 435 hand-colored engravings in four
     volumes between 1826 and 1838.

Audubon colors dive in through your retina
like a searchlight
roving shadowlessly up and down the brain   15

until you turn away.
And you do turn away.
There is nothing to see.

You can look at these true shapes all day and not see the bird.
Audubon understands light as an absence of darkness,   20
truth as an absence of unknowing.

It is the opposite of a peaceful day in Hokusai.[1]
Imagine if Hokusai had shot and wired 219 lions
and then forbade his brush to paint shadow.

"We are what we make ourselves," Audubon told his wife   25
when they were courting,
In the salons of Paris and Edinburgh

where he went to sell his new style
this Haitian-born Frenchman
lit himself   30

as a noble rustic American
wired in the cloudless poses of the Great Naturalist.
They loved him

for the "frenzy and ecstasy"
of true American facts, especially   35
in the second (more affordable) octavo edition (*Birds of America*, 1844)

—2000

---

1   *Hokusai* Katsushika Hokusai (1760–1849), Japanese painter and engraver, known in the
     West for such works as *Thirty-Six Views of Mount Fuji*.

Dana Gioia
b. 1950

Thanks for Remembering Us

The flowers sent here by mistake,
signed with a name that no one knew,
are turning bad. What shall we do?
Our neighbor says they're not for her,
and no one has a birthday near.
5   We should thank someone for the blunder.
Is one of us having an affair?
At first we laugh, and then we wonder.

The iris was the first to die,
enshrouded in its sickly-sweet
10   and lingering perfume. The roses
fell one petal at a time,
and now the ferns are turning dry.
The room smells like a funeral,
but there they sit, too much at home,
15   accusing us of some small crime,
like love forgotten, and we can't
throw out a gift we've never owned.

—1983

Planting a Sequoia

All afternoon my brothers and I have worked in the orchard,
Digging this hole, laying you into it, carefully packing the soil.
Rain blackened the horizon, but cold winds kept it over the Pacific,
And the sky above us stayed the dull grey
5   Of an old year coming to an end.

In Sicily a father plants a tree to celebrate his first son's birth—
An olive or a fig tree—a sign that the earth has one more life to bear.
I would have done the same, proudly laying new stock into my father's orchard,
A green sapling rising among the twisted apple boughs,
10   A promise of new fruit in other autumns.

But today we kneel in the cold planting you, our native giant,
Defying the practical custom of our fathers,
Wrapping in your roots a lock of hair, a piece of an infant's birth cord,
All that remains above earth of a first-born son,
A few stray atoms brought back to the elements.   15

We will give you what we can—our labour and our soil,
Water drawn from the earth when the skies fail,
Nights scented with the ocean fog, days softened by the circuit of bees.
We plant you in the corner of the grove, bathed in western light,
A slender shoot against the sunset.   20

And when our family is no more, all of his unborn brothers dead,
Every niece and nephew scattered, the house torn down,
His mother's beauty ashes in the air,
I want you to stand among strangers, all young and ephemeral to you,
Silently keeping the secret of your birth.   25

—1991

Andrew Hudgins
b. 1951

At Chancellorsville: The Battle of the Wilderness[1]

He was an Indiana corporal
shot in the thigh when their line broke
in animal disarray. He'd crawled
into the shade and bled to death.
5   My uniform was shabby with
continuous wear, worn down to threads
by the inside friction of my flesh on cloth.
The armpit seams were rotted through
and almost half the buttons had dropped off.
10   My brother said I should remove
the Yank's clean shirt: "From now on, Sid,[2]
he'll have no use for it." Imagining
the slack flesh shifting underneath
my hands, the other-person stink
15   of that man's shirt, so newly his,
I cursed Clifford from his eyeballs to
his feet. I'd never talked that way before
and didn't know I could. When we returned,
someone had beat me to the shirt.
20   So I had compromised my soul
for nothing I would want to use—
some knowledge I could do without.
Clifford, thank God, just laughed. It was good
stout wool, unmarked by blood.

---

1   *At ... Wilderness* Eventually included in *After the Lost War: A Narrative* (1988), this poem
is one of Hudgins's dramatic monologues in the voice of Sidney Lanier (1842–81), an in-
novative and well-known Georgia poet. Lanier and his brother Clifford were Confederate
soldiers who fought at the Battle of Chancellorsville in May 1863, an important Confed-
erate victory. Lanier's reputation as a significant poet endured until World War II, after
which point he largely fell from view. Scholars are now returning to his work as a window
into the Civil War era as well as for Lanier's complex theories about poetry as a form of
music. The title of this poem also alludes metaphorically to The Battle of the Wilderness,
fought in May 1864.
2   *Sid* Sidney Lanier.

By autumn, we wore so much blue[1]
we could have passed for New York infantry.

25

—1981

November Garden: An Elegy

The zinnias—cut-and-come-again—
are dry as Mother's hair. They crush
beneath my hand. The lilies, though,

are further gone than that, sunk down
into their bulbs, as Mother has
gone underground. Each spring they burst

5

into their almost human flesh—
white blooms like all they've ever made.
But not the same. A different bud

dyed with the same returning color.
The marigolds, though, cannot withdraw.
They're hybrids. They don't seed. Next year

10

they won't be back. And so they flower,
the withered blooms beside the red
ones that seem garish now, and cheap.

15

I pick the browns off. The reds
bloom grimly through a dozen frosts
to the first hard freeze. They cannot stop.

—1984

---

1   *blue* Union forces in the Civil War generally wore blue uniforms, while the Confederacy
     wore gray. "Blue" and "gray" became symbolic colors that represented the warring ar-
     mies and their opposing causes. Often desperate for supplies, including clothing, soldiers
     sometimes took what they could from corpses.

Rita Dove
b. 1952

Persephone, Falling[1]

One narcissus among the ordinary beautiful
flowers, one unlike all the others! She pulled,
stooped to pull harder—
when, sprung out of the earth
5 on his glittering terrible
carriage, he claimed his due.
It is finished. No one heard her.
No one! She had strayed from the herd.

(Remember: go straight to school.
10 This is important, stop fooling around!
Don't answer to strangers. Stick
with your playmates. Keep your eyes down.)
This is how easily the pit
opens. This is how one foot sinks into the ground.

—1988

---

1   *Persephone, Falling* In Greek mythology, Persephone was the daughter of Zeus and
Demeter and became the wife of Hades, god of the underworld. Because Persephone was
so beautiful and desired by the male gods of Olympus, Demeter took her to Earth and
kept her hidden for protection. One day as Persephone was out gathering flowers, Hades
leapt from a crack in the earth and dragged her with him to the underworld.

Mary Ruefle
b. 1952

Why I Am Not a Good Kisser

Because I open my mouth too wide
Trying to take in the curtains behind us
And everything outside the window
Except the little black dog
Who does not like me
So at the last moment I shut my mouth.   5

Because Cipriano de Rore[1] was not thinking
When he wrote his sacred and secular motets[2]
Or there would be only one kind
And this affects my lips in terrible ways.   10

Because at the last minute I see a lemon
Sitting on a gravestone and that is a thing, a thing
That would appear impossible, and the kiss
Is already concluded in its entirety.

Because I learned everything about the beautiful   15
In a guide to the weather by Borin Van Loon,[3] so
The nature of lenticular clouds and anticyclones[4]
And several other things dovetail in my mind
& at once it strikes me what quality goes to form
A Good Kisser, especially at this moment, & which you   20
Possess so enormously—I mean when a man is capable
Of being in uncertainties, Mysteries & doubts without me
I am dreadfully afraid he will slip away
While my kiss is trying to think what to do.

Because I think you will try to read what is written   25
On my tongue and this causes me to interrupt with questions:

---

1   *Cipriano de Rore* Flemish madrigal composer (c. 1515–65).
2   *motets* Choral music.
3   *guide ... Borin Van Loon An Instant Guide to the Weather* (2000) by Eleanor Lawrence and
     Borin Van Loon; *Borin Van Loon* British artist and illustrator (b. 1953).
4   *lenticular clouds* Lens-shaped clouds; *anticyclones* High-pressure wind moving in a cir-
     cular pattern; the opposite of a cyclone, which is created by low-pressure wind.

A red frock? Red stockings? And the rooster dead?
Dead of what?

Because of that other woman inside me who knows
30 How the red skirt and red stockings came into my mouth
But persists with the annoying questions
Leading to her genuine ignorance.

Because just when our teeth are ready to hide
I become a quisling[1] and forget the election results
35 And industrial secrets leading to the manufacture
Of woolen ice cream cones, changing the futures
Of ice worms everywhere.

Can it be that even the greatest Kisser ever arrived
At his goal without putting aside numerous objections—

40 Because every kiss is like throwing a pair of doll eyes
Into the air and trying to follow them with your own—

However it may be, *O for a life of Kisses*
Instead of painting volcanoes!

Even if my kiss is like a paintbrush made from hairs.
45 Even if my kiss is squawroot, which is a scaly herb
Of the broomrape family parasitic on oaks.
Even if a sailor went to sea in me
To see what he could see in me
And all that he could see in me
50 Was the bottom of the deep dark sea in me.[2]

Even though I know nothing can be gained by running
Screaming into the night, into the night like a mouth,
Into the mouth like a velvet movie theater
With planets painted on its ceiling
55 Where you will find me, your pod mate,
In some kind of beautiful trouble
Over moccasin stitch #3,
Which is required for my release.

—2002

---

1   *quisling* Enemy collaborator during military occupation.
2   *Even if ... sea in me* Allusion to popular children's rhyme.

Mark Doty
b. 1953

Charlie Howard's Descent[1]

Between the bridge and the river
he falls through
a huge portion of night;
it is not as if falling

is something new. Over and over   5
he slipped into the gulf
between what he knew and how
he was known. What others wanted

opened like an abyss: the laughing
stock-clerks at the grocery, women   10
at the luncheonette amused by his gestures.
What could he do, live

with one hand tied
behind his back? So he began to fall
into the star-faced section   15
of night between the trestle

and the water because he could not meet
a little town's demands,
and his earrings shone and his wrists
were as limp as they were.   20

I imagine he took the insults in
and made of them a place to live;
we learn to use the names
because they are there,

---

1   *Charlie Howard's Descent* Charles O. Howard (1961–84) was a gay man from Bangor,
     Maine, who was murdered because of his sexual orientation. Howard and a friend were
     on a bridge crossing Kenduskeag Stream when they were attacked by three teenage boys.
     His friend escaped, but the asthmatic Howard couldn't outrun them and was thrown into
     the water where he subsequently drowned.

25   familiar furniture: *faggot*
      was the bed he slept in, hard
      and white, but simple somehow,
      queer something sharp

      but finally useful, a tool,
30   all the jokes a chair,
      stiff-backed to keep the spine straight,
      a table, a lamp. And because

      he's fallen for twenty-three years,
      despite whatever awkwardness
35   his flailing arms and legs assume
      he is beautiful

      and like any good diver
      has only an edge of fear
      he transforms into grace.
40   Or else he is not afraid,

      and in this way climbs back
      up the ladder of his fall,
      out of the river into the arms
      of the three teenage boys

45   who hurled him from the edge—
      really boys now, afraid,
      their fathers' cars shivering behind them,
      headlights on—and tells them

      it's all right, that he knows
50   they didn't believe him
      when he said he couldn't swim,
      and blesses his killers

      in the way that only the dead
      can afford to forgive.

—1987

Gjertrud Schnackenberg
b. 1953

The Paperweight

The scene within the paperweight is calm,
A small white house, a laughing man and wife,
Deep snow. I turn it over in my palm
And watch it snowing in another life,

Another world, and from this scene learn what   5
It is to stand apart: she serves him tea
Once and forever, dressed from head to foot
As she is always dressed. In this toy, history

Sifts down through the glass like snow, and we
Wonder if her single deed tells much   10
Or little of the way she loves, and whether he
Sees shadows in the sky. Beyond our touch,

Beyond our lives, they laugh, and drink their tea.
We look at them just as the winter night
With its vast empty spaces bends to see   15
Our isolated little world of light,

Covered with snow, and snow in clouds above it,
And drifts and swirls too deep to understand.
Still, I must try to think a little of it,
With so much winter in my head and hand.   20

—1982

Kim Addonizio
b. 1954

First Poem for You

I like to touch your tattoos in complete
darkness, when I can't see them. I'm sure of
where they are, know by heart the neat
lines of lightning pulsing just above
5 your nipple, can find, as if by instinct, the blue
swirls of water on your shoulder where a serpent
twists, facing a dragon. When I pull you
to me, taking you until we're spent
and quiet on the sheets, I love to kiss
10 the pictures in your skin. They'll last until
you're seared to ashes; whatever persists
or turns to pain between us, they will still
be there. Such permanence is terrifying.
So I touch them in the dark; but touch them, trying.

—1994

Louise Erdrich
b. 1954

Dear John Wayne[1]

August and the drive-in picture is packed.
We lounge on the hood of the Pontiac
surrounded by the slow-burning spirals they sell
at the window, to vanquish the hordes of mosquitoes.
Nothing works. They break through the smoke screen for blood.   5

Always the lookout spots the Indians first,
spread north to south, barring progress.
The Sioux or some other Plains bunch
in spectacular columns, ICBM missiles,
feathers bristling in the meaningful sunset.   10

The drum breaks. There will be no parlance.
Only the arrows whining, a death-cloud of nerves
swarming down on the settlers
who die beautifully, tumbling like dust weeds
into the history that brought us all here   15
together: this wide screen beneath the sign of the bear.

The sky fills, acres of blue squint and eye
that the crowd cheers. His face moves over us,
a thick cloud of vengeance, pitted
like the land that was once flesh. Each rut,   20
each scar makes a promise: *It is
not over, this fight, not as long as you resist.*

Everything we see belongs to us.

A few laughing Indians fall over the hood
slipping in the hot spilled butter.   25
The eye sees a lot, John, but the heart is so blind.

---

1   *John Wayne* American film actor (1907–79) associated especially with the Western genre.

Death makes us owners of nothing.
He smiles, a horizon of teeth
the credits reel over, and then the white fields

30 again blowing in the true-to-life dark.
The dark films over everything.
We get into the car
scratching our mosquito bites, speechless and small
as people are when the movie is done.
35 We are back in our skins.

How can we help but keep hearing his voice,
the flip side of the sound track, still playing:
Come on, boys, we got them
where we want them, drunk, running.
40 *They'll give us what we want, what we need.*
Even his disease was the idea of taking everything.
Those cells,[1] burning, doubling, splitting out of their skins.

—1984

Indian Boarding School: The Runaways

Home's the place we head for in our sleep.
Boxcars stumbling north in dreams
don't wait for us. We catch them on the run.
The rails, old lacerations that we love,
5 shoot parallel across the face and break
just under Turtle Mountains. Riding scars
you can't get lost Home is the place they cross.

The lame guard strikes a match and makes the dark
less tolerant. We watch through cracks in boards
10 as the land starts rolling, rolling till it hurts
to be here, cold in regulation clothes.
We know the sheriff's waiting at midrun
to take us back. His car is dumb and warm.
The highway doesn't rock, it only hums

---

1   *Those cells* Wayne died of cancer.

like a wing of long insults. The worn-down welts   15
of ancient punishments lead back and forth.

All runaways wear dresses, long green ones,
the color you would think shame was. We scrub
the sidewalks down because it's shameful work.
Our brushes cut the stone in watered arcs   20
and in the soak frail outlines shiver clear
a moment, things us kids pressed on the dark
face before it hardened, pale, remembering
delicate old injuries, the spines of names and leaves.

—1984

Carol Ann Duffy
b. 1955

Little Red-Cap[1]

At childhood's end, the houses petered out
into playing fields, the factory, allotments
kept, like mistresses, by kneeling married men,
the silent railway line, the hermit's caravan,
5 till you came at last to the edge of the woods.
It was there that I first clapped eyes on the wolf.

He stood in a clearing, reading his verse out loud
in his wolfy drawl, a paperback in his hairy paw,
red wine staining his bearded jaw. What big ears
10 he had! What big eyes he had! What teeth!
In the interval, I made quite sure he spotted me,
sweet sixteen, never been, babe, waif, and bought me a drink,

my first. You might ask why. Here's why. Poetry.
The wolf, I knew, would lead me deep into the woods,
15 away from home, to a dark tangled thorny place
lit by the eyes of owls. I crawled in his wake,
my stockings ripped to shreds, scraps of red from my blazer
snagged on twig and branch, murder clues. I lost both shoes

but got there, wolf's lair, better beware. Lesson one that night,
20 breath of the wolf in my ear, was the love poem.
I clung till dawn to his thrashing fur, for
what little girl doesn't dearly love a wolf?
Then I slid from between his heavy matted paws
and went in search of a living bird—white dove—

25 which flew, straight, from my hands to his open mouth.
One bite, dead. How nice, breakfast in bed, he said,
licking his chops. As soon as he slept, I crept to the back

---

1   *Little Red-Cap* "Little Red Cap" (1812) is the Brothers Grimm's version of the story first
recorded by Charles Perrault as "Little Red Riding-Hood" (1697).

of the lair, where a whole wall was crimson, gold, aglow with books.
Words, words were truly alive on the tongue, in the head,
warm, beating, frantic, winged; music and blood.   30

But then I was young—and it took ten years
in the woods to tell that a mushroom
stoppers the mouth of a buried corpse, that birds
are the uttered thought of trees, that a greying wolf
howls the same old song at the moon, year in, year out,   35
season after season, same rhyme, same reason. I took an axe

to a willow to see how it wept. I took an axe to a salmon
to see how it leapt. I took an axe to the wolf
as he slept, one chop, scrotum to throat, and saw
the glistening, virgin white of my grandmother's bones.   40
I filled his old belly with stones. I stitched him up.
Out of the forest I come with my flowers, singing, all alone.

—1999

Salome[1]

I'd done it before
(and doubtless I'll do it again,
sooner or later)
woke up with a head on the pillow beside me—whose?—
what did it matter?   5
Good-looking, of course, dark hair, rather matted;
the reddish beard several shades lighter;
with very deep lines around the eyes,
from pain, I'd guess, maybe laughter;
and a beautiful crimson mouth that obviously knew   10
how to flatter ...
which I kissed ...
Colder than pewter.
Strange. What was his name? Peter?

---

1 *Salome* Member of the Herodian Dynasty and daughter of Herod II and Herodias (c.
   14–62), Salome is reputed to be the daughter who performed a dance for Herod II in
   exchange for which she requested the head of the prophet John the Baptist on a platter.

15 Simon? Andrew? John?[1] I knew I'd feel better
     for tea, dry toast, no butter,
     so rang for the maid.
     And, indeed, her innocent clatter
     of cups and plates,
20   her clearing of clutter,
     her regional patter,
     were just what I needed—
     hungover and wrecked as I was from a night on the batter.[2]

     Never again!
25   I needed to clean up my act,
     get fitter,
     cut out the booze and the fags and the sex.
     Yes. And as for the latter,
     it was time to turf out the blighter,
30   the beater or biter,[3]
     who'd come like a lamb to the slaughter
     to Salome's bed.

     In the mirror, I saw my eyes glitter.
     I flung back the sticky red sheets,
35   and there, like I said—and ain't life a bitch—
     was his head on a platter.

                                                    —1999

---

1   *Peter ... John?* Four of Christ's apostles.
2   *on the batter* Slang for drinking binge.
3   *beater or biter* Slang for a disagreeable, contemptible person.

Patricia Smith
b. 1955

Skinhead[1]

They call me skinhead, and I got my own beauty.
It is knife-scrawled across my back in sore, jagged letters,
it's in the way my eyes snap away from the obvious.
I sit in my dim matchbox,
on the edge of a bed tousled with my ragged smell,   5
slide razors across my hair,
count how many ways
I can bring blood closer to the surface of my skin.
These are the duties of the righteous,
the ways of the anointed.   10

The face that moves in my mirror is huge and pockmarked,
scraped pink and brilliant, apple-cheeked,
I am filled with my own spit.
Two years ago, a machine that slices leather
sucked in my hand and held it,   15
whacking off three fingers at the root.
I didn't feel nothing till I looked down
and saw one of them on the floor
next to my boot heel,
and I ain't worked since then.   20

I sit here and watch niggers take over my TV set,
walking like kings up and down the sidewalks in my head,
walking like their fat black mamas *named* them freedom.
My shoulders tell me that ain't right.
So I move out into the sun   25
where my beauty makes them lower their heads,
or into the night
with a lead pipe up my sleeve,

---

1   *Skinhead* Subculture often associated, as here, with racism, homophobia, and white su-
    premacy movements.

a razor tucked in my boot.
30 I was born to make things right.

It's easy now to move my big body into shadows,
to move from a place where there was nothing
into the stark circle of a streetlight,
the pipe raised up high over my head.
35 It's a kick to watch their eyes get big,
round and gleaming like cartoon jungle boys,
right in that second when they know
the pipe's gonna come down, and I got this thing
I like to say, listen to this, I like to say
40 *"Hey, nigger, Abe Lincoln's been dead a long time."*

I get hard listening to their skin burst.
I was born to make things right.

Then this newspaper guy comes around,
seems I was a little sloppy kicking some fag's ass
45 and he opened his hole and screamed about it.
This reporter finds me curled up in my bed,
those TV flashes licking my face clean.
Same ol' shit.
Ain't got no job, the coloreds and spics got 'em all.
50 Why ain't I working? Look at my hand, asshole.
No, I ain't part of no organized group,
I'm just a white boy who loves his race,
fighting for a pure country.
Sometimes it's just me. Sometimes three. Sometimes 30.
55 AIDS will take care of the faggots,
then it's gon' be white on black in the streets.
Then there'll be three million.
I tell him that.

So he writes it up
60 and I come off looking like some kind of freak,
like I'm Hitler himself. I ain't that lucky,
but I got my own beauty.
It is in my steel-toed boots,
in the hard corners of my shaved head.

I look in the mirror and hold up my mangled hand,   65
only the baby finger left, sticking straight up,
I know it's the wrong goddamned finger,
but fuck you all anyway.
I'm riding the top rung of the perfect race,
my face scraped pink and brilliant.   70
I'm your baby, America, your boy,
drunk on my own spit, I am goddamned fuckin' beautiful.

And I was born

and raised

right here.   75

—1992

Li-Young Lee
b. 1957

Persimmons

In sixth grade Mrs. Walker
slapped the back of my head
and made me stand in the corner
for not knowing the difference
5   between *persimmon* and *precision*.
How to choose

persimmons. This is precision.
Ripe ones are soft and brown-spotted.
Sniff the bottoms. The sweet one
10   will be fragrant. How to eat:
put the knife away, lay down newspaper.
Peel the skin tenderly, not to tear the meat.
Chew the skin, suck it,
and swallow. Now, eat
15   the meat of the fruit,
so sweet,
all of it, to the heart.

Donna undresses, her stomach is white.
In the yard, dewy and shivering
20   with crickets, we lie naked,
face-up, face-down.
I teach her Chinese.
Crickets: *chiu chiu*. Dew: I've forgotten.
Naked: I've forgotten.
25   *Ni, wo*: you and me.
I part her legs,
remember to tell her
she is beautiful as the moon.

Other words
30   that got me into trouble were

fight and *fright*, *wren* and *yarn*.
Fight was what I did when I was frightened,
Fright was what I felt when I was fighting.
Wrens are small, plain birds,
yarn is what one knits with.   35
Wrens are soft as yarn.
My mother made birds out of yarn.
I loved to watch her tie the stuff;
a bird, a rabbit, a wee man.

Mrs. Walker brought a persimmon to class   40
and cut it up
so everyone could taste
a *Chinese apple*. Knowing
it wasn't ripe or sweet, I didn't eat
but watched the other faces.   45

My mother said every persimmon has a sun
inside, something golden, glowing,
warm as my face.

Once, in the cellar, I found two wrapped in newspaper,
forgotten and not yet ripe.   50
I took them and set both on my bedroom windowsill,
where each morning a cardinal
sang, *The sun, the sun.*

Finally understanding
he was going blind,   55
my father sat up all one night
waiting for a song, a ghost.
I gave him the persimmons,
swelled, heavy as sadness,
and sweet as love.   60

This year, in the muddy lighting
of my parents' cellar, I rummage, looking
for something I lost.
My father sits on the tired, wooden stairs,
black cane between his knees,   65
hand over hand, gripping the handle.

He's so happy that I've come home.
I ask how his eyes are, a stupid question.
All gone, he answers.

70 Under some blankets, I find a box.
Inside the box I find three scrolls.
I sit beside him and untie
three paintings by my father:
Hibiscus leaf and a white flower.
75 Two cats preening.
Two persimmons, so full they want to drop from the cloth.

He raises both hands to touch the cloth,
asks, *Which is this?*

This is persimmons, Father.

80 *Oh, the feel of the wolftail on the silk,*
the strength, the tense
precision in the wrist.
I painted them hundreds of times
eyes closed. These I painted blind.
85 *Some things never leave a person:*
scent of the hair of one you love,
the texture of persimmons,
in your palm, the ripe weight.

—1986

Kathy Fagan
b. 1958

Road Memorial

The crucifix bent nearly parallel
to earth, the plastic cherubs poised, mid-lim-
bo, under each arm of the cross's T

were meant to make the unseen visible:
X marks the spot where Jesus called our Jim-   5
bo home, and were erected solemnly,

in prayer, while semis shuddered half a mile
away and small things moved inside the berm
grass. They were not then the sorry junk we see,

ephemera nodding toward eternity,   10
til nodding off completely, once and for all.
The highway is a public place and we,

a people dying for a sign. Simple-
ton angels posed in imbecile poses: some-
one thought they'd keep the lost one company,   15

like giving to a fussy child a doll
to help it sleep, to dream the pleasant dreams
of the oblivious. And look! A teddy

bear for Baby, wreath for Mom, and twistied
to the fence they raised when Junior jumped   20
the overpass, helium balloons.

This crap from Wal-Mart could outlast us all,
which in our grief is no small com-
fort, since death lasts so much longer, and has no form.

—2007

Jackie Kay
b. 1961

In My Country

Walking by the waters
down where an honest river
shakes hands with the sea,
a woman passed round me
5 in a slow watchful circle,
as if I were a superstition;

or the worst dregs of her imagination,
so when she finally spoke
her words spliced into bars
10 of an old wheel. A segment of air.
"*Where do you come from?*"
"Here," I said. "Here. These parts."

—1991

Olena Kalytiak Davis
b. 1963

The Lyric "I" Drives to Pick Up Her Children from School: A Poem in the Postconfessional Mode[1]

"i" has not found, started, finished "i's" morning poem,
the poem "i" was writing about "i" having sex with the man "i" left her husband for
the night before or maybe just this morning.
a sex poem, so to speak, so to say, so as to lay ...   5
a foundation for ...
what???????

SEX

i lost my sex/poem!
how did it go?   10
i know it was called

SEX

something about my bosky acres,
my unshrubb'd down
'bout all being tight and yare   15

(bring in tiresias?)
did you say soothe?
tiresias, who lies fucking more?
whoops.

~~*who likes fucking more?*~~   20

---

1   In order not to overburden particularly allusion-heavy poems like this one with excessive
    notation, this edition runs them with minimal notes. The poem thus retains its appear-
    ance as the poet wrote it, and readers can investigate terms as they choose on their own.

("bring in // the old thought // [allen grossman doing yeats]
that life prepares us for // what never happens")

today (the color of) my sex
was lavender then yellow
25 *gold then muted mossy grey and green*

i bid my lover
lower
i bid my lover shhhhhhh

i bid my lover
30 *linger*

i bid my
lover, go

lover, go!
(see!)

35 *i bid my lover stay*
away

"i" notices it is almost time to pick up her children from school!
"i" realizes she has gotten nowhere, nowhere near it, much less inside it,
wasted another morning, can't fucking write a poem to save "i's" life, oh
40 well,
"i" is, at least, "working".
"i" pulls on her tight jeans, her big boots, her puffy parka.
"i" remote-starts her car.
"i's" car is a 1995 red toyota 4-runner with racing stripe that doesn't have
45 enough power for "i".
"i's" car stereo also doesn't have enough power for "i".
"i" drives cross town listening to dylan, who has plenty of power for "i".
"i" wonders how why dylan isn't "i's" man.
"i" gets some looks from some lesser men, some in better, more powerful
50 trucks, even though "i's" dirty dirty-blonde hair is covered by a woolen cap.
"i" feels the power of being a single mom in a red truck.
"i" knows it is not enough power.
"i" thinks "i am the man, i suffered, i was there".
"i" is almost broke, but

"i" thinks "i live more in a continuous present that i enjoy".   55
"i" thinks "amor fati".
"i" notices the chugach mountains.
"i" notices the chugach mountains sometimes look good and sometimes
bad.
"i" remembers that yesterday the chugach mountains looked desolate and   60
dirty and roadblocky.
"i" notices the chugach mountains look particularly beautiful today covered
in sun and snow.
"i" almost thinks "bathed in sun and snow" but stops herself.
"i" feels that "i" can maybe find, really start, really finish her sex poem   65
tomorrow.
"i" likes the dubus thing about adultery having a morality of its own.
"i" also likes "human drama".
"i" really enjoyed "i ♥ huckabees".
"i" thought sex was overrated for a long time, then not for a year and a half,   70
and now, again.
"i" gives, well, has given, good head.
"i" takes it like a man.
"i" thinks there should be a new "new sexualized and radicalized poetry of
the self",   75
"i" knows the "single-minded frenzy of a raving madman" but,
"i" mostly keeps her head.
"i" remembers that "as long ago as 1925, boris tomashevsky, a leading
russian formalist critic, observed that the 'autobiographical poem' is one that
mythologizes the poet's life in accordance with the conventions of his time.   80
it relates not what has occurred but what should have occurred, presenting
an idealized image of the poet as representative of his literary school".
"i" wants to be a man like marjorie perloff, helen hennessy vendler, boris
tomashevsky.
"i" thinks, on the other hand, "i mean i like in art when the artist doesn't   85
know what he knows in general; he only knows what he knows specifically".
"i" thinks: "that mantel piece is clean enough or my name isn't bob
rauschenberg".
"i" just wishes "i" could talk more smarter theory, no
"i" just wishes "i" could write more smarter poems, no   90
"i" thinks "WHY I AM A POET AND NOT A ...".
"i" thinks "KALYTIAK DAVIS PAINTS A PICTURE".
"i" wants to include the word *coruscate* in it, and, possibly, a quote from
rudolf steiner.

95   "i" wishes she could remember abrams's definition of the structure of the
greater romantic lyric, but that it presents "a determinate speaker in a
particularized, and usually localized, outdoor setting, whom we overhear
as he carries on, in a fluent vernacular which rises easily to a more formal
speech, a sustained colloquy, sometimes with himself or with the outer
100 scene, but more frequently with a silent human auditor, present or absent"
and that "the speaker begins with a description of the landscape" and that
"an aspect or change of aspect in the landscape evokes a varied but integral
process of memory, thought, anticipation, and feeling which remains closely
intervolved with the outer scene" and that "in the course of this meditation
105 the lyric speaker achieves an insight, faces up to a tragic loss, comes to a
moral decision, or resolves an emotional problem." and that "often the
poem rounds upon itself to end where it began, at the outer scene, but with
an altered mood and deepened understanding which is the result of the
intervening meditation" evades her.
110 "i" wants to say "silent human auditor, are you absent or present?" but "i"
knows "i" makes, has made, that move too often.
    "i" knows "i" is alone in her red truck.
    "i" reconsiders, perhaps it is like giving good head?
    "i" thinks *his his he himself*, but not too bitterly, then
115 "i" thinks "i", then,
    "i" thinks "you".
    "i" has not told her lover that "i" is not in love with him any longer, but "i"
knows he knows, must know.
    "i" has not told her lover that "i" had a long conversation with "i's"
120 x-husband on the phone last night.
    "i" thinks "my sidestepping and obliquities".
    "i" thinks love **is** what went wrong.
    "i" feels elizabeth bishop reprimanding "i".
    "i" thinks like a gentle loving firm almost slap but really just a squeeze of,
125 not on, the hand from a, the, mother neither one of them had for very long,
long enough.
    "i" has not thought of "i's" dead mother in a long time.
    "i" thinks of jonatham letham[1] and his dead mother and his wall of books.
    "i" thinks of mark reagan and his walls and walls of books, and how his
130 landlord, fearing collapse, made him move to the bottom floor.
    "i" thinks of doug teter and his smaller, but still, wall of books.
    "i" thinks of jude law.
    "i" thinks jude law probably doesn't know how to read.

---

1   *letham* Jonathan Lethem, contemporary novelist (b. 1964).

"i" knows that no lover can be her "objective correlative", still
"i" thinks "so true a lover as theagenes".   135
"i" thinks "so constant a friend as pylades".
"i" thinks "so valiant a man as orlando".
"i " thinks "so right a prince as xenophon's cyrus".
"i" thinks "so excellent a man in every way as virgil's aeneas".
"i" notices dylan is almost done singing "to ramona".   140
"i" loves "everything passes, everything changes, just do what you think you
should do".
"i" thinks dylan is singing to "i".
"i" thinks he means now, and now, and now; daily.
"i" is almost there.   145
"i" wonders if "i's" meditation is too long, has gotten away from "i".
"i" thinks it should take precisely as long as the ride: 15 minutes tops; well,
30 in a snowstorm.
"i" knows it is not snowing.
"i" wonders if "i" should at this point even refer to "i's" meditation.   150
"i" thinks "man can embody truth but he cannot know it".
"i" thinks "especially under stress of psychological crisis".
"i" thinks what's worse, anaphora or anaphrodesia?
"i" thinks of the diaphragm still inside her.
"i" shutters at the audacity of her sex.   155
"i" is exactly on time to pick up her daughter.
"i" must wait another 45 minutes to retrieve her son.
"i" will try and remember to remove it promptly when they get back to "i's"
house, i.e., home.
"i" has fucked with the facts so "you" think she's robert lowell.[1] (*but whoever*   160
saw a girl like robert lowell?)
"i" doesn't care if "you", silent human auditor, present or absent, never heard
of, could give a flying fuck about, robert lowell.

—2005

---

1   *robert lowell* Davis plays here with the image of Robert Lowell (p. 451) as "confessional"
    poet.

Sherman Alexie
b. 1966

After the Trial of Hamlet, Chicago, 1994

Did Hamlet mean to kill Polonius? Diane and I sit at a table
with the rich, who have the luxury to discuss such things
over a veal dinner. The vegetables are beautiful! We have just come
from the mock Trial of Hamlet, which is more a fund-raiser
5 and social gathering, but we must render a verdict. I am here

because I wrote a book which nobody here has read, a book
that Diane reads because she loves me. My book has nothing
to do with Hamlet. My book is filled with reservation Indians.
Maybe my book has everything to do with Hamlet. The millionaire
10 next to me sets down one of his many forks to shake my hand.

He tells me the poor need the rich more than the rich need the poor.
Abigail van Buren[1] eats corn at the next table. I read this morning
she has always believed homosexuality is just as genetically determined
as heterosexuality. Finally. Somebody tells the truth. Dear Abby
15 can have all the corn she wants! I'll pay. She wears a polka-dot dress

and is laughing loudly at something I know is not funny.
Did Hamlet really see his father's ghost? Was there a ghost? Was Hamlet
     insane
or merely angry when he thrust his sword through
that curtain and killed Polonius? The millionaire tells me
20 taxicab drivers, shoe shine men, waiters, and waitresses exist

only because the rich, wearing shiny shoes, often need to be driven
to nice restaurants. A character actor walks by with a glass of wine.
I recognize him because I'm the type of guy who always recognizes
character actors. He knows that I recognize him but I cannot tell
25 if he wants me to recognize him. Perhaps he is afraid that I am

---

1   *Abigail van Buren* Pen name of the "Dear Abby" advice columnist Pauline Esther Fried-
man.

confusing him with another character actor who is more famous or less
  famous.
He might be worried that I will shout his name incorrectly
and loudly, transposing first and last names, randomly inserting
wild syllables that have nothing to do with his name.
Did Hamlet want to have sex with his mother Gertrude? Was Hamlet mad   30
  with jealousy

because Claudius got to have sex with Gertrude? When is a king
more than a king? When is a king less than a king? Diane is beautiful.
She wears red lipstick which contrasts nicely with her brown skin.
We are the only Indians in Chicago! No, we are the only Indians
at the Trial of Hamlet. I hold her hand under the table, holding it   35

tightly until, of course, we have to separate so we can eat our food.
We need two hands to cut our veal. Yet Diane will not eat veal.
She only eats the beautiful vegetables. I eat the veal and feel guilty.
The millionaire tells me the rich would love a flat tax rate. He talks
about interest rates and capital gains, loss on investments   40

and trickle-down economics. He thinks he is smarter than me.
He probably is smarter than me, so I tell him insecurely that I wrote a book.
I know he will never read it. My book has nothing to do
with Polonius. My book is filled with reservation Indians. Maybe it has
  everything
to do with Polonius. A Supreme Court Justice   45

sits at the head table. He decides my life! He eats rapidly. I want to know
  how
he feels about treaty rights. I want to know if he feels
guilty about eating the veal. There is no doubt in my mind
the Supreme Court Justice recognizes the beauty of our vegetables.
Was Hamlet a man without logical alternatives? Did he resort   50

to a mindless, senseless violence? Were his actions those of a tired
and hateful man? Or those of a righteous son? The millionaire introduces
  his wife,
but she barely acknowledges our presence. Diane is more
gorgeous, though she grew up on reservations and once
sat in a tree for hours, wishing she had lighter skin. Diane wears   55

a scarf she bought for three dollars. I would ask her to marry me right
now, again, in this city where I asked her to marry me the first time.
But she already agreed to marry me then and has, in fact, married me.
Marriage causes us to do crazy things. She reads my books. I eat veal.
60   Was Hamlet guilty or not by reason of insanity for the murder of Polonius?

The millionaire tells me how happy he is to meet me. He wishes me
luck. He wants to know what I think of Hamlet's case. He tells me Hamlet,
insane or not, is responsible for what he did. There is always something
beautiful in the world at any given moment. When I was poor I loved
65   the five-dollar bills I would unexpectedly find in coat pockets. When I feel

tired now, I can love the moon hanging over the old hotels of Chicago.
Diane and I walk out into the cold November air. We hail a taxi.
The driver is friendly, asks for our names, and Diane says, I'm Hamlet,
and this is Hamlet, my husband. The driver wants to know where we're
    from
70   and which way we want to go. Home, we say, home.

                                                              —1996

Terrance Hayes
b. 1971

Jumpschool

... the high came when you found you'd landed safely
—Jimi Hendrix,[1] 101st Airborne

Today there is no war,
only this crowd of people,
green and idle as weeds,
watching the helicopter rise:
My parents, fatally proud   5
& camera-ready,
crewcut medics smoking

by an ambulance, a few boys
wrestling in the grass.
I remember reading   10
Jimmy Hendrix left jumpschool
with bad ankles & a cheap
guitar, and think now
of the few wild years he lived

teasing Death the way he'd tease   15
his fans: singing loud on manic
knees; acid bobsledding
his veins, fingers & teeth
strumming Stratocaster flames.
I am trying to understand danger: 20
those summers my baby-brother

backflipped from diving boards,
and the wheel of his body
turned me dizzy;
those nights he was reckless   25

---

1   *Jimi Hendrix* Hendrix (1942–70) was an American songwriter and guitarist. He was
    briefly trained as a paratrooper in the US army.

on roller-coasters twisting
like barbed wire
across amusement parks.

Now, as soldiers fall
30 from the chopper, banging
their helmets on sun,
rocks in an odd constellation,
I feel the earth beneath my shoes.
Their chutes open wide
35 as Hendrix's giant hands,

around me, people begin to cheer,
my father holds binoculars
to my mother's eyes.
I won't breathe until he lands,
40 my brother, black
as an eighth note drifting
against the sky.

—2006

LANGUAGE POETS

A collective avant-garde movement in poetics that arose in the 1960s, Language poetry countered and overturned "official" establishment ideas about poetry, including the ways publishing companies, universities, and other cultural authorities defined poetry for the public. Often collaborating as writers, readers, and publishers of each other's work (via small presses and journals they founded), Language poets rejected the common assumption that the voice of a poem should represent a (great) poet-speaker who either conveys personal emotional experience or who hands down inspired wisdom or a moral or a message. (See "Romanticism" and "confessional poetry" in the Glossary for two examples.) By contrast, Language poets took as their subject the poem's own medium: language.

By the time the Language movement began, paradigm-shifting twentieth-century linguistics scholarship had demonstrated that language is a system of meanings that works through shared social conventions—not because words are somehow "true" labels inherently tied to or accurately describing particular things in the "real world." Since words are always unstable and multi-layered, language generates new and different meanings for different people in different situations, a slipperiness that both enables and blocks communication. These challenging gaps and alternate paths of signification became one of Language poetry's primary subjects. (See Charles Bernstein, "A Test of Poetry," below.)

Working *with*, exploring, and dramatizing (rather than sidestepping) these fundamental qualities of language, Language poems left some readers disoriented or even angry. As had other poets before them, Language poets worked with techniques of defamiliarization (see Glossary), artistic methods crafted to make language strange in order to open new doors of perception. Language poet Bruce Andrews argued that the "routine" operations of language are bred into us as social creatures born into a particular sociopolitical world. For him, the disruptions that Language poetry enacted challenged social and political norms.

Developing a vast and innovative array of forms and techniques, Language poets worked with fragments, digressions, and discontinuities; repetitions; gaps; the inclusion of borrowed or "found" language from other (often "non-poetic") sources (see Kenneth Goldsmith, "DAY," below); incorporation of silence, self-commentary, and instructions (as in Jackson Mac Low, below); modes of performance; disrupted communication; and typographically distinct (or illegible) uses of the page. The very discomfort and mystification readers might experience is a crucial part of Language poetry, which depends heavily on a concept of engaged and attentive readers whose participation is central to the meaning of the poem.

The initial Language movement fostered an ongoing and diverse experimental body of work by later poets, now often called "Language poetries." Scholar Oren Izenberg observes that "the Language poets have succeeded in securing a widespread contemporary consensus that to write with a heightened awareness of language as medium is among the most vital currents in poetic art."

Many readers new to Language works will find it helpful to think about questions like the ones that follow. First, answer them by relying on your initial reaction to these poems, and then approach them again by drawing specific comparisons with any other poems of your choice in this volume.

What *kind* of "poem" is the one I'm reading?
How does it compare to other poems I've read or liked?
What does it do differently?
How does it meet or defy my expectations?
What kinds of language does it incorporate?
How does it use the page?
How does it conceive of the reader's role?
What seem to be its definitions of a "poet," a "poem," and "poetic language"?

Jackson Mac Low
1922–2004

from *Daily Life*

How to Make Poems from a DAILY LIFE List

I. Prepare a list such as the following:

DAILY LIFE 1

6 August 1963

1	A.	I'm going to the store.	Black Ace
2	B.	Is the baby sleeping?	Black Two 5
3	C.	I'd better take the dog out.	Black Three
4	D.	What do you want?	Black Four
5	E.	Let's have eggs for breakfast.	Black Five
6	F.	Has the mail come yet?	Black Six
7	G.	I'll take the garbage down.	Black Seven 10
8	H.	Is there anything you need downstairs?	Black Eight
9	I.	I'll see you.	Black Nine
10	J.	Shall I turn the light on?	Black Ten
11	K.	I'll take the bottles back.	Black Jack
12	L.	Did somebody knock on the door?	Black Queen 15
13	M.	I'm going to close the window.	Black King
14	N.	Is the baby crying?	Red Ace
15	O.	Hello, sweety-baby!	Red Two
16	P.	What's that red mark on him?	Red Three
17	Q.	I'm going to lie down & rest my back for awhile.	20 Red Four
18	R.	What did you say?	Red Five
19	S.	Look how this plant has grown!	Red Six
20	T.	Have you fed the cat & dog?	Red Seven
21	U.	I'm going to make some coffee.	Red Eight
22	V.	Do you want some ginger beer?	Red Nine 25
23	W.	I wish it wasn't always so noisy.	Red Ten
24	X.	Is it all right if I turn on the news?	Red Jack
25	Y.	What's the matter with the baby?	Red Queen
26	Z.	Have half a banana.	Red King

30 II. Employ one of the following methods:

1. *Letters*. This is the method first used by the author when he conceived the idea of a DAILY LIFE list as a source for poems, plays, &c. (6 August 1963), & except for one poem, it is the only method he has used up to the present time (8 January 1964). One selects (or allows chance or circumstance to select) a
35 name, phrase, sentence, title, or any other limited series of words, & translates each successive letter into the sentence corresponding to it on a DAILY LIFE list. The end of a word produces the end of a strophe, e.g., translating the title DAILY LIFE into the sentences of DAILY LIFE 1, one gets:

DAILY LIFE

40 What do you want?
I'm going to the store.
I'll see you.
Did somebody knock on the door?
What's the matter with the baby?

45 Did somebody knock on the door?
I'll see you.
Has the mail come yet?
Let's have eggs for breakfast.

Obviously, if one wants a poem having the same number of lines in every
50 strophe, one must choose a series of words having the same number of letters in each word.

2. *Numbers*. One selects a source of digits, such as a random digit table or a telephone book, & translates the digits, taken in pairs, in any of a number of ways. The simplest way is to use only the first 25 sentences of a list & to make
55 a correspondence chart for all possible pairs of digits (see next page for such a chart). [Since there are exactly 100 possible pairs of digits, the number of different lines corresponding to the digit pairs must divide evenly into 100. That's why all 26 lines in the Daily Life list cannot be used, but only 25. (The Letters and Playing Cards methods, in contrast, allow use of all 26 lines in
60 the Daily Life list.)—A.T.] One can use single digits (0 being taken as 10) or pairs of digits to determine the number of strophes in a poem & the number of lines in each successive strophe. (If one wants the same number of lines in every strophe, one need use only 2 digits: one for the number of strophes & one for the number of lines in every strophe.)

25-place correspondence chart for digit pairs:

01	26	51	76	09	34	59	84	17	42	67	92
02	27	52	77	10	35	60	85	18	43	68	93
03	28	53	78	11	36	61	86	19	44	69	94
04	29	54	79	12	37	62	87	20	45	70	95
05	30	55	80	13	38	63	88	21	46	71	96
06	31	56	81	14	39	64	89	22	47	72	97
07	32	57	82	15	40	65	90	23	48	73	98
08	33	58	83	16	41	66	91	24	49	74	99
								25	50	75	00

Using a 5-place random digit table, one may get the series 94736 24128. The first digit, 9, determining the number of strophes in a poem; the 2nd digit, 4, determining the number of lines in the first strophe; & the last 8 digits, taken in pairs translated into 01 to 25 thru the correspondence table, determining the successive lines of the first strophe; one gets as the first strophe of a nine-strophe poem:

73–23 I wish it wasn't always so noisy.
62–12 Did somebody knock on the door?
41–16 What's that red mark on him?
28–03 I'd better take the dog out.

Other methods may also be used to translate numbers into a DAILY LIFE list to produce poems. For instance, one may dispense with a correspondence table & only use pairs from 01 to 26, disregarding all other combinations of digits. Or one may use as a source a *mixed* series of numbers & letters, as the author did the 2nd time he used DAILY LIFE 1 as a source (15 August 1963), when he translated the series (found on a slip of paper clipped from the top of a printer's galley): "8–8 Caled w 8 Spt Hvy x 16 RAU (1) Dec. 19 6535" using the digits singly except when a pair formed a number between 10 & 26.

3. *Playing Cards.* One method for using playing cards is to shuffle, draw one card to determine number of strophes (1 to 13, taking Ace as 1 & Jack, Queen & King as 11, 12 & 13; or 1 to 26, using the correspondences of numbers to card colors & denominations appearing on the list). Then draw as many cards as strophes to determine the number of lines in each successive strophe (or draw only one card, if one wants to have the same number of lines in every strophe). Finally, shuffle & draw a single card for each line of the poem, shuffling between every 2 draws, or at least fairly frequently. Other methods of using playing cards may also be used.

4. *Other Methods.* Still other methods may be devised to use lists of sentences from daily life as sources of poems. For instance, several alternative lists may be used at the same time with some chance determinant selecting which list 105 is to be used as the source for any particular line of a poem. &, of course, readers may make their own list(s), using them alone or together with one or more of the author's lists. What wd make such a poem a realization of DAILY LIFE is the use of one or more lists of sentences from daily life as source(s) for poems or other literary works. (The author has already written an essay 110 describing a method for using such lists as sources for dramatic presentations [August 1963].)

—1964

from "Is That Wool Hat My Hat?"[1]

for two, three, or four voices

Four voices is optimum, but two or three can perform this. All four words in each column (or the top two or three) are to be spoken simultaneously, following an even beat. One performer (or a separate conductor) should beat time throughout. Do *not* use a metronome.

5 1. Is   that wool hat   my   hat? Is   that wool hat
   2. Is   that wool hat   my   Is   that wool hat   my
   3. Is   that wool hat   my   hat? Is   that wool hat
   4. Is   that wool hat   my   hat? Is   that wool hat

   1. my   hat? Is   that wool hat   my   hat? Is   that
10 2. Is   that wool hat   my   Is   that Is   that Is
   3. my   hat? Is   that wool hat   my   hat? my   hat?
   4. my   hat? Is   that wool hat   my   hat? Is   that

   1. wool hat   my   hat? Is   that wool hat   my   hat?
   2. that is   that Is   that is   that wool hat   my
15 3. is   that my   hat? Is   that my   hat? Is   that
   4. wool hat   my   hat? Is   that wool hat   my   hat?

   1. Is   that wool hat   my   hat? wool wool wool hat
   2. hat? is   hat   hat   hat   wool hat   my   hat? wool

---

1 This excerpt reproduces five four-line sections of the complete poem's 35 sections. The complete poem is available on the companion website.

3.	my	hat?	Is	that	my	hat?	Is	that	my	hat?	
4.	wool	hat	wool	hat	wool	hat	wool	hat	wool	hat	20

1.	hat	hat	hat	hat	Is	that	wool	hat	my	Is
2.	hat	my	wool	hat	my	wool	hat	my	wool	hat
3.	Is	that	that	wool	hat	my	hat?	Is	that	wool
4.	my	hat?	Is	wool	hat	my	hat?	Is	wool	hat

Notes and Performance Instructions for "*Is That Wool Hat My Hat?*"

This piece came about in the following way: During the 12th International Sound Poetry Festival, held at Washington Square Church in New York during April 1980, I came to the April 13th session wearing a navy blue wool hat ("watch cap"). Richard Kostelanetz had also walked over to the church for the performance, wearing a similar hat.

At the church door I met my friend the writer/clairvoyant Hannah Weiner and we chatted a while. Then during intermission I talked with other people, but just before I took my seat, Hannah came over to me and handed me a wool hat similar to my own, which she'd found on the floor after the chairs in the church were shifted. Having seen me wearing such a hat before the program, she had assumed that I'd dropped mine and that this was it.

I'd gotten in just as someone began performing, so I had no opportunity to tell her it wasn't mine—Hannah had taken a seat not very near me—so I just held the hat in my hand, meaning to turn it in later to the "lost & found," and gave my attention to the performer.

Then, somewhat suddenly, Richard Kostelanetz, who was sitting behind me, leaned over and asked, "Is that wool hat *my* hat?" Having often seen Richard wearing such a hat, I assumed it was his, and handed it to him. But his rhythmical question stuck in my mind, so that night I composed this piece for speakers.

As I wrote it, I decided to make four superimposed parts, each composed of repetitions of the question and of parts of it. I used a die to decide how many of the six words of the question were to be repeated each time. As a result, the four parts sometimes coincide exactly, but often the four speakers are saying four entirely different words at the same time.

Performance Instructions

It is best that the piece be performed by four speakers—where possible, by two men and two women. But it may be performed by other combinations of speakers and/or by fewer than four (three or two). I've never tried it with fewer than three other speakers, but others may find such a performance rewarding, and circumstances may sometimes dictate a smaller number of speakers than four.

55   Either one of the performers should act as a "time-beater," or a fifth person should act as conductor. The beat should be very precise—almost metronomic, although a metronome should never be used—and neither too fast nor too slow. I've usually performed it about "One Word = MM.132," but others may wish to read it slightly faster or slower. However, it oughtn't go *much* faster or
60 slower than this.

       Each four words lined up vertically should be spoken precisely at the same time. However, if a speaker mistakenly skips or repeats a word of the like, that speaker should go on from wherever the mistake was made—with no break and *certainly* no attempt to correct the mistake. If somehow the speaker can
65 skip or the like to get back to the proper alignment, that would be good—but never at the cost of the beat.

       The words should be spoken moderately loudly, but never over-emphatically. In some performances after the work's premiere (18 April 1980, during the same festival), speakers got louder and louder, some practically *barking*
70 the words. Such things must be avoided; moderate loudness at a precise beat is what's needed.

       The best way to end the performance is for the conductor's left hand to be raised straight up—while the right hand continues beating time—at the beginning of the last "system" (group of four lines), and then brought down
75 swiftly at the end of that system.

       If through an error one speaker has reached the end of the piece before the others, that speaker should reread the words of the last line until the conductor's left hand comes down.

       All speakers should stop precisely as the conductor's hand falls.

score: 13–14 April 1980
notes & instructions: 5 December 1980
New York

Lyn Hejinian
b. 1941

from *Writing Is an Aid to Memory*

28.

we are parting with description
termed blue may be perfectly blue
goats do have damp noses
that test and now I dine drinking with
others   5
adult blue butterfly for a swim with cheerful birds
I suppose we hear a muddle of rhythms in water
bond vegetables binder thereof for thread
and no crisp fogs
spice quilt mix   10
know shipping pivot
sprinkle with a little melody
nor blot past this dot mix
now for a bit and fog of bath rain
do dot goats   15
swift whipper of rice
a type as cream
into a froth
ranking a time when rain looms
I part the swim and width whereas   20
hob for swing yard note
product in the woody weeds
trees in the foreshortening
a source "draws" shortening
by an inkspot over the four rivers   25
darkness ficing no flaw pink
the stain whose at him stuff suggested
is visible as follows (cone in space)
old waters
this morning over fringed crop involving   30
quantity
it lasts into the empty sky shopping and glittering

I can picture the marked page
          poke beauty
                    sunset like a pack of dogs
                    swaying with daylight
it is late afternoon and I hurry
          my fault of comfort
                    the streets of traffic are a great success

—1978

Michael Davidson
b. 1944

Et in Leucadia Ego[1]

For Chris Dewdney[2]

So they get this and we're coming off some it's like and
then I went so he goes well hey and how you doing?

He went with this scene he was on my you know some
scene he was well I go then said fuck it.

Hey how you what's up hey you *see* wait a minute you did   5
no way I *see* this you know all right you know no way.

What it does is *see* it has this thing I don't know I know it
won't what's it want it has some stuff you know like.

Fuck that I mean well fuck no he did some fucking thing
so I go fuck no he comes back fuck that no way so fuck I   10
split he split.

Sure really are you sure oh sure really can you believe oh
really I can't believe you for really oh really oh sure.

Yeah then I went yeah he went there yeah then I yeah
over to and yeah so he yeah and oh yeah I came back yeah   15
and he oh yeah who I.

Do it do it Oh Kay hey wait for all right do it Oh Kay do it
hey wait don't do it it's my it's my don't do it.

—1985

---

1   *Et in Leucadia Ego* A play on the Latin phrase "Et in Arcadia ego," or "In Arcadia I am."
    Leucadia is a beach community in California.
2   *Chris Dewdney* Canadian poet (b. 1951).

Ron Silliman
b. 1946

from *The Chinese Notebook*

79. I am continually amazed at how many writers are writing the poems they believe the person they wish they were would have written.

80. What if writing was meant to represent all possibilities of thought, yet one could or would write only in certain conditions, states of mind?

81. I have seen poems thought or felt to be dense, difficult to get through, respaced on the page, two dimensional picture plane, made airy, "light." How is content altered by this operation?

82. Certain forms of "bad" poetry are of interest because inept writing blocks referentiality, turning words and phrases in on themselves, an autonomy of language which characterizes the "best" writing. Some forms of sloppy surrealism or pseudo-beat automatic writing are particularly given to this.

83. Designated art sentence.

84. One can use the inherent referentiality of sentences very much as certain "pop" artists used images (I'm thinking of Rauschenberg,[1] Johns,[2] Rosenquist,[3] etc.) to use as elements for so-called abstract composition.

85. Abstract v. concrete, a misleading vocabulary. If I read a sentence (story, poem, whatever unit) of a fight, say, and identify with any spectator or combatant, I am having a vicarious experience. But if I experience, most pronouncedly, this language as event, I am experiencing that fact directly.

86. Impossible to posit the cat's expectations in words. Or Q's example— the mouse's fear of the cat is counted as his believing true a certain English

---

1   *Rauschenberg* Robert Rauschenberg (1925–2008), American painter and sculptor.
2   *Johns* Jasper Johns (b. 1930), American painter.
3   *Rosenquist* James Rosenquist (b. 1933), American painter.

sentence. If we are to speak of things, we are proscribed, limited to the external, or else create laughable and fantastic fictions.

87. Story of a chimpanzee taught that certain geometrical signs stood for words, triangle for bird, circle for water, etc., when presented with a new object, a duck, immediately made up the term "water bird."

88. That writing was "speech" "scored." A generation caught in such mixed metaphor (denying the metaphor) as that. That elaboration of technical components of the poem carried the force of prophecy.

89. Is any term now greater than a place-holder? Any arrangement of weighted squares, if ordered by some shared theory of color, could be language.

90. What do nouns reveal? Conceal?

91. The idea of the importance of the role of the thumb in human evolution. Would I still be able to use it if I did not have a word for it? Thought it simply a finger? What evidence do I have that my right and left thumbs are at least roughly symmetrical equivalents? After all I don't really use my hands interchangeably, do I? I couldn't write this with my left hand, or if I did learn to do so, it would be a specific skill and would be perceived as that.

92. Perhaps as a means of containing meaning outside of the gallery system, the visual arts have entered into a period where the art itself exists in a dialectic, in the exchange between worker, critic, and worker. Writing stands in a different historical context. Fiction exists in relation to a publishing system, poetry to an academic one.

93. At Berkeley, when I was a student, graduate students in the English Department liked to think of themselves as "specialized readers."

94. What makes me think that form exists?

95. One possibility is my ability to "duplicate" or represent it. As a child, I could fill in a drawing as though it and color existed.

96. I want these words to fill the spaces poems leave.

97. The assumption is, language is equal if not to human perception per se, then to what is human about perception.

98. Good v. bad poetry. The distinction is not useful. The whole idea assumes a shared set of articulatable values by which to make such a judgment. It assumes, if not the perfect poem, at least the theory of limits, the most perfect poem. How would you proceed to make such a distinction?

—1977

Rae Armantrout
b. 1947

Soft Money

They're sexy
because they're needy,
which degrades them.

They're sexy because
they don't need you.

They're sexy because they pretend
not to need you,

but they're lying,
which degrades them.

They're beneath you
and it's hot.

They're across the border,
rhymes with dancer—

they don't need
to understand.

They're content to be
(not *mean*),

which degrades them
and is sweet.

They want to be
the thing-in-itself

and the thing-for-you—

Miss Thing—

but can't.

25   They want to be you,
     but can't,

which is so hot.

—2010

Charles Bernstein
b. 1950

A Test of Poetry[1]

What do you mean by *rashes of ash?* Is *industry*
systematic work, assiduous activity, or ownership
of factories? Is *ripple* agitate lightly? Are
we *tossed in tune* when we write poems? And
what or who *emboss with gloss insignias of air?*   5

Is the *Fabric* about which you write in the epigraph
of your poem an edifice, a symbol of heaven?

Does *freight* refer to cargo or lading carried
for pay by water, land or air? Or does it mean
payment for such transportation? Or a freight   10
train? When you say a *commoded journey*
do you mean a comfortable journey or a good train
with well-equipped commodoties? But, then, why
do you drop the 'a' before *slumberous friend?* And
when you write, in "Why I Am Not a Christian"   15
You always throw it down / But you never
pick it up—what is *it??*

In "The Harbor of Illusion", does *vein*
refer to a person's vein under his skin or
is it a metaphor for a river? Does *lot*   20
mean one's fate or a piece of land?
And does *camphor* refer to camphor trees?
Moreover, who or what is *nearing.* Who or
what has *fell?* Or does *fell* refer to the
skin or hide of an animal? And who or what has   25
stalled? Then, is the *thoroughfare of*
noon's atoll an equivalent of *the template?*

---

1   *A Test of Poetry* Bernstein described the persona in this poem as a Chinese translator
    working on a poem in English replete with American cultural references. Bernstein in-
    cludes multiple allusions to his earlier works "The Voyage of Life," "Why I Am Not a
    Christian," "The Harbor of Illusion," "Fear of Flipping," and "No Pastrami."

In "Fear of Flipping" does *flipping* mean
crazy?

30 How about *strain*, does it mean
a severe trying or wearing pressure or
effect (such as a strain of hard work),
or a passage, as in piece of music?
Does *Mercury* refer to a brand of oil?[1]

35 In the lines
shards of bucolic pastry anchored
against cactus cabinets, Nantucket buckets
could we take it as—pieces of pies
or tarts are placed in buckets (which
40 are made of wood from Nantucket)
anchored against cabinets (small
rooms or furniture?) with cactus?

What is *nutflack*?[2]

I suppose the *caucus of caucasians*
45 refers to the white people's meeting
of a political party to nominate candidates.
But who is Uncle Hodgepodge?
And what does *familiar freight*
to the returning antelope mean?

50 You write, *the walls are our floors*.
How can the *walls* be floors if the floors
refer to the part of the room which forms
its enclosing surface and upon which one
walks? In *and the floors, like balls,*
55 *repel all falls*—does *balls* refer to
nonsense or to any ball like a basket ball
or to guys? Or to a social assembly for
dancing? *Falls* means to descend
from higher to a lower

---

1   *Mercury ... oil* From "Fear of Flipping": "It's the strain, two liters of Mercury and never /
     enough flotation devices."
2   *nutflack* From "Fear of Flipping": "Sadly / to state a grew-quite-a-lot-since-last-look,
     nut- / flack visage advancing the caucus of Caucasians."

or to drop down wounded or dead?   60
But what is *the so-called overall
mesh?*

Is the *garbage heap* the garbage heap
in the ordinary sense? Why does
garbage heap exchange for *so-called*   65
overall mesh? Since a *faker* is
one who fakes, how can
arbitrary reduce to *faker?*

Who or what are disappointed
not to have been?   70

Does *frames* refer to form, constitution,
or structure in general? Or to a
particular state, as of the mind?

In the sentence,
If you don't like it   75
colored in, you can always xerox it
and see it all gray
—what is *it?* What does
colored in mean?

A few lines later you write,   80
You mean, image farm when you've got bratwurst—
Does *bratwurst* refer to sausage?
Does the line mean—the sausage
you saw reminded you of a farm which you imagined?

Does *fat-bottom boats* refer to boats with thick bottoms?   85
Is *humble then humped* used to describe the actions of one
who plays golf?[1] In the phrase *a sideshow freak*—
the *freak* refers to a hippie? *Sideshow* refers to secondary
importance? Or an abnormal actor in the sideshow?
Then, who or what is *linked* with *steam of pink.* And   90
how about *the tongue-tied tightrope stalker*—

---

1   *humped ... golf* In golf, the swing problem also known as early extension is sometimes
     called "humping the goat."

does the *stalker* refer to one who is pursuing
stealthily in the act of hunting game? The stalker
is a witness at first and then a witless witness?

95 You write *The husks are salted*:
what kind of nut husks can be salted for eating?
What does *bending* mean—to become curved,
crooked, or bent? Or to bow down in submission
or reverence, yield, submit? Does *bells*
100 refer to metallic sounding instruments or
a kind of trousers?

Just a few lines later you have the phrase
Felt very poured. Who felt poured? Toys?
Is *humming* in the sense of humming a song?
105 *Stepped into* where? *Not being part of* what?

In "No Pastrami" *(Walt! I'm with you in Sydney / Where
the echoes of Mamaroneck howl / Down the outback's
pixilating corridors)*—does the *pastrami* refer
to a highly seasoned shoulder cut of beef? Is
110 *Mamaroneck* a place in the U.S.[1] where wild oxes howl?
I take it *corridors* refers to the passageway
in the supermarket? Could I read the poem as—
The speaker is doing shopping in a supermarket
in Sydney; he is walking along the eccentric
115 passageways among the shelves on which goods
are placed; he does not want to buy the pastrami
as he seems to have heard the echoes of wild oxes
howling in the U.S. while he addresses Walt Whitman?[2]

In "No End to Envy", does the envy refer to admire or
120 in the bad sense?

                                                    —1999

---

1   *place in the U.S.* Mamaroneck, New York.
2   *Walt Whitman* American poet (1819–92) (see p. 169).

Harryette Mullen
b. 1953

Denigration

Did we surprise our teachers who had niggling doubts about the
picayune brains of small black children who reminded them of
clean pickaninnies on a box of laundry soap?[1] How muddy is the
Mississippi compared to the third-longest river of the darkest
continent?[2] In the land of the Ibo, the Hausa, and the Yoruba,   5
what is the price per barrel of nigrescence?[3] Though slaves, who
were wealth, survived on niggardly[4] provisions, should inheri-
tors of wealth fault the poor enigma for lacking a dictionary?
Does the mayor demand a recount of every bullet or does city
hall simply neglect the black alderman's district? If I disagree   10
with your beliefs, do you chalk it up to my negligible powers of
discrimination, supposing I'm just trifling and not worth con-
sidering? Does my niggling concern with trivial matters negate
my ability to negotiate in good faith? Though Maroons,[5] who
were unruly Africans, not loose horses or lazy sailors, were   15
called renegades in Spanish, will I turn any blacker if I renege
on this deal?

—2002

---

1   *picayune* Small; *pickaninnies* Racist term for black children; *clean ... soap* The package
     for Fairbank's Gold Dust Washing Powder, a brand introduced in 1889 and lasting till
     well into the twentieth century, depicted two black children. The racist "pickaninny"
     stereotype, and other racist stereotypes rooted in the legacy of slavery, were common in
     marketing in the US.
2   *third-longest river* Niger River; *darkest continent* Dark Continent is an archaic phrase
     used to describe Africa.
3   *Ibo ... Yoruba* Ethnic groups from various regions in Nigeria; *nigrescence* Blackness.
4   *niggardly* Meager.
5   *Maroons* Runaway slaves who managed to establish independent communities in places
     where they were not likely to be recaptured, such as swamps or highlands.

Dim Lady[1]

My honeybunch's peepers are nothing like neon. Today's special at Red Lobster is redder than her kisser. If Liquid Paper is white, her racks are institutional beige. If her mop were Slinkys, dishwater Slinkys would grow on her noggin. I have seen table-
5 cloths in Shakey's Pizza Parlors, red and white, but no such picnic colors do I see in her mug. And in some minty-fresh mouthwashes there is more sweetness than in the garlic breeze my main squeeze wheezes. I love to hear her rap, yet I'm aware that Muzak has a hipper beat. I don't know any Marilyn Monroes.
10 My ball and chain is plain from head to toe. And yet, by gosh, my scrumptious twinkie has as much sex appeal for me as any lanky model or platinum movie idol who's hyped beyond belief.

—2002

---

1   *Dim Lady* See Shakespeare's Sonnet 130, p. 17.

Kenneth Goldsmith
b. 1961

from DAY[1]

A2

A2 L+ THE NEW YORK TIMES, FRIDAY, SEPTEMBER 1, 2000 B
Cartier
Must®Tank®
Watch
Vermeil. Quartz.
Small. $1,425.
Large 1,500.
©1999 Cartier, Inc.
Visit our temporary location 711 Fifth Avenue at 56th Street (212)
753-0111
Trump Tower, Fifth Avenue at 56th Street (212) 308-0840
Madison Avenue at 69th Street (212) 472-6400
The Mall at Short Hills, Short Hills, New Jersey (973) 467-9005
what to wear
when the world
is watching
units per hour
ROLEX
OYSTER PERPETUAL
SUPERLATIVE CHRONOMETER
OFFICIALLY CERTIFIED
COSMOGRAPH
DAYTONA
ROLEX
DAYTONA COSMOGRAPH
Oyster Perpetual Certified Chronometer
18K yellow or white gold with deployable

---

1 Of his ambitious book-length poem *Day*, Goldsmith wrote: "On Friday, September 1, 2000, I began retyping the day's *New York Times*, word for word, letter for letter, from the upper left hand corner to the lower right hand corner, page by page." A conceptual poet, Goldsmith often explores what he calls "uncreative writing." The poem's epigraph is Truman Capote's comment on Jack Kerouac: "That's not writing. That's typing."

fliplock clasp on strap.

$14,550

30   NOW OPEN AT WORLD TRADE CENTER

TORNEAU NEW YORK • PALM BEACH • BAL HARBOUR •

SOUTH COAST

PLAZA • HOUSTON

SINCE 1900

35   Torneau TimeMachine: 57th at Madison • Madison at 52nd St. •

Madison at 59th St.

Seventh at 34th St. • World Trade Center • Garden City, LI: Roosevelt

Field • 212•758•6234

News Summary

40   INTERNATIONAL A3-12

Missile Test Delay Likely; No Decision on Deployment

The Pentagon will probably postpone the next test of a national missile
defense system until January, administration officials said. Any decision to
deploy the missile shield now seems certain to pass from President Clinton
45   to his successor. A1

China Official Sued In U.S.

Five veterans of the Tiananmen Square democracy movement are suing
Li Peng, chairman of the National People's Congress, in federal court in New
York. They accuse him of human rights abuses arising from his role in the 1989
50   crack-down that killed hundreds of civilians in Beijing. A6

Volkswagen Mexico Strike Ends

Workers at Volkswagen Mexico negotiated a raise of more than double the
inflation rate, ending a two-week battle that included a walkout at the Puebla
factory, the only one in the world that produces Beetles. A4

55   France Proposes Tax Cuts

France proposed a large package of tax cuts, nudged by Germany and
probably providing an example to Italy. The proposed cuts, totaling roughly
$16 billion over three years, are part of a wave of similar measures being
enacted across Europe, as governments react to increased tax revenue from
60   expanding economies and declining unemployment. A12

Inquiry on Liechtenstein Courts

A government-sponsored inquiry into whether Liechtenstein is a center
for money laundering found shortcomings in how the principality's justice
system handles the issue with some cases idle for years. A4

65   Religious Leaders Pledge Peace

Participants at the four-day Millennium World Peace Summit of Religious
and Spiritual Leaders in New York signed a detailed statement pledging to
work for world peace. A12

World Briefing A8
SCIENCE/HEALTH
Mass Extinctions Foreseen
Global warming could wipe out many species of plants and animals by the end of the 21st century, the World Wide Fund for Nature, known in the United States as the World Wildlife Fund, warned in a report. A3

—2003

SONGS

Lyrics to songs typically circulate in multiple versions, as indeed has been the case throughout the long history of the song-poem. The texts that follow draw on multiple sources: liner notes; official lyrics posted on artist websites; crowdsourced versions; and variants by artists themselves, for example, in cases where songs as performed differ from liner notes. Such variants and the responses to them by fans are part of the active lives of songs in circulation.

2Pac

Changes

Ooh yeah

Come on come on
I see no changes, wake up in the morning and I ask myself,
Is life worth living
5 Should I blast myself
I'm tired of bein' poor and even worse I'm black
My stomach hurts, so I'm lookin' for a purse to snatch
Cops give a damn about a negro
Pull the trigger, kill a nigga, he's a hero
10 Give the crack to the kids who the hell cares
One less hungry mouth on the welfare
First ship 'em dope and let 'em deal to brothers
Give 'em guns, step back, watch 'em kill each other
It's time to fight back that's what Huey said
15 Two shots in the dark now Huey's dead
I got love for my brother but we can never go nowhere
unless we share with each other
We gotta start makin' changes
Learn to see me as a brother 'stead of two distant strangers
20 And that's how it's supposed to be
How can the Devil take a brother if he's close to me
I'd love to go back to when we played as kids
But things changed, and that's the way it is

Come on come on
25 That's just the way it is
Things'll never be the same

That's just the way it is
Aww yeah

That's just the way it is
Things'll never be the same
That's just the way it is
Aww yeah

I see no changes, all I see is racist faces
Misplaced hate makes disgrace to races
We under
I wonder what it takes to make this one better place
Let's erase the wasted
Take the evil out the people, they'll be acting right
'Cause both black and white are smokin' crack tonight
And only time we chill is when we kill each other
It takes skill to be real, time to heal each other
And although it seems heaven sent
We ain't ready to see a black President, uh
It ain't a secret don't conceal the fact
The penitentiary's packed, and it's filled with blacks
But some things will never change
Try to show another way but they stayin' in the dope game
Now tell me what's a mother to do
Bein' real don't appeal to the brother in you
You gotta operate the easy way
"I made a G today"
But you made it in a sleazy way
Sellin' crack to the kids
"I gotta get paid"
Well hey, well that's the way it is

Come on, come on
That's just the way it is
Things'll never be the same
That's just the way it is
Aww yeah

That's just the way it is
Things'll never be the same
That's just the way it is
Aww yeah

65 We gotta make a change
    It's time for us as a people to start making some changes
    Let's change the way we eat, let's change the way we live
    And let's change the way we treat each other
    You see the old way wasn't working so it's on us to do
70 What we gotta do to survive

    And still I see no changes, can't a brother get a little peace
    There's war on the streets and the war in the Middle East
    Instead of war on poverty
    They got a war on drugs so the police can bother me
75 And I ain't never did a crime I ain't have to do
    But now I'm back with the facts givin' 'em back to you
    Don't let 'em jack you up, back you up, crack you up and pimp smack you up
    You gotta learn to hold ya own
    They get jealous when they see ya with ya mobile phone
80 But tell the cops they can't touch this
    I don't trust this, when they try to rush I bust this
    That's the sound of my tool
    You say it ain't cool, but mama didn't raise no fool
    And as long as I stay black I gotta stay strapped and I never get to lay back
85 'Cause I always got to worry 'bout the payback
    Some buck that I roughed up way back
    Comin' back after all these years
    Rat-a-tat-tat-tat-tat

    That's the way it is

90 That's just the way it is
    Things'll never be the same
    That's just the way it is
    Aww yeah

    That's just the way it is
95 Things'll never be the same
    That's just the way it is
    Aww yeah

    Some things'll never change

—1998

Animal Collective

Peacebone

(Bonefish)

A Peacebone got found in the dinosaur wing
Well I've been jumping all over, but my views are slowly shrinking
I was a jugular vein in a juggler's girl
I was supposedly leaking the most interesting colors

While half of my fingers are dipped in the sand   5
You progress in letters but you're used to cooking broccoli
The other side of takeout is mildew on rice

And an obsession with the past is like a dead fly
And just a few things are related to the old times
Then we did believe in magic and we did die   10
It's not my words that you should follow, it's your insides
You're just an inside. Adjust your insides. You're just an inside.

I bet the monster was happy when we made him a maze
Cause he don't understand intentions and he just looks at your face
I bet the bubbles exploded to tickle the bath   15
And all the birds are very curious, all the fish were at the surface

With half of me waiting for myself to get calm
I'm like a pelican at red tide
I'm a corpse, I'm not a fisherman and
A blow out does not mean I will have a good night   20

Cause an obsession with the past is like a dead fly
And just a few things are related to the old times
When we did believe in magic and we did die.
It's not my words that you should follow, it's your inside
Adjust your insides. You're just an inside   25

Well I start in a hose and I'll end in a yard
When I feel like I'm stealing I can't keep myself from hearing God

Only the taste of your cooking can make me bow on the ground
It was the clouds that carved the mountains
30 It was the mountains that made the kids scream

Oh well she bore all her parts but
She never was found
You think I'll carve a path through New York
and be an artist, but are you anything
35 Then you find out that you can't ask a baby to cry

And an obsession with the past is like a dead fly
And just a few things are related to the old times
When we did believe in magic and we did die.
It's not my words that you should follow, it's your insides
40 You're just an inside. Adjust your insides. You're just an inside.

—2007

The Antlers

Two;
or, I Would Have Saved Her If I Could[1]

In the middle of the night I was sleeping sitting up, when a doctor came
to tell me, "Enough is enough." He brought me out into the hall (I could
have sworn it was haunted), and told me something that I didn't know
that I wanted to hear: That there was nothing that I could do to save you,
the choir's gonna sing, and this thing is gonna kill you. Something in my   5
throat made my next words shake, and something in the wires made the
light bulbs break. There was glass inside my feet and raining down from the
ceiling, it opened up the scars that had just finished healing. It tore apart the
canyon running down your femur, (I thought that it was beautiful, it made
me a believer.) And as it opened I could hear you howling from your room,   10
but I hid out in the hall until the hurricane blew. When I reappeared and
tried to give you something for the pain, you came to hating me again, and
just sang your refrain:

You had a new dream, it was more like a nightmare. You were just a little
kid, and they cut your hair, then they stuck you in machines, you came   15
so close to dying. They should have listened, they thought that you were
lying. Daddy was an asshole, he fucked you up, built the gears in your head,
now he greases them up. And no one paid attention when you just stopped
eating. "Eighty-seven pounds!" and this all bears repeating.

"Tell me when you think that we became so unhappy, wearing silver   20
rings with nobody clapping. When we moved here together we were so
disappointed, sleeping out of tune with our dreams disjointed. It killed me
to see you getting always rejected, but I didn't mind the things you threw,
the phones I deflected. I didn't mind you blaming me for your mistakes,
I just held you in the doorframe through all of the earthquakes. But you   25
packed up your clothes in that bag every night, and I would try to grab your
ankles (what a pitiful sight.) But after over a year, I stopped trying to stop
you from stomping out that door, coming back like you always do. Well no
one's gonna fix it for us, no one can. You say that, 'No one's gonna listen,

---

1   Writer Peter Silberman's official version of the lyrics, available at The Antlers' website,
     employs this prose-poetry form.

30 and no one understands.' So there's no open doors, and there's no way to get
through, there's no other witnesses, just us two.

There's two people living in one small room, from your two half-families
tearing at you, two ways to tell the story (no one worries), two silver rings
on our fingers in a hurry, two people talking inside your brain, two people
35 believing that I'm the one to blame, two different voices coming out of your
mouth, while I'm too cold to care and too sick to shout.

You had a new dream, it was more like a nightmare. You were just a little
kid, and they cut your hair. Then they stuck you in machines, you came
so close to dying. They should have listened, they thought that you were
40 lying. Daddy was an asshole, he fucked you up, built the gears in your head,
now he greases them up. And no one paid attention when you just stopped
eating. "Eighty-seven pounds!" and this all bears repeating.

—2009

Arcade Fire

Modern Man[1]

So I wait my turn, I'm a modern man
and the people behind me they can't
understand. Makes me feel like ...
Makes me feel like ...
So I wait in line, I'm a modern man   5
and the people behind me they can't
understand. Makes me feel like ...
Something don't feel right.

Like a record that's skipping,
I'm a modern man.   10
And the clock keeps ticking,
I'm a modern man. Makes me feel
like ... Makes me feel like ...

In my dream I was almost there
then they pulled me aside and said   15
you're going nowhere. They say we
are the chosen few but we waste it
and that's why we're still waiting ...

... On a number from the modern man
Maybe when you're older you will   20
understand, why you don't feel
right, why you can't sleep at night
now.

In line for a number but you don't
understand, like a modern man.   25
In line for a number but you don't
understand, like a modern man.

Oh I had a dream, I was dreaming
and I feel I'm losing the feeling.

---

1   We reprint these lyrics and their typography from the liner notes.

30 Makes me feel like ... like something
    don't feel right.

    I erase the number of the modern
    man, wanna break the mirror of the
    modern man. Makes me feel like ...
35 Makes me feel like ...

    <u>In my dream I was almost there
    Then they pulled me aside and said
    you're going nowhere. I know we are
    the chosen few but we waste it and</u>
40 <u>that's why we're still waiting.</u>

    <u>In line for a number but you don't
    understand, like a modern man.
    In line for a number but you don't
    understand, like a modern man.</u>
45 <u>If it's alright, then how come you
    can't sleep at night.
    In line for a number but you don't
    understand, like a modern man.</u>

    I'm a modern man
50 I'm a modern man
    I'm a modern man
    I'm a modern man

—2010

Bright Eyes

First Day of My Life[1]

This is the first day of my life,
I swear I was born right in the doorway.
I went out in the rain, suddenly everything changed,
They're spreading blankets on the beach.
Yours is the first face that I saw,   5
I think I was blind before I met you.
Now I don't know where I am, I don't know where I've been
But I know where I want to go.

And so I thought I'd let you know
That these things take forever,   10
I especially am slow.
But I realize that I need you
And I wondered if I could come home.

Remember the time you drove all night
Just to meet me in the morning.   15
And I thought it was strange you said everything changed,
You felt as if you'd just woke up.
And you said "This is the first day of my life,
I'm glad I didn't die before I met you.
But now I don't care I could go anywhere with you   20
And I'd probably be happy."

So if you want to be with me,
With these things there's no telling,
We just have to wait and see.
But I'd rather be working for a paycheck   25
Than waiting to win the lottery.
Besides maybe this time is different,
I mean I really think you like me.

—2005

---

1   We reprint these lyrics from the published sheet music.

Jim Carroll

People Who Died[1]

Teddy sniffing glue he was 12 years old
Fell from the roof on East Two-nine
Cathy was 11 when she pulled the plug
On 26 reds and a bottle of wine
5 Bobby got leukemia, 14 years old
He looked like 65 when he died
He was a friend of mine

Those are people who died, died
Those are people who died, died
10 Those are people who died, died
Those are people who died, died
They were all my friends, and they died

G-berg and Georgie let their gimmicks go rotten
So they died of hepatitis in upper Manhattan
15 Sly in Vietnam took a bullet in the head
Bobby OD'd on Drano on the night that he was wed
They were two more friends of mine
Two more friends that died
I miss 'em—they died

20 Those are people who died, died
Those are people who died, died
Those are people who died, died
Those are people who died, died
They were all my friends, and they died

25 Mary took a dry dive from a hotel room
Bobby hung himself from a cell in The Tombs
Judy jumped in front of a subway train
Eddie got slit in the jugular vein
And Eddie, I miss you more than all the others,

---

1   This song is an homage to the poem of the same title by Ted Berrigan (p. 541).

And I salute you brother   30
This song is for you my brother

Those are people who died, died
Those are people who died, died
Those are people who died, died
Those are people who died, died   35
They were all my friends, and they died

Herbie pushed Tony from the Boys' Club roof
Tony thought that his rage was just some goof
But Herbie sure gave Tony some bitchen proof
Hey, Herbie said, Tony, can you fly?   40
But Tony couldn't fly ... Tony died

Those are people who died, died
Those are people who died, died
Those are people who died, died
Those are people who died, died   45
They were all my friends, and they died

Brian got busted on a narco rap
He beat the rap by rattin' on some bikers
He said, hey, I know it's dangerous,
but it sure beats Rikers
But the next day he got offed   50
by the very same bikers

—1980

Common

I Used to Love H.E.R.

Yes, yes, y'all and you don't stop
To the beat y'all and you don't stop
Yes yes, y'all and you don't stop
1, 2, y'all and you don't stop
5 Yes, yes, y'all and you don't stop
And to the beat Com Sense'll be the sure shot
Come on

I met this girl, when I was ten years old
And what I loved most she had so much soul
10 She was old school, when I was just a shorty
Never knew throughout my life she would be there for me
On the regular, not a church girl she was secular
Not about the money, no studs was mic checkin' her
But I respected her, she hit me in the heart
15 A few New York niggaz, had did her in the park
But she was there for me, and I was there for her
Pull out a chair for her, turn on the air for her
And just cool out, cool out and listen to her
Sittin' on a bone, wishin' that I could do her
20 Eventually if it was meant to be, then it would be
Because we related, physically and mentally
And she was fun then, I'd be geeked when she'd come around
Slim was fresh yo, when she was underground
Original, pure untampered and down sister
25 Boy I tell ya, I miss her

Yes, yes, y'all and you don't stop
To the beat y'all and you don't stop
Yes yes, y'all and you don't stop
1, 2, y'all and you don't stop
30 Yes, yes, y'all and you don't stop
And to the beat Com Sense'll be the sure shot,
Come on

Now periodically I would see
Ol girl at the clubs, and at the house parties
She didn't have a body but she started gettin' thick quick   35
Did a couple of videos and became Afrocentric
Out goes the weave, in goes the braids beads medallions
She was on that tip about stoppin' the violence
About my people she was teachin' me
By not preachin' to me but speakin' to me   40
in a method that was leisurely, so easily I approached
She dug my rap, that's how we got close
But then she broke to the West Coast, and that was cool
Cause around the same time, I went away to school
And I'm a man of expandin', so why should I stand in her way   45
She probably get her money in L.A.
And she did, stud, she got big pub but what was foul
She said that the pro-black was goin' out of style
She said Afrocentricity was of the past
So she got into R&B hip-house bass and jazz   50
Now black music is black music and it's all good
I wasn't salty, she was with the boys in the hood
Cause that was good for her, she was becoming well rounded
I thought it was dope how she was on that freestyle shit
Just havin' fun, not worried about anyone   55
And you could tell by how her titties hung

Yes, yes, y'all and you don't stop
To the beat y'all and you don't stop
Yes yes, y'all and you don't stop
1, 2, y'all and you don't stop   60
Yes, yes, y'all and you don't stop
And to the beat Com Sense'll be the sure shot,
Come on

I might've failed to mention that the shit was creative
But once the man got you well he altered her native   65
Told her if she got an energetic gimmick
That she could make money
And she did it like a dummy
Now I see her in commercials, she's universal
She used to only swing it with the inner-city circle   70
Now she be in the burbs lickin' rock and dressin' hip

And on some dumb shit when she comes to the city
Talkin' about poppin' Glocks servin' rocks and hittin' switches
Now she's a gangsta rollin' with gangsta bitches
75 Always smokin' blunts and gettin' drunk
Tellin' me sad stories, now she only fucks with the funk
Stressin' how hardcore and real she is
She was really the realest before she got into showbiz
I did her, not just to say that I did it
80 But I'm committed
But so many niggaz hit it
That she's just not the same lettin' all these groupies do her
I see niggaz slammin' her, and takin' her to the sewer
But I'ma take her back hopin' that the shit stop
85 Cause who I'm talkin' bout y'all is hip-hop

Yes, yes, y'all and you don't stop
To the beat y'all and you don't stop
Yes yes, y'all and you don't stop
1, 2, y'all and you don't stop
90 Yes, yes, y'all and you don't stop
And to the beat Com Sense'll be the sure shot, come on

I used to love her
I used to love her
I used to love her
95 I used to love her

I think you're overstepping your bounds just a little bit
I can't do this anymore

—1994

The Coup

Strange Arithmetic[1]

[Dedicated to revolutionary teachers around the world]

History has taught me some strange arithmetic
Using swords, prison bars, and pistol grips
English is the art of bombing towns
While assuring that you really only blessed the ground
Science is that honorable, useful study   5
Where you contort the molecules and then you make that money
In mathematics, dead children don't get added
But they count the cost of bullets comin out the automatic

Teacher
My hands up   10
Please, don't make me a victim
Teachers
Stand up
You need to tell us how to flip this system

Economics is the symphony of hunger and theft   15
Mortar shells often echo out the cashing of checks
In Geography class, it's borders, mountains and rivers
But they will never show the line between the takers and givers
Algebra is that unique occasion
In which a school can say that there should be a balanced equation   20
And then Statistics is the tool of the complicit
To say everybody's with it and that you're the only critic

Teacher
My hands up
Please, don't make me a victim   25
Teachers
Stand up
You need to tell us how to flip this system

---

1   We reprint these lyrics from the liner notes.

Social Studies, the goliath to tackle
30 Which turns into a sermon on simplicity of shackles
Physics is to school you on the science of force
'Cept for how to break the hell out the ghetto, of course
Home Ec can teach you how to make a few sauces
And accept low pay from your Walmart bosses
35 If your school won't show you how to fight for what's needed
Then they're training you to go through life and get cheated

Teacher
My hand's up
Please, don't make me a victim
40 Teachers
Stand up
You need to tell us how to flip this system

—2012

Drake

Hotline Bling[1]

You used to call me on my
You used to, you used to
Yeah

You used to call me on my cell phone
late night when you need my love,   5
call me on my cell phone
late night when you need my love.
And I know when that hotline bling,
that can only mean one thing.
I know when that hotline bling,   10
that can only mean one thing.

Ever since I left the city,
you got a reputation for yourself now.
Everybody knows and I feel left out.
Girl you got me down, you got me stressed out.   15
'Cause ever since I left the city,
you started wearin' less and goin' out more.
Glasses of champagne out on the dance floor,
hangin' with some girls I've never seen before.

You used to call me on my cell phone
late night when you need my love,   20
call me on my cell phone
late night when you need my love.
I know when that hotline bling,
that can only mean one thing.
I know when that hotline bling,   25
that can only mean one thing.

Ever since I left the city, you, you, you,
you and me we just don't get along.
You make me feel like I did you wrong,
going places where you don't belong   30

---

1   We reprint these lyrics from the published sheet music.

Ever since I left the city,
You, you got exactly what you asked for.
Running out of pages in your passport,
35   hanging with some girls I've never seen before.

You used to call me on my cell phone
late night when you need my love,
call me on my cell phone
late night when you need my love.
40   And I know when that hotline bling,
that can only mean one thing.
I know when that hotline bling,
that can only mean one thing.

These days, all I do is
45   wonder if you're bendin' over backwards for someone else.
Wonder if you're rollin' over backwards for someone else,
doin' things I taught you, gettin' nasty for someone else.
You don't need no one else,
you don't need nobody else, no.
50   Why you never alone
Why you always touchin' road?
Used to always stay at home, be a good girl.
You was in a zone. Yeah.
You should just be yourself.
55   Right now you're someone else.

You used to call me on my cell phone
late night when you need my love,
call me on my cell phone
late night when you need my love.
60   And I know when that hotline bling,
that can only mean one thing.
I know when that hotline bling,
that can only mean one thing.

Ever since I left the city ...
65   Ever since I left the city ...
Ever since I left the city ...
Ever since I left the city ...

—2015

Florence and the Machine

Delilah[1]

Driftin' through the halls with the sunrise,
Holdin' on for your call.
Climbin' up the walls for that flashlight,
I can never let go.

Cause I'm gonna be free and I'm gonna be fine,   5
Holdin' on for your call.
Cause I'm gonna be free and I'm gonna be fine,
Maybe not tonight.

Now the sun is up and I'm goin' blind,
Holdin' on for your call.   10
Another drink just to pass the time,
I can never say no.

Cause I'm gonna be free and I'm gonna be fine,
Holdin' on for your call.
Cause I'm gonna be free and I'm gonna be fine,   15
Maybe not tonight.

It's a different kind of danger and the bells are ringin' out
And I'm callin' for my mother as I pull the pillars down
It's a different kind of danger and my feet are spinnin' 'round
Never knew I was a dancer 'til Delilah showed me how   20

Too fast for freedom,
Sometimes it all falls down.
These chains never leave me,
I keep draggin' them around.

Now I'm dancin' with Delilah and her vision is mine.   25
Holdin' on for your call.
A different kind of danger in the daylight,
I can never let go.

---

1   We reprint these lyrics from the published sheet music.

Took anything to cut you I can find,
30 Holdin' on for your call.
A different kind of a danger in the daylight.
Can't you let me know?

Now it's one more boy and it's one more line,
Holdin' on for your call.
35 Takin' the pills just to pass the time,
I can never say no.

I'm gonna be free and I'm gonna be fine,
Holdin' on for your call.
Cause I'm gonna be free and I'm gonna be fine,
40 but maybe not tonight.

It's a different kind of danger and the bells are ringin' out.
And I'm callin' for my mother as I pull the pillars down.
It's a different kind of danger and my feet are spinnin' 'round.
Never knew I was a dancer 'til Delilah showed me how.

45 Now I'm dancin' with Delilah and her vision is mine.
Holding on for your call
A different kind of danger in the daylight
I can never let go
Anything to cut you I can find
50 A different kind of danger in the daylight
Can't you let me know?

Strung up, strung out for your love
Hang in, hung up, it's so rough
I'm rung and ringing out
55 Why can't you let me know?

Strung up, strung out for your love.
Hang in, hung up, it's so rough.
I'm rung and ringin' out
Why can't you let me know?

60 It's a different kind of danger and the bells are ringin' out.
And I'm callin' for my mother as I pull the pillars down.

It's a different kind of danger and my feet are spinnin' 'round.
Never knew I was a dancer 'til Delilah showed me how.

It's a different kind of danger and the bells are ringin' out.
And I'm callin' for my mother as I pull the pillars down.   65
It's a different kind of danger and my feet are spinnin' 'round.
Never knew I was a dancer 'til Delilah showed me how.

Too fast for freedom,
Sometimes it all falls down.
These chains never leave me,   70
I keep draggin' them around.

Too fast for freedom,
Sometimes it all falls down.
These chains never leave me,
I keep draggin' them around.   75

—2015

Lady Lamb

Hair to the Ferris Wheel[1]

Take me by the arm to the altar, take me by the collar to the cliff, take me
by the waist to the water, take me by the hair to the ferris wheel, take me by
the wrist to the river, take me by the braid down to my grave. Love is selfish,
love goes tic-toc-tic, love knows jesus, apples & oranges. It's a zoo in your
5   room when you part your lips & you long to kiss like you won't exist come
the morning time, come the sunrise. & all I'd like to do this afternoon is
to drag the mattress up to the roof: hushed tones in the ears of the airplane
next to you. Let's crawl all over one another likes crows on a carcass, like
ants on a crumb starving only starving only for the taste of tongues. Love
10 is selfish, love goes tic-toc-tic, love knows jesus, apples and oranges. Take
me by the arm to the altar, take me by the collar to the cliff, take me by the
waist to the water, take me by the hair to the ferris wheel, take me by the
wrist to the river, take me by the braid down to my grave.

—2013

---

1   Author Aly Spaltro (Lady Lamb) employs this prose-poetry form for these lyrics on her
website.

Margot & the Nuclear So and So's

Real Naked Girls

Real naked girls
You could go around the world but I've brought them to you
They have real naked skin
There's a priest on your shoulder don't bother with him
'Cause this skin belongs to you   5
So use it as you choose
Oh your blues

There was dark crimson blood
It had covered the carpets, the screams were distorted
And that old Christian judge   10
Gave out fifty to life like he was handing out chocolate
But it's too late to flee
But you can help me breathe
Through this gruesome scene
Gruesome   15

But it's too late to flee
But you can help me breathe
Through this gruesome scene
Gruesome scene
Gruesome   20

—2008

Mountain Goats

Moon Over Goldsboro[1]

I went down to the gas station
For no particular reason
Heard the screams from the high school
It's football season

5   Empty lot the station faces
Will probably be there forever
I climbed over the four-foot fence
I was trying to sever the tether

Moon in the sky
10   Cold as a stone
Spend each night in your arms
Always wake up alone

I laid down in the weeds
It was a real cold night
15   I was happy 'till the overnight attendant
Switched on the floodlight

Walking home, I was talking to you under my breath
Saying things I would never say directly
I heard a siren on the highway up ahead
20   Kinda wished they'd come and get me

Frost on the sidewalk
White as a bone
Tried to get close to you again
Always wake up alone

25   And as I was crossing our doorstep
I hesitated just a moment there

---

1   We reprint the version of this song printed as a poem in *Measure: A Review of Formal Poetry* (Volume 7, Issue 2).

Remembered the day we moved into our small house
'Till the vision got too vivid to bear

You were almost asleep
Halfway undressed
I lay right down next to you   30
Held your head against my chest

And a guy with any kind of courage
Would maybe stop to think the matter through
Maybe hold you still and raise the question   35
Instead of blindly holding onto you

But we crank up the heat
And you giggle and moan
Spend all night in the company of ghosts
Always wake up alone   40

—2006

Nas

NY State of Mind

Yeah, yeah
Ayo, black, it's time, word (Word, it's time, man)
It's time, man (Aight, man, begin)
Straight out the fucking dungeons of rap
5 Where fake niggaz don't make it back

Rappers I monkey flip em with the funky rhythm I be kickin'
Musician, inflictin' composition
of pain I'm like Scarface sniffin cocaine
Holdin a M-16, see with the pen I'm extreme, now
10 Bulletholes left in my peepholes
I'm suited up in street clothes
Hand me a nine and I'll defeat foes
Y'all know my steelo with or without the airplay
I keep some E&J, sittin' bent up in the stairway
15 Or either on the corner bettin' Grants with the cee-lo champs
Laughin' at baseheads, tryin' to sell some broken amps
G-Packs get off quick, forever niggaz talk shit
Reminiscin' about the last time the Task Force flipped
Niggaz be runnin' through the block shootin'
20 Time to start the revolution, catch a body head for Houston
Once they caught us off guard, the Mac-10 was in the grass and
I ran like a cheetah with thoughts of an assassin
Pick the Mac up, told brothers, "Back up," the Mac spit
Lead was hittin' niggaz, one ran, I made him backflip
25 Heard a few chicks scream my arm shook, couldn't look
Gave another squeeze heard it click yo, my shit is stuck
Try to cock it, it wouldn't shoot now I'm in danger
Finally pulled it back and saw three bullets caught up in the chamber
So now I'm jettin' to the building lobby
30 and it was filled with children probably couldn't see as high as I be
(So whatchu sayin'?) It's like the game ain't the same
Got younger niggaz pullin' the triggers bringin' fame to they name
and claim some corners, crews without guns are goners
In broad daylight, stickup kids, they run up on us
35 Fo'-fives and gauges, Macs in fact

Same niggaz'll catch a back to back, snatchin' yo' cracks in black
There was a snitch on the block gettin' niggaz knocked
So hold your stash 'til the coke price drop
I know this crackhead, who said she gotta smoke nice rock
And if it's good she'll bring ya customers in measuring pots, but yo   40
You gotta slide on a vacation
Inside information keeps large niggaz erasin' and they wives basin'
It drops deep as it does in my breath
I never sleep, cause sleep is the cousin of death
Beyond the walls of intelligence, life is defined   45
I think of crime when I'm in a New York state of mind

New York state of mind
New York state of mind
New York state of mind
New York state of mind   50

Be havin' dreams that I'm a gangster—drinkin' Moets, holdin' Tecs
Makin' sure the cash came correct then I stepped
Investments in stocks, sewin' up the blocks
to sell rocks, winnin' gunfights with mega cops
But just a nigga, walkin' with his finger on the trigger   55
Make enough figures until my pockets get bigger
I ain't the type of brother made for you to start testin'
Give me a Smith and Wesson I'll have niggaz undressin'
Thinkin' of cash flow, buddah and shelter
Whenever frustrated I'm a hijack Delta   60
In the PJs, my blend tape plays, bullets are strays
Young bitches is grazed each block is like a maze
Full of black rats trapped, plus the Island is packed
From what I hear in all the stories when my peoples come back, black
I'm livin' where the nights is jet black   65
The fiends fight to get crack I just max, I dream I can sit back
and lamp like Capone, with drug scripts sewn
Or the legal luxury life, rings flooded with stones, homes
I got so many rhymes I don't think I'm too sane
Life is parallel to Hell but I must maintain   70
and be prosperous, though we live dangerous
cops could just arrest me, blamin' us, we're held like hostages
It's only right that I was born to use mics
and the stuff that I write, is even tougher than dice

75 I'm takin' rappers to a new plateau, through rap slow
    My rhymin' is a vitamin held without a capsule
    The smooth criminal on beat breaks
    Never put me in your box if your shit eats tapes
    The city never sleeps, full of villains and creeps
80 That's where I learned to do my hustle had to scuffle with freaks
    I'm a addict for sneakers, twenties of buddah and bitches with beepers
    In the streets I can greet ya, about blunts I teach ya
    Inhale deep like the words of my breath
    I never sleep, 'cause sleep is the cousin of death
85 I lay puzzle as I backtrack to earlier times
    Nothing's equivalent, to the New York state of mind

    New York state of mind
    New York state of mind
    New York state of mind
90 New York state of mind

                                                    —1994

The National

Mistaken for Strangers[1]

You have to do it running but you do everything that they ask you to
cause you don't mind seeing yourself in a picture
as long as you look faraway, as long as you look removed
showered and blue-blazered, fill yourself with quarters
showered and blue-blazered, fill yourself with quarters   5

You get mistaken for strangers by your own friends
when you pass them at night under the silvery, silvery citibank lights
arm in arm in arm and eyes and eyes glazing under
oh you wouldn't want an angel watching over
surprise, surprise they wouldn't wannna watch
another uninnocent, elegant fall into the unmagnificent lives of adults   10

Make up something to believe in your heart of hearts
so you have something to wear on your sleeve of sleeves
so you swear you just saw a feathery woman
carry a blindfolded man through the trees
showered and blue-blazered, fill yourself with quarters   15
showered and blue-blazered, fill yourself with quarters

You get mistaken for strangers by your own friends
when you pass them at night under the silvery, silvery citibank lights
arm in arm in arm and eyes and eyes glazing under
oh you wouldn't want an angel watching over   20
surprise, surprise they wouldn't wannna watch
another uninnocent, elegant fall into the unmagnificent lives of adults

You get mistaken for strangers by your own friends
when you pass them at night under the silvery, silvery citibank lights
arm in arm in arm and eyes and eyes glazing under
oh you wouldn't want an angel watching over   25
surprise, surprise they wouldn't wannna watch
another uninnocent, elegant fall into the unmagnificent lives of adults

—2007

---

1   The lyrics for the following two songs were provided by the artist.

Green Gloves

Falling out of touch with all my
friends are somewhere getting wasted,
hope they're staying glued together,
I have arms for them.

5   Take another sip of them,
it floats around and takes me over
like a little drop of ink in a glass of water

Get inside their clothes
with my green gloves
10   watch their videos, in their chairs.
Get inside their beds
with my green gloves
Get inside their heads, love their loves.

Cinderella through the room
15   I glide and swan cause I'm the best slow dancer
in the universe

Falling out of touch with all my
friends are somewhere getting wasted,
hope they're staying glued together,
20   I have arms for them.

Get inside their clothes
with my green gloves
watch their videos, in their chairs.
Get inside their beds
25   with my green gloves
Get inside their heads, love their loves.

Now I hardly know them
and I'll take my time
I'll carry them over, and I'll make them mine.

30   Get inside their clothes
with my green gloves
watch their videos, in their chairs.
Get inside their beds
with my green gloves
35   Get inside their heads, love their loves.

—2007

Neutral Milk Hotel

The King of Carrot Flowers, Part One[1]

When you were young you were the king of carrot flowers and how you built
a tower tumbling thru the trees in holy rattlesnakes that fell all around your
feet and your mom would stick a fork right into daddys shoulder and dad
would throw the garbage all across the floor as we would lay and learn what
each other's bodies were for and this is the room one afternoon i knew i could   5
love you and from above you how i sank into your soul into that secret place
where no one dares to go and your mom would drink until she was no longer
speaking and dad would dream of all the different ways to die each one a little
more than he could dare to try

—1998

---

1   We reprint these lyrics from the liner notes, where they appear in this prose-poetry form.

Radiohead

Kid A

I slip away
I slipped on a little white lie

We've got heads on sticks
You've got ventriloquists
5 We've got heads on sticks
You've got ventriloquists

Standing in the shadows at the end of my bed
Standing in the shadows at the end of my bed
Standing in the shadows at the end of my bed
10 Standing in the shadows at the end of my bed

The rats and children follow me out of town
The rats and children follow me out of their homes
Come on kids

—2000

Sharon Van Etten

Love More

Chained
To the wall of our room
Yeah you chained me like a dog in our room
I thought that's how it was
I thought that we were fine   5
Then the day was night
You were high you were high when I was doomed and dying for
With no life
With no light

Tied to my bed   10
I was younger then I had nothing to spend
But time on you
But it made me love it made me love it made me love more
It made me love it made me love it made me love more

Do what you said, the words she said left out   15
Over into the sky where I'll soon fly
And she took the time
To believe in, to believe in
What she said

She made me love she made me love she made me love more   20
She made me love she made me love she made me love more
More
More
More
More   25
More
More
More
More
More   30
More

—2010

Sleater-Kinney

Call the Doctor[1]

they want to socialize you
they want to purify you
they want to dignify, and analyze and terrorize you

this is love and you can't make it
5 in a formula or shake me
i'm your monster i'm not like you
all your life is written for you

(look out they want what you know
steal a kid break a heart steal the show
10 Peel back the skin see what's there
i'll never show you what's in here)

your life is good for one thing
you're messing with what's sacred
they want to simplify your needs and likes
15 to sterilize you

this is love and you can't make it
in a formula or break it
i'm your monster i'm just like you
all my life is right before you

20 (don't need you to explain the pain
i can prove to you it's all fake
she's dead but she can stand she can walk
call the doctor miracle she can talk)

call the doctor
25 call the doctor
call the doctor
call the doctor
call the doctor

---

1   We reprint these lyrics from the liner notes.

call the doctor
call the doctor
call the doctor   30

this is love and you can't break it
in a formula or make me
i'm no monster i'm just like you
all my life is right before me   35

(this is not really me at all
stunt girl daring twirls watch me fall
carbon copy same body different hearts
can't tell anymore the real parts)

—1996

The Smiths

Ask[1]

Shyness is nice, but
Shyness can stop you
From doing all the things in life
That you'd like to
5 So, if there's something you'd
like to try
If there's something you'd
like to try
ASK ME - I WON'T SAY "NO" - HOW COULD I?

10 Coyness is nice, but
Coyness can stop you
from saying all the things in
Life that you'd want to
So, if there's something you'd
15 like to try
If there's something that you'd
like to try
ASK ME - I WON'T SAY "NO" - HOW COULD I?

Spending warm, Summer days indoors
20 Writing frightening verse
To a buck-toothed girl in Luxembourg

ASK ME, ASK ME, ASK ME
ASK ME, ASK ME, ASK ME

Because if it's not Love
25 Then it's the Bomb
That will bring us together

—1986

---

1   We reprint these lyrics from the liner notes. As sung on "Louder than Bombs," the song
     ends with the lines "Nature is a language—can't you read?"

St. Vincent

Cruel

Bodies, can't you see what everybody wants from you?

Forgive the kids, for they don't know how to live
Run the alleys, casually

Cruel
Cruel

Bodies, can't you see what everybody wants from you?
For you could want that, too

They could take or leave you
So they took you, and they left you
How could they be casually

Cruel
Cruel
Cruel
Cruel

Bodies, can't you see what everybody wants from you?
If you could want that, too, then you'll be happy

You were the one waving flares in the air
So they could see you
And they were a zephyr
Blowing past ya
Blowing fastly so they can't see ya

Cruel
Cruel
Cruel
Cruel
Cruel
Cruel
Cruel
Cruel

—2011

Stars

Personal

Wanted
Single F
under 33
must enjoy the sun
5 must enjoy the sea
Sought by single M
Mrs. Destiny
Send photo to address
is it you and me?

10 Reply to single M
My name is Caroline,
cell phone number here
call if you have the time
28 and bored
15 grieving over loss
sorry to be heavy
but heavy is the cost
heavy is the cost

Reply to Caroline
20 Thanks so much for response
These things can be scary
Not always what you want
How about a drink?
The St. Jude Club at noon?
25 I'll phone you first I guess
I hope I see you soon

I never got your name
I assume you're 33
Your voice it sounded kind
30 I hope that you like me
When you see my face
I hope that you don't laugh

I'm not a film-star beauty
I sent a photograph
I hope that you don't laugh   35

Note to single M
Why did you not show up?
I waited for an hour
I finally gave up
I thought once that I saw you   40
I thought that you saw me
I guess we'll never meet now
It wasn't meant to be
It wasn't meant to be
I was sure you saw me   45
but it wasn't meant to be

Wanted
Single F
under 33
must enjoy the sun   50
must enjoy the sea
Sought by single M
nothing too heavy
send photo to address

Is it you or me?   55
Is it you or me?
Is it you or me?
Is it you or me?
[repeats]

                                               —2007

Sun Kil Moon

Ben's My Friend[1]

woke up this mornin' august 3rd it's been a pretty slow and uneventful sum-
mer went to visit a friend in santa fe went to new orleans and went to see my
family woke up this mornin' and it occurred i needed 1 more track to finish up
my record but i was feelin' out of fuel and uninspired laid in my bed too long
5   a little down a little tired i met my girl and we walked down to union street i
was scattered and my head was in a bunch of places i bought a 350 dollar pair
of lampshades and we ate at perry's and i ordered crab cakes blue crab cakes
she said i seem distracted and asked what was goin' on with me i said i can't
explain it and it's a middle-aged thing she said okay and ate her eggs benedict
10   and i looked at the walls cluttered with sports bar shit got on the phone and i
called my mother i called my father i talked a little bit with my sister she's got
a new boyfriend, he's a deer hunter and she's gettin' used to venison and my
dad's still fightin' with his girlfriend about his flirtin' with the girls at panera
bread my mom was good but sounded out of breath i worry so much about
15   her i worry to death the other night i went and saw the postal service ben's my
friend but gettin' there was the worst tryin' to park and gettin' up the hill and
find a spot amongst the drunk kids starin' at their cells stand at the back of
the crowd of 8,000 i thought of ben and when i met him in 2000 at a festival
in spain we were on the small stage then i didn't know his last name now he's
20   singin' at the greek and he's bustin' moves and my legs were hurtin' and my
feet were too i called him later, said i'll skip the backstage hi/bye but thanks
for the nice music and all the exercise and we laughed and it was alright there's
a thin line between a middle-aged guy with a backstage pass and a guy with
a gut hangin' around like a jack-ass everybody there was 20 years younger at
25   least i'll leave it at this not my fondest memory i carried my legs back down
the hill gave my backstage passes to two cute asian girls and drove to my place
near tahoe i got in my hot tub and thought well that's how it goes and it was
quiet and i was listenin' to the crickets and ben's still out there, sellin' lotsa
tickets and though i'm content there's a tinge of competitiveness but ben's my
30   friend and i know he gets it within a couple of days my meltdown passed back
to the studio doin' 12 hour shifts singin' a song about one thing or an another
another day behind the microphone this summer this tenderloin summer

—2014

---

1   We reprint these lyrics from the liner notes, where they appear in this prose-poetry form.

Talking Heads

Heaven[1]

Everyone is trying to get to the bar.
The name of the bar, the bar is called Heaven.
The band in Heaven plays my favorite song.
They play it once again, they play it all night long.

Heaven is a place where nothing ever happens.   5
Heaven is a place where nothing ever happens.

There is a party, everyone is there.
Everyone will leave at exactly the same time.
It's hard to imagine that nothing at all
could be so exciting, could be so much fun.   10

Heaven is a place where nothing ever happens.
Heaven is a place where nothing ever happens.

When this kiss is over it will start again.
It will not be any different, it will be exactly the same.
It's hard to imagine that nothing at all   15
could be so exciting, could be so much fun

Heaven is a place where nothing ever happens.
Heaven is a place where nothing ever happens.

—1979

---

1   We reprint these lyrics from the liner notes.

Toadies

Possum Kingdom

Make up your mind
Decide to walk with me
Around the lake tonight
Around the lake tonight
5   By my side
By my side

I'm not gonna lie
I'll not be a gentleman
Behind the boathouse
10 I'll show you my dark secret

I'm not gonna lie
I want you for mine
My blushing bride
My lover, be my lover, yeah

15 Don't be afraid
I didn't mean to scare you
So help me Jesus

I can promise you
You'll stay as beautiful
20 With dark hair
And soft skin
Forever
Forever

Make up your mind
25 Make up your mind
And I'll promise you
I will treat you well
My sweet angel
So help me Jesus

Give it up to me   30
Give it up to me
Do you wanna be
My angel
Give it up to me
Give it up to me   35
Do you wanna be
My angel
Give it up to me
Give it up to me
Do you wanna be   40
My angel
So help me

Be my angel
Be my angel
Be my angel   45

Do you wanna die?
Do you wanna die?
Do you wanna die?
Do you wanna die?
Do you wanna die?   50
Do you wanna die?
Do you wanna die?
Do you wanna die?

Well I promise you
I will treat you well   55
My sweet angel
So help me Jesus
Jesus
Jesus
Jesus   60

—1993

Weezer

Tired of Sex

I'm tired, so tired
I'm tired of having sex (so tired)
I'm spread so thin
I don't know who I am (who I am)

5 Monday night I'm making Jen
Tuesday night I'm making Lynn
Wednesday night I'm making Catherine
Oh, why can't I be making love come true?

I'm beat, beet red
10 Ashamed of what I said (what I said)
Oh I'm sorry, here I go
I know I'm a sinner
But I can't say no (say no)

Thursday night I'm making Denise
15 Friday night I'm making Therese
Saturday night I'm making Louise
Oh, why can't I be making love come true?

Tonight I'm down on my knees
Tonight I'm begging you please
20 Tonight, tonight, oh please
Oh, why can't I be making love come true?

—1998

More Poems in Conversation

On the Æolian Harp

Slavery

Metapoetics: The Example of Birdsong

Animals

Nature and Eco-Poetics

"Dialect" and Spoken Language

Parents, Children, Families, "Home"

Realism v. Romance

Intimates and Strangers

More Experiments in Dramatic Lyric

Love and "Love Songs"

Ideas of the Beyond

Self and Society

Breakups

Genders and Sexualities

Some "Popular" Poets

What Is Poetry?

Poets and songwriters have explored diverse answers to this question for centuries. Compare how the poems in this section conceive of poetry. Consider questions like these: How does each poem understand its purpose(s)? What does each consider to be apt subject matter for a poem? What kinds of language does each poem employ? How does each poem imagine its speaker and its possible audiences?

Glossary

Accent: in poetry the natural emphasis (stress) speakers place on a syllable.

Accentual Verse: poetry in which a line is measured only by the number of accents or stresses, not by the number of syllables.

Accentual-Syllabic Verse: poetry in which a line is measured by the number of syllables and by the pattern of accented (stressed) and unaccented (unstressed) syllables. This is the most common metrical system in traditional English verse.

Aesthetes: members of a late nineteenth-century movement that valued "art for art's sake," that is, for its purely aesthetic qualities as opposed to other values such as moral content or intellectual stimulation.

Allegory: a narrative with both a literal meaning and a secondary, often symbolic, meaning or meanings. Allegory frequently employs personification to give concrete embodiment to abstract concepts or entities, such as feelings or personal qualities. It may also present one set of characters or events in the guise of another, using implied parallels for the purposes of satire or political comment.

Alliteration: the grouping of words with the same initial consonant (e.g., "break, blow, burn, and make me new"). See also *assonance* and *consonance*.

Alliterative Verse: poetry that employs alliteration of stressed syllables in each line as its chief structural principle.

Allusion: a reference, often indirect or unidentified, to a person, thing, or event. A reference in one literary work to another literary work, whether to its content or its form, also constitutes an allusion.

Ambiguity: an "opening" of language created by the writer to allow for multiple meanings or differing interpretations. In literature, ambiguity may be deliberately employed by the writer to enrich meaning; this differs from any unintentional, unwanted ambiguity in non-literary prose.

Anachronism: accidentally or intentionally attributing people, things, ideas, and events to historical periods in which they do not and could not possibly belong.

Analogy: a broad term that refers to our processes of noting similarities among things or events. Specific forms of analogy in poetry include *simile* and *metaphor*.

Anapest: a metrical foot containing two unstressed syllables followed by one stressed syllable: xx / (e.g., underneath, intervene).

Antistrophe: from Greek drama, the chorus's countermovement or reply to an initial movement (*strophe*). See *ode*.

Apostrophe: a figure of speech (a *trope*; see *figures of speech*) in which a writer directly addresses an object—or a dead or absent person—as if the imagined audience was actually listening.

Archetype: in literature and mythology, a recurring idea, symbol, motif, character, or place. To some scholars and psychologists, an archetype represents universal human thought-patterns or experiences.

Assonance: the repetition of identical or similar vowel sounds in stressed syllables in which the surrounding consonants are different: for example, "shame" and "fate"; "gale" and "cage"; or the long "i" sounds in "Beside the pumice isle...."

Atmosphere: see *tone*.

Aubade: a poem that greets or laments the arrival of dawn.

Ballad: a folk song, or a poem originally recited or sung to an audience, which tells a dramatic story based on legend or history.

Ballad Stanza: a quatrain typically composed of alternating lines of iambic tetrameter and iambic trimeter that rhyme *abcb* or sometimes *abab*. See *hymn meter*.

Baroque: powerful and heavily ornamented in style. "Baroque" is a term from the history of visual art and music sometimes also applied to literary styles.

Bathos: an anticlimactic effect brought about by a writer's descent from an elevated subject or tone to the ordinary or trivial.

Black Comedy: humor based on death, horror, or any incongruously macabre subject matter.

Blank Verse: unrhymed lines of iambic pentameter. (A form introduced to English verse by Henry Howard, Earl of Surrey, in his translation of parts of Virgil's *Aeneid* in 1547.)

Bombast: inappropriately inflated or grandiose language.

Broken Rhyme: a kind of rhyme in which a multisyllablic word splits at the end of a line and continues onto the next, creating an end rhyme with the split syllable.

Burlesque: satire of a particularly exaggerated sort, which ridicules its subject by emphasizing its vulgar or ridiculous aspects.

Caesura: a pause or break in a line of verse occurring where a phrase, clause, or sentence ends, and indicated in scansion by the mark ||. If it occurs in the middle of the line, it is known as a "medial" caesura.

Canon: in literature, those works commonly accepted as culturally authoritative or important. In practice, "canonical" texts or authors are those that are discussed most frequently by scholars and taught most frequently in university courses.

Canto: a sub-section of a long (usually epic) poem.

Canzone: a short song or poem, with stanzas of equal length and an *envoy*.

Caricature: an exaggerated and simplified depiction of character; the reduction of a personality to one or two telling traits at the expense of all other nuances and contradictions.

Carpe Diem: Latin phrase often translated as "seize the day." The idea of enjoying the moment is a common one in Renaissance love poetry. See, for example, Marvell's "To His Coy Mistress."

Catalexis: the omission of unstressed syllables from a line of verse. (Such a line is referred to as "catalectic.") In iambic verse the first syllable of the line is usually omitted; in trochaic, the last. For example, in the first stanza of Housman's "To an Athlete Dying Young" the third line is catalectic: i.e., it has dropped the first, unstressed syllable called for by the poem's iambic tetrameter form: "The time you won your town the race / We chaired you through the market-place; / Man and boy stood cheering by, / And home we brought you shoulder-high."

Chiasmus: a *figure of speech* (a scheme) that reverses word order in successive parallel clauses. If the word order is A-B-C in the first clause, it becomes C-B-A in the second, as in Donne's line "She is all states, and all princes, I" ("The Sun Rising").

Classical: originating in or relating to ancient Greek or Roman culture. The term also typically implies a strong sense of formal order.

Common Measure: see *hymn meter*.

Conceit: an unusually elaborate metaphor or simile that extends beyond its original *tenor and vehicle* in a particular poem to become a key analogy for the larger poem (see, for example, Donne's "The Flea"). Ingenious or fanciful images and comparisons were especially popular with the *metaphysical poets* of the seventeenth century, giving rise to the term "metaphysical conceit."

Concrete Poetry: an experimental form, most popular during the 1950s and 1960s, in which the layout of printed type creates a visual image of the poem's key words or ideas. See also *pattern poetry*.

Confessional Poetry: a term initially coined to describe the work of Robert Lowell. The first-person speakers of confessional poetry explore intensely personal subjects that often transgress social taboos about self-exposure. For Lowell and the initial confessional poets (also see Sylvia Plath and Anne Sexton), notable subjects included such topics as mental illness, family disorder and trauma, alcoholism, and other subject matter crossing social boundaries of propriety and intimacy. Confessional poems are not simply direct records of personal experience, although readers often relate to them in this way; they are crafted forms of artistic performance. Social ideas about what might be "transgressive" subject matter change at different points in history.

Connotation: the implied, often unspoken meaning(s) of a given word, as distinct from its denotation, or literal meaning. Connotations may have highly emotional undertones and are usually culturally specific.

Consonance: the pairing of words with similar initial and ending consonants, but with different vowel sounds (live/love, wander/wonder). See also *alliteration*.

Convention: aesthetic approach, technique, or practice accepted as characteristic and appropriate for a particular form. It is a convention of certain sorts of plays, for example, that the characters speak in blank verse, of other sorts of plays that characters speak in rhymed couplets, and of still other sorts of dramatic performances that characters frequently break into song to express their feelings.

Couplet: a pair of rhyming lines, usually in the same meter. If they form a complete unit of thought and are grammatically complete, the lines are known as a closed couplet. See also *heroic couplet*.

Dactyl: a metrical foot containing one strong stress followed by two weak stresses: / xx (e.g., muttering, helplessly). A minor form known as "double dactyls" makes use of this meter for humorous purposes, e.g., "jiggery pokery" or "higgledy piggledy."

Defamiliarization: artistic effect designed to make language strange in order to open new doors of perception. The term originated with Russian formalist Viktor Shklovsky in 1917. Artistic effects of defamiliarization block routine and clichéd responses to language and art, pushing readers out of automatic and habitual behaviors and into new arenas of insight.

Denotation: see *connotation*.

Dialogue: words spoken by characters to one another. (When a character is addressing him or herself or the audience directly, the words spoken are referred to as a *soliloquy*.)

Diction: word choice. Diction in a literary work (for example, slang idioms, formal speech, scientific or political terminology, and so on) contributes significantly to the tone and effect of the text.

Didacticism: aesthetic approach emphasizing moral instruction.

Dimeter: a poetic line containing two metrical feet.

Dirge: a song or poem that mourns someone's death. See also *elegy* and *lament*.

Dissonance: harsh, unmusical sounds or rhythms that writers may use deliberately to achieve certain effects. Also known as cacophony.

Dramatic Irony: this form of *irony* occurs when an audience has access to information not available to the character.

Dramatic Monologue: a poem in which a single speaker typically addresses a silent listener. The speaker may be an historical personage (as in some of Robert Browning's dramatic monologues), a figure drawn from myth or legend (as in some of Tennyson's), or an entirely imagined figure (as in Webster's "A Castaway").

Dub Poetry: a form of protest poetry originating in Jamaica, with its roots in dance rhythms, especially reggae, and often accompanied in performance by drums and music. See also *rap*.

Duple Foot: a duple foot of poetry has two syllables. The possible duple forms are *iamb* (in which the stress is on the second of the two syllables), *trochee* (in which the stress is on the first of the two syllables), *spondee* (in which both are stressed equally), and *pyrrhic* (in which both syllables are unstressed).

Eclogue: now generally used simply as an alternative name for a pastoral poem. In classical times and in the early modern period, however, an eclogue (or *idyll*) was a specific type of pastoral poem—a dialogue or dramatic monologue involving rustic characters. (The other main sub-genre of the pastoral was the *georgic*.)

Elegiac Stanza: a quatrain of iambic pentameters rhyming *abab*, often used in poems meditating on death or sorrow. The best-known example is Thomas Gray's "Elegy Written in a Country Churchyard."

Elegy: a poem that formally mourns the death of a particular person (e.g., Tennyson's "In Memoriam") or in which the poet meditates on other serious subjects (e.g., Gray's "Elegy"). See also *dirge*.

Elision: omitting or suppressing a letter or an unstressed syllable at the beginning or end of a word, so that a line of verse may conform to a given metrical scheme. For example, the three syllables at the beginning of Shakespeare's Sonnet 129 are reduced to two by the omission of the first vowel: "Th' expense of spirit in a waste of shame." See also *syncope*.

Ellipsis: the omission of a word or words necessary for the complete grammatical construction of a sentence, but not necessary for our understanding of the sentence.

End-Rhyme: see *rhyme*.

End-Stopped: technical term for a line of poetry that ends with punctuation such as a comma or period, an effect that flags the line as a grammatical unit of meaning. For example, in this couplet from Pope's "Essay on Criticism," both lines are end-stopped: "A little learning is a dangerous thing; / Drink deep, or taste not the Pierian spring." Compare with *enjambment*.

746 POEMS: A CONCISE ANTHOLOGY

Enjambment: technical term for the "running-on" of the sense from one line of poetry to the next, with no pause created by punctuation (contrast *end-stopped*). Poets use enjambment to create many effects of meaning. For example, enjambed lines can carry one implication at the line break and then acquire an additional meaning once the following lines complete the utterance. Some poets use enjambment to enhance the feeling of conversational speech.

Envoy (Envoi): a stanza or half-stanza that forms the conclusion of certain French poetic forms, such as the *sestina* or the ballade. It often sums up or comments upon what has gone before.

Epic: a lengthy narrative poem, often divided into books and sub-divided into cantos. Epic generally celebrates heroic deeds or events, often in a lofty and grand style, as in Spenser's *The Faerie Queene* and Milton's *Paradise Lost*.

Epic Simile: an elaborate simile, developed at such length that the *vehicle* of the comparison momentarily displaces the *tenor* or primary subject with which it is being compared. See *tenor and vehicle*.

Epigram: a very short poem, sometimes in closed couplet form, characterized by pointed wit.

Epigraph: a quotation placed at the beginning of a work to indicate the theme.

Epithalamion: a poem celebrating a wedding. The best-known example in English is Edmund Spenser's "Epithalamion" (1595).

Epode: the third part of an *ode*, following the *strophe* and *antistrophe*.

Ethos: the perceived character, trustworthiness, or credibility of a writer or narrator.

Euphemism: mode of expression through which aspects of reality considered to be vulgar, crudely physical, or unpleasant are referred to indirectly rather than named explicitly. A variety of euphemisms exist for the processes of urination and defecation; *passed away* is often used as a euphemism for *died*.

Euphony: pleasant, musical sounds or rhythms—the opposite of *dissonance*.

Eye Rhyme: see *rhyme*.

Feminine Rhyme: see *rhyme*.

Figures of Speech: deliberate, highly concentrated uses of language to achieve particular purposes or effects. There are two kinds of figures: *schemes* and *tropes*. Schemes involve changes in word-sound and word-order, such as *alliteration* and *chiasmus*. Tropes play on our understandings of words to extend, alter, or transform meaning, as in *metaphor* and *personification*.

Fixed Forms: poems that follow prescribed rules of pattern in meter, rhyme, number of lines per stanza, and so on. Examples include the *sonnet, haiku, ottava rima, sestina,* and *villanelle*. (Also called "closed forms." "Fixed" or "closed" forms contrast with "free" or "open" forms.)

Found Language or Found Poetry: the incorporation or reappropriation of language from another source (hence, "found," as in "found elsewhere than in this text you are reading") into a poem. Found language is often aggressively mundane, as from a pamphlet, product label, or internet blog, rather than from a "high-culture" source like a work of canonical literature. In the latter case, we often use the term *allusion*: the fact of two different terms depending on whether the source is from "high" rather than "popular" or "low" culture is significant in itself, and poets indeed often incorporate found language to challenge boundaries between "high" and "low" culture and to dismantle the putative differences between original and appropriated language. Kenneth Goldsmith's *Day* is a poem composed entirely of found language.

Free Verse: poetry that does not adhere to any regular or prescribed patterns of meter, line length, or rhyme scheme. (See *fixed forms*.) Free verse is not formless; however, it rejects traditional fixed forms in order to carve out new shapes and new rhythms often of the poet's own design. (Free-verse forms are also called "open forms").

Genre: a term for the classifications or types of literary work. Multiple genre terms apply to any individual text. For example, works in the genres of poetry, drama, and prose fiction also fall under sub-genres such as epic, comedy, romance, fantasy, and so on.

Georgic: (from Virgil's *Georgics*) a poem that celebrates the natural wealth of the countryside and advises how to cultivate and live in harmony with it.

Ghazal: derived from Persian and Indian precedents, the ghazal presents a series of thoughts in closed couplets usually joined by a simple rhyme scheme such as: *a/a b/a c/a d/a, ab bb cb eb fb*, etc.

Gothic: in architecture and the visual arts, a term used to describe styles prevalent from the twelfth to the fourteenth centuries, but in literature a term used to describe work with a sinister or grotesque tone that seeks to evoke a sense of terror.

Grotesque: literature characterized by a focus on extreme or distorted aspects of human behavior or psychology.

Haiku: a Japanese poetic form composed of three unrhymed lines typically of five, seven, and five syllables presenting a precise, concentrated image.

Heptameter: a line containing seven metrical feet.

Heroic Couplet: a pair of rhymed iambic pentameters, a form common in seventeenth- and eighteenth-century poems and plays on heroic subjects.

Hexameter: a line containing six metrical feet.

Horatian Ode: inspired by the work of the Roman poet Horace, an ode that is usually calm and meditative in tone and homostrophic (i.e., having regular stanzas) in form. Keats's odes are English examples.

Hymn: a song whose theme is usually religious, in praise of divinity. Literary hymns may praise more secular subjects.

Hymn Meter: the meter of traditional church hymns, typically a quatrain form with alternating four-stress and three-stress iambic lines that rhyme *abab* or *abcb*. A form of *ballad stanza*; also called "common measure."

Hyperbole: a *figure of speech* (a *trope*) that deliberately exaggerates or inflates meaning to achieve particular effects, such as the irony in A.E. Housman's claim (from "Terence, This Is Stupid Stuff") that "malt does more than Milton can / To justify God's ways to man."

Iamb: the most common metrical foot in English verse, containing one unstressed syllable followed by a stressed syllable: x / (e.g., between, achieve).

Idyll: traditionally, a short pastoral poem that idealizes country life, conveying impressions of innocence and happiness.

Image: a representation of a sensory experience or of an object that can be known by the senses.

Imagery: the range of images in a given work.

Imagism: a free-verse, modernist poetic movement that arose in the nineteen-teens to represent emotions or impressions through spare language focused on direct and compressed treatment of the subject. Imagists intended to counter a long tradition of elaborate "poetic" rules, diction, and forms.

Incantation: a chant or recitation of words that are believed to have magical power. A poem can achieve an "incantatory" effect through a compelling rhyme scheme and other repetitive patterns.

Interlocking Rhyme: see *rhyme*.

Internal Rhyme: see *rhyme*.

Intertextuality: the relationships between one literary work and other literary works. A literary work may connect with other works through *allusion*, *parody*, or *satire*, or in a variety of other ways.

Irony: the use of irony draws attention to a gap between what is said and what is meant, or what appears to be true and what is true. Types of irony include verbal irony (which includes *hyberbole*, *litotes*, and *sarcasm*), *dramatic irony*, and structural irony (in which the gap between what is "said" and meant is sustained throughout an entire piece, as when an author makes use of an unreliable narrator or speaker).

Lament: a poem that expresses profound regret or grief either because of a death, or because of the loss of a former, happier state.

Language Poetry: a collective avant-garde movement in poetics that arose in the 1960s and that remains influential today. Language poets countered and overturned familiar ideas about poetry, including the common conception that a poem should present the wisdom or emotional experience of a first-person speaker. Instead, Language poets worked aggressively with the poem's medium—language. They experimented with fragments, digressions, and discontinuities; repetitions; gaps; *found language* from other (often "non-poetic") sources; silence, self-commentary, and instructions (as in Jackson Mac Low, "'Is That Wool Hat My Hat?'"); modes of performance; disrupted communication; and typographically distinct or illegible uses of the page.

Litotes: a *figure of speech* (a *trope*) in which a writer deliberately uses understatement to highlight the importance of an argument or to convey an ironic attitude.

Lyric: today the term "lyric" typically indicates a poem, usually short, expressing an individual speaker's personal feelings or private thoughts. "Lyrics" were originally songs performed with accompaniment on a lyre. Definitions of the term "lyric" have varied substantially at different points in history.

Madrigal: a lyric poem, usually short and focusing on pastoral or romantic themes and often set to music.

Masculine Ending: a metrical line ending on a stressed syllable.

Masculine Rhyme: see *rhyme*. An alternative term is hard landing.

Metaphor: a *figure of speech* (in this case, a *trope*) that compares two unrelated things or actions without the use of "like" or "as."

Metaphysical Poets: a group of seventeenth-century English poets, notably Donne, Cowley, Marvell, and Herbert, who employed unusual, difficult imagery and *conceits* in order to develop intellectual and religious themes. The term was first applied to these writers to criticize their use of philosophical and scientific ideas in poems.

Metonymy: a *figure of speech* (a *trope*), meaning "change of name," in which a writer refers to an object or idea by substituting the name of another object or idea closely associated with it: for example, the substitution of "crown" for monarchy, "the press" for journalism, or "the pen" for writing. *Synecdoche* is a kind of metonymy.

Meter: the pattern of stresses, syllables, and pauses that constitutes the regular rhythm of a line of verse. Poetry in the English language includes, but is not limited to, a long tradition of accentual-syllabic meter. See *accent*, *accentual-syllabic*, *caesura*, *elision*, and *scansion*. For some of the better-known meters, see *iamb*, *trochee*, *dactyl*, *anapest*, and *spondee*. See also *monometer*, *dimeter*, *trimeter*, *tetrameter*, *pentameter*, and *hexameter*.

Mock-Heroic: a style applying the elevated diction and vocabulary of epic poetry to low or ridiculous subjects. An example is Alexander Pope's "The Rape of the Lock."

Modernism: in the history of literature, music, and the visual arts, a movement that began in the early twentieth century, characterized by a thorough-going rejection of then-dominant artistic conventions. Modernist poetry overturned conventions of form, diction, and subject matter.

Monologue: an extended speech by a single speaker or character in a poem or play. Unlike a *soliloquy*, a dramatic monologue has an implied listener.

Monometer: a line containing one metrical foot.

Mood: this can describe the writer's attitude, implied or expressed, toward the subject (see *tone*); or it may refer to the atmosphere that a writer creates in a passage of description or narration.

Motif: pattern formed by the recurrence of an idea, image, action, or plot element throughout a literary work, creating new levels of meaning and strengthening structural coherence. The term comes from music, where it describes recurring melodies or themes. See also *theme*.

Narration: the process of disclosing information, whether fictional or non-fictional.

Neoclassical: term often used to describe literature of the British Restoration and eighteenth century periods, strongly influenced by ancient Greek and Roman models.

Nonsense Verse: light, humorous poetry that contradicts logic, plays with the absurd, and invents words for amusing effects. Lewis Carroll is one of its best-known practitioners.

Octave: also known as "octet," the first eight lines in certain forms of sonnet, notably the *Italian/Petrarchan*, in which the octet rhymes *abbaabba*. See also *sestet* and *sonnet*.

Octosyllabic: a line of poetry with eight syllables, as in iambic tetrameter.

Ode: originally a classical poetic form, used by the Greeks and Romans to convey serious themes. English poetry has evolved three main forms of ode: the Pindaric (imitative of the odes of the Greek poet Pindar); the Horatian (modeled on the work of the Roman writer Horace); and the irregular ode. The Pindaric ode has a tripartite structure of *strophe, antistrophe*, and *epode* (meaning turn, counterturn, and stand), modeled on the songs and movements of the Chorus in Greek drama. The Horatian ode is more personal, reflective, and literary, and employs a pattern of repeated stanzas. The irregular ode, as its name implies, avoids a recurrent stanza pattern, and is sometimes irregular in line length also (for example, Wordsworth's "Ode: Intimations of Immortality").

Onomatopoeia: a *figure of speech* (a scheme) in which a word "imitates" a sound or in which the sound of a word seems to reflect its meaning.

Ottava Rima: an eight-line stanza, usually in iambic pentameter, with the rhyme scheme *abababcc*. For an example, see Yeats's "Sailing to Byzantium."

Oxymoron: a *figure of speech* (a *trope*) in which two words whose meanings seem contradictory are placed together; we see an example in Shakespeare's *Twelfth Night*, when Orsino refers to the "sweet pangs" of love.

Pantoum: linked quatrains in a poem that rhymes *abab*. The second and fourth lines of one stanza are repeated as the first and third lines of the stanza that follows. In the final stanza the pattern is reversed: the second line repeats the third line of the first stanza, the fourth and final line repeats the first line of the first stanza.

Parody: a close, usually mocking imitation of a particular literary work, or of the well-known style of a particular author, in order to expose or magnify weaknesses. Parody is a form of *satire*—that is, humor that may ridicule and scorn its object.

Pastiche: a discourse that borrows or imitates other writers' characters, forms, style, or ideas, sometimes creating something of a literary patchwork. Unlike a *parody*, a pastiche can be intended as a compliment to the original writer.

Pastoral: in general, pertaining to country life; in prose, drama, and poetry, a stylized type of writing that idealizes the lives and innocence of country people, particularly shepherds and shepherdesses. See also *eclogue, georgic, idyll*.

Pastoral Elegy: a poem in which the poet uses the pastoral style to lament the death of a friend, usually represented as a shepherd. Milton's "Lycidas" provides a good example, including its use of such conventions as an invocation of the muse and a procession of mourners.

Pathetic Fallacy: a form of *personification* that attributes human emotions to the natural world: for example, rain clouds "weeping." John Ruskin coined the term in 1856 to describe the common "fallacy" or "falseness" in Western poetry and painting of projecting human feelings onto the external world.

Pathos: the emotional quality of a discourse or its power to appeal to audience emotions, especially feelings of pity or sorrow aroused by images of pain, suffering, or loss.

Pattern Poetry: a predecessor of modern *concrete poetry* in which the shape of the poem on the page is intended to suggest or imitate an aspect of the poem's subject, as in George Herbert's "Easter Wings."

Pentameter: verse containing five metrical feet in a line.

Performance Poetry: poetry composed primarily for oral performance, often very theatrical in nature. See also *dub poetry* and *rap*.

Persona: the assumed identity or "speaking voice" in a literary work. The term "persona" literally means "mask." See *voice*.

Personification: a *figure of speech* (a *trope*), also known as "prosopopoeia," in which a writer refers to inanimate objects, ideas, or non-human animals as if they were human, or creates a human figure to represent an abstract entity such as Philosophy or Peace.

Phoneme: a linguistic term denoting the smallest unit of sound that it is possible for the speaker of a given language to distinguish. The words *fun* and *phone* each have three phonemes, though one has three letters and one has five.

Point of View: the perspective from which the voice of a poem (or other work of literature) speaks. A first-person perspective uses *I* and *me*, whereas a third-person perspective uses *he, she, they*, and so on.

Postmodernism: in literature and the visual arts, a movement influential in the late twentieth and early twenty-first centuries, sometimes now called "literature of the present." With roots in the work of poststructuralist French philosophers such as Jacques Derrida and Michel Foucault, postmodernism is heavily theoretical and self-reflexive. Like modernism, postmodernism embraces difficulty. More broadly, postmodernism rejects "metanarratives" rooted in concepts of absolute truth or value. Postmodernism reacted to modernism and extended its innovations as modernism had done with its own prior traditions.

Prose Poem: a type of poem that uses prose formats (such as paragraphs rather than line breaks or stanzas) yet is written with the kind of attention to language, rhythm, and cadence that characterizes verse.

Prosody: the study and analysis of meter, rhythm, rhyme, stanzaic pattern, and other devices of versification.

Protagonist: the central character in a literary work.

Prothalamion: a wedding song; a term coined by the poet Edmund Spenser, adapted from *epithalamion*.

Pun: a play on words, in which a word with two or more distinct meanings, or two words with similar sounds, may create humorous ambiguities. Also known as "paranomasia."

Pyrrhic: a metrical foot containing two weak stresses.

Quantitative Meter: a metrical system used by Greek and Roman poets, in which a line of verse was measured by the "quantity," or length of sound, of each syllable. A foot was measured in terms of syllables classed as long or short.

Quantity: duration or how long it takes to speak the syllables in a poem, one of the elements of sound that create effect. Thomas Campion's line "There is a Garden in her face" and Thomas Hardy's line "Down their carved names the rain drop ploughs" both contain eight syllables, but Hardy's line takes much longer to say and creates a heavy feeling.

Quatrain: a four-line stanza.

Quintet: a five-line stanza. Sometimes given as "quintain."

Rap: originally a term for informal conversation, "rap" now describes a style of performance poetry that skillfully crafts rhyme, pattern, and beat, often with musical accompaniment, and sometimes improvised. (See Nas and 2Pac in this volume.)

Realism: in literary works, realism is a type of writing that aims to depict real life, often in stark contrast to other modes of writing such as fantasy, romance, and the *gothic*. "Realist" approaches have shifted dramatically from one age to the next, and particular writers have approached ideas about "realism" in highly divergent ways. For example, some have presented photographic-style descriptions of exterior "reality," while others have tried to trace the contours of interior or psychological "reality."

Refrain: one or more words or lines repeated at regular points throughout a poem, often at the end of each stanza or group of stanzas. Sometimes a whole stanza may be repeated to create a refrain, like the chorus in a song.

Rhyme: the repetition of identical or similar sounds, usually in pairs and generally at the ends of metrical lines.

    End Rhyme: a rhyming word or syllable at the end of a line.

    Eye Rhyme: rhyming that pairs words whose spellings are alike but whose pronunciations are different: for example, though/slough.

    Feminine Rhyme: a two-syllable (also known as "double") rhyme. The first syllable is stressed and the second unstressed: for example, hasty/tasty. See also *triple rhyme*.

    Interlocking Rhyme: the repetition of rhymes from one stanza to the next, creating links that add to the poem's continuity and coherence.

    Internal Rhyme: the placement of rhyming words within lines so that at least two words rhyme with each other.

    Masculine Rhyme: a correspondence of sound between the final stressed syllables at the end of two or more lines, as in grieve/leave, ar-rive/sur-vive.

    Slant Rhyme: an imperfect or partial rhyme (also known as "near" or "half" rhyme) in which the consonant sounds of stressed syllables match but the vowel sounds do not, as in spoiled/spilled, taint/stint.

    Triple Rhyme: a three-syllable rhyme in which the first syllable of each rhyme-word is stressed and the other two unstressed, as in lottery/coterie.

    True Rhyme: a rhyme in which everything but the initial consonant matches perfectly in sound and spelling.

Rhyme Royal: a stanza of seven iambic pentameters, with a rhyme-scheme of *ababbcc*. Also known as the Chaucerian stanza, as Chaucer was the first English poet to use this form. See also *septet*.

Rhythm: patterns of sound that exhibit some degree and kind of regularity or repetition played against variations and discernible as a pattern that interests and appeals to the human brain. *Meter* is a subset of rhythm.

Romanticism: a major social and cultural movement, originating in Europe, that shaped much of Western artistic thought in the late eighteenth and nineteenth centuries. Opposing the ideal of controlled, rational order often valued during the Enlightenment, Romanticism in poetry and other arts emphasized spontaneous self-expression, emotion, and personal experience and privileged the "natural" over the conventional or the artificial.

Rondeau: a 15-line poem, generally octosyllabic, with only two rhymes throughout its three stanzas, and an unrhymed refrain at the end of the ninth and fifteenth lines, repeating part of the opening line.

Sarcasm: a form of *irony* (usually spoken) in which the meaning is conveyed largely by the tone of voice adopted; something said sarcastically is meant to imply its opposite.

Satire: literary work designed to make fun of or seriously criticize its subject.

Scansion: the formal analysis and description of patterns of meter and rhyme in poetry.

Scheme: see *figures of speech*.

Septet: a stanza containing seven lines.

Sestet: a six-line stanza. A sestet forms the second grouping of lines in an *Italian/Petrarchan sonnet*, following the octave. See *sonnet* and *sestina*.

Sestina: an elaborate unrhymed poem with six six-line stanzas and a three-line *envoy*.

Setting: the time, place, and cultural environment in which a story or work takes place.

Simile: a *figure of speech* (a *trope*) which makes an explicit comparison between a particular object and another object or idea that is similar in some (often unexpected) way. A simile always uses "like" or "as" to signal the connection. Compare with *metaphor*.

Soliloquy: in drama, a speech in which a character, usually alone, reveals his or her thoughts, emotions, and/or motivations without being heard by other characters. Hamlet's "To be, or not to be" speech is a famous example.

Sonnet: a highly structured poem, normally written in 14 lines of iambic pentameter. Four major variations of the sonnet include:

Italian/Petrarchan: named for the fourteenth-century Italian poet Petrarch, its octave rhymes *abbaabba*, followed by a sestet rhyming *cdecde, cdcdcd*, or other variants. Usually, a turn in argument takes place between the octave and sestet.

Miltonic: developed by Milton and similar to the Petrarchan in rhyme scheme, but eliminating the turn after the octave, thus giving greater unity to the poem's structure of thought.

Shakespearean: often called the English sonnet, its form includes three quatrains and a couplet. The quatrains rhyme internally but do not interlock: *abab cdcd efef gg*. The turn in argument may occur after the second quatrain, but is usually revealed in the final couplet. Shakespeare's sonnets are the best-known examples.

Spenserian: Edmund Spenser developed the form in his sonnet cycle *Amoretti*. Features three quatrains linked through interlocking rhyme and a separately rhyming couplet: *abab bcbc cdcd ee*.

Spenserian Stanza: a nine-line stanza, with eight iambic pentameters and a concluding 12-syllable line, rhyming *ababbcbcc*.

Spondee: a metrical foot containing two strong stressed syllables: // (e.g., blind mouths).

Sprung Rhythm: a modern variation of *accentual verse*, created by the English poet Gerard Manley Hopkins. Rhythms are determined largely by the number of strong stresses in a line, without regard to the number of unstressed syllables. Hopkins felt that sprung rhythm more closely approximated the natural rhythms of speech than did conventional meter.

Stanza: any lines of verse that are grouped together and separated by a space from other similar groups. In metrical poetry, stanzas share metrical and rhyming patterns; however, stanzas may also be formed on the basis of thought, as in irregular odes. Conventional stanza forms include the *tercet*, the *quatrain*, *rhyme royal*, the *Spenserian stanza*, the *ballad stanza*, and *ottava rima*.

Stress: see *accent*.

Strophe: a *stanza*. In a Pindaric *ode*, the *strophe* is the first stanza, followed by an *antistrophe*, which presents the same metrical pattern and rhyme scheme, and finally by an *epode*, differing in meter from the preceding stanzas. Upon completion of this "triad," the entire sequence can recur.

Style: a distinctive or specific use of language and form.

Sublime: a concept, popular in eighteenth-century England, that sought to capture the qualities of grandeur, power, and awe inherent in or produced by raw nature or great art; higher and loftier than something merely beautiful.

Substitution: a deliberate change from the dominant pattern of stresses in a line of verse to create emphasis or variation. Thus the first line of Shakespeare's sonnet "Shall I compare thee to a summer's day?" is decidedly iambic in meter (x/x/x/x/x/), whereas the second line substitutes a *trochee* (/x) in the opening foot: "Thou art more lovely and more temperate."

Subtext: implied or suggested meaning.

Surrealism: an artistic mode that explores elements from life and nature according to a logic more typical of dreams than waking life. Isolated aspects of surrealist art may create powerful illusions of reality, but the effect of the whole is usually to disturb or question our sense of reality rather than to confirm it.

Syllabic Verse: poetry in which the length of a line is measured solely by the number of syllables, regardless of accents or patterns of stress.

Syllable: one unit of spoken language, as defined by the sound system of a given language. Some syllables consist of a single *phoneme* (e.g., the word *I*, or the first syllable in the word *u*-nity) but others may be made up of several phonemes (as with one-syllable words such as *lengths*, *splurged*, and *through*). By contrast, the much shorter words *ago*, *any*, and *open* each have two syllables.

Symbol: in literature, something that points beyond itself to suggest one or more associated meanings. For example, the image of a rose may call forth associations of love, passion, transience, fragility, youth, and beauty, among others.

Syncope: in poetry, the dropping of a letter or syllable from the middle of a word, as in "trav'ller." Such a contraction allows a line to stay within a metrical scheme. See also *catalexis* and *elision*.

Synecdoche: a kind of *metonymy* in which a writer substitutes the name of a part of something to signify the whole: for example, "sail" for ship or "hand" for a member of the ship's crew.

Syntax: the ordering of words in a sentence.

Tenor and Vehicle: paired terms for two core elements of a metaphor: the thing described or meant (tenor) and the language that conveys that meaning (vehicle). Tenor and vehicle work in complex interaction to create layers of meaning, particularly in poetic language.

Tercet: a group, or stanza, of three lines, often linked by an interlocking rhyme scheme as in *terza rima*. See also *triplet*.

Terza Rima: an arrangement of *tercets* interlocked by a rhyme scheme of *aba bcb cdc ded*, etc., and ending with a couplet that rhymes with the second-last line of the final tercet (for example, *efe, ff*). See, for example, Percy Shelley's "Ode to the West Wind."

Tetrameter: a line of poetry containing four metrical feet.

Theme: in general, an idea explored in a work through character, action, and/or image.

Tone: a text's attitude toward a given subject or audience, expressed through an array of literary devices such as *diction*, *figures of speech*, and rhythmic devices. Compare *mood*.

Tragedy: originally, a serious narrative recounting the downfall of the protagonist, usually a person of high social standing. The term now applies to a wide variety of literary forms in which the tone is predominantly dark and the narrative does not end happily.

Trimeter: verse containing three metrical feet in a line.

Triolet: a French form that requires the poet to work deftly within the constraints of only eight lines and only two rhymes (*abaaabab*). The first line repeats at lines four and seven; the second line repeats in line eight. See *fixed forms.*

Triple Foot: poetic foot of three syllables. The possible varieties of triple foot are the *anapest* (in which two unstressed syllables are followed by a stressed syllable), the *dactyl* (in which a stressed syllable is followed by two unstressed syllables), and the mollossus (in which all three syllables are stressed equally). English poetry tends to use *duple* rhythms (see *iamb* and *trochee)* far more frequently than triple rhythms.

Triplet: a group of three lines with the same end rhyme, much used by eighteenth-century poets to vary or punctuate the flow of couplets. See also *tercet.*

Trochee: a metrical foot containing one strong stress followed by one weak stress.

Trope: any *figure of speech* that plays on our understandings of words to extend, alter, or transform "literal" meaning. Common tropes include *metaphor, simile, personification, hyperbole, metonymy, oxymoron, synecdoche,* and *irony.* See also *figures of speech.*

Turn: (Italian "volta") the point in a sonnet where the mood or argument changes. The turn typically occurs between the octave and sestet, i.e., after the eighth line, or in the final couplet, depending on the kind of sonnet.

Unreliable Narrator: a narrator whose reporting or understanding of events invites questioning from the reader. Narrators may be considered unreliable if they lack sufficient intelligence or experience to understand events or if they have some reason to misrepresent events.

Vers libre: French for *free verse.*

Verse: a general term for works of poetry, usually referring to poems that incorporate conventional metrical structures. The term may also describe a stanza (as in some song forms).

Villanelle: a poem usually consisting of 19 lines, with five three-line stanzas (*tercets*) rhyming *aba*, and a concluding quatrain rhyming *abaa.* The first and third lines of the first tercet a repeat at fixed intervals. See, for example, Dylan Thomas's "Do Not Go Gentle into That Good Night."

Voice: the qualities of a poem's language that lead us to imagine that a particular speaker is addressing us as readers. "Voice" is an oral term linked to the long history of poems as art works for performance, recited or sung aloud and heard by audiences rather than read. Different kinds of poems invoke and manipulate effects of voice in different ways (as in *lyric, romanticism, dramatic monologue, found language*).

Volta: See *turn*.

Zeugma: a *figure of speech* (*trope*) in which one word links semantically to two ideas that follow in the same sentence but connects to each in a different way, often to comic or ironic effect. For example, a verb may govern two objects, as in Pope's line "Or stain her honour, or her new brocade."

Permission Acknowledgments

POEMS

Diane Ackerman. "Sweep Me through Your Many-Chambered Heart," from *Jaguar of Sweet Laughter: New & Selected Poems* by Diane Ackerman. Copyright © 1991 by Diane Ackerman. Used by permission of Random House, an imprint and division of Random House LLC. All rights reserved. Any third party use of this material, outside of this publication, is prohibited. Interested parties must apply directly to Penguin Random House LLC for permission.

Kim Addonizio. "First Poem for You," from *The Philosopher's Club*. BOA Editions, 1994. Copyright © Kim Addonizio; reprinted with permission.

Sherman Alexie. "After the Trial of Hamlet, Chicago, 1994," from *The Summer of Black Widows*. Copyright © 1996 by Sherman Alexie. Reprinted by permission of Hanging Loose Press.

Agha Shahid Ali. "Postcard from Kashmir," from *The Half-Inch Himalayas*. Copyright © 1987 Agha Shahid Ali. Reprinted by permission of Wesleyan University Press. "The Wolf's Postscript to 'Little Red Riding Hood,'" from *The Veiled Suite: The Collected Poems*. Copyright © 1987 by Agha Shahid Ali. Used by permission of W.W. Norton & Company, Inc.

Maya Angelou. "Still I Rise," from *And Still I Rise*. Copyright © 1978 by Maya Angelou. Used by permission of Random House, an imprint and division of Random House LLC. All rights reserved. Any third party use of this material, outside of this publication, is prohibited. Interested parties must apply directly to Random House LLC for permission.

Rae Armantrout. "Soft Money," from *Money Shot*. Copyright © 2011 Rae Armantrout. Reprinted by permission of Wesleyan University Press.

John Ashbery. "Paradoxes and Oxymorons," from *Shadow Train*. Copyright © 1980, 1981 by John Ashbery. "Soonest Mended," from *The Double Dream of Spring* by John Ashbery. Copyright © 1966, 1970 by John Ashbery. Reprinted by permission of Georges Borchardt, Inc., on behalf of the author.

Margaret Atwood. "Death of a Young Son by Drowning," from *The Journals of Susanna Moodie*. Copyright © 1976 by Oxford University Press. Reprinted by permission of Houghton Mifflin Harcourt Publishing Company. All rights reserved.

W.H. Auden. "Musée des Beaux Arts," "The Unknown Citizen," "Funeral Blues," and "September 1, 1939," from *W.H. Auden Collected Poems*. Copyright © 1940 and renewed 1968 by W.H. Auden. Used by permission of Random House, an imprint and division of Penguin Random House LLC. All rights reserved.

Reprinted by permission of Curtis Brown, Ltd. "miss rosie," "wishes for sons," and "the lost baby poem," from *The Collected Poems of Lucille Clifton*. Copyright © 1987 by Lucille Clifton. Reprinted with the permission of The Permissions Company, Inc., on behalf of BOA Editions Ltd., www.boaeditions.org.

Billy Collins. "Lines Composed Over Three Thousand Miles from Tintern Abbey," from *Picnic, Lightning*. Copyright © 1998. Reprinted by permission of the University of Pittsburgh Press.

Gregory Corso. "BOMB" and "Marriage," from *The Happy Birthday of Death*. Copyright © 1960 by New Directions Publishing Corp. Reprinted by permission of New Directions Publishing Corp. Copy text of "BOMB" courtesy of the Rare Books & Manuscripts Library of The Ohio State University Libraries.

Hart Crane. "At Melville's Tomb" and "Recitative," from *The Complete Poems of Hart Crane*, edited by Marc Simon. Copyright © 1933, 1958, 1966 by Liveright Publishing Corporation. Copyright © 1986 by Marc Simon. Used by permission of Liveright Publishing Corporation.

Stephen Crane. Copy texts of poems from *The Black Riders and Other Lines* and *War is Kind* are used by courtesy of the Rare Books & Manuscripts Library of The Ohio State University Libraries.

Robert Creeley. "The Language" and "America," from *The Collected Poems of Robert Creeley, 1945–1975*. Copyright © 1967 and 1969 by Robert Creeley. Reprinted with the permission of The Permissions Company, Inc., on behalf of The Estate of Robert Creeley. "The Pattern," from *The Collected Poems of Robert Creeley, 1945–1975*, University of California Press, 1982. Reprinted with the permission of the University of California Press via Copyright Clearance Center, Inc.

Countee Cullen. "Yet Do I Marvel" and "From the Dark Tower," from *My Soul's High Song: The Collected Writings of Countee Cullen*. Doubleday, 1991. Reprinted with the permission of The Amistad Research Center at Tulane University, New Orleans, Louisiana.

E.E. Cummings. ["in Just-"], copyright © 1923, 1951, © 1991 by the Trustees for the E.E. Cummings Trust; copyright © 1976 by George James Firmage. ["l(a"], copyright © 1958, 1986, 1991 by the Trustees for the E.E. Cummings Trust. ["may I feel said he"], copyright © 1935, © 1963, 1991 by the Trustees for the E.E. Cummings Trust; copyright © 1978 by George James Firmage. ["i like my body"], copyright © 1923, 1925, 1951, 1953, © 1991 by the Trustees for the E.E. Cummings Trust; copyright © 1976 by George James Firmage. ["the Cambridge ladies who live in furnished souls"], copyright © 1923, 1951, © 1991 by the Trustees for the E.E. Cummings Trust; copyright © 1976 by George James Firmage. From *Complete Poems: 1904–1962* by E.E. Cummings, edited by George J. Firmage. Used by permission of Liveright Publishing Corporation.

Michael Davidson. "Et in Leucadia Ego," from *The Landing of Rochambeau*. Burning Deck Press, 1985. Reprinted with the permission of Michael Davidson.

Olena Kalytiak Davis. "The Lyric 'I' Drives to Pick up Her Children from School: A Poem in the Postconfessional Mode," from *The Poem She Didn't Write and Other Poems*. Copyright © 2014 by Olena Kalytiak Davis. Reprinted with the permis-

Jackie Kay. "In My Country," from *Darling: New and Selected Poems*. Bloodaxe Books, 2007. Reprinted with permission of Bloodaxe Books, on behalf of the author. www.bloodaxebooks.com.

Weldon Kees. Excerpts from "Five Villanelles," "Sestina: Travel Notes," "Robinson at Home," "Aspects of Robinson," "Relating to Robinson," and "Robinson," from *The Collected Poems of Weldon Kees*, edited by Donald Justice. Copyright © 1962, 1975 by the University of Nebraska Press; copyright renewed 2003 by the University of Nebraska Press. Reprinted by permission of the University of Nebraska Press.

Jack Kerouac. Excerpts from "Mexico City Blues," copyright © 1959 by Jack Kerouac. Used by permission of Grove/Atlantic, Inc. Any third party use of this material, outside of this publication, is prohibited.

Kenneth Koch. "One Train May Hide Another," "Variations on a Theme by William Carlos Williams," and "Mountain," from *The Collected Poems of Kenneth Koch*. Copyright © 2005 by The Kenneth Koch Literary Estate. Used by permission of Alfred A. Knopf, an imprint of the Knopf Doubleday Publishing Group, a division of Random House LLC. All rights reserved. Third party use of this material is prohibited. Interested parties must apply directly to Random House LLC for permission.

Yusef Komunyakaa. "Blue Light Lounge Sutra for the Performance Poets at Harold Park Hotel" and "Facing It," from *Pleasure Dome*, copyright © 2001. Reprinted by permission of Wesleyan University Press.

Philip Larkin. "Church Going," "Talking in Bed," "This Be the Verse," and "The Old Fools" from *The Complete Poems of Philip Larkin*, edited by Archie Burnett. Copyright © 2012 by The Estate of Philip Larkin. Reprinted by permission of Farrar, Straus and Giroux, LLC.

Li-Young Lee. "Persimmons," from *Rose*. Copyright © 1986 by Li-Young Lee. Reprinted with the permission of The Permissions Company, Inc., on behalf of BOA Editions Ltd., www.boaeditions.org.

David Lehman. "The Difference between Pepsi and Coke" and "First Offense," from *An Alternative to Speech*. Princeton University Press, 1986. Reprinted with permission.

Denise Levertov. "What Were They Like?" from *Poems 1960–1967*. Copyright © 1966 by Denise Levertov. "The Day the Audience Walked Out on Me, and Why," from *Poems 1968–1972*. Copyright © 1970 by Denise Levertov. Reprinted by permission of New Directions Publishing Corp.

Philip Levine. "Animals Are Passing from Our Lives," from *New Selected Poems*. Copyright © 1992 by Philip Levine. Reprinted by permission of Wesleyan University Press.

Audre Lorde. "Hanging Fire" and "Outside," from *The Black Unicorn*. Copyright © 1978 by Audre Lorde. Used by permission of W.W. Norton & Company, Inc.

Charles Olson. "Rufus Woodpecker" and "As the Dead Prey Upon Us," from *The Collected Poems of Charles Olson*. University of California Press, 1997. Reprinted with the permission of the University of California Press via Copyright Clearance Center, Inc.

George Oppen. "Latitude, Longitude," and "The Forms of Love," from *New Collected Poems*. Copyright © 1975 by George Oppen. "Psalm," from *New Collected Poems*, copyright © 1965 by George Oppen. Reprinted by permission of New Directions Publishing Corp.

Sylvia Plath. "Daddy" and "Lady Lazarus," from *Ariel*. Copyright © 1961, 1962, 1963, 1964, 1965, 1966, by Ted Hughes. Reprinted by permission of HarperCollins Publishers. "Ariel," from *Ariel*. Copyright © 1965 by Ted Hughes. Reprinted by permission of HarperCollins Publishers. "Mushrooms," from *The Colossus*. Copyright © 1957, 1958, 1959, 1960, 1961, 1962 by Sylvia Plath. Used by permission of Alfred A. Knopf, an imprint of the Knopf Doubleday Publishing Group, a division of Penguin Random House LLC. All rights reserved. Any third party use of this material, outside of this publication, is prohibited. Interested parties must apply directly to Penguin Random House LLC for permission.

Stan Rice. "The Strangeness," from *Red to the Rind*. Copyright © 2002 by Stan Rice. Used by permission of Alfred A. Knopf, an imprint of the Knopf Doubleday Publishing Group, a division of Penguin Random House LLC. All rights reserved. Any third party use of this material, outside of this publication, is prohibited. Interested parties must apply directly to Penguin Random House LLC for permission.

Adrienne Rich. "Aunt Jennifer's Tigers," copyright © 2002, 1951 by Adrienne Rich; "Living in Sin," copyright © 2002, 1955 by Adrienne Rich; "A Valediction Forbidding Mourning," copyright © 2002 by Adrienne Rich, copyright © 1971 by W.W. Norton & Company, Inc. "Diving into the Wreck," copyright © 2002 by Adrienne Rich; copyright © 1973 by W.W. Norton & Company, Inc., from *The Fact of A Doorframe: Selected Poems 1950–2001*. Used by permission of W.W. Norton & Company, Inc.

Theodore Roethke. "Root Cellar," copyright © 1943 by Modern Poetry Association, Inc.; "I Knew a Woman," copyright © 1954 by Theodore Roethke; "My Papa's Waltz," copyright © 1942 by Hearst Magazines, Inc.; from *Collected Poems*. Used by permission of Doubleday, an imprint of the Knopf Doubleday Publishing Group, a division of Random House LLC. All rights reserved. Any third party use of this material, outside of this publication, is prohibited. Interested parties must apply directly to Random House LLC for permission.

Mary Ruefle. "Why I Am Not a Good Kisser," from *Tristimania*. Carnegie Mellon University Press, 2004.

Gjertrud Schnackenberg. "The Paperweight," from *Supernatural Love: Poems 1976–1992*. Copyright © 2000 by Gjertrud Schnackenberg. Reprinted by permission of Farrar, Straus & Giroux, LLC.

Anne Sexton. "Sylvia's Death," from *Live or Die*. Copyright © 1966 by Anne Sexton; renewed 1994 by Linda G. Sexton. Reprinted by permission of Houghton Mifflin

SONGS

WEBSITE

Solutions to the Exeter Book Riddles:

23, penis or onion (rose has also been suggested); 33, iceberg; 81, fish and river.

Index of First Lines

Index of Authors and Titles